Imagery

and

ALLAN PAIVIO
University of Western Ontario
London, Ontario

Verbal Processes

LEA LAWRENCE ERLBAUM ASSOCIATES, PUBLISHERS
Hillsdale, New Jersey

To my wife Kathleen
and my children Sandra, Anna Lee, Heather, Eric, and Karina

Lawrence Erlbaum Associates, Inc., Publishers
365 Broadway
Hillsdale, New Jersey 07642

Library of Congress Catalog Card Number 73-150787

Printed in the United States of America

Preface

In this book I have attempted to present a systematic theoretical and factual account of the role of higher mental processes in human learning and memory, and certain aspects of the psychology of perception and language. The major orienting theme of the book is its dual emphasis on nonverbal imagery and verbal processes (inner speech) as memory codes and mediators of behavior. Based on recent experimental evidence, the conceptual approach in a sense represents an integration of prebehavioristic and behavioristic views concerning the nature of thought.

The book is intended both as a textbook and as a theoretical monograph. Beginning with a theoretical orientation, I soon became convinced that I could not adequately convey the scope of the approach without an extensive review of the research literature in the various areas it encompasses. Moreover, the skepticism which behaviorism justifiably fostered in regard to the mentalistic concept of imagery still persists to some extent among experimental psychologists, and it is unlikely to be completely dispelled without overwhelming empirical evidence demonstrating that the construct can have real scientific value. I have done my best to present such evidence, with the result that the book is somewhat longer than I had originally intended, but at the same time perhaps more useful than it might otherwise have been as a textbook and reference book for psychology students. It is most relevant as a textbook for graduate and upper-division undergraduate courses in human learning, memory, psycholinguistics, and cognitive processes. It could also serve as supplementary reading in courses on perception. I have assumed throughout that the reader has some familiarity with the basic facts in the various areas—of the level provided, for example, by introductory courses in learning and perception, or a course in general experimental psychology.

ALLAN PAIVIO

London, Ontario
July 1971

Acknowledgements

It is a pleasure for me to express my gratitude to the many people who in one way or another have contributed to the book or to the enterprise on which it is based. These include the graduate students and former graduate students whose names appear throughout the book as collaborators in the studies that grew out of the ideas we shared and who, individually or in seminars, have commented on drafts of various chapters—Professors Frank D. Colman, Stephan A. Madigan, Herb M. Simpson, A. Dan Yarmey, John C. Yuille, and Dr. Padric C. Smythe; more recently, Carole Ernest, Ian Begg, Kalman Csapo, Brian O'Neill, Ronald Philipchalk, and Ted Rowe. I am grateful also to Professor Doreen Kimura, Professor Zenon Pylyshyn, Dr. Colin Berry, Andrew Feldmar, and Peter Skehan, who read and commented on sections of the book. It was my good fortune, too, that Professor Ralph Haber read the entire preliminary manuscript on behalf of Holt, Rinehart and Winston, and I was able to take advantage of his counsel in preparing the final draft.

Many of the key studies reported in this book grew out of a research program that has been supported financially by the National Research Council of Canada (Grant APA 87), the University of Western Ontario Research Fund and the University's Summer Supplements program. The scope of the research program would have been severely restricted without their support.

A number of people have provided clerical and other assistance. Mrs. Helen Smith expertly typed an early mimeographed draft of the book and most of the final manuscript. Mrs. Patricia Butler and Mrs. Ann Anas proofread the various drafts and helped compile the references. Typing and general clerical assistance were ably provided by Mrs. Elizabeth Wilkins.

Above all I am grateful to my wife, who has been patient and encouraging over the years when I devoted much of my "spare" time during evenings and weekends to writing. Moreover, despite her own busy life, she found time to contribute specifically to the book by typing early drafts of several chapters and part of the final manuscript. This book is affectionately dedicated to her and to my children.

In addition to the individuals mentioned above and the sources noted in the figure legends, credit is due the following for permission to reproduce or adapt material:

Figure 4.1. Reprinted with permission of authors and publisher: From Robinson, J. S., Brown, L. T., & Hayes, W. H. Test of effects of past experience on perception. *Perceptual and Motor Skills,* 1964, **18,** 953–956.

Figure 4.2. Adapted from Pritchard, R. M., Heron, W., & Hebb, D. O. Visual perception approached by the method of stabilized images. *Canadian Journal of Psychology,* 1960, **14,** 67–77.

Figure 4.3. From Tees, R. C., & More, L. K. Effect of amount of perceptual learning upon disappearances observed under reduced stimulation conditions. *Perception and Psychophysics,* 1967, **2,** 565–568.

Figure 4.4. From Wapner, S., & Werner, H. *Perceptual development.* Worcester, Mass.: Clark University Press, 1957.

Figure 4.5. From Dick, A. O., & Mewhort, J. K. Order of report and processing in tachistoscopic recognition. *Perception and Psychophysics,* 1967, **2,** 573–576.

Figure 4.6. From Kimura, D. Functional asymmetry of the brain in dichotic listening. *Cortex,* 1967, **3,** 163–178. Reproduced by permission of the author.

Figure 5.1. From Hershenson, M., & Haber, R. N. The role of meaning in the perception of briefly presented words. *Canadian Journal of Psychology,* 1965, **19,** 42–46.

Figure 5.2. From Standing, L., Sell, C., Boss, J., & Haber, R. N. Effect of visualization and subvocalization on perceptual clarity. *Psychonomic Science,* 1970, **18,** 89–90.

Figure 5.3. From Posner, M. I., & Mitchell, R. F. Chronometric analysis of classification. *Psychological Review,* 1967, **74,** 392–409. Copyright 1967 by the American Psychological Association, and reproduced by permission.

Figure 5.4. From Posner, M. I., & Keele, S. W. Decay of visual information from a single letter. *Science,* 1967, **158,** 137–139. Copyright 1967 by the American Association for the Advancement of Science.

Figure 5.5. From Posner, M. I., Boies, S. J., Eichelman, W. H., & Taylor, R. L. Retention of visual and name codes of single letters. *Journal of Experimental Psychology Monograph,* 1969, **79** (1, Pt. 2). Copyright 1969 by the American Psychological Association, and reproduced by permission.

Figure 5.6. From Haber, R. N., & Nathanson, L. S. Processing of sequentially presented letters. *Perception and Psychophysics,* 1969, **5,** 359–361.

Figure 5.7. From Brooks, L. R. The suppression of visualization in reading. *Quarterly Journal of Experimental Psychology,* 1967, **19,** 289–299.

Figure 5.8. From Brooks, L. R. Spatial and verbal components of the act of recall. *Canadian Journal of Psychology,* 1968, **22,** 349–368.

Figure 7.2. From Vanderplas, J. M., & Garvin, E. A. The association value of random shapes. *Journal of Experimental Psychology,* 1959, **57,** 147–154. Copyright 1959 by the American Psychological Association, and reproduced by permission.

Figure 7.3. From Feuge, R. L., & Ellis, H. C. Generalization gradients in recognition memory of visual form: The role of stimulus meaning. *Journal of Experimental Psychology,* 1969, **79,** 288–294. Copyright 1969 by the American Psychological Association, and reproduced by permission.

Figure 7.5. From Noble, C. E. Meaningfulness and familiarity. In C. N. Cofer and B. S. Musgrave (Eds.), *Verbal behavior and learning.* Copyright 1963 by McGraw-Hill. Used with permission of McGraw-Hill Book Company.

Figure 7.8. From Paivio, A., & Madigan, S. A. Noun imagery and frequency in paired-associate and free recall learning. *Canadian Journal of Psychology,* 1970, **24,** 353–361.

Figure 7.10. From Koeppel, J. C., & Beecroft, R. S. The conceptual similarity effect in free recall. *Psychonomic Science,* 1967, **9,** 213–214.

Figure 7.11. From Paivio, A., Yuille, J. C., & Rogers, T. B. Noun imagery and meaning-

fulness in free and serial recall. *Journal of Experimental Psychology*, 1969, **79**, 509–514. Copyright 1969 by the American Psychological Association, and reproduced by permission.
Figure 7.12. From Paivio, A., Rogers, T. B., & Smythe, P. C. Why are pictures easier to recall than words? *Psychonomic Science*, 1968, **11**, 137–138.
Figure 7.14. From Paivio, A., & Smythe, P. C. Word imagery, frequency, and meaningfulness in short-term memory. *Psychonomic Science*, 1971, **22**, 333–335.
Figure 7.15. From Wickens, D. D., & Clark, S. Osgood dimensions as an encoding class in short-term memory. *Journal of Experimental Psychology*, 1968, **78**, 580–584. Copyright 1968 by the American Psychological Association, and reproduced by permission.
Figures 7.16 and 7.17. From Paivio, A., & Csapo, K. Concrete-image and verbal memory codes. *Journal of Experimental Psychology*, 1969, **80**, 279–285. Copyright 1969 by the American Psychological Association, and reproduced by permission.
Figures 8.3 and 11.1. From Paivio, A., Smythe, P. C., & Yuille, J. C. Imagery versus meaningfulness of nouns in paired-associate learning. *Canadian Journal of Psychology*, 1968, **22**, 427–441.
Figure 8.6. From Paivio, A., and Madigan, S. A. Imagery and association value in paired-associate learning. *Journal of Experimental Psychology*, 1968, **76**, 35–39. Copyright 1968 by the American Psychological Association, and reproduced by permission.
Figure 8.7. From Yuille, J. C., Paivio, A., & Lambert, W. E. Noun and adjective imagery and order in paired-associate learning by French and English subjects. *Canadian Journal of Psychology*, 1969, **23**, 459–466.
Figure 8.9. From Asch, S. E., & Ebenholtz, S. M. The principle of associative symmetry. *Proceedings of the American Philosophical Society*, 1962, **106**, 135–163.
Figure 9.1. From Kiess, H. O. Effects of natural language mediators on short-term memory. *Journal of Experimental Psychology*, 1968, **77**, 7–13. Copyright 1968 by the American Psychological Association, and reproduced by permission.
Figure 9.2. From Bower, G. H., & Clark, M. C. Narrative stories as mediators for serial learning. *Psychonomic Science*, 1969, **14**, 181–182.
Figure 10.1. Reprinted with permission of author and publisher: From Smith, R. K., & Noble, C. E. Effects of a mnemonic technique applied to verbal learning and memory. *Perceptual and Motor Skills*, 1965, **21**, 123–134.
Figure 10.2. From Senter, R. J., & Hauser, G. K. An experimental study of a mnemonic system. *Psychonomic Science*, 1968, **10**, 289–290.
Figure 10.4. From Bugelski, B. R. Images as mediators in one-trial paired-associate learning. II: Self-timing in successive lists. *Journal of Experimental Psychology*, 1968, **77**, 328–334. Copyright 1968 by the American Psychological Association, and reproduced by permission.
Figure 10.6. From Paivio, A. Effects of imagery instructions and concreteness of memory pegs in a mnemonic system. *Proceedings of the 76th Annual Convention of the American Psychological Association*, 1968, 77–78. Copyright 1968 by the American Psychological Association, and reproduced by permission.
Figure 11.2. From Yuille, J. C., & Paivio, A. Latency of imaginal and verbal mediators as a function of stimulus and response concreteness-imagery. *Journal of Experimental Psychology*, 1967, **75**, 540–544. Copyright 1967 by the American Psychological Association, and reproduced by permission.
Figure 11.4. From Yuille, J. C., & Paivio, A. Imagery and verbal mediation instructions in paired-associate learning. *Journal of Experimental Psychology*, 1968, **78**, 436–441. Copyright 1968 by the American Psychological Association, and reproduced by permission.
Figures 11.5 and 11.6. From Paivio, A., and Yuille, J. C. Changes in associative strategies and paired-associate learning over trials as a function of word imagery and type of learning set. *Journal of Experimental Psychology*, 1969, **79**, 458–463. Copyright 1969 by the American Psychological Association, and reproduced by permission.
Figure 11.7. From Paivio, A., & Foth, D. Imaginal and verbal mediators and noun concreteness in paired-associate learning: The elusive interaction. *Journal of Verbal Learning and Verbal Behavior*, 1970, **9**, 384–390.
Figure 11.12. Epstein, W., Rock, I., & Zuckerman, C. B. Meaning and familiarity in associative learning. *Psychological Monographs*, 1960, **74** (4, Whole No. 491). Copyright 1960 by the American Psychological Association, and reproduced by permission.
Figure 12.2. From Katz, J. J., & Fodor, J. A. The structure of a semantic theory. *Language*, 1963, **39**, 170–210. Copyright 1963 by the Linguistic Society of America.

Figure 12.3.   From Miller, G. A., & Isard, S. Some perceptual consequences of linguistic rules. *Journal of Verbal Learning and Verbal Behavior*, 1963, **2**, 217–228.

Figure 13.3.   From Reynolds, J. H. Cognitive transfer in verbal learning: II. Transfer effects after prefamiliarization with integrated versus partially integrated verbal-perceptual structures. *Journal of Educational Psychology*, 1968, **59**, 133–138. Copyright 1968 by the American Psychological Association, and reproduced by permission.

Figure 13.4.   From Sachs, J. S. Recognition memory for syntactic and semantic aspects of connected discourse. *Perception and Psychophysics*, 1967, **2**, 437–442.

Figure 13.5.   From Begg, I., & Paivio, A. Concreteness and imagery in sentence meaning. *Journal of Verbal Learning and Verbal Behavior*, 1969, **8**, 821–827.

Figure 13.6.   From Paivio, A. Imagery and deep structure in the recall of English nominalizations. *Journal of Verbal Learning and Verbal Behavior*, 1971, **10**, 1–12.

Figure 14.4.   From Pettifor, J. L. The role of language in the development of abstract thinking: A comparison of hard-of-hearing and normal-hearing children on levels of conceptual thinking. *Canadian Journal of Psychology*, 1968, **22**, 139–156.

Excerpts from Frances A. Yates, *The art of memory* (Chicago: University of Chicago Press; London: Routledge & Kegan Paul, 1966), pp. 2, 4, 6–8, 9–10, 22, 24–25, 35–36. Copyright 1966 by the University of Chicago Press. Reprinted by permission of the publishers.

Contents

ix

14

INDIVIDUAL DIFFERENCES IN SYMBOLIC HABITS AND SKILLS, 477

15

EXTENSIONS AND SPECULATIONS, 525

1
Introduction

A remarkable trend is emerging in major areas of psychological inquiry. The trend involves a renewed interest in mentalistic concepts, among which imagery and meaning are central. It is remarkable because such concepts, once prominent in psychology, became anathema in American psychology shortly after the turn of the century. The negative attitude is generally attributed to the behavioristic revolution, and the main issues and developments will be considered primarily in that context. However, in view of the attention given to human learning and memory in this book, it is important to note that the negative influence was not restricted to behaviorism proper, but stemmed also from the rote learning tradition established by Ebbinghaus in 1885. This approach was no less objective than Watson's behaviorism. Ebbinghaus abandoned the introspective method and sought to minimize effects attributable to pre-experimental associative habits and meaning (both mentalistic concepts in that prebehavioristic era) in order to reveal the factors responsible for the formation of new memory associations. The latter goal was to be achieved especially by the introduction of the nonsense syllable as the unit for the experimental study of memory. The main features of the Ebbinghaus approach persisted in rote learning experiments with little change for more than seventy years (see Irion, 1959).

The approach has unquestionably yielded important information concerning effective variables in a variety of tasks, but most of the problems originally investigated by Ebbinghaus remain essentially unsolved today. The slow development of theoretical understanding can be attributed partly to the complexity of human learning and memory. In addition, however, it is possible that the attempts (largely unsuccessful, as it turned out) to control rather than systematically investigate the contributions of meaning and the correlated associative habits from the outset had a retarding effect on theoretical developments in the field. Be that as it may, the situation is changing rapidly. The change is manifested in an accumulating research literature on such variables as meaningful-ness, mediation processes, and organizational factors in learning and memory. But these departures from the Ebbinghaus tradition have also shown a bias in the theoretical approach to the mental mechanisms presumed to be the basis of such phenomena: Verbal processes were emphasized while nonverbal imagery was almost totally ignored. The verbal emphasis arose directly from behaviorism and extended beyond memory to the related problems of meaning, association, perception, and thought in general. The emphasis contrasts sharply with the yeoman's role played by mental imagery over a period of 2500 years in the interpretation of such phenomena. It contrasts also with the consideration given to imagery in the present volume. Does this conceptual revival reflect real theo-retical and empirical progress in psychology or is it merely a passing, reactionary trend? That question is the orienting theme of the book. It may not be answered entirely to the reader's satisfaction, but he will at least find considerable evidence and argument to weigh. To indicate why the question arises at all, it is neces-sary to review the relevant historical developments and controversial issues lead-ing up to the present state of affairs.

Mental Images versus Mental Words

Statements concerning the functions of mental imagery in such phenom-ena as meaning and memory appeared in early Greek writings, and the funda-mental ideas then expressed persisted in associationism and structuralism up to the time of Watson's persuasive attack on mentalistic concepts. Around 500 B.C., the poet Simonides aptly summarized the essence of the imagery hypothesis of linguistic meaning in the phrase "Words are the images of things" (Bowra, 1961, p. 363). Some 2500 years later, William James similarly described the static meaning of concrete words as consisting of "sensory images awakened" (1890, p. 265), and Titchener (1909) extended this view to encompass abstract terms as well.

The image appeared in theories of memory in two forms. First, as manifested in Plato's "wax tablet" model, imagery was the prototype of stimulus-trace the-ories of memory (see Gomulicki, 1953), according to which perceptions and thoughts are impressed on the mind as on a block of wax, to be remembered and known as long as the image lasts. Second, as associative imagery it was assumed to play a mediational role in various memory techniques, which appar-ently originated with Simonides and were thereafter elaborated by philosophers and teachers of rhetoric as a practical art (see Yates, 1966, and Chapter 6 in this book). This associative view holds that memory images could be evoked by stimuli with which the imaged objects or events have been associated in the past, and that these images could themselves combine associatively, as in the "association of ideas." The image theory of meaning can be regarded as a logical extension of such associationistic views to the domain of language, with words presumably serving as the cues for the arousal of the memory image. Common-sense experience continues to make the acceptance of such views compelling. Occasionally, when I have been required to list the names of my colleagues from memory, I have found myself visualizing the hallways in which their offices are located, systematically moving past these offices, then picturing and naming the occupants. Shepard described a similar personal observation as follows: ". . . if I am now asked about the number of windows in my house, I find that I must *picture* the house, as viewed from different sides or from within different rooms, and then count the windows presented in these various mental images. No amount of purely verbal machinations would seem to suffice" (1966, p. 203). The crucial point about such experiences is that the eliciting question and the behavioral expression of recall may be entirely verbal, but the mediating mechanism apparently consists of nonverbal imagery associatively evoked by the words.

It is necessary only to add that such views were extended by the structuralists to the interpretation of perception as a combination of sensations and memory images, and to thought in general as the manipulation of mental images, and the story is complete. Memory, meaning, association, perception, thought—all of these in one way or another implicated mental imagery as a crucial mechanism.

It is precisely such views that were rejected by Watson (1913). Partly on philosophical grounds and partly on the basis of experimental evidence then available on the issue, he concluded that mental images are mere ghosts, without functional significance. The image theory of memory was shaken by findings that revealed that images are not faithful reproductions of reality, even for those individuals who claim "photographic" memories (e.g., Fernald, 1912). Furthermore, the Würzburg experiments yielded abundant evidence that thinking may go on without reportable conscious content in the form of concrete-object or verbal images (see Humphrey, 1951; Mandler & Mandler, 1964). Experimental data thus raised serious questions concerning both the representational (memory) and associative or mediational (thought) functions that traditionally had been attributed to images, and such findings apparently prompted Watson to conclude that imagery had no functional significance. Moreover, the concept was unacceptably subjective and was to be banished along with the rest of the mentalistic baggage that introspectionism produced.

In Watson's approach, the functions that had been attributed to images in thought and memory became the burden of words—verbal responses—or their gestural substitutes (e.g., Watson, 1930, pp. 265–268). Verbal recollections of remembered objects and events are simply habits, learned responses that occurred originally in the particular setting being described and are re-evoked later by cues that originally accompanied their occurrence. To the extent that thought is involved in such behavior, as when one thinks about the original events before responding, the mediating process is also verbal, that is, it consists of talking to oneself. Meaning, too, was to be viewed in terms of the organized verbal and nonverbal responses that a given object evokes in an individual.

Contemporary Status of the Controversy

Watson's stand on imagery and the factors leading up to it effectively suppressed interest in the concept, particularly in America. This was reflected in a marked reduction in the number of empirical studies involving the concept in comparison with the volume of research that followed Galton's pioneering studies on individual differences in imagery in 1880 and continued until a few years after Watson's attempted *coup de grâce*. As the interest in imagery declined, an emphasis on verbal processes quite in accord with Watson's views increasingly dominated empirical and theoretical approaches to problems of meaning and mediation processes in verbal learning, memory, association, and language (see Goss, 1961). The meaningfulness of verbal units came to be defined most often in terms of such measures as association value (Glaze, 1928) or meaningfulness (*m*; Noble, 1952a), which assume that verbal associations are the basis of meaning. Consistent with this definition, effects of meaningfulness on associative learning and memory were interpreted in terms of the availability of implicit verbal associates as potential mediators of stimulus-response connections, as in the associative probability or "grapnel" theory (Glanzer, 1962; Underwood & Schulz, 1960, p. 296)—the greater the number of verbal associations that item A evokes, the greater the probability that one of these associations will provide a common link between A and B. A similar verbal emphasis has been generally apparent in research on mediated transfer and generalization, organizational factors in memory and language, and so-called "natural language" mediators (e.g., Adams, 1967; W. A. Bousfield, 1961; Cofer, 1965; Deese, 1965; J. J. Jenkins, 1963). Even in perception, higher-order coding processes have been interpreted as primarily verbal in nature (e.g., Glanzer & Clark, 1963a; Haber, 1966). Explicitly or implicitly, the dominant view in America has been that effective meaning and mediational phenomena generally are founded on verbal associative mechanisms. The possibility that nonverbal imagery may be functionally involved was generally ignored and occasionally rejected for reasons that echo Watson's original objections to the concept.

The logical argument   The current attitude toward imagery and the reasons for it have been summarized recently by Deese (1965) in reference to association and language. The arguments apply generally to the phenomena being considered here and, because they express a rather general viewpoint, they merit careful consideration. Thus:

> The modern experimental psychologist works almost exclusively with linguistic associations for the good reason that these provide controllable material for his laboratory studies; he ignores the extra existence of perceptual imagery. Without necessarily denying either their reality or their importance, the contemporary psychologist finds images difficult to manage in empirical study. Partly for this reason and partly for others, association theory in modern

psychology has become a theory of the succession of elements in verbal behavior (p. 4).

This is one of the classical behavioristic arguments—imagery is subjective and inferential, words are objective and manageable. It constitutes a valid case against imagery if the interests of contemporary psychologists remained at the empirical level, but they obviously do not. As Deese goes on to say:

> We study associations in order to make inferences about the nature of human thought. . . . *The whole of the current concern is with the associative properties of explicit verbal behavior as a model for the implicit verbal process of thought* (1965, p. 4, italics added).

With that the empirical superiority of words over images ends, for implicit verbal processes are no less inferential than perceptual images. One might argue that it is more direct and, therefore, more parsimonious to infer a verbal mediating process when the response is verbal, but this follows only if one assumes a one-to-one relation between the overt associative reaction and the mental process that caused it. Such an assumption would be unsound, for one can respond verbally to pictures as well as to words and so, by analogy, one's verbal response could just as logically be mediated by a "mental picture" as by "mental words" (that is, implicit verbal representations). Both are pure inferences and which one it is more logical to infer in research concerned with such problems depends on the total set of conditions in a given study, not merely on the mode of the overt response. The problem is empirical as well as logical, and it is the experimenter's burden to devise conditions that will permit him to make reasonable inferences about the nature of the effective underlying processes independent of their particular behavioral expression.

The factual argument Watson's second major objection to the concept of imagery, which also persists in contemporary discussions (e.g., R. W. Brown, 1958), was based on the lack of factual evidence that images have any functional significance, even in memory tasks where vivid images should be most useful. The conclusion that images have no relation to memory because they do not accurately reflect reality is unjustified, however, simply because all memory is imperfect. Bartlett (1932) clearly recognized the inaccuracy but did not find it necessary therefore to conclude that the concept of memory is unnecessary, nor that images have no function in relation to it. Instead, his conclusion was that remembered events are partly constructions rather than faithful reproductions of reality. The imageless thought experiments likewise did not indicate that images had no mediational function, only that complex mental operations could occur without conscious content. Images were, in fact, reported frequently in those experiments, and Humphrey (1951) concluded from this that the Würzburg psychologists underplayed the significance of imagery as inferred from the reports of their subjects. Moreover, inferences concerning the function of imagery were based almost exclusively on individual differences in the reported vividness of images, a defining operation that still fails to reveal the functional significance of imagery as clearly as other objective procedures, as will be seen later.

Finally, just as verbal mediation processes are no less inferential than images, so too are they open to the same factual criticisms: Verbal associative memory is imperfect, and conscious verbal processes were absent in imageless thought (Humphrey, 1951). Should we conclude from such observations that the concept of verbal mediation is without scientific value? I presume that few would want to do so and we must accordingly reject such a conclusion in regard to imagery as well. The problem in the case of both of these postulated processes is to clarify their functions, that is, to determine the conditions under which mental images and mental words are aroused and to identify the nature of their effects on overt behavior. *Both are theoretical constructs and whether or not it is useful to postulate either, or both, depends on the adequacy of the defining operations and the research procedures used to test the properties that have been theoretically attributed to them.*

Revival of the image   Perhaps partly for the reasons just discussed and partly because the concept is somehow a valid reflection of mental processes, Watson's attack did not succeed in burying "the image." Research concerned explicitly with mental imagery continued to appear sporadically in psychological literature even during the most arid period in the 1920s and thirties, and the classical problems associated with imagery continued to be discussed in influential textbooks of the day (e.g., Woodworth, 1938). In addition, concepts with essentially the same functional properties as imagery turned up in behavioristic writings. Perhaps the most obvious example is Tolman's (e.g., 1932, 1948) cognitive approach to behavior theory, in which such terms as expectancy, sign learning, and cognitive maps substituted for the various functions that had been attributed earlier to mental images. Hull's (1931) fractional anticipatory goal response (r_g-s_g) mechanism and Osgood's (1953) elaboration of it under the label of representational mediation process are functionally parallel to Tolman's sign-Gestalt-expectation and, on close inspection, all of the concepts can be seen to retain some of the cognitive flavor of the imagery concept. Perhaps this was only to be expected. As pointed out by Morgan (1943) and Hebb (1949), mental variables have been repeatedly thrown out because there was no place for them in stimulus-response psychology, but they repeatedly find their way in again in one form or another because they are necessary to a full account of behavior.

Thus it is not surprising that we find the concept of imagery reappearing essentially in its pristine form but with its respectability enhanced by a behavioristic cloak. On the basis of results from experimental investigation involving a classical conditioning paradigm, Leuba (1940) felt justified in referring to images as conditioned sensations. Skinner (1953) similarly discussed visual imagery as "conditioned seeing." The possibility has even been suggested that conditioned images may play a mediational role in classical conditioning involving lower animals (Mowrer, 1960; Sheffield, 1965). The most elaborate treatment of this kind can be found in Beritoff's (1965) analysis of aspects of higher vertebrate behavior in terms of images, although in it he distinguished "image-driven" behavior from conditioned reflexes. Other theorists with diverse interests (e.g., Arnheim, 1969; Bruner, Olver, & Greenfield, 1966; Greenwald, 1970; Hebb, 1966, 1968; Holt, 1964; M. J. Horowitz, 1967; G. A. Miller, Galanter, & Pribram, 1960; Singer, 1966; Tomkins, 1962) have also devoted considerable attention to the concept without necessarily placing it into the framework of classical conditioning, which is itself but poorly understood theoretically.

At the empirical level, the experimental study of dreaming as introduced by Aserinsky and Kleitman (1953) has drawn attention to imagery in a manner that is relevant not only to dream phenomena but also to the problem of nonverbal mediation of verbal behavior. The reality of imagery and the validity of the dream report as evidence of imagery are assumed in such research, with the implication that descriptive verbal behavior (the dream report) is caused by nonverbal central events (the dream image). Behavioral effects are also attributed to verbally aroused imagery in Wolpe's (1958) approach to psychotherapy.

The view that images may have functional significance in behavior after all extends to the phenomena that are most relevant here, namely, meaning and mediation processes in perception, verbal learning, memory, and language. Osgood (1953, 1961) has consistently argued in favor of nonverbal mediating processes in his theory of meaning, where meaning is identified with the conditioned capacity of a sign (e.g., a word) to arouse a fractional component of the reaction pattern originally evoked by a stimulus object. Staats (1961) has shown that imagery could be incorporated into the model by interpreting an image as the fractional component of the original sensory response to an object, which can become conditioned to a word and represent its denotative meaning. Essentially the same idea has been proposed independently by Mowrer (1960) and by Sheffield (1961). Except in their adoption of conditioning as the explanatory mechanism, such a view appears to differ little from the ancient view that "words are the images of things." That we may indeed have come around full circle in our theorizing is evidenced further by an increasing recent interest in research on the possible role of mediating imagery specifically in verbal learning and memory (see Paivio, 1969). While the trend is unlikely to result in a return to the "wax tablet" model of memory or the naive view of associative imagery that was characteristic of the earlier period, it reflects the vitality of the concept and the compelling nature of the phenomena that led to its revival.

But old fads also have a habit of returning, and if imagery proves to be no more than that after a hard look, we must be prepared to reject it once more. The ultimate question to be faced concerns the scientific usefulness of postulating such a process. This question can be answered only within a framework based on an empirical foundation and constructed according to a theoretical blueprint. Imagery, like all inferential concepts, can have functional significance only to the extent that it can be differentiated from other concepts theoretically, and to the extent that these distinctive theoretical properties are open to empirical test. It is essential, therefore, to compare and contrast the concept of imagery with other concepts that have distinct theoretical properties and at the same time can be distinguished operationally from imagery. Within the limitations of present knowledge, this is the approach followed in the present volume, the aim of which is to compare and contrast the roles of imagery and of verbal symbolic processes in relation to a variety of psychological phenomena.

AN OVERVIEW OF THE PRESENT APPROACH

The emphasis throughout is on the functional significance of the two postulated processes, with interest centered on imagery because verbal processes have received the lion's share of the attention in recent psychological research and theory. Restricting our conceptual treatment to images and verbal processes does not imply that these are the only modes of representation and mediation. Reference has already been made to Osgood's theory, which assumes that the mediation process may involve anything from implicit muscular responses to cortical reactions, and multiple modes of representation have been explicitly postulated by a number of other theorists whose views are reviewed in Chapter 2. Although relevant problems are considered from time to time, no attempt will be made to include a systematic treatment of the possible contributions of emotional and motivational processes to the various phenomena. This omission may seem regrettable in view of the emphasis given to affective meaning in Osgood's approach to psycholinguistics, and the importance ascribed to motivational factors in directed thinking by Berlyne (1965). However, the main concern here is with cognitive processes that directly serve a symbolic, representational function and other processes or functions will be considered only in passing.

The theoretical approach   Images and verbal processes are viewed as alternative coding systems, or modes of symbolic representation, which are developmentally linked to experiences with concrete objects and events as well as with language. In a given situation, they may be relatively directly aroused in the sense that an object or an event is represented in memory as a perceptual image and a word as a perceptual-motor trace, or they may be associatively aroused in the sense that an object elicits its verbal label (or images of other objects) and a word arouses implicit verbal associates or images of objects. In addition, it is assumed that chains of symbolic transformations can occur involving either words or images, or both, and that these can serve a mediational function in perception, verbal learning, memory, and language.

The arousal and mediation functions of both processes, but of images particularly, are theoretically coordinated to an abstract-concrete dimension of stimulus meaning or task characteristics. The more concrete or "thing-like" the stimulus or the task situation, the more likely is it to evoke memory images that can be functionally useful in mediating appropriate responses in that situation. Verbal processes presumably are less dependent on concreteness for their arousal and functioning, hence their *relative* usefulness accordingly increases as the task becomes more abstract. Stated differently, both symbolic modes are readily aroused and can be functionally useful when the situation is relatively concrete, whereas verbal processes will be differentially favored when the situation is relatively abstract. Many situations likely involve an interaction of imaginal and verbal processes, however, and the latter would necessarily be involved at some stage whenever the stimuli or responses, or both, are verbal, as is the case with most of the phenomena that are relevant here.

A second postulated distinction is made in terms of the relative efficiency of the symbolic modes as parallel and sequential processing systems. To oversimplify for the moment, visual imagery is regarded primarily as a parallel processing system, specialized for the storage and symbolic manipulation of information concerning spatially organized objects and events. The verbal system, on the other hand, is specialized for sequential processing, as in serial memory tasks, by virtue of its auditory-motor nature. Finally, the systems are distinguished in terms of a static-dynamic dimension, with imagery viewed as the more dynamic process, capable of flexible and swift symbolic transformations. (These statements are appropriately qualified in Chapter 2.)

The empirical approach   The theoretical approach is tied to an empirical one involving three converging operations on the independent variable side, all conceptually linked by the postulated imaginal and verbal symbolic processes. These include (1) *stimulus characteristics,* with particular emphasis on their abstractness-concreteness and verbal associative meaning; (2) *experimental manipulations* such as differential task instructions, presentation rates, and task demands; and (3) *individual differences* in imaginal and verbal associative abilities. All of these are designed to affect the availability or accessibility of one or other of the symbolic systems in a given task. On the dependent variable side, physiological reactions as well as overt behavioral effects are predicted from the independent variables, the predictions frequently including complex interactions of two or more variables.

Our goal of differentiating the two symbolic processes is an extraordinarily difficult empirical problem at best, but is especially so when the theoretical goal is the explanation of *verbal* behavior, for here it is difficult to rule out verbal mediation as the most parsimonious interpretation and at the same time isolate whatever contribution may have been made by imagery. Thus the key issue is whether or not it is necessary, or at least useful, to postulate both kinds of symbolic processes, nonverbal as well as verbal, to account for effects that have been observed in a variety of situations.

Plan of the Book

The book expands on the above approach by defining and elaborating on the theoretical properties of the postulated symbolic processes and then reviewing empirical evidence relevant to those properties, their behavioral implications, and the general usefulness of the model as a theoretical approach to the analysis of the psychological phenomena in question.

The basic concepts are defined in Chapter 2, which is concerned with the nature and development of imagery and verbal symbolic processes. Chapter 3 deals with the relation between meaning and the symbolic processes, in anticipation of the subsequent chapters in which meaning is one of the predictors of experimental results. The remaining chapters deal in turn with perception, memory, associative learning, mediated learning, language, individual differences in symbolic habits and skills, and, finally, theoretical implications of the basic approach for such problems as creativity and education.

2
Development and Functions of the Symbolic Systems

Nonverbal imagery and verbal processes are distinguished here primarily in terms of their functions as symbolic systems, although an assumed relationship between the two processes and visual and auditory sensory modalities has functional implications that are important to later discussions. In the classical approach to imagery, initiated empirically by Galton (1883) and explored by subsequent investigators particularly in relation to individual differences, the term image was used to refer to consciously-experienced mental processes rather generally and distinctions were drawn in terms of the sensory modality (visual, auditory, kinesthetic, and so on) of the image as revealed by introspection. Verbal thought processes were usually regarded as auditory images of words or as proprioceptive sensations from implicit verbal responding, or both, and occasionally as visual images of words. Images of nonverbal objects and events, on the other hand, usually implied visual imagery because of the dominance of visual sense experience, but nonverbal events obviously could involve other modalities as well. Some writers (e.g., Pear, 1927) simply distinguished between verbal and nonverbal imagery, although this terminology confounds distinctions based on modality and those based on symbolic systems, as when reference is made to "visualizers" and "verbalizers" (e.g., Golla, Hutton, & Walter, 1943). Presumably the intended distinction is between nonverbal (visual) and verbal (auditory-motor?) thinking, but this is not clear from the terms. At any rate, some preliminary definitions will help avoid confusions that might arise in subsequent discussions, although appropriate qualification of the terms will still be necessary from time to time. Ultimately, however, we shall rely primarily on operational rather than verbal definitions of the postulated processes. Moreover, introspective awareness will be viewed simply as one possible behavioral manifestation of those processes, rather than as an essential feature of their definition, contrary to the classical approach and some contemporary approaches to imagery (e.g., Richardson, 1969).

Preliminary Definitions

The terms image and imagery will generally be used to refer to concrete imagery, that is, *nonverbal* memory representations of concrete objects and events, or nonverbal modes of thought (e.g., imagination) in which such representations are actively generated and manipulated by the individual. This will usually be taken to mean *visual* imagery, although it is clear that other modalities (e.g., auditory) could be involved and when they are, this must be specified. Imagery, so defined, will be distinguished from *verbal* symbolic processes, which will be assumed to involve implicit activity in an auditory-motor speech system. Thus, although the emphasis is on a distinction between verbal and nonverbal symbolic modes, a correlation presumably exists between symbolic and sensory modality. The contingency is important, for it is the basis of one of the functional distinctions to be postulated between imaginal and verbal processes, namely, their differential capacity for spatial representation and parallel processing on the one hand, and serial representation or sequential processing on the other.

The symbolic and sensory distinctions become confounded in the case of printed words that can be visually imagined, and nonverbal auditory patterns, such as melodies, which apparently are represented (stored) in a nonverbal auditory system. Such instances are more than trivial exceptions, but by using appropriate qualifiers, they can be discussed without confusion and without sacrificing the convenience of using the term imagery in its generally accepted sense of nonverbal visual imagery. Similarly, verbal processes as a *functional* symbolic system are assumed to be auditory-motor in nature, even when the verbal input is visual or the task requires one to generate visual images of letters or words.

The term *image* requires qualification also when the reference is to specific types of imagery, such as the afterimage, the eidetic image, and the rapidly fading perceptual trace, which Sperling (1960) calls an image and Neisser (1967), iconic memory. Use of the same label to identify so many different phenomena can be criticized, but I do not regard it as a sufficiently serious problem to warrant substitution of unique neologisms in every case for a familiar term that can be readily qualified when precision is necessary.

The balance of the chapter deals with the development of, and functional distinctions between, the symbolic modes. We begin with a discussion of the factors or mechanisms that might be responsible for the original acquisition of images and verbal processes into the psychological repertoire of the individual.

ACQUISITION MECHANISMS

What factors are essential to the original acquisition of nonverbal images and verbal thought processes? We are far from knowing the answer to this important question at the present time, but certain possibilities can be suggested that essentially represent specific applications of general theoretical approaches to learning and long-term memory. The relationship of both modes, but imagery in particular, to perception and perceptual learning will become apparent in later sections as well.

Simple exposure to stimulus patterns, classical conditioning, and operant conditioning are theoretical alternatives that have been proposed, in somewhat different ways, as explanations of the genesis of each symbolic mode.

Perceptual Exposure

The wax tablet model is at once the oldest theory of the origin of images and the oldest form of the stimulus-trace theory of memory (Gomulicki, 1953). According to this interpretation, sensory experiences are impressed on the mind and the record endures more or less permanently, depending on such characteristics as the physical intensity and vividness of the stimulus input. The theory was rejected early in the twentieth century, but it persists tenaciously in contemporary thinking. Penfield (1954) has presented some of the most dramatic evidence for such a view. Electrical stimulation of the exposed temporal cortex of epileptic patients evoked memories that were described as rivaling perceptions in their vividness. On the basis of these results, Penfield concluded that the temporal cortex of man contains an "experiential recording mechanism" wherein is formed a permanent record of the stream of consciousness—all the events of which a man was once aware.

Beritoff (1965) has similarly suggested that an integrated image or mental representation—a "psychoneural complex"—may be generated in an animal as a result of a single exposure to a situation. The evidence for accurate long-term storage of this kind is lacking, however. The kind of setting Penfield has used could provide the necessary behavioral information to test the theory, but an additional requirement that has been unsatisfied is an objective record of the remembered events as they were originally experienced. The best evidence from psychological research suggests that such memory traces are formed and can be scanned for information immediately after stimulus exposure but that they are of brief duration (e.g., Sperling, 1960). Penfield holds that very little of the experiential record can be voluntarily reactivated, however, and thus the view seems testable only by use of stimulating electrodes.

A perceptual exposure theory of the acquisition of verbal symbolic processes follows directly from the preceding discussion to the extent that one accepts the assumption that such processes are represented as auditory traces of speech (one's own as well as that of others). It is also implicit in the suggestion that "casual observation" on the part of the learner might partly explain the rapid onset of speech (and presumably the capacity for verbal thought), and that a critical developmental stage might be involved much as in the phenomenon of imprinting (Lenneberg, 1967).

Classical Conditioning

The wax tablet or trace theories of imagery can be distinguished from associative theories, which are concerned with the conditions that determine the arousal of memory images. Traditional associationism was such a theory and it has its contemporary counterparts. Beritoff, for example, assumes a simple contiguity principle in his proposal that "The psychoneural complex [i.e., image] can be easily reproduced under the influence of only one component of the corresponding environment or a stimulus closely related to the environment (1965, p. 2)." He also distinguished the processes involved in image formation and association from those responsible for the establishment of conditioned reflexes, although the processes may also become related. Thus "image driven behavior may become automatized, carried out according to the principle of a chain conditioned reflex (p. 7)." This differs from the more commonly expressed view that images are sensory responses that can become conditioned to stimuli associated with the original sensory experience, following the principles of classical conditioning (Ellson, 1941a, 1941b; Leuba, 1940; Mowrer, 1960; Sheffield, 1961; Skinner, 1953; Staats, 1961). The conditioning approach runs into problems with such phenomena as dreams, where it is difficult to conceptualize the nature of the conditioned stimuli that would have to be postulated as the elicitor of the dream image. On the other hand, even if one argues that images do not necessarily follow conditioning principles in their genesis, it is nevertheless possible to maintain that they are *conditionable* as associative sensory reactions to stimuli, such as words, that accompanied their original arousal. Sensory conditioning (e.g., Brogden, 1947) would be the appropriate acquisition model in this case. As will be seen in subsequent chapters, such a conceptualization of imagery is relevant to the interpretation of meaning and certain perceptual phenomena, as well as associative learning and memory generally.

In regard to the origin of verbal symbolic processes, the early circular-reflex theory of speech development as proposed by F. H. Allport (1924) was a conditioning theory supposedly of the Pavlovian variety. The infant's tendency to repeat his own sounds, as in "lalling," was viewed as the unconditioned reflex. Through conditioning, adult speech sounds acquire the same capacity to elicit vocalization. However, it can now be seen that speech (including implicit speech) might be more appropriately analyzed in terms of operant conditioning, since the stimulus for the original vocal response that sets off the reflex is indeterminate. Contemporary conditioning approaches in any case tend to apply the classical conditioning model primarily to the acquisition of linguistic meaning (Osgood, 1953; Staats, 1968). To the extent that imagery, defined as a conditioned sensory response, can be regarded as one kind of meaning reaction, classical conditioning provides the theoretical mechanism for a linkage between verbal processes and imagery. The issue is discussed more fully in Chapter 3.

Motor Components of the Symbolic Processes and the Role of Operant Conditioning

A third approach to the interpretation of image formation emphasizes motor processes in addition to sensory input. Piaget (1962) and Piaget and Inhelder (1966) have argued that imagery consists of internalized imitation, paralleling the motoricity involved in perceptual exploration, in which movements "imitate" the contours of the perceived figure. This interpretation is in striking agreement with Hebb's (1949) neuropsychological theory, in which eye movements are assumed to play an important role in the establishment of the cell assemblies that are postulated to be the basis of perception and ideational processes, including imagery. Hebb proposed informally that eye movements remain important in the arousal of imagery—a view upon which he has recently elaborated (Hebb, 1968). We shall have more to say about that later. In the present context, such an approach raises the question of the mechanism responsible for "building in" the motor component. A possible answer is suggested by Skinner's (1953) analysis of the role of operant conditioning in the development of private events such as images. In addition to describing visual imagery in terms of classical conditioning ("conditioned seeing"), he extends the concept of "operant seeing" to the level of private responses, for which the controlling variables are operant reinforcement and deprivation (see also N. E. Miller, 1959), and which may include a mixture of discriminative and manipulative covert behavior. As we shall see presently, such a viewpoint has particularly important implications regarding the functions that can be attributed to images, for it frees them from the theoretical limitations of the wax tablet and photographic image models, which imply that images are static and inflexible.

Skinner's operant reinforcement approach to the acquisition of private behavior applies even more obviously to thought as implicit speech. Verbal thinking begins (is reinforced) as overt operant behavior and becomes covert because controlling stimuli are inadequate or because covert behavior is easier, or because it avoids punishment, and so on (Skinner, 1957, Chapter 19). Our concern here is not with the validity of particular features of this approach, but with the general view that instrumental conditioning can be a mechanism responsible for verbal thinking. In any event, the assumption that verbal symbolic processes include a motor component, if only at the level of the motor cortex, is a common one and it has been given persuasive theoretical expression in the motor theory of speech perception proposed by Liberman and his associates (Liberman, Cooper, Shankweiler, & Studdert-Kennedy, 1967). Operant reinforcement can be viewed as playing a role in the development of such a system even if it is not the entire story.

We have briefly considered three theoretical interpretations that have been proposed for the acquisition of imaginal and verbal symbolic modes—passive perceptual exposure, classical conditioning, and operant conditioning. Until basic research provides a basis for choosing among these and other alternatives, we will find it useful to accept all three as working hypotheses.[1] We turn now to a discussion of the nature and development of imagery and verbal processes as functional symbolic systems. This will include a detailed consideration of three overlapping functional distinctions: (a) concrete versus abstract, (b) static versus dynamic, and (c) parallel versus sequential processing. Evidence on the developmental sequence of these proposed functions is most plentiful in relation to concreteness-abstractness and will be discussed primarily in that context.

CONCRETENESS-ABSTRACTNESS OF FUNCTIONING

The concept of concreteness-abstractness has been variously defined in psychological literature, and it will be helpful to begin by clarifying these definitions. Three classes of definitions sharing a common core of meaning can be identified. Most often the dimension is defined as a characteristic of stimuli, especially words. According to this usage, abstractness refers to the directness with which the stimulus denotes particular objects or events and is equated with specificity-generality of terms or subordination-superordination of conceptual categories (R. W. Brown, 1958). The "abstraction ladder" of the general semanticists (Hayakawa, 1949) expresses this kind of definition in terms of levels of abstraction, where higher levels involve increasing omission of reference to the characteristics of particular objects. An increasing order of abstraction is represented, for example, by the progression from the experienced object "cow" to the words *Bessie, cow, livestock, farm-assets, asset,* and *wealth,* in which references to particular attributes of "Bessie the cow" are increasingly omitted. This is the kind of definition that will be most commonly adopted here, although it will be seen in the discussion of meaning in Chapter 3 that abstractness-concreteness and generality-specificity are not necessarily equivalent when operationally defined in terms of subjects' responses, nor does linguistic abstractness-concreteness necessarily reflect an underlying psychological dimension in a one-to-one fashion.

The concept has also been used to refer to task characteristics, thereby im-

---

[1] To this list should be added E. J. Gibson's (1969) perceptual learning theory, which emphasizes an active discovery of distinctive features rather than the passive absorption of stimulus information implied by the perceptual exposure theory. Moreover, it differs from the motor and operant conditioning theories in its de-emphasis of external reinforcement in perceptual learning. Especially relevant in the present context is Gibson's proposal (pp. 150–153) that the discovery of distinctive features, achieved while looking for differences between objects, precedes and is perhaps necessary to the formation of adequate memory images.

plying stimulus-response relations with relatively more emphasis on the response side than is implied by the stimulus definition. Concrete tasks presumably involve characteristics demanding particular kinds of responses, whereas abstract tasks demand others. The definition of abstractness in this sense is more complex than the stimulus definition and is generally implicit except in studies of concept formation, where abstraction explicitly refers to the process of responding to (identifying) some common feature of a series of stimuli and ignoring the varying, irrelevant features. This use of the term essentially represents the dictionary definition of its verb form—to abstract is to "take from"—and is implicit also in the stimulus definition of abstractness. Thus the understanding of a general or superordinate concept requires the recognition only of the common features of the referents of more specific, subordinate terms. Or, in the case of abstractness at the level of pictorial representation, a line drawing is more abstract than a photograph in that the artist has included only essential features of the concrete situation represented in greater detail by a photograph.

Another way of viewing the task definition is that abstraction requires the manipulation of spatially and temporally remote events—not simply storing such events in memory, but manipulating the symbolic components (perhaps along with concrete aspects of the task that confronts the individual) in the interests of the demands of the situation. In these terms, the more abstract the task, the more it requires taking account of the dimensions of space and time beyond the here and now. This use of the term, too, can be related to the stimulus definition in that the more abstract the task, the more it involves reacting to something other than the immediate concrete situation. Thus we may generally define task abstractness in terms of the degree to which the successful completion of the task requires the manipulation and integration of stimulus information not immediately available to the senses. It can be seen that this definition includes those features of a task that have been used to investigate symbolic processes in lower animals as well as man, such as the delayed reaction situation and the temporal maze (W. S. Hunter, 1913; for a review of such studies and their significance, see Osgood, 1953).

A third approach defines concreteness-abstractness in terms of the psychological characteristics or reaction tendencies of the individual. The best-known example of this class of definition is that of Goldstein and Scheerer (1941), who distinguish between abstract and concrete attitudes particularly in reference to the symptoms of aphasia. In the extreme concrete attitude the person tends to react to the unique details of the concrete thing or situation as it is immediately given, as opposed to the abstract attitude in which the person is able to generalize and react on the basis of features that are not present in the situation but must be provided symbolically by the individual. The concrete attitude is diagnosed by tests that require the subject to match colors or patterns on the basis of the general category to which they belong (for example, to select from the Holmgren color yarns those strands that belong to a given color category such as red). Concreteness would be identified by a relative inability to pull together a sample of reds varying in hue, apparently because each is unique, slightly different from any other.

The Goldstein-Scheerer definition of the abstract attitude has been criticized for its ambiguity and lack of precision (e.g., R. W. Brown, 1958), but this is not the point here. What is relevant is that it illustrates a general approach in which the concept of abstractness is related to the psychological functioning of the individual, which is essential if the concept is to have any psychological significance. To be consistent with the stimulus and task definitions, the behavioral definition of abstractness must differentiate concrete and abstract in terms of response dimensions that correlate with independently defined stimulus or task characteristics. Once defined in terms of stimulus-response relations, abstractness-concreteness can be extended to refer to individual differences in dispositional characteristics—tendencies to respond more or less consistently in ways that are generally appropriate to concrete (or abstract) situations despite variations in the stimulus or task.

The major theme to be elaborated on in the following sections concerns the relationships between imaginal and verbal symbolic processes and the concrete-abstract dimension of stimulus attributes, task attributes, and psychological functioning. It will be argued that imagery develops as a symbolic capacity or mode of thought through the individual's perceptual-motor experiences with concrete objects and events, and remains particularly functional in dealing symbolically with the more concrete aspects of situations. Verbal processes develop through language experience, including associative experiences involving words and concrete objects, as in the act of reference, as well as through intraverbal associative experiences. Like imagery, verbal thought remains functional in coping with concrete situations but surpasses imagery in its capacity to deal with abstract tasks requiring the integration and manipulation of spatially and temporally remote objects or events, or tasks involving abstract reasoning. This is not to be taken as a rigid dichotomy of symbolic modes, for it will be suggested that imagery, too, may be abstract and schematic and that it apparently can serve abstract functions, although usually only in interaction with verbal processes.

Given the definitions of abstractness that were presented above, it is simply asserting a truism to say that modes of symbolic representation evolve within the individual from the more concrete to the more abstract. That is, the developing individual becomes increasingly able to deal with abstract symbols, problems that require taking account of or integrating information about temporally and spatially remote objects and events, and so on. Somewhat less obvious and of special interest here is the relationship between concreteness-abstractness of symbolic functioning and the nature and development of imaginal and verbal modes of representation. The problem has a long history, but we shall be concerned here with what has been said by psychologists who have made empirical as well as theoretical attempts to deal with aspects of the complex issue. In discussing the problem, I shall emphasize particularly the contributions of Bruner, Piaget, Werner, and Binet.

Bruner's Views on the Development of Abstract Modes of Representation

Bruner (1964; Bruner, Olver, & Greenfield, 1966) is most explicit in describing the sequential emergence of three modes of representation: enactive (or motor), ikonic (imagery), and symbolic (verbal). At first the child knows and copes with his world through habitual patterns of action—action schema that serve to guide action itself. According to Bruner, this system is limited because a schema is linked to particular acts that are temporally (serially) organized and under the immediate control of environmental stimuli. In this sense the enactive mode of representation is highly concrete. Gradually the schema becomes abstracted from a particular act and the second (ikonic) stage emerges, in which the child can represent the world to himself by an image or spatial schema that is relatively independent of action. It is a more abstract system than the enactive in that behavior can be organized in more flexible ways— anticipations, detours, and substitution to meet changed conditions are possible. The limitation of this system is that it is tied to the "surface of things"—relatively vivid sensory features of objects—rather than to more abstract, invariant features.

The limitations of the enactive and ikonic modes are assumed to be surmounted in symbolic representation, the third stage, which Bruner views as "protosymbolic activity that supports language and all other forms of symbolization" (Bruner et al., 1966, p. 31). Despite the reference to "other forms of symbolization," however, Bruner's discussion centers almost exclusively on language. The properties of language that he sees as suggesting the general properties of human symbolic functioning include such "design features" (Hockett, 1960) as semanticity, arbitrariness (the symbols do not resemble their referents), productivity (new utterances can be formed through grammatical rules), and displacement. All of these suggest the abstractness of the verbal symbolic system, but the last does so in particular, for it refers to the capacity of language to represent objects and events that are remote in space and time. In addition, linguistic signs have the properties of *category* and *hierarchy*—they refer to categories, not only specific instances, and the categories can be hierarchically organized—features of abstraction that were emphasized earlier in this chapter. These and other characteristics of symbolic functioning make for the greatest freedom in dealing effectively with abstract problems and concepts.

A comparison of the ikonic and symbolic modes of representation is most relevant for our purposes, and we shall briefly indicate the kind of experimental evidence that illustrates the functional distinctions proposed by Bruner and his collaborators (Bruner et al., 1966). One series of studies was concerned with the development of equivalence judgments from age six to nineteen. Object names and pictures were used as stimuli, and subjects were asked to state how different items are alike or different, or to group items that were alike in some way. Interest centered on changes in the features that are used as the basis for establishing equivalence. The results indicated that six-year-olds grouped more often according to perceptual attributes such as color, size, shape, and place of things, whereas older children grouped more often according to functional attributes or linguistically based superordinate features. The authors relate the findings to the growth of ikonic and symbolic modes of representation:

> Equivalence for the six-year-old reflects a basis in imagery, both in what he uses as a basis for groupings and in how he forms his groups. From age six on, linguistic structures increasingly guide what and how things will be judged alike. With the development of symbolic representation, the child is freed from dependence upon moment-to-moment variation in perceptual vividness and is able to keep the basis of equivalence invariant (p. 84).

Another experiment indicated that there is no difference between children of the ages five, six, and seven in their ability to replace objects taken from a matrix or to rebuild a scrambled matrix. However, with a single member transposed (e.g., an object formerly in the southwest corner put in the southeast corner), the seven-year-olds were able to construct the matrix, but hardly any of the youngest children could do so. The latter seemed to be dominated by a memory image of the original matrix. The older children are apparently freed from such ikonic dominance, presumably (according to Bruner) because of the more advanced level of development of their verbal symbolic capacities, which permits them to produce transformations guided by verbal rules. These findings illustrate the interaction of task abstractness and representational mode in that the more concrete tasks such as rebuilding the matrix, with which imagery presumably can be effective, were solved equally well by five-year-olds and by the older children. The more abstract transposition task, requiring symbolic spatial manipulation, was solved better by the more verbal, older children.

These examples will suffice to illustrate Bruner's views on the development and functions of modes of representation. We will have occasion to return to these views and the supporting evidence again in this and later chapters. Here we may note, in summary, certain features of the approach that are particularly relevant to subsequent discussions of the functions of the symbolic systems:

(1) Bruner regards language as the most specialized system of symbolic activity, although he recognizes also that images and motor activities can serve symbolic functions.

(2) He discusses the interaction of the systems, but the treatment sometimes leaves the impression of transition from one discrete stage to another rather than the growth of cognitive systems in which interaction or fusion might be the rule.

(3) Images tend to be treated as relatively concrete and static, without reference to the possibility that they may evolve into more abstract and dynamic forms.

(4) Imagery is viewed as a "rather sluggish mode of representation," whereas (verbal) symbolism is an "extraordinarily swift system" (p. 40).

As we shall see, others have differed in their theoretical orientations regarding these points, and the views that I will ultimately propose are also in fundamental disagreement with several aspects of Bruner's approach. This is not to say that the disagreements in any way diminish the value of his contribution to the understanding of these complex problems.

Piaget's Views on the Development of Functional Abstractness in Imagery

Piaget, like Bruner, views the development of symbolic capacities in terms of increasing abstractness of functioning in that the child's understanding of abstract concepts such as causality and time develops gradually. Furthermore, images and words are coordinated to concreteness-abstractness in the sense that images designate concrete objects in terms of their perceptual and figural properties, whereas words can signify concepts—relations, classes, numbers (Piaget & Inhelder, 1966, pp. 450–451). Piaget and Bruner differ, however, in their emphasis on certain characteristics of imagery. Whereas Bruner minimizes the symbolic nature of imagery (the "ikonic" or image stage being distinguished from the "symbolic," as we have noted above), Piaget has consistently emphasized their symbolic nature (Piaget, 1962; Piaget & Inhelder, 1966)—images are essential for representing and effectively thinking about concrete features of the perceptual world. Images and words thus complement each other in their distinct symbolic functions.

Piaget differs from Bruner also in his emphasis on development changes in imagery that make it increasingly functional in an abstract sense. The definitive statement of these views and the related empirical evidence have been presented recently by Piaget and Inhelder (1966). Imagery, as we have already noted, is defined as "internalized imitation," developing from imitative acts, including perceptual exploration (in which the contours of a perceived figure are followed). Images are therefore characterized by their motoricity. The authors emphasize the versatile nature of imagery, asserting that normal adults can imagine static objects, movements, known transformations (e.g., dividing a square into two equal triangles), or even anticipate in imagery novel transformations. At the outset they accordingly classify imagery into a major dichotomy between *reproductive* and *anticipatory* images, with the former further divided into static, moving (cinétique), and transformational reproductive images, and the latter into anticipatory images of movements and transformations. Their research program was directed specifically at providing evidence on the ontogenetic development of imagery with respect to these functional distinctions.

The experimental procedures were designed in such a manner as to require the subject to fulfill task requirements by the use of mental images. Thus the tests of simple reproductive imagery included estimations of the length of a metal rod by drawn reproductions, by a multiple-choice test, and by reproduction of the length with the fingers. The experimental manipulations included the presence or absence of the rod, imagined spatial displacements or rotations of the rods before the reproductions, and so on. The investigation of reproductive images of movement required subjects to imagine the outcome of a displacement, as when the upper member of two vertically adjacent squares is moved to the right or the left, or when a rod pivoted at one end is rotated in a manner corresponding to the movements of the hands of a watch or of one's arms. Reproductive images of transformation were studied by such methods as having the subject indicate the length that would result if an arc-shaped wire is straightened out, that is, when it had undergone a transformation of form.

All of the tasks concerned with reproductive images were intended to involve perceptual features that were more or less familiar to the subjects. The investigations of anticipatory imagery, on the other hand, were conducted using tasks in which the relevant elements were not familiar but required the subject to anticipate novel changes. Thus anticipatory images of transformation were studied using compound patterns that could be folded to yield a novel relationship among the elements. For example, two squares or triangles were joined at the folding axis in such a manner that turning one figure over onto the other resulted in a simple contiguity (e.g., two horizontally adjacent squares), an intersection, or a complete superposition of the two figures. The subject's task was to anticipate (e.g., by a drawing) the resulting transformation.

Other studies were concerned with spatial imagery and the correlation between mental images and operations as inferred from reactions to the typical Piaget-type problems of conservation. In the latter case, for example, subjects were asked to anticipate, presumably by imagined representations, the changes in the level of water when it is poured into jars of different shapes before the change is actually demonstrated.

A major general finding from this series of studies was that the hypothesized dichotomy between reproductive (especially static) images and anticipatory images was confirmed. The authors repeatedly emphasize the functional role of anticipatory imagery, not only in tasks involving anticipations, but in those involving reproductions of movements and transformations as well. Regarding developmental changes, the capacity for the static reproductive imagery was found in children much before the age of seven or eight, but anticipatory imagery, as reflected in the degree of success in the other tasks, became functional only after that age. Such imagery apparently develops along with concrete operations and may be dependent on it, as judged by the conservation tasks, where the ability to anticipate appeared after conservation at least in the case of tasks that Piaget and Inhelder regard as relatively novel for the child (on more familiar problems, such as conservation of liquid, anticipations preceded conservation).

The authors conclude that the evolution of imagery displays only two decisive stages and a single general division. The first stage is the appearance of imagery, marking the beginning of symbolic function, at the age of one and a half to two years. The second "decisive moment," emerging at seven to eight years, is the establishment of anticipatory images. These two major periods correspond to the preoperative stage (before seven–eight years) and to the operative stage, in terms of Piaget's developmental sequence. The imagery of the first of these two

periods remains essentially static and consequently inept in representing movements and transformations and all the more so in the anticipation of unfamiliar
processes. The capacity for anticipatory imagery permits the reconstruction of
dynamic processes and the foreseeing of new consequences. This developmental
change is dependent on the anticipation of execution or performance and is
possible only because the anticipatory imagery derives from imitative acts and
therefore consists of internalized imitation.

What is the import of this for our discussion of concrete and abstract symbolic
functions? The major point is that the ontogenetic evolution of imagery is associated with an increasing capacity for coping with tasks that by definition are
relatively abstract. The anticipation of transformations, for example, essentially
involves an ability to manipulate (mentally) the components of a stimulus
situation in order to conceptualize the not-here and not-now—clearly a highly
abstract function although carried out in the context of a concrete situation.
In this respect, Piaget and Inhelder attribute greater functional abstractness to
imagery than we interpreted Bruner to have done. It should be noted, however,
that there is a remarkable parallel in the ages marking the emergence of anticipatory images, in the case of Piaget, and the symbolic (linguistic) system, in the
case of Bruner. This can be interpreted to mean that the role of anticipatory
images might be given greater emphasis in Bruner's conceptualization of symbolic representation. On the other hand, Piaget and Inhelder gave little consideration to the possible contribution of language to the solution of the imagery
problems given to their subjects, although they obviously recognize such a role.
It is likely that both positions are correct, i.e., that developmental changes in
abstract functioning are accompanied by developmental changes in both the
verbal symbolic system and in imagery, and that the two systems interact in
some manner that remains to be understood.

Werner and Kaplan on the Development of
Abstract Symbolization

Werner and Kaplan (1963) discuss developmental changes relevant to
the present discussion in terms of progressive "distancing" between symbolic
vehicle and referential object. The authors apply the concept of distancing to
the external form (e.g., object and word) and the internal (cognitive) form of
both components. From a primitive level of functioning, in which inner and
external forms of both vehicle and referent are scarcely distinguished from each
other, there is an increased differentiation (distancing) as the individual develops, so that the object, external symbol, and inner representation become
increasingly distinct. This involves increased abstractness in the meaning of a
referent itself, as well as in the symbols and cognitive representations, and the
linkage between symbol and referent is carried through their inner form. Thus:

> As the inner form of the referent becomes more abstract so too must the inner
> form or inner dynamic schema constituting the symbolic vehicle. An abstract
> reference therefore requires a vehicle in which the inner form is not inti-

mately tied to the external form. . . . Indeed . . . the more "primitive" a [symbolic] medium, . . . the more difficult it is to employ the medium for the representation of relatively abstract concepts or abstract conceptual relations; the only way such a task can be meaningfully executed is by concretizing the referent (pp. 48–49).

The authors later describe research illustrating such concretizing of the time dimension through the nonverbal media of expressive lines and visual imagery. A study (p. 425 ff.) concerned with imagery is particularly interesting and relevant here because it illustrates one way in which imagery can serve abstract functions. Subjects under hypnosis were asked to transform a series of sentences into imagery. Later, when awake, they described their images. Each of four groups of four sentences contained the same verb, but the tenses varied. For example, one group included the sentences *He fights, He is fighting, He fought,* and *He will fight.* The subject's task was to represent, in his images, the agent ("he"), the action ("running," etc.) and the temporal locus of the agent's action. Six principal means for referring to temporality were identified: agent characteristics, agent state or posture, situational elements, phases of a natural event, spatial relation of the agent's action to the situational context, and qualities inherent in the medium. For example, *He fought* was represented variously by "an old man with a broken leg," a "soldier lying dead," etc.; *He will run* by "an empty track . . .," and so on. In general, the means of reference to time were intimately fused with the means for referring to action—about-to-begin-running, just-finished-fighting, thinking-all-the-time, etc. Furthermore, in most instances the image was relatively personal and idiosyncratic, in contrast with the communal (conventional) nature of language. Finally, it is particularly noteworthy that the subjects' descriptions indicate that the images serving the abstract functions are highly specific in their content. Comparable findings were obtained in a later study involving compound sentences expressing thought relations (see Chapter 13).

Concerning nonverbal media, Werner and Kaplan conclude that imaginal and linear representation are genetically early forms of symbolization, with imagery being the more primitive. The linear medium provides a more abstract medium (lines rather than concrete pictures). However, "it is only at levels of linguistic codification that one observes a progression towards the attainment of full-fledged means for the differential articulation of the various aspects of an event" (p. 438). Nevertheless, their observation that subjects can represent abstract dimensions such as time in visual imagery, however idiosyncratic or personal, is of considerable theoretical interest in relation to the functions that can be attributed to images.

Binet's Study of the Development of Abstract Images

That similar modifications in the characteristics of modes of representation occur in adults as a function of specific experience is suggested by a study of chess players by Binet (1966 translation). From his observations of blindfolded chess games and interviews with the players, Binet concluded that the blindfold game depends on the interaction of visual and verbal memory. The visual image is, however, more an "act of imagination" rather than of memory, constructed from verbal information supplied by the announcer of the game. Particularly significant is the observation that the imaginal representation of the chessboard decreases in clarity of detail as the player's experience increases. Binet divides players into three categories according to experience. The first group, "plain amateurs," tell Binet that they

> . . . imagine the chessboard exactly as if they were actually looking attentively at the board and the pieces. They retain a veritable mental photograph in which the board appears clearly with its black and white squares, and all the pieces are present in color and with their characteristic shapes. Some players . . . carry this individualization of the image to such an extreme as to visualize even the imperfections, the nicks and scratches of their own set (p. 156).

Binet notes, however, that many of these subjective accounts are exaggerated, that insignificant details are lacking in the image, which therefore represents a first degree of abstraction.

Abstraction becomes more important in Binet's second category of chessplayers. Their representation of the chessboard is still visual but the image is unclear, impressionistic, and simplified. This shift toward abstractness of imagery proceeds further in the case of the third category, whose visual images "are stripped of all material and concrete baggage" (p. 158). All color disappears and the chessmen are distinguished simply as friend or foe. Concrete details are unimportant but the geometry of the situation—the direction of movement of a piece and the number of the square where it must stop—is retained. These players utilize visual memory, but "it lacks . . . concrete, pictorial quality. Though visual, it is an abstract kind of memory . . . a geometrical memory" (p. 160). Occasional players carry the abstraction still further, apparently proceeding with little or no reportable imagery. Thus, "the experienced player leaves the concrete visual image of the chessboard to the mere amateur; to put it mildly, such a view is useless and naive. In general, the good player depends surely on abstract memory" (p. 161).

Although not derived from controlled experiments, the preceding evidence is remarkable. It is based on astute observations of numerous chess games and interviews with many players of varying levels of proficiency, whose reports, Binet notes, are in fundamental agreement with each other. The evidence goes beyond casual anecdote in suggesting that imagery evolves toward more abstract, simple, and schematic forms as a function of repeated experience with a particular task. The differential experience is reflected in individual differences in the reliance on and concreteness of the imagery.

The changes described by Binet appear to demonstrate schematization of memory based upon repeated experience with a particular task. Such schematic or generic images have long been assumed to be part of man's symbolic repertoire and their nature and function received detailed treatment in the early literature on thinking (see Humphrey, 1951, Chapter 9). Recently Hebb (1968) has argued for the plausibility of such images, and proposed a speculative theoretical model in terms of hierarchies of cell assemblies representing the physiological substrate of levels of abstraction. A related idea is the concept of schema as used in the sense of a representation for a class of objects or a generalized situation (Woodworth, 1938), as distinguished from Bartlett's (1932) more general use of the term. Such memory schemata have been described and investigated as representations that encode redundant aspects of the environment, making for economical information storage (e.g., Attneave, 1954, 1957; Edmonds & Evans, 1966; Oldfield, 1954). Although the form of the abstract representation remains uncertain, recent experimental evidence indicates that the schematic information can be abstracted very efficiently from instances stored in memory (Posner & Keele, 1968). The "generic image" may be one manifestation of such schema in conscious thought. Abstractness of imagery in this sense is to be distinguished, of course, from the idea that specific images can have an abstract function, as suggested in Werner and Kaplan's discussion of the concretization of abstract concepts.

Concreteness-Abstractness of Verbal Processes

The ontogenetic development of symbolic processes from concrete to abstract has been discussed so far in terms of a shift from imaginal to verbal modes of representation, and of imagery from relatively static and concrete to more flexible, creative, and schematic forms. A comparable genesis of verbal symbolic processes can be inferred from the evidence that language progresses in the direction of greater abstractness as the child develops. R. W. Brown (1957), for example, compared adult and child vocabularies and found that the nouns used by children are more likely to be concrete and "picturable" than are the nouns used by adults. Such a developmental sequence is, in fact logically inevitable since the learning of abstract words depends on the prior acquisition of "object-words," which Russell has defined, "logically, as words having meaning in isolation, and, psychologically, as words which have been learnt without its being necessary to have previously learnt any other words" (1940, p. 65). The evolution from concrete to abstract has been postulated not only in relation to the psychological but to the historical progression of language as well (see R. W. Brown, 1958; Werner & Kaplan, 1963). Of course, such statements gloss over many complexities. It is recognized, for example, that language development within the individual is not simply a unidirectional progression toward greater abstractness, for descriptive language also becomes increasingly differentiated and specific as the child develops. From the word *dog,* he moves to a mastery of labels for different types of dogs as well as an understanding of the concept *mammal.* Thus verbal processes apparently become increasingly efficient both as a descriptive system for concrete objects and events and as a means of expressing abstract ideas.

It can be concluded that modes of representation generally evolve toward more abstract and flexible forms—from concrete to more abstract imagery, overlapping with the emergence of verbal symbolic processes, which in turn become more abstract (as well as more differentiated and precise). This is not to suggest that one symbolic mode is *replaced* by another, although this has sometimes been implied, as we shall see later. Instead, it may be assumed that new modes are added to the symbolic repertoire of the individual and that their utilization is a function of situational demands, just as their original development presumably occurred in the interests of utility. Furthermore, it is likely that the modes continually interact in their functioning. These points are aptly summarized by Reitman (1965) as follows:

> Human information processing . . . may be taken as basically perceptual, with words and language operating upon the basic perceptual system. We describe the world and react to verbal descriptions by calling up, constructing, and manipulating percepts. Anyone who has watched pre-verbal children cope with their environment has evidence of the power and effectiveness of these nonverbal information-processing capabilities. Whether or not some people process information without a perceptual component (employing, if you like, imageless thought), it is likely that a great deal of human thinking makes use of perceptually coded cognitive elements and processes for manipulating them, even in cases involving what we usually think of as abstract concepts. . . . The acquisition of language, in other words, ought not to be thought of as abolishing the underlying perceptual system which . . . evidently continues to guide judgments, decisions, and behavior and otherwise to serve as an operating substrate for thought (pp. 250–251).

We are far from having more than an elementary understanding of the nature and development of such interacting symbolic systems, although the studies described above represent important advances in that direction and guide the theoretical speculations that are necessary.

To summarize the concrete-abstract functional distinction, the developmental studies inspired by Piaget, Bruner, and Werner all involved the assumption that images are specialized for the representation of concrete objects and events, whereas inner speech is functionally useful in dealing with abstract problems, concepts, and relationships. Some of the evidence discussed above supports the theoretical distinction in a relative sense and it will be retained as a working hypothesis in subsequent chapters dealing with problems of meaning, association, and memory. That this cannot be a rigid functional distinction is indicated on the one hand by the apparent development of relatively abstract (schematic) images and concretization of abstract ideas in the form of specific images, and on the other hand by the fact that words can represent concrete objects and events in addition to describing relationships and abstract ideas. Despite the overlapping functions, however, images can represent concrete perceptual features of situations in a way that cannot be accomplished by means of words, as evidenced by such examples as counting from memory the number of windows in one's house (Shepard, 1966). Conversely, images are of little or no functional significance in dealing with highly abstract concepts, although they may play a heuristic part in some instances, as Reitman's discussion suggests.

STATIC VERSUS DYNAMIC FUNCTIONS

A number of major theorists from William James to the present have distinguished between representational processes that have a static function and processes that fulfil the dynamic function of transitions from one specific thought to another. A clear statement of such a distinction and a review of the analogous views of other writers is presented by Berlyne (1965), who distinguished between *situational* and *transformational* thoughts. Situational thoughts represent stages in ongoing problem solving behavior or thought, whereas transformational thoughts refer to processes that effect a transition between the represented situations. The former, it may be noted, could represent intermediate stages in a sequence of thoughts leading to some ultimate (symbolic or real) goal, or they could represent the ultimate goal itself, the attainment of which terminates a particular symbolic or overt response sequence. In both instances, the situational thoughts will be seen as serving as "sign-posts" which guide the symbolic processes or give thinking the direction that Berlyne particularly emphasizes. In the case of the representation of a goal, the motivational function of the symbolic process and the relation of the present distinction to such classical theoretical concepts as primary process thinking, expectations, fractional anticipatory goal responses, and the like, becomes apparent. The discussion thus deals with problems of rather general theoretical significance, although the present aim is to provide a framework within which the specific problems of verbal learning, memory, and language will later be conceptualized.

Like so many of the seminal ideas in contemporary psychology, this one was anticipated by William James (1890), specifically in his chapter on the stream of thought. The relevant distinction is between the "substantive part" and the "transitive part" of the stream as developed in the following passage, which is concerned with the moment-to-moment alterations in the rate of change in ongoing thought:

> This difference in the rate of change lies at the basis of a difference of subjective states of which we ought immediately to speak. When the rate is slow we are aware of the object of our thought in a comparatively restful and stable way. When rapid, we are aware of a passage, a relation, a transition *from* it, or *between* it and something else. As we take, in fact, a general view of the wonderful stream of our consciousness, what strikes us first is this different pace of its parts. Like a bird's life, it seems to be made of an alternation of flights and perchings. The rhythm of language expresses this, where

every thought is expressed in a sentence, and every sentence closed by a period. The resting-places are usually occupied by sensorial imaginations of some sort, whose peculiarity is that they can be held before the mind for an indefinite time, and contemplated without changing; the places of flight are filled with thought of relations, static or dynamic, that for the most part obtain between the matters contemplated in the periods of comparative rest.

Let us call the resting-places the "substantive parts," and the places of flight the "transitive parts," of the stream of thought. It then appears that the main end of our thinking is at all times the attainment of some other substantive part than the one from which we have just been dislodged. And we may say that the main use of the transitive parts is to lead us from one substantive conclusion to another (Vol. I, p. 243).

The static-dynamic conceptual distinction appears in various forms in more recent psychological theories. The properties of the "life space" as developed by Lewin (e.g., see Cartwright, 1959) included situational cognitive states, conceptualized as psychological regions and goals. Transformational processes, on the other hand, are implicit in the concept of locomotion, which refers to symbolic movement, as when the symbolized person changes regions within the life space.

The distinction appears also in the final version of Tolman's "purposive behaviorism." In the original form of his theory (see MacCorquodale & Meehl, 1954) the S-S unit, or expectancy, explicitly included situational components and implied a transformational construct. Thus expectancy was defined as a cognitive event having relational properties: when one pattern of stimulation ("sign") is followed by another ("significate"), a relation develops between them "cognitively, centrally, perceptually," which is the knowledge that behaving in a certain way to the sign will eventuate in the significate. Sign and significate, the static components of the cognitive construct, were specified, but the behavioral (transformational) component was left implicit. MacCorquodale and Meehl's (1954) suggested formalization of the theory and Tolman's (1959) final statement of it explicitly introduced transformational processes into the cognitive construct. The S-S unit was extended to include an intermediary (implicit) response between the sign and significate. Thus the construct became $S_1R_1S_2$—the S_1 component referring to the elicitor, R_1 the reaction class, and S_2 the expectandum (or significate). In their principle of mnemonization, MacCorquodale and Meehl suggest what role experience plays in the development of the central process: it develops not only as a result of perceptual experience with objects in the environment but also as a result of responding in relation to those objects. Their emphasis on the role of contiguous perceptual and motor experience in the development of an expectancy, and the implicit motor component in the definition of the construct itself, are remarkably similar to the way imagery specifically has been conceptualized by Piaget and Inhelder (1966), Skinner (1953), and Hebb (1968).

The parallel can be seen particularly in the case of Piaget and Inhelder (1966). As noted earlier, the major developmental change in imagery that they emphasized was that between static images and images of movement and trans-formation. They noted that imagery prior to the ages of seven or eight years is characterized by a static quality where movement is represented only by imagi-nation of successive stages of the act; later, imagery is more flexible, capable of representing movements and transformations, and characterized especially by its anticipatory quality. The earlier imagery may be based on passive percep-tion, but the later imagery is founded on imitative acts and can be conceptualized as internalized imitation. Such imagery is perceptual in the sense that percep-tion itself involves an act of imitation, as when eye movements trace the con-tours of a figure. The important feature of this analysis is that the more mature imagery incorporates *the implicit motor components of imitative acts in its capacity to symbolize movements and transformations.* Anticipatory imagery is possible only because it contains within it the anticipation of execution, or performance. So conceptualized, anticipatory imagery appears to be quite analogous to Tolman's expectancy construct with the response component included.

A comparable emphasis on implicit motor components in imagery, expressed in behavioristic terms, occurs in Skinner's (1953) treatment of "private seeing" as an aid to "private problem solving." The symbolic processes involved in the following example include highly active visual imagery, implicit manipulation of the imaged object, and implicit verbal responding to it.

> In the following problem . . . behavior is usually facilitated by private seeing. "Think of a cube, all six surfaces of which are painted red. Divide the cube into twenty-seven equal cubes by making two horizontal cuts and two sets of two vertical cuts each. How many of the resulting cubes will have three faces painted red, how many two, how many one, and how many none?" It is possible to solve this without seeing the cubes in any sense—as by saying to oneself, "A cube has eight corners. A corner is defined as the intersection of three faces of the cube. There will therefore be eight pieces with three painted faces. . . ." And so on. But the solution is easier if one can actually see the twenty-seven small cubes and count those of each kind. This is easiest in the presence of actual cubes, of course, and even a sketchy drawing will provide useful support; but many people solve the problem visually without visual stimulation.
>
> Private problem-solving usually consists of a mixture of discriminative and manipulative responses. In this example one may *see* the larger cube, *cut* it covertly, *separate* the smaller cubes covertly, *see* their faces, *count* them sub-vocally, and so on. In mental arithmetic one multiplies, divides, transposes, and so on, seeing the result in each case, until a solution is reached. Pre-sumably much of this covert behavior is similar in form to the overt manipu-lation of pencil and paper; the rest is discriminative behavior in the form of seeing numbers, letters, signs, and so on, which is similar to the behavior which would result from overt manipulation (p. 273).

Both Piaget's and Skinner's approaches to imagery are highly reminiscent of views expressed earlier by the proponents of the motor theory of thought (see, for example, Humphrey, 1951; McGuigan, 1966). The difference appears to be that neither Piaget nor Skinner insist that the "internalized imitation" or "private seeing" need be manifested in peripheral motor reactions. The same is true of Hebb's (1949) informal statements, noted earlier, concerning the role of eye movements in the generation of images. His observation was that eye movements (or imagined movements) *facilitate* the formation of a clear image of a pattern such as a triangle, not that they are completely necessary for it. Evidence on these points is provided by eye-movement records, which have been found to correlate with the direction of reported activity in dreams (Dement, 1965) as well as during waking imagery (Antrobus, Antrobus, & Singer, 1964). However, Singer (1966) also reports an absence of eye movements during day-dreamlike thought, much as Perky (1910) had found for images of imagination. Thus explicit movements are sometimes appropriately associated with imagery and sometimes not, posing an interesting problem concerning the precise function of motor responses during thought, which will be considered further in a later context. What is relevant here is the conclusion that a motor component (implicit or explicit) appears to be generally characteristic of images of movement, and of the transformations involved in the generation of an integrated figural image or the solution of more complex problems requiring visual thinking. The motor component somehow facilitates the transition from one substantive part of the stream of thought to another.

Thus far we have considered only the properties of imagery in relation to static and dynamic functioning. What are the capacities and relevant characteristics of verbal processes in this regard? It is possible to analyze the function of language in a fashion paralleling the analysis of imagery. Concrete nouns and noun phrases, like static images, fulfill a representational function—they symbolize objects and situations. Action verbs or verb phrases effect transitions in the stream of thought by virtue of their capacity to represent movement and change. The latter, like images of action, have a "motor" component, but in the case of words that component is entirely semantic, emerging, for example, as an activity dimension in factor analytic studies of meaning (Osgood, Suci, & Tannenbaum, 1957). This static-dynamic distinction in verbal processes has validity in the obvious and rather trivial sense that it refers to conventional distinctions in form class and grammar. Whether it has *psychological* significance in relation to problems of learning and memory is the important question—one that will be considered in due course (see especially Chapter 11)—but a possible theoretical limitation must also be faced.

Berlyne (1965), who accepts the usefulness of words as situational (that is, labeling) responses, rather surprisingly argues that verbal processes are deficient in their capacity to represent transformations. This follows specifically from his interpretation of transformational thoughts as derivatives of overt responses that have been effective in producing environmental change. Words cannot do this except through social mediation, that is, by influencing the behavior of other individuals. Berlyne cites no direct evidence for such a functional limitation in verbal patterns of thought and, on the face of it, the contention does not seem reasonable, especially since he adopts the view that images can represent transformations. Why should images be attributed with such a capacity and verbal processes not? The answer apparently lies in the motor components that are assumed by Berlyne to be part of the derivational history of images for essentially the same reasons that have been discussed here. Nevertheless, his arguments are not sufficient justification for attributing a transformational limitation to verbal processes, for images as symbolic processes include at most a motor *component*. Such covert responses may originally have been effective overt responses that produced changes in the stimulus field, but the perceptual experiences that must have accompanied the responses, and from which the images must partly derive, could have had no such effect in a direct sense. Verbal responses (and verbal thoughts) can, and obviously do, accompany motor responses that effect environmental change, and the two may become associatively linked through such experience just as sensory images and their motor components are assumed to do. There appears to be no logical reason for assuming that these components are differentially effective in later transformational thinking when the accompanying (active) symbolic system is verbal than when it is perceptual (i.e., imaginal). The motor component may somehow be more *intrinsic* to images of movement and transformation than to verbal symbolizations of action, but it is difficult to see how this in itself would make the former a more effective vehicle of thought.

In a sense Berlyne's view of the relative efficacy of images and words seems directly contrary to Bruner's assertion, noted earlier in this chapter, that imagery is a sluggish mode of representation because of its "lag and slow transformability" (Bruner et al., 1966, p. 40), whereas verbal symbolism is an "extraordinarily swift system." Assuming that the statement applies to the dynamic, active, function of the symbolic modes as it is being discussed here, I must reject Bruner's contention and agree partly with Berlyne. Images appear to be effective modes of representing static situations as well as changes in situations. Indeed, subjective reports of their role in creative thinking (surely the ultimate in transformation thought) suggest that imagery is the very basis of swift creative leaps of imagination (Rugg, 1963). We will later have occasion to see the relevance of this viewpoint for the conceptualization of associative learning as well.

With respect to verbal processes, on the other hand, my position is a compromise between Bruner's and Berlyne's. I assume that the verbal system can serve both a static, or representational, function and the dynamic function involved in transformational or transitive phases of the stream of thought. However, neither images nor words ordinarily act as independent processes but interact continually in both functions. A static situation may be identified (labeled) verbally and then transformed into imagery in order to facilitate concrete symbolic manipulation of the elements of the situation; a concrete situation may be given nonverbally, perceptually, and new (potential) relations among the elements may be conceived verbally, and so on. Which mode will be functionally dominant in a given situation will depend on the nature and demands of the situation. One of the important determining characteristics, already considered, is the abstractness-concreteness of the situation or task: Imagery is particularly functional when the task is relatively concrete, and verbal processes become increasingly necessary for both the "flights" and the "perchings" of the stream of thought as the task is more abstract. These functional differences are presumably related to the differential availability of images and verbal processes in abstract task situations (see Chapter 3).

Another important determinant of the "preferred" mode is whether the task is a sequential one as opposed to one in which the elements are simultaneously given or in which the elements can at least be dealt with independently of each other. This leads to a consideration of the symbolic modes in terms of their relative efficacy as parallel and sequential processing systems—a distinction closely related, as we shall see, to the static-dynamic one just considered.

PARALLEL VERSUS SEQUENTIAL PROCESSING

Visual perception is characterized by its spatial properties. The receptors and higher neural elements of the visual system are spatially organized, capable of receiving, transmitting, and processing information simultaneously given in a spatial array. Stated another way, the functional elements of the system are spatially parallel and it is accordingly viewed as a *parallel processing* system. To the extent that visual imagery is analogous to visual perception, it can be similarly regarded as a symbolic system specialized for parallel processing of information. It involves what Susanne Langer (1942) termed presentational or *nondiscursive symbolism*.

Auditory perception, on the other hand, is a system specialized for dealing with temporally (serially) organized stimulus patterns. To the extent that the verbal symbolic system is linked to the auditory sensory modality, it must therefore be characterized as a sequential processing system. This is most obvious when we are dealing with auditory speech input. However, the verbal system is also sequentially organized as a symbolic system by virtue of its syntactical nature: the grammar of a language involves a temporal ordering of its elements. Thus, ". . . all language has a form which requires us to string out our ideas even though their objects rest one within the other; as pieces of clothing that are actually worn one over the other have to be strung side by side on the clothesline. This property of verbal symbolism is known as *discursiveness* . . ." (Langer, 1948 reprint, pp. 65–66). There is, of course, flexibility in the sequential ordering to the extent that different grammatical transformations can be used for saying the same thing, but within any acceptable alternative, the information conveyed (the meaning of the pattern) depends on what came before and what is yet to come in the sequence. The difference in meaning between "The boy hit the girl" and "The girl hit the boy" results from a different ordering of the words. In this fundamental sense, the verbal symbolic system must be viewed as a sequential processing system.

The above distinction between visual and verbal system is generally recognized and we can accept it as valid up to a point but in need of qualification. Neisser (1967) distinguishes between systems that are spatially parallel and ones that are operationally parallel. The former is characteristic of the visual system specifically, as already discussed, in that simultaneously given information can be processed over a broad area of the retina, and Neisser gives other illustrations in connection with pattern recognition systems generally. An array of tuning forks, for example, operates as a parallel recognition system for frequency in that a tone sounded near the array is accessible to the array and in a sense "compared with" the whole array at once, but causes vibration only in the fork with a similar resonating frequency. The other sense of the principle of parallel processing is the functioning of systems that are operationally parallel—items of information can be processed or operations carried out independently of one another. The defining property of such a system is not simultaneity of functioning, as in the case of spatially parallel systems, but rather that the functioning of any element in the system does not depend on the outcome of the functioning of another. They may function serially, one at a time, but independently.

Neisser also distinguishes between serial and sequential processing. An activity can be spatially serial, as in the case of reading letters from a tachistoscopic display from left to right or vice versa. The term sequential processing, however, refers to the manner in which a process is organized—it is sequential when the successive steps involved in its functioning are interdependent, the outcome at one point determining the next step in the sequence.

Neisser's analysis helps to clarify the functional properties of imaginal and verbal symbolic systems. Visual imagery can now be interpreted as a parallel processing system in both the spatial and the operational sense, with a potential capacity for serial processing by virtue of the dynamic properties discussed in the preceding section. These characteristics can be informally demonstrated by an observation that, as far as I have been able to determine, anyone can easily verify. Consider the following task: Form an image of an upper-case block letter such as $\mathbb{E}$, and from the image, count the angles or corners beginning, say, at the upper right-hand corner of the middle bar, moving counterclockwise. I find that I am able to do this easily and accurately beginning at any point, moving in either direction. I have presented others with the task and they find it equally easy, with any letter of the alphabet.

A number of points should be noted. The most obvious one is that the task involves parallel processing in the spatial sense. But it is operationally parallel as well, in that one can begin the counting at any part of the imagined outline and move in either direction—there is independence at least with respect to the starting point and direction of the mental operation. The independence is limited, however, in that maximal efficiency is obtained only if one moves around the figure systematically, imposing serial processing on a spatial pattern. This is not a limitation on the *scanning* of the imagined figure; one can move about the figure freely from any corner to another, indicating complete operational independence with respect to the elements of the implicit perceptual task. Doing so in the case of the counting operation, however, imposes an additional load on memory in that it is difficult to keep track of what corners have and have not been counted. Serial processing minimizes the memory load in that it is necessary only to remember where on the imagined figure the counting was begun. Beyond this, the counting operation itself (as distinct from the imaging) involves sequential processing, for the elements of the numerical series are interdependent.

Let us compare this example with one used by Hebb (1966, 1968) to illustrate the serial properties of imaging. The task is to form a visual image of a moderately long word, such as *university,* and from the image read off the letters, first in one direction, then the other. The speed of the operation is typically much faster in the left to right direction than in the reverse. This is not a limitation on perceptual scanning, Hebb argues, since the speed of reading off the letters from the printed word itself is almost as efficient in either direction. Hebb interprets this evidence to mean that a mental image cannot be considered analogous to a photographic image. Instead, it involves a process with a directional component corresponding to the direction of the perceptual and motor experiences originally involved in a task, in this instance reading and spelling. Given an equal amount of experience in the right-to-left direction, the imagery task presumably would be equally easy in either direction. While not readily apparent from the task of reading off the letters from a printed word, the directional limitation does appear to be characteristic of perception, as indicated by tachistoscopic recognition studies involving stimulus arrays presented across the fixation point. The findings from such studies seem interpretable, at least partly, in terms of reading habits (see the discussion by Hebb, 1966). The problem is complex, however, and will receive more attention in Chapter 4.

The present view is in agreement with some aspects of Hebb's analysis of imagery and in disagreement with others. Considering the task of counting the corners of an imagined block letter in terms of Hebb's analysis, one could argue that the original perception of actual block letters involves parallel processing in that eye fixations jump around from point to point more or less at random, rather than in a particular direction sequentially. Accordingly, parallel processing of the image is also possible. The difference between Hebb's treatment and mine is in the emphasis here on a separate sequential processing system. In Hebb's analysis, imagery could be said to carry a *directional tag* derived from the original perceptual activity on which it is based. (A general model of sequential memory incorporating such a feature has been proposed recently by Bryden, 1967). Serial ordering in this sense is an intrinsic part of the imagery process itself. In addition, however, I assume that serial or sequential processing can be *superimposed* on the imagery. This seems to be the case in the corner counting example, where the numerical component of the task is sequentially organized but the scanning process otherwise is not. The task of reading off the letters from a word image similarly requires sequential processing because it incorporates a sequentially organized verbal system to such a degree that nonsequential scanning is difficult. Indeed, it is possible that, instead of first generating a word image and then reading off the letters, one must first say the letters to oneself in order to generate the image (see further below). The greater difficulty of processing the image from right to left could thus be explained in terms of the greater difficulty of spelling words backward, rather than any directional bias in the visual image per se.

Turning now specifically to the verbal symbolic system, we find that it involves parallel as well as sequential processing features. It is not spatially parallel, since it is functionally linked to the auditory-motor system, but it is operationally parallel with respect to its lexical features: Words appear to be *relatively* independent in their availability as units. So, too, are phrases and sentences as integrated grammatical units. It is sequentially organized with respect to the phonetic components (e.g., syllables) of its word units and, as already noted, the arrangement of words within the grammatical units. Taken together, these features result in the hierarchical structure so characteristic of language (see G. A. Miller, Galanter, & Pribram, 1960); it is comprised of units within higher-order units. In a sense, there is considerable freedom of choice or independence of the units at any level—one is free to say what one wants and there are many different ways of saying it. But at any level of the organizational structure, the *meaning* of what is said is largely determined by the sequential arrangement of the units. Thus the verbal system as a whole functions always *both* as an operationally parallel and as a sequential processing mechanism, although the two functional characteristics can be separated experimentally for analytic purposes.

The postulated superiority of the verbal system for the processing of sequential information is illustrated rather directly by the results of recent experiments on serial processing in visual and speech imagery by Weber and his associates (Weber & Bach, 1969; Weber & Castleman, 1970). These investigators required their subjects to run through the alphabet mentally, either by speaking the letters silently (speech imagery) or by visualizing them appearing one at a time, as on a movie screen (visual imagery). They found that processing time was much faster for speech imagery (about six letters per second) than for visual imagery (about two letters per second). They concluded that the two imagery modes differ fundamentally in the manner in which they process information. The present analysis specifies the essential difference: The speech system is specialized for processing of verbal sequences such as the alphabet, the visual-image system is not. Indeed, it may be more accurate to say that the alphabet *is* a self-contained sequential unit stored in the speech system in such a manner that each letter name readily arouses the name of the next letter in the sequence. The letters are visual entities that can be generated sequentially only under the control of the sequentially-organized speech system. In other words, the letters must first be named implicitly before the images can be generated in correct sequence. Weber and Castleman (1970) recognized the latter possibility, but concluded that this could not account entirely for the difference in processing rates, since estimated visual imagery remained slower than verbal imagery even when the time for the latter was subtracted out as a component of visual imagery time. However, they overlooked the possibility that it may take more time to generate an image to a letter name than it does to name the next letter in the verbal sequence. The former involves an associative relationship between symbolic systems, the latter, between the organized components within one symbolic system. Such distinctions will be discussed fully in the context of a theory of meaning to be presented in the next chapter.

To summarize the proposed functional distinction for both imagery and verbal processes, imagery is basically a parallel processing system in both the spatial and the operational sense. It is capable of sequential processing as well if a response sequence is intrinsic to the imagery (e.g., imagining oneself walking down a familiar road or street, passing familiar buildings and other "signposts" in their natural sequence), or if its elements are linked to sequential operations involving the verbal system (e.g., counting corners of an imaged letter). The verbal system, on the other hand, functions in an operationally parallel manner as well as sequentially. Imaginal and verbal systems thus overlap fully in regard to the capacity for operationally parallel functioning; they are differentiated with respect to spatial processing, which is characteristic only of imagery, and sequential processing, which is relatively more characteristic of the verbal system. These theoretical distinctions have important implications for the analysis of the symbolic systems in relation to perception, memory, and language, as will be seen in subsequent chapters.

OVERLAP OF THE THREE FUNCTIONAL DISTINCTIONS

The distinction between imaginal and verbal processes in terms of parallel and sequential functioning overlaps with both the concrete-abstract and the static-dynamic distinction considered earlier. The spatial characteristics of imagery reflect its likeness to visual perception of concrete objects and events. That imagery is a parallel processing symbolic system in the spatial sense is therefore tantamount to saying that it is specialized for dealing with concrete tasks. The verbal system, on the other hand, is at once sequential and abstract in the case of its capacity to represent numerical order. Such instances of functional overlap do not make the distinctions identical, however; the verbal system is *semantically abstract* in the case of verbal units that represent the concepts *truth, time, goodness,* and so on, yet *operationally parallel* in that the abstract words can be used independently of one another. Conversely, concrete terms must be processed sequentially when their combined meaning depends on a grammatical context, as when one is verbally describing a concrete situation. Again, spatially parallel visual imagery can contribute to the solution of abstract problems as well as concrete ones, or represent abstract concepts (albeit idiosyncratically), as indicated by examples given in the section on the abstract-concrete functional distinction.

These considerations serve to make the general point that the functional distinctions are themselves conceptually distinct, although they overlap within the two symbolic systems. The relations among the functions vis-à-vis the two symbolic systems can be informally summarized as follows: imagery is relatively better than the verbal system for representing and coping with the concrete aspects of a situation, with transformations, and with parallel processing in the spatial sense. The verbal system is superior in abstract and sequential processing tasks.

Interaction of the symbolic modes and functions   Obviously the symbolic systems normally do not function independently of each other, nor in one capacity only. They must be assumed to interact continually in any but the simplest of tasks. Situations may be represented imaginally, but their elements organized verbally; verbal stimuli may arouse associative verbal responses from storage systems that appear to be organized either in parallel or sequentially, as suggested by the distinction between paradigmatic (substitutive) and syntagmatic (sequential) processes in language (Jakobson & Halle, 1956), but words may also arouse nonverbal images of static objects as well as of action and transformation; and so on.

One important hypothesis concerning the interaction of the processes is that images are particularly effective in promoting rapid associations while verbal processes give them direction. Something of this kind has been suggested, for example, by Rugg in connection with the requisites of the creative act, which are said to include "a well-filled storehouse of imagery to guarantee richness and freedom of association, and of ordered key concepts to guarantee organization of thought" (1963, p. 311). Imagery is characteristic of autistic thinking in general and in that context is free of logical restraints; verbal processes superimposed on such imagery presumably contribute order and direction. These hypothesized, mutually supportive functions of images and words can be viewed as a consequence of the relative weighting of parallel processing and sequential processing features in the two systems: Imagery, having both spatially and operationally parallel properties, is likely to be characterized by freedom and speed of association, whereas the sequentially organized verbal system is capable of providing organization to the associative process.

These general theoretical views will be expressed in the form of more specific hypotheses, and their empirical implications explored throughout the remainder of the book.

3
Meaning and the Symbolic Processes

This chapter presents a systematic approach to the persistent and controversial problem of meaning. The problem is central to our concern with imaginal and verbal symbolic processes because these are inferentially linked to semantic attributes of nonverbal and verbal stimuli and responses. The problem involves empirical and theoretical considerations. Empirically, stimulus attributes constitute one class of defining operation by means of which imaginal and verbal processes might be differentiated. Theoretically, specification of the inferred relations between the stimulus attributes and the symbolic processes is an essential step toward a more general understanding of the functional significance of the latter. In effect, the operational-theoretical aspects of the approach to meaning are involved, sometimes along with other operations and theoretical assumptions, in the prediction of perception, learning, memory, and language. Accordingly, the present discussion of meaning will be restricted mainly to issues that are directly relevant to these later concerns, although in the course of the discussion we will touch on problems of more general significance.

The problem of meaning is not only relevant to subsequent topics, but inevitably overlaps with them. The inseparability of meaning from other substantive areas in psychology has been emphasized by others. Osgood (1953), for example, concludes that meaning and perception together "occupy the no man's land of central mediation" (p. 195); F. H. Allport (1955) notes that meaning runs through nearly all psychological processes, giving them a common aspect and a kind of unity. This pervasiveness of meaning implies that it somehow has priority, requiring consideration before other phenomena can be adequately discussed. On the other hand, meaning itself depends upon the other processes. This can be clearly seen in the relation between memory and meaning. Whatever its other defining characteristics, meaning implies at the very least that there is information in memory storage that contributes to a sense of familiarity when one is presented with a "meaningful" stimulus. Memory processes are more fundamental, therefore, than meaning. Nevertheless, meaning is given priority here as a topic of discussion because it enters into the prediction of the particular phenomena that are the main concern of this book. Any overlap in the consideration of basic processes that cut across the different areas will serve only to emphasize their interdependence as psychological phenomena.

The chapter is divided into three major sections. The first deals with the traditional psychological approaches to meaning, thereby placing the present approach in the proper historical context. This is followed by a discussion of the two-process theory of meaning to be adopted here. Finally, specific indices will be proposed for the operational definition and measurement of the various theoretical dimensions of meaning.

TRADITIONAL APPROACHES TO THE PSYCHOLOGY OF MEANING

The psychological literature on the problem has been concerned almost exclusively with the meaning of verbal material (e.g., see the review by Creelman, 1966). That nonverbal signs and objects themselves have meaning has been recognized but for some reason their explicit and systematic consideration in relation to problems of meaning has been generally neglected. F. H. Allport's (1955) treatment is a notable exception. He defines meaning as "the process by which one perceives the concrete character of objects and situations" (p. 531) and orients his discussion of the "unsolved problem" of meaning around that definition. He states (p. 573) that, if we are to discover the true nature of meaning, we should address ourselves to the basic problem of the meaning of objects rather than word signs. Word signs constitute a separate meaning problem—their meaning is wholly contingent upon the earlier formed object-meaning, and the question is how that meaning is able to recur in the object's absence. We must eventually direct our attention to both aspects of the problem but, because it has received most attention, we shall review the most relevant psychological approaches to the problem of linguistic meaning.

The general approaches to the problem have included an emphasis on one or another of the following: (1) meaning as some kind of implicit reaction that words arouse, including evoked imagery, nonverbal conditioned reactions, and verbal associative responses; (2) a functional-behavioristic approach, which stresses only the relations between verbal stimuli and overt responses; and (3) meaning as a dispositional concept.

Implicit-Reaction Theories

Meaning as evoked imagery Traditional associationistic psychology equated meaning with ideas or images: the meaning of a word is the mental image it arouses. As noted in Chapter 1, such an interpretation of linguistic meaning dates back to antiquity. The Greek poet Simonides (circa 500 B.C.), whose name figures most prominently in the origin of imagery mnemonic systems (see Chapter 6), seems also to have expressed the imagery theory of meaning in the apt phrase "Words are the images of things."[1] The theory was implicitly accepted and passed on by philosophers and psychologists, including particularly the British empiricists, and reached its most explicit and extensive expression with Titchener (1909). This view has been the topic of repeated controversy and a review of the main issues will be instructive because the theory is to be proposed here once more in a modified form.

One of the most contentious problems has been whether images can be abstract. Titchener's discussion succinctly identifies the problem and its classical origin. Following a description of his own visual images as a "picture gallery . . . of impressionistic notes" occurring whenever he reads or hears descriptive verbal material, and which, for him at least, are the "vehicles of logical meaning," he goes on to say:

> [This description] leads us . . . to a very important question,—the old question of the possibility of abstract or general ideas. You will recall the main heads of the controversy. Locke had maintained that it is possible to form the general idea, say, of a triangle which is "neither oblique nor rectangle, neither equilateral, equicrural, nor scalenon; but all and none of these at once." Berkeley replied that "if any man has the faculty of framing in his mind such an idea of a triangle, as is here described, it is in vain to pretend to dispute him out of it, nor would I go about it. . . . For myself, I find indeed I have a faculty of imagining, or representing to myself, the ideas of those particular things I have perceived, and of variously compounding and dividing them . . . [but] I cannot by any effort of thought conceive the abstract idea above. . . . The idea of man that I frame to myself must be either of a white, or a black, or a tawny, a straight, or a crooked, a tall, or a low, or a middle-sized man." The dispute has lasted down to our own day. Hamilton calls the Lockean doctrine a "revolting absurdity." Huxley finds it entirely acceptable. "An anatomist who occupies himself intently with the examination of several specimens of some new kind of animal, in course of time acquires so vivid a conception of its form and structure, that the idea may take visible shape and become a sort of waking dream. But the figure which thus presents itself is generic, not specific. It is no copy of any one specimen, but, more or less, a mean of the series,"—a composite photograph of the whole group.

Titchener then suggests a resolution to the controversy, which he says involves a confusion of logic and psychology. It is incorrect to speak of an abstract or general process in consciousness (i.e., the idea or image). Only the logical meaning, of which the process is a vehicle, can be abstract; the process itself may vary in form:

---

[1] Although we can make only passing reference to the idea here, it may be more than incidentally relevant that Simonides' poetry, like his mnemonic system, was especially rich in imagery (Bowra, 1961).

Locke and Huxley, now, believed that abstract meaning is represented in consciousness by abstract or composite imagery; Berkeley and the other Nominalists believed that imagery is always individual and concrete, and that abstract meaning is accordingly represented by the abstract term, the general name. But here is no alternative for psychology. Imagery might be strictly reproductive in form, and yet—for a certain type of mental constitution—be the psychological equivalent of an abstract meaning; and, again, imagery might be vague and indefinite, and yet be the psychological equivalent of an individual, particular meaning. The issue, in its psychological formulation, is an issue of fact. Is wordless imagery, under any circumstances, the mental representative of meaning? And if it is, do we find a correlation of vague imagery with abstract and of definite imagery with particular meaning (pp. 15–16)?

The discussion has a familiar ring. In Chapter 2 we considered evidence that suggested that imagery might serve abstract functions in two ways: The imagery itself could be schematic and abstract, or abstract referents might be concretized, represented by specific images. In the present context these alternatives are applied specifically to the problem of linguistic meaning. The issue is not closed and I will later return to a more detailed consideration of factual evidence on the kinds of empirical questions Titchener raised.

A closely related issue, which arose as an empirical problem early in the century, concerned the independence of meaning and image. Betts, for example, concluded on the basis of his own research as well as that of others (e.g., Binet) that logical meanings and images are independent "except for the accident of association, by which a meaning may call up an image equally well with an image calling up a meaning" (1909, p. 94). The problem of which comes first, meaning or image, was investigated by Moore (1915) using a reaction time task in which concrete nouns were the stimuli and subjects were set to respond when either meaning or image was aroused. His findings indicated that meaning was aroused more quickly than was an image. Tolman (1917) repeated the experiment, however, and from his results concluded that individuals differ in whether meaning or image comes first. While the majority of his subjects, like Moore's, showed longer reaction time under the image set, one group of subjects consistently responded more quickly under the image than under the meaning set. Moreover, they reported that visual images came before meaning. Tolman suggested the compromise view that meaning depends upon image but is itself distinct from the latter.

Two related points may be noted concerning this controversy. First, it was essentially a specific form of the imageless thought issue in that meaning independent of imagery is impalpable, without sensory content. Titchener himself tentatively (and one suspects, reluctantly) suggested (p. 178 ff.) that meaning perhaps need not be conscious at all, but may be "carried" in purely physiological terms. A second implication of the argument (essentially a corollary of the first) is that meaning might better be viewed as an organismic disposition rather than an aroused state or response.

The controversy persists. In a thorough review and critique of imagery-as-meaning, R. W. Brown (1958) recently discussed three major difficulties with the theory that the "click of comprehension" of a word is the occurrence of an image when the word is heard. The first difficulty is the classical one, discussed above, that images are of particular objects whereas words can be generic or abstract in reference. A second is essentially equivalent to the imageless-thought argument: Many people report a lack of mental images for terms they understand and use appropriately. And third, of the people who do report mental images, most do not report the kind of image that could explain the ability to identify referent instances, which again argues for the independence of meaning and image. These arguments must be reconsidered in the context of the theoretical approach to meaning that will be proposed later, for despite the objections the view that meaning and imagery are somehow related is tenacious. We encounter it again in the following section.

Meaning as a nonverbal conditioned reaction   A second version of the general interpretation of meaning as some kind of implicit nonverbal reaction appeared in conditioning theories. It was first proposed by Watson (1930), who substituted implicit muscular (especially vocal or gestural) responses for images. Occurring first as overt and then as implicit responses to objects themselves, by Pavlovian conditioning they transfer to words and constitute their meaning. The most explicitly stated, general, and productive elaboration of this kind of approach is Osgood's (1953) theory of meaning as a representational mediation process. It evolved most directly from Hull's (1943) concept of the "pure stimulus act" whose function it is to produce self-stimulation that can mediate further overt responses. The fractional anticipatory goal response, on which Osgood based his conception of meaning, was a specific instance of such an act.

Osgood's theory states that objects arouse a complex pattern of reactions, some of which are "detachable" and therefore conditionable to other stimuli ("signs") such as words, which are repeatedly associated with the objects. The arousal of these fractional components of the original pattern of responses together with the self-stimulation resulting from those responses constitutes the meaning of the sign. The implicit responses are representational because they are a part of the pattern originally evoked by the object itself; they are mediational in that they serve to mediate overt responses, including ones never associated directly with the original object. The essential components of the paradigm follow the sequence, $S-r_m-s_m-R$, where S is the eliciting sign, r_m-s_m comprises the mediating process (reaction plus self-stimulation), and R is the overt (mediated) response.

Osgood's model is general in that the meaning reaction is not defined in terms of any particular response system—it may be peripheral, autonomic, or entirely cortical. In practice, however, the research stemming from the approach has emphasized affective reactions, perhaps largely because of the properties of the semantic differential, which Osgood and his coworkers (e.g., Osgood, Suci, & Tannenbaum, 1957) have developed for the measurement of meaning. The instrument consists of a series of bipolar adjectival scales such as *good-bad,* usually graded into seven steps, on which a given concept is rated. Numerous factor-analytic studies have consistently yielded three strong factors labeled evaluative (defined by scales such as good-bad, and pleasant-unpleasant), potency (e.g., weak-strong, soft-hard), and activity (e.g., active-passive, fast-slow). The relation between these dimensions of meaning and dimensions of emotion or feeling has been pointed out by Bugelski (1960). Wundt's three dimensions of feeling, for example, were pleasant-unpleasant, tense-relaxed, and excited-calm, which bear an obvious correspondence to Osgood's evaluative, potency, and activity factors, respectively.

Nevertheless, the representational mediation process is not limited in principle to affective meaning but is intended to be quite general in nature. Although Osgood did not explicitly make this suggestion, it seems reasonable that imagery could be considered an aspect of meaning or one kind of meaning reaction within the theory. A. W. Staats (1961, 1968) has proposed just such an analysis, with images regarded as representing the denotative meanings of signs. Such meaning is acquired through classical conditioning, in which sensory responses evoked by an object transfer to verbal stimuli occurring in contiguity with the object. Images thus are conditioned sensations for which words function as conditioned stimuli, and which can serve a mediational function in Osgood's sense. Essentially the same view of imagery has been presented independently by Mowrer (1960) and Sheffield (1961). A more detailed consideration of these views and of the supporting evidence will be presented later on. They are mentioned in this context to show how the imagery theory has tenaciously persisted and become incorporated into conditioning theories of linguistic meaning.

In view of the possibility of encompassing imagery within the theory, it is not surprising that Osgood's mediation hypothesis and other conditioning theories are open to the same criticisms as the older image theory of meaning and consequently "have retreated under the pressure to the same sanctuary—the central nervous system. Assuming that words must have immediate effects, and plagued by the shortages of overt effects, the conditioning theorist has revised his conception of meaning from overt response to implicit and eventually mediated response. Finally, behavioral meanings are found cheek-by-jowl with imaginal meaning inside the organism—neither revealed in action nor available to introspection" (R. W. Brown, 1958, p. 102). More recently, Fodor (1965a) has questioned mediation theories of meaning on formal grounds. To account for linguistic reference, such theories must assume that the mediating response, r_m, is in a one to one correspondence with the observable response. Given this assumption, mediation theories have no advantage over simple S-R theories, since the postulated mediating response is theoretically redundant. Osgood (1966) and Berlyne (1966) replied to the charges, the former arguing, for example, that he accepts the assumption of a part-to-whole relation between r_m and the total behavior to the thing signified, but not between r_m and the response to the sign (e.g., the name of the significate). Greater flexibility is therefore possible than Fodor assumes. The issues have not been resolved and for present purposes they need not be considered in more detail, since the theoretical viewpoint to be adopted here is not mainly a response-based mediation theory.

Verbal-associative approaches to meaning   Osgood's theory stresses nonverbal reactions—the fractional components of the total pattern originally evoked by the stimulus object—as the basis of meaning. Contrasted with this approach are the associative definitions and theories that place their emphasis on the pattern of verbal associates a word evokes. These approaches reflect the joint influence of the Ebbinghaus tradition, early word association research, and Watson's behaviorism. They have been concerned with two aspects of the problem of meaning—the conceptualization and measurement of (*a*) the amount of meaning, i.e., *meaningfulness,* and (*b*) interword associative relations, i.e., *associative* or *structural* meaning.

Meaningfulness   When it became apparent that the nonsense syllables invented by Ebbinghaus were not devoid of meaning, various attempts were made to measure their meaningfulness in terms of association value. Glaze (1928) first defined association value as the percentage of subjects who had an association to a syllable within a given time interval. Similar or modified methods were subsequently developed by others (e.g., Hull, 1933; Krueger, 1934; Witmer, 1935; G. Mandler, 1956).[2] Noble (1952a) extended the basic approach to real words. He formally defined meaning as a relation between stimulus and response, coordinating (but not equating) this definition with Hull's (1943) habit strength construct. His operational definition of the meaningfulness (*m*) of a word or other sign accordingly was specified as the average number of continuous written associations given to the item in a standard time period (in his original study, one minute) by a group of subjects.

Noble's reference to his method as a measure of meaning has instigated various criticisms (e.g., Osgood, 1961), many of which can be avoided by consistent use of the term *meaningfulness* rather than *meaning.* Noble (1963) has in any case defended himself ably against such criticisms and his method has been widely used in studies of the effects of meaningfulness in verbal learning and memory. The underlying assumption in such research is that the implicit verbal associations indexed by *m* potentially serve to mediate associations between verbal items that are not directly associated with each other. The assumption is linked to the associative probability (Underwood & Schulz, 1960) or "grapnel" theory (Glanzer, 1962), the essentials of which were suggested by William James (1890, Vol. I, p. 662). The theory states that the greater the number of associates elicited by a verbal item, the greater the probability that one of these items will "hook up" with another. Although later I shall have occasion seriously to question the mediating efficacy of verbal associations, as indexed by *m,* in verbal learning research (see especially Chapter 8), the theory is appealing and

---

[2] The various methods have been reviewed and described by Underwood and Schulz (1960) and Goss and Nodine (1965).

particularly relevant to a more general conceptualization of the functional role of verbal associative processes.

Associative meaning Noble's *m,* like earlier measures of association value, was intended as a quantitative index of what might be termed potency of associative meaning of single words. Other approaches have been concerned with measuring interword associations involving two or more words, thereby yielding a relational or structural definition of meaning and mediating mechanisms, which is implicit in such concepts as associative probability. Verbal associative structure, or organization, refers to such associative relations among words. The limiting instance is the two-word relationship: *A* and *B* constitute an associative structure to the extent that they are associates of each other. Larger structures involve not only more items but the possibility of mediated relations among items—*A* and *B* may not be directly related as associates, but might share a common association with *C.* The associative relations may vary in strength according to how commonly items occur as associates to one another (as determined by word association norms, Palermo & Jenkins, 1964) or how many associates they share in common (associative overlap). The meaning of a word within this approach can be defined in terms of its location within an associative hierarchy, and two items may be regarded as similar in meaning to the extent that they share associative responses in common.

Such an associative-structural approach has been adopted by many psychologists in the investigation of problems of language behavior and of associative learning and memory (for recent statements and reviews, see, e.g., Creelman, 1966; G. Mandler, 1968; Pollio, 1968). One of the first to investigate such problems systematically was Deese, who has reviewed the issues and his own research in a recent book (1965). His views are particularly relevant here because he is explicit in relating the verbal associative approach to the concept of meaning. He emphasized that meaning can be variously defined and that the empirical problems associated with the concept are broader than those raised by verbal associations alone. Specifically, he defines the meaning of a form as given by the potential distribution of responses to that form (p. 41), and argues further that verbal associative meaning is the largest subset of such a distribution that it is possible to obtain empirically by any technique (p. 43). His empirical program included the development of an index of *interitem associative strength,* which expresses quantitatively the direct associative relations within a group of words, that is, the extent to which the words tend to evoke each other as associates. Thus, a matrix is set up in which the same words serve as row headings (stimuli) and as column headings (responses). Each cell of the matrix contains the proportion of time a particular column word occurs as a response to a particular row word. The index is the sum of the matrix, which expresses the number of interconnections common to the entire group of words. Deese was able to show that this index is predictive of such behavioral phenomena as the ease with which the set of words can be learned in free recall.

Deese's index and numerous other measures of interword associations are concerned with direct (single step) associative links between words. It is possible also to quantify interword relations in terms of all of the common (mediating) associations as a measure of associative overlap between two or more words. Various measures of both kinds of relatedness have been described by G. R. Marshall and Cofer (1963). Generally these are based on discrete free association data, but such measures could also be based on continuous associations as yielded by Noble's (1952a) production method for measuring m. Associative overlap data of this kind have been considered in relation to verbal learning, for example by Wimer (1963). The findings from such research will not be reviewed at this point. What is relevant here is the assumption in all of this research that meaning is a verbal associative phenomenon and that it is possible to measure associative (meaning) similarity in terms of common response elements. Furthermore, while the empirical data are observable responses, most of the investigators who adopt this approach have been concerned with making inferences about the underlying, covert associative processes (Deese, 1965, p. 4), and their research accordingly is directly relevant to the present interest in verbal symbolic mechanisms.

Some have even taken the extreme position, at least in regard to verbal behavior, that the mediating mechanism is entirely verbal. Such a view has been explicitly expressed by W. A. Bousfield (1961), who questioned the usefulness of the concept of meaning, particularly as the concept has been used by Osgood, while espousing the verbal associative view of mediating mechanisms. A basic term in his analysis is the *representational response,* which resembles but is distinguished from Osgood's concept of the representational mediation process. The representational response to a stimulus word is not a meaning response in Osgood's sense, but rather the immediate, implicit or observable emission of the word itself as a response—the stimulus word *man* evokes the implicit response *man.* Further implicit associations may then occur as responses to the representational stimulus, i.e., feedback stimulation from the representational response, and function as mediators in such situations as those involving verbal (semantic) generalization. The measurement of meaning using Osgood's semantic differential scales is simply a special case of word associations, where the polar adjectives are themselves part of the associative hierarchy to the concept being rated. If the association with one of the polar terms is strong, the rating will be polarized toward that term. Thus, the word *evil* will be rated at the bad end of the *good-bad* scale because evil elicits bad as a fairly strong associate. Where the association to both polar terms is weak or equal, the rating will occupy a neutral position on the scale.

In a reply to W. A. Bousfield, Osgood (1961) agreed that implicit verbal chaining can function as a mediating mechanism, but he took strong exception to the view that it is the only mechanism and that the concept of meaning is superfluous. He cites research evidence in support of his view that nonverbal processes, too, can mediate verbal behavior and argues that the concept of meaning is crucial to the understanding of such behavior.

The debate is of considerable interest because it bears on a central issue of this book—*if verbal associative mechanisms are sufficient to account for verbal behavior, all nonverbal representational processes, including imagery, are unnecessary.* Obviously I do not accept such a view, and abundant evidence to the contrary will be presented throughout the sections on learning and memory along with evidence indicating the role played by verbal associative structure in such phenomena. In regard to the specific issue of meaning as a nonverbal representational process versus meaning as verbal associative structure, a resolution was suggested by A. W. Staats and C. K. Staats (1959). They distinguished word meaning in Osgood's sense from a word's verbal associates. Measures of the two are correlated, however, and this was interpreted to be a result of word-word contiguities in experience, which strengthen the connection between a word and its associates and, in addition, results in the meaning of the associates becoming conditioned to the word. Accordingly, the associates tend to have the same meaning as the words as measured by the semantic differential. Staats and Staats further asserted that words would not acquire meaning through word associations per se. Words originally acquire meaning through systematic pairing with aspects of the environment—a point that will be reemphasized later in the context of the present approach to meaning.

It should also be noted that models of linguistic meaning have recently been proposed that resemble the associative-structural approach in that they emphasize semantic structure or networks, but that do not make use of associationistic concepts (Katz & Fodor, 1963; Quillian, 1967). However, it has not been demonstrated that these models generate psychological predictions that an associationistic model could not handle, and it may be that no fundamental theoretical distinctions exist.

Skinner's Functional Approach to Meaning

Behavioristic approaches to meaning have tended to stress the response side of a stimulus-response relation. J. B. Watson (1930) stated such a viewpoint as follows: "experimentally determine all the organized responses a given object can call forth in a given individual, and you have exhausted all possible 'meanings' of that object for that individual" (p. 355). As previously noted, Noble (1952a) formally defined meaning as a relation between stimulus and response. His operational definition of meaningfulness, however, emphasizes the response side of the relation, that is, m is defined in terms of the number of responses evoked by a word. Similarly, meaning as associative structure is defined in terms of relations specified by responses to stimulus items. In all of these instances, the response emphasis was extended to inferences concerning implicit responses as the basis of meaning. Skinner's (1957) position contrasts with such accounts of meaning. He states that ". . . meaning is not a property of behavior as such but of the conditions under which behavior occurs. Technically, meanings are to be found among the independent variables in a functional account, rather than as properties of the dependent variable. When someone says that he can see the meaning of a response, he means that he can infer some of the variables of which the response is usually a function" (pp. 13–14). The meaning of a word is accordingly specified by the conditions under which it occurs and, apart from such a functional account, nothing further need be said about meaning.

While espousing a pure functional behaviorism, however, Skinner not only makes use of the concept of covert verbal behavior, especially in his discussion of thinking, but also explicitly recognizes images ("conditioned seeing") and emotions as reactions to verbal stimuli. Moreover, such processes appear to play a mediational role in Skinner's analysis of verbal behavior that differs in no essential way from the role of representational (meaning) responses in Osgood's theory (cf. Jakobovits, 1966). Semantically mediated generalization is involved, for example, in his analysis of metaphor and metonymy in language. Thus he concedes that the metaphorical extension involved in a phrase such as "Juliet is the sun" might have been mediated by an emotional response that both the sun and Juliet evoked in Romeo. Nevertheless, Skinner's approach generally differs from other behavioristic accounts of verbal behavior in its emphasis on identifying the environmental events that control such behavior.

Meaning as a Behavior Disposition

R. W. Brown's (1958) critique of imagery and implicit response theories of meaning ultimately rests on the argument that the mediating reactions that supposedly are the basis of meaning are pushed inside the organism where they cannot be identified. In the face of such difficulties, Brown prefers an approach proposed earlier by C. Morris (1946) and Stevenson (1944) in which meaning is viewed as a behavior disposition. Thus "the meaning of a linguistic form appears to be the total disposition to make use of and react to the form" (p. 109). Brown urges that psychologists focus on the behavior itself and leave the central (implicit) reaction to others. In an empirical study of linguistic meaning, however, one cannot deal with total behavior dispositions but must concentrate on those particular behaviors that are somehow fundamental to the full disposition. The two best examples of such behavior, he suggests, are the ability to name referents and the ability to react to names as signs of referents. It is with those that the theories of meaning begin.

To summarize this brief review of relevant psychological approaches to the problem, linguistic meaning was long identified with mental images: The "click of comprehension," to use Brown's phrase, is the image evoked by a word. Subsequently meaning was interpreted as a conditioned response—originally evoked by the object, the response transfers via classical conditioning to the word. Originally the reference was to overt responses, but with Watson these were pushed back into the organism as implicit responses, both nonverbal and verbal. Nonverbal implicit responses, the fractional components of the total response pattern originally evoked by the object, are emphasized by Osgood as the basis of meaning, whereas implicit interword associations are stressed by the association theorists. From different points of departure, Skinner and

Brown reject the traditional approaches, the former choosing to define the problem of meaning in terms of a functional analysis of verbal behavior, and the latter, in terms of behavior dispositions.

THE PRESENT APPROACH TO MEANING

In this section is presented a systematic theoretical and empirical analysis of meaning, which assumes that there is no fundamental disagreement among the approaches described above. Meaning is obviously a theoretical construct whose "meaning" is assigned to it. Explicitly or implicitly, the various psychological approaches assume covert processes as part of that meaning, although they differ in the locus and specificity of the assumed processes.

The analysis of meaning that I will propose is a specific expression of the more general theoretical orientation of the book, which coordinates imaginal symbolic processes with concrete stimuli and symbolic tasks involving them, and verbal symbolic processes with both concrete and abstract stimuli or tasks. It differs from the majority of the contemporary approaches described above in at least two respects: (1) its acceptance of nonverbal imagery as a representational and associative reaction system that reflects the dominant or "core" meaning of certain classes of stimuli; and (2) its explicit emphasis on the meaning of concrete objects or their pictorial representations, as well as words. Since the analysis deals with meaning in terms of implicit reactions, we will first consider R. W. Brown's (1958) objection to such an approach and his conclusion that psychologists should view meaning as a response disposition.

Meaning: Disposition or Aroused State?

Brown's insistence that meaning is a response *disposition* rather than a covert reaction of some kind involves a distinction that is generally accepted between organismic dispositions and aroused states. The distinction is unlikely to provoke argument if it is so understood. Anxiety, for example, is treated both as a dispositional trait, or readiness to react with anxiety, and as the aroused state itself, the two being empirically distinguished by different operations (e.g., trait questionnaires *versus* physiological reactions). Inasmuch as Noble treats meaning as analogous to Hull's habit construct, he regards it as a disposition, and his m index presumably measures the *average* strength of that disposition within a given sample of subjects. To say that words have a given m value refers to their acquired "capacity" to evoke the overt responses definitive of the underlying disposition. This logical argument applies equally to approaches such as Osgood's, although the distinction between disposition and aroused state has not always been made explicit.

The term *meaning* will be used here in both ways, and with reference both to the characteristics of stimuli and of covert as well as overt reactions. An S-R relationship is theoretically implied, but whether the emphasis is on the stimulus side, response side, or inferred (mediating) reaction should always be clear from the context. Mainly we are concerned with psychological meaning of stimuli, which, theoretically, refers to the capacity of words and nonverbal objects and signs *consistently to arouse covert and overt reactions* of certain kinds. Therefore, when we speak of word meaning, we are referring to the relevance of the word as a stimulus for the activation of a correlated disposition within the person. Meaning reactions are the *aroused,* covert (inferred) or overt expressions of the organismic dispositions. For present purposes, it is unnecessary to speculate extensively about the nature of the organismic disposition, although an analysis such as Hebb's (1949, pp. 130–134), in terms of cell assemblies and phase sequence capable of forming new associations (meanings) and having connections with various afferent and motor systems, would be an acceptable *kind* of approach. In agreement with the general position of theorists such as Osgood (1953), and Werner and Kaplan (1963), I assume that the aroused meaning process evoked by a word or other symbol is an organismic reaction with affective or motor (including verbal) or imaginal components, or all of these at once, mediated by the neural-dispositional meaning structures activated by the symbol and the situation in which it occurs. The meaning reaction may be covert and not expressed in overt action (as in thinking, daydreaming, etc.), or it might mediate behavior. Furthermore, the mediating reaction may be unconscious, not verbalizable, or it may be short-circuited, in either case resulting in behaviors not preceded by reportable mental content (e.g., "imageless thought"). This analysis explicitly assumes that the meaning reaction aroused by a stimulus is variable, as Titchener had proposed in his discussion of imagery-as-meaning and as Hebb (1949) has suggested more recently in his neuropsychological account of conceptual activity. According to Hebb:

> The implication of [the analysis] is that a concept is not unitary. Its content may vary from one time to another except for a central core whose activity may dominate in arousing the system as a whole. To this dominant core, in man, a verbal tag can be attached; but the tag is not essential. The concept can function without it, and when there is a tag it may be only part of the "fringe": sometimes aroused with the dominant subsystem, sometimes not. The conceptual activity that can be aroused with a limited stimulation must have its organized core, but it may also have a fringe content, or meaning, that varies with the circumstances of arousal (p. 133).

The assumption that the meaning of concepts is not entirely fixed to some extent meets objections such as R. W. Brown's (1958) and Fodor's (1965a, 1965b) to implicit reaction and image theories of meaning—the meaning state aroused by a symbol could be an image, a covert verbal response, an emotion, or none of these, depending on the stimulating conditions (see further below). Nevertheless, some reactions to particular symbols are more consistent than others and it is these that define the dominant ("core") psychological meanings of the concepts.

Imaginal and Verbal Coding Processes and Levels of Meaning

The organismic reactions that are the psychological basis of stimulus meaning can be regarded as a series of transformations and elaborations of the incoming stimulus information. While not always related explicitly to the concept of meaning, such an approach to information transmission within the individual is accepted rather generally in contemporary psychology. Various terms such as coding, mediation, information processing, etc., have been used to label the relevant processes, and numerous theoretical models in psychology are based on some kind of hierarchical elaboration of the properties of such concepts. Osgood's mediational theory is a prime example, particularly the hierarchical version (Osgood, 1957) in which he postulates different levels of organization within the nervous system, viz., projection, integration, and representation. Hebb's (1949) neuropsychological theory also involves processes at different levels of organization in regard to both the distinction between sensation and perception and the elaboration of the latter in terms of the integration of the cell assemblies that are assumed to be the basis of perception into superordinate structures (pp. 95–98). Hebb (1968) has explicitly applied this idea of hierarchical processes involving first-order and higher-order assemblies to the analysis of abstraction in imagery and thought, with obvious implications for the concept of meaning (to be considered later).

Levels of transformation, or coding, are also assumed in other contemporary approaches to perception and memory, in which the postulated processes range from short-duration sensory storage of the stimulus input, through short-term, to long-term memory systems with various theoretical properties (for relevant discussions, see Atkinson & Shiffrin, 1968; Neisser, 1967). Specific aspects of such models and pertinent empirical findings are surveyed at various points throughout this book. What is relevant at this point is the general assumption in all of these approaches that incoming stimulus information is transformed and elaborated within the organism. The initial stimulus representation fades rapidly, but a coded trace of some kind remains available. Pylyshyn and Agnew (1963) have presented a useful analysis of coding processes in perception and memory in such terms. They postulate that a stimulus sets up a representation that undergoes a continuous process of transformation as it interacts with the organism and its long-term memory. This results in "information overlap" or "system redundancy," whose extent at any time is referred to as the level to which the stimulus representation has been coded. The level reached depends, among other things, upon the rate of coding, which in turn depends on the availability of various mediating processes involved in the system. The implications of the model for perception and immediate memory are based on the further assumption that different responses require different levels of coding.

The present theoretical analysis is a specific interpretation of the nature of the coding processes involved at different levels of the processing of stimulus information. The levels might be continuous, as Pylyshyn and Agnew suggest, but for present purposes it will simplify matters to postulate four discrete levels, of which the last three will be discussed in detail. The first level is the sensory storage system referred to above, which is assumed to retain relatively untransformed information for a brief period following stimulus presentation. Such a system has received most attention in vision following Sperling's (1960) research on the "short-duration visual image." Recently, however, Crowder and Morton (1969) have presented evidence for a similar acoustic system, which they refer to as "precategorical acoustic storage." These sensory storage systems will not be viewed as related to meaning inasmuch as the properties of the transient trace presumably are unaffected by operations that define meaning. All further levels, however, do involve processes that are theoretically and operationally linked to meaning. These levels of meaning reactions will be described here as (*a*) the *representational process* (or representational meaning), (*b*) *referential associative reactions* (or referential meaning), and (*c*) *associative chains or structures* (or associative meaning). Each level involves either imaginal or verbal symbolic processes, or both, and the analysis applies to nonverbal as well as to verbal stimuli.

The representational-process level refers to hypothetical symbolic representations that are stored in long-term memory as concrete memory images in the case of objects and as implicit auditory-motor representations in the case of verbal stimuli. At this level, objects and words as stimuli simply activate the corresponding representational processes within the individual. The referential-meaning level refers to the first level of associative reaction, which presumably requires the establishment of a connection between the representational image and the representational verbal process corresponding to a particular concept. At this level, therefore, an object or a picture evokes its implicit or explicit verbal label, and a verbal stimulus may evoke the corresponding representational image. The reactions in each case are referential or denotative in nature. The third (associative) level refers to sequences or patterns of associative reactions involving words, or images, or both. It includes associative meaning in the sense of intraverbal associations (Deese, 1965) and in addition incorporates the assumption of imaginal chains and structures, or transformational chains involving both symbolic modes (cf. Berlyne, 1965) as possible associative reactions. It can be seen that the three postulated levels of meaning vary according to the degree to which a given verbal or nonverbal stimulus is "connected with something else" (cf. Bartlett, 1932, pp. 44–45). This feature of the model relates it closely to the abstractness-concreteness dimension of stimulus meaning, as will be seen presently.

Each of the levels will now be considered in more detail, emphasizing the distinctive criterial properties of each, with preliminary supporting evidence for the distinctions and their psychological significance.

Representational processes and meaning   This level of meaning corresponds intuitively to familiarity in that the familiar has meaning for the individual in the most elementary sense of "knowing" the stimulus. Familiarity implies that some organismic representation of a stimulus is "available." Further associative connections may be lacking, however, in which case the stimulus has no higher-order (referential or associative) meaning. Noble's (1963) statement that the meaningful is always familiar but the familiar is not always meaningful (in the sense of having acquired the capacity to evoke associative reactions) is relevant here, although the present assumption is that the availability of a representational process in response to a stimulus is the first stage in the development of psychological meaning. The term *availability* is used here in somewhat the same sense as item availability has been used by a number of theorists (see L. M. Horowitz, Norman, & Day, 1966; Steinfeld, 1967), with the difference that it is operationally linked to indices of familiarity (see below) rather than recall probability, which, in its strict sense, is relevant only to verbal material.

The processes involved in representational meaning have their parallels in a number of theoretical systems, some of which were mentioned above. At the level of neuropsychological theory, the representational process can be regarded as corresponding to Hebb's cell assembly—"the simplest instance of a representative process (image or idea)" (1949, p. 60). The concept is similar to Osgood's representational mediation process, except that I consider it desirable to keep symbolic representation separate from mediation, which can take place only when associations develop between representations. Furthermore, the assumed properties of the process are more specific here than in Osgood's theory. In the case of the verbal representation, the process corresponds rather directly to W. A. Bousfield's (1961) concept of the representational response, which refers to the implicit or explicit emission of the word itself as the initial reaction to a verbal stimulus. Processes at this level appear to correspond also to images as defined by Simon and Feigenbaum (1964) in their information-processing (computer simulation) theory of verbal learning. Thus:

> An image is the informational representation of an external stimulus configuration that the learner has stored in memory. [It] is comprised of the information the learner knows about, and has associated with, a particular stimulus configuration (p. 386).

The images are constructed by a computer program (the Elementary Perceiver and Memorizer, or EPAM) as information stored in the form of symbols at the terminal nodes of a "discrimination net." Incoming stimulus information (which can be from different sensory modalities) is sorted through the net to a terminal and is compared with the image (if any) stored at that terminal. If the two are similar, the stimulus has been successfully recognized and is called "familiar." The present concern is not with the properties or usefulness of the model as a whole, but rather with the theoretical and empirical properties of the image. It is theoretically coordinated to familiarity as a variable, which is empirically manipulated by varying the number of exposures to the stimulus configuration. Thus familiarization is the critical variable in the image-building process in EPAM and could be so regarded in the case of the development of representational meaning as viewed here, although other variables may be important as well.

Another relevant feature of the image in EPAM is that it may be elementary or compound. The former corresponds to stimuli whose characteristics may be noticed but which are not decomposable into more elementary familiar stimuli. The compound image has elementary or other compound images as its components. Just what is to be regarded as elementary is specified in EPAM, but the problem remains to be considered in the case of the present concept of the representational process. One implication of this feature of the EPAM analogy is clear: *Although representational meaning is regarded here as a primary level in the progressive elaboration of stimulus information, it cannot be assumed that the underlying processes are simple or that the level is relatively undifferentiated.* Instead, we must assume that varying degrees of generalization can take place and are somehow incorporated into the structure of the representational image or verbal process. The problem will be discussed again later in the context of acquisition mechanisms, particularly with reference to representational imagery.

We are faced with difficult conceptual problems in the case of the verbal representational process. In the first place, what constitutes a verbal representational unit? Does it correspond to a phoneme? A syllable? A word? For practical purposes it will generally be assumed that the representational unit corresponds to a word. This is in agreement with Osgood's (1963) proposal that the word is the characteristic unit of perceptual forms in language, as well as similar proposals by certain linguists who are willing to assign special status to the word as a unit of linguistic analysis (e.g., Uhlenbeck, 1967). Theoretically, however, the unit can be conceptualized as varying in size depending on what has been experienced as the functional unit in speech. Higher-order units may be comprised of lower-order units, yielding in some cases a hierarchical compound in which the elements are relatively independent, functionally in parallel at all levels. For example, *rainbow* presumably involves a representation distinct from those corresponding to *rain* and *bow*. The experiences responsible for the different levels of representation may be entirely distinct in such instances—*rainbow* is not simply an associative derivative of *rain* and *bow*, but a separate word. In other cases, however, unitization in G. A. Miller's (1956) sense may occur through repeated associative contiguities of lower-order elements that are sequentially organized and retain their individual significance as words even in the compound, as in the expression *back and forth*.

Further problems concern the sensory-motor systems involved in verbal representations. Although it was defined earlier as an auditory-motor process, we must recognize that the motor involvement may be minimal when the process is activated as an implicit "echoic response" (Skinner, 1957) to auditory verbal stimuli, and that auditory stimulation is not essential for the arousal of the process once the individual has learned to read. Rather than being simple, then, the verbal representational process must be viewed as undergoing considerable associative elaboration during its development. The auditory-motor connection may itself reflect an early stage of such elaboration. Thus it is clear that verbal understanding developmentally precedes verbal production and, indeed, the latter stage may not be achieved at all, as in the case of certain individuals with an inborn disability to produce speech who nevertheless appear to have full understanding of the meaning of speech sounds (Lenneberg, 1967, Chapter 7). Such evidence suggests that speech must initially be represented largely in an auditory system, or in any case not in a speech *motor* system unless one assumes that the connections between auditory and motor-neural systems are biologically "wired-in," as implied in the Liberman et al. (1967) motor-theory of speech perception. If this view were accepted, we could postulate that speech production simply involves the acquisition of the necessary peripheral motor connections to a pre-established auditory-motor cortical system. However, there is too little factual evidence in this area to warrant extensive speculation concerning the nature of the verbal representational system at a level where verbal understanding is possible without speech production. We must fall back on the general theoretical assumption that it is auditory-motor in nature, at least in normal subjects of speaking age.

When the verbal representational process is activated by a visual rather than an auditory verbal stimulus, we must assume that intermodal association is involved. An auditory-motor verbal representation is already available in the case of the auditorily familiar word, and an association develops with a visual word-image (or visual representations of lower-order units, such as letters and syllables) as the child acquires the grapheme-to-phoneme transformational skill involved in reading. Or, the auditory-motor representation may develop along with a visual representation when the individual implicitly responds to a visual pattern in the course of learning a new word by reading. The mechanism in the latter case must be especially complex, involving the ability actively to construct new psychological structures from old elements (cf. Neisser, 1967). Despite the necessity of postulating visual as well as auditory-motor representations to account for reading, however, it will be assumed that the *functional* verbal representational system is auditory-motor in nature. This implies that the arousal of the system is less direct when the stimulus word is visual than when it is auditory.

The above discussion indicates that the concept of a representational meaning process without higher-order associative properties is largely an idealized simplification. Generally it must be assumed that representational processes merge continuously with those involved theoretically in referential and associative meaning. Nevertheless, "pure" representational processes might be approximated by such experimental techniques as familiarization trials involving nonsense forms, and the availability of these processes can be operationally indexed by such procedures as familiarity ratings that have been found to be a positive function of familiarization trials (e.g., Noble, 1963—see further below).

Referential associative reactions and meaning The second level of meaning theoretically involves the development of interconnections between imaginal and verbal representational processes, which are reflected in the ability to name objects or their pictorial representations on the one hand, and in behavioral indicators of the image aroused by the name of an object (drawing a picture of the object would be one criterial response) on the other. As in the case of representational meaning, the conception appears straightforward and it makes contact with proposals by others. Especially relevant is R. W. Brown's (1958) discussion of meaning as a behavioral disposition, in which he specifies the ability to name new instances of a referent and the ability to react to a name as a sign of the referent as behaviors that are "functionally central" to a meaning disposition. It is these two abilities with which theories of meaning begin (p. 109). Such meaning reactions are central also to the present conception of referential meaning, but our assumptions concerning the underlying processes are more specific. Brown rejects the usefulness of images and other implicit reactions in the analysis of meaning and prefers to view meaning simply as a disposition—a response potential without any substantial character. In the present approach, however, such dispositions are assumed to have specific properties, being reflected in *implicit* labeling responses to referent stimulus objects, and evoked mental images to the names of the referent objects. Analogous *overt* reactions, such as those involved in the defining operations for referential meaning, to be described later, presumably can occur only when a link has been established between the two classes of representational processes.

Theoretically, the referential linkage may be symmetrical or asymmetrical, depending on the conditions of acquisition. Familiar objects and their labels may be experienced together in such a manner that the name evokes an image as readily as the object elicits its name, or the associative experiences may be such that verbal and imaginal referential reactions are differentially available to the referent stimuli. The nature of the relationship has important implications for areas ranging from perception to psycholinguistics, but especially in regard to performance in memory and associative learning tasks involving verbal and pictorial stimuli (Chapters 7 and 8).

Associative meaning Whereas referential meaning involves associative reactions that "stay close" to the referent, associative meaning presumably involves the development of associative connections or an associative structure involving different referents or conceptual categories. The associative structure might be entirely intraverbal, in which case the analysis of processes at this level would not differ in any essential way from the traditional verbal-associative approaches to meaning (e.g., W. A. Bousfield, 1961; Deese, 1965) as outlined earlier. The present view, however, extends the idea of associative structure to include images as well as words.

Associative connections presumably can become established among imaginal representational processes alone, thereby resulting in organized systems of imagery analogous to verbal associative structures, with the important difference that the organization in the former case is, theoretically, spatial rather than sequential. In a sense the meaning of any complex object could be viewed in such terms—that is, the representational image, as described above, may consist of clusters of elementary images corresponding to components of an object, which in turn may be organized into higher-order structures comprised of the already established object images, and so on. Two points should be noted concerning such a conceptualization. First, the structures thus envisaged are assumed to be associatively organized—indeed, such a view seems unavoidable given the analogy with perceptual structures. Just as the unitary features of a complex object cannot be clearly perceived at once but must be viewed by successive fixations, so too might a representational image involve successive awareness of components of the object. The processing of the image may be said to "run off" associatively (but not necessarily in any particular sequence, since the image system is not assumed to be organized sequentially) even in the case of unitary object-representations, and all the more so when the associative structure involves different objects rather than the components of one.

The second important point to be noted is that such associative structures may be *hierarchically* organized, presumably because the components of objects and classes of objects as perceptually experienced are themselves hierarchically arranged. Thus, for example, the component parts of individual persons and of groups of persons are not experienced as a random arrangement at any level of complexity, but as components with relatively stable and predictable arrangements in higher-order perceptual structures. Such features as the eyes and nose of an individual are arranged in a particular way in a face, faces on bodies of whole individuals, groups of individuals in "clusters" at a table, and so on (cf. Allport, 1955, pp. 551–566). Handel and Garner (1966) referred to such hierarchical perceptual structures as nested sets, in which a stimulus is perceived as belonging to a subset, which is in turn part of one or more other subsets, and so on (see also Imai & Garner, 1968). The point seems straightforward, but it deserves special emphasis because it has often been overlooked and even denied. Bruner et al. (1966), for example, suggested that hierarchical organization is characteristic of linguistic symbolic structures but not of iconic representations. The present argument is that hierarchies are characteristic of *perceptual* experiences and, therefore, of imagery as well. Indeed, it could be argued that linguistic (semantic) hierarchies develop only because the perceptual world actually contains corresponding, discriminable categories independent of language.

The preceding argument does not deny the involvement and central importance of language in associative structures. In fact, it is assumed that associative meaning generally involves both classes of representational processes. In the case of familiar objects, this implies the establishment of associative connections between imaginal representations and verbal representations corresponding to those objects. Two conceptual elements such as *boy* and *girl* would accordingly involve an associative structure comprising four "elementary" representational systems, two imaginal and two verbal, and their interconnections at the referential (word-image) and associative (e.g., word-word) levels. Which components are most strongly connected presumably depends on the nature of prior experience, as discussed below, and which component will occur as an implicit or explicit associative reaction to a stimulus in a given situation would depend on a variety of factors including the *Aufgabe,* as emphasized long ago by the Würzburg psychologists. Associative chains or structures involving both systems may follow predictable patterns yet to be discovered. For example, verbal associations may give direction to an associative chain, as suggested previously in the discussion of the functional properties of the symbolic modes (Chapter 2). Such direction might include a limitation on the range of associations that can occur to a given stimulus even when imagery is involved. The stimulus word *fruit,* for example, may evoke names of particular fruits entirely by virtue of its position as the superordinate member of a particular intraverbal associative structure, or because it first evokes a memory image of a basket of fruit whose spatially organized contents are "read off" verbally. In the latter case, the stimulus word might guide the associative reactions by maintaining attention on the fruit basket rather than on other images that might be aroused, such as an imagined table on which the basket rests. It will require unusual experimental ingenuity to tease apart the contributions of verbal and imaginal determinants of such complex associative reactions. The evidence to be presented later in relation to such problems as paired-associate learning and language reveal both the difficulties and the theoretical usefulness of the conceptualization.

It was proposed above that some associative structures may be entirely verbal in nature, as the verbal association theorists generally assume. It will be argued in the following section that such a condition would be approximated in the case of the associative meaning of highly abstract words, relational words, function words, and nonsense syllables.

Abstractness-Concreteness and Levels of Meaning

The relation to be proposed between the above conceptualization and the abstract-concrete dimension of stimulus meaning is a specific expression of the more general theoretical approach of the book, according to which imaginal symbolic processes are functional particularly with concrete stimuli and symbolic tasks involving them, and verbal symbolic processes are functional with both concrete and abstract stimuli and tasks. What follows is essentially an elaboration of views I have previously summarized elsewhere (Paivio, 1966, 1969). Concreteness is formally defined in terms of directness of sensory reference and, for present purposes, this can be taken to mean a dimension extending from highly abstract words (e.g., *truth*), to concrete words (e.g., *house*), to pictures and objects, in increasing order of concreteness. Psychologically, concreteness can be defined in terms of the ease with which the stimulus evokes an image of an object or objects, or simply as the "picturability" of a stimulus. Objects or their pictorial representations obviously arouse images directly and pose no conceptual problem in this context. Concrete terms presumably derive their meaning through association with concrete objects and events as well as through contextual association with other words, and thereby acquire the capacity to evoke nonverbal images and verbal processes as associative reactions. Abstract terms, on the other hand, derive their meaning largely through intraverbal experiences and more effectively arouse verbal associative than imaginal processes, although the latter could also occur as reactions to some abstract terms. Concrete and abstract words are thus distinguished primarily on the basis of their differential capacity to evoke concrete images as associative reactions, not on their verbal associative meaning (although it will be seen later that concrete words also are somewhat favored in terms of the latter). This view is basically an old one, at least in its broad lines. An essential aspect appears, for example, in William James' (1890) interpretation of "static" meaning: "The static meaning, when the word is concrete, as 'table,' 'Boston,' consists of sensory images awakened; when it is abstract, as 'criminal legislation,' 'fallacy,' the meaning consists of other words aroused, forming the so-called 'definition' " (Vol. I, p. 265). The present analysis differs from that of James only in its explicit assumption that concrete words readily evoke verbal associates as well as images.

The concreteness dimension cannot be fully equated with levels of meaning as described above, although a partial correlation is assumed. Both concrete and abstract words obviously must develop appropriate verbal representations, so they are not differentiated at that level. Referential meaning refers primarily to objects, their pictures, and relatively concrete words, since highly abstract concepts such as truth, justice, and religion are, strictly speaking, not picturable. It is difficult in any case to conceive of an object or picture that would be reliably coded by such terms; conversely, abstract words are unlikely to evoke images that have sufficient communality to be called referent images. This is not to deny a relation between abstract labels and concrete situations, or images of such situations, but I would assume that such relations fall at the level of associative chaining rather than referential meaning. The word *religion* may evoke an image of a church as an associative reaction, and a picture of a church might arouse *religion* as an associate, but both are likely to be mediated by the implicit verbal associate *church*. This would be an instance of concretization of an abstract referent as described in Chapter 2. The analysis implies that abstract terms are primarily meaningful in the verbal-associative sense, with images possibly occurring as secondary associations to concrete verbal associates in an associative chain. However, images might conceivably occur directly as associative reactions to abstract stimulus terms as a result of idiosyncratic associative frequency in experience: The word *liberty,* for example, may promptly evoke an image of the Statue of Liberty, especially for persons raised in New York City. Such a reaction would not differ in principle from the imaginal reaction occurring to a more concrete word such as *dog,* which could vary in content according to one's experiences with particular breeds of dogs. The analysis, therefore, does not imply any absolute difference in the nature of the symbolic associative reactions that can occur to concrete and abstract terms, but only that there are differences in the probabilities involved—images are more likely to be directly evoked by concrete than by abstract words. In addition, it is possible that any images aroused by abstract or denotatively general words are somehow more abstract than the images aroused by more concrete and specific terms (see further below).

The discussion thus far has been restricted to nouns, but it extends readily to other classes of words. It can be argued that verbs, adjectives, prepositions, and so on, are relatively more abstract than concrete nouns because their meaning depends on the verbal context created by the sentence. They can evoke images only by being concretized as an attribute, action, or relation involving an imagined object, such as a *tall* tree, a boy who *runs,* or the *in*side of a house as imaginal associations to the words *tall, run,* and *in,* respectively. It is conceivable that these images might be evoked relatively directly by such words, if presented individually as stimuli, but I would assume that the primary mechanism is by verbal chaining, e.g., *tall* first evokes the verbal associate *tree* and together they evoke the image of a tall tree. There is precious little direct evidence on the problem, although it is researchable. Ordinarily, of course, the concrete verbal context would be provided by a sentence containing a concrete noun together with its qualifiers, action words, and so on. In such instances, the imaginal meaning reaction is determined by the sentence as a whole (cf. Bugelski, 1969). If the concrete noun is missing, the subject must concretize the referent in his imagery, as in the Werner and Kaplan (1963) studies mentioned earlier. Such interpretations of sentence meaning will be discussed further in Chapter 13.

What are the implications of this analysis for nonsense syllable stimuli? Obviously they can have verbal associative meaning, as reflected in their association values, but can they have "imaginal association value"? The preceding analysis suggests that they can, again through verbal mediation. For example, JAQ may be encoded as JACK and then as the image of a person named Jack. The initial verbal-associative phase has been investigated in a number of studies of coding processes in learning and memory, and one implication of the assumed second (imaginal) phase formed the basis of an experiment by Paivio and Madigan (1968). A study by Imae (1968) is particularly relevant in the present context because it showed that subjects were able to classify nonsense syllables into seven parts of speech (noun, verb, etc.). Moreover, some of the nonsense words that were classified relatively consistently as nounlike were further classified according to their concreteness-abstractness, and this variable was predictive of incidental recall—the subjects remembered more of the concrete-noun than of the abstract-noun type syllables. Presumably the two types would also differ in their image-evoking value, which has been found to be the major effective correlate of concreteness among actual nouns, but this implication has not been directly tested. These studies are mentioned here to indicate that the theoretical speculations are plausible and testable; they will be discussed in more detail later (Chapters 7 and 8). I hasten to add that the present discussion is not intended to imply that imagery is a common associative reaction to nonsense syllables in experimental studies in which they have been used as units. The occurrence of imagery may instead require priming by instructional sets or verbal contexts. Nonsense syllables would therefore be particularly "abstract" in the sense that imagery is an improbable associative reaction, but they are obviously also low in verbal associative meaningfulness.

Meaning as image   We must now reconsider the old controversy. Any suggestion that the meaning of a word could be represented as an image must take account of the classical argument that images are specific, whereas *all* words (even "concrete" ones) are abstract in meaning. I have already noted R. W. Brown's (1958) restatement of this argument as a primary basis for rejecting the image theory of meaning. More recently, Fodor (1965b) has aired essentially the same issue, phrased in terms of the mediational role attributed to images in the production and understanding of language. Thus, "an image of a particular dog cannot be the mediator for the abstract term 'dog' if only because images are unalterably individual while the term is generic. (Should the image that mediates the understanding of 'dog' be a Poodle or a Chow? And if it is a Poodle-image that mediates 'dog,' what image mediates Poodle?)" (Fodor, 1965b, p. 385). The argument is not valid for at least two reasons. First, if we accept the arguments and general evidence considered earlier, images are not necessarily highly specific forms of symbolic representation but may be schematic and abstract, at least to an extent short of the "hopeless jumble" that would result if the generic image were to be a truly representative "composite portrait" (R. W. Brown, 1958, p. 88). However, even if we assume that the representational image is relatively specific, Fodor's arguments are logically wrong, as can be seen by making explicit the analogy between visual image and pictorial representation (or object, for that matter). Following Fodor's reasoning, generic labels should not occur as responses to specific pictures (how can a Poodle-picture mediate the response "dog"?). Moreover, we would have difficulty explaining the choice of a specific object to represent the generic class (should a person who is asked to draw a "dog" represent it as a Poodle or a Chow?). The position taken here is that the reactions, whether covert or overt, nonverbal or verbal, are *associative* reactions that depend for their occurrence not only on the particular stimulus to which one reacts but also upon one's past experience with particular dogs and their labels and upon the situational context (verbal or other) in which the stimulus occurs. Thus the word *dog* can arouse different images in different people and in a given person on different occasions, and the image is somehow representative of the specific meaning of the word for that person at that time. This is not to say that meaning *is* an image—the term "meaning" has broader meaning than that, as I have noted earlier. The claim is that images can occur as associative reactions to words, that these images can be dynamic and variable rather than being fixed "portraits" (as Brown seems to assume in his discussion), and that they can mediate language behavior. Furthermore, their arousal is more probable in the case of concrete than abstract terms, as indicated by evidence presented below.

The arguments advanced by Fodor to some extent seem to involve the same confusion between logical definition of word meaning and individual (psychological) reaction to words that Titchener noted in reference to the classical issue of abstract images and meaning. The abstract properties of objects are verbal and these are reflected in the conventional definition of the labels for the referents, e.g., the abstract (verbal) definition of the word triangle. The individual reaction, too, might be verbal and conventional, but it could also be a private image that occurs to the word and is capable of mediating further overt reactions to it. In the latter case, it seems appropriate to say that the psychological meaning of the term is manifested in the image it arouses.

Preliminary evidence for the two-process theory of concrete and abstract meaning Early evidence consistent with the above theory can be found in Galton's (1883) pioneering study of association, in which he made some remarkable observations concerning the nature of associated "ideas" as a function of stimulus word type. He identified three main groups of associative reactions: (1) *verbal,* e.g., imagined sounds of words as in verbal quotations, (2) *sense imagery,* most frequently visual imagery, and (3) *"histrionic" representations,* in which he experienced a "nascent sense of some muscular action," as in pantomiming an attitude. (These classes of associative ideas, it may be noted, show a striking parallel to Bruner's (1964) categories of modes of representation if we equate histrionic representations with Bruner's "enactive" mode.) Galton found that these reactions were related to the quality of the stimulus words involved, which he had categorized into three groups or "series." His data, summarized in Table 3-1, indicated that imagery occurred most frequently to

Table 3-1

Percentages of Different Associative Reactions to Three Classes of Stimulus Words. From Galton, 1883.

Stimulus Type	ASSOCIATION		
	Sense Imagery	Histrionic	Purely Verbal
"Abbey" series	43	11	46
"Abasement" series	32	33	35
"Afternoon" series	22	25	53

concrete stimulus words (his "abbey" series), verbal associative reactions occurred most often to abstract words (his "afternoon" series), and histrionic representations were aroused most often by the "abasement" series (attitudinal words?). Histrionic representations aside for the moment, it should be noted that the dominant meaning of concrete terms was expressed as often in evoked imagery as in "purely verbal" ideas, whereas the associative meaning of abstract terms was predominantly verbal. Galton's empirical observations are thus fully in accord with the present analysis of concrete and abstract meaning. However, such a theory was not explicitly stated by Galton nor did his research in any sense constitute a systematic exploration of the implications of such an approach, as has been done in recent studies that will be considered throughout the book.

The following study is particularly relevant in the present context. The two-process theory suggests that the latency of an associated image to a stimulus word should be longer when the word is abstract than when it is concrete, whereas verbal associative latency should be less affected by variation in concreteness. This prediction was tested (Paivio, 1966) by presenting subjects with concrete and abstract stimulus nouns and requiring them to press a key either when a mental image or an implicit verbal associate occurred to the word. The results are presented in Figure 3-1, where it can be seen that reaction times were longer to abstract than concrete words under both the verbal and imaginal associative instructions but, as predicted, the difference was much greater under the imagery set.

While the finding is consistent with the two-process interpretation, it could be argued alternatively that the effects were mediated entirely by verbal processes: Abstract nouns may simply arouse a longer covert verbal response chain under imagery instructions. Such an interpretation fails to account for the interaction between stimulus concreteness and instructional set, for if imagery instructions simply increase covert verbalization, why would they not increase imaginal reaction time to concrete words as much as to abstract? Direct evidence on the role of verbalization in such a situation was incidentally obtained in another study (Simpson & Paivio, 1968), an aspect of which required the subject to press a key when an image occurred to a stimulus word, with or without a subsequent description of the image. The key press latency increased significantly when verbalization was required, but it did so equally for concrete and abstract stimulus words. This finding indicates that differential (covert) verbalization alone cannot account for the interaction obtained in the Paivio (1966) study,

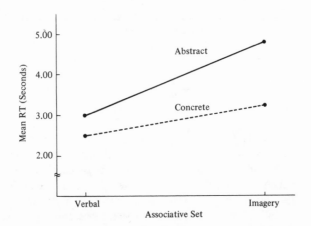

FIGURE 3-1. Mean reaction time (RT) in seconds as a function of associative set, and abstractness-concreteness of stimulus words. Adapted from Paivio (1966).

and it indirectly enhances the plausibility of the view that both imaginal and verbal mediators were involved.

Further evidence on the relationship between linguistic abstractness-concreteness and verbal and imaginal symbolic processes will be considered later in this chapter in the context of measures of meaning, and more intensively in subsequent chapters on learning and memory. We turn first to a consideration of possible factors in the development of meaning as it has been conceptualized above.

Mechanisms in the Development of Meaning

The most self-evident statement that can be made concerning the development of representational, referential, and associative meaning is that it must involve some kind of experience with objects, words, and their interrelations. The precise nature of the necessary experiences is by no means clear, however. The possible mechanisms include at least the three suggested in Chapter 2, viz., perceptual exposure, classical conditioning, and instrumental conditioning.

Perceptual exposure   Imaginal and verbal representations may develop initially through simple exposure to objects and spoken words, as suggested by the ancient wax tablet model and its contemporary versions as proposed by Beritoff (1965) and Penfield (1954). Both Beritoff and Penfield proposed that images might be stored as a consequence of a single exposure to the stimulus situations. The results of recognition experiments by Nickerson (1965) and Shepard (1967) might be taken as supporting such a view. Subjects were shown, once, as many as 600 pictures, which were then used in a recognition test along with a set of new items. An astounding 95 percent or more of the test stimuli were correctly recognized as old or new. However, the content of each item was already familiar to the subjects in the general sense and it is not known whether completely unfamiliar stimulus patterns would be similarly retained. Repetition must in any case have important effects on the availability of a representational system. Noble (1963) found that familiarity ratings of stimulus patterns were a positive function of the number of familiarization trials, indicating operationally that representational availability is a function of exposure frequency. However, Hebb's (1968) argument that perceptual exploration of a complex object is essential before the object is perceived as a single entity and before its components can be imaged clearly, suggests that passive sensory experience may be an insufficient condition for the unitization of perceptual elements into an image. This view is consistent also with Piaget's conceptualization of imagery as internalized imitation, as already noted in the preceding chapter. The development of a representational image, therefore, does not fit the wax tablet analogy, according to which experience somehow impresses itself on a passive "organ of the mind." It presumably results instead from active serial exploration of the features of an object, the consequence of which is a multifaceted image that also can be "scanned" serially because it incorporates a motor component.

Similarly, verbal representational systems presumably do not result ordinarily from passive auditory experience alone, but from such experience coupled with the motor activity involved in the production of the verbal units (cf. Liberman et al., 1967). It may be that *speech* motor activity is not absolutely essential, however, but that any activity correlated with the auditory pattern could become part of the verbal-representational meaning process. Such a conceptualization may provide an explanation for those individuals described by Lenneberg (see above) who have full understanding of speech sounds without being able to produce them. The verbal representational processes may indeed include sequentially organized motor components, but ones derived from nonarticulatory rather than articulatory behavioral experience, such as might be involved in the manipulation of objects occurring contiguously with the hearing of a speech sound.

Classical conditioning   The picture presented by the preceding analysis is one in which object or word meaning is linked to complex associative processes, the components of which derive from sensory-motor contiguities of experience. A somewhat similar conceptualization of object-meaning, expressed in terms of classical conditioning mechanisms, has been proposed by Sheffield (1961). His analysis begins with assumed sensory and perceptual "responses" that are completely central in locus and that need not have any motor components. They are subject to learning principles (association by contiguity) and are assumed to have both cue properties and response properties. Sensory responses and perceptual responses are distinguished in the theory. The former term refers to the innate sensory responses elicited by immediate sensory stimulation; the latter refers, in addition, to other sensory responses that have been conditioned to the immediate stimulation in past experience. Perceptual responses are thus relevant not only to our discussion of the representational meaning of concrete objects but also to our later discussion of referential and associative meaning. In Sheffield's terms, the perceptual responses permit complete representation of a distinctive stimulus in its absence or when only some of its stimulus aspects are directly sensed. His analysis runs as follows:

> If a set of n sensory responses, R_{s1}, R_{s2}, R_{s3}, . . . R_{sn}, are elicited by different aspects of a given stimulus *object*, they will become conditioned to each other in the course of exploration of the object, which stimulates first with one aspect, then with another, and so forth, as it is examined, manipulated, sensed with different modalities, etc. Thus an object like an orange is smelled, touched, hefted, peeled, tasted, etc., giving rise to a succession of distinctive sensory responses which become conditioned to each other as cues. In the great variety of experience provided when a child becomes familiar with an orange, practically every stimulus aspect has sometimes preceded, sometimes followed, and sometimes occurred simultaneously with every other aspect, giving rise to a conditioned (perceptual) response pattern which is unique for oranges as objects and which can be elicited in relatively complete form by only one unique aspect of the orange. . . . This "cross-conditioning" mecha-

nism accounts for the "filling-in" property of perceptual behavior in which a fragment of a total stimulus-pattern "redintegrates" the whole (1961, pp. 16–17).

Sheffield's analysis involves an old view of perception as a combination of sensory stimulation and images associatively aroused by that stimulation, which will be discussed further in Chapter 4. The significance of the analysis in the present context is that the conditioned perceptual responses contribute to the unique representational meaning that distinguishes one object from another. The total perceptual response may be "fairly labile, shifting from moment to moment in the particular constellation of conditioned sensory responses that constitute the momentary perception of the object," but at any moment the set of responses "would be sufficient to provide a constellation unique to the actual object" (p. 17). This parallels Hebb's analysis of the meaning of concepts, cited earlier: "The conceptual activity that can be aroused with a limited stimulation must have its organized core, but it may also have a fringe content, or meaning, that varies with the circumstances of arousal" (1949, p. 133). Although couched in different language, Sheffield's interpretation corresponds also to Hebb's analysis of the genesis of object-percepts and object-images in that it assigns importance to associative experiences involving the components of a complex object.

The conditioning approach extends directly to the interpretation of the referential meaning of words in terms of conditioned imagery. Sheffield goes on to say that "a complete perceptual response can be elicited by a conditioned stimulus in the absence of any of the stimulus aspects of the perceived object" (p. 17), the most common case being that in which the perceptual response of an object becomes conditioned to its verbal label. The cue for the perceptual response in this case is completely neutral, unrelated to the stimulus object except through conditioning. This is the basis of the meaning of all symbolic systems, including especially language. Mowrer (1960) and A. W. Staats (1961, 1968) have independently proposed the same view of imagery-as-meaning. They regard images as conditioned sensory responses, i.e., fractional components of the total sensory response to objects that have become conditioned to words and that constitute their denotative meaning in the psychological sense. The process may include both first-order conditioning, in which the object itself is the UCS, or higher-order conditioning involving denotatively meaningful words as the UCSs (see further below).

Classical conditioning is also applicable in a straightforward manner to the interpretation of the acquisition of labeling responses as the referential meaning of objects or pictures. One possibility is that a verbal representational response is already available to the spoken sound, and that the response later becomes conditioned to the sight of the referent object, which also has already acquired representational (imaginal) meaning. Such a situation could be achieved in the laboratory by presenting familiarization trials with visual and verbal nonsense patterns as units prior to their copresentation as paired associates, but it is probably a rare occurrence in real life. A more likely situation is one in which both representational and referential meanings are acquired together, as when a child sees a new object and simultaneously hears its name spoken for the first time. This would correspond closely to the sensory conditioning paradigm (e.g., Brogden, 1947) but would be more complex if we assume in addition that there is transfer from previous experience such that the child is immediately able to produce an implicit or explicit echoic response, i.e., imitate the speech sound.

The classical conditioning model can be extended further to encompass aspects of associative meaning. Just as the sensory reactions to components of a complex object become associated to produce the characteristic percept of the object as a unit, according to Sheffield's analysis, so too would the perceptual representations (images) of different objects, perceived contiguously, become conditioned to each other and constitute links in a chain of visual imagery or components of a spatially organized compound image. Similarly, the processes by which verbal associative chains develop through interword experiences may include sensory conditioning, where the stimulus elements are all verbal; or, compound chains involving both imaginal and auditory-verbal representational units may develop through multiple object-word and word-word contiguities in experience.

Although already complex, an analysis based entirely on first-order classical conditioning is still insufficient. It seems apparent from everyday experience that the denotative meaning of concrete words can be acquired entirely at a verbal level, through verbal descriptions of a named object rather than through direct contact with it. This is what Osgood (1953) terms assign learning, and for which he has proposed higher-order conditioning as the acquisition mechanism (p. 704). The theoretical possibility has been explored most extensively by A. W. Staats (e.g., 1968, Chapter 3). Assuming that descriptive words have already acquired denotative (referential) meaning, i.e., they are capable of evoking conditioned sensory responses (images), the components of such images can become conditioned to a new word when the latter is merely defined verbally. For example, a person unfamiliar with a jellyfish may be told that it is mottled, gelatinous, averages about eighteen inches across, and so on. Such a description, Staats argues, would elicit grossly appropriate sensory responses that become conditioned to the word *jellyfish* and constitute its denotative meaning.

Instrumental conditioning   Instrumental, or discriminative operant, conditioning must also play an important role at every stage of meaning acquisition. Imitative (echoic) responses and other verbal associative responses to a stimulus word may be shaped by reinforcements contingent on the responses. Shaping procedures could presumably act also to reinforce verbal responses of reduced intensity under some conditions (cf. Skinner, 1957), creating the implicit motor component of the verbal representational process. The motor components of images that have been emphasized by Hebb, Piaget, and Skinner might similarly involve operant reinforcement in their genesis. These arguments have already been presented in Chapter 2. The only special feature of the present analysis is the emphasis on the stimulus conditions to which the sensory and motor reactions become conditioned: the reactions define the representational, referential, and associative meaning of the objects and words that elicit them.

A Critique and Further Evidence

Some criticisms of specific features of the approach have already been discussed. Other issues remain to be considered, among which the plausibility of the conditioning approaches to meaning-as-imagery is crucial because conditioning theories carry a particularly heavy burden in what they are required to explain. Like the older interpretation of meaning in terms of imagery, the more specific, behavioristic interpretation of images as conditioned sensations has been criticized as an approach to word meaning. Ausubel (1965), for example, has argued that it strains credulity to apply the classical conditioning model to such a phenomenon and he suggests a more cognitive approach, the essence of which is that the individual somehow acquires knowledge about the world. Unfortunately, the force of such criticisms is weakened by the vagueness of the cognitive approach and by the absence of supporting evidence. The conditioning model has the advantage of being relatively explicit and testable, and there is some empirical evidence to support its validity in the present context. Leuba (1940), using hypnosis, found that subjects will report the smell of creosote when a bell is rung if the bell had previously been rung a number of times while he was actually smelling creosote. In an extension of the study, Leuba and Dunlap (1951) obtained similar results when subjects were simply asked to imagine the conditioned stimulus. For example, a hypnotized subject was presented repeatedly with the sound of a doorbell paired with a pin prick on one hand. When subsequently asked to imagine hearing a doorbell, the subject reported that when he did so, he felt a sharp·pain in the area that had previously been pricked. Imagery was accordingly interpreted as conditioned sensations. Similar findings were obtained by Ellson (1941a, 1941b), who interpreted the sensory experiences as hallucinations produced by sensory conditioning. Such findings are open to alternative interpretations, such as acquiescense to what the subjects thought was expected of them, but they are at least consistent with the conditioning interpretation of imagery-as-meaning, including imaginal chaining. In this instance, the verbal instructions apparently evoked the imagined sound of a doorbell, which in turn elicited the pain experience.

Evidence for the role of operant conditioning as well as classical conditioning variables, which incidentally suggests one function served by the motor components of associative responses, has been presented by Hefferline and Perera (1963). When their subject occasionally emitted an invisibly small thumb twitch (detected by electromyography), he received a tone, which in turn served as a signal to press a key. After several conditioning sessions, the tone was progressively diminished to zero. The subject nevertheless continued to press the key whenever he emitted a thumb twitch, and he reported that he still heard the tone. The procedure apparently involved a mixture of classical and instrumental conditioning elements and resulted in reported experiences interpreted as being in keeping with the literature on experimentally produced images, conditioned sensations, and hallucinations. While word meaning is not directly involved, the data are generally relevant to the issue of associative (especially imaginal) chaining in that the thumb twitch apparently served as the cue for the auditory image of the tone as well as for the overt key press. Assuming that such response-produced cues would be effective in visual imagery as well, the finding suggests that one function of the motor component of an image is to provide feedback stimulation that would trigger a further sensory response, and so on, in an imagery chain.

Suggestive evidence of such a process in the visual modality can be found in a study by I. Kohler (1964). The relevant finding was that negative after-images resulting from the prolonged wearing of colored filters occurred subsequently in response to eye movements, apparently as a result of sensory conditioning in which motor feedback from eye movements functioned as the CS for the negative afterimage (the CR). The evidence at least makes it plausible that a similar mechanism might operate in relation to visual mental images as well—eye movements may facilitate the generation of imagery in some circumstances by providing proprioceptive retrieval cues, acquired through conditioning. The evidence from eye-movement data in dream research (see Chapter 2) is relevant to the same point. Such conditioning would be highly probable in the case of eye movements in particular because they are intimately linked with the perceptual act, but we can go further and assume that correlated motor feedback from any response system could acquire a similar function. This would be especially true of one's own speech activity, which in many circumstances could be correlated with perceptual experience, resulting in the conditioning of visual images to implicit speech so that one can produce images by "talking to oneself." It need not be assumed that peripheral mechanisms are involved at every stage—connected segments of associative imagery may "run off" entirely at the central level, as would be assumed on the basis of Hebb's model (facilitation of cell-assembly activity by other assemblies) as well as the sensory conditioning model proposed by Sheffield (see above). Such imagery chains may be reflected in such reports as daydreaming without eye-movements (Singer, 1966). But, we are wandering somewhat afield. The point here is that conditioning provides a possible mechanism by which imaginal and verbal processes come to be evoked by verbal or nonverbal stimuli as associative chains, in which motor and sensory feedback play a modulating or regenerative role as conditioned stimuli once the process has been initiated by an associatively meaningful object or word.

Higher-order conditioning also has some empirical support as a mechanism in the development of denotative meaning from a study by Staats, Staats, and Heard (1959). Their basic procedure involved pairing a nonsense syllable (the CS) with a series of words that presumably elicit a particular common sensory meaning (the UCS words), then testing by a rating-scale procedure to see if the nonsense syllables had acquired the relevant kind of denotative meaning. Some syllables were paired with UCS words that had *angular* sensory meaning, e.g., square, box, roof; others were paired with words of *round* sensory meaning, e.g., coil, globe, hub. Ratings of the nonsense syllables following the conditioning trials indicated that they had significantly acquired the appropriate class of denotative meaning. This study is open to a criticism that applies generally to findings obtained using the paradigm originated by C. K. Staats and A. W. Staats (1957), i.e., that classical conditioning in the usual sense is not involved, but subjects see it instead as a problem-solving situation and give the expected ratings because they have become aware of the associative relations involved in the experiment (see Hare, 1964). Nevertheless, if subjects did indeed develop specific images (e.g., of a square, box, etc.) as associative reactions to a particular nonsense syllable, and these reactions mediated the appropriate rating (angularity), the data would support an interpretation of imaginal associative meaning in terms of associative experience occurring entirely at a verbal level. The problem deserves further investigation not only using the Staats paradigm but also using members of a class of objects or their pictures as the "UCS" items. Such studies could yield evidence bearing on the problem of the genesis of the meaning of general or abstract words (cf. Posner & Keele, 1968).

Despite the supporting evidence, the conditioning model encounters general difficulties that must be recognized. Granted that sensations can be conditioned and that this might occur to a limited degree in the case of verbal stimuli, classical conditioning seems inadequate to explain the productive quality and flexibility of imagery as an associative reaction to language. The images aroused by verbal cues often appear too complex and creative for them to have been acquired on the basis of actual contiguities in experience. Thus one can imagine objects and events that have never been experienced as percepts. The elements may be familiar, but their combination as images may be quite novel, not explainable in terms of actual associative experiences as demanded by the conditioning model. Something analogous to primary stimulus generalization might further such an explanation, but it would be strained and lacking in empirical support. In this respect imagery is similar to language, which is characterized especially by its productivity—one can say things that have never been said before, using old and familiar elements. Both imagery and verbal processes seem to require some kind of generative mechanism that will construct the content of the imagery or the verbal output from stored schemata, as emphasized by Bartlett (1932) in the case of memory, and more recently by Neisser (1967) in the case of cognitive processes generally. The nature of such a mechanism is unknown, although a neuropsychological theory such as Hebb's may eventually be sophisticated enough to cope with the phenomena. In any event, conditioning as it is presently understood in the laboratory setting is probably insufficient as a theoretical explanation for language-evoked images. Moreover, there is at the present time considerable uncertainty concerning the mechanisms involved in classical conditioning itself, although it is reasonably well understood operationally (cf. Kimble, 1961, Chapter 3), and for that reason alone it seems premature to use the concept as a complete explanation of image acquisition. An associative principle of some kind nevertheless must be involved at some stage, and conditioning *variables* must be relevant to the eventual understanding of associative imagery. We have at least seen some evidence that images are conditionable in the methodological sense and to that extent conditioning contributes to the conceptualization of concrete meaning.

Direct evidence on the development of effective concreteness   The tone of the preceding discussion reflects the remarkable lack of evidence on the precise conditions necessary for the development of different levels of meaning. Even the common assumption that the referential meaning of concrete words develops through their association with objects appears not to have been tested in any rigorous way until recently, perhaps because the problem seems trivial. Triviality implies, however, that we should have no difficulty demonstrating the acquisition of such meaning experimentally, and this has not been the case. As part of his doctoral research, Philipchalk (1971) carried out a long series of experiments on the problem in our laboratory using effectiveness in memory tasks as the major criterion of image-arousing capacity. It has been firmly established that the imagery value or concreteness of nouns is the best predictor of how easily they will be learned in a variety of tasks (see Chapters 7 and 8). Thus any imagery that a new word acquires experimentally should be reflected in its learnability, relative to control words, in subsequent learning tasks. An initial series of experiments involved repeated passive pairing of nonsense syllables with pictures of familiar objects. Syllables so treated were no more effective in subsequent memory and learning tasks than were syllables that the subjects had seen the same number of times without picture associates. Thus it appears that passive associative experience is insufficient to produce effective concreteness, or at least it is inefficient in this regard.

Nonsense syllables acquired effective concreteness, however, when subjects were required to respond appropriately to them during training. After two trials in which the syllables were presented along with pictures, concrete nouns, or abstract nouns, each syllable was presented alone and the subject was required to produce a rough drawing of the pictured object or to write the word with which the syllable had been paired. The picture or word then appeared, confirming or disconfirming the subject's response. This procedure was repeated for ten trials, during which the subjects responded with increasing accuracy and the speed of their anticipatory responses became asymptotically fast. The syllables were then paired with meaningful response words in a subsequent learning task. Provided that the subjects were also encouraged to use the associations learned in the first phase, learning in the second phase proved to be best for pairs in which the syllable member had previously been associated with pictures, next best for those previously associated with concrete nouns, and poorest for those that had been associated with abstract nouns. This is precisely the ordering that has been found for the referent stimuli themselves: Pictures are superior to concrete nouns, which in turn are more effective than abstract nouns, as stimuli in paired-associate learning (see Chapter 8).

A further experiment showed that overt responding was not required in the meaning-acquisition phase to produce the effect. Merely telling the subject to try to think about the picture or word that was to follow when the syllable appeared alone resulted in the same ordering of syllable effectiveness in the subsequent learning task. A tentative conclusion from this series of studies is that effective concreteness does not develop merely as a result of the passive pairing of word and object, but requires the active (overt or covert) generation of an image of the referent when the word is presented alone, coupled with subsequent reinforcement by the appearance of the object itself. To the extent that this conclusion proves to be valid, the acquisition of imagery-as-meaning would conform more closely to the discriminative operant conditioning paradigm than to sensory conditioning.

THE MEASUREMENT OF MEANING

This section is concerned with the measurement of the semantic stimulus attributes that are directly relevant to the theoretical views expressed in the preceding sections, and to the research to be described in subsequent chapters. The emphasis will be on criterial measures of the different theoretical levels of associative meaning and, more specifically, on the scaling of stimuli in terms of their concreteness, image-evoking value, and verbal associative meaningfulness, although attention will be given to other relevant dimensions as well. In addition, we will examine the relations among various scaled attributes in the light of expectations generated by the semantic theory.

Criterial Measures of Levels of Meaning

Representational meaning   The defining operations for representational meaning should reflect the availability of the imaginal and verbal representations corresponding to particular nonverbal and verbal stimulus units. Measures of familiarity and recognizability are most obviously relevant, since the responses required of the subject presumably do not depend on associative connections with other representational units. Specific operations would include familiarity ratings, frequency counts (e.g., Thorndike & Lorge, 1944), perceptual recognition thresholds, and reaction time for recognition responses. In the case of the last two, overt verbal responses would be appropriate (although not essential) if the stimulus is verbal but not if it is nonverbal, since the latter would theoretically involve an extra mediating step, or transformation, from imaginal to verbal representation. The theoretical validity of such measures is indicated by their relation to frequency of perceptual exposure to the stimuli, which presumably is a major determinant of the availability of the representational process. Thus, familiarization training and word frequency are directly related to the familiarity of the stimuli as measured by ratings (e.g., Noble, 1963), and to perceptual recognition thresholds as measured by various experimental procedures described in the next chapter. A further implication is that the criterial measures of this level of meaning of a particular stimulus unit should not be sensitive to associative connections with other units nor to associative experiences, provided that familiarity with the unit itself is controlled. These criterial features have implications that are relevant to our consideration of the relations among different scaled attributes, and for our later analysis of certain perceptual threshold and recognition phenomena.

Referential meaning   The defining operations for referential meaning are those that reflect the availability of an image as an associative response to a word, and of a verbal representation to a nonverbal stimulus. The former would be most directly measured by indices of the latency of image arousal to a word. This has been done empirically using the reaction time for a key press that indicates when the subject experienced an image (Paivio, 1966), and by the time taken to begin a simple line drawing of an object suggested by a stimulus word (Dominowski & Gadlin, 1968). The time required to judge a word and a subsequently presented object as being "same" or "different" would also be an appropriate index under conditions on which the subject expects the second stimulus to be an object rather than a word (cf. Posner, Boies, Eichelman, & Taylor, 1969; Tversky, 1969). The availability of a verbal representation should be indicated by the codability of an object. A number of such indices have been used, but the time taken to name an object may be regarded as the criterial measure. Since this presumably involves an extra coding step (the object must first arouse a representational image, i.e., it must be recognized), naming latency for an object should be longer than the time it takes to read the verbal label of the object. This is precisely what experimental data show (e.g., Fraisse, 1960, 1964, 1968). Moreover, consistent with the present analysis, Fraisse (1960) suggested that a supplementary coding of the "concrete sign" is involved and the subject must make a transition from the sign to the word.

The codability of colors has been measured in terms of intersubject agreement on naming color chips by R. W. Brown and Lenneberg (1954) and Lantz and Stefflre (1964). These investigators also used brevity of verbal descriptions of the stimuli by subjects as an index of codability, as did Glanzer and Clark (1963a) in the case of black and white figures and binary numbers. Still another index of codability is communicational accuracy, i.e., "the accuracy with which a verbal label applied to a stimulus by one person can be used by a second to identify the stimulus in the array" (Koen, 1966; Lantz & Stefflre, 1964), which especially takes into account the social nature of referential meaning. Note that intersubject agreement and communicational accuracy can be viewed as controlled *association commonality* measures, comparable to commonality indices in free association research. This operational analogy is important because it also establishes a bridge between these codability indexes and naming latency.

The relation is suggested by the finding that associative latency to a stimulus correlates negatively with response commonality (Woodworth & Schlosberg, 1954, p. 61; Laffal, 1955). With respect to referential associations, this means that the greater the amount of intersubject agreement on the name, the more quickly it should occur as a response to a nonverbal stimulus, presumably because the group data reflect the number of alternative labels and the dominance of a particular labeling response within the individual's repertoire of names for a given object.

The analysis can be extended to referent images. As suggested earlier in the discussion of meaning-as-imagery, a particular label might evoke a number of alternative images. For example, the word *dog* could arouse an image of either a Poodle or a Chow, depending on the person's past experiences with dogs and the context in which the word occurs. The alternative referent images may constitute a hierarchy that can vary in number and relative availability of the alternatives, and the latency of image arousal to a given label may be a function of these two parameters. The associative data necessary for testing such a view do not exist although they could be readily obtained by such procedures as presenting subjects with a concrete word and requiring them to generate drawings, or to choose the most representative referent from a series of alternative pictures.

One implication of the analysis is that the relative latencies of verbal and imaginal and referential reactions could vary, depending on the nature of their respective hierarchies. Only suggestive evidence is presently available on the problem. In an experiment to be discussed more fully in Chapter 5, Posner et al. (1969) found evidence suggesting that subjects can generate usable "visual information" about a letter within a period of .75 to 1 second after the letter name has been presented auditorily. Considering the visual letter as the referent object, the time can be taken as an estimate of the latency of the arousal of a referent image. This can be compared with faster naming latency—approximately .45 seconds—obtained by Morin, Konick, Troxell, and McPherson (1965) for visually presented letters. The difference must be interpreted cautiously because of the different methods involved. However, assuming that the data accurately reflect at least the direction of the difference, it could be interpreted in terms of the relative uncertainty of the implicit label and the referent images. A given letter of the alphabet can be visually represented (imaged) in several forms (e.g., B, b, ℓ) but each form has the same name ("be"). The difference in referential reaction time may be due to the greater number of possible alternatives in the case of the letter image as compared to the letter name. Other data suggest that the two classes of referential reactions need not differ in latency. Tversky (1969) used schematic faces with well-learned names as stimuli in a successive comparison task in which a single name or face was followed by another and the subject responded "same" if they had the same name and "different" if they did not. As in the case of the Posner et al. study just mentioned, the conditions of the experiment were such that latencies for generating images to the names or implicit names to faces could be inferred from the data. The results suggested that the two classes of referential reactions generally had comparable arousal latencies, approximating .64 seconds for well-practiced subjects under certain conditions.

The data from the above studies are rather indirect estimates of the latencies of referential reactions. Simpson (1970) used the more direct method of having subjects press a key when they "had an image" to a stimulus word (cf. Paivio, 1966). In addition, he estimated arousal time for a representational response to the same words by requiring subjects to press the key as soon as they recognized the word. Subjects in one phase of the experiment were tested repeatedly with the same word list until their reaction reached an asymptotic speed. As expected, the image latencies were again faster to concrete than to abstract nouns, but recognition time did not differ for the two classes. Thus Simpson succeeded in separating verbal representational and imaginal referential reactions operationally. Subtracting the recognition from the image response time yielded a value of approximately .60 seconds as an estimate of image latency to concrete words. This value, like the estimates from the other methods described above, has important implications for research in which images (or implicit labels) are assumed to play a mediational role, since it suggests a lower limit for the time required for a useful (potential) mediator to be elicited by a stimulus (see later chapters). Such a technique could be used systematically to estimate arousal latencies for all of the postulated levels of meaning reactions to different types of stimuli.

Since referential meaning reactions presumably depend upon representational meaning, although not vice versa, variables affecting the latter should also affect the former. That this may be so is suggested by Oldfield's (1966) finding that labeling speed for pictures of objects correlates positively with the Thorndike-Lorge frequency of their verbal labels. The direction of any causal chain is, of course, indeterminate in these data, so they are only suggestive. A "pure" index of referential meaning should also be independent of higher-level associative meaning. We shall later consider evidence relevant to that expectation as well.

Associative meaning   The third, associative, level of meaning is theoretically defined by operations related to the availability of associative linkages between representational processes corresponding to different referents or conceptual classes. These may involve associations between mental images, or "mental words," or mental images and words. Most of the empirical work has, of course, involved procedures designed to measure interverbal associations. A criterial measure, common also to representational and referential meaning, is the latency of verbal associative arousal, which has been directly measured frequently in the case of verbal stimuli (e.g., Hall & Ugelow, 1957; R. C. Johnson, 1964), and occasionally in the case of objects or their pictures (e.g., Karwoski, Gramlich, & Arnott, 1944). To make the situations comparable for verbal and pictorial stimuli, the subject in the latter case is required to respond with a verbal associate other than the name of the object. Since this again involves an extra step, one would expect the verbal associative reaction time to be longer when the stimulus is nonverbal, and this is indeed the case (e.g., Karwoski et al. 1944). Karwoski et al. suggest that the differences in reaction time result because a further process, often an image, intervenes between the stimulus and the response when the former is an object, which also is consistent with the present view.

Association value as originally measured by Glaze (1928) is an analog of associative reaction time, being based on the percentage of subjects who were able to think of an associate to a particular nonsense syllable in a brief time interval. R. C. Johnson (1964) obtained a product-moment correlation of —.80 between mean reaction time and Archer (1960) association values for 80 items. Noble's (1952a) m also involves a timed task, but it requires continuous associations and is, therefore, the most direct index of the number of associative connections between an item and other items. Although the overt response is verbal, however, it is by no means certain that the mediating processes also are verbal. This and other features of m will be considered in greater detail below, for it is a central variable in much of the research on learning and memory in subsequent chapters.

The verbal associative meaning of nonverbal stimuli has been quantified in a number of studies. Vanderplas and Garvin (1959a) defined the association value of random shapes in the same way as nonsense syllables were scaled by Glaze (1928), i.e., the percentage of subjects who gave associative responses to each form. Wimer and Lambert (1959), and Dominowski and Gadlin (1968) measured the meaningfulness of objects and pictures, respectively, in terms of Noble's m. It is interesting that no difference was found in either study between the mean m values for the nonverbal stimuli and the m of their corresponding noun labels.

Qualitative aspects of the verbal associations to pictures and their labels have also been studied occasionally. Otto (1962) found qualitative differences in the nature of the associations to groups of verbal and pictorial stimuli, sensory responses being relatively favored to pictorial representations in the case of certain stimulus groups, although not to others. Dominowski and Gadlin (1968) found that category names elicited fewer adjectives than either object names or pictures, possibly reflecting the "thinglike" characteristics of the latter two. Associations to the pictures and their names were very similar.

We turn now to a more detailed consideration of procedures that have been used to scale items on relevant dimensions specifically for the purpose of providing lists of items that would be useful in research. Attention will center on the degree to which the various empirical variables constitute "pure" measures of the theoretical dimensions outlined above, and to what extent they are confounded with other semantic characteristics.

Word Concreteness and Imagery

To the extent that imaginal processes are coordinated with abstractness-concreteness, a scaling of items on that dimension would define their capacity to evoke images. Objects and pictures are highly concrete by definition, but variation in concreteness is possible even at this level. Iscoe and Semler (1964) varied concreteness in terms of object-picture comparisons in learning. Jakobovits and Lambert (1964) compared objects, clear photographs, underexposed photographs, and line drawings in a study of semantic satiation. Bousfield, Esterson, and Whitmarsh (1957) compared colored with black and white drawings in a recall study. These studies all involved variation in concreteness entirely at the level of object representations. Although there has been no extensive scaling of such stimuli on concreteness, nor any systematic attempts to explore the effects of the dimension on behavior, the studies mentioned suggest directions that such enterprises might take. The paucity of work on the problem represents a gap that should be filled, particularly in view of its potential relevance to the understanding of abstract images, or nonverbal schemata.

More research has been concerned with the scaling of words on abstractness-concreteness and imagery. The balance of the discussion will be devoted to the problems that have arisen in that connection. Gorman (1961) categorized 1061 nouns as unambiguously concrete or abstract, according to the assessment of two judges. Concreteness was defined in terms of the directness of reference to things (including mythical creatures) and was distinguished from the general-specific dimension of meaning. That is, Gorman assumed that both concrete and abstract words can vary in specificity. The predictive validity of her scale was supported by a recognition memory experiment, which showed that recognition is higher for concrete than for abstract words. The value of Gorman's word list is somewhat restricted by her use of a dichotomous scale rather than one with finer gradations, and a general definitional problem is involved in that a dictionary definition of concreteness would not have psychological significance in those instances where a subject is unfamiliar with the conventional meaning of a word. These features were not involved in the procedure followed by Spreen and Schulz (1966), who used ratings of a group of subjects to scale 329 familiar nouns (Thorndike-Lorge frequency values of A) on a 7-point concreteness scale. Concreteness was defined in terms of reference to sense experience, and the judges did not use dictionaries.

The above studies provided no direct evidence on the relation of concreteness to imagery. Such data were first obtained by Paivio (1965) in the context of a PA learning experiment. Sixteen concrete and 16 abstract nouns from Gorman's list were rated by a group of subjects on a 5-point imagery scale. On the assumption that the usefulness of stimulus-evoked imagery as a mediator of verbal associations would depend on how readily an image is aroused, imagery was defined in terms of the ease or difficulty with which the word arouses a mental image (picture, sound, etc.). In effect, the scale was intended as a crude measure of the latency of stimulus-evoked imagery, i.e., the availability of referent images to words. The results showed that there was no overlap in the imagery (I) values of the concrete and abstract nouns, the former exceeding the latter in every case.

The high correlation between I and concreteness obtained in the initial study

(Paivio, 1965) was confirmed with larger samples of words in subsequent studies. In the most extensive of these, Paivio, Yuille, and Madigan (1968) obtained normative data on the concreteness, imagery, and m for 925 nouns of varying Thorndike-Lorge frequencies. Concreteness was defined as in the Spreen and Schulz study, and each word was rated on a 7-point abstract-concrete scale. Imagery was defined as by Paivio (1965), and each word was rated on a 7-point Low Imagery-High Imagery Scale. The correlation between the attributes was .83, and the correlations between scale values obtained from independent groups were .94 for both c and I, indicating considerable intersample stability of the variables. A subsample of 245 words appeared also in Gorman's list. The point-biserial correlation between her dichotomous values and seven-point concreteness is .87, indicating essential equivalence of the two measures for those purposes in which a dichotomous categorization suffices. Ninety words also appeared in Spreen and Schulz's list, and the correlation between their c values and those of Paivio et al. is .97. W. P. Brown and Ure (1969) and Walker (1970) reported comparably high correlations between their c and I ratings, respectively, and those of Paivio et al. These relations indicate that concreteness and imagery can be reliably indexed by different groups of judges using somewhat different scaling procedures. Furthermore, c and I substantially measure the same underlying variable, any discrepancy probably being due to the scaling instructions and to the distinction between conventional (dictionary) meaning and psychological meaning.

Paivio et al. found that discrepancies in I and c values occurred only for certain classes of words. One group included words like *ghost* and *phantom,* which were rated relatively abstract but high I, suggesting that the subjects were responding on the basis of object-character when rating on c, and sense experience involving, e.g., pictorial referents when rating on I. This did not occur for Gorman (1961), whose judges were instructed to rate fictitious creatures as concrete. Another group of words rated as abstract but relatively high I were affect labels and other terms implying sense experience other than visual-auditory, e.g., *anger, happiness,* etc. A smaller group of words showed the contrasting pattern in which c exceeds I. These are mainly uncommon words such as *antitoxin, armadillo,* etc., which presumably are recognized as names of "things," hence their high c ratings, but the things have been infrequently experienced, hence the low I.

Concreteness and imagery have also emerged as a single dimension in two factor-analytic studies of semantic dimensions. Paivio (1968) used group data to scale 96 nouns on 30 variables, including indices of concreteness and imagery. A factor analysis of the correlations among these variables yielded six factors, including a strong concreteness-imagery factor, which loaded highly on rated concreteness, tangibility, I, and vividness of imagery. Imaginal reaction time scores for the nouns also loaded highly on this factor, supporting the interpretation of it as a measure of the availability of referent images. Frincke (1968) also factor-analyzed the intercorrelations among a substantial number of characteristics of 74 nouns, including ratings of clearness of imagery and concreteness. Imagery and concreteness correlated .92. The factor analysis revealed two common factors, one of which Frincke called imagery-concreteness. In anticipation of later chapters, it may be noted that both studies found imagery-concreteness to be the best predictor of verbal learning scores.

Form class and imagery   The above studies involved only nouns. In unpublished research at Western University, we have obtained imagery ratings for 1318 words of various form classes using the Paivio et al. (1968) procedure. In descending order of magnitude, the mean I ratings for the different classes are as follows: nouns, 4.60; adjectives, 3.52; verbs, 3.30; pronouns, 3.03; adverbs, 2.41; and function words (a, about, against, etc.), 1.79. The noun class includes both concrete and abstract nouns. The concrete nouns far exceed other word classes in imagery level, but abstract nouns, adjectives, and verbs overlap on this attribute. These data will be relevant to later discussions of verbal learning and memory.

Interrelations between Imagery-Concreteness and Verbal-Associative Meaningfulness

While imagery-concreteness clearly emerged as a factor in the above studies, other nominal characteristics show some correlation with the imagery and concreteness variables and these relations are theoretically interesting. This is especially true of $m,$ as already mentioned, because it is an index of verbal associative meaningfulness and its relation to empirical measures of imagery and concreteness would accordingly confound the interpretation of the latter variables in terms of nonverbal processes.

Lambert (1955) was the first to show that concrete nouns exceed abstract in m and his finding has been confirmed in subsequent research with large samples of words. Gorman (1961) did not obtain m data for her sample, but Spreen and Schulz (1966) did so in theirs and found a correlation of .70 between c and m. Paivio, Yuille, and Madigan (1968) obtained correlations of .56 between c and $m,$ and .72 between I and m. Similarly, both Paivio (1968) and Frincke (1968) found substantial (and comparable) loadings of m on the imagery-concreteness factor. If we ignore for the moment the possibility that some entirely different process accounts for these relations, they can be interpreted alternatively to mean that imagery influences verbal associations, or that verbal (mental) associations influence the imagery and concreteness ratings, or that both processes are involved to some degree. The issue cannot be fully resolved, but there is suggestive evidence that imagery may be a determining factor in the relatively greater number of associations elicited by the concrete, high-imagery nouns.

Correlational data in the Paivio (1968) study unexpectedly showed that m correlated more highly with imaginal RT $(-.58)$ than with verbal RT $(-.30)$ when both latency measures involved the same response, a key press. The finding is difficult to reconcile with the view that m is determined entirely by the availability of verbal associations, but it is consistent with the interpretation that both are involved as components of an associative chain. That is, a concrete noun may evoke an object image that suggests a further imaginal associate that can be labeled verbally, and so on. Such imaginal "clusters" would be expected to occur as a result of associations of the referent objects in perceptual experience. Of course, purely verbal chains would be expected as well. This suggestion is generally consistent with the finding that continuous word responses tend to occur in clusters, or "bursts," of semantically related and associatively related words (Matthews, 1967; Pollio, 1964), but there is no way of distinguishing the possible contributions of mental images and mental words in such data.

Additional evidence that aids in the interpretation of the variables can be found in the nature of the relations between I, c, and m in the Paivio, Yuille, and Madigan study. The correlations indicated that m is more closely related to I ($r = .72$) than to c ($r = .56$). This difference is largely attributable to the evaluative-emotional items (affection, agony, anger, gaiety, pleasure, etc.) mentioned earlier, on which I and c differ. Most of the items in that group are rated as relatively abstract but not low on m or I. The addititional independence of m from both I and c is due mainly to items with low values on the last two. That is, many items can be found that are low in imagery and concreteness but relatively high in verbal associative meaningfulness. The relation is consistent with the developmental view, expressed earlier, that abstract items derive their meaning largely from intraverbal experience and that this is reflected in evoked verbal associations (i.e., m) but not necessarily evoked imagery. Highly concrete items, on the other hand, presumably are associated with both concrete-sensory and verbal experience, which are reflected in their high I and m values. These relationships between c and I on the one hand and m on the other appear precisely analogous to that suggested by A. W. Staats and C. K. Staats (1959) in the case of meaning and m—imagery-concreteness and m are "correlated but separate." We shall see later that this separation is empirically reflected in differential effects in verbal learning tasks.

Other Relevant Correlates

Familiarity and frequency   Various other word characteristics have been studied in relation to imagery-concreteness and meaningfulness. Familiarity is of particular interest because it was specified above as a criterial measure of the availability of representational processes but not of referential or associative meaning reactions. Nevertheless, the latter two are dependent on representational meaning (although not vice versa), so that some relationship would be expected between their empirical indices. The correlations between familiarity and imagery-concreteness are typically low, however. Paivio (1968) found no loading of either rated familiarity or Thorndike-Lorge frequency on the concreteness-imagery factor. Earlier, Paivio (1965) did find that concrete nouns exceeded abstract in auditory familiarity (as well as imagery) although the two classes of words were equated on frequency, and Paivio, Yuille, and Madigan (1968) obtained a small but significant correlation of .23 between I and frequency for their total sample of 925 nouns. Frincke (1968) unexpectedly found a moderate *negative* correlation between familiarity ratings and the imagery-concreteness factor, but he concludes that his finding is atypical. It may be concluded that, within the frequency ranges sampled, there is a slight positive relation between I and the familiarity of nouns. If the range were extended to include more extremely rare words, the correlation would be expected to increase, since both the verbal representations (presumably the determinants of familiarity) and referent images (the determinants of imagery ratings) would be relatively unavailable even in the case of concrete nouns.

The correlations between m and indices of familiarity has generally been slightly to moderately positive. Paivio, Yuille, and Madigan (1968) obtained a correlation of .33 between m and frequency for the 925 nouns. Paivio (1968) found m to correlate .21 and .23 with frequency and rated familiarity, and Frincke (1968) found m, frequency, and familiarity to load moderately (.54 or higher) on a "meaningful-familiarity" factor. However, Matthews (1965) failed to obtain a clear relation between m and word frequency. The above studies involved relatively familiar nouns. Noble (1953) reported a considerably higher correlation between m and rated familiarity for the 96 dissyllables from his original list (Noble, 1952a), which is not surprising since the list includes words that occur very infrequently in print, as well as nonsense words. The relation was nonlinear, however, familiarity being a negatively accelerated positive function of m. Noble (1963) also reported a rank-difference correlation of .83 between Thorndike-Lorge frequency and the m values of 60 words from the m-scale list.

The low correlation between the familiarity measures and m scores for words other than those in Noble's list and the curvilinear relation obtained by Noble for the latter indicate that the relations cannot be interpreted in terms of a single causal factor. Since familiarity has been shown to be a hyperbolic function of experimentally induced frequency of exposure (Noble, 1963, p. 103), Noble interprets familiarity and m to be related via the frequency factor, but he also concludes that frequency alone is insufficient to create associative meaningfulness—what is needed in addition is associative experience. This additional factor, according to Noble, creates an asymmetrical relationship: The meaningful is always familiar, but the familiar is not always meaningful (in the associative sense). It should be noted, however, that in the Paivio, Yuille, and Madigan normative sample of 925 nouns and in the Matthews (1965) study, some low-frequency words produced as many associates as high-frequency words, indicating that the highly meaningful is not necessarily highly familiar. Matthews suggests, and provides some evidence in support of, the hypothesis that associations in such instances may be given by a controlled chaining method. A low-frequency stimulus such as "mare" may evoke a high frequency associate such as "horse," which in turn generates further associates appropriate to the original stimulus. This interpretation involves the same general principle as suggested in the earlier discussion of the possible role of images (as well as verbal mediators) as part of an associative chain that might mediate the overt associations to concrete stimulus words.

Generality-specificity   Linguistic specificity has often been treated as equivalent to, or at least part of, the broader abstractness-concreteness continuum (e.g., R. W. Brown, 1958; Darley, Sherman, & Siegel, 1959; Hayakawa, 1949; Paivio, 1963). Spreen and Schulz (1966) took this ambiguity into account and had their 329 nouns rated for specificity as well as for concreteness. Their correlational analysis indicated that concreteness and specificity correlated only .38 when the contribution of other variables was partialed out. In agreement with this relative independence, specificity emerged as a factor separate from concreteness-imagery in the Paivio (1968) factor-analytic study. The results are somewhat puzzling because they would not be theoretically expected and because specificity and concreteness have been found to have similar effects on paired-associate learning (Paivio, 1966; Paivio & Olver, 1964). It is possible that the results are an artifact of the scaling procedures, but no firm explanation can be offered.

Emotionality   Emotionality was included as a semantic dimension in the factor-analytic study (Paivio, 1968) because of Skinner's (1957, p. 158) suggestion that concrete terms are more likely to be associated with specific affective stimuli and therefore have greater emotional effects than abstract terms. This interpretation was not borne out by the data, inasmuch as emotionality correlated *negatively* ($-.54$) with concreteness as well as rated imagery ($-.32$). Yuille (1968) confirmed the relation. Also consistent with these data is the finding that abstract words are associated with higher physiological arousal, as indexed by the GSR (Butter, 1970; M. G. Smith & Harleston, 1966) and pupillary dilation (Paivio & Simpson, 1966), than are concrete words. It may be recalled, too, that the possibility was suggested in the preceding chapter that emotional arousal may be an important factor in image acquisition. The data reviewed here suggest, however, that emotional arousal is not a necessary condition inasmuch as high-imagery words were, on the average, rated less emotional than low-imagery words. These findings cannot be regarded as definitive, but they are suggestive and worth pursuing by experimental techniques.

Semantic differential factors   Three factors, labeled evaluation, activity, and potency have shown up consistently in semantic differential investigations of connotative meaning (Osgood et al., 1957). Pivotal scales for these factors were included in Paivio's factor-analytic study in order to determine their relations to the concreteness and imagery variables. The three factors did not emerge clearly from the analysis, possibly because not enough representative scales were included. Good-bad, the pivotal scale for the evaluative factor (Osgood et al., 1957, p. 52), loaded most highly on a familiarity factor. This finding that the familiar is good is consistent with the findings of R. C. Johnson,

Thomson, and Frincke (1960) and Zajonc (1968). Active-passive, Osgood's pivotal scale for oriented activity, loaded most highly on a factor that seemed more appropriately labeled "impressiveness" than "activity," being defined as it was by such rating scales as impressiveness, interest, complexity, and colorfulness. Hard-soft, definitive of the semantic differential potency factor, had its highest loading on the specificity factor in the Paivio (1968) study. None of the pivotal scales from Osgood's factors loaded on the imagery-concreteness factor. Frincke (1968) found similar independence of imagery-concreteness and goodness as defined by two scales. These results make it clear that the dominant meaning factor being emphasized here (i.e., imagery-concreteness) is quite independent of the semantic differential factors that have been the subject of so much attention in recent years. Osgood et al. (1957, p. 65) do suggest that the tangible-intangible and substantial-insubstantial scales might reflect a separate dimension, but none of their studies included enough relevant scales to permit it to emerge as a group factor as it did in Paivio's and Frincke's studies (see also Di Vesta & Walls, 1970).

Thus a gap is filled, for the semantic differential factors can be regarded as exhausting the major portion of connotative meaning, whereas imagery-concreteness may be viewed as defining intensity of denotative meaning. The underlying psychological processes appear also to differ, connotative meaning involving affective (e.g., pleasant-unpleasant) and motor (e.g., active-passive) components, whereas denotative meaning involves cognitive imagery and (as indicated by the moderate loading of m on the imagery-concreteness factor) verbal associative processes.

A further general relation may be noted. The average polarity of the ratings (deviation from the midpoint of each scale) on 15 different semantic differential-type scales in the Paivio study loaded moderately (.46) on the imagery-concreteness factor as well as on two other factors. Frincke similarly found that evaluative scale polarity scores loaded moderately on both the imagery-concreteness and meaningful-familiarity factors. Thus semantic differential polarity seems to qualify as a general index of intensity of meaning.

SUMMARY

To summarize, a theoretical approach to meaning has been proposed in which mental images and words are regarded as major psychological reactions to objects and verbal stimuli. These reactions are the substance of an analysis involving three hypothetical levels of associative meaning: representational, referential, and associative chaining. *Representational meaning* implies that a mental representation or code (an image or word) corresponding to an object or verbal stimulus has been stored and is "available" for further psychological processing. The availability of a representation would be indexed by familiarity or recognition responses to the stimulus itself. *Referential meaning* implies an association *between* imaginal and verbal representations corresponding to the same referent, so that the object can evoke its verbal label and the label can arouse the object image. The defining operations include indices of the codability of objects and the image-evoking value of verbal stimuli. *Associative meaning* refers to chains or clusters of associations involving words, images, or both and is analogous to traditional verbal associative approaches with the difference that imaginal associative processes are recognized and given considerable weight in the analysis. Theoretically, such associative meaning implies associations between different classes of representational processes of either symbolic modality. However, most available operations tend to be restricted to the assessment of verbal associations alone.

Abstractness-concreteness of meaning was analyzed in terms of the associative model. Defined in terms of directness of sensory reference, concreteness is assumed to be psychologically differentiated primarily in terms of how readily or how directly images are available as associative reactions to the stimuli. Objects or pictures are highly concrete by definition. Concrete terms such as *house* readily evoke both images and words as associative (meaning) reactions, whereas abstract words such as *truth* more readily arouse only verbal associations. The meaning of the latter is primarily intraverbal. This is not an absolute distinction, however, since images could be aroused indirectly, secondarily, by the primary verbal association to an abstract stimulus, and might conceivably be aroused directly, depending on the nature of prior word-object associative experiences as well as the situational context. A similar analysis extends to function words and even nonsense syllables.

Simple perceptual exposure with or without exploratory motor activity, classical conditioning, and operant conditioning were discussed as possible mechanisms in the integration of the features of complex objects and words into unitary images and verbal representations, and the development of the associations between representations involved in referential and associative meaning. The meaning of concrete words is assumed to derive from associative experiences involving both objects and words, while that of abstract terms derives mainly from word-word associations.

Various scaling operations that define imaginal and verbal associative meaning and abstractness-concreteness were also reviewed. Investigations of the interrelations among specific measures of word meaning revealed that imagery-concreteness is a major semantic component, at least of nouns, and could be regarded generally as an index of intensity of denotative meaning. Aspects of the relations among the empirical variables are also consistent with the theoretical model.

The model has extensive implications, many of which have been tested at various stages of the development of the model itself in studies to be considered in subsequent chapters. Other studies indirectly provide relevant evidence. In general, imaginal and verbal processes are assumed to be functional as memory codes and associative mediators in situations in which the items vary in their concreteness. Performance is assumed to vary as a function of the availability of either, or both, of the symbolic codes, where availability is manipulated by varying stimulus meaning as defined in the present chapter or by experimental procedures such as different instructional sets, stimulus presentation rates, and so on. The mediational function of images and verbal processes in response to stimuli varying appropriately in meaning is relevant not only to isolated stimulus units or pairs of units but to connected discourse, including natural language, and they are implicated most intimately in perceptual phenomena, as we shall see in the following chapter.

4

Perception and the
Symbolic Processes:
Effects of Meaning

The consideration of empirical evidence on the functional significance of the symbolic processes begins appropriately with perceptual phenomena. Both processes, but especially imagery, are generally assumed to be related to perception in their developmental origin and in their functional properties. In addition, many traditional and contemporary approaches to perception have included the theoretical view that the symbolic processes modify or interact with sensory input to determine perceptual experience. We shall first review what has been said by these theorists concerning the matter, together with preliminary supporting evidence. This is followed by a statement of the theoretical position to be adopted here—essentially a restatement of the views presented in the preceding chapters as they apply to perceptual phenomena. The implications are then evaluated in the light of selected evidence, reviewed in two parts. The present chapter will be concerned with studies of the effects of stimulus meaning, whereas Chapter 5 deals primarily with effects of the experimental arousal of the symbolic processes on perception.

Imagery and Perception

The relation between perception and imagery is introspectively most obvious in the case of dreams, which we unhesitatingly identify as visual experiences sometimes rivaling "real" perception in their vividness. That waking imagery similarly involves perceptual mechanisms has been assumed by various theorists. Indeed, it has been suggested directly that perception itself involves the activation of neural patterns, or schemata, or cell assemblies that are the basis of imagery as well (Bruner, 1957; Hebb, 1949, 1968; Pribram, 1960; J. G. Taylor, 1962; Tomkins, 1962). According to such an approach, perception consists of some kind of matching process involving sensory input and the neuronal model. Bruner, for example, likens perceptual identification to the "determination of a fit between a model and some sample that is being matched to it" (1957, p. 344). The theoretical identity of perception and imagery is plainly expressed by Tomkins in regard to the conscious experience of perception:

> It is our belief that the afferent sensory information is not directly transformed into a conscious report. What is consciously perceived is *imagery* which is created by the organism itself. Psychologists from Galton to Freud have investigated imagery without appreciating its full significance. The world we perceive is a dream we learn to have from a script we have not written. It is neither our capricious construction nor a gift we inherit without work. Before any sensory message becomes conscious it must be matched by a centrally-innervated feedback mechanism (1962, p. 13).

Such accounts imply a template model of the perceptual process, but the fit between image and percept can also be expressed in another manner. Neisser (1967), following Bartlett's (1932) approach to memory, interprets visual perception and visual imagery as constructive processes involving the synthesis of visual information. From perceptual experience the perceiver continually constructs a model or schema of the world around him. In dreams and in waking images the same kind of constructive process is assumed to occur with the difference that the representational processes are somehow activated in the absence of "adequate" stimulation. The process may thus be described as having "autogenetic properties" (Bruner, 1957, p. 349) or as a learned skill in which "central sending produces the conscious image in the absence of afferent support" (Tomkins, 1962, p. 13). The same notion has been described by Hebb (1963) as the "semiautonomous process," meaning, in his theoretical language, that cell assembly activity can be centrally initiated, although requiring periodic sensory support for its maintenance.

The kind of theoretical approach suggested above is basically very old, its classical version being the structuralist view that perception is a combination of sensations (stimulation of receptors) and memory images (recollections of previous sensations). It has not been acceptable to all perceptual theorists. J. J. Gibson has consistently rejected all such approaches, denying that the concept of imagery has any validity or usefulness (Gibson, 1966). Hochberg (1964) similarly asserted that the doctrine of memory images that developed through association of sensations is without supporting evidence and is inapplicable to perceptual phenomena. The objections are not unequivocal, however, for Gibson nevertheless admits the validity of such phenomena as hallucinations and discusses them in terms of internal excitations of the nervous system (J. J. Gibson, 1966, pp. 316–317). Furthermore, Hochberg (1968) has recently modified his theoretical position to include the role of memory structures in perception. Following a consideration of evidence that indicated that successive brief glimpses ("momentary glances") of the parts of a figure will yield a structured perception of the entire pattern, Hochberg postulates an integrative component in visual processing, which he refers to as a *schematic map*. He suggests that such maps are built up from previous experience as well as from the successive views of a given object or scene, and that they function as the "glue" by which the successive glimpses are joined into a single perceptual structure. The relevance of such views to the present discussion is evident in Hochberg's concluding statement: "If you try translating the above into the old words: momentary glance into 'sensation,' schematic map into 'image,' and perceptual structure into 'perception,' the fit is very good indeed. The units and measures have changed, but the main features . . . are surprisingly close to those outlined by Helmholtz, Wundt and Titchener" (1968, p. 330).

The above theoretical views included two related propositions or assumptions: first, that imagery and visual perception involve similar processes, and second, that imagery and sensation interact to determine perceptual phenomena. The second proposition is a major theme of this chapter, and evidence relevant to it will be considered later. A brief summary at this point of some experimental support for the first assumption will establish a firmer basis for the later discussions. That waking imagery may be indistinguishable from unclear perceptions was demonstrated in the classic experiment by Perky (1910), whose subjects accepted faint projections of objects as being the products of their imagination. This finding has been replicated and extended recently in a series of studies by Segal and her associates (e.g., Segal, 1968; Segal & Nathan, 1964), aspects of which will be considered in detail later on. Essentially the same general point emerges from a study by Barber (1959a), in which some subjects reported negative afterimages of "hallucinated" colors following a "minimal hypnotic induction procedure." Similar results were obtained with other subjects when they were asked to imagine colors without the hypnotic procedure. The perceptual nature of the phenomenon is strongly suggested by the fact that the subjects were unable to define or name complementary colors. However, further research on the mechanism involved is clearly needed, as Barber points out.

Additional objective evidence relating imagery and· perception is provided by the finding that eye movements appropriate to the perception of a situation accompany dream imagery as described by the subject (Dement, 1965), as well as waking imagery as defined by instructions to imagine situations or perceptual tasks (e.g., Antrobus, Antrobus, & Singer, 1964; Berlyne, 1965, pp. 140–144). A study by Deckert (1964) in particular provides rather unequivocal evidence of the perceptual nature of imagery in that subjects who were asked to imagine a beating pendulum developed smooth pursuit movements of a frequency comparable to that of a previously visualized real pendulum, rather than saccadic movements, which would be normally expected with eye movements in the absence of a moving object. Deckert suggests that the necessary prerequisite for such eye movements is the development of an appropriate cerebral image. The finding supports an "outflow" theory of eye movement control, with the control presumably initiated by the central activity (imagery).[1]

---

[1] A recent study by Graham (1970) failed to replicate Deckert's finding, so this particular interpretation must now be regarded as questionable.

Verbal Processes and Perception

Like visual imagery, verbal symbolic processes are theoretically linked to perception in two senses. A direct relation is implied by the interpretation of verbal processes as involving auditory (or auditory-motor) mechanisms. Verbal processes accordingly would be expected to have some of the functional properties of the auditory system, just as visual images appear to be functionally similar to visual perception. The second relationship is that implied in the assumption that verbal processes have a determining influence on perceptual experience regardless of the modality of the latter. This assumption is at least partly the basis of Whorf's (1956) hypothesis of linguistic determinism, which is concerned in the most general sense with the influence of language on non-verbal cognitive processes, including perception. Bruner's (1957) categorization theory of perception is similar to the Whorfian hypothesis. Bruner hypothesized that perception *is* an act of categorization, so that an object is perceived only after it has been appropriately classified. Furthermore, these categories are primarily linguistic. Thus the Whorfian and Brunerian theories both imply that perceptual phenomena are at least partly mediated by verbal mechanisms.

Haber (1966), in a review of the effects of set on perception, also suggests that many of the reported effects can be explained in terms of encoding processes. His analysis takes cognizance of the persistence of memory for stimuli, after the stimuli and their short-term memory have terminated. During the presence of a stimulus or its short-term memory, the stimulus is encoded into previously learned linguistic units, usually words, and such encoding mediates reorganization of the memory process. Haber reports several experiments that suggest that effects of set and other variables interact with the coding strategy adopted by the subject. Other investigators also have applied encoding processes to a wide range of perceptual problems. Particularly interesting here because it explicitly incorporates only verbal mediation processes, is Glanzer and Clark's (1963a) "verbal-loop" hypothesis, which states essentially that performance on a perceptual task depends on the length of the chain of covert verbalization demanded by the task. If, as in most perceptual tasks, there is either limited exposure of the stimulus or some delay between exposure and final response, then those stimuli that elicit a long verbalization will be handled less accurately than those that elicit short verbalization. Stimulus complexity is thus identified with the length of the subject's verbalization. The implications of the above views will be examined presently in the context of experimental studies of perception.

IMAGINAL AND VERBAL PROCESSES IN PERCEPTION: THE PRESENT APPROACH

The approach to be taken to perceptual phenomena here combines some of the general features of the views mentioned above with more specific hypotheses concerning the functional properties of the two postulated symbolic systems.

In addition, specific operational approaches to the definition and manipulation of the symbolic processes will be emphasized.

The most general theoretical statement that might be made on the basis of the views already summarized above is that imaginal and verbal processes interact with stimulus conditions to determine perceptual phenomena. Beyond this, however, we must be able to specify the nature of the interaction and the conditions that influence it. The theoretical assumption that perception and the symbolic processes involve the same mechanisms suggests that imagery or verbal symbolic processes could either facilitate, interfere with, or have no effect on perceptual experience or the performance of a perceptual task, depending on the availability or accessibility of the symbolic processes and their relevance to the perceptual task. Availability and accessibility are assumed to be a function of stimulus meaning, as hypothesized in the preceding chapter, experimental conditions (to be specified in Chapter 5), and individual differences in symbolic habits (to be considered in Chapter 14). Task relevance has the following implications: Any facilitation of perceptual task-performance would be expected to occur only when the aroused image or verbal process is congruent with the process aroused by the target stimulus; otherwise the effect may be one of interference if the symbolic modality is the same as the perceptual modality involved in the task, and simple distraction if the symbolic and perceptual modes differ. The specific implications of this general theoretical statement will be spelled out in the context of the relevant research.

Some Preliminary Issues

It is necessary first to limit the range of the perceptual phenomena to be considered and to specify the particular classes of operations that will define the symbolic processes assumed to influence those phenomena.

The problem of defining perception has been given detailed consideration in writings devoted to the field of perception more generally than is the case in the present book (e.g., F. H. Allport, 1955; Dember, 1960; Epstein, 1967; Hebb, 1949; Neisser, 1967). No comparable treatment can be given the problem here, but certain aspects of it cannot be avoided. The distinction between perceptual and memory phenomena is a central issue. What determines whether a particular behavioral effect belongs properly in one category rather than the other? The problem has two facets, one involving long-term memory and the other, short-term memory. In regard to the former, Zuckerman and Rock (1957) argued that perception should be distinguished from recognition, identification, and interpretation, all of which involve factors derived from past experience. Such factors can enrich or modify perception, but they do not explain the "innate organization" in visual perception when an object is perceived for the first time. While it is important to recognize the distinction, it does not represent a serious problem here inasmuch as we are specifically interested in the contributions of long-term memory processes in perception.

The other aspect of the problem, that of distinguishing between perception and short-term memory, arises from the fact that many so-called perceptual tasks involve a memory component in the form of a delay between stimulus exposure and the response (e.g., recognition threshold studies), or between the viewing of one stimulus and another to which the first is being compared (e.g., perceptual discrimination studies). One solution to the problem is to restrict perceptual tasks to ones in which the delay is absent or minimal. Thus, if a discrimination problem is involved, the to-be-compared stimuli should be viewed simultaneously (cf. F. H. Allport, 1955, pp. 329–330). Unfortunately, such a restriction would rule out successive discrimination as a perceptual research problem, and even the study of form perception would be difficult because such perception ordinarily requires successive fixations of the features of a pattern, thereby implicating short-term memory (cf. Hochberg, 1968).

Closely related to the memory issue is the problem of distinguishing between effects operating at the input side of perception, involving the "appearance" of things, and those attributable to output or response mechanisms. This issue has been particularly important in studies of the effects of set on perception, where the theoretical alternatives have been the "perceptual tuning" hypothesis, which assigns the effects to the perceptual system itself, and different versions of the "response" hypothesis, according to which set operates either on the memory trace or on responses occurring to the perceptual experience (Haber, 1966).

The attitude adopted here in regard to these issues is one that is rapidly coming to the fore in perceptual research (e.g., Neisser, 1967). Rather than attempt to eliminate memory or response factors from perception, it is useful to think in terms of a continuum of *information processing,* which involves perceptual, memory, and response processes in different degrees, depending on temporal and other relevant factors. The problem is to distinguish conceptually between the different processes, to identify the controlling variables, and to specify the nature and locus of their effects over the time course of information processing.

Our discussion of the problem will be restricted to research findings that contribute most directly to the understanding of the role of the symbolic processes in perception and that can be meaningfully related to subsequent discussions of learning and memory. In effect, this means that we will be concerned primarily with the same classes of independent variables as the studies reviewed in later chapters. These variables include (*a*) relevant dimensions of stimulus meaning, particularly familiarity, abstractness-concreteness, and associative meaningfulness; and (*b*) experimental manipulation or arousal of the symbolic processes by such methods as instructional sets, associative "priming," and variations in task difficulty and concreteness. Effects of these classes of variables will be considered in relation to recognition and detection thresholds, perceptual stability, functional (right-left) asymmetries in perception, certain memory tasks in which perceptual variables are prominent, and so on. The emphasis throughout the remainder of this chapter and the following one will be on the theoretical specification of the *differential* functional characteristics of imaginal and verbal symbolic systems in relation to perception.

STUDIES OF THE EFFECTS OF STIMULUS MEANING

Meaning was defined in Chapter 3 in terms of the associative processes that are reliably evoked by a stimulus, three levels of meaning being distinguished in such terms. Representational meaning refers to the availability of a symbolic representation (mental image or word) corresponding to the stimulus unit, so that the stimulus has some degree of familiarity and will elicit a recognition response. Referential meaning implies a higher-order associative process involving a linkage between an object-image and the name of the object, so that the referent object can evoke a labeling response and the name, an object image. Finally, associative meaning involves further associative connections between different images, words, or both. The analysis has interesting implications regarding perceptual phenomena. *It implies that the availability of processes at any given level, and hence any effects attributable to them, would depend not only on the pre-experimentally defined meaning of the stimulus items but also upon such variables as their relevance for the required response and the time available for their operation as a result of stimulus durations or memory factors. Meaning should be unimportant if little memory load is involved and no representational (labeling) response is required. If the task demands only an immediate recognition of the stimulus, its familiarity should be important, but higher levels of meaning should be irrelevant. Higher-order associative meaning may be effective, however, if sufficient time is available for the associative processes to be evoked·during the perceptual task.*

Perceptual Thresholds and Meaning

Familiarity   Evidence relevant to the above hypothesis is provided by comparisons of the effects of different stimulus and response variables on perceptual thresholds. One of the most reliable findings in the area is that familiar stimuli are correctly identified at briefer (or with fewer) tachistoscopic exposures than are unfamiliar stimuli (e.g., see Dember, 1960). This is consistent with the generalization that ease of recognition depends on the availability of a memory representation, and an appropriate verbal label if recognition must be indicated by naming. Some recent studies have shown that familiarity is unimportant when such factors are minimized. Robinson, Brown, and Hayes (1964) compared the effects of familiarity on same-different and identification thresholds. The former involves presentations of pairs of stimuli whose components may be identical or different and the subject judges them as "same" or "different." Robinson et al. reasoned that the same-different method yields effects that can be termed "perceptual" because it avoids the memory and response factors involved in recognition or identification procedures. Using both methods, they obtained duration thresholds for letters varying in familiarity according to their frequency of occurrence and their physical orientation (normal versus reversed). The results, presented in Figure 4-1 for the letter orientation conditions, showed

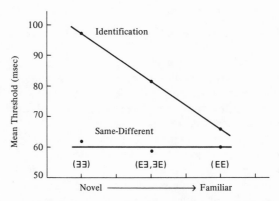

FIGURE 4-1.   Mean same-different and identification thresholds for letter pairs varying in familiarity of orientation. From Robinson, Brown, and Hayes (1964).

the usual facilitating effect of familiarity on identification, but the familiarity variables had no effect on same-different thresholds.

Experiments reported by Hochberg (1968) show the same lack of effect of familiarity on same-different judgments for pairs of words when the comparison is direct or simultaneous, but they also revealed that familiarity becomes important when the comparison is indirect or successive and hence involves short-term memory. In the direct condition, the two words appeared close together; in the indirect condition they were separated horizontally so that both could not be seen foveally with one fixation. The results showed no measurable effect of familiarity (meaning, pronunciability, orientation) when the comparison was direct. When it was indirect, however, the number of tachistoscopic glances needed in order to judge whether the words were the same or different was greater for the unfamiliar than for the familiar words.

It can be concluded from these findings that the familiarity, or representational meaning, of verbal stimulus patterns has no effect on perceptual thresholds when memory is not a factor in the task. Familiarity becomes important, however, when memory is involved, as it is in indirect or successive comparison that involves short-term memory, and in a recognition task where the stimulus must be "compared" with a long-term memory image or (in Hochberg's terms) schematic map. These findings leave open the question of the role of higher-order referential and associative meaning in perceptual threshold studies. The present position is that such meaning is unimportant even in recognition tasks unless they involve labeling, memory, or associative factors. The hypothesis will be examined in the light of the literature on verbal codability, concreteness, and meaningfulness variables in perceptual threshold research.

Verbal codability   Kimura (1963) reported that subjects with lesions of the right temporal lobe are impaired relative to controls in the tachistoscopic perception of unfamiliar, but not of familiar, nonverbal stimuli. She discussed the findings in terms of Hebb's cell assembly theory but also suggested that "verbal identifiability" may be a crucial concomitant of familiarity. Her reasoning apparently was that no differences occurred with familiar material because the neural representations correlated with familiarity are located in the language center, that is, in the left (undamaged) hemisphere. The permanent neural representation of unfamiliar stimuli, on the other hand, may not be extensively elaborated in that hemisphere and the right hemisphere accordingly plays a more important role in the perception of unfamiliar stimuli.

The neuropsychological implications are not in question here. The central issue is whether verbal identifiability is indeed crucial to the "rapid visual identification" of familiar nonverbal stimuli, as Kimura suggests. The alternative suggested here is that familiarity should be critical independent of verbal codability unless an associative or memory component is involved in the task. In Kimura's study, each stimulus was presented for a constant (brief) exposure time, followed by a recognition test in which the subject was given a card containing all the stimuli presented during that test series. He was required to say the number of, or point out, the object he had been presented. The procedure introduces a delay between stimulus presentation and response that might have been bridged by holding the verbal label in a short-term memory store in the case of familiar objects. The verbal label need not have played any role whatever in the discriminative perception of the stimulus. The question must remain open, however, since it apparently has not been adequately investigated in the context of recognition threshold research. Related studies on the effects of acquired distinctiveness of cues have been concerned with discrimination and recognition memory rather than perceptual thresholds as the dependent variable (see Epstein, 1967, Chapter 6). Thus they do not provide an answer to the present question, although they are relevant to the general issues with which we are concerned and will be considered in detail later (Chapter 7).

Word concreteness and meaningfulness   On the basis of the evidence reviewed in the preceding chapter, it is assumed here that the major effective variable differentiating concrete and abstract words is the availability of referent images: The former readily evoke images, the latter do not. Concreteness, so defined, should be irrelevant to immediate perceptual recognition of a word because the arousal of the effective meaning component depends upon prior recognition of the eliciting word. Precisely the same conclusion applies to verbal associative meaningfulness, or *m*. To argue otherwise would require one to postulate a perceptual mechanism that is sensitive to meaning independent of word recognition. I consider such a mechanism unnecessary and implausible in the present context as it has been found by others (e.g., Eriksen, 1958; Neisser, 1967, pp. 126–134; Zuckerman and Rock, 1957) in relation to the issue of perceptual defense, "semantic subception," and other effects related to the connotative meaning of words and experiential variables generally. What are the facts in regard to concreteness and *m*?

Winnick and Kressel (1965) used concrete and abstract words varying in frequency from Gorman's (1961) list in a visual recognition threshold experiment and found no differences in duration thresholds for the two categories, but did find the usual effect for word frequency. J. A. Taylor (1958) investigated the effects of meaning and frequency of exposure on duration thresholds. Meaning was experimentally manipulated by preliminary training involving 15 exposures of nonsense syllable stimuli, each accompanied by a picture of a familiar common object. This procedure can be interpreted as an attempt to produce concrete meaning experimentally, although it obviously does not parallel the associative experience ordinarily involved in the learning of concrete words, either in amount or in quality. Frequency was varied by giving the same number of exposures to the nonsense syllables alone. The results showed that, while both procedures reduced duration thresholds relative to a control list, frequency and meaning conditions did not differ. The findings of both of the above studies are consistent with the hypothesis that representational meaning (familiarity) is important to tachistoscopic recognition, but higher-order referential meaning (concreteness) is not.

Other studies do not support the negative conclusion regarding concreteness. Riegel and Riegel (1961) correlated visual duration threshold data for words with a number of word characteristics, including frequency and abstractness-concreteness. Positive correlations were obtained for both of these variables, with concreteness emerging as the best single predictor of thresholds. Spreen, Borkowski, and Benton (1967) similarly found superior auditory recognition for more concrete words than for less concrete words under conditions of masking noise. Thus concreteness has been found to be ineffective in two threshold experiments and positively effective in two others. An attempted resolution of the ambiguity will be considered presently.

Verbal associative meaningfulness (m) has also been proposed as a variable that would be relevant to tachistoscopic recognition performance. While Noble (1953) did not explicitly make such a prediction, he did suggest that stimuli acquire both m and familiarity (f) as some monotonic function of frequency, and that endowing stimuli with m or f "may constitute one unambiguous definition of Thorndikian 'identifiability,' which in turn may be related to such current notions as 'pre-differentiated structure,' 'distinctiveness,' 'cue-value,' and 'recognizability' " (p. 97). Thus, m and f were lumped together with the implication that m defines properties that should be relevant to immediate perceptual recognition. Kristofferson (1957), apparently basing his study on the above assumptions, investigated the effects of m and rated familiarity on visual duration thresholds for 20 words from Noble's (1952a) list. Both variables correlated substantially and about equally with thresholds. Unfortunately, m and familiarity were completely confounded since the two correlated .97 (Spearman's rho, calculated from his data) in the sample used. Whether *number of associations* per se, as measured by m, has any effect was thus left indeterminate. However, R. C. Johnson, Frincke, and Martin (1961) obtained a small but significant effect of word m on thresholds when frequency was controlled.

Meaningfulness has been ineffective in other studies. Inasmuch as concreteness and m covaried in the Winnick and Kressel (1965) study described above, their failure to obtain any effect of concreteness on thresholds applies to m as well. E. J. Gibson, Bishop, Schiff, and Smith (1964) found recognition thresholds, as measured by the relative brightness of the exposure field, to be higher for meaningful trigrams such as IBM and FBI than for relatively meaningless but pronounceable syllables such as MIB and BIF. Meaningfulness was measured by a rating scale and its relation to associative meaningfulness (m) is therefore uncertain, but it seems improbable that m would be higher for the low-meaningful items than for the high-meaningful items. It seems reasonable to conclude, therefore, that pronunciability had a stronger positive effect on ease of recognition than did meaningfulness, however the latter is defined. If correct, this conclusion is highly relevant here, for it implies that pronunciability is effective because it reflects the availability and accessibility of corresponding verbal representational processes. Such availability could be a function of the frequency with which the pronounceable syllables have been heard, spoken, and seen as integrated components of words. As in the case of concreteness, however, the empirical status of m needs clarification before any further theoretical speculation is justified.

Paivio and O'Neill (1970) attempted to resolve some of the ambiguity concerning the effectiveness of both imagery-concreteness and m in tachistoscopic recognition, comparing the effects of these variables with that of familiarity. Two sets of nouns were selected from the Paivio, Yuille, and Madigan (1968) list. In one set, m was held constant while imagery-concreteness and frequency were factorially varied so that half the words were high on imagery and concreteness, and half were low on these variables. Half of the words of each imagery level were high in frequency of usage, and half were low frequency according to the Thorndike-Lorge (1944) word count. The other set involved similar factorial variation of m and frequency, with I and C held constant. Tachistoscopic duration thresholds were determined for each word using the ascending method of limits. The mean threshold values are presented in Table 4-1. As may be seen, the results for both lists revealed the typical positive relation between frequency and thresholds, i.e., the more familiar words were significantly easier

Table 4-1

Mean Tachistoscopic Recognition Thresholds for Words in Milliseconds as a Function of Word Frequency (F), Imagery (I), and Meaningfulness (m). From Paivio and O'Neill (1970).

	High F	Low F
High I	17.13	25.50
Low I	16.88	20.50
High m	16.25	20.63
Low m	20.50	28.63

to identify. The relation between m and ease of recognition also was positive, confirming the findings of Kristofferson (1957) and R. C. Johnson et al. (1961). The effect of I-C was significantly *negative,* however, words low on imagery-concreteness being more readily identified than ones that are high on this attribute. This unexpected result is inconsistent with the results obtained by the Riegels and, to a lesser degree, with those of Winnick and Kressel.

It seemed possible that familiarity may not have been adequately controlled in the Paivio and O'Neill experiment by the selection of words on the basis of their Thorndike and Lorge frequencies. This was suggested by the fact that several subjects, upon recognizing the stimulus word *perception* spontaneously commented that they had just been studying the topic of perception in their introductory psychology course. The mean threshold for this word, which was classified in the experiment as abstract and relatively infrequent, was lower than that for any other member of that class. Thus, in one case at least an abstract word was unusually easy to identify because it was unexpectedly familiar. To determine the possible role of such uncontrolled familiarity, the original experimental subjects rated each of the stimulus words in the experiment on familiarity, using a seven-point scale. Mean familiarity scores were obtained for each word and correlations computed between the familiarity, mean threshold, imagery, and m values for the words. In the case of the list in which imagery was varied, rated familiarity correlated $-.48$ with I, and $-.58$ with thresholds. When rated familiarity was partialed out, a correlated of .28 between I scores and thresholds was reduced to zero, whereas the correlation between familiarity and thresholds was essentially unaffected by partialing out I. The apparent effect of concreteness on thresholds in the original analysis could thus be explained entirely in terms of uncontrolled familiarity.

In the case of the m-varied list, mean familiarity ratings correlated .40 with m and $-.54$ with thresholds. With familiarity partialed out, a correlation of $-.45$ between m and thresholds was reduced to $-.29$. With m held constant, however, the correlation between familiarity and thresholds was still a substantial $-.44$. Thus the possibility remained that m may have a small independent effect, although familiarity accounted for much more of the variance in thresholds. The small but significant effect of m was confirmed in two further experiments.

In summary, although firm conclusions cannot yet be drawn from the relatively few recognition threshold studies that have involved variables that can be taken to define imaginal or verbal associative meaning, relative support emerges for the hypothesis that such meaning is not a potent variable affecting immediate perception. Positive effects have been obtained only inconsistently, and the Paivio and O'Neill results swung the balance of the evidence in favor of the conclusion that imagery-concreteness is ineffective and, although m was consistently related to thresholds, its effect is small relative to that of frequency-familiarity.[2] By contrast, the effects of imagery in particular have been very

---

[2] These conclusions have been recently confirmed and extended by O'Neill (1971) in a series of experiments involving dichotic listening tasks.

consistent and strong in learning and memory tasks. The bulk of the evidence on the latter effects will be considered in later chapters. To emphasize the point, however, it may be noted that the conclusion is directly supported by two of the studies reviewed here. While Winnick and Kressel (1965) failed to find any effect of concreteness (or its correlate, m) on recognition thresholds, they did find that subsequent free recall for the words that had been used in the tachistoscopic recognition phase, without any further exposure to them, was higher in the case of concrete than abstract words. In addition, the concrete words were superior as items in a separate paired-associate learning experiment. E. J. Gibson et al. (1964) similarly found that, while pronunciability was more effective than meaningfulness in perceptual recognition, meaningfulness was the better predictor of retention as measured by both recognition and free recall.

The present position is also favored theoretically. No one seems to have proposed a reasonable mechanism that would indicate how referential or associative meaning might contribute to perceptual recognition at fast exposure speeds when associative and memory factors are minimized. Until such a mechanism is made explicit, the present position remains that such meaning cannot affect perceptual recognition because the stimulus must first evoke the appropriate representation before any further associative verbal process or image can be aroused. Evocation of the former should be sufficient for perceptual identification without the arousal of the latter, and familiarity alone should be the relevant stimulus attribute. The majority of the studies reviewed here are consistent with the hypothesis, but a few exceptions remain unexplained.

Perceptual Stability and Meaning

Under certain conditions of reduced stimulation, visual objects exhibit perceptual instability, which is characterized by the disappearance and intermittent reappearance of the object or some portion of it. This has been observed when the image is stabilized on the retina by means of an optical projection system attached to a contact lens (see Pritchard, Heron, & Hebb, 1960), when a luminous target is viewed under conditions of reduced illumination (McKinney, 1963), when a target is defocused (McKinney, 1966b), and when it is viewed as a prolonged afterimage (Bennet-Clark & Evans, 1963). Experiments using these techniques have demonstrated that the image tends to fragment and disappear in perceptual units of varying size and complexity. Since meaning and past experience are apparently among the more potent determinants of such unit effects, the phenomenon is of unusual interest here. The most relevant findings will be reviewed in the present theoretical context.

Pritchard et al. (1960), summarizing the effects that were consistently reported by their subjects, noted that a meaningful figure or part of a figure is visible longer than a meaningless one. This can be illustrated by references to the three stimulus patterns shown in Figure 4-2. The left panel (a) shows a meaningless curve on the left and a profile of a face on the right. When seen with the apparent fixation point being midway, the meaningless curve faded faster and was absent more often than the face. The pattern shown in Figure 4-2b

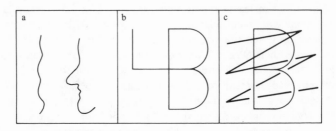

FIGURE 4-2.   Examples of visual stimuli used by Pritchard, Heron, and Hebb (1960).

includes a "4," a "B," and a "3." The fading of parts of the figure was not random—when any part was present, it almost always included one or more of the symbols as complete units. Figure 4-2c shows a meaningless line superimposed over the letter B. The line acted independently of, and faded more frequently than, the "B." When the hatching was present, the "B" was seen as a separate entity nearer the observer. Pritchard (1961) reported further that when entire words are presented, the partial fragmentation of letters can cause different words to be perceived. For example, BEER yielded the products PEER, PEEP, BEE, and BE. Meaningless groups of letters such as EER were less likely to be reported, indicating again that the fragmentation involves perceptual units related to meaning.

McKinney (1963) reported similar findings using luminous targets viewed under conditions of reduced illumination. Hart (1964) questioned the claim that results obtained using this technique reveal perceptual units or meanings, suggesting on the basis of his own data that disappearances are related instead to the meaningful way that subjects see and fixate the figures. Schuck, Brock, and Becker (1964) were able to demonstrate, however, that meaningful disappearances are not artifacts of the manner of fixation but indeed reflect meaningful perceptual units. Furthermore, Clarke and Evans (1964) conclude that qualitatively similar, structured or meaningful fragmentation occurs under three different viewing conditions, i.e., monocular viewing under reduced illumination, stabilized retinal images, and viewing of prolonged afterimages. The different techniques differ in the degree to which fine tremor is controlled and in some aspects of the physiological mechanisms that may be involved (Evans, 1967), but they nevertheless yield comparable results to which common theoretical interpretations can be applied.

Theoretical interpretations of perceptual fragmentation   Pritchard et al. (1960) believe that the reported phenomena lead inevitably to the conclusion that perceptual elements, as distinct from sensory elements, exist in their own right. These organized entities are often simpler than the wholes emphasized in Gestalt theory, and when complex, they appear to be syntheses of simpler ones but capable also of functioning as units. The findings were interpreted as supporting the general features of Hebb's (1949) cell-assembly theory and certain specific hypotheses within it. Thus, "meaning in the theory is activity in a set of interconnected assemblies which, as a more complex system, can be active longer" (Hebb, 1963, p. 18). That a meaningful (more complex?) object remains visible longer than a meaningless one is understandable in such terms.

The data are also generally consistent with the level of theorizing (without particular neuropsychological assumptions) presented in the preceding chapters. Specifically, the findings support the idea of a hierarchically organized meaning system that was suggested as the basis of representational and associative images. Representational images were interpreted as consisting of clusters of elementary images corresponding to components of an object, which in turn may be organized into higher-order associative structures comprised of the already-established object-images, and so on. Such a system could be conceptualized in terms of lower-order and higher-order assembly activity (Hebb, 1968), conditioned perceptual responses (Sheffield, 1961), or as elementary and compound images within the framework of a computer-simulation model (Simon & Feigenbaum, 1964) without affecting the relevance of the data.

In stating that the findings are consistent with the imagery theory of meaning, however, we must be clear about what is being claimed. The observed fragmentation is perceptual and the relationship to imagery is based on the assumption that perception and imagery are linked by common underlying mechanisms. The nature of those mechanisms is inferred from the reported *perceptual* experience and in the present context we have thus far established no direct inferential link to imagery in terms of operations that define that concept. Some direct evidence can be found in figural completion phenomena reported by Pritchard et al. An irregular amoebalike outline figure loses one of its limbs and a transient closure is occasionally reported. One observer reported that a slightly irregular hexagon became definitely regular. These are interpreted by the authors as clear cases of the production of a better figure, in the Gestalt sense of goodness of form. More dramatic from our point of view is the hallucinatory addition of an eye to the profile in Figure 4-2a, which was reported by two observers viewing different profile figures. Such reports come closer to defining imagery than do the reports of fragmentation alone in that the former imply the production of a perceptual experience in the absence of corresponding "adequate" stimulation.

Inferences should also be possible on the basis of stimulus meaning, but the necessary information is lacking in the above studies in that meaning is undefined. A profile face and a meaningless wavy line differ simultaneously in concreteness, familiarity, and verbal meaning. How much do the different dimensions of meaning contribute to the observed effects? The same question applies to words and one can inquire further whether the effects involving verbal stimuli depend only on their visual form, or whether there are additional effects that could be attributed more specifically to the sequential and other properties of the auditory-motor language system. To what extent, furthermore, are the reported phenomena centrally determined and to what extent do they reflect response variables? The available research is insufficient to provide any firm answers, but the following studies are at least relevant to these questions.

McKinney (1966b) used the defocusing technique to investigate the effect of verbal identifiability on perceptual stability. The subjects fixated on geometric patterns that were presented either as "letters" or as "designs." The letter condition was intended to encourage implicit naming; the designs condition, to inhibit naming. The distinction was achieved by instructions and by presenting nonletter patterns along with the letters in the case of the designs condition. The results showed that the targets were more stable (that is, they exhibited less fragmentation) when recognized as familiar letters than when not associated with a verbal label.

McKinney interpreted his results as support for the contention that a verbal label generally facilitates perceptual recognition, relating this conclusion specifically to Kimura's (1963) interpretation of familiarity effects in tachistoscopic recognition. The generalization may not be warranted for reasons already discussed in relation to tachistoscopic studies, where it was suggested that the pattern must be recognized before the label is evoked. Whether or not codability is facilitative will depend upon the time available in the task for associative (memory) factors to operate. Such conditions are favorable in the perceptual stability situation, where the subject views the stabilized target continuously and has ample time to name it implicitly. In terms of the processes I assume to be involved in referential meaning, *the implicit naming response may associatively arouse the representation corresponding to the geometric pattern. The greater stability under the name condition could thus be interpreted as a regenerative process in which perceptual integrity is maintained through feedback from the naming response.*

Two further possibilities are suggested by Hebb's theory, each assigning more weight directly to central factors. One interpretation is that the facilitation in the name condition is entirely central: A geometric pattern perceived as a letter is more meaningful in the sense of arousing more complex assembly activity, which maintains activity (hence perceptual stability) for a longer period than when the pattern is viewed as a meaningless design. The second Hebbian alternative involves the concept of attention, which, within the theory, is conceptualized as involving facilitation of cell assembly activity by activity in neighboring assemblies. In this instance, implicit labeling may keep the subject's attention on the geometric pattern longer, thereby maintaining perceptual stability by the facilitative action of other (nontarget) assemblies. The data do not permit a choice between the alternatives, which are relevant here as specific hypotheses concerning the mechanisms whereby verbal symbolic processes might affect perceptual stability.

Other recent studies of the fragmentation phenomenon provide evidence of factors that might be involved in the development of compound representational processes or associations between representational units. Tees and More (1967a) investigated the effects of perceptual learning experience involving the contiguous presentation of digit pairs upon the frequency of their joint disappearances under the McKinney (1963) luminous stimulus conditions. The target stimuli were pairs of discriminally different digits, e.g., 85. The perceptual learning experience consisted of the repeated presentation of digit strings varying in length, within which the critical pairs were periodically embedded. The target digits were paired different numbers of times for different groups. In an attempt to restrict the associative experience to stimulus (rather than stimulus-response) pairing, the subjects were not required to report the digits during the training phase. Instead, they were asked only to count the number of digits in each string. The results showed that, as a result of such associative experience, the target stimuli disappeared together more frequently than without such association when presented along with a third digit in the test situation. Moreover, as can be seen in Figure 4-3, the extent to which the two "operated" together was a linear function of the frequency of the previous joint occurrence.

Tees and More interpreted the results as support for the contiguity hypothesis of the development of a cell assembly. In less specific terms, a compound symbolic representation is apparently formed as a result of contiguous exposure to the elements of the compound. The finding was extended in a further study in which Tees and More (1967b) demonstrated that contiguity of two letters in prior *auditory* perceptual learning experience (during which they were presented as components of words that were spelled out) resulted in their joint disappearance in the subsequent visual test. This was viewed as evidence for intermodal perceptual learning.

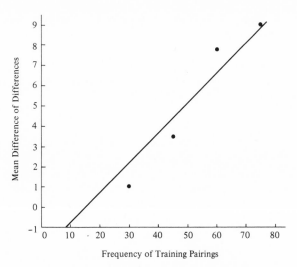

FIGURE 4-3. Linear trend for disappearances (calculated as the mean difference of differences between disappearances before and after perceptual learning) as a function of the number of preconditioning pairings. From Tees and More (1967a).

Despite the care with which Tees and More controlled response variables in an attempt to restrict the learning experience in each study to simple perceptual contiguity, an alternative explanation is possible. The perceptual learning phase can be viewed as being comprised of an intentional and an incidental learning component, the latter involving the crucial independent variable in the experiments. The subjects might well have become aware of the critical pair, such awareness being manifested as a discriminating (implicit) verbal response. Such a common response could serve to mediate the increased perceptual stability in the subsequent test, as the verbal labels apparently did in the McKinney (1966b) experiment described above. Such an interpretation does not reduce the importance of the empirical findings, but the proposed mechanism is quite different from that suggested by Tees and More.

The plausibility of a verbal mediating mechanism is supported by the results of a study by Donderi and Kane (1965). They investigated perceptual stability using a stimulus pattern comprised of three circles of unequal diameter, two of which the subject had learned to label "A" and one of which the subject had learned to label "B" in a preliminary learning phase. The subjects were required to report disappearances. The results showed that circles assigned the same label were more likely to fragment simultaneously than were two with dissimilar names. The finding is particularly interesting here because it represents positive evidence for verbal mediation in perception, paralleling mediational effects observed in verbal learning research to be considered later. Donderi and Kane in effect used an acquired stimulus equivalence mediation paradigm, in which two circles, C_1 and C_2, became functionally equivalent as stimuli as a result of their association with a common response, "A." Thus, stage 1 learning involved a C_1-A association, and stage 2, C_2-A. Acquired stimulus equivalence is evidenced by the similar perceptual response (fragmentation) they evoke as stimuli under reduced stimulation conditions.

In summary, the perceptual stability phenomenon appears to be unusually sensitive to meaning and associative processes generally. The influence of verbal referential meaning (codability) and verbal mediating processes is most clearly demonstrated in two instances. Familiarity and imagery are presumably involved in other instances, but they tend to be operationally confounded with each other and with verbal meaning generally. Suggestive evidence has been obtained for the effect of perceptual contiguities on the development of compound representational systems, but the data are open to alternative interpretations in terms of verbal mediating responses. The effective variables hopefully can be teased apart and the alternative hypotheses tested by further research. The present theoretical approach generates predictions that could be tested in such research. Associative factors apparently have time to operate in the experimental settings that are typically used to investigate perceptual stability. Associative imagery should thus be associated with high stability—for example, concrete nouns should be stable longer than abstract nouns even when familiarity and verbal associative meaning are controlled. Such an outcome would be theoretically important, for it would strain attempts to explain the effect in terms of verbal mechanisms alone and at the same time increase the plausibility that nonverbal representational processes are somehow involved.

The necessary research has not been done and the postulated dimensions of meaning and the assumed underlying processes remain relatively undifferentiated in terms of the functions that we have attributed to them.

Dynamic Characteristics of Stimulus Meaning in Perception

Thus far we have been concerned with general dimensions of meaning without reference to more specific qualitative aspects. Concreteness, for example, was defined in terms of the directness of reference to concrete objects and events, ignoring the dynamic properties of the referents. Perceptual effects attributable to such properties would provide evidence that the underlying representational processes aroused by the stimulus include the dynamic components, and that such components indeed have functional significance, as was suggested in the discussion of dynamic as compared to static representations in Chapter 2.

A number of studies have revealed such effects, the majority of these stemming from Wapner and Werner's (e.g., 1957) sensory-tonic field theory of perception, and the related organismic theory of symbolization as presented by Werner and Kaplan (1963). The research is summarized in both of the above works. The relevant series of experiments was concerned with the effects of directional properties of pictured objects. Thus, if a picture of a bird flying to the left is placed in the objective median plane, the observer perceives the object as displaced in the direction of flight, with the result that the apparent median plane shifts to the right. Similar effects are obtained with pictures of pointing hands: When the hands are pictured as pointing to the left or right, the apparent median plane shifts significantly in the direction opposite to the pointing. When the hands are pictured as pointing up or down, the apparent horizon shifts in the opposite direction—for example, when the "directional dynamics" is down, the apparent horizon is located relatively upward.

Other experiments investigated the effects of directional dynamics connoted by words. Luminescent words were presented to subjects in the dark so that they appeared to be suspended in space. Some words referred to upward movement (climbing, rising), others to downward movement (falling, plunging). A word was first placed at the objective (horizontal) eye level of the observer and then shifted up or down at his request until it appeared to him to be at his eye level. The earlier experiments summarized by Wapner and Werner (1957, pp. 30–31) did not yield significant effects, but such effects apparently were obtained more recently (Chandler, as cited in Werner and Kaplan, 1963, p. 28). Thus, to be located at the subject's apparent eye level, "climbing" and "raising" had to be placed at a spatial position below "lowering" and "dropping." These studies deserve careful replication because the reported effects of word meaning are theoretically important, but their reliability appears to be uncertain.

The directional characteristics of pictured objects are also reflected in perceived movement. Experiment 6 reported by Wapner and Werner (1957) involved a comparison of the apparent velocity of a pictured object having a dynamic quality (e.g., a running mouse) with that of the same object pictured as static (e.g., a sitting mouse). Five different pairs of pictures were used, two of which are reproduced in Figure 4-4. Each stimulus was presented to the subject as a series of identical pictures 1 inch apart on a continuously-moving belt. The static object, serving as the standard, was presented in one window at a constant speed. The dynamic counterpart was presented in a window to the left or right of the standard and its velocity (in a "forward" direction) could be adjusted by the subject until it appeared to be moving at the same speed as the standard. A velocity setting lower than that of the standard would indicate that the figure with the directional dynamics was perceived as moving faster than the static figure. This is what in fact occurred, with the effect varying as a function of age: The youngest subjects adjusted the dynamic figure at a relatively slow speed, and the adjusted speed increased steadily with age until it approximated the standard for the 16–19 year groups. For children at least, then, the apparent motion of a pictured object is manifested in a perceptual effect.

Other investigators have reported a similar effect with adult subjects. G. D. Jensen (1960) found that it was significantly easier to induce a stationary silhouette figure of an airplane to move forward than backward. The study was repeated by Brosgole and Whalen (1967) with the addition of certain appropriate controls. Motion was induced by displacing the target relative to a vertical line. The amount of induced motion was indicated by a counteractive adjustment by the subject. The results of one experiment showed that induced forward motion was significantly greater than apparent backward movement and greater than the movement of a control stimulus (rectangle) in the same direction. The effect was destroyed, however, when the target was surrounded by a frame. The experimenters interpreted this to mean that the frame imparted a meaning of its own that tended to override that contributed by the target. In any event, while the effective variables require further research, under some conditions the results are consistent with those predicted and obtained by

FIGURE 4-4.   Examples of static and dynamic pictures from Wapner and Werner (1957).

Wapner and Werner for directional dynamics and are presumably interpretable in similar terms.

Interpretation of directional dynamics   Werner and Kaplan discuss the effects attributable to directional dynamics in terms of their organismic theory of meaning: "Organism-environment transactions . . . affect perceptual organization of symbolic vehicles as they do that of objects" (1963, p. 29). The directional dynamics inherent in stationary pictures or in the meanings of the words as a result of past experience may be said to exert a directional "pull" consistent with the dynamic meaning of the stimulus. In our terms, such meaning is manifested in dynamic visual imagery, which in turn influences perception. The effects are probably related to Kohler's (1964) finding that, following prolonged wearing of yellow-blue spectacles, changes in the position of head and eyes resulted in corresponding negative afterimages, apparently because the sensory feedback from muscular contractions became conditioned to the afterimages (see Chapter 3). Moreover, the reverse effect also occurred: Yellow and blue surfaces in the visual field induced the subject to assume an "appropriate eye position." The directional dynamics inherent in stationary pictures may similarly involve a learned association between characteristics of the object and proprioceptive activity previously associated with viewing similar objects in motion.

The phenomena and the above interpretations are also consistent with Hebb's (1949) theoretical analysis, in which motor components are assumed to accompany perceptual processes and the visual imagery as a function of perceptual learning, as already noted in Chapter 2. For example, the eye movements associated with reading presumably become an intrinsic component of the cell assemblies and phase sequences hypothesized to be the representational basis of visual letters and words. One implication of Hebb's theory is that a directional bias is associated with the visual processing of verbal material quite analogous to the directional dynamics postulated by Werner and his collaborators for static pictures.

Effects relevant to Hebb's hypothesis are considered along with other effects and hypotheses in the following section in the context of lateral asymmetries in perception. Such asymmetries, more than most of the perceptual effects considered up to this point, provide evidence of functional distinctions between verbal and nonverbal symbolic representations.

Meaning and Left-Right Asymmetries in Perception

The left and the right visual fields and the two ears are not equivalent in all perceptual tasks, but display lateral asymmetries related in particular to the verbal-nonverbal distinction in stimulus meaning and to certain characteristics of the task. In the case of vision, the research has typically involved rapid tachistoscopic presentation of stimulus material either simultaneously to the right and the left of a central fixation point, or successively (and randomly), to the right or the left field. With the simultaneous method, both verbal material such as letters (Heron, 1957) and nonverbal material such as geometrical forms or binary strings of open and closed circles (e.g., Bryden, 1960; Harcum & Dyer, 1962) are reported more accurately from the left than from the right visual field. With successive presentation to one or the other field, however, recognition of verbal material is easier when it is exposed to the right field (e.g., Bryden & Rainey, 1963; Forgays, 1953; Heron, 1957; Mishkin & Forgays, 1952; Terrace, 1959), whereas nonverbal geometrical forms and nonsense figures are recognized equally easily in either field (e.g., Bryden, 1960; Heron, 1957; Kimura, 1966; Terrace, 1959).

Comparable results have been obtained with auditory stimuli, although the conditions under which the effects are observed differ. When normal speech sounds such as spoken digits are simultaneously presented to the two ears, the sounds arriving at the right ear are more accurately recognized than those arriving at the left (Kimura, 1961, 1964). The right-ear superiority also obtains for nonsensical "verbal" sounds such as reversed playback of recorded speech (Kimura & Folb, 1968). On the other hand, recognition of nonverbal auditory patterns, i.e., melodies, is superior in the left ear. These asymmetries are not obtained with the successive method (stimuli arriving successively at one or the other ear), so the effective conditions are reversed for the visual and the auditory modes. The same generalization is nevertheless justified in the case of both modes: The representational processes that mediate perceptual recognition must differ in some crucial way for verbal stimuli and certain nonverbal stimuli.

What are the possible differentiating mechanisms? The theoretical controversies have been oriented around two classes of interpretations. One, relevant primarily to the visual phenomena, emphasizes factors involved in the processing of the perceptual trace immediately following exposure. The second attributes both auditory and visual effects to functional asymmetries of the two cerebral hemispheres. We shall first consider the postexposure processing factors that have been suggested as explanations of visual asymmetries. These factors include implicit motor components and scanning habits intrinsic to the perceptual process itself, habitual order of reporting items, and memory factors.

Postexposural scanning, order of report, and memory factors   Consistent with Hebb's (1949) general approach to the role of motor components in perceptual processes, Heron (1957) interpreted both the simultaneous and the successive fixation data in terms of a "postexposural process" comprised of eye-movement tendencies acquired while learning to read. One characteristic movement in reading is the left-to-right scanning involved in reading a line; another is the jumping movement back to the beginning of the next line. In tachistoscopic word perception, the implicit movement processes are assumed to operate on the postexposure trace to determine the perceptual report in a manner analogous to the effect of the overt eye movements while actually reading. When an array of letters appears simultaneously to the left and to the right of fixation, the left-moving tendency toward the beginning of the array overrides the scanning tendency to the right, resulting in greater left-field accuracy because of a primacy effect. When the verbal stimuli appear only on one side of the fixation point, accuracy is greater for the right field because the two movement tendencies complement one another rather than conflict—that is, the tendency to begin from the left side of the line and the reading movement coincide when the entire line is to the right. Heron suggested further that these eye movements are specific to letter material.

It should be noted particularly that the emphasis in this conceptualization is on dynamic processes intrinsic to the visual system paralleling the "directional dynamics" inherent in pictorial representations of familiar objects according to the Wapner and Werner studies cited earlier. In Heron's interpretation, continuity is assumed between perceptual processing (reading) and the processing of immediate memory images (postexposural scanning). The continuity extends further to "mental" images in Hebb's (1968) analysis of visual word-images that can be processed more efficiently in a left-to-right direction (see the discussion in Chapter 2). The concept of a visual-verbal representational system that includes experientially determined motor components and encompasses perception, immediate memory, and imagery is parsimonious and integrative. Many of the relevant findings are consistent with the hypothesis, whereas others introduce complications that at the very least demand an elaboration of the postulated mechanisms.

Bryden (1961) reasoned that the postexposure process might manifest itself in appropriate overt eye movements. In support of this, he found a significant relation between the locus of recognition and eye movements occuring after the exposure of the material. He suggested that such eye movements may indeed facilitate recognition but also pointed out that the movements might be a result of recognition rather than the other way around. Similar results and interpretations were reported by Crovitz and Daves (1962).

Heron's suggestion that the movement tendency is specific to verbal material is not supported by the results obtained with simultaneous presentation of material to the left and right of fixation, inasmuch as the left-field superiority has been found also for nonverbal stimuli (Bryden, 1960; Bryden & Rainey, 1963; Harcum & Dyer, 1962). Furthermore, L. G. Braine (1968) found that Israeli students, who read from right to left, also showed greater accuracy under the simultaneous method for tachistoscopic material appearing in the left field. She suggested that the asymmetries are not primarily due to reading habits, although such habits may have influenced the results, since the "left effect" was less strong and consistent than would be expected for a comparable American group (see Harcum & Friedman, 1963). The results with the simultaneous method of presentation thus indicate a general bias favoring recognition of material to the left of fixation. Such a bias can be interpreted generally in terms of motor habits associated with perception, but such habits could be reflected specifically in either a selective perceptual "attentiveness" to one side of a spatial pattern, as L. G. Braine (1968) implies, or a tendency for subjects to report objects from left to right (Bryden, 1960).

When order of report has been manipulated, the findings have served to differentiate verbal and nonverbal processes even in the case of simultaneous tachistoscopic presentation to both visual fields, and have suggested a specific interpretation of the trace systems corresponding to verbal material. Bryden (1960) found in one experiment that subjects generally tended to report both letters and geometric forms in a left-to-right order. The greater left-field accuracy could therefore be interpreted in terms of the early reporting of material on the left, coupled with the assumption of a rapidly fading perceptual trace that has faded below threshold before the material on the right can be reported (cf. Sperling, 1960). This interpretation was supported by the results of another experiment in which, immediately after stimulus exposure, subjects were instructed to report the material either from left to right or from right to left. Geometrical forms appearing in the left field were better identified when the order of report was from left to right, whereas those in the right field were better identified when the report was from right to left. The order of report, however, did not affect the position in which letters were easiest to recognize: Regardless of order, left-field recognition was superior. In the case of letters, moreover, subjects frequently reported that they had to repeat the letters to themselves in a left-to-right order before they were able to report them in the opposite direction.

On the basis of these results, Bryden suggested that the trace systems that are excited when letters are tachistoscopically exposed are "polarized" in a left-to-right direction. Thus letters situated in any position facilitate traces corresponding to letters situated to the right of them, while they exert little if any facilitation on the traces corresponding to letters situated to the left. No such polarization is postulated in the case of forms. Bryden contrasts his viewpoint with that of Lashley (1951), who proposed a scanning mechanism that determines the serial order of responses but is independent of the specific traces (e.g., of letters) to be scanned. Bryden suggested instead that the directional bias is intrinsic to the traces of alphabetic material. Such stimuli may be said to carry a "directional tag" as part of their representational meaning, so that perceptual processing of letter sequences is facilitated in one direction and hindered in the other. Bryden (1967) has recently elaborated on his model in relation to the general problem of the sequential organization of behavior.

The polarization hypothesis, like Heron's postexposure scanning hypothesis, was intended to be applicable to the tachistoscopic recognition of alphabetic material generally. Recent evidence indicates, however, that the directional bias in the accuracy and order of the perceptual report is affected specifically by the associative characteristics and physical spacing of the verbal stimuli. Mewhort (1966) found this to be the case with eight-letter pseudowords varying in their sequential redundancy: More letters were recognized when they more closely resembled the letter sequences found in English words (fourth-order approximations) than when their arrangement was random (zero-order approximations to English). Moreover, the fourth-order pseudowords were more often reported in a left-to-right order. Increased spacing of the letters also impaired recognition of fourth-order but not zero-order approximations, suggesting that the subject's ability to make use of redundancy was disrupted. Specifically, Mewhort argued that redundant materials are "chunked" into easier-to-recall units (cf. G. A. Miller, 1956), and that spacing slows down sequential scanning enough so that such materials fade from short-term memory before they can be chunked. Low-redundancy materials presumably are not chunked, hence the lesser effect of spacing. In a similar study, Dick and Mewhort (1967) used alpha-numeric sequences comprised of four letters and four numbers as stimuli. They found that grouping, redundancy, and order of report variables had significant effects on letter accuracy but not on number accuracy. The results for the order-of-report variables are illustrated in Figure 4-5. The findings for alphabetic material were interpreted in terms of sequential information processing, or a "sequential operator," coupled with short-term memory processes. More flexibility is suggested in the case of number-processing, presumably because numbers are not similarly linked to sequential dependencies in experience. The results were confirmed and extended by Bryden, Dick, and Mewhort (1968), who found that the processing of numbers in the recognition task is more flexible than that of letters but somewhat less flexible than that of geometric forms in terms of the relative ease and accuracy of right-to-left and left-to-right processing.

Further qualifications of both the scanning and polarization hypotheses are suggested by other findings. Harcum and Finkel (1963) presented English words (e.g., PRACTICE) and their left-right mirror images (e.g., ƎϽITϽAЯꟼ) successively to the right and the left of fixation. They found that the letters of normally printed words were, as usual, more accurately perceived to the right of fixation, but the letters of the reversed words were more accurately perceived

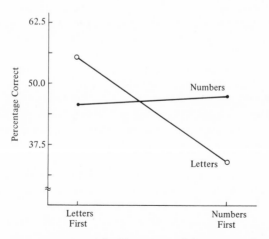

FIGURE 4-5. Percentage of items correctly reported as a function of the order of report. From Dick and Mewhort (1967).

when they appeared to the left. They argued that the directional characteristics of the letters affected the direction of the perceptual scanning process. The conclusion was verified and extended in subsequent research (e.g., Harcum, 1966). Bryden (1966), however, presented evidence suggesting that directional scanning may be important only with multiple-letter material. In one experiment he presented single letters to one or the other side of fixation, in their normal orientation or as mirror images. When subjects saw only one of the two types of material, both types were better identified in the right visual field. The Harcum-Bryden exchange centered on the adequacy of the directional postexposural scanning as compared to the cerebral-dominance interpretation of left-right differences in tachistoscopic recognition, which will be considered below. At this point, the results serve to indicate the insufficiency of both the left-to-right scanning and polarization mechanisms, for the directional bias is obviously affected by the physical orientation and number of letters presented to the subject.

Sequential verbal processing   The theoretical mechanisms discussed above—postexposural scanning, trace polarization, sequential operator—apparently refer specifically to visual processes. They assume that the determinants of laterality effects are to be found directly in the characteristics of the visual representations corresponding to printed letters. It could be argued alternatively that the directional bias and laterality effects observed in the different studies for visually presented alphabetic material are explainable primarily in terms of the auditory-motor verbal system, which is presumably specialized for sequential processing of stimulus information. Visual receiving centers may identify printed letters or words as verbal stimuli and determine the starting point and direction in which the visual array will be processed. The processing itself, however, is controlled by the speech system as sequentially ordered naming responses. The left-to-right directional bias may simply reflect the habitual order of verbal processing (i.e., the sequential properties of English are reflected in a left-to-right spatial order in print), which imposes directionality upon the postexposure scanning of a spatial array rather than the other way around, as seems to be implied by the visual hypotheses. The effects of redundancy and spacing found by Mewhort (1966) and Dick and Mewhort (1967) are consistent with the verbal-process interpretation if we assume that the visual (spatial) pattern is transformed into a temporal sequence. Redundancy and spatial proximity of the letter sequences simply permit a faster readout of information by the sequentially organized verbal system before the visual trace has faded. Presumably for the same reason, the verbal processing of mirror-image letter sequences in the Harcum and Finkel study is facilitated by a right-to-left scan, especially in the case of meaningful words that can be appropriately spelled only in that direction. Bryden and Rainey's (1963) finding of right-field superiority with successive presentation for pictures of familiar objects as well as for letters, although not for geometric forms, has been attributed (Bryden, 1966) to the fact that the drawings could be readily labeled, which also would be consistent with the verbal-process hypothesis under discussion. Finally, Ayres (1966) and Winnick and Bruder (1968) obtained evidence suggesting that left-field dominance for horizontal material is an artifact of order of reporting (see also Merikle, Lowe, & Coltheart, 1970). All of these findings strongly implicate verbal sequential processing in the visual laterality effects.

The above theoretical issue turns on the relative primacy of visual and verbal processes in word perception, and the research does not permit an unequivocal choice between the alternatives. Clearly, directional scanning, sequential reporting, and associative factors acquired while learning to read play an important role in either case and serve to differentiate effects for verbal material from those for nonverbal material such as geometric forms. The laterality effects also implicate an entirely different theoretical viewpoint, to be considered next.

Functional asymmetry of the cerebral hemispheres Kimura (1961) found for both normal subjects and preoperative patients that, when different digits were presented simultaneously to the two ears through earphones, more digits were accurately reported for the right ear. Her interpretation was that the right ear has stronger connections with the left hemisphere than does the left ear, and that speech is generally represented in the left hemisphere. (The reverse results would be expected and were in fact obtained in the case of patients with known right-hemisphere speech representation.) Kimura suggested that a similar relation between perceptual asymmetry and hemispheric dominance might be found in the case of visual recognition of verbal material. Stimuli presented to each hemifield project impulses to the visual receiving area in the opposite side of the brain. Accordingly, verbal material in the right visual field, which first excites the left (speech-dominant) hemisphere, should be perceived more accurately than material presented to the left field. Such an effect may be overshadowed by the strong effects of reading habits in the case of sequential arrays presented to both fields simultaneously; hence no support emerges for hemispheric dominance from studies employing such a procedure. In the case of successive presentation to one or the other field, however, right-field superiority is generally observed with verbal stimuli but not with nonverbal stimuli such as geometric forms. These findings are consistent with the view that perception of verbal stimuli is particularly dependent on the dominant hemisphere.

Kimura's (1964) finding of right-ear superiority for digits and left-ear superiority for melodies could be interpreted alternatively in terms of the relative familiarity of the digits. Kimura (in press) reported an experiment that appears to resolve the issue. Melodies were played in dichotic pairs to a group of experienced music listeners, who were asked to hum the melodies they heard. The results showed clear left-ear superiority especially when both melodies of a pair were familiar to the subject. Furthermore, the same subjects showed the typical right-ear superiority for digits. Kimura concluded that familiarity per se does not appear to be a critical factor in hemispheric specialization of function. The conclusion is supported further by the observation that recognition of familiar faces is more often impaired by right- than by left-hemisphere lesions (Hecaen, as reported by Kimura, in press). Thus the left hemisphere apparently plays a dominant role in the perception of verbal stimuli, whereas the right hemisphere is favored in the case of nonverbal auditory patterns and certain nonverbal visual stimuli. These asymmetries are illustrated by Kimura's neuroanatomical schema for auditory stimuli, shown in Figure 4-6.

How are these hemispheric distinctions to be interpreted? Since the stimuli that are processed primarily by the left hemisphere appear to be sounds producible by the speech musculature and visual stimuli (letters, words, familiar objects) that can be named, it could be argued that the perceptual effects involving such stimuli are critically dependent on the activity of motor centers subserving verbal behavior (Kimura, in press). Such an interpretation would be consistent with the motor theory of speech perception (Liberman et al., 1967). For our purposes, however, it is not necessary to accept only the motor interpretation. What is important is the general conception of a verbal representational system, located in the left hemisphere, which influences the perceptual processing of verbal stimuli. It may do so even in the case of multiunit visual stimuli by virtue of its sequential processing characteristic, which imposes a directional bias on the visual scanning and reporting of such a series in the manner described above. Or, the scanning mechanism and the "verbal sequential operator" may be independent mechanisms, both with their control centers in the speechdominant hemisphere, and both participating in a coordinated fashion in the processing of visual-verbal stimulus sequences.

The right-hemisphere system that subserves perception of nonverbal stimuli appears to be characterized by different attributes. It does not appear to have any intrinsic directional bias, although some directionality may be imposed on perceptual processing because of general left-attending (L. G. Braine, 1968) or left-to-right reporting habits already discussed. It has been suggested that the right-hemisphere perceptual mechanisms involve activity more nearly repre-

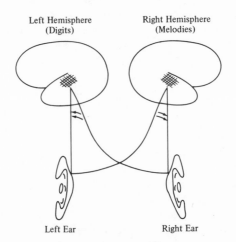

FIGURE 4-6.   Neuroanatomical schema for the auditory asymmetries. Arrows represent occlusion of ipsilateral impulses by contralateral pathways. From Kimura (1967).

sentative of the stimulus input than is the case with the left-hemisphere (e.g., Kimura, in press), or more diffuse representation, which is especially functional in the perception of spatial patterns (Semmes, 1968). The evidence and the interpretations suggest a representational system specialized for parallel processing in the spatial sense. It is tempting to identify such a system as the substrate of concrete (nonverbal) imagery generally, incorporating stored information from different modalities, or involving, in Neisser's (1967) terms, mechanisms for generating such information. The motor processes associated with visual imagery, for example, could be conceptualized as "concrete" in the sense that they are derived from the exploration of concrete objects and spatial patterns generally. The proprioceptive feedback from such activity could be viewed as part of the total stimulus input that is stored in some form and subsequently expressed as a fusion of visual-motor imagery.

Empirical and theoretical uncertainties in laterality effects   The preceding analysis is frankly speculative and its uncertainty is increased by some dissonant evidence concerning the perceptual asymmetry phenomena on which the analysis is based. Overton and Wiener (1966) investigated left-right field differences in recognition-threshold behavior using a monocular rather than a binocular viewing condition for English words. They found the typical right-field superiority, but this was attributable to the effects in the left eye only and more specifically to the extreme left portion of the left eye. They concluded that no current explanation can account satisfactorily for their data. However, Goodglass and Barton (1963) and Barton, Goodglass, and Shai (1965) obtained right-field superiority for both eyes, although the latter study did tend to show that the disparity between fields was greater in the case of the left eye, in agreement with Overton and Wiener. McKinney (1966a) used the perceptual stability phenomenon to investigate left-right field differences in the stability of nonalphabetic material presented simultaneously to both fields. The results indicated greater fragmentation in the left visual field, i.e., the right field showed superior stability. This finding is inconsistent with the tachistoscopic recognition data for simultaneous presentation, where left-field superiority is generally found regardless of the nature of the material. It suggests left-hemisphere dominance, but this interpretation is inconsistent with the earlier suggestion that such asymmetry is associated with verbal stimuli. In another study, McKinney (1967) again found greater stability for a nonverbal target in the right visual field under the simultaneous presentation condition. Consistent with the Overton and Wiener results for tachistoscopic recognition of words under monocular viewing conditions, McKinney found the laterality effect for the left eye but not the right. He suggested a dual interpretation in terms of the combined effect of cerebral dominance and greater sensitivity of the temporal as compared to the nasal hemiretina. The data and the suggested interpretations obviously require some modification of the theoretical views expressed earlier, but the direction such modifications should take is not clear at this time.

Stimulus meaning is implicated in issues raised by other data. It will be recalled that Kimura (1961) found right-ear superiority for the recognition of dichotically presented digits, and interpreted the effect in terms of left-hemisphere dominance in the perception of verbal stimuli. We also noted, however, that Dick and Mewhort (1967) found grouping, redundancy, and order of report to affect letter but not number accuracy in tachistoscopic recognition. It appears that number processing is "verbal" in the auditory situation but "nonverbal" in the visual. This discrepancy may be consistent with findings obtained with patients in whom the hemispheres have been surgically disconnected (Sperry, 1968). Four of six subjects were able correctly to add or multiply pairs of numerals presented to the left field, indicating right-hemisphere processing, although the answer in these instances could not be directly expressed verbally. Thus both hemispheres apparently have representation for numbers, but only the "talking hemisphere" can process them verbally. Any clarification this might suggest, however, is offset by the further finding that such patients can also comprehend words presented to the left field (hence the right hemisphere), provided that the response is nonverbal, e.g., searching out the named object by touch. The limits of such right-hemisphere verbal functioning remains to be determined.

A final problem is raised by the results of studies of the effects of word abstractness on laterality effects for dichotically presented words. Borkowski, Spreen, and Stutz (1965), and Jones and Spreen (1967) found better recall for concrete words, suggesting an effect of referential imagery. If concrete imagery is associated with the right hemisphere, as suggested above, one might expect the usual right-ear superiority for words to be less in the case of concrete than abstract words. However, the results showed clear right-ear superiority for both classes of words, suggesting either that nonverbal imagery was not involved or that such imagery (at least when it is verbally evoked) involves both hemispheres equally and enhances recall of concrete words in either ear. Another possibility is that the laterality effect for words is primarily a perceptual effect, as Kimura (in press) has argued, and is therefore unaffected by associative variables, whereas the superior recall of concrete words in both ears is a memory effect to which the imagery meaning component can contribute. The latter interpretation is consistent with the theory proposed at the outset of the present review of perceptual phenomena, where it was suggested that effects attributable to associative processes would depend in part on the time available for their operation. These issues and the suggested interpretations obviously cannot be resolved on the basis of empirical evidence that is currently available.

SUMMARY

In this chapter we have examined evidence relevant to the proposition that perceptual phenomena are determined by the interaction of sensory input and the symbolic processes, the latter being defined here in terms of stimulus meaning. Meaning was conceptualized in terms of the stored representational and associative processes aroused by a stimulus, and it was hypothesized that the effect of meaning variables would depend on the memory load and other temporal factors involved in the perceptual task. In addition, the level of meaning was expected to be important. Much of the experimental evidence is consistent with these hypotheses. Simple classification of stimuli as "same" or "different" is unaffected even by familiarity when both stimuli are simultaneously in view. With increased temporal separation of the stimuli, familiarity facilitates matching. Tachistoscopic recognition thresholds are consistently affected by familiarity, at least when the stimulus must be identified verbally, indicating the importance of the availability of a representational response. The majority of studies concerned with the role of higher-level associative meaning (e.g., concreteness, meaningfulness) have indicated that such meaning is relatively unimportant to the recognition process if familiarity is controlled.

Perceptual stability as measured by the fragmentation phenomenon is strongly affected by meaning in general. The differential effects of particular dimensions of meaning are yet to be systematically investigated, however, and the theoretical interpretation of the findings remains unclear. Meaning is also an important determinant of right-left asymmetries of perception. Under specifiable presentation conditions, verbal stimuli presented to the right visual field or to the right ear are perceived more accurately than those presented to the left visual field or the left ear. Differential accuracy is not obtained for nonverbal visual stimuli such as geometrical patterns, however, and accuracy for nonverbal (musical) sounds is better in the left ear than in the right. These findings suggest different hemispheric representations for verbal and nonverbal stimuli. Order of report (right-to-left versus left-to-right) and sequential redundancy of stimulus elements also have more effect on the accuracy of reporting briefly presented verbal than nonverbal stimulus arrays, supporting the view that verbal symbolic processes have a strong sequential component that is absent in the representational system corresponding to nonverbal stimuli. The next chapter examines further experimental evidence on the perceptual implications of such functional distinctions between the symbolic systems.

5

Perception and the Experimental Arousal of the Symbolic Processes

In this chapter we will consider studies involving instructional sets, associative "priming," and other experimental procedures that can be interpreted as affecting the arousal of imaginal or verbal symbolic processes in perceptual tasks. The theory that perception and the symbolic processes involve common patterns of neural activity suggests that the arousal of the symbolic activity could enhance, modify, or interfere with a perceptual task depending on the congruency or compatibility between the symbolic and the perceptual activity. Imagery, for example, would be expected to facilitate perception only when the imagery aroused, by whatever means, is congruent with the perceptual image aroused by the target stimulus; otherwise the effect should be one of interference. These speculations are similar to those proposed by Bruner and Postman in their hypothesis theory of perception (see F. H. Allport, 1955, Chapter 15) or in the categorization theory subsequently presented by Bruner (1957). However, Bruner particularly emphasized the theoretical role of linguistic categories in perception and a similar orientation is evident in Haber's (1966) review of the effects of set on perception. Such research is especially pertinent here, and we shall consider the findings with specific emphasis on nonverbal as well as verbal symbolic or coding processes, as these are aroused by various experimental sets.

FACILITATIVE AROUSAL OF THE SYMBOLIC PROCESSES

Repeated Exposure of a Stimulus

The most direct method for arousing representational processes that would be congruent with subsequent perceptual input is the repeated presentation of the same stimulus. This is involved in the traditional procedure for determining visual recognition thresholds by the method of limits, but repetition and exposure duration are confounded in such studies. Haber (1966, 1967) discussed several studies in which he and his associates presented the same stimulus repeatedly at the same tachistoscopic exposure speed for a given group of subjects. Subjects were asked to report only letters that they recognized clearly, rather than total words, a procedure that Haber views as a superior index of perception as phenomenal experience because it is less affected by guessing strategies than is the method of reporting whole words. The results of these studies indicated that the clarity of letters increased markedly over repeated presentations, even when few or none of the letters could be seen on the initial exposure, demonstrating the "growth" of a percept as a function of repetition.

The clarity of the percept was shown to be influenced by a number of variables. Prior exposure to a stimulus word, so that the subject had no doubt about what the stimulus was going to be, increased the clarity of the letters (Haber, 1965). This would be a trivial demonstration but for the fact that clarity increased slowly and at about the same rate with repetition whether the subject knew the word or not. Only the average level of clarity differed for the two treatments. The same study demonstrated higher clarity for frequent English words than for rare words when the subject did not know the word ahead of time, but no difference between rare and frequent words when he did know the word. These results led Haber to conclude that the effects of word frequency are probably mediated by response processes, such as differential availability of the high frequency words when the stimulus is unknown. However, the similarity of the growth function under all conditions was interpreted as evidence that the repetition variable had its effect directly on perceptual processes.

Hershenson and Haber (1965) found, similarly, that clarity of letters was higher for English words than for Turkish words, but that the increase of clarity with repetition was comparable for the two classes—if anything, the rate of increase was slightly faster for the Turkish words. These effects are shown for three different exposure durations in Figure 5-1. A suggested interpretation was that meaning may contribute to two antagonistic effects on perception, a facilitatory part comprised of feedback to the perceptual system from an organized cognitive structure corresponding to English words, and an inhibitory effect resulting from incorrect guesses or hypotheses about the stimulus when the subject knows the population of possible stimuli. An alternative explanation in terms of response processes was rejected on the grounds that subjects were trained to report only letters they perceived and did in fact report that the letters become unambiguously clear with repeated trials. This conclusion appears inconsistent with that suggested in the case of the frequency effect, above, where the same procedure was followed yet the effect of word frequency on letter clarity (without prior exposure to the word) was attributed to response processes.

The apparent inconsistency may involve an assumed meaning-frequency distinction. An "organizational structure" exists for the meaningful English words,

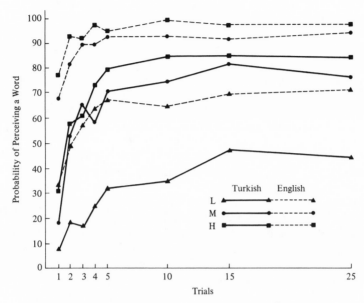

FIGURE 5-1. The probability of perceiving Turkish and English words as a function of low (20 msec), medium (25 msec), and high (30 msec) exposure durations and repeated exposure trials. From Hershenson and Haber (1965).

whether rare or frequent, but not for the meaningless Turkish words. Thus, although familiar letter units are involved in all cases, there can be no feedback from word meaning in the case of Turkish words. On the face of it, this explanation seems contrary to my earlier suggestion in Chapter 4 that associative meaning should have no effect on recognition thresholds because there is no time for associative processes to feed back to the perceptual system and thereby affect recognition directly. Here the distinction between *word* perception and *letter* perception becomes relevant. My assertion referred to effects of word meaning on perceptual recognition of the word as a unit, whereas Hershenson and Haber are referring to the effects of word meaning on the perceived clarity of the letter units comprising the word. In the latter situation, word perception is credited only when the subject has reported seeing all of the letters clearly, although he may have been able to guess the identity of the word earlier from partial information. It would not be surprising, therefore, to find that knowledge of the identity of the word, by whatever means, facilitates perception of the letter units, e.g., by attentional mechanisms, hence the higher clarity scores for English than for Turkish words or for rare than for frequent words when there is no prior knowledge of the word; and for expected words than for unexpected words regardless of frequency. Meaning in the sense of referential or associative processes aroused by the word-unit need not be invoked to explain such effects, however, only the idea of a compound representational unit whose availability affects the perception of its components.

The analysis once more raises the issue, introduced in the last chapter, of the effects of different kinds of meaning, and again the available data do not permit a resolution of the problem. The Hershenson and Haber study confounds familiarity and higher-order referential or associative meaning, i.e., English words exceed Turkish on all of these for the subjects tested. Furthermore, the subjects' expectations were not manipulated in that study by prior exposure of the words as was done in the Haber study, in which frequency was a variable. Perhaps such treatment would eliminate any difference between Turkish and English words as it did in the case of rare and frequent words. If it does, a response-process interpretation would be equally applicable to both sets of findings or to neither.

Further studies are in any case called for that compare the traditional method of limits and Haber's clarity procedure on perceptual recognition as a function of different dimensions of meaning, including concreteness, meaningfulness, frequency, and sequential redundancies of letter strings. Concreteness and meaningfulness would reveal whether the associative meaning of a word could affect perceived clarity of letter units, whereas sequential redundancy would reveal effects attributable to the degree of organization, or unitization, of multiple-letter strings in the relative absence of referential or associative meaning of the string. In addition, the reported clarity of entire words needs to be compared with letter clarity. As Neisser (1967) suggests in a comparable analysis of Haber's (1965) word frequency data, genuine visual effects would be expected only if the cognitive unit with which the subject is familiar or for which he has been set is the unit actually used for his "visual synthesis"—Neisser's term for the process that generates visual perception. Accordingly, "word frequency may only affect the perceptual experience of a subject who is trying to see whole words, but not one who is trying to make out individual letters" (p. 123).

Information is presently available on one of the above issues. Hershenson (1969) found that the perceptibility of repeatedly exposed letter arrays increased significantly as a function of the percentage of redundancy of the letter sequences. That is, clarity increased as the sequences increased in their order of approximation to the statistical structure of English. However, the effect was small, especially in the second of two experiments, in which the subjects had memorized the stimuli prior to the perceptual task. Hershenson accordingly interpreted the finding as providing only suggestive support for the view that memory structure (the subject's knowledge of the English language) enhances the percept of a stimulus that approximates that structure. In our terms, the finding means that the degree of unitization of the representational system corresponding to a letter sequence has at best only a slight influence on the perceptibility of the lower-order (letter) units of the compound structure when response processes are controlled.

Further interesting findings using the repeated-presentation procedure were reported by Dainoff and Haber (1967). They found an increase of clarity with repetition for single-letter stimuli comparable to that obtained for words. Furthermore, errors in naming letters always involved confusion with a letter that looked the same rather than with one that sounds the same. This finding differs from short-term memory studies in which errors are attributable to acoustic similarity even when the items are presented visually (see Chapter 7 for a review of these studies). Dainoff and Haber suggest that such studies involve a high memory load, thus requiring active rehearsal in an auditory information storage system, whereas their study involved low memory load with a resultant absence of interference from acoustic encoding. This interpretation is fully consistent with the present view that the associative processes evoked by a stimulus (in this case, the labeling reaction to a letter) should have no effect on perceptual recognition unless memory load is high.

Effects of visual imagery and naming sets on perceptual clarity   The facilitating effect of prior knowledge of the test stimulus on perceptual clarity (Haber, 1965; Hershenson, 1969) can be interpreted to mean that such knowledge involves arousal of symbolic representations corresponding to the stimulus. Telling the subject what the stimulus will be or prefamiliarizing him with the stimulus list in effect "primes" the relevant representational systems. However, the results do not reveal the nature of the effective underlying process—it could be verbal (i.e., auditory-motor) or imaginal (i.e., visual).

An experiment by Standing, Sell, Boss, and Haber (1970) provided some direct evidence on the issue. The study was concerned with the effect of instructions designed to arouse imaginal and verbal symbolic processes on the perceived clarity of letter stimuli. The subjects were shown five flashes of a single letter under each of six conditions. In five of them, the subject was told the letter before the first exposure and then was asked to visualize it during the flashes (i.e., to "hold a visual image of the test letter in his consciousness"), to subvocalize the letter silently to himself, to visualize another letter (also told to him), to subvocalize another letter, or to do nothing. The sixth condition provided no prior knowledge of the letter to be flashed. After each presentation, the subject rated the clarity of the stimulus on a 5-point scale. The results, presented graphically in Figure 5-2, showed that the greatest clarity occurred when the subject imagined or subvocalized the letter being presented and the least when he imagined a different letter.

The similarity of the effects of visualization and subvocalization suggests that the latter provided cues that generated visual imagery, i.e., the letter name evoked a referent image. This interpretation is favored by Dainoff and Haber's (1967) conclusion that acoustic factors do not affect visual processes directly, which implies that subvocalization should not have affected letter clarity directly but only indirectly via imagery. This view is also supported by a study by Posner et al. (1969), to be described in a later section, which showed that subjects can generate usable "visual information" concerning a letter when the name of the letter is presented auditorily.

Assuming the above interpretation to be correct, the effects of the instructional sets are fully in accord with the view that the arousal of symbolic activity

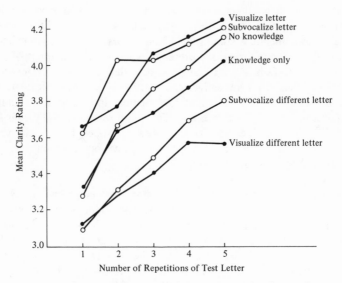

FIGURE 5-2.   Mean rated clarity of test stimuli over five repeated flashes for six experimental conditions. From Standing, Sell, Boss, and Haber (1970).

enhances perception when that activity is congruent with the perceptual process aroused by the target stimulus itself, whereas interference results when the two are incongruent. This conclusion assumes more generally that visual imagery and perception involve a common underlying process. The fact that instructional set and repetition did not interact, i.e., clarity increased at about the same rate for all six conditions (Figure 5-2), could be interpreted as further support for such identity of processes. That is, the effects of set and repetition are additive, as though they are two ways of influencing the same central process. We shall see later that studies of other perceptual phenomena lead to the same conclusion.

Haber (1967) interprets the findings described above in terms of an analogy between Hebb's (1949) theory of the ontogenetic growth of a cell assembly as a function of perceptual experience, and the "microgenetic" development of a percept during the experimental task. The clarity of a percept is a function of the degree of arousal of the previously established cell assemblies and phase sequences corresponding to a stimulus. The arousal of such processes is affected by the properties of the stimulus (duration, intensity, etc.), by the prior arousal of related processes by sets given to the subject, and by repetition of the stimulus itself. In the terminology adopted here, the effects would be described in terms of the prior availability of a symbolic representational system corresponding to the stimulus, and the "priming" of such a process by various experimental procedures. Repeated presentation of the same stimulus is the limiting instance in which the stimulus and representational process are directly correlated. The method used by Haber and his associates directly assesses the availability of a unitary representational process only in the case of single-letter stimuli. When entire words are presented and the subject is asked to report perceived letters, the procedure involves hierarchical processes such that the stimulus may be adequate to evoke a representational response at the word level (i.e., the subject "knows" the word), although not all of the lower-order components (letters) have yet been evoked or, in Neisser's terms, visually synthesized. In a real sense, the Haber procedure involves contextual-associative variables (i.e., letter-letter or word-letter associations) whose precise influence in the experimental situation is not fully known at present, although a few of the studies reviewed above provide some information on such issues. We turn now to a consideration of other studies in which word perception has been investigated as a function of more indirect associative priming.

Associative Priming

The term "associative priming" stems from the word association research, where it refers to the modifying effect of contextual stimuli on associations to a given stimulus word (see Cofer, 1967). For example, presenting the words *devil, fearful,* and *sinister* along with the critical word *dark* influences the nature of the associative responses given to the latter. Such procedures have also been used to encourage subjects to use particular mediators in paired-associate learning (see Chapter 9).

Rouse and Verinis (1962) gave their subjects one word to fixate, and a second word was flashed in the same place at increasing durations. The associative relatedness of the two words was varied. The results showed that recognition time for associated test words was significantly less than for nonassociated test words. The results were attributed to "a general associative set which activates a large number of associates, enabling the *S* to guess the flashed word with only a partial perception. If the pair is nonassociated, the flashed word is not among those activated, so recognition is not aided but hindered" (p. 303). Thus the effect seems explainable in terms of verbal response processes. Consistent with such an interpretation, Tulving and Gold (1963) conceptualized tachistoscopic word recognition as a situation in which the subject has to select a previously learned response from a set of alternative responses. Information from various sources can be utilized to aid selection. They conducted several experiments in which recognition thresholds for target words were correlated with measures of information content and degree of congruity with their pre-exposural contexts. The contexts were sentences of varying length that were either congruous or incongruous with the subsequent target word. Thus the sentence item "The actress received praise for being an outstanding . . ." is a congruous context for the target word *performer* but not for *collision*. Tulving and Gold hypothesized that the recognition threshold varies inversely with the amount of relevant information provided by the context. Their results were fully consistent with the hypothesis. The length of the context, or the amount of information conveyed by the context, was unimportant in itself, but its relevance was crucial. In their Experiment III, for example, the correlation between visual duration threshold and the degree of congruity between context and the target word was —.93, whereas the correlation between thresholds and the amount of information conveyed by the context was only —.35. The results are consistent with those obtained by Rouse and Verinis. Both sets of results indicate that relevant associative priming facilitates tachistoscopic recognition, presumably through its effect on the availability of a verbal identifying response. Samuels (1969) has recently presented further confirmatory evidence of the facilitative effect of associative priming on word recognition.

Priming and perceptual organization   A study by Steinfeld (1967) demonstrated that verbal associative priming can also facilitate the perceptual organization of ambiguous stimuli. The study essentially replicated an earlier one by Leeper (1935), with corrections for certain shortcomings in the latter. The target stimulus was a fragmented figure of a "ship" from the Street (1931) Gestalt completion test. Prior to being shown the figure, one group of subjects was given relevant verbal information, i.e., they were read a story about the sinking of a liner. Another group was read an irrelevant story, and a third group was read no story. Following the initial treatment, the figure was exposed until the subjects recognized the ship. The results of two such experiments showed that the group that had been read the relevant story recognized the ship much more quickly than either the irrelevant or no-story control groups. The latter two did not differ significantly, although the mean recognition time was somewhat longer for the irrelevant story group in both experiments.

Steinfeld's results, like those of Tulving and Gold, demonstrate a facilitative effect of relevant associative priming, but the effect in this case appears to be more directly on perceptual rather than verbal processes. Noting the similarity between his results and priming effects in other studies, Steinfeld raises the question of how an auditory (verbal) stimulus can facilitate a perceptual reorganization of a visual stimulus. The present answer is that the story evoked relevant visual imagery that, combined with the partial information provided by the fragmented stimulus, resulted in a complete percept of the object.

Evidence of perceptual reorganization resulting from nonverbal rather than verbal priming was obtained in a widely cited experiment by Wallach, O'Connell, and Neisser (1953). The stimulus was the shadow pattern cast by a wire figure, which was perceived as two-dimensional by a control group. The experimental group first saw the shadow when the wire was being rotated, a procedure that produced figural transformations that resulted in a kinetic depth effect. When subsequently exposed to the stationary pattern, these subjects continued to perceive it as three-dimensional. Spontaneous reversals of the figure and changes in the perceived size of its parts suggested that the effect was indeed a perceptual rather than a verbal phenomenon. This effect, too, is interpretable in terms of the priming of visual imagery: Long-term memory images of three-dimensional wire figures presumably were aroused by the stationary pattern when primed by the more effective dynamic pattern.

Priming by Experimental Sets and Stimulus Alternatives

Numerous studies have investigated priming effects using instructional sets indicating which of several attributes of a compound stimulus is to be noted, and by presenting multiple stimulus alternatives, among which is the test stimulus. The effect of such information has generally been to facilitate perceptual accuracy. Whether the effect is one of perceptual "tuning" or some manner of response facilitation has been a central issue in these studies, as it has been in the other problem areas considered up to this point. Haber's (1966) review provides a general coverage of the research on the problem and we shall restrict our attention to a few studies that are especially pertinent. In an attempt to distinguish between perceptual processes and verbal responses in tachistoscopic recognition, Neisser (1954) presented subjects a list of words to study, indicating that some of them would later be shown tachistoscopically. Some were in fact shown, but other target stimuli were homonyms of other words on the study list. Facilitation was obtained for the original words but not for the homonyms. Since the latter require the same response but only the former were facilitated, Neisser concluded that the effect was one of perceptual enhancement. Subsequently, however, Neisser (1967, pp. 118–121) reformulated the distinction between perception and response as a difference between visual processes and verbal processes. The former refers to what was *seen* and is interpreted as a product of figural synthesis; the latter refers to inner speech (auditory synthesis). He concedes that the set effects in his experiment could have involved response bias in the sense that subjects' reports are mediated by such verbal processes.

Haber (1966) suggests a similar interpretation of Neisser's results in terms of encoding. Perceptual processing requires a translation of the visual image of the stimulus into some kind of memorial trace after the stimulus terminates. The product of coding differs for the members of homonym pairs and occurs more quickly for words the subject expects to see, hence the facilitated perception of the latter without the corresponding homonyms being affected. This explanation is consistent with Haber's general theoretical approach to perceptual processing and applies to set effects in particular. What is the nature of this encoding process? Although he does not deny the possibility that some nonlinguistic code may be used by some subjects, especially in the case of nonlinguistic stimuli, Haber suggests that "encoding into words is the most probable basic strategy" (p. 346). Encoding as used by Haber and verbal processes as used by Neisser appear, therefore, to be essentially similar mechanisms, although Haber places relatively more emphasis on memory processes as a defining feature of encoding. Thus encoding of words that one expects to see may be faster than that of unexpected words, resulting in different memory codes that permit a distinction between the two even when the unexpected word is a homonym of the expected one.

It is important to note that the memory factor in Haber's encoding concept is not simply a fading memory trace of the physical stimulus pattern. The distinction is a central issue in a series of studies involving instructional sets to attend differentially to particular attributes of multidimensional stimuli. Lawrence and LaBerge (1956) used stimulus cards containing number, color, and shape as attributes. All three attributes were to be reported, but the relative value of reporting each attribute correctly was manipulated in such a manner that all attributes received equal value, or one attribute was emphasized by offering the subject relatively more money for reporting it rather than the other attributes correctly. The order in which the attributes were to be reported was also varied in the case of a group with equal set for the three attributes. Lawrence and LaBerge found that set increased accuracy for the emphasized attribute and decreased it for the other two. Furthermore, accuracy with the equal set was greater for items reported early than for ones reported later. They accordingly interpreted the set effect in terms of fading memory combined with order of report—an explanation already familiar to us from the discussion in the last chapter of order-of-report effects for tachistoscopically presented material (cf. Bryden, 1960).

Harris and Haber (1963) repeated the experiment with the modification that each subject was tested under all set conditions, with a free order of report on half the trials and a forced order on the other half, even in the case where the attention instructions emphasized one attribute. They found that order of report could not account for the set effect, inasmuch as the critical attribute was more accurately reported whether it was reported early or late. The Lawrence and LaBerge interpretation was therefore rejected.

In the same experiments, Harris and Haber (1963) and Haber (1964a) demonstrated the importance of encoding processes as a determiner of set effects. They had observed earlier that subjects spontaneously encoded the stimulus material into words and rehearsed the message prior to report. Furthermore, two different encoding strategies were used. One was an *objects* code, in which the stimulus was separated into objects on the left and right (for example, one red triangle, three blue stars); the other, a *dimensions* code, in which the stimulus was separated into three dimensions (for example, red blue, triangle star, one three). Harris and Haber emphasized the linguistic distinction between the two strategies: The dimensions code could be varied without disturbing the strategy, whereas the objects code has its order of encoding fixed by the rules of English syntax (we say "one red triangle," but not "red one triangle," for example). They investigated the effects of these strategies systematically by training subjects to use one or the other strategy. Effects of both set and order of report were obtained, but these variables interacted with coding strategy in such a manner that the differential accuracy for emphasized or first-reported attributes as compared to incidental or later-reported attributes was greater in the case of dimensions than objects coders. These findings were consistent with the hypothesis that objects coders, presumably constrained by English word-order habits, could not easily give special treatment to the emphasized dimension. The results also showed that the objects coders were generally more accurate in their reports. A third study (Haber, 1964b), in which the subjects were required to verbalize overtly their encoding and rehearsal of the stimulus, revealed that objects coders began encoding and completed the encoding faster than did the dimensions coders. The latter also made more errors during the rehearsal process after the initial encoding. From these data, Haber (1966) concluded that the two strategies differ in speed of encoding and resistance to errors during rehearsal, and that these differences account for many of the effects of set that had been observed in prior research, including the Neisser (1954) experiment already mentioned.

A similar coding theory has been proposed by Glanzer and Clark (1963a). Their verbal-loop hypothesis asserts that subjects faced with a perceptual task such as the recall of a visual array encode the information verbally and then translate the verbal information into a final response. The length of the covert "verbal loop" is critical in much the same sense as speed of encoding in Haber's analysis—the shorter the verbalization required by the perceptual task, the more accurate the performance. The hypothesis has been supported by evidence showing the predicted relations between verbal code length and measures of perceptual difficulty and organization (e.g., Glanzer & Clark, 1963b, 1964). Glanzer and Fleishman (1967) also investigated the effect of encoding training on recall of tachistoscopically presented binary numbers. The expectation that training in efficient codes (ones that minimize the number of words that encode the input) should improve perceptual performance was not supported. Instead, imposing a code on the subject impaired tachistoscopic performance. The authors suggest that an additional encoding step may have been added to the information processing and there was insufficient time to complete the encoding in such a fast, visual task. In serially presented auditory memory tasks, where more time is available, similar encoding has been found to facilitate performance (Pollack & Johnson, 1965). This interpretation is fully consistent with the general assertion made earlier that the effect of mediating mechanisms in perceptual tasks depends on the time available for their operation.

An alternative to the verbal encoding hypothesis   Apart from Haber's (1966) passing reference to possible nonverbal mechanisms, the encoding processes described above are assumed to be based exclusively on verbal mediation. An alternative analysis, which stresses nonverbal as well as verbal processes, will now be considered with reference to Haber's views in particular.

The main point to be emphasized is that the critical difference between the objects and dimensions codes may be one of concreteness-abstractness of the task and its effect on imagery processes, rather than word-order habits alone. Subjects using the objects code are simply required to attend to the stimuli as concrete objects, whereas those using the dimensions code are required to pay particular attention to the abstract properties of the objects. Accordingly, the objects code may be relatively more effective because it is associated with more efficient arousal of nonverbal (imaginal) memory representations of the stimulus objects, which include the attributes as intrinsic components of the representation. The process of abstraction involved in the dimensions encoding, on the other hand, requires an immediate translation of the stimulus into verbal form, which may indeed take longer than the verbalization involved in objects encoding, but it also takes the subject's attention away from the concrete stimulus. Moreover, it provides less effective (implicit) verbal cues for *regeneration* of images corresponding to the concrete objects than does the objects code. Thus, "red blue; two four; star circle" is less likely to evoke appropriate concrete images than is "two red circles, four blue stars." The superiority of the objects code therefore can be attributed, first, to more effective arousal of concrete symbolic representations by the stimulus itself because the subject is set to attend primarily to the objects as figural entities rather than to their abstract attributes (regardless of the emphasized dimension); and, second, to more effective maintenance of such representations by the verbalization resulting from the concrete (objects) set. The difference between this interpretation and Haber's is in the present emphasis on the functional properties of nonverbal processes rather than the verbal symbolic system alone.

While the implications of the present analysis have not been independently tested using the appropriate perceptual tasks, evidence from several sources is consistent with the hypothesis. Studies to be reviewed later indicate that concrete, high-imagery stimuli are consistently superior to abstract stimuli in a variety of associative and memory tasks even when the availability of verbal associative processes is controlled (Chapters 7 and 8). The perceptual effects under consideration are consistent with such data if it is assumed that objects and dimensions coding strategies differ in the degree to which concrete as compared to abstract (verbal) characteristics serve as the functional stimulus for recall.

Further suggestive clues can be found directly in the results of the experiments by Haber and his associates when considered in conjunction with findings from other sources. While dimensions coders showed differential accuracy for the emphasized dimension, objects coders showed little difference in accuracy of reporting emphasized and incidental dimensions. It will be recalled that Haber attributed the difference to speed of verbal encoding, with the faster objects code permitting more effective transformation of the rapidly fading visual memory image of the stimulus into a verbal code. This explanation seems insufficient if the stress remains on verbal mediation. Haber (1966, p. 344) notes that the afterimage of the stimulus persists for perhaps several hundred milliseconds after the offset of the stimulus (values approximating 300 msec have been obtained by different experimenters using several different procedures; see Haber & Standing, 1969). This time span seems too brief to permit verbalization of the stimulus from the trace even in the case of the well-practiced syntax associated with the objects code. The evidence bearing on this point derives from studies of reaction time for naming responses (e.g., Fraisse, 1964; Morin et al., 1965), already mentioned in Chapter 3. The RTs vary as a function of various factors, such as discriminability and number of alternatives, but the average estimates range upward from about 450 msec for stimulus units such as geometric figures. While this estimate is for overt naming, it seems unlikely that the implicit naming response would occur in less than 300 msec (cf. Landauer, 1962). Moreover, the RT value is for a single unit, not for the elements of a stimulus containing a number of codable units as in the Haber experiments. The inevitable conclusion is that some figural representation of the stimulus pattern other than the visual afterimage must be evoked by the stimulus, and that this representation must persist well beyond 300 msec if it is to mediate the appropriate verbal report.

Evidence for such persistent and usable visual images is provided by the following data. Free verbal recall scores are higher for pictures than for their verbal labels (see Chapter 7). The fact that this occurs despite the more direct availability of the verbal code when the stimulus is a word suggests that the differential recall results from retention of nonverbal information over a period of minutes at least. Posner and Konick (1966) present data indicating that short-term retention of visual location and kinesthetic distance is primarily through imagery rather than through verbal codes, and that about 64 percent of the information in the image is retained over a 10-second interval even when the interval is filled with an interpolated task. Thus useful visual information apparently persists long enough to permit verbal processing of stimuli in the encoding experiments under discussion. A third finding is even more directly pertinent to the encoding studies. In a series of experiments to be discussed in more detail below, Posner and his associates have been able to estimate the rate of decay of visual information using a matching task in which identity judgments for pairs of letters are based either on physical identity (e.g., AA) or only on name identity (e.g., Aa). One of several experiments by Posner, Boies, Eichelman, and Taylor (1969) showed that the rate of decay of visual information within a one-second retention interval was reduced by a procedure designed to keep the subject's attention on the physical form of the letter rather than on its name. While the conditions of the experiments are not comparable, the results provide evidence for a visual "rehearsal" mechanism that may be applicable to the Haber and Harris data. The relevant argument is that the objects encoding set used by Haber and Harris encourages the subject to attend to the physical object-characteristics of the complex stimulus, thereby preserving a usable visual image; conversely, the dimensions code draws attention to the abstract attributes of the stimulus, thereby encouraging verbalization rather than visual rehearsal and resulting in rapid decay of the visual information. Consistent with such an interpretation is the equivalent performance of objects coders with respect to emphasized dimensions and their relative freedom from order-of-report effects, as though they were able to rely on a read-out from a persisting visual (spatial) representation. By contrast, the dimensions coders apparently relied more directly on verbalization, which encodes the visual information sequentially and hence results in differential accuracy for first-reported and emphasized attributes.

Further relevant evidence is found in a study by Ernest and Paivio (1969) in which subjects with high imagery ability, as measured by spatial ability tests and questionnaires, were superior to low-imagery subjects in remembering the incidental components of a compound stimulus, although no differences were obtained for components to which the subject's attention had been directed during a learning task. Considered in greater detail in Chapter 14, these results are relevant here because they provide evidence that the use of imagery is associated with accurate incidental memory without any compensatory loss of intentional memory. The finding is analogous to the equivalent accuracy for emphasized and incidental dimensions shown by Haber's studies, strengthening the inference that an imagerylike process was involved in that case as well.

The above findings reveal effects attributable to the arousal of both verbal and visual coding processes by set instructions and other appropriate cues, but the experiments generally were not designed to differentiate the two mechanisms and did not do so clearly. The studies by Posner and his associates were cited as providing support for a visual memory process in perception. Such experiments make ingenious use of a technique that may enable us to distinguish between different kinds of mental processes, including those assumed to be involved at the different levels of associative meaning described in previous sections. We shall now consider that approach in some detail.

Perceptual and Symbolic Processes in Classification Tasks

The discussion of stimulus meaning and perception in Chapter 4 included a reference to research reported by Hochberg (1968) in which a perceptual matching task was used to investigate effects of familiarity. The findings revealed that same-different judgments were unaffected by familiarity when the two stimuli could be viewed simultaneously or nearly so. With longer interstimulus intervals, the identity judgment was faster for familiar than for unfamiliar stimuli. Hochberg concluded that the effects of prior learning are to be found in the "schematic map" that is stored in memory and not in the contents of the "momentary glance." The matching technique thus distinguished between effects attributable to the physical stimulus per se and higher levels of cognitive processing based on stored information. Neisser and Beller (1965) expressed the same distinction in terms of the depths at which a stimulus can be examined. They showed that an item search based on memory examination (looking for a proper name) took longer than one based on physical attributes (e.g., looking for K). The difference in latencies can be taken as reflecting the latency of the memory process. Such an analysis takes advantage of the subtractive method of Donders (Boring, 1950, pp. 147–149) in which the duration of a mental process was estimated from the difference in reaction times to tasks differing in complexity. For example, by subtracting simple RT from discrimination RT, Donders presumably obtained the time for the discrimination. Despite criticisms that have been directed at it, the subtractive method promises to be an extraordinarily sensitive approach to the study of internal events.

The method has been systematically extended by Posner and his associates to the analysis of "depth of processing" in a variety of classification tasks. The basic approach, described in detail by Posner and Mitchell (1967)[1], involves presentation of pairs of stimulus items such as letters, to which the subject must respond "same" or "different" as quickly as possible. The identity match can be based on various characteristics. Posner and Mitchell compared three different levels of complexity, where the stimuli were held constant but the level of processing was varied by instructional sets. Thus "same" was defined in terms of *physical identity*, where both letters (for example) are capitals or both are small (e.g., AA or aa), *name identity* (e.g., Aa), and *rule identity* (e.g., both vowels). The findings revealed that the matching response is generally faster when the two letters are physically identical than when they only have the same name, and those based on a common name were in turn faster than those based on a common rule (see Figure 5-3). The extra time at the second as compared to the first level presumably reflected the time required to "look up" the names of the letters, while the further increase at the third level suggests that the subjects may first derive the names of the letters before determining whether they are both vowels or both consonants. The authors are careful to point out, however, that the increasing times for the three levels might result from processes that operate either serially or in parallel, or some combination of both.

Posner and Mitchell also found, in agreement with Hochberg (1968) and Robinson et al. (1964), that the rate of matching on the basis of physical identity did not change with the familiarity of the stimulus pair. They note that this cannot logically be true for the higher levels where identity is a mediated phenomenon established by learning. The effect of learning, however, appears to be a stable one involving long-term memory processes, inasmuch as there was little evidence that the relationships between the levels changed with practice over the course of the experiment.

Posner and Mitchell conceptualize the different levels of processing as a hierarchical tree structure with three processing nodes corresponding to the basis on which the match is made. The tree diagram is depicted in Figure 5-3. In terms of the conceptual system adopted here, the operations can be viewed as defining levels of task abstractness. The first node involves the most concrete task, in which subjects are directed to respond according to the physical attributes of the stimulus. The second node involves a higher level of abstraction in which the common characteristic of the stimuli is defined by their name. This level of processing therefore can be viewed as involving the referential meaning of letters. Further abstraction is involved at the third level, where identity is based on a more general rule. The processing times, which varied between 450 and 900 msec depending on the node, reflect the differential difficulty of dif-

---

[1] Further detailed reviews of the extension of Donders' method to the investigation of processing stages have been presented recently by Posner (1970) and Sternberg (1968).

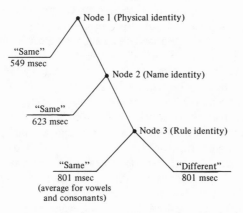

FIGURE 5-3. Tree diagram showing three processing nodes corresponding to the basis on which the same-different match is made. The mean RTs for "same" responses are shown for each node, as well as the overall mean for "different" responses. Adapted from Posner and Mitchell (1967).

ferent levels of task abstractness. The mechanisms may also differ, the first level presumably involving visual processes without any significant contribution from either visual memory processes (imagery) or the verbal symbolic system, whereas the other two levels involve verbal processes in varying degree.

Decay and generation of visual information in classification tasks   A further series of studies provided evidence concerning the rate of decay of visual information in the classification task. Posner and Keele (1967) used the subtraction technique to examine the persistence of usable visual information in memory by delaying the presentation of the second letter for varying intervals. They found that, immediately after presentation, the physical identity (AA) match was about 80 msec faster than the name identity (Aa) match, and that this difference was reduced to about zero when the presentation of the second letter was delayed by 1.5 sec. The reduction in the physical-name difference over time was interpreted as reflecting the rate of decay of visual information. The decay function is shown in Figure 5-4. This basic finding was replicated and extended by Posner et al. (1969), who showed that the rate of decay of visual information within a one-second interval could be reduced by keeping the subject's attention on the physical form of the letter rather than on its name, thus providing evidence for a visual "rehearsal" mechanism discussed earlier in relation to the Haber and Harris encoding experiments.

In another experiment, Posner et al. investigated the generation of visual information. They reasoned that when a subject is presented the first letter auditorily and the second visually, and he knows in advance whether the sec-

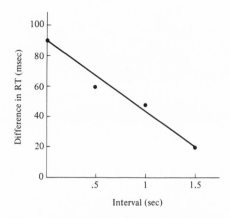

FIGURE 5-4. Decay function for
visual information obtained by subtracting
physical from name identity RT. Adapted
from Posner and Keele (1967).

ond will be capital or small, he may be able to generate the visual information
of the opposite case. If this occurs, the subject should show as efficient matching
for audiovisual as for visual physical identity pairs, and superior to visual name
identity pairs. This is precisely what happened with practiced subjects. The data
for the two critical conditions of the experiment are presented in Figure 5-5,
where it can be seen that, at an interstimulus interval of approximately .75 to 1
second, subjects were able to match a new visual letter as rapidly when the first
letter was auditory as when it was visual. They were never able to do so at a
zero delay interval. These data suggest a latency of .75 to 1 second for the
arousal of a visual image by an auditory verbal stimulus, i.e., a letter image
by its name.

Since the subjects were similarly able to produce information that underlies
the detection of more than one letter, Posner et al. suggested that the generated
material may not be in the form of a spatial image, but should be viewed instead
as a program for analyzing visual features. Regardless of the terminology, however, the evidence suggests that the generated information contains usable figural
information of the kind generally attributed to visual images. Perhaps the only
distinction is that the conditions in the Posner et al. experiment do not allow
sufficient time for the generation of a representation that is consciously experienced and reportable as a visual image, although it has the functional characteristics of the latter. The distinction between visual information and imagery
thus appears to parallel that between imaginal (concrete) meaning and imagery,
discussed in Chapter 3, where imagery was viewed as an associative manifestation of an underlying meaning disposition. The issue will come up again in
subsequent chapters, where the term imagery will be used to refer to a memory
code or associative mediator that provides spatially parallel information that

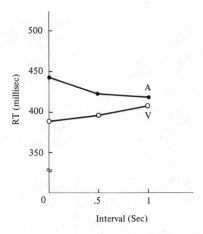

FIGURE 5-5. RTs for "same" responses when the first stimulus is either auditory (A) or visual (V) and the second stimulus is visual and always uppercase. The data are for practiced subjects (i.e., from the last two of four experimental days). Adapted from Figure 4 in Posner, Boies, Eichelman, and Taylor (1969).

can mediate overt responses without necessarily being consciously experienced as a visual image.

The evidence that subjects can generate useful visual information on the basis of verbal cues makes it possible to argue that some of the previously discussed effects of set on visual recognition of letters and words could be interpreted in similar terms. Long, Reid, and Henneman (1960), for example, found that informing subjects beforehand that the stimulus to be flashed was one of two particular letters resulted in greater accuracy than if the set was given only after the flash. Subjects informed beforehand might have made use of generated visual information against which to match the subsequent stimulus, just as in the Posner et al. experiment. A Donders-type classification study by Sternberg (1967) provides evidence directly relevant to such an interpretation. Subjects were visually presented either an intact or a degraded digit and were required to indicate whether or not the digit was one of a set of positive alternatives, varying in number, which had been auditorily presented prior to the exposure of the test stimulus. From the different reaction-time functions for intact and degraded stimuli over set size, Sternberg was able to infer that the test stimulus was encoded as a visual memory-representation and that the match was made on that basis rather than on the basis of a name code. He suggested that the auditorily presented positive set need not have been similarly retained as visual representations; instead, the members of the set may have been converted into such a form as required. The suggestion implies generation of visual information from auditory-verbal input and is directly applicable to the results obtained by Long et al. Perhaps the latter imply something similar in their suggestion that set increased perceptual accuracy by augmenting the discrimination of important stimulus elements. The hypothesis could be extended to words, although the extension is particularly speculative because a more complex visual image must be assumed.

To summarize up to this point, we have been considering effects of experimental sets that facilitate perception, presumably by arousing symbolic processes that are congruent with the perceptual activity itself or by preserving the information provided by the stimulus until the discriminative response can be made. The most direct priming of perception is by means of repeated presentation of the same stimulus, resulting in a gradual growth of a clear percept. Indirect priming has been achieved by the prior presentation of words or sentences that are associatively related to the stimulus, or by instructional sets that direct the subject's attention to particular aspects of the stimulus or that reduce the stimulus alternatives. The crucial issue has been whether the effects involve some manner of direct "tuning" of the visual system itself, or facilitate the encoding of the stimulus into a memory system that is less subject to rapid decay and loss of stimulus information. The evidence suggests that perceptual tuning is plausible in the case of repeated presentation, but that memory coding systems are involved in set effects generally. Verbal coding that permits rehearsal of the coded stimulus information has been stressed by Haber and other theorists and is undoubtedly operative. In addition, however, evidence was presented that visual imagery—evoked by the stimulus or generated by the subject, or both—can be effectively utilized in perceptual tasks.

INTERFERING INTERACTIONS OF PERCEPTUAL AND SYMBOLIC ACTIVITY

The preceding sections were concerned with experimental procedures that have a facilitating effect on perception, presumably because the symbolic processes aroused by the set are somehow congruous with the perceptual input or because they increase the probability of responding appropriately. The next section, by contrast, deals with interfering effects of cognitive activity on perception, and vice versa. The phenomena again range from the short-term events that occur during the initial stages of information processing immediately after stimulus presentation, to the longer-term events involved in relatively continuous perceptual and symbolic tasks.

Backward Masking

The perception of a brief visual display can be interrupted or modified by a second stimulus presented a moment later. This phenomenon has been variously termed backward masking, erasure, or metacontrast, depending on the nature of the masking stimulus and the resulting effect. Of particular interest here is the case where the mask itself is a patterned figure (visual noise). A detailed consideration of the problems associated with the phenomenon is unnecessary for our purposes (for reviews see Kahneman, 1968; Neisser, 1967, pp. 22–35; Raab, 1963; Weisstein, 1968) and our attention will center on a few relevant issues. Haber (1968) points out that the critical issue is what happens during the interval between the onset of the target stimulus and the visual noise. One interpretation (e.g., Eriksen, 1966) is that the masking stimulus combines in some way with the test stimulus so that its representation is degraded—that is, its brightness, contrast, and so on, suffer as a result of the mask. An alternative interpretation (e.g., Sperling, 1963) is that the mask interrupts the information processing that began with the initial registration of the stimulus. The former viewpoint stresses a temporal summation of the sensory effects of the two stimuli; the latter, an active extraction of information from a representation of the stimulus.

Haber and Nathanson (1969) investigated the problem using sequential presentation of the letters of a word, each letter arriving in the same retinal location. They assumed that each successive letter would act to stop the processing of the previous one and that processing time could therefore be computed as the time from the onset of a letter to the onset of the next. By varying the "off" time between letters, stimulus duration and processing time could be varied independently. They used five "on" times ranging from 10 to 150 msec per letter and five similar off times. The subject reported the letters he was sure he saw correctly after the last letter had appeared. The results showed that, for every on-off combination summing to the same processing time, the ratio of on time to off time could be varied as much as 15:1 without changing the performance. This finding seems inconsistent with the sensory interpretation, according to which short off times should favor temporal summation and hence result in greater masking effects than would longer times. It is consistent, however, with the information processing interpretation, according to which the important variable is the total processing time from the onset of the first stimulus to the onset of the interfering mask. Neither on time alone nor off time alone is important as long as the on time is sufficient for initial registration of the stimulus and arousal of its short-term visual image, for which as little as 19 msec was sufficient in the Haber and Nathanson experiment, as well as in earlier experiments by Sperling (1963), in which multiple-letter displays were used.

The important point here is not the inadequacy of the sensory interpretation (it may be sufficient for simpler problems), but the positive evidence that the processing of information within a brief interval can be stopped by subsequent visual noise. The backward masking technique thus provides a method for assessing the rate at which information can be extracted from the stimulus as a function of such variables as the amount of information in the display, stimulus meaning, and so on. Sperling (1963), for example, found that the number of letters that a subject could correctly report from a brief exposure increased at the rate of about one letter per 10 msec delay of the noise field for the first three or four letters of an array. This finding suggested that the short-term visual image could be scanned at a rate of 10 msec per letter. Beyond four letters the required processing time per unit increased sharply. The sequential presentation of letters in the Haber and Nathanson experiment yielded much greater values of 65 to 110 msec per letter, depending on the length of the word (see Figure 5-6), indicating that sequential presentation resulted in less efficient processing than the simultaneous presentation method. These comparisons suggest that, although the output phase of the information processing is necessarily serial in both situations, the spatially parallel input involved in simultaneous presentation has an overall advantage over sequential input. The reason may be that the former arouses a unitary visual image containing spatially organized letter information that can be scanned efficiently, whereas the latter does not provide a usable image and performance is almost entirely dependent upon sequential verbal encoding, which is limited by the speed at which letters can be implicitly named.

Neisser's (1967, pp. 33–35) critical discussion of the rate of readout from the icon (his term) is relevant here. He considers it extremely unlikely that items can be processed at the rate of 10 msec per item, or 100 per second, as

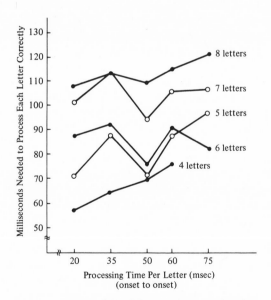

FIGURE 5-6. Mean exposure duration needed to process a letter as a function of processing time per item, for words of different lengths. From Haber and Nathanson (1969).

proposed by Sperling, because it is much faster than estimates by other methods and because it would be useless under normal conditions (the potential readout during the 200 msec or so that eyes are stationary would far exceed memory span). Therefore he prefers the interpretation that the processing of the icon does not end at the moment the mask is presented, as Sperling suggested, but continues for some time thereafter. The *subjective* duration of the image may indeed terminate with the onset of the masking stimulus, but the figural information the image contains can still be read. The fact that the fast processing rates held only for the first three or four items is perhaps consistent with this conclusion in that it may reflect the limits of the figural information retained by the subject after the mask. Neisser's analysis is also generally in agreement with the suggestion made earlier in connection with the encoding of visual information under different set conditions, as well as with the analysis in the preceding paragraph.

Implicated here is the problem of the relative information processing capacities of a parallel-processing system involving vision and visual imagery, and the sequential-processing verbal system that must be involved in the verbal readout. Some direct evidence on the latter point comes from an experiment by Mewhort, Merikle, and Bryden (1969), who used the backward masking technique to demonstrate that familiar (high redundancy) letter sequences are input to memory faster than are random letter strings and that the input mechanism proceeds sequentially from left to right. These results are consistent with the view that performance in such a task is mediated at least partly by the sequentially organized verbal symbolic system. This problem will be considered again in the context of studies of short-term memory in Chapter 7.

Stimulus meaning and backward masking effects   The effects of meaning on the rate of information processing is an obvious problem for investigation by the method of backward masking. Little systematic research is yet available, although the Mewhort et al. (1969) study just mentioned can be interpreted as providing some evidence on the effect of representational meaning (familiarity) on processing rate. Further suggestive evidence was provided by D. A. Allport (1968), who used Sperling's (1963) method to investigate the rate of assimilation of visual information for digits and a vocabulary of four Landolt rings (simple ring figures with a break in each). Subjects used the names "up," "down," "left," and "right" to indicate the position of the break in each ring. Strings of each type of stimulus were presented tachistoscopically with varying delays of the masking stimulus. The results for digits (a mean of 11.4 msec per item) were similar to those obtained by Sperling for letters, but the processing of information from the Landolt rings occurred two to three times more slowly (30.5 msec per item). The difference was not reduced by practice. Allport considered cue redundancy and familiarity (the accessibility of a naming response) as possible explanations, favoring the latter. Although the interpretation of these data remains uncertain, Allport's study, like that of Mewhort et al., shows the potential usefulness of the backward masking technique for the investigation of meaning.

Effects of Interpolated Activity

The backward masking studies generally have not used masking stimuli that require active processing, although they could do so. The Haber and Nathanson experiment, for example, involved the assumption that each succeeding letter of a series masks the preceding one. In such a case, the effect of any visual noise created by the mask is confounded with the effect of the processing activity demanded by the information it contains. The following studies involve different procedures and longer time intervals than the masking studies, but they are relevant to the general problem of the effect of interpolated symbolic activity on perceptual processing, and vice versa.

Posner and Konick's (1966) experiment on the retention of visual and kinesthetic information, discussed earlier, yielded the conclusion that information about distance was stored primarily in a visual code. It also showed that reading and recording visually presented digits during the retention interval had little effect on the level of retention, whereas adding or classifying the digits had a much greater effect. One experiment by Posner et al. (1969) pursued the implications of the finding using the same-different reaction time technique. The first of two letters was presented tachistoscopically for 1 second, followed by a .5 second interpolated interval and then by the second letter for 2 seconds. Reaction time was measured from the onset of the second letter. The interpolated activity consisted of a blank field, a random noise field (small black and white squares), or two pairs of digits grouped around the central fixation, the upper pair of which had to be added. As in the previously discussed experiments in this series, physical identity (e.g., AA) and name identity (e.g., Aa) matches were compared.

The results showed that the interpolated noise and addition conditions had overall effects of slowing down reaction time, but visual noise alone did so equally for both physical and name identity conditions. Thus the mask appeared only to delay the processing of the second stimulus without affecting the presence of visual information specifically. The usual superiority of the physical identity over the name identity matching was almost entirely lost with the interpolated addition task, however, indicating that this task had a more detrimental effect on the preservation of visual than on name information. The authors favor the interpretation that the addition task interferes with the attention that the subject gives to processing visual aspects of the letter, thereby increasing the rate of decay of visual information relative to blank or visual noise conditions, or the visual rehearsal condition described previously. They consider it unlikely that the number stimuli had a greater *visual* effect than the mask field, and this is probably true if the reference is to the numbers and the noise field as physical stimulus patterns. We shall see later, however, that the interference effects depend on the relation between the modalities that are "tied up" by the perceptual and symbolic components of a task.

Effects of Prior and Concurrent Symbolic Activity on Perception

A number of studies suggest that incongruent imagery or verbal activity aroused by prior experimental sets can modify or interfere with perception. We have already encountered such effects in the earlier section on perceptual clarity, where we saw that the clarity of flashed letters suffered when subjects were asked to image or to subvocalize a letter other than the one that was presented (Standing et al., 1970). The general problem will now be considered more fully.

Bruner and Postman (1949) gave subjects a set to see normal playing cards, then showed them cards in which colors and suits disagreed (e.g., black hearts). Many subjects reported the cards as they normally would appear (e.g., red hearts), but others reported seeing a compromise such as purple hearts. The latter finding suggests that the perception of the stimulus was modified by the arousal of memory images corresponding to normal playing cards. Although alternative interpretations of the findings are possible, numerous other studies have similarly suggested that memory color can influence color perception (see the review by Epstein, 1967, Chapter 4, and the more recent experiment by Herring & Bryden, 1970).

Eliava (1962) reported experiments on "ustanovka" (set or attitude) that included three variants of a basic experiment. In one experiment, subsequent to multiple tachistoscopic exposure of the same picture, a picture having a completely different object content was presented (the first picture was omitted in a control condition). In a second experiment, four different pictures of the same object content preceded the new object. In the third, the subjects were repeatedly asked to imagine a woman in an old-style red crinoline, then a picture of a decanter of red wine was presented repeatedly. The control condition involved no prior imagination of the woman. The results from all three experiments showed that the perception of the object was in some way influenced by the activity preceding perception. Moreover, adequate perception was achieved only gradually. These findings, discussed by the author in terms of the concepts of attitude, set, personality, and categorization, are consistent with the more specific interpretation that the arousal of imagery modified subsequent perception, inasmuch as the "set" operations can be regarded as definitive of imagery. Bruner and Potter (1964) found comparable interfering effects on perception when a fuzzy picture was gradually focused and subjects were required to describe what they thought the picture was during the period of increased focus. The authors discussed the finding in terms of misclassifications that are tested against the fuzzy picture, which implies that the effective symbolic activity was verbal. However, the results also could be interpreted more simply in terms of the arousal of imagery incongruent with the actual object. The effect, according to this view, would be analogous to the findings that the content of imagery can be influenced by prior exposure to a subliminal visual stimulus (Fiss, Goldberg, & Klein, 1963), and by a concealed figure in a perceptually dominant stimulus (Eagle, Wolitzky, & Klein, 1966).

Daydreaming and perception Highly relevant here is Singer's (1966) discussion of daydreaming and perception as involving an interaction of environmental and internal sources of stimulation, which compete for "channel space." The phenomenon is familiar to anyone who has had the experience of driving on a highway absorbed in thought and later having no recollection of the scenery along the way. My own impression of such instances runs as follows. To the extent that my daydreaming consists of visual imagery, I can attend to internal visual experiences while responding appropriately to those features of the external environment necessary for carrying out the routine task of driving. At the same time, I remain unaware of irrelevant visual stimulation, however compelling such stimulation might be if my attention is directed to it. The daydreaming is sharply reduced, however, or entirely absent when I am driving in crowded traffic conditions, where it is clearly adaptive for the external channel to have priority over the inner. Antrobus and Singer (1964) obtained experimental evidence consistent with such observations: Signal detection during behavior (spontaneous, free associative speech) analogous to daydreaming was inferior to detection during a more monotonous counting task. Conversely, Antrobus, Singer, and Greenberg (1966) found in one experiment that increasing the rate of signal presentation or increasing the memory load in the task reduced the number of reported task-irrelevant thoughts in general and visual images in particular. Thus, whether imagery or perceptual activity has priority appears to depend on the difficulty of the perceptual task.

The Perky phenomenon as a signal detection problem Segal and Gordon (1968) have taken a similar approach to the Perky (1910) phenomenon in terms of signal detection. Perky's conclusion was that images are indistinguishable from faint stimuli inasmuch as subjects who were asked to imagine an object such as a banana usually failed to detect a supraliminal stimulus simulating the object but did report an appropriate image. In signal detection terms, the failure to report the stimulus represents a "miss" of a signal. This could be due to the difficulty of distinguishing the signal from the internal "noise" created by imaging, or to the subject's guessing strategy when he has been instructed to expect images. Segal and Gordon investigated the problem by manipulating the subject's expectancies and the brightness of the projected stimulus, and then using signal detection measures as a basis for interpreting the data. In one experiment, a naive (Perky) condition was compared with an informed condition in which subjects were told that slides might be projected while they were forming images of objects they were asked to image. In both conditions slides were projected in some trials and not on others, and subjects were required to report whether or not such a projection had occurred. In another experiment, a discrimination condition without imagery and a stimulus intensity variable were added to the design. The results showed that guessing strategy varied considerably and that brighter signals were more detectable. However, even when stimulus brightness was held constant and the effects of guessing strategy were partialed out statistically, sensitivity (d'), a measure of the subject's ability to discriminate a signal-plus-noise from noise alone, was still affected by the subject's expectancy. Thus d' was highest for the discrimination condition, significantly lower for the informed imagery condition, and lowest for the naive imagery condition. These experiments supported the conclusion that imaging activity interferes with perception by raising the level of internal noise, thereby altering the signal-to-noise ratio.

It remained uncertain in the above study as in others we have considered whether the effect was specifically attributable to visual imagery as distinguished from verbal thinking or some more general factor such as attention. The uncertainty was reduced in a further experiment by Segal and Fusella (1970), which involved auditory as well as visual signals and imagery. They found that the detection of visual signals was hindered more by visual than by auditory imagery and, conversely, that auditory perception was hindered more by auditory than by visual imagery, indicating that the effects are modality specific to a significant degree. Segal's experiments thus provide some of the best evidence we have that imagery and perception are continuous modes of experience.

Visual versus verbal perceptual-symbolic systems   The studies considered thus far were not designed to distinguish between verbal processes and imagery in perceptual tasks. Strong evidence that visual perception and visual imagery "tie up" one system, and speech perception and verbal thinking another, has been presented in a series of studies by L. R. Brooks. One series of four experiments (Brooks, 1967) demonstrated a conflict between reading verbal messages and imagining the spatial relations described by the messages, but not between listening to the same messages and visualization. A description of two of the experiments will illustrate the general approach and the main findings. In one experiment, subjects were presented with a series of messages that described the spatial relations depicted in the diagram shown in Figure 5-7 but that were not actually accompanied by the diagram. The messages went as follows: "In the starting square put a 1. In the next square to the *right* put a 2. In the next square *up* put a 3," and so on. Different sequences of transitions (up, down, right, left) were used in different messages. Some of the messages were spoken to the subject and others were spoken but accompanied by the simultaneous exposure of a typewritten copy of the message. A control series of nonsense messages had the same form as the spatial one but did not convey a spatial meaning. These were formed by substituting the words *quick, slow, good, bad,* for the words *right, left, up, down.* The subject's task in each case was to repeat the message verbatim after its presentation. The results showed that subjects made more errors after reading the spatial messages than after listening to them, whereas the reverse was true in the case of the nonspatial nonsense

		3	4
	1	2	5
		7	6
		8	

FIGURE 5-7. A sample of the experimental material used by Brooks (1967). The spatial message in this case would read, "In the starting square put a 1. In the next square to the *right* put a 2. In the next square *up* put a 3," etc. The nonsense material would read, "In the starting square put a 1. In the next square to the *quick* put a 2. In the next square to the *good* put a 3," etc. From Brooks (1967).

messages. Brooks concluded that reading interferes with the generation of an internal representation of the spatial relations.

A second experiment demonstrated a similar conflict between reading and visualizing (i.e., visual imagery) during output instead of input: Underlining the key words of the spatial message on a written copy, which requires reading the message, took much longer than did a spoken output of the message. The same comparison for nonsense material was nonsignificant. It is of considerable interest, furthermore, that most subjects in the experiment reported that they "pictured the pattern" described by the spatial material and that they referred to this pattern during output. Conversely, all subjects reported that they learned the nonsense material by noticing sequential patterns in the key words and that at output these word patterns "just came." Those descriptions suggest an active monitoring of a spatially parallel visual representation (not necessarily a clear image) in the one case and retrieval from a sequentially organized verbal storage system in the other.

The same general notion that verbal and spatial information are handled in distinct, modality-specific manners was supported by a further series of experiments (Brooks, 1968) in which conflict was induced between overt responding and the act of recall. The first experiment is representative. In one task, the subject was presented a sentence such as "a bird in the hand is not in the bush."

His task was to categorize each word sequentially, from memory, as a noun or a non-noun. Thus, the above sentence would produce the sequence, "no, yes, no, no, yes, no, no, no, no, yes." This could be done in one of three ways, (1) saying "yes" and "no," as indicated, (2) tapping with the left hand for each noun and the right hand for each non-noun and (3) pointing to a "y" for each noun and an "n" for each non-noun on an output sheet on which the letter "y" was repeated as a vertical series on the left and "n" on the right (the letters being staggered to force close visual monitoring or pointing). Brooks reasoned that, if the sentence is recalled in a specifically articulatory manner, then concurrently *saying* something should provide difficulties not present when the same information is signaled by pointing or tapping.

The other task involved analogous categorization of the corners of simple block diagrams of letters, such as the "F" shown in Figure 5-8. The subject looked at the letter and then, from memory, categorized each corner as a point on the extreme top or bottom, or as a point in between. Starting at the asterisk and proceeding clockwise as indicated in the example, he would produce the sequence "yes, yes, yes, no, no, no, no, no, no, yes." The same output modes were used as in the case of sentences. The reasoning in the case of the diagram, however, was that if the "F" is recalled in a specifically visual or spatial manner, then concurrently looking at a different array should lead to difficulties not present when the information is signaled in a different manner.

If the expected conflicts are present in both tasks, speaking should be the slowest form of output when categorizing sentences, and visually monitored pointing should be the slowest form when categorizing the line drawings. As

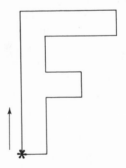

FIGURE 5-8.   A sample of the simple block diagrams used by Brooks (1968). The asterisk and arrow show the subject the starting point and direction for both reproduction and categorization.   F r o m Brooks (1968).

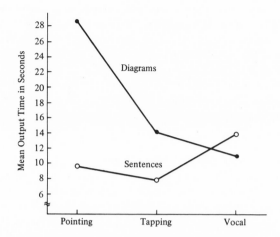

FIGURE 5-9. Mean output time for diagrams and sentences as a function of form of the output. Based on data in Brooks (1968).

can be seen from the interaction shown in Figure 5-9, both predictions were strongly confirmed. All subjects showed a longer average time for vocal output than for the other two modes in the case of sentences, and longer average time for the pointing output than for the other two in the case of the diagrams. Furthermore, the subjects' introspective reports were consistent with the conflict interpretation. They reported that they "could say the sentences to themselves" while tapping or pointing but not while saying "yes" and "no." The diagrams could be "pictured" while the subjects were saying "yes" and "no" but not while they were trying to point. The other experiments in the study confirmed the general conclusions and ruled out a number of possible alternative interpretations. Experiment III, for example, showed clearly that the disruptive effect of pointing in the case of recall of the diagram was attributable to the visual monitoring of the movement and not to movement per se. Thus the conflict apparently resulted from the involvement of a common visual-spatial control mechanism in both the memory and the perceptual-motor (output) components of the task. However, another experiment (VII) showed that the recall of the spatial information from the diagrams also conflicts with *tactually* monitored movement, leading Brooks to suggest that the conflict involves a more general spatial system rather than the visual modality specifically.

The Boundaries of the Perceptual-Symbolic Systems

Brooks discusses his findings in terms of "modality-specific processing" and raises the question of the boundaries of such "modalities." In one form or another, the issue has come up repeatedly in this chapter and the preceding one. Our initial orientation was that visual perception and imagery involve common processes, distinct from the auditory-motor processes comprising speech and verbal thought. Singer and his associates referred to daydreaming and perception as competing for "channel space." Segal concluded that imagery and perception are continuous "modes of experience." These conceptualizations all imply a commonality between perceptual and symbolic modalities. Brooks (1968) suggests that the boundaries of such a hypothetical system obviously cannot be identified with any traditional sensory or motor system. This is indicated especially by the finding that both tactual and visual monitoring conflict with the same type of recall. It is supported too by informal observations, e.g., that speech and musical information are probably handled relatively independently despite common sensory and motor components. On the other hand, Segal and Fusella's (1970) results indicate that the continuity of perception and imagery is indeed sense-specific to a significant degree.

In considering the defining features, or boundaries, of these perceptual-symbolic systems, it will be instructive to begin by examining the concept of a general spatial system, which Brooks suggested as the mediator of the conflict between the recall of spatial information from the diagrams and *both* visually and tactually monitored movement. The example is important because it implicates separate sensory modalities in a common symbolic function of spatial information processing. What is the nature of such a spatial system? The precise theoretical answer hinges on the relationship between vision and touch. Similarities between the two perceptual modes, often pointed out by others, have been emphasized recently by J. J. Gibson (1962). When viewed as "channels for information-pickup, having active and exploratory sense organs," they provide the same information and yield the same phenomenal experiences with respect to some aspects of the spatial properties of objects, surface perception, etc. It is readily understood, in general terms at least, how the functional similarities could arise from correlated visual-tactual experiences with object and spatial information. J. J. Gibson (1966, pp. 283–284) has expressed this idea as a "registering of covariant inputs" from different organs over time. He does not speculate, however, about the nature of the representational system that might develop as a result of such correlated inputs, and in particular he eschews the kind of interpretation that I find congenial, namely, one expressed in terms of imagery. In developing this viewpoint, we encounter general issues involving form discrimination and intermodal transfer that go beyond the scope of this book and, in referring to research on such problems, our attention will center only on what is most directly relevant to the present issue.

Transfer of training in form discrimination from vision to touch and the reverse has been clearly demonstrated (see, e.g., Eastman, 1967; Lobb, 1965), providing evidence that the two modalities do indeed yield common perceptual information. The effects are generally positive with easy perceptual conditions, where discrimination training in one modality facilitates subsequent relearning of forms in the other. However, interference has been demonstrated in more difficult experimental circumstances, where a form is first experienced in one modality and subsequently must be discriminated from transformations of it in either the same or the other sensory modality. Lobb (1968) has reviewed several studies in which prior visual experience in particular increased the subsequent likelihood of tactually mistaking transformations for primaries. After considering several alternative explanations, Lobb suggested that the visual interference may result from a learned "perceptual response (image)." Fragmentary stimuli in the tactual modality could evoke the complete image, which may tend to occlude minor distortions in the tactual stimulus and increase the probability of discrimination failure. Consistent with this interpretation, Lobb (1970) demonstrated strong positive crossmodal transfer of discrimination learning from vision to touch but no transfer in the reverse direction. The important point here is the general implication that tactual discrimination is mediated by visual memory of the prior stimulus, the mediating mechanism being conceptualized in a manner similar to Sheffield's (1961) analysis of conditioned perceptual responses (see the discussion in Chapter 3, above). A number of other investigators (e.g., Hyman, 1966; Scholtz, 1958; Worchel, 1951; Zigler & Northrup, 1926) have similarly concluded that visual imagery plays an important role in tactual form perception. Subjects' reports provided direct evidence for the imagery interpretation in a recent study by Scagnelli (1969). In the experimental task, the subjects were given information about unfamiliar geometric designs, visually, haptically, or verbally and then they attempted to find each design in a visual embedding field. Questionnaire data revealed that, for the majority of subjects, visual imagery was the most important "internal medium" for recalling shapes that had been presented haptically or verbally. This was taken as evidence for the view that imagery is the key representational process underlying the representational system for all three input modes in his experiment. Attneave and Benson (1969) likewise suggested that spatial location is represented primarily in visual terms, even when based on input from tactual stimulation.

It can be concluded that there is considerable empirical and theoretical support for the general idea that tactual form discrimination may involve visual imagery. It is possible to argue, therefore, that the interference Brooks observed between recall of spatial information from diagrams and tactually monitored movement is attributable to visual imagery rather than to some kind of superordinate spatial system.

The above viewpoint is consistent with the theoretical properties that were attributed to imagery in earlier chapters, where imagery was seen to include a strong motor component that contributes to its usefulness in transformational thinking. The motor component may include eye-movement tendencies as emphasized by Hebb, and more general "internalized imitation" as proposed by Piaget. In the case of the tactual monitoring of spatial location, the motor component is explicit, but it does not thereby become disengaged from its visual covariate. Instead, the latter continues to accompany it in the form of visual imagery, presumably as a result of a lifetime of correlated visual-tactual experience. This is not to say that the two components might not become "disengaged" as a result of special training, just as vision and touch as perceptual modalities apparently do in the case of such skilled activities as typing while simultaneously following a line of print, or playing a piano while following a sheet of music. The components can go on in parallel but not without special practice, as evidenced by the "hunt and peck" typist who can type from a copy only by attending alternately to the print and the typewriter keys. The analysis suggests that, with extended practice, tactually monitored movement in the Brooks-type experiment might become similarly independent of the imagined tracing of a spatial diagram, so that a conflict would not be evident.

The other modality in the Brooks studies obviously corresponds to the verbal symbolic system. It is analogous to the concept of a superordinate spatial system in several respects. Like the latter, the verbal system is to some extent functionally independent of specific sensory-motor channels: Verbal information can be given by auditory or visual input, and the processing output can be in the form of speech or writing. Nevertheless, as we have repeatedly suggested, the symbolic system may be basically auditory-motor in nature in the sense that the effect of visual-verbal input is mediated by the auditory-motor language system. Thus, the spatial and verbal modalities may be basically independent as sensory-motor systems, as well as in their functioning as symbolic systems, although at the same time they obviously share sensory and motor channels and are interconnected. That they share sensory channels is evidenced by the conflict between reading spatial messages and visualizing the relations. Their functional independence is indicated by the absence of conflict between listening to the same messages and visualizing. Their interconnectedness is suggested by evidence that spatial images can be generated from verbal input, and verbal descriptions can be mediated by spatial images.

In general, then, the boundaries of the two symbolic modalities appear to be defined by the attributes of the imaginal and verbal systems. Although not linked to highly specific sensory or motor channels, they are closely related to more general perceptual-motor systems comprised of visual and haptic processes on the one hand, and the mechanisms of speech perception and production on the other. Whether *nonverbal* auditory perception and imagery comprise an entirely separate channel or are part of a more general system that is specialized for processing nonverbal (concrete) information, whatever its specific sensory origin, is one of many questions that arise in this context. The initial conceptual preference with respect to mental processes, as specified in Chapter 2, was to differentiate concrete imagery regardless of sensory origin from verbal processes. This need not be only a dichotomy, however, since it is possible to conceive of concrete information processing as a general system with subdivisions corresponding to more specific perceptual modalities. Some of the findings reviewed in the last chapter and the present one are consistent with such a conceptual distinction. Thus the differential right-left asymmetries of perception for verbal and nonverbal stimuli, regardless of sensory mode, suggest a general division between concrete-imaginal and verbal symbolic processes. Segal and Fusella's (1970) findings with the Perky phenomenon, on the other hand, suggest further sense-specific subdivisions within the system that subserves perception and imagery for concrete stimulus events. We will be in a position to evaluate these theoretical speculations further in subsequent chapters.

SUMMARY

The effect of experimental arousal of the symbolic processes on perception may be facilitative or interfering, depending on the particular combination of variables involved. Perceptual recognition and clarity are facilitated by repeated presentation of the to-be-recognized stimulus or by prior exposure to stimuli that are associatively related to the target stimulus. Instructional sets that reduce the number of stimulus alternatives or direct attention to particular attributes of a stimulus also have been shown to increase perceptual accuracy. A major theoretical question in such research has been whether the effect is on perception per se (perceptual "tuning") or on response processes. In most instances this resolves itself into a question of the role of visual as compared to verbal processes in perceptual recognition. One theoretical approach has stressed verbal coding as a means of preserving the information in a rapidly fading visual trace. Recent evidence indicates, however, that stimulus information can also be stored as visual images for longer periods than had been supposed, and that such figural information can be actively generated by the individual.

Interference occurs (a) when a stimulus flash is closely followed by a second (masking) stimulus, which apparently stops the processing of the information in the first; (b) when the imagery or verbal process aroused by a prior experimental set is incongruent with the content of the to-be-perceived stimulus; and (c) when the symbolic activity competes for or "ties up" the channel or modality that is involved in the perceptual task, e.g., visual imagery interferes with the detection of a visual stimulus, and reading or spatial monitoring of output interferes with visual imagery. These studies raise questions concerning the identification of the precise components of interpolated symbolic activity that are detrimental to particular perceptual tasks and, more generally, the specification of the defining attributes or boundaries of the postulated perceptual-symbolic modalities.

Further information on the relationships between symbolic processes and perception is provided by studies in which the former class of variables is defined by measures of individual differences in imagery and verbal processes. These will be considered in Chapter 14. Prior to that, however, we must extend our consideration of the time span of information processing directly to learning and memory.

6
Learning and Memory: Classical Mnemonic Systems

Our discussion of memory and learning begins with a review of mnemonic techniques in which mental imagery played a central role. The treatment is mainly historical and nonempirical but nevertheless relevant because the assumptions on which the mnemonic systems were founded bear directly on important theoretical issues concerning memory. Those assumptions in effect constitute hypotheses about the mechanisms of memory and associative learning. Some of these will be recognized as having obvious counterparts in contemporary theories and as such they have been frequently subjected to experimental study. Other assumptions, while familiar, do not appear in such theories and their implications have only recently begun to be tested, perhaps because they are only now being recognized. Some of the main issues and relevant empirical evidence have been reviewed relatively briefly elsewhere (Paivio, 1969). The present chapter presents a more detailed and extended introduction to the topic, relating insights inherent in the mnemonic systems to contemporary theoretical notions. Subsequent chapters deal with empirical evidence bearing on the issues.

THE MNEMONIC SYSTEM OF SIMONIDES

Simonides was introduced in Chapter 1 as the inventor (circa 500 B.C.) of a mnemonic system involving imagery as its major memory mechanism. In the following review of the basic principles involved in the technique, I have relied on Frances Yates' (1966) recent book *The Art of Memory,* which contains the most complete coverage of the historical background of the topic that is currently available in any single source (for briefer accounts, see I. M. L. Hunter, 1964; Middleton, 1887).

153

The memory principles were purportedly suggested to Simonides by a personal episode. He was chanting a lyric poem at a banquet when he was called out by a message. During his absence the roof of the banquet hall fell in, crushing and mangling the guests so that they could not be identified. Simonides remembered the places at which they had been sitting and could thus indicate to relatives which were their dead. On the basis of this experience, Simonides formulated a memory technique in which he stressed the importance of orderly arrangement as an aid to memory, and how this could be achieved through images for localities, or places, and images for to-be-remembered facts or things.

No description of the technique by Simonides himself has survived. What has come down to us are descriptions in Latin treatises on rhetoric by Cicero and Quintilian, and in an anonymous work, the *Ad Herennium*. As suggested by those sources, the technique was taught to students of rhetoric as a practical skill that could be applied to the memorization of long speeches. Being learned, such a skill was referred to as "artificial" memory, as distinguished from the "natural" memory we are born with. The basic principles of "artificial" memory then expressed have survived essentially unchanged up to the present time, although the later memory treatises introduced variations in regard to specific features of the technique.

In *De oratore,* Cicero summarized the general purpose behind the use of localities and images as memory aids as follows:

> . . . persons desiring to train this faculty [of memory] must select places and form mental images of the things they wish to remember and store those images in the places, so that the order of the places will preserve the order of the things, and the images of the things will denote the things themselves, and we shall employ the places and images respectively as a wax writing-tablet and the letters written on it (in Yates, 1966, p. 2).

Rules for Places and Images

The efficiency of the system of places and images was to be maximized by following certain rules that were apparently well known to students of rhetoric and accordingly were only outlined by Cicero and Quintilian. The most detailed description of the rules was given in the anonymous *Ad Herennium* and, in summarizing the rules for our purposes, I can do no better than to quite directly from Yates' account of that source.

> A *locus* is a place easily grasped by the memory, such as a house, an intercolumnar space, a corner, an arch, or the like. Images are forms, marks or simulacra . . . of what we wish to remember. For instance if we wish to recall the genus of a horse, of a lion, of an eagle, we must place their images on definite *loci*.
>
> The art of memory is like an inner writing. ". . . the places are very much like wax tablets or papyrus, the images like the letters, the arrangement and disposition of the images like the script, and the delivery is like the reading."

If we wish to remember much material we must equip ourselves with a large number of places. It is essential that the places should form a series and must be remembered in their order, so that we can start from any locus in the series and move either backwards or forwards from it. If we should see a number of our acquaintances standing in a row, it would not make any difference to us whether we should tell their names beginning with the person standing at the head of the line or at the foot or in the middle. So with memory loci. "If these have been arranged in order, the result will be that, reminded by the images, we can repeat orally what we have committed to the loci, proceeding in either direction from any locus we please."

The formation of the loci is of the greatest importance, for the same set of loci can be used again and again for remembering different material. The images which we have placed on them for remembering one set of things fade and are effaced when we make no further use of them. But the loci remain in the memory and can be used again by placing another set of images for another set of material. The loci are like the wax tablets which remain when what is written on them has been effaced and are ready to be written on again.

In order to make sure that we do not err in remembering the order of the loci it is useful to give each fifth locus some distinguishing mark. We may for example mark the fifth locus with a golden hand, and place in the tenth the image of some acquaintance whose name is Decimus. We can then go on to station other marks on each succeeding fifth locus.

It is better to form one's memory loci in a deserted and solitary place for crowds of passing people tend to weaken the impressions. Therefore the student intent on acquiring a sharp and well-defined set of loci will choose an unfrequented building in which to memorise places.

Memory loci should not be too much like one another, for instance too many intercolumnar spaces are not good, for their resemblance to one another will be confusing. They should be of moderate size, not too large for this renders the images placed on them vague, and not too small for then an arrangement of images will be overcrowded. They must not be too brightly lighted for then the images placed on them will glitter and dazzle; nor must they be too dark or the shadows will obscure the images. The intervals between the loci should be of moderate extent, perhaps about thirty feet, "for like the external eye, so the inner eye of thought is less powerful when you have moved the object of sight too near or too far away" (Yates, 1966, pp. 6–8).

The ordinary method involved "real places" based on the person's experiences. However, if a person feels that he does not have enough good loci directly from experience, he can construct them in his imagination. This distinction between real and imaginary places also appeared in later modifications of the technique.

The rules for images specified, first, that there are two kinds of images, one for "things" and the other for "words." In this context, "things" (*res*) refers to the subject matter of the speech—the arguments, notions, facts—and the images were intended to remind one of the "things." The "words" are the language in which the "things" are expressed and memory for words involved finding images to remind one of every word. The following passage describes the rules for choosing memorable images:

> Now nature herself teaches us what we should do. When we see in every day life things that are petty, ordinary, and banal, we generally fail to remember them, because the mind is not being stirred by anything novel or marvellous. But if we see or hear something exceptionally base, dishonourable, unusual, great, unbelievable, or ridiculous, that we are likely to remember for a long time. Accordingly, things immediate to our eye or ear we commonly forget; incidents of our childhood we often remember best. Nor could this be so for any other reason than that ordinary things easily slip from the memory while the striking and the novel stay longer in the mind. A sunrise, the sun's course, a sunset are marvellous to no one because they occur daily. But solar eclipses are a source of wonder because they occur seldom, and indeed are more marvellous than lunar eclipses, because these are more frequent. Thus nature shows that she is not aroused by the common ordinary event, but is moved by a new or striking occurrence. Let art, then, imitate nature, find what she desires, and follow as she directs. . . .
>
> We ought, then, to set up images of a kind that can adhere longest in memory. And we shall do so if we establish similitudes as striking as possible; if we set up images that are not many or vague but active [imagines agentes]; if we assign to them exceptional beauty or singular ugliness; if we ornament some of them, as with crowns or purple cloaks, so that the similitude may be more distinct to us; or if we somehow disfigure them, as by introducing one stained with blood or soiled with mud or smeared with red paint, so that its form is more striking, or by assigning certain comic effects to our images, for that, too, will ensure our remembering them more readily. The things we easily remember when they are real we likewise remember without difficulty when they are figments. But this will be essential—again and again to run over rapidly in the mind all the original places in order to refresh the images (*Ad Herennium*, cited in Yates, pp. 9–10).

Sweeping psychological assumptions as well as more specific principles of memory are contained in the system and the rules advocated for its practical application. To indicate their contemporary relevance, these assumptions and principles will be summarized and discussed in terms of current theoretical concepts that seem to be clearly implied in the early theory.

General Psychological Assumptions in the Mnemonic System

Continuity of perception and thought   The ancient theory assumed that perception, imagination, and thought are continuous modes of experience. The discussions of the rules for places begin with real places, which are distinguished by their memorability as *perceptual* experiences to the rhetoric student moving through a building intent on forming a series of memory localities. It is the places themselves that should be deserted, of moderate size, and so on. But it is clearly implied, too, that these attributes carry over to the *memory* for the places—they are to be remembered in order; it is *images* of things that are placed on the *loci,* and if necessary it is possible to construct such places entirely in one's imagination. Thus the discussion moves freely between the perceptual level of "real" experience and the mental world of memory loci and images, anticipating the contemporary emphasis on the commonality of perceptual and symbolic modalities as discussed in the last chapter.

The wax-tablet theory of memory   The wax tablet metaphor is explicitly stated in each of the Latin treatises on the memory system—the places are like wax tablets, from which the images can be read off as though they were letters. Whether this basic assumption was also introduced into the mnemonic system by Simonides or added later by teachers of rhetoric as a result of other influences is uncertain. According to Gomulicki (1953), the earliest recorded reference to the metaphor is in Plato and it was used also by Aristotle, but both were undoubtedly familiar with the mnemonic system and it is possible that their use of the wax tablet analogy in their respective theories of memory came from earlier sources. In any case, as Yates notes, "[the metaphor] . . . connects the mnemonic with ancient theory of memory, as Quintilian saw when, in his introduction to his treatment of the mnemonic, he remarked that he did not propose to dwell on the precise functions of memory, 'although many hold the view that certain impressions are made on the mind, analogous to those which a signet ring makes on wax' " (1966, pp. 35–36). This assumptive basis of the mnemonic system is implicit in the above-stated assumption of the continuity of perception and thought, and it may help explain the following emphasis in the system.

The emphasis on visual processes   An emphasis on the advantages of the visual system is apparent in all aspects of the mnemonic technique from the perceptual to the imaginal level, and the origin of this emphasis, too, has been attributed to Simonides:

> It has been sagaciously discerned by Simonides or else discovered by some other person, that the most complete pictures are formed in our minds of the things that have been conveyed to them and imprinted on them by the senses, but that the keenest of all our senses is the sense of sight, and that consequently perceptions received by the ears or by reflexion can be most easily retained if they are also conveyed to our minds by the mediation of the eyes (Cicero, cited in Yates, p. 4).

Thus Simonides' invention of the mnemonic "rested, not only on his discovery of the importance of order in memory, but also on his discovery that the sense of sight is the strongest of all the senses." Yates (p. 28 ff.) sees this as a common theme throughout Simonides' various contributions, for he also is said to have "called painting silent poetry and poetry painting that speaks."

Thus he saw "poetry, painting and mnemonics in terms of intense visualization." It is interesting that this emphasis, perhaps derived from the mnemonic system, is basic also to the Aristotelian theory of imagination, memory, and thought. He stated that it is impossible to think without a mental picture, and used the images of mnemonics to illustrate his statements about imagination and thought. Memory, too, he interpreted as a collection of mental pictures from sense impressions of things past. Mnemonic theory and the Aristotelian theory of knowledge can thus be regarded as the sources of the emphasis on visualization that dominated psychological theories of memory and thought up to the beginning of this century.

Symbolic transformations   The mnemonic system implies a sequence of symbolic transformations from words to images and back to words, particularly in the context of rhetoric. A speech presumably was prepared first in its verbal form; then the main points were transformed into concrete (imaginal) symbols placed on memory loci. Subsequently, during the delivery of the speech, the speaker imagined the places sequentially (presumably using verbal cues that designate the order of the topics—see further below) and was thereby reminded of the symbolic images of "things" deposited there. The images in turn were assumed to generate the overt verbal output. In addition, he may have endeavored to use "images of words" to remind him of the specific words in his speech.

The complexity of these features was not lost on the early critics of the technique. Quintilian agreed that images may be useful for reproducing the names of objects in order because material things call up images. But the "notions" involved in the parts of speech do not do so, and images for them accordingly must be invented. Moreover, even passing over the fact that it is impossible to find any "likeness" to represent certain words, such as conjunctions, "how can such an art grasp a whole series of connected words?" Assuming further that we could find images for everything and use an infinite number of places to recall words ". . . will not the flow of our speech inevitably be impeded by the double task imposed on our memory? For how can our words be expected to flow in connected speech, if we have to look back at separate forms for each individual word?" In view of these difficulties with the method, Quintilian concluded that his "precepts will be of a simpler kind," consisting of the intensive use of ordinary rote learning, supplemented by visualization of the pages on which the words are written and of the individual lines on it (cited in Yates, pp. 24–25).

Quintilian thus grasped the complexity of the symbolic transformations involved in the mnemonic technique and the difficulties they pose in regard to the mediation of verbal behavior. The difficulties were noted by others in subsequent centuries, and we shall see that they continue to plague us today in the context of the experimental study of imagery in associative learning and memory (Chapter 10).

Principles of Memory in the System

The preceding section was concerned with general psychological principles that seemed to have been accepted by the ancient teachers of the art of memory. The present section is concerned with more specific memory principles that were suggested or implied in relation to the technique. The discussion again emphasizes the contemporary relevance of the ancient principles.

Organization Simonides emphasized the importance of orderly arrangement as a mnemonic aid, and the images of places were intended to serve that end; hence the instruction by the Latin orators that the places should form a series and must be remembered in their order. However, this is no sequentially constrained system—the memory information is spatially parallel: Just as we could name our acquaintances in any order if they are standing in a row, so too can we name the images in our ordered memory loci in any order.

This combination of sequential and spatial features was inherent in the mnemonic imagery if the places were appropriately chosen. Quintilian advocated "a spacious house divided into a number of rooms. Everything of note therein is diligently imprinted on the mind, in order that thought may be able to run through all the parts without let or hindrance." The first "notion" to be remembered "is placed, as it were, in the forecourt; the second, let us say, in the atrium; the remainder are placed in order all round the impluvium, and committed not only to bedrooms and parlours, but even to statues and the like." When the memories are to be reviewed, "one begins from the first place to run through all, demanding what has been entrusted to them, of which one will be reminded by the image" (from Yates, p. 22).

The principle is obviously paralleled by the stress on organizational processes in contemporary psychological theories of memory, although these have generally involved a verbal rather than a visual emphasis (see Chapter 7). A notable exception is Köhler's (1929) interpretation of associative learning in terms of perceptual organization, which he illustrated using mnemonic imagery in learning word pairs as an example of the principle in action. Experiments on memory organization reported by G. Mandler (1967) also involved a procedure reminiscent of the ancient mnemonics: His subjects were literally required to place to-be-remembered items into separate slots according to conceptual categories determined by the subject.

Chunking, another contemporary organizational principle (G. A. Miller, 1956), also had its counterpart in the suggestion by the author of the *Ad Herennium* that it is useful to give each fifth locus a distinguishing mark so that we will not err in remembering the order of the loci.

Association The principle of association is implicit in some descriptions of the system, but it was explicitly expressed by Quintilian as follows:

. . . it is an assistance to the memory if localities are sharply impressed upon the mind. . . . For when we return to a place after considerable absence, we not merely recognize the place itself, but remember things that we did there, and recall the persons whom we met and even the unuttered thoughts which passed through our minds when we were there before (1953 translation, p. 221).

It should be noted that the principle of association in this context included the important (implicit) assumption that associations between concrete objects are particularly strong. Once "notions" are concretized and their images deposited in the places, the association is firm. This assumption, along with the assumed superiority of the visual modality, may be at the heart of the symbolic transformation that was central to the system—specifically, the concretization of the verbal ideas of a speech. We shall return later to a more detailed discussion of this important point.

Rehearsal   In addition to the "art" of mnemonics, the necessity of rote learning was clearly recognized and advocated. The author of *Ad Herennium* thus referred to learning verse by heart. However, in the rules for images of things described above, the author also "advocated running over in the mind all the original places in order to refresh the images." This implies *visual* rehearsal of the kind discussed in the preceding chapter in relation to Posner's research on classification tasks.

Retrieval cues   The images of places were intended as retrieval cues in the mnemonic system. In addition, however, explicit ordinal cues were provided by the method described by Quintilian, in which the images are sequentially deposited in and retrieved from ordered places, apparently by verbal cues that initiated the sequence. It is said that the phrases "in the first place," "in the second place," etc., used in dividing a discourse into topics, derive from the mnemonic system (Middleton, 1887).

Interference   The system included a variety of principles related to conditions of interference or its absence. That the memory places can be used over and over again implies a remarkable freedom from proactive interference. However, to avoid interference, the places should not be too much like each other, "for their resemblance to one another will be confusing." They should not be too small, "for then an arrangement of images will be overcrowded." Distinctiveness is emphasized in the instructions referring to lighting and separation of the places, and so on.

Novelty   An emphasis on novelty overrides all other features of the rules for images. We remember what is "exceptionally base; dishonourable, unusual, great, unbelievable, or ridiculous," whereas "ordinary things easily slip from memory." Thus we should set up images that are active, exceptionally beautiful or ugly, disfigured or comical. This rule, too, can be related to the principle of interference or its converse, distinctiveness, and along with the rule for ordered places it was given the greatest emphasis in all of the imagery mnemonic systems to follow.

VARIANTS AND APPLICATIONS OF
THE BASIC TECHNIQUE

The ancient rules for places and images were rather general, the student of rhetoric being encouraged to invent his own places and images after having learned the method. Only a few specific examples are therefore available in the Latin sources, among which Quintilian is most explicit. He devoted his attention mostly to the "architectural" method, in which the natural divisions of a house or public building provide the necessary variety of locations, as indicated above. He also mentioned a long journey, going through a city, and pictures as a source of the ordered places. We can guess that the mnemonic use of a journey involved visualizing oneself moving along a familiar road that includes places or "sign-posts" such as houses, trees, and the like. The to-be-remembered items are imagined at these prominent locations and retrieved by "retracing" the route.

Quintilian's examples of images of things refer to the symbolic use of concrete objects to represent general notions. Thus the symbolic "sign," may be "drawn from a whole 'thing,' as navigation or warfare, or from some 'word';
. . . let us suppose that the sign is drawn from navigation, as, for instance, an anchor; or from warfare, as, for example, a weapon" (in Yates, 1966, p. 22). These symbolic images then are "placed" in the various locations in accordance with the principle of achieving an ordered arrangement in memory, and serve to remind one of the general notions to be covered in a speech.

Over the subsequent centuries, innumerable variations of the basic technique were developed by religious leaders, philosophers, and professional mnemonists, although the architectural method remained the most common. In the Middle Ages, scholastic philosophers such as Albertus Magnus and Thomas Aquinas transformed the ancient rules for images and places and advocated that they be used for remembering abstract notions related to ethics or morality. Yates suggests, for example, that the remembering of Paradise and Hell lay behind the scholastic interpretation of the "artificial" memory. Memory treatises stemming from this tradition explicitly applied the rules to such an end, often accompanied by illustrative diagrams. Thus Romberch, a sixteenth-century German Dominican, discussed Hell as being divided into many places that we remember with inscriptions on them. The places of Hell could thus be regarded as memory *loci* that varied according to the sins punished therein.

Such a use of the imagery mnemonic may have been expressed rather generally in both the visual arts and the writing and rhetoric of the period. Grotesque figures symbolizing the virtues and vices, such as Charity and Envy, presumably reflected the ancient instruction to form images that are striking and novel. Verbal "pictures" may have been similarly drawn by the preachers of the day for the same practical end of providing images that would serve as reminders of the points of a sermon on sin. For example, Ridevall, an English friar of the fourteenth century, described the "image of a prostitute, blind, with mutilated ears, proclaimed by a trumpet (as a criminal), with a deformed face, and full of disease. He calls this 'the picture of Idolatry according to the poets' " (Yates, p. 96). In the same context, Yates (p. 95) suggests that Dante's poem *Inferno* perhaps could be regarded as a kind of memory system for memorizing Hell and its punishments with striking images on orders of places. To the extent that the interpretation is correct, the phenomena represent a later manifestation of the common visual theme that Simonides had perceived in poetry, painting, and mnemonics.

These developments are relevant to the interpretation of imagery and meaning as discussed in Chapter 3, for they illustrate the compelling nature of the conceptual relations between pictorial representation, word imagery, and visual (mental) imagery. For the most part these relations were accepted uncritically by the early proponents of the memory art, as was the assumption that imagery in any of these forms somehow facilitates the memory. To what extent and under what conditions these assumptions are justified is one of the major empirical-theoretical issues in forthcoming chapters.

Printed memory treatises began to appear in the fifteenth century and continued to appear with increasing frequency into the nineteenth century. It would serve no useful theoretical purpose here to consider even a representative sample of these, since they generally followed the Latin sources in advocating rules for places and images, as already indicated. However, it will be instructive to review some of the forms these rules took with a view to noting any systematic modifications of psychological interest.

Astrological Images and Occult Memory Systems

The signs of the zodiac were first used as a memory device by Metrodorus, a Greek teacher of rhetoric who still lived in Cicero's time and was quoted by the latter. The divisions of the zodiac were divided into an ordered series of places (perhaps 360 in all), each with its particular image. Romberch, the German Dominican, in 1520 published a memory treatise part of which included a place system based on the zodiacal system of Metrodorus and another based on the "spheres of the universe." The latter comprised the spheres of the elements, the planets, the fixed stars, the celestial spheres, and the nine orders of angels forming an ascending ordered series of places for the imagined "things" of Paradise and Hell (Yates, p. 115). Such astral systems of places were incorporated into occult, or magical, memory systems presented by the Hermetic philosophers, Giulio Camillo and Giordano Bruno in the sixteenth century, and Robert Fludd in the seventeenth. These astral systems were combined with elaborate architectural mnemonics.

Camillo developed a memory theater that was actually concretized and exhibited as a wooden structure filled with images. What is of particular interest to us is the extraordinarily systematic, hierarchical nature of the system and the fact that it was intended for the purpose of encompassing a highly abstract body of mysticoreligious and earthly knowledge. Reconstructed from a published manuscript, the Theatre is described by Yates as follows:

> The Theatre rises in seven grades or steps, which are divided by seven gang-ways representing the seven planets. The student of it is to be as it were a spectator before whom are placed the seven measures of the world "in spet-taculo," or in a theatre. And since in ancient theatres the most distinguished persons sat in the lowest seats, so in this Theatre the greatest and most im-portant things will be in the lowest place. . . . On each of its seven gangways are seven gates or doors. These gates are decorated with many images. . . . The solitary "spectator" of the Theatre stands where the stage would be and looks toward the auditorium, gazing at the images on the seven times seven gates on the seven rising grades. . . . [Camillo] is using the plan of a real theatre, . . . but adapting it to his mnemonic purposes. The imaginary gates are his memory places, stocked with images (pp. 136–137).

This mnemonic structure with seven as the unit at each level is tantalizingly analogous to current hierarchical models of the organization of memory based on the limits of the immediate memory span (e.g., G. Mandler, 1967). The "magical number seven" in the case of Camillo's theater, however, derives from the seven pillars of Solomon's House of Wisdom, which Camillo chose as the foundation of his system.

Yates infers from a description of the Theatre that under the images on the gates were drawers or boxes containing masses of papers on which were speeches relating to the subjects recalled by the images. She suggests (pp. 144–145) that Camillo "had hit upon a new interpretation of memory for 'things' and 'words' by storing written speeches under the images." The Theatre thus "begins to look like a highly ornamental filing cabinet. But this is to lose sight of the grandeur of the Idea—the Idea of a memory organically geared to the universe."

What was the "grand Idea" that was to be encompassed by Camillo's hierar-chical memory system? A detailed account of the influence behind the system and of its content is not relevant for our purposes, but a general sketch will help us to appreciate the scope and abstractness of the body of knowledge it was intended to cover. The system was a reflection of the occult philosophical tradition of the Renaissance, based on an amalgamation of Egyptian (Hermetic), Jewish (the Cabala), and Christian religious influences coupled with a neo-platonic philosophy. The technique was intended to grasp and unify, within a single memory system, all natural and supernatural knowledge—"terrestrial, celestial, and supercelestial." Moreover, it was a magical system whereby the memory draws its power from divine powers of the cosmos—this being achieved through the use of talismanic imagery. Thus, like the engraved images of the talisman, which were usually of stars and were supposed to draw magical power from astral spirits, the memory system would have, "or be supposed to have, the power of unifying the contents of memory by basing it upon . . . images drawn from the celestial world. The images of Camillo's Theatre seem to be supposed to have in them something of this power, enabling the 'spectator' to read off at one glance, through 'inspecting the images,' the whole contents of the universe" (Yates, p. 155).

Psychologically we find here a hierarchically organized *visual* memory system, the contents of which can be read off at a glance. The perceptual organization is given by the spatial organization of the Theatre as described above. The *conceptual* hierarchical structure is determined, however, by the symbolic nature of the images, which can be appreciated only when they are transformed into a verbal form. Let us briefly examine this symbolic hierarchy.

The basic images, constituting one dimension of the structure, are given by the "seven planets," which are easily grasped as memory images because they are strikingly differentiated from each other and because they have affective appeal (expressing the tranquility of Jupiter, the anger of Mars, etc.), in keeping with the ancient rules for images. These planet images, being of the first order of importance, are placed on the first grade—the lowest seats of the Theatre. As a dimension, however, the planet series is also represented by the gangways at each of the six upper grades.

The symbolic theme of each grade cuts across the planet dimension. The general meaning of the second level is depicted on all gates by a banquet image, symbolically representing the first day of creation in terms of Homeric mythology—a banquet given to the gods, which are the emerging elements of creation. The third grade is depicted by a cave, symbolizing a further stage in creation where the elements are mixed to create things, after the fashion of the Homeric Cave in the Odyssey in which nymphs were busy weaving and bees going in and out. And so on, with different symbols at each subsequent grade representing the creation of man's soul, the union of soul and body, his natural activities, and finally his arts and sciences, religion, and law. The more specific content at each level is given by the intersecting planetary series. Jupiter, for example, symbolizes the element of air. The Banquet grade in this series contains the image of Juno suspended, depicting air as a simple element; the same image under the Cave means air as a mixed element, and so on.

Thus Camillo clearly employed the ancient art of memory, following the prescribed rules and using a building divided into memory places with memory images. However, it has been transformed into an occult religious art.

The occult memory art was given its most elaborate and systematic expression in several works by Bruno. His aim, like Camillo's, apparently was to encompass and unify the world of appearance and the supercelestial world of ideas, using the memory tradition and astrological notions. The intermediaries between the two levels were to be magical star-images organized according to the associative structure of astrology. The grand aim was no less than that of grouping, coordinating, and unifying all the multiplicity of earthly phenomena within memory through the organization of significant images that derive magical power from the stars. Through the celestial images, the confused plurality of things becomes unity.

I will not attempt to deal with the complexities of the various attempts by Bruno to achieve his aims. We may note, however, that, along with the astrological and the more traditional architectural memory art, he adopted features of a system developed by Ramon Lull (or Raymond Lully) in the thirteenth and fourteenth centuries. Lull made use of letter notations for the to-be-remembered concepts. One form in which these were set out involved a system of concentric circles that could be revolved to produce different combinations of concepts. According to a source cited by Middleton,

> . . . certain general terms which are common to all the sciences, but principally those of logic, metaphysics, ethics, and theology, are collected and arranged according to the caprice of the inventor. An alphabetical table of such terms was provided; and subjects and predicates taken from these were respectively inscribed in angular spaces upon circular papers. The essences, qualities and relations of things being thus mechanically brought together, the circular papers of subjects were fixed in a frame, and those of predicates were so placed on them as to move freely, and in their revolutions to produce various combinations of subjects and predicates; whence would arise definitions, axioms, and propositions, varying infinitely, according to the different applications of general terms to particular subjects" (1887, p. 10).

Bruno combined Lull's method with the traditional imagery mnemonic. "He put the images of the classical art on the Lullian combinatory wheels, but the images were magic images and the wheels were conjuring wheels" (Yates, p. 211). The "sub-celestial elemental world" was to be influenced by manipulating the star-images on the Lullian wheels. To achieve this end, Bruno's system, like Camillo's Theatre, was hierarchical in nature, with the stars, the earthly things, and all arts and sciences symbolized by images on different wheels. It was thus that Bruno hoped to coordinate in memory the "multiplicity of appearances" in the phenomenal world.

Bruno's last works on memory (Yates, p. 295 ff.) include an encyclopaedic memory system in which he uses a "double picture" combining the "round" (Lullian) celestial system with the "square" (architectural) system composed of memory rooms. The latter consisted of twenty-four rooms each divided into nine memory places, with further divisions into "fields" and "cubicles." Everything in the physical world—plants, stones, animals—and all the arts, sciences, and human activities were to be represented in these rooms by images. The round celestial system juxtaposed with the square plan (perhaps as a round building encompassing a square one) contained the celestial figures and images which were to animate, organize, and unify the detailed places and images contained in the memory room.

Psychological implications of the Brunian System   Its occult aspects aside, Bruno's system probably represents the most ambitious attempt ever made to achieve organization in memory through the use of imagery. The traditional rules for places and images and the principle of order find expression in it in varied and complex forms. The places and images are arranged in spatial, hierarchical structures in which the components differ qualitatively (e.g., the "round" and the "square" systems) as well as being ordered in terms of level. Order is provided by the overlearned intrinsic sequential arrangement of places (the signs of the zodiac and numerous other schemes) as well as by the Lullian alphabetic coding system. Moreover, the system incorporates what was a new addition to mnemonics by Lull: Rather than being a static system of places and images, it is a dynamic system in which the static elements can be combined and recombined by rotating the Lullian concentric wheels to yield different combinations of "subjects and predicates." Considered at the symbolic level of memory, this feature of the system can be seen as corresponding to transformational thinking involving the manipulation of images in an extraordinarily systematic and creative way. It is indeed a grand scheme, entirely speculative with respect to its implicit assumptions concerning the "power" of human memory, but perhaps containing within it remarkable insights concerning the quality and capacity of organizational processes in memory.

An occult memory system similar to Bruno's was presented by Robert Fludd in England early in the seventeenth century. It combined a "round" memory scheme comprised of magical celestial images with a "square" art involving images of concrete things—men, animals, inanimate objects. The square system notably made use of a theater as a memory place system, perhaps a distorted reflection of Shakespeare's Globe Theatre (Yates, Chapter XVI). Its doors and columns properly spaced and variously colored to make them more distinctive, constitute the memory loci. Generally, however, despite its great complexity, Fludd's theater memory system adds no new mnemonic elements to the ones already considered, and we need not go into it in further detail.

Verbal Mnemonics

The techniques we have considered generally involved verbal processes at least implicitly, and some involved explicit use of abstract verbal mnemonics. In particular, Lull made use of a system of letter notation and geometrical figures rather than images in the classical sense, although the letter system was embedded in spatial diagrams and figures contributing to an overall hierarchical symbolic structure. The letter system was based on abstract concepts such as goodness, greatness, eternity, and power, which derived from religious conceptions of the names or attributes of God. These attributes were designated by letters. One form in which they were used was the concentric combinatory wheels, already described. Lull also used them in relation to the "ladder of creation" of the Middle Ages, graded in levels from God at the top, to the angels, stars, man, animals, and so on, in descending steps. The abstract, alphabetically coded symbol system repeated itself at each level, appropriately applied to the subject matter of that level. Thus, the attribute of Bonitas, designated by B, meant the Bonitas of God, the bonitas of angels, the bonitas of man, etc., when applied to the respective levels (Yates, p. 179). Lull also used a tree diagram as a kind of place system, but with letters and other abstract labels, rather than images, on the roots, branches, and leaves. The system worked at different levels of abstract classification, with his particular letter code as a constant that could be applied to any subject.

An influential movement based on logical (verbal) principles was begun by Peter Ramus in the sixteenth century. The general goal behind the movement was the simplification of teaching methods, which was to be achieved in large part through better ways of memorizing subjects. Toward this end, Ramus rejected the old art of memory and substituted a new method involving "dialectical order." A subject was set out in schematic form descending from general to more specific aspects in a series of dichotomized classifications. The schematic presentation thus consisted essentially of a hierarchical tree structure with binary branching at each node. From this the ramifications (literally, the branchings) of the subject were to be memorized. Memorizing from such a schematic layout (the Ramist epitome) involves spatial visualization, but the content is clearly abstract and verbal in form.

The Ramist method differs drastically from the Brunian system of places and images, and it is of considerable (although incidental) interest that these opposed systems were the center of a lively controversy in England during the latter part of the sixteenth century (Yates, Chapter XII). According to Yates, it was basically a religious controversy. Alexander Dicson, a disciple of Bruno, advocated the classical memory system, including the use of images that are striking, active, unusual, and emotion-arousing. William Perkins, a Puritan preacher, vigorously opposed such a system of places and images on the grounds that it is impious because the animation of images arouses passion—"depraved carnal affections!" A second reason was more rational: Such a system imposes on memory the triple task of remembering the places, the images, and then the point one wishes to recall. The Ramist method was to be preferred because it was emotionally neutral and because logical order was presumably a more efficient method of remembering than were the inept images.

Yates suggests also that Perkins' endorsement of the Ramist method and his opposition to the Brunian imagery system represented an inner iconoclasm corresponding to the earlier outer iconoclasm—an attack on idolatry of the mind. Just as the outer images of the church had been smashed and defaced, so the inner images of the art of memory were to be removed by the adoption of the abstract method of dialectical order. This may be part of the explanation of the popularity of Ramism in Protestant countries like England.[1]

---

[1] An analogy between the Renaissance controversy involving mnemonic systems and the later rejection of images in behavioristic psychology may be noted. Behaviorism in general represented a "protestant reformation" movement in psychology, and Watson's rejection of imagery and his concomitant emphasis on verbal processes as the mechanism of thought (including memory) in particular bears a striking resemblance to Perkins' earlier rejection of Brunian memory and his advocation of Ramism. The implications of the comparison may be of considerable historical interest, but they will not be pursued here.

The Lullian and Ramian emphasis on verbal coding in mnemonics apparently had a lasting influence on the mnemonic art, for aspects of their systems commonly appeared in the methods taught by later professional mnemonists.

Methods of the Professional Mnemonists

Mnemonic systems taught by professional mnemonists from the seventeenth century onward generally involved variations of the traditional method of places and images. In addition, however, the mnemonic experts introduced techniques for remembering sequences of numbers, such as historical dates. A few representative examples will suffice to illustrate the principles involved (for a summary of such techniques, see Middleton, 1887). Earlier versions had been taught in which concrete symbols represented numerals, for example, a candle or a dart for 1, a swan or a goose for 2, etc., but a letter-coding system introduced by Winckelman in 1648 became the basis of many of the later techniques. The numerals were represented by letters of the alphabet, and these in turn were used to form words that coded the to-be-remembered number sequence. The letter-numeral associations obviously were to be well learned, as was the technique of translating the letter code into words and the words back into numbers. A rather complicated sequence of encoding and decoding is therefore involved in such techniques, the difficulty of which would depend on the extent to which the particular technique made use of some natural or prelearned relationship between numerals and letters, or letters and meaningful words. Some mnemonists were rather arbitrary in this regard, but most took advantage of visual or acoustic similarity. Gregor von Feinaigle, one of the most famous of the professional mnemonists, lectured on the art in Europe early in the nineteenth century, and his system was published by his students. The following summary is based on an English version published in 1813. The system as a whole involved an elaborate combination of the method of places and images and a numeral-alphabet-word code.

The place system   The locality or place system consisted of the imaginal division of rooms into a hierarchically ordered set of memory places. The floor and the four walls provided general locations, each of which was divided further into a matrix of nine compartments, numbered as follows:

1	2	3
4	5	6
7	8	9

These were to be explicitly named the first place, second place, and so on. In addition, each wall was numbered, and a tenth square was located on the ceiling over each wall to permit a systematic decimal progression from one wall to the next, yielding an ordered series of 50 memory places to a room. The layout of the first of two rooms is illustrated in Figure 6-1. To visualize the system, imagine yourself standing on the floor. The first wall is to your left, the second straight ahead, the third to your right, and the fourth behind you. The squares on the floor represent the numbers 1–9. The square on the ceiling over the first wall is numbered 10, initiating the numerical series, 10–19, on the wall below; over the second wall is the 20 square; and so on. Fifty is represented by an extra square on the ceiling and provides the transition to a second memory room.

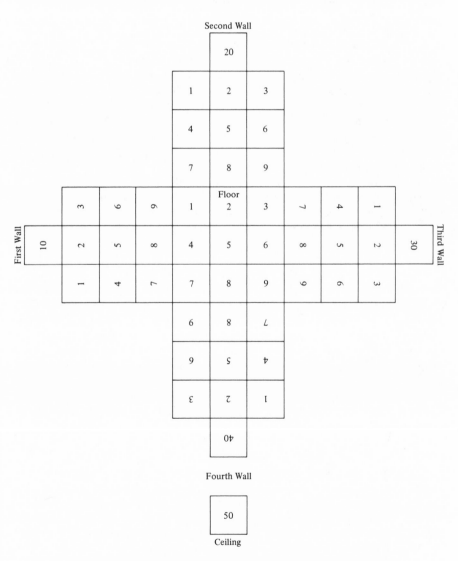

FIGURE 6-1.   Memory locations in the first room. After Feinaigle (1813).

The floor of the second room is denominated the fifth wall; the wall on the left, the sixth, etc., places thus being provided in the same manner as in the first room for the numbers 51–100.

The hierarchical system can be easily summarized. All the numbers up to 50 are found in the first room, and those from 51 to 100 in the second. Having found the room, the left-hand figure of a number denotes the wall and the right-hand figure will show the place. An ordered set of memory places is thus provided that can be used for remembering numerical information (e.g., dates) as well as more concrete information about "things." We shall consider examples after the other features of the technique have been summarized.

Concrete number symbols   Feinaigle's expositor goes on to say that the method as outlined thus far (as well as the number-letter code, to be considered later) is not sufficient. It provides only an intellectual order; numbers have been localized, but the realities are wanting. Implied here is the ancient assumption that concrete situations are particularly potent as memory cues. Indeed, not only was the memory system introduced with a reference to the importance of orderly arrangement, but it was also stated explicitly that "Sensible objects have a powerful effect in recalling to the mind the ideas with which it was occupied when those ideas were presented" (1813, p. 32). Such "realities" or "sensible objects" were accordingly added to the place system by filling the squares with pictures of objects that appropriately symbolize the numbers. The student will be "materially assisted in the remembrance of his *places*, or localities" (p. 51), provided that the figures in the two rooms are permanently fixed in memory. In effect, what is being advocated here is concretization of the abstract, spatial-numerical place system.

The place symbols for the first room are shown in Figure 6-2. The system obviously follows earlier ones in taking advantage of physical similarity and prelearned symbolic meaning. The cardinal number 1, in the "first place" of the floor location, is represented by the Tower of Babel, 2 by a swan (hence resembling the numeral 2), 6 by the Horn of Plenty, 11 by the Pillars of Hercules, and so on. The student was instructed to memorize the visual symbols along with their names, and their numerical locations so that he could readily identify the room, wall, and place of any symbol corresponding to it. This, then, would constitute mastery of the locality component of Feinaigle's technique—a numerically and spatially ordered set of object images, together with their names, which would serve as the permanent memory loci for new to-be-remembered information.

The verbal code   The number-letter-word code was incorporated into Feinaigle's memory system to facilitate the recall of numbers. Figures and letters were viewed merely as "signs of signs" and hence difficult to remember. The "elements of words" must therefore be sought. Toward this end, consonants were selected as the appropriate units because they were regarded as the "principle parts" of words, whereas vowels serve only as connectors.

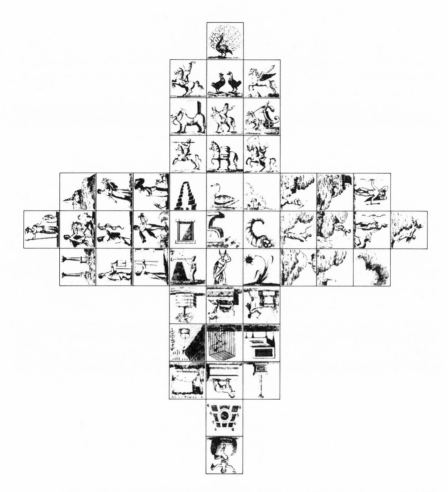

FIGURE 6-2.   Place images for the first room in Feinaigle's mnemonic system. For example, the number 1 in the "first place" of the floor location is represented by the Tower of Babel, 2 by a swan, 6 by the Horn of Plenty, 11 by the Pillars of Hercules, etc. From Feinaigle (1813).

The letters were chosen on the basis of their visual or acoustic similarity to numbers, as follows:

1	2	3	4	5	6	7	8	9	0
t	n	m	r	L	d	hard c	b,h,v	p,f	s,x,z
						k,g,q	w		

The number 1 was represented by t because it resembles the numeral; n represented 2 because it has two downstrokes; m has 3 downstrokes; the letter r occurs in the word four and its translation-equivalent in a number of languages; L was used as a numerical letter for 50, hence its assignment to 5; d resembles the reversed number 6; and so on.

The translation into words is easily achieved by introducing vowels, which are ignored for the purpose of the code. The number 32, for example, could be represented by the word *man,* the *m* and the *n* denoting the appropriate digits. The words *tin, ton,* and *tan* could be used to denote 12; *rum* stands for 43; *mouse* for 30; and so on. Typically, a single word was used to represent a two-digit number, only the first two consonants being used for the code. Additional words were added in the case of longer numbers.

Feinaigle advocated further that the words be associated with images, which were to be connected together by arranging them in order in the different places of the memory room. Accordingly, the words used for coding numbers were all concrete words—names of objects that could be readily visualized. (Feinaigle's expositor seems to advocate different sequencing methods in this context, one involving the code words placed in their respective places, the other involving an imaginal action sequence comprised of the referents of the words: a *bat* is seen flying after a *mouse,* which shelters itself under a *cap,* etc., where the number sequence is given by the words *bat, mouse, cap.*) Thus even abstract number information was to be concretized and represented by images, indicating that the entire mnemonic system was based on imagery. This feature has been retained among the techniques advocated by contemporary writers of memory improvement books. An example is the "hook method" taught by Furst (1948).

Applications of the system   Feinaigle applied his technique to the memorization of chronological events, history (for which purpose more rooms were added, representing centuries), geography, language, and the like. For example, to remember William the Conqueror, the first of the succession of kings of England, the word "willow" was suggested. This was to be imaged as a willow tree upon the Tower of Babel (the symbol for the first memory location), indicating William I. That he was the conqueror was symbolized by hanging some laurel upon the willow tree. The date of the conquest (1066) is given by the word *dead* (symbolized by the laurel being dead), the consonants d, d standing for 66, with the 1000 being understood. This is a relatively simple example and the system became increasingly complex as it was applied to more complex information. Nevertheless, the same principles were followed in the extensions, combining abstract numerical and verbal information with concrete spatial and symbolic imagery in what can be regarded as a systematic use of symbolic transformational chains.

A number of mnemonists subsequently attempted to improve on Feinaigle's number-alphabet code. No new principles were involved, however, and the variations need not be considered here. Others emphasized verbal devices that, although not new in principle, deserve special mention because of their relevance to current mnemonic techniques and mediation paradigms. A German mnemonist, Kothe (Middleton, 1887, p. 36), in 1848 introduced the method of associating two unrelated words by using common associates as mediators. Thus the words, "wine-Jacob," could be connected by the verbal associative chain, "wine-cellar-staircase-ladder-Jacob." The technique was advocated by later mnemonists as well and obviously represents an early anticipation of the chaining mediation paradigm involving natural language associations (see Chapter 9).

The systematic use of rhymes as mnemonic aids is the other verbal device to be noted. The mnemonic value of the rhythm and rhyme of poetry has long been recognized, and indeed poetry may have originated as a memory aid (see discussion in Chapter 13). The technique was incorporated into mnemonic systems that also involved the usual features, such as alphabetic coding and imagery, by a number of eighteenth-century mnemonists. Brayshaw and Stokes, for example, applied the method in England to the memorization of the facts and dates of history, geography, and other subjects (Middleton, p. 37 ff.). Rhyming was also incorporated into a system that provided a number-word-image code without the mediating letter stage. Perhaps because of its relative simplicity, the basic method has survived to the present and has recently been the subject of experimental research. We shall review it, therefore, as a "modern" mnemonic system.

A MODERN VERSION OF THE PLACE-IMAGE TECHNIQUE

Around 1879, in England, John Sambrook introduced a system in which rhyming syllables and words were used to represent numerals. As described by Middleton (p. 49 ff.), one was represented in the system by such words as *gun, son,* and *come*; two by *you* or *crew*; three by *free, feet, street*; four by words in which *r* is prominent, as in *for, our, more*; five by *thrive, hive, night, time*; six by syllables and words with the gutteral sound of *g, k, x,* and *q*, as in *sick, fix, mix*; seven by words with the fricatives, *f* and *v*, as in *drift* and *raft*, as well as *sh, ch, s,* and *z*; eight by *gate, weight, stake*, etc.; nine by *hymn, hen, dine, mind*; and zero by words with the long *o* sound, as in *note* or *boat*. Numbers higher than nine were expressed by compound words; for example, *banjo* for ten (one-o), *common* for eleven (one-one), etc. Sambrook combined the above with other devices including the locality method and applied it to the "usual range of subjects."

Essentially the same technique has been taught more recently in the context of a public speaking course and textbook by Dale Carnegie (1937), with the modification that it is advocated for use in recalling associated verbal material and not for the memorization of dates or other numerical information. Moreover, the use of imagery is explicitly recommended. A rhyme scheme suggested by Carnegie (any rhyming words can be substituted), for memorizing twenty items, is as follows: *one-run, two-zoo, three-tree, four-door, five-beehive, six-sick, seven-heaven, eight-gate, nine-wine, ten-den, eleven-a football eleven, twelve-shelve, thirteen-hurting, fourteen-courting, fifteen-lifting, sixteen-licking, seventeen-leavening, eighteen-waiting, nineteen-pining,* and *twenty-Horn of Plenty.*

Mental pictures corresponding to the critical words are advocated as the key to memory. Thus, for "run" we might visualize a race horse; for "zoo," a bear cage in the zoo; for "heaven," a street paved with gold and angels playing on harps, etc. Having learned the number-picture scheme, the system is used for remembering a series of objects, or the points of a talk, by visualizing the to-be-recalled item in some bizarre association with the peg image: the first object riding a race horse, the second being sniffed by the bear in the zoo, the third in the top of a tree, and so on. The objects can then be recalled easily in any order, or so it is claimed, given the numbers as cues for the associated images.

Despite changes in the specific features of the technique, it obviously retains the essential features of Simonides' original mnemonic system of places and images. The latter also involved an ordered sequence of familiar, imagined locations, so that recall could be prompted by the cues "in the first place," "in the second place," etc., which were intended to generate the visual images of the objects or "notions" that had been placed there. The present system differs in that it takes advantage of rhyming words as image-evoking cues, but the principles are the same in all respects, including the claim that bizarreness of imagery is particularly beneficial to memory. It is of incidental interest, moreover, to note the persistence of the practical application of Simonides' memory technique to the art of public speaking!

Psychological Implications of the Rhyme-Image Mnemonic

The attention of many psychologists was recently drawn to the one-run (or one-bun) technique by G. A. Miller, Galanter, and Pribram (1960), who discussed it as a memory "plan" that helps the memorizer to retrieve material much as a librarian locates books labeled by a code. The coding analogy is equally applicable to all versions of the basic technique of places and images, but the present version, although complex, is analytically somewhat simpler than many of its predecessors. Operationally, the procedure involves numerical, verbal, and imaginal coding: One first learns a number-word rhyme, then practices visualizing objects or situations suggested by the cue words *bun, zoo, tree,* etc. Then, given a list of items to memorize, one numbers them in sequence and forms a compound image involving the first object and a bun, the second one and a zoo animal, or a shoe, etc. On a recall trial, the compound image is presumably reinstated by a numerical cue and at least a portion of the image is decoded into the appropriate verbal response. In brief, although apparently simple in practice, the rhyming technique is psychologically complex, involving multiple stages of symbolic transformation or coding, from words to images and back to words. The technique also involves, implicitly, the psychological assumptions characteristic of all of the imagery mnemonic techniques. These have been listed earlier and, in review, we need summarize only those that are most critical and unique to the mnemonic systems.

One critical assumption is that concrete objects are easier to remember than words. This was more-or-less explicitly stated by a number of mnemonists, but it is also implicit in the technique itself—if it were not, why bother to make the transformation from words to concrete images at all? Closely related to the preceding is the assumption that concrete objects or situations are particularly effective as retrieval cues for associated material, otherwise why the pains to translate numbers into words that suggest "sensible things"? The third (overriding) assumption is that visual images of the concrete situations can function as effective mediators, even in the case of verbal material. This general assumption subsumes more specific ones: that the images can be associatively aroused by instructions and by verbal cues; that they can be "read off" verbally; and that their novelty or bizarreness is important.

The above features and many others, although supported by anecdotal evidence, remained assumptions in the mnemonic technique as practiced by its professional advocates over the centuries. The principles of the system constitute a kind of psychological theory about the nature of memory, particularly in relation to verbal behavior. Although some of the principles and assumptions were critically examined by individuals as far back as Quintilian, they have been almost totally neglected by psychologists until recently. Thus they have not been subjected to a detailed scientific analysis. Such an analysis is attempted in the following chapters, most specifically in Chapters 10 and 11. The issues and the empirical information to be reviewed stand on their own, but the mnemonic technique forms a convenient point of departure and an orienting vehicle throughout. We shall see that the ancients were right on a number of important points and wrong on others, and that the recent research findings and theoretical views provide the basis for a more sophisticated interpretation of why mnemonic techniques work than has been possible up to now. In turn, the research on mnemonics contributes to the general theoretical understanding of the nature of memory.

7
Stimulus Attributes and Memory

This chapter deals with the effects of item attributes in learning and memory situations other than paired associates, which will be considered in the next chapter. As in the discussion of perception in Chapter 4, comparisons will be made between variables related to the different theoretical levels of meaning— representational, referential, and associative. Attention centers on imagery-concreteness, however, because it is conceptually related most directly to imagery as a symbolic process. The variable also provides a convenient reference point around which the discussion of memory can be organized, consistent with the emphasis given to imagery throughout this book.

As suggested in the preceding chapter, the imagery mnemonic systems were based on the implicit assumption, among others, that concrete objects and events, or their verbal surrogates, are easier to remember than more abstract stimuli. In anticipation it can be stated that the assumption is borne out by the facts, but that conclusion alone does not take us very far in the theoretical understanding of the relationship between the symbolic processes and memory. To further our theoretical understanding, we will seek answers to the following questions: What are the relative effects of different empirical dimensions of meaning on different kinds of memory tasks? What theoretical mechanisms are most probably involved? More specifically, what inferences can we make regarding the functional significance of imaginal and verbal processes in memory tasks from an analysis of the empirical relations between meaning attributes and performance?

These questions will be considered in the context of a detailed review of relevant experimental findings. Because the review encompasses a number of different memory tasks, variables, and issues, it will be helpful to begin by providing a general orienting framework within which the details can be viewed. Accordingly, the major empirical conclusions arising from the research will be presented at the outset, together with the main features of a theoretical model that appears to be consistent with much of the data—indeed, some of the most pertinent findings have been generated by it. The model is not intended to be a complete theory of memory but is concerned instead with the functional roles of imaginal and verbal processes as memory codes. The evidence will show that such distinctions must be assumed in order to explain the consistent and striking findings that have emerged from the relevant research, and that similar ideas therefore must be incorporated into any contemporary theory of memory that aims at comprehensiveness.

The critical reader will be able to evaluate the conclusions and the orienting conceptual model in the light of the detailed evidence that follows. Supplementary theoretical principles and alternative hypotheses will be discussed along with research on recognition memory, free verbal recall, serial learning, and various short-term memory tasks. An experiment specifically designed to test some implications of the dual coding model will then be presented. Finally, the theory will be discussed in relation to other current conceptions of memory.

EMPIRICAL AND THEORETICAL OVERVIEW

The relevant memory tasks can be distinguished according to whether they require the subject to retain item information, order information, or both. Recognition memory and free recall, for example, involve only memory for items and not their order, whereas immediate memory span and serial reconstruction involve memory for sequential order, but the items themselves are either overlearned at the outset or are provided by the experimenter and need not be stored. Serial learning is intermediate in the sense that the subject ordinarily must learn and retain the list items as well as their sequential order over repeated trials. Some consistent generalizations are possible when the learning and memory tasks are conceptualized in this manner. In tasks that require the subject to remember the items but not their sequential order, the meaning attribute that most consistently and strongly predicts recall is abstractness-concreteness, or imagery value: Objects and pictures are better remembered than concrete nouns, which in turn are superior to abstract nouns. Other meaning dimensions such as frequency-familiarity and associative meaningfulness are either relatively ineffective or inconsistent in their effects. Frequency, for example, sometimes has negative effects in such tasks. Conversely, abstractness-concreteness is ineffective in tasks that require the subject to remember only the sequential order of items. Pictures are in fact inferior to words in sequential memory tasks under conditions in which the verbal labels of the pictures are not readily available to the subject.

The results generally suggest that nonverbal imagery alone or both imagery and verbal processes contribute to the memorability of items, but that verbal meaning alone is crucial to sequential memory. These conclusions oversimplify the factual picture somewhat and they need to be buttressed with additional evidence, but they are not inconsistent with any of the data presently available. The conclusions and the data on concreteness effects are also consistent with the dual-coding hypothesis, which we shall consider next. The model is not relevant to the less-consistent and weaker effects of other meaning attributes, such as frequency and meaningfulness, and our discussion of possible interpretations of their effects will be postponed to the sections in which the research is reviewed in detail.

Ideas already discussed in previous chapters are extended to memory phenomena in the dual-coding model. It involves assumptions concerning the availability of nonverbal imagery and verbal mechanisms as memory codes, and a hypothesized functional distinction between them.

Availability of Imaginal and Verbal Codes

The theoretical assumptions are concerned with the differential availability of images and verbal processes as a function of the concreteness dimension, analyzed in terms of levels of meaning as discussed in Chapter 3. Pictures, if familiar and easily named, are meaningful both at the representational and the referential levels; that is, they readily arouse both a concrete memory representation (image) and a verbal label. The availability of the verbal code is relatively lower, however, because an extra transformation is involved—it must be associatively aroused after the nonverbal representation has been activated by the picture. Of course, the verbal code would be even less available if the pictures are unfamiliar or ambiguous. In the case of relatively familiar concrete and abstract words, the verbal code is directly and equally available (in theoretical terms, they are equivalent in verbal representational meaning), but the concrete words are more likely to evoke images because they are higher in referential meaning. These assumed differences are illustrated in Figure 7-1, which depicts the degree of availability of each code by the number of plus $(+)$ signs assigned to each level of concreteness.

Empirical support for, and a rough quantification of, the assumptions are provided by reaction time data discussed in Chapter 3 in connection with the defining operations for the different levels of meaning. Words can be read faster

Stimulus	Coding System	
	Imagery	Verbal
Picture	+++	++
Conc. Word	+	+++
Abstr. Word	−	+++

FIGURE 7-1.   Availability of two coding systems as a function of stimulus concreteness; degree of availability is indicated by the number of plus $(+)$ signs.

than objects can be named (e.g., Fraisse, 1964, 1968; Morin et al. 1965), indicating the higher availability of the verbal code in the former case. The latency of image arousal is faster for concrete words than for abstract words, as indicated by key-press reaction time data (Paivio, 1966) and by pupillary reactions when subjects image to word stimuli (e.g., Paivio & Simpson, 1968). Furthermore, comparison of average reaction times in the different experiments suggests that image arousal to words is slower than verbal coding of words or familiar pictures, although the data were not obtained under identical conditions and this assumption must therefore be regarded as tentative. No comparable data are available on image arousal to picture stimuli, but it can be assumed that the latency would be no greater than that involved in the implicit reading of a word.

A ranking of the availability, or arousal probability, of each code for the different stimuli can be inferred from these data, and is reflected in the number of plus signs shown in Figure 7-1. Image arousal in the case of pictures and verbal coding in the case of words have the highest availability, the verbal code to pictures second, imagery to concrete words third, and images to abstract words fourth. Thus the summative availability of *both* codes is highest in the case of pictures, intermediate for concrete nouns, and least for abstract nouns.

The effect of concreteness on memory is hypothesized to be a function of the availability of one or the other code, or both of them, the precise effect depending on the nature of the task and the functional utility of imaginal and verbal codes in different tasks, as discussed in the following section.

Parallel and Sequential Memory Storage

The hypothesis concerning the functional distinction between the symbolic (memory) codes is related to the relative capacity of visual images and verbal processes as parallel and sequential information processing systems (see the discussion in Chapter 2). Visual memory images are assumed to be functionally related to visual perception—an assumption strongly supported by evidence reviewed in Chapter 5 (e.g., Brooks, 1968; Segal & Fusella, 1970). Imagery, therefore, is basically a parallel-processing system in both the spatial and the operational senses. It is not specialized for serial processing unless linked to an integrated (symbolic) motor response system, such as might be involved in imaginally tracing the outline of a block letter or some other familiar figure (see Chapter 2); or imagining oneself moving along a familiar route containing sequentially arranged "signposts," as advocated in one version of Simonides' technique of places and images; or unless the imagery is linked to a sequentially organized verbal system, as in other versions of the mnemonic system, including the one-bun, two-shoe technique discussed in the preceding chapter.

The verbal system, on the other hand, is assumed to be specialized for serial or sequential processing by virtue of the temporal nature of the auditory-motor speech system. It undoubtedly functions also as an operationally parallel system, however, in that verbal units can be processed independently of each other (cf. Neisser, 1967).

The analysis implies that both codes can be functional in tasks involving retention of item information, since even in free verbal recall the appropriate verbal response presumably can be retrieved from either code provided that the image can be readily decoded. The probability of remembering an item would thus be a direct function of the availability of both codes. In effect, this is a *coding redundancy* hypothesis: Memory increases directly with the number of alternative memory codes available for an item. In the case of concreteness, the increase in the number of items remembered as we go from abstract words, to concrete words, to pictures would thus be interpreted as reflecting the differential availability of concrete imagery as a supplementary coding system, since the availability of the verbal code does not increase with concreteness. The precise manner in which imagery might operate to facilitate item recollection is open to alternative interpretations, however, and these will be discussed later in connection with the detailed findings for the relevant tasks.

The inverse implication of the analysis is that imagery should not be functional in sequential memory tasks, and that performance in such tasks should therefore be related only to the availability of the verbal code.

Inasmuch as the imaginal and verbal codes are functionally differentiated in the theory primarily in terms of their relative efficiency as spatial and sequential information processing systems, the greatest differential effects should occur in tasks involving memory for spatial as compared to sequential information. Some evidence on this distinction was reviewed in Chapters 4 and 5, e.g., briefly presented letter arrays can be reported more efficiently from left to right than the reverse, presumably because such stimuli are coded and retrieved verbally, whereas nonverbal arrays can be reported equally easily in either direction, presumably because they are stored as visual images. Very little comparable evidence will be considered here because the majority of relevant studies deal with memory tasks involving retention of discrete items or their sequential order but not spatial information. Spatial organization constitutes one possible interpretation of the facilitative effect of imagery in free recall, but it will be seen that direct evidence is generally lacking at the present time. For these reasons, the assumed special capacity of the image system for storing and processing spatial information receives less emphasis in the present chapter than it deserves. This situation will be corrected in subsequent chapters, where spatial integration becomes a central concept in the interpretation of the effects of imagery in associative learning tasks.

We turn now to the detailed review of the effects of semantic stimulus attributes in memory tasks, beginning with recognition memory.

RECOGNITION MEMORY

Recognition memory tasks are generally the least complex of the tests of memory because no particular identifying response is required of the subject. He need indicate only whether a stimulus is "old" or "new"—that is, whether it was previously presented or not. Because the response is relatively unimportant, recognition memory is sometimes considered as lying closer to the perceptual side of learning and memory mechanisms, while memory tasks in which overt responses are crucial are presumed to involve response mechanisms to a relatively greater degree (see Adams, 1967). We might accordingly expect that recognition memory would be particularly sensitive to the effects of perceptual variables, such as distinctiveness, and perceptual processes, such as imagery. In addition, it should depend (almost by definition) on the familiarity of the stimulus. It will be seen, however, that verbal meaning alone has been regarded by some as the crucial basis of perceptual distinctiveness and familiarity, and hence of recognition.

Stimulus Concreteness and Recognition Memory

Pictures versus words   Recognition memory has been investigated using pictures and words varying in their concreteness or imagery (I) value. One of the most dramatic demonstrations of memory capacity was first reported by Shepard in 1959 at a scientific meeting and was subsequently published in 1967. Subjects looked through an inspection series of about 600 stimuli selected from a larger population. They were then tested for recognition memory using a test series of "old" stimuli paired with "new" stimuli not previously exposed to them. The inspection series for one group of subjects consisted of 612 pictures selected to be individually of "high salience and memorability." The rate of presentation was self-paced. The inspection series was immediately followed by a test of 68 pairs, presented a pair at a time, and the subject was asked to indicate which one of each pair was the old picture. Another group was similarly presented an inspection series of 540 English words, 270 of which were "frequent" (occurring 100 or more times per million according to Thorndike & Lorge, 1944), and 270 were "rare" (occurring less than once per million). The test series consisted of 60 pairs, with the familiarity of the members of pairs being systematically varied. A third group was similarly presented sentences.

The results showed remarkably high recognition memory for all stimulus types, but highest for pictures. The medians of the percent correct on the immediate test were 98.5, 90.0, and 88.2 for pictures, words, and sentences respectively. The picture superiority is probably reliable, although a statistical comparison was reported only for pictures and sentences. Picture recognition was also tested for different subsets of stimuli after varying intervals of up to 120 days. Performance declined markedly, but even after one week memory for the pictures was nearly equivalent to that found for the verbal material.

Comparable results have been reported for pictures by Nickerson (1965) using a somewhat different procedure. A set of 600 pictures was presented one at a time, without responses to the first 200. Thereafter, the subject responded by indicating whether each stimulus was new or old. Old items were periodically interspersed with new, following the procedure introduced by Shepard and Teghtsoonian (1961). The results showed that 95 percent of the responses were correct, with variation above and below as a function of the lag between the first and the second presentation of an item. The performance was thus generally comparable to that obtained by Shepard. A subsequent experiment (Nickerson, 1968) also showed a systematic loss of retention as a function of retention interval.

Shepard's procedure was repeated by Standing, Conezio, and Haber (1970), with results that were even more dramatic. In one experiment, five subjects were shown 2560 photographs for 10 seconds each over a period of 2 or 4 days. This was followed by 280 test trials, in which 280 pictures drawn from the original 2560 were paired with 280 new items drawn from a larger pool. Recognition scores averaged 90.5 percent correct, indicating retention of over 2000 items, some for as long as three days. Other experiments showed that reducing time to one second per picture and reversing the orientation of the picture in the test situation did not impair recognition appreciably. The orientation of the pictures also was retained well above chance, although not as well as the identity of the pictures.

These experiments demonstrate remarkably high recognition memory for pictures. Shepard's study also demonstrates picture superiority relative to words, although this effect is difficult to interpret because both nouns and adjectives were used. Thus it is uncertain whether pictures are better recognized because of their picturability or because they are implicitly labeled by concrete-noun responses during presentation, given the possibility that such verbal responses are easier to remember than adjectives and any abstract nouns that might have appeared in the word list. In brief, perhaps the effect is related to differential verbal responses rather than picturability.

Such an interpretation seems unlikely on the basis of other studies (Fozard & Lapine, 1968; J. R. Jenkins, Neale, & Deno, 1967; Paivio & Csapo, 1969) in which higher recognition memory was obtained for pictures of familiar objects than for their concrete-noun labels. Jenkins et al. also included conditions in which the inspection series consisted of pictures while the test series consisted of the verbal labels of the pictures, or vice versa. The results showed that recognition was better when pictures were used in both inspection and test phases than when either (or both) consisted of words, indicating that subjects were not simply encoding the pictures as words in the former case. Further evidence on this point appeared in the Paivio and Csapo experiment, to be reviewed in detail later. At this point we may conclude that the superior recognition memory for pictures is related to their pictorial quality rather than to the verbal labels they evoke.

Concrete versus abstract words   The positive effect of concreteness extends to variation within words alone. Jampolsky (1950) found slightly better recognition and a much lower number of false recognitions for concrete words than for abstract words. Gorman (1961), having categorized nouns as concrete and abstract on the basis of judges' ratings (see Chapter 3), also found recognition memory to be much better for the concrete nouns.

Gorman had controlled for frequency in her study, but neither experiment took m into account. Inasmuch as m correlates substantially with noun concreteness and I (see Chapter 3), the effective attribute is indeterminate in both studies. Working in our laboratory, Olver (1965) attempted to vary concreteness (as well as I) and m independently in memory experiments. She was able to achieve only limited control over the variables because the necessary normative data on word attributes were available for only a relatively small sample of nouns at the time. Therefore, imagery-concreteness and m were somewhat confounded. Despite this, the results showed that concreteness had a highly significant positive effect independent of m and frequency.

It can be concluded from the above studies that recognition memory is a direct function of stimulus concreteness: Recognition increases from abstract words, to concrete words, to pictures. These findings are generally consistent with the interpretation that concreteness is related somehow to distinctiveness, or differentiation, and such an explanation was suggested in each of the studies reviewed. Unless we can specify the mechanisms that underlie distinctiveness, however, the concept remains no more than a redundant descriptive label for the facts themselves. Since the availability of nonverbal imagery, but not that of verbal processes, increases with concreteness, imagery can be assumed to be the basis of the distinctiveness and recognizability of concrete stimuli, especially pictures. Verbal mechanisms could be a critical determinant of stimulus distinctiveness and recognition memory performance in the case of other variables, and both processes may be involved in still others, as the dual-coding hypothesis implies. Systematic evidence is not available at this time on all of these possibilities, but the relative importance of verbal and imaginal processes at different levels of meaning can be evaluated to some extent by comparing the potency of other stimulus attributes with that of imagery-concreteness.

Verbal Meaning and Recognition Memory for Nonverbal Stimuli

The effects of verbal referential meaning as defined, for example, by measures of verbal codability, and of verbal associative meaningfulness (e.g., association value) have been investigated frequently in recognition memory experiments involving nonverbal stimuli. This research is relevant here because it permits us to evaluate the extent to which verbal processes contribute to the distinctiveness and memorability of such stimuli, and to compare the effectiveness of verbal mechanisms with that of imagery as inferred from the research on concreteness, reviewed above, and occasional studies to be considered here.

Verbal referential meaning   Studies that we would interpret as being concerned with verbal referential meaning have appeared under such rubrics as linguistic determinism, stimulus predifferentiation, and acquired distinctiveness of cues. All of these concepts have been investigated particularly with reference to the effect of distinctive verbal labels on recognition memory (other memory tasks have been used as well but are not relevant here).

The term *linguistic determinism* identifies Whorf's (1956) hypothesis that language determines thought in the sense that it codes and categorizes the environment for the individual. Verbal labels facilitate perceptual discrimination and memory for the coded units. The hypothesis was investigated by R. W.

Brown and Lenneberg (1954), who tested recognition memory for colors that varied in their verbal codability. Codability was measured by intersubject agreement in naming the color—a highly codable color is one that is given the same label by a number of subjects, whereas a low-codability color is variously named by different subjects (see the discussion of measures of referential meaning in Chapter 3). In agreement with the Whorfian hypothesis, recognition memory was better for highly codable colored chips than for less codable ones.

Not all studies have yielded positive support for the hypothesis, however (see Lenneberg, 1961), and Lantz and Stefflre (1964) sought to clarify matters by adding communicational accuracy as a measure of codability. Communicational accuracy was indexed by the accuracy with which subjects could identify colors on the basis of descriptions of the colors given by other subjects. Lantz and Stefflre found that this measure was superior to naming agreement as a predictor of recognition memory for colors. Indeed, with communicational accuracy partialed out statistically, naming agreement was essentially unrelated to recognition.

Ignoring the issue of which index is the more appropriate measure of verbal referential meaning, these studies indicate that such meaning does play a role in recognition memory for nonverbal stimuli. A study reported by Stuart Klapp (1969) suggests, however, that the effect of verbal referential meaning may be specific to subjects who have poor imagery, or visual memory, as measured by a test of memory for shapes. He found a high correlation of .89 between recognition memory for colors and communication accuracy scores for the colors in the case of subjects scoring low on memory for shapes, whereas the corresponding correlation was only .26 for high-scoring subjects. Thus subjects with poor visual imagery apparently had to rely on verbal coding in order to recognize colors, whereas high imagery subjects did not. This finding is important because it suggests that verbal coding *can* be used to facilitate recognition of nonverbal stimuli, but is not essential for such recognition. Unfortunately, Klapp failed to obtain the same relations in a subsequent study, and any generalizations from the data must remain tentative.

The color codability research involved a correlational approach in which advantage has been taken of pre-experimentally established differences in referential meaning. Other studies, generally related to the acquired distinctiveness or predifferentiation hypothesis, have attempted to manipulate verbal codability by experimental pretraining. The transfer of such training has been tested in various perceptual discrimination and recognition memory tasks (for a recent review, see Epstein, 1967). Our concern here is with the latter. Other experiments have varied verbal coding by procedures designed to encourage or discourage labeling of familiar pictures during their presentation.[1]

The hypothesis of acquired distinctiveness of cues was formulated by N. E.

---

[1] Strictly speaking, these predifferentiation and labeling experiments belong with other experimental studies of verbal mediation processes (Chapter 9), but they will be discussed here because of their special relevance to the problem of verbal meaning and recognition memory.

Miller and Dollard (1941) in the context of the concepts of stimulus differentiation and generalization. It states that learning to respond with distinctive labels to similar stimuli reduces the generalization of responses from one stimulus to another by producing cues that increase the difference in the stimulus patterns. In the present context, this represents a specific hypothesis concerning the mechanism by which verbal referential meaning might have its effect. Although more specific, it also expresses essentially the same point as the Whorfian hypothesis. Since recognition memory is affected by the discriminability of the stimulus alternatives used in an experiment (see Adams, 1967), it follows from the hypothesis that acquired distinctiveness training—attaching distinctive verbal labels to stimuli—should enhance recognition memory in a subsequent test.

What are the facts? The experiments on the problem have yielded inconsistent results. Hake and Eriksen (1956) gave some subjects practice using letters of the alphabet as discriminative responses, while others were not given such training. Subsequently, all subjects were given a predifferentiation task consisting of paired-associate learning in which nonsense-form stimuli were paired with the letters as responses. Different numbers of letters were used with different groups, so that some subjects had a different letter paired with each nonsense form while others learned common letter responses to different stimuli. Presumably, the greater the number of different responses in the list, the greater should be the acquired distinctiveness and the more recognizable the stimuli. The results were negative: Neither the preliminary practice using the letters as discriminative responses nor the number of alternative responses used in the paired-associates task had any overall effect on a subsequent recognition task in which the predifferentiated forms had to be selected from an equal number of new but similar forms. Vanderplas and Garvin (1959b) varied the amount of practice in the predifferentiation task along with stimulus complexity and meaningfulness (to be discussed later). The stimuli consisted of random shapes scaled for complexity according to the number of inner and outer points they contain (Attneave, 1957; Vanderplas & Garvin, 1959a). Examples of the shapes are shown in Figure 7-2. The pretraining involved 2, 4, 8, or 16 paired-associate learning trials with nonsense syllables as responses. On the recognition test, the shapes were presented along with similar variations. The results showed no effect of the level of predifferentiation practice on recognition memory. Santa and Ranken (1968) similarly found that learning names for novel shapes had no effect on simple recognition memory for the shapes, although naming did facilitate performance in other memory tasks to be discussed later.

Positive effects of labels on recognition memory have been obtained in other studies. Ellis and Muller (1964), using a design similar to that of Vanderplas and Garvin, varied shape complexity, level of practice, and type of pretraining. A distinctiveness training condition involved paired-associate learning with the nonsense forms as stimuli and meaningful words as responses. An observation training condition consisted of exposure to the forms without labeling, and an equivalence training condition required the subjects to learn the label "wide" for half the stimuli and "narrow" for the other half. The results

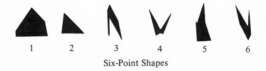

1   2   3   4   5   6

Six-Point Shapes

1   2   3   4   5   6

Twenty-Four Point Shapes

FIGURE 7-2.   Examples of random shapes at different levels of scaled complexity. Adapted from Vanderplas and Garvin (1959a).

showed that equivalence training resulted in poorer performance than either of the other two conditions on the subsequent recognition memory task. Practice and complexity interacted in such a manner that the facilitating effect of increasing practice was greater for the more complex forms. Complexity and type of training also interacted, with observation training resulting in better performance for simple forms and labeling (distinctiveness) resulting in better recognition for the more complex forms. Epstein (1967), discussing the contrasting results of Vanderplas and Garvin (1959b), and Ellis and Muller, with respect to the practice variable, suggested that the difference might be due to the greater meaningfulness of the responses (words as compared to low-association-value trigrams) used by Ellis and Muller during pretraining. The effect of the meaningfulness of the label would be to enhance the strength of the association between the shapes and the labeling responses, presumably making the label more available as a differentiating response to the form in the recognition task.

Further evidence on the effect of coding, among other variables, was obtained by H. J. Clark (1965) using subjective reports as a measure of coding. The experiment was concerned with recognition memory for random shapes varying in association value and complexity. Complexity was varied according to the number of points each shape contained, the simple forms containing 4 or 6 points while the complex contained 16 or 24. These were selected from the pool published by Vanderplas and Garvin (1959a). Coding was determined by a questionnaire that asked subjects to indicate how often they named the forms in order to remember them. In the recognition task, the subjects viewed 10 forms once and subsequently were required to identify the forms in a forced-choice task in which the forms were paired randomly with 10 new ones.

The results showed that subjects reported coding complex forms significantly more often than simple forms. A correlational analysis also showed that coding was significantly related to recognition accuracy in the case of complex forms but not in the case of simple forms. The simple forms apparently were difficult to code for recognition, and subjects claimed that they relied on remembering an "uncoded image of the entire contour of the form" (1965, p. 594). On the other hand, they found verbal coding necessary for accurate recognition of the complex forms. Clark suggested that perhaps the contours of simple forms can be stored, while the contours of complex forms cannot.

Experiments involving familiar objects or their pictures have yielded variable effects on recognition memory of procedures designed to encourage labeling. Positive results were obtained under certain conditions in a widely cited study by Kurtz and Hovland (1953), and in a recent experiment by Wilgosh (1970). Kurtz and Hovland showed elementary school children an array of 16 familiar objects. As the experimenter pointed to each object, half of the subjects found and encircled the name of the object on a sheet of printed names, while saying the name aloud. The other half merely circled the picture of the object on a sheet of pictures. Some of the subjects from each condition were given a recognition test one week later involving the 16 original objects and 16 new objects, half presented as printed names and half as photographs. The results revealed superior recognition on the part of the subjects that had verbalized the objects during their presentation, but this was true mainly on the verbal test. With photographs as the test stimuli the verbalization group made significantly fewer errors, but they were not superior to the nonverbalization groups in number of correct responses. Wilgosh (1970) found that providing subjects with verbal labels facilitated recognition memory for pictures of familiar objects in the case of four- and eight-year-old children but not adults. The facilitative effect was obtained even when the children could not distinguish between correct and incorrect alternatives on the basis of verbal labels alone, since pairs of recognition alternatives were identifiable by the same labels. The latter finding led Wilgosh to reject such response-oriented explanations as differential rehearsal of the labels (e.g., Flavell, Beach, & Chinsky, 1966). She suggested instead that the words influenced the subjects to process or store pictorial information more effectively, perhaps by directing their attention to the distinctive features of the pictures.

Negative effects of naming have been reported by others. W. C. H. Prentice (1954) investigated the effect of verbal labels on the nature of recognition errors, following a procedure introduced by Carmichael, Hogan, and Walter (1932). Carmichael et al. showed that presenting names along with ambiguous figures resulted in memory reproductions that resembled the objects referred to by the labels. Prentice did not find a similar selective effect of labels on recognition errors and concluded that the labels influenced the activity of reproducing the figures rather than the subjects' perception or memory of them. Bahrick and Boucher (1968) found naming to have detrimental effects on visual recognition memory for familiar objects: Subjects who were required to call out the names of pictured objects as they were presented over nine trials made fewer correct responses on a recognition test given two weeks later than did subjects not given instructions to verbalize. In agreement with the Santa and Ranken

(1968) results mentioned earlier, verbalization facilitated performance in another memory task (in this case, free recall—see later).

It can be concluded from the above results that verbal labels do not consistently facilitate recognition memory for nonverbal stimuli, although such labels can be helpful under certain conditions. The general nature of those conditions can be inferred from some of the findings. Klapp (1969) found that codability of colors correlated highly with recognition memory for the colors in the case of subjects with poor visual memory but not subjects with good visual memory. Amount of pretraining with distinctive labels had no effect in the Vanderplas and Garvin (1959b) study, in which the labels were meaningless trigrams, whereas practice was effective (especially with more complex stimuli) in the Ellis and Muller (1964) study, in which the labels were meaningful words. Finally, Clark found that reported coding predicted recognition accuracy for complex forms but not for simple forms. The emerging pattern is that verbal coding may be effectively used when such codes are readily available and when the subjects find it difficult to store the nonverbal information in memory either because they have poor visual memory or because the stimulus is complex. However, verbal coding need not be resorted to if (a) the subject has good visual memory, (b) the stimuli are simple shapes or familiar objects that can be stored as uncoded images, or (c) the verbal code (e.g., a nonsense syllable) is not readily available in the subject's response repertoire.

Verbal associative meaning   Several of the studies reviewed above under referential meaning also included association value as a variable. Perhaps it would be more appropriate to regard that variable as a measure of referential rather than associative meaning, since the stimuli were nonsense shapes and the instructions used to obtain the defining associative responses to the items (Vanderplas & Garvin, 1959a) encouraged the subjects to label the stimulus or some component of it. Be that as it may, the findings for association value will be summarized and discussed in this section along with those for other measures of verbal meaningfulness of shapes.

Vanderplas and Garvin (1959b) found no main effect of the association value of nonsense shapes on recognition memory. In a later study, however, Vanderplas, Sanderson, and Vanderplas (1964) did obtain a significant effect, as did H. J. Clark (1965) in the experiment described above and in a subsequent replication (H. J. Clark, 1968). High-association-value stimuli were easier to recognize in each case. H. J. Clark (1965) also found that reported coding was positively related to association value for complex forms but not for simple forms. Since coding was also related to recognition memory for complex forms, the data are consistent in suggesting that verbal (referential and associative) meaning facilitates recognition memory for such stimuli. The results are inconsistent for simple forms, however, since association value facilitated their recognition but coding did not. Clark suggested that perhaps the simple forms of high association value had characteristics that allowed images of their contours to be remembered more efficiently than the contours of simple forms with low association value. Perhaps the former resembled concrete objects more than did the latter and were more memorable for that reason.

Ellis, Muller, and Tosti (1966) compared the effects of three different measures of associative meaningfulness on shape recognition. The stimuli were 6-point and 24-point random shapes selected from Vanderplas and Garvin (1959a; see Figure 7-2). One measure of meaning was association value, as defined by the percentage of subjects reporting an association. Another was associative frequency, defined in terms of the average number of associations given in one minute, which resembles Noble's (1952a) m index for verbal stimuli, with the difference that Ellis et al. instructed their subjects to state what each stimulus "looked like" rather than to respond with verbal associations generally. The third measure was associative consistency, which refers to the degree of consistency with which subjects assigned labels to the shapes; for example, if half of the subjects said that a particular shape looked like a "crab," then that shape would have an associative consistency value of 0.5 (cf. associative commonality). These variables were independently varied over high and low values using different sets of items.

The experiment involved eight trials of predifferentiation training in which the subjects learned meaningful labels as responses to the shapes. This was followed by a recognition test in which the original shapes were presented along with new variants of them. The results showed positive effects of meaningfulness that depended on the type of measure used: the number of correct recognitions increased with association value for shapes of either level of complexity, and with associative consistency when the shapes were simple but not when they were complex. In contrast, associative frequency had no effect on shape recognition. Thus, association value most consistently predicted recognition performance, whereas associative frequency entirely failed to do so.

A subsequent study provided some information on the basis of the differential effects of association value and associative frequency. Feuge and Ellis (1969) gave their subjects paired-associate practice in labeling or observing a set of random shapes, followed by a recognition test consisting of those shapes and distortions of them that varied systematically in their degree of similarity to the original shapes. Interest lay in the effect of the two measures of stimulus meaning on generalization gradients, i.e., the frequency of recognition responses to stimuli varying in their similarity to the shapes used in pretraining. The results, plotted in Figure 7-3, showed contrasting effects for the two measures of meaning. In the case of association value, the generalization gradient was steeper for shapes of high rather than low meaningfulness, i.e., the distortions were more often mistaken for the original when they were low in association value. Conversely, the gradient was steeper when associative frequency was low rather than high, indicating a greater tendency to make recognition errors in the case of high-associative-frequency items.

Feuge and Ellis interpreted their findings in terms of stimulus distinctiveness. High-association-value shapes are stimuli to which subjects have a strong tendency to give a single associate. This single dominant associate enables the subject

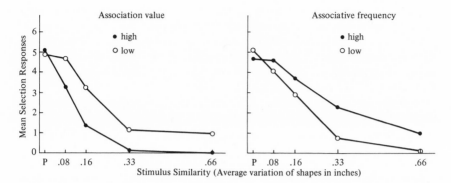

FIGURE 7-3. Gradients of generalization in recognition of visual form, plotted as the mean number of selection responses in the recognition test as a function of stimulus similarity and two measures of stimulus meaning (association value vs. associative frequency). P refers to the prototype shape used in pretraining. From Feuge and Ellis (1969).

to focus on more of the distinguishing characteristics of the shape during pretraining; consequently, such stimuli will be relatively distinct from the original prototypes and less likely to be confused with them during the recognition test than shapes of low association value. On the other hand, high-associative-frequency shapes lead to greater variability in the manner in which the subject attempts to encode a shape over successive trials. This increased variability may reduce the effectiveness of encoding, thereby leading to poorer recognition of the prototypes and hence greater generalization to other similar stimuli than is the case with shapes of low associative frequency. Note that the latter interpretation could be rephrased in terms of associative interference, thereby relating the research on shape recognition to verbal recognition memory studies (to be reviewed later) in which false recognitions have been attributed to implicit associative reactions (e.g., Underwood, 1965).

What theoretical significance do these findings and interpretations have in the present context? The results indicate that the verbal associative meaningfulness of nonverbal stimuli, as measured by association value or associative consistency, is generally related positively to recognition memory. As in the case of the effects of predifferentiation training (where such effects have been obtained), the favored interpretation is in terms of the contribution of verbal associative processes to stimulus distinctiveness. An alternative interpretation is possible, however: The verbal reactions that define associative meaningfulness of shapes may simply reflect the degree to which the shapes resemble concrete objects. Recall that Vanderplas and Garvin (1959a) asked their subjects to label the shapes, and Ellis et al. (1966) were even more explicit in requiring subjects to state what the stimuli looked like. Therefore, high association value or associative consistency might indicate that the stimuli tend to be readily perceived as definite objects, whereas high associative *frequency* could reflect ambiguity in the things suggested by such stimuli. According to this view, then, the variation in recognition scores as a function of level of meaningfulness would be attributed to the concrete properties of the shapes and the underlying non-verbal symbolic processes rather than to verbal associative processes directly. A more likely alternative is that imaginal and verbal processes contribute to the effects, the relative weight and nature of their contributions depending upon the precise conditions of the experiment. Such possibilities have already been mentioned above in connection with H. J. Clark's (1965) findings and the research on verbal referential meaning.

The theoretical alternatives remain to be directly tested, but at this point it appears that nonverbal processes are more important in visual recognition memory than are verbal processes. This conclusion is suggested by an overall comparison of the effectiveness of imagery-concreteness and the variables that define verbal meaning: The former consistently show a positive relation to recognition memory scores in different experiments but measures of verbal meaning do not. Further support for this view comes from a series of experiments on short-term memory for visual figures conducted by R. L. Cohen and Granström (1970), who concluded from their results that verbal information is unnecessary in visual recognition memory although it plays a part in reproduction.

Frequency and Familiarity in Recognition Memory

Frequency and familiarity measures operationally define representational meaning, i.e., the availability of a verbal or imaginal representational system corresponding to a word or an object. Recognition memory might be expected to be a direct function of the availability of such representations and thus, of stimulus familiarity. The empirical data seem inconsistent with this expectation, however, at least in the case of words.

In the previously described study on recognition memory for words, sentences, and pictures, Shepard (1967) systematically varied the frequency of the old and the new words of the test pairs so that all possible combinations of frequent and rare words were included. His results showed that subjects were better able to recognize old words when they were rare (92.5 percent correct) than when they were frequent (84.4 percent correct). The frequency level of the new word did not have a significant effect, although the difference tended to be in the same direction as in the case of the old words. Gorman (1961) and Olver (1965) similarly found highly significant negative effects of frequency. Moreover, in both studies the contrasting effects of frequency and concreteness were independent. Within either concrete or abstract nouns, recognition scores were higher for relatively low frequency words than for the more commonly occurring words. Gorman's data for both variables are shown in Figure 7-4.

Schulman (1967) obtained comparable frequency effects using a signal detection approach in which subjects gave confidence ratings on a 6-point scale rather than simple binary decisions of old or new. The inspection series consisted of 100 words read to the subjects. The test series consisted of 200 words that included the original 100. Half of the old and the new words were relatively

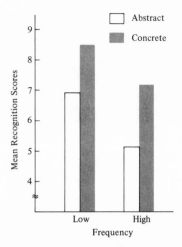

FIGURE 7-4. Mean recognition memory scores for abstract and concrete nouns of high and low frequency. Based on data in Gorman (1961).

frequent and half were rare. The results showed that recognition memory was markedly superior for the rare words.

Comparable data on frequency or familiarity effects among nonverbal stimuli would be theoretically interesting, but the problem has not been systematically investigated, and studies with relevant information have generally involved confounding of familiarity with other dimensions of meaning. For example, Hochberg and Galper (1967) used Shepard's recognition procedure with photographs of upright and inverted faces. Recognition memory scores were significantly higher for the more familiar upright faces, apparently contradicting the word-frequency data. However, inverted faces probably differ from upright faces in a number of respects besides their familiarity, and one of these could be the effective dimension. It is possible, for example, that faces are recognized on the basis of particular distinguishing features that are less readily discriminated when the faces are inverted (cf. Scapinello & Yarmey, 1970; Yin, 1969). The differential recognition memory for the two types of faces would accordingly be explainable in terms of perceptual similarity. The difference could also be interpreted in terms of verbal coding, since the upright faces are probably easier to label than the inverted ones. These and other possibilities need to be explored before further speculation is warranted.

Distinctiveness as an explanation of the word frequency effect   The negative effect of word frequency is consistent with a differentiation or distinctiveness hypothesis of recognition memory and has been so interpreted in the above studies. Thus, both Gorman and Shepard suggested that high-frequency words may be more subject to interference from other words in the subject's language repertoire. Shepard proposed alternatively that not all of the rare words included in his study were unfamiliar to any given subject. Perhaps only a quarter of those in the inspection series were truly strange, and they might have been better remembered because they were unusual or because they stood out as being in the minority. The latter essentially expresses a distinctiveness or novelty effect, analogous to the "von Restorff" phenomenon (see W. P. Wallace, 1965). Schulman proposed a similar explanation in terms of associative overlap: Rare words should tend to be more distinctive semantically, since they should share fewer associations than do common words. Why a novel or distinctive stimulus should be better recognized is by no means explicitly answered by such formulations, however, since it is the *memory of the previous exposure* that is to be explained, not the discriminability of items per se. Presumably novelty or rareness somehow enhances the memorability of the single exposure given to the stimulus during the inspection trial. In terms of a habit or memory trace interpretation (see Adams, 1967), recognition occurs when a response, associatively aroused by a stimulus during its original presentation, is re-evoked by the stimulus during the test trial. Interference occurs when the response generalizes to a new item in the test series. Such generalization, or lack of it, constitutes one possible interpretation of the "distinctiveness" of rare words and the effect of this variable on recognition: The verbal responses evoked by rare words during the inspection series are likely to be re-evoked by the same words and not by others during the test trial. The responses evoked by familiar words are relatively more likely to generalize to other stimuli occurring in the test trial. This interpretation is basically similar to the one offered by Feuge and Ellis (1969) to account for the negative effect of associative frequency on shape recognition.

The familiarity- or frequency-increment hypothesis An alternative explanation can be suggested on the basis of two sources of information, one stemming from data on the relation between familiarity and exposure frequency, the other from research on verbal discrimination learning. In a study already described in Chapter 3, Noble (1954) exposed meaningless words different numbers of times to subjects, who then rated the words on familiarity. He obtained a hyperbolic function relating familiarity to frequency of exposure. The relation is shown in Figure 7-5, where it can be seen that familiarity rises sharply with frequency up to about five exposures and then levels off. It could be argued in this case that the leveling of the curve reflects a ceiling effect determined by the restricted (5-point) rating scale used for measuring familiarity. However, Arnoult (1956) obtained a similar function for nonsense shapes but with a much lower asymptote (the lower curve in Figure 7-5). Thus, familiarity indeed appears to be a non-artifactual increasing, negatively accelerated function of exposure frequency.

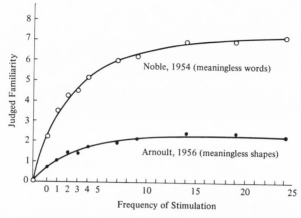

FIGURE 7-5.   Functions relating ratings of familiarity to frequency of stimulus exposure. From Noble (1963).

What is the significance of the frequency-familiarity relationship for the interpretation of the recognition memory data? Adams (1967, p. 250) suggested that Noble's familiarity function can be interpreted as a relationship between frequency of stimulation and recognition, and that the negative relation between word frequency and recognition memory obtained by Gorman (1961) and Shepard (1967) is therefore contradictory to the work of Noble and Arnoult. That is, Noble's familiarity hypothesis would predict that high-frequency words should be better recognized than low-frequency words, whereas the opposite was found. This does not necessarily follow, however, since Noble's procedure for measuring familiarity differs in a crucial way from the recognition memory procedure. The former reflects a long-term memory process. The familiarity rating is in effect an estimate of the frequency with which the subject has been exposed to the word in pre-experimental situations. The recognition memory experiment, on the other hand, involves relatively *short-term* memory for an event that occurred within the experimental setting. The subject is required to indicate whether or not a given stimulus had in fact been presented during the study trial, not to estimate its long-term familiarity.

This important distinction, considered in conjunction with Noble's familiarity-frequency function, suggests a possible resolution of the apparently paradoxical negative effect of word frequency in recognition memory. Briefly stated, the hypothesis is that the *probability of correct recognition is a direct function of the relative increment in stimulus familiarity that results from a single exposure to the target stimulus.* The signal that elicits the recognition response is a *change* in familiarity from a pre-experimental baseline. The negatively accelerated positive function obtained by Noble shows that the subjective (rated) familiarity of infrequently experienced stimuli increases sharply with one exposure; after

10 or so exposures, however, one additional exposure to the stimulus increases its familiarity only slightly. Given these effects, it follows from the hypothesis that infrequent stimuli will be easier to recognize than frequent stimuli because the familiarity of the former is increased relatively more by the single exposure occurring during the inspection phase of a recognition memory experiment.

Essentially the same hypothesis arises as a corollary from a theory of verbal discrimination learning proposed by Ekstrand, Wallace, and Underwood (1966), although they emphasize the concept of frequency rather than familiarity. In verbal discrimination learning, the subject is presented with pairs of stimulus words and one member of each pair is arbitrarily designated as "correct" by the experimenter. The subject must learn to discriminate the correct member from the incorrect member over repeated trials. Ekstrand et al. proposed that the primary basis for the discrimination is the relative frequency of the paired words. The correct word accumulates "frequency points" over trials more rapidly than does the incorrect word because of such factors as differential (implicit) rehearsal favoring the former. The authors also proposed that the frequency increments may be relative to the baseline frequency of the word: The lower the initial frequency, the greater the increment resulting from a further exposure (or response) to the word. This Weber-function corollary was intended to apply particularly to *experimental* frequency, but Ekstrand et al. also suggested that it might apply to the background frequency of the word as indexed, for example, by the Thorndike-Lorge word count.

The relevance of the frequency theory of discrimination learning for recognition memory can be readily appreciated. The forced-choice procedure (e.g., Shepard, 1967) is particularly similar to discrimination learning in that the subject must choose between the correct old item and the incorrect new item. This might be done on the basis of the relative frequency of the two items because greater frequency has accrued to the old item as a result of exposure to it during the inspection trial (Underwood & Freund, 1970). Moreover, the Weber-function corollary implies that rare words might accumulate differential frequency faster and would thus be easier to recognize than frequent words, as indeed they are. The interpretation itself has not been directly tested in recognition memory experiments, however, and the indirect evidence from verbal discrimination learning is not encouraging. Paivio and Rowe (1970) investigated the effects of word frequency (as well as imagery and m) on verbal discrimination and found only a nonsignificant trend favoring low-frequency words. Thus the relative frequency hypothesis as applied to background frequency was not supported. Note, however, that the ineffectiveness of word frequency in discrimination learning contrasts with the consistent negative effect of that variable in recognition memory. It could be argued, therefore, that the latter is somehow more sensitive to relative frequency increments than is verbal discrimination learning. The proposal remains speculative, however, and we must conclude that there is more empirical support at present for the associative-interference than for the relative-frequency-increment interpretation of the negative effect of word frequency. The plausibility of the former is enhanced further by the clear demonstration of verbal associative interference in studies described below.

Associative Meaning of Words in Recognition Memory

In her investigation of concreteness and frequency, Olver (1965) attempted also to vary associative meaningfulness (m). Because of the relatively small word sample and a substantial correlation between concreteness and m, it was possible to vary m only over a relatively restricted range within both concrete and abstract nouns. The results showed no main effect attributable to independent variation in m. The study obviously needs to be repeated before firm conclusions can be drawn, but the absence of an effect is at least consistent with results obtained for other memory tasks (see below) using more adequate word lists. A negative effect might in fact be predicted for m, since increasing the number of associations presumably could increase the likelihood of associative interference (see further in Chapter 8).

Interfering effects attributable to specific (implicit) associative reactions have in fact been demonstrated in a number of studies. In an experiment by Underwood (1965), 200 words were read to subjects and the subject was required to indicate whether or not it had been read earlier. The list included five different classes of critical stimulus words that were presumed to elicit specified implicit associative reactions. The assumed associative response words were also presented later in the list. Examples of the stimulus words and their associates (taken from association norms), respectively, are *bottom, top*; *rough, smooth*; *butter, bread*; *maple, tree*; and *barrel, round*. Words presumably not associated with preceding words in the list were included as controls.

The results showed that, for three of the five classes of implicit response words, false recognition was much higher than for control words. The frequency with which the critical stimulus words were presented was also varied, and it was found that the greater the frequency, the greater the likelihood of false recognition. Underwood interpreted this to be a function of the frequency of elicitation of the implicit associative reactions. His general theoretical explanation of the effect was that the occurrence of implicit associative responses to the critical stimulus words when originally presented resulted in a later confusion between implicit associative reactions and representational responses, where representational response is used in the Bousfield sense discussed in Chapter 3, i.e., the immediate response to the word as it is perceived.

Results consistent with the above were also obtained by W. P. Wallace (1967) and by Anisfeld and Knapp (1968). The latter also considered the directionality of the associates. False recognition errors were obtained when the preceding words in the list associatively elicited the subsequent test words and when the associative relation was bidirectional. The errors did not occur when only the test words elicited the preceding words. Consistent with interference theory, these studies show clearly that specific verbal associative (meaning) reactions can be a source of confusion in recognition memory.

Summary of Research on Recognition Memory and Meaning

Some empirical generalizations can be made reasonably confidently on the basis of the findings reviewed above. Stimulus concreteness has consistently shown a positive effect, pictures being easier to recognize than their concrete noun labels, and concrete nouns in turn being superior to abstract nouns. Frequency, when varied within words, has an equally consistent negative effect—rare words are easier to recognize than common words. Verbal referential meaning (e.g., codability) and associative meaning have inconsistent effects, although the positive effects can be related with some predictability to situations in which recognition memory is difficult on the basis of nonverbal stimulus information alone. In other instances, nonverbal information apparently suffices.

The findings implicate both nonverbal and verbal symbolic processes, and different levels of associative meaning. The superiority of pictures over words and the absence of any facilitative effect of verbal coding on recognition memory for visual forms and pictures in some studies suggest that nonverbal representational images can function effectively as memory codes. The superiority of concrete over abstract words suggests that referent images, associatively evoked by the concrete nouns, facilitate recognition memory. Verbal associative processes are implicated in those instances where labeling responses and association value enhance recognition memory, although imagery is not ruled out as an alternative or supplementary explanation even in those instances.

The positive effects of imaginal and verbal referential and associative meaning and the negative effect of word frequency perhaps can be explained in terms of the single concept of distinctiveness, operating through nonverbal and verbal processes. Where imagery is involved, it may have its effect by providing a perceptual basis for differentiation. What is recognized is a distinctive perceptual image—directly aroused as a representational image by a nonverbal pattern, or indirectly as a referential image by a word, and re-evoked when the stimulus reappears during the recognition test.

The negative effect of frequency, on the other hand, may be restricted to words and to verbal representational processes only, as suggested by the independence of this effect from that of imagery-concreteness and (perhaps) verbal associative meaning. Distinctiveness in this case might be interpreted in terms of the familiarity-increment hypothesis: What makes the rare word stand out as familiar in the recognition memory test is the increment in the strength of the underlying verbal representation resulting from the previous exposure. At present, however, this interpretation lacks empirical support. An alternative interpretation, applicable also to the positive effects of verbal referential or associative meaning of nonverbal stimuli, is that distinctiveness is based on the uniqueness of the verbal reactions to a particular to-be-recognized stimulus, so that mediated associations do not result in false recognition. Such a conceptualization is supported by the studies of Underwood (1965), W. P. Wallace (1967), and Anisfeld and Knapp (1968).

Recognition memory and perceptual recognition compared   The data clearly indicate that recognition memory cannot be equated with perceptual recognition. The former is positively affected by imagery-concreteness and verbal associative meaning, and negatively affected by frequency. Conversely, perceptual recognition was shown in Chapter 4 to be relatively unaffected by the imagery and verbal associative variables, but consistently related *positively* to word frequency. Apparently associative processes evoked by the target stimulus can be functional in the memory task where they cannot in the perceptual task. The fact that frequency is positively related to perceptual thresholds and negatively to recognition memory is consistent with the view that the former depends only on the availability of the representational response to the stimulus (hence its familiarity), whereas recognition memory depends upon an increase in the availability of the representation (i.e., an increase in familiarity) as a result of one exposure. The latter interpretation may be applicable also to Haber's (1965) findings, discussed in Chapter 5, that frequency was related to perceptual clarity only when the subject was not shown the words beforehand. Perhaps the effect of that exposure was to increase substantially the familiarity of low-frequency words with little effect on the asymptotically familiar high-frequency words, thereby reducing pre-experimental differences in the availability of the representational systems that underlie the perception of high- and low-frequency words. In this instance, perceptual clarity and recognition memory would be comparable because both are affected by short-term memory processes occurring within the experimental situation. The hypothesis is speculative but presumably testable.

FREE VERBAL RECALL

Whereas verbal identifying responses are not required in recognition memory tasks, they are essential in free recall. It would be expected, therefore, that free recall performance would be relatively more dependent upon the verbal symbolic system. In the obvious sense that the study of free recall is restricted to materials that can be named, the expectation is borne out by definition. Within the limitations imposed by task characteristics, however, there is evidence that nonverbal processes can also play a crucial mediational role in free recall. This conclusion is based on comparisons of different meaning attributes, whose relative effects in free recall are strikingly similar to their effects in recognition memory. However, there are notable differences to be considered as well.

Item Concreteness and Imagery in Free Recall

Picture-word comparisons   The effect of "picturability" has been more frequently investigated in free recall than in recognition memory, and the effect is consistently positive. In what must be one of the earliest experimental studies of free recall, Kirkpatrick (1894) tested recall for a number of different lists of items, including the names of objects and the actual objects. His subjects were students ranging in age level from third grade primary school to college. For both sexes at every age level, average recall was highest for the objects. Calkins (1898) essentially replicated Kirkpatrick's findings using pictures of objects rather than the actual objects. Moore (1919) compared memory for objects, pictures, and written and spoken words. He found immediate recall to be better for objects than for pictures and better for pictures than for words. Although he used only four subjects, the general superiority of objects and pictorial representations over words is consistent with the earlier and later findings.

W. A. Bousfield, Esterson, and Whitmarsh (1957) presented for recall nouns alone, nouns along with uncolored pictures of their referents, and nouns with their colored pictures. Recall was found to be least for the words alone and highest for the colored pictures. Superior recall for either objects or pictures as compared to their verbal labels has also been obtained by Kaplan, Kaplan, and Sampson (1968), Lieberman and Culpepper (1965), Paivio, Rogers, and Smythe (1968), Sampson (1970), and Scott (1967). Apparently the only exception to this general pattern of results appeared in a study by Ducharme and Fraisse (1965). Children between the ages of seven and nine years found words easier to memorize than pictures of the words' referents, whereas adults did better with pictures. Even the negative finding has been offset recently by Cole, Frankel, and Sharp (1969), who found objects or pictures consistently easier to recall than words for children in grades 1 through 9.

The evidence overwhelmingly supports the general conclusion that objects or their pictures are easier to recall than their verbal labels. The finding is of uncommon theoretical interest because the required response is verbal in both cases and the to-be-remembered name should be more readily available when the stimulus is a word rather than a picture. Since it is not, verbal processes alone seem insufficient to account for the finding. The finding is consistent with the ancient assumption that concrete objects make a particularly deep impression on the organ of memory—they are more vivid and memorable than words. Without some elaboration, however, this is simply a redundant description rather than an explanation of the effect. A number of alternative hypotheses will be considered after a review of the effects of variation in imagery-concreteness at the word level, and of other dimensions of meaning.

Effects of word concreteness and imagery   The effects of word concreteness are again completely consistent and positive. Stoke (1929) found recall to be higher for concrete nouns than for abstract nouns. The finding has been confirmed in recent studies (e.g., Dukes & Bastian, 1966; Olver, 1965; Winnick & Kressel, 1965), in which group ratings have been used to define abstractness-concreteness. Others have obtained superior recall for nouns rated high on measures of imagery than for nouns rated low on imagery. Bowers (1931, 1932) reported a positive correlation between recall scores for words and their rated visual and kinesthetic imagery values. Tulving, McNulty, and Ozier (1965) found better recall for words rated high than for ones rated low in vividness, where vividness was defined in terms of "the ease with which you can picture something in your mind" when presented the word—a measure that is operationally similar to Paivio's (1965) word-imagery index. Concreteness and imagery are so highly correlated (.83 in the 925-word normative sample of Paivio, Yuille, & Madigan, 1968) that they can be taken as essentially defining the same variable. Even so, Paivio (1968) found rated imagery to be superior to rated concreteness as a predictor of free recall, supporting the conclusion that the effective empirical variable is best defined by ratings of the image-evoking capacity of words.

The three levels of concreteness compared under intentional and incidental instructions, and immediate and delayed recall   The potency of the effect over three levels of concreteness and its generality across variations in experimental conditions were demonstrated in a recent, unpublished study by Paivio and Csapo. The experiment involved pictures of objects, their concrete noun labels, and abstract nouns as stimuli (examples of each stimulus type are shown in Figure 7-6). Recall was tested under short-term and long-term retention conditions, and intentional or incidental instructions. Subjects were presented a homogeneous list containing 72 items of one of the three classes. Under the incidental condition, subjects were told that the experiment was concerned with the accuracy of identifying pictures (or words) when they are shown very briefly. Each item was exposed by projector for a duration of .063 sec., which had been found previously to permit completely accurate recognition (Paivio & Csapo, 1969). The balance of a 5-second interitem interval was used by the subject to write down the name of the picture or the word that had been flashed. After the list had been presented, half the subjects were dismissed and asked to return the following week, ostensibly for a second experiment. The other half were unexpectedly asked to recall the items they had been shown. The dismissed group were similarly tested for incidental recall a week later.

Under the intentional instructions, the procedure was the same as above, except that the subjects were informed prior to list presentation that they would later be asked to recall the items.

Recall for the picture groups was scored on the basis of the labels given to the pictures by each subject during the original presentation. The means for all groups are shown in Figure 7-7, where the most notable effect is the striking superiority of picture recall. After the 5-minute retention interval, roughly 50 percent of the 72 pictures were correctly recalled under both incidental and intentional learning conditions, as compared to about half that in the case of concrete words and still fewer in the case of abstract. Even after one week, pictures were recalled as well as concrete nouns were after 5 minutes, a result consistent with Shepard's for recognition memory. Intentional recall was higher on the average than incidental recall, but the difference tended to be smaller in the case of pictures. Although the interaction of stimulus attribute by incidental-intentional conditions was not significant, the trend does suggest that concrete

Pictures	Concrete Words	Abstract Words
	Piano	Justice
	Snake	Ability
	Clock	Ego
	Pencil	Moral
	Lobster	Bravery
	Cigar	Amount
	Star	Theory
	House	Freedom
	Pipe	Grief

FIGURE 7-6. Examples of pictures, concrete nouns, and abstract nouns used as stimulus items in the free recall experiment by Paivio and Csapo.

(visual) memory may be less affected than verbal memory by motivational factors. The issue will come up again in subsequent discussions (see especially Chapter 10).

It can be concluded that there is a completely reliable orderly progression in free recall performance as a function of concreteness, with objects or pictures being easiest, concrete (high-imagery) words intermediate, and abstract (low-imagery) words most difficult to recall. The finding is consistent with the view that nonverbal imagery is of major importance even when recall must be verbally expressed. Before elaborating on this interpretation and considering alternative ones, however, it is important to determine the potency of the effect of con-

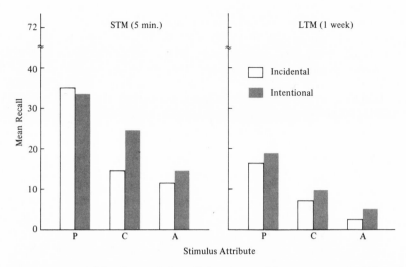

FIGURE 7-7.   Free verbal recall for pictures (P), concrete words (C), and abstract words (A) after different retention intervals and under intentional or incidental learning conditions.

creteness-imagery relative to other meaning attributes. The comparisons involve verbal stimuli only, and the important variables, as before, are the criterion indices of verbal representational meaning and verbal associative meaning, namely, frequency-familiarity and meaningfulness, respectively.

Frequency-Familiarity Compared with Word Imagery

The effects of frequency and familiarity are inconsistent across experiments. High-frequency words have been found easier to recall than low-frequency words, in a number of studies (e.g., W. A. Bousfield & Cohen, 1955; Deese, 1960; Hall, 1954; Murdock, 1960). While consistent with what would be generally expected (cf. Adams, 1967, pp. 156–157), the finding is not the rule. Peters (1936) found no effect of frequency on recall. In a factor-analytic study involving various dimensions of meaning, Paivio (1968) also found essentially no correlation between free recall and either Thorndike-Lorge frequency (which varied over the range of 1 to more than 100 occurrences per million in the word lists) or ratings of familiarity and "usualness." In the case of the rating measures, the direction of the relation was in fact negative. Frincke (1968) similarly obtained no correlation between frequency and free recall, and found a negative correlation of —.33 between rated familiarity and recall.

The Frincke and Paivio data may conceal a curvilinear relation, which was not tested for in those studies. Winnick and Kressel (1965) tested for recall of concrete and abstract words immediately after subjects had provided written associations (m data) to the words. They obtained a significant interaction of abstractness-concreteness by frequency, so that recall was slightly better for high-frequency words when they were concrete, and very slightly superior for low-frequency words when they were abstract. Dukes and Bastian (1966) also found a significant interaction of the two variables, but the pattern differed somewhat from that of Winnick and Kressel: Low-frequency words were easier to recall than high-frequency words when the nouns were abstract, but frequency had no effect when the nouns were concrete. The consistent aspect of both studies was that frequency was negatively related to recall within abstract words but not within concrete words. A clearer interaction was obtained by Paivio and Madigan (1970) using mixed lists containing concrete and abstract nouns of high and low frequency. Subjects learned two 32-item lists of this kind, each presented for 10 trials. The results are presented in Figure 7-8, which shows that concrete nouns were consistently easier to recall than abstract nouns regardless of frequency. However, high-frequency words were easier to recall than low-frequency words when they were concrete, whereas low-frequency words were superior on the first five trials when they were abstract. Considered along with the somewhat similar patterns obtained by Winnick and Kressel and Dukes and Bastian, this interaction can be regarded as a reliable finding for mixed lists. Comparable studies are needed using homogeneous lists, but at this point it can be concluded that the effects of frequency-familiarity vary from negative, to zero, to positive in different experiments and as a function of variation on word concreteness.

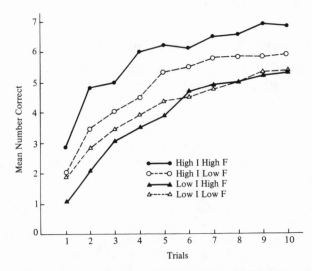

FIGURE 7-8.   Free recall learning over 10 trials as a function of noun imagery (I) and frequency (F). From Paivio and Madigan (1970).

The interaction of frequency and concreteness remains to be explained, and an attempt will be made later to do so. The relevant point here is that frequency alone in no way explains the more potent and consistently positive effect of word imagery-concreteness.

Associative Meaningfulness and Imagery Compared

Dukes and Bastian (1966) and Tulving et al. (1965) held m and rated meaningfulness, respectively, constant; thus there is no question that the positive effects of concreteness and vividness they obtained were independent of meaningfulness. Paivio (1967) found that a slight correlation between free recall and m was reduced to zero when I was partialed out, whereas I correlated significantly with recall when m was similarly controlled. Frincke's (1968) study yielded entirely comparable results for imagery-concreteness and m.

The above studies did not insure that m and I were varied over equivalent ranges. This was done by Paivio, Yuille, and Rogers (1969). The two attributes were varied over high and low levels, with the difference in levels being roughly equated according to standard score units based on the respective distributions of the two variables in the pool of 925 nouns from which the lists were selected. One experiment involved 24-item lists that were mixed with respect to attribute level; that is, one list included high- and low-I nouns equated on m, and the other, high- and low-m nouns with I held constant. A second experiment involved 12-item lists homogeneous in regard to attribute and level (e.g., one list consisted entirely of high-I nouns, etc.). Both experiments revealed positive overall effects for the two variables. The most important finding, however, was an interaction of attribute by level, which occurred in both experiments. The interactions are shown in Figure 7-9, where it can be seen that the positive effect of

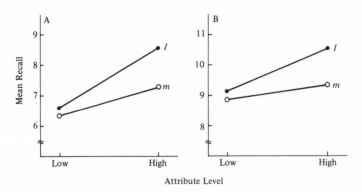

FIGURE 7-9. Interactions showing greater effect of low-high variation in I than of m on free recall in experiments involving lists mixed with respect to the levels of an attribute (A) and with lists homogeneous in both attribute and level (B). Based on data in Paivio, Yuille, and Rogers (1969).

I is greater than that of *m* in each case. In fact, the difference between low and high *m* words was significant only in Experiment I.

It is clear from the above experiments that *I* is a more potent variable than *m* in free recall. As we shall see, this is particularly important when it comes to the interpretation of the effects, since *m* has been regarded as a measure of potential mediating associations in verbal learning, and such associations have been thought to have only facilitative effects in free recall, as compared to the interfering effects that have been postulated for them in recognition memory (see above) and in paired-associate learning (see Chapter 8).

In summary, the effect of imagery-concreteness on free recall cannot be attributed to the processes that specifically underlie measures of either frequency-familiarity or *m*. Other obvious semantic attributes such as emotionality, semantic differential meaning dimensions, distinctiveness, and the like are also ruled out inasmuch as these were included in the factor-analytic study by Paivio (1968) and were found not to be related to recall (see also Frincke, 1968). The major fact to be explained, then, is the singular and consistent positive effect of imagery-concreteness in free recall. Alternative possible interpretations are examined in the following sections.

Physical Stimulus Characteristics as a Possible Explanation of the Memorability of Pictures

It might be argued that the superiority of pictures in free recall is due to some physical characteristic of pictorial stimuli, such as vividness or multiplicity of cues, which might enhance their memorability. An analysis of this kind was presented by Bousfield et al. (1957) to account for the superiority they found for pictures presented along with words, as compared with words alone. They suggested that a written name is a well-established response to the appropriate sign (word or picture) and becomes conditioned to the data sheets, which function as conditioned stimuli for the written response during a recall trial. Conditioning was presumably a function of the compounding of elements in the unconditioned stimulus when pictures, especially colored ones, accompanied the stimulus words. In actual fact, their experimental procedure does not fit the classical conditioning model satisfactorily and an explanation in such terms therefore does not appear superior to one based on the ancient wax tablet metaphor, according to which one might say that concrete stimuli simply make a particularly deep impression on memory. Nevertheless, it could be argued that some physical characteristic, such as compounding of elements or vividness, is the effective variable even if the precise psychological mechanism for such an effect is uncertain.

The above interpretation was tested by Paivio, Rogers, and Smythe (1968), who compared recall for uncolored (outline) pictures of objects, colored pictures, uncolored words (the labels of the pictures), and colored words. Maximum variation in colors was used across stimuli, and the word colors exactly matched the colors of the corresponding (referent) pictured objects. Different groups were presented unmixed lists of the different stimulus modes. It was reasoned that either the stimulus vividness hypothesis or the multiplicity-of-cues hypothesis would predict superior recall for the colored versions of the pictures or words. While the results showed higher recall for pictures than for words, the effect of color was nonsignificant and in a direction contrary to expectation. It appears, therefore, that concreteness in the sense of object character is sufficient to facilitate recall and that added color cues are irrelevant or redundant. The negative trend for color seems somewhat discrepant with that of W. A. Bousfield et al. (1957), who found better recall for words presented together with colored rather than uncolored pictures. They did not include a picture condition without the accompanying names, so that direct comparisons with the Paivio et al. experiment are difficult, but an explanation in terms of compounding of elements or physical vividness in any case does not suffice to account for the findings and is inapplicable to the imagery effect at the word level.

The Dual-Coding Hypothesis and Free Recall

The effects of imagery-concreteness can be alternatively interpreted in terms of the dual-coding hypothesis presented at the beginning of the chapter. However, that model provides only a general framework within which further specific alternatives can be considered. Since imagery increases with concreteness but verbal meaning does not, it is possible that the effect on recall is due entirely to imagery. As concreteness increases, the subject is increasingly likely to store the item as an image, and recall is enhanced because the image is somehow more memorable than the verbal code. Inasmuch as we are dealing here with verbal recall, it must be assumed at the same time that the image can be readily transformed into the verbal code during retrieval. This poses no problem within the theory, since it states that the two coding systems are interconnected at the level of referential meaning. In effect, the image can be named in the same way as the object itself, since in both cases the reactions are presumably mediated by their interconnected representations (Chapter 3). What remains unanswered within the hypothesis is why images should be superior to words as memory codes. Until a reasonable mechanism can be suggested, the hypothesis does no more than restate the fact that pictures are easier to recall than words. We shall return to this issue later.

Another possibility within the dual-coding framework is the coding redundancy hypothesis: Recall increases with concreteness because the items are increasingly likely to be stored in *both* the verbal and the nonverbal code, or at least experienced in both forms. Thus concrete words not only are read or heard but some of them also evoke referent images; familiar pictures are perceived (images are aroused), and implicit labeling is highly probable particularly if the subject knows that verbal recall will be required. The increased availability of both codes increases the probability of item recall because the response can be retrieved from either code—one code could be forgotten during the retention interval, but verbal recall would still be possible provided that the other is retained. This interpretation relates the concreteness effect to another phenomenon. Bevan, Dukes, and Avant (1966) reported three experiments that showed that variation in the specific stimuli that represented an object class enhanced recall of that class. For example, more names of familiar objects, such as "apple," and "shoe," were recalled when photographs of two different specimens (e.g., a red apple and a yellow apple) were presented than when a single specimen was presented twice. The dual-coding interpretation of the concreteness effect implies an analogous phenomenon at the implicit level. If a subject generates an image to a concrete word or implicitly labels a picture, he is essentially exposed to two very different representatives of the same object class. The appropriateness of the analogy can be questioned but, to the extent that it is valid, our understanding of the concreteness effect is broadened even if the stimulus (or code) variation effect itself is not thereby explained. Since the interpretation of the latter remains uncertain (Daves & Adkins, 1969), as does the validity of the analogy, we need not pursue the matter further.

The image-superiority and coding-redundancy interpretations have not been directly compared in research to date, but the latter tends to be favored because the stimulus variation effect provides an empirical analogue and because other evidence suggests that the availability of both codes enhances recall of pictures. Procedures designed to encourage verbalization of familiar pictures during their presentation have been shown to enhance subsequent verbal recall of pictures (e.g., Bahrick & Boucher, 1968; Kurtz & Hovland, 1953; Wilgosh, 1970), although verbalization generally has little or no effect on recognition memory, at least with adult subjects (see above). The effect on recall cannot be interpreted solely in terms of verbal mechanisms, for we have already seen that verbal recall is higher when the stimulus items are presented as pictures than when they are presented as words. Considered together, these data indicate that recall increases from abstract words, to concrete words, to pictures presented alone, to pictures-plus-verbalization. The progression is consistent with hypothesis that recall is a function of the increasing availability of both codes, as the redundancy hypothesis suggests. Note that this hypothesis implies independent storage systems for the imaginal and verbal codes corresponding to the same object. Bahrick and Boucher (1968) considered such independent storage as improbable in relation to their recall and recognition data, but it certainly cannot be rejected here on the basis of the evidence that is presently available. The problem will be discussed again later in the context of a study by Paivio and Csapo (1969), which was explicitly designed to test some implications of the dual-coding model for free recall as well as for other memory tasks.

The alternative interpretations of the modus operandi of the two coding systems in free recall pertain to storage or retention mechanisms. One proposal attributes the recall effects to qualitative differences (images are easier to remember than words), the other to quantitative differences (two codes are better than one). Neither hypothesis has anything to say about memory processes per se, i.e., storage, retention, or retrieval mechanisms, which may be differentially involved in the functioning of the two codes in free recall as well as in other memory tasks. Alternative interpretations of such mechanisms will be considered next.

Organization versus Independent Storage of Items

One of the most important theoretical problems that has arisen in connection with free recall learning concerns the form in which items are stored (see Tulving, 1968). According to the organization (or interdependence) hypothesis, items beyond immediate memory span are not recalled as independent units; instead some kind of associative principle operates to reduce the memory load involved in recall by facilitating interitem organization or clustering of items into higher-order memory units. According to the independence hypothesis, free recall is a function of the response strength or the availability of the items as independent units—the recall of one item is not dependent on the recall of other items in a list. Because an understanding of these hypotheses is important to later discussions and because they are of interest in their own right, they will be discussed in some detail.

The organization hypothesis   The concept of organization has already been discussed in relation to meaning and perception under such rubrics as structural or associative relationships. Even more directly relevant to the present discussion was the centrality of organization as a memory principle in the ancient mnemonic systems and their successors, as we saw in the last chapter. Simonides stressed the importance of an orderly arrangement of memory places, and the author of the *Ad Herennium* advocated that every fifth place be marked in some distinctive fashion so that we will not err in remembering the order of the loci. Subsequent proponents of mnemonic systems, such as Camillo, Bruno, and Feinaigle, developed elaborate models in which hierarchical organization was a dominant feature. These memory treatises anticipated modern psychological views on organizational factors in memory, but there is a striking difference in the symbolic elements that have been emphasized—while the ancients primarily stressed nonverbal images, the contemporary emphasis has been almost exclusively on verbal mechanisms as the basis of organization. It is the adequacy of the latter as an explanation of the effects of stimulus attributes on free recall that we shall examine here, for the conceptual and methodological tools have been most fully developed in that context.

Central to the contemporary approaches are the concepts of *clustering* and *subjective organization* of recall. Clustering was defined by W. A. Bousfield (1953) as the occurrence of sequences of related items in the free recall of a randomly ordered list. Relatedness is specified by the experimenter in terms of such characteristics as membership in a common conceptual category, interitem associations based on association norms, synonymity, parts of speech, and so on. The typical experimental approach involves the presentation of a list containing two or more subsets of items from different categories, such as animals and countries, or different sets of associatively rated items, etc. The amount of clustering is measured in terms of the extent to which items from a given subset are recalled in immediately adjacent positions, as compared to the number of such sequential occurrences that would be expected by chance (see A. K. Bousfield & W. A. Bousfield, 1966).

Clustering measures have the advantage in that they can be calculated on the basis of a single free recall trial. Tulving (e.g., 1962, 1968) saw their main disadvantage as being the fact that they are experimenter-defined and therefore underestimate the degree of organization that might actually have occurred. Even when the presented list consists of words from different conceptual categories, a subject's recall might reflect an organizational basis that cuts across those categories. Such organization would not be detected by the typical cluster analysis. Tulving accordingly developed a measure he calls subjective organization, which is defined in terms of consistency of output orders on successive free recall trials, occurring despite variations in the order of presentation of items from trial to trial. A modified form of Tulving's method was developed by W. A. Bousfield, Puff, and Cowan (1964), who proposed the term intertrial repetition to refer to the sequential ordering effect described by Tulving. (For a comparison of the two methods, see Puff & Hyson, 1967.) Variants of these and other measures of organization have been developed but will not be discussed here except where they have been employed in relevant experiments.

The significance of clustering and subjective organization is twofold. First, the amount of organization is related to various characteristics of the items presented for recall. A. K. Bousfield and W. A. Bousfield (1966), for example, list 15 characteristics that have been found in groups of sequentially occurring items in different experiments. These include interitem associations, mediated interitem associations, grammatical sequences, alphabetical sequences in the initial letters of words, similarity of connotative meaning, von Restorff effects, and so on. Second, with some exceptions, the measures of organization have been found to correlate with the number of words recalled (see Tulving, 1968), as have the item characteristics that affect organization (see below). The relevant point here is that many of the variables that affect organization are dimensions of meaning, and it can be asked whether the potency of concreteness in free recall, as well as the effects (or lack of effects) of the other attributes with which we are concerned, might also be mediated through organizational processes. Before confronting that issue directly, the theoretical views and evidence concerning such processes will be examined in more detail.

Theoretical interpretations of the factors underlying organization and recall have emphasized either conceptual categories or associative relations as the basis of the effects. Bousfield originally interpreted category clustering in terms of the activation of superordinate structures by the subordinate instances represented in the list. The occurrence of items such as dog, cat, and lion, for example, would activate the superordinate "animal." During recall, the retrieval of one item would activate the superordinate structure, which would then activate the other subordinates, resulting in the clustered recall of items belonging to the same conceptual category. The alternative view is the already-familiar verbal association hypothesis. J. J. Jenkins and Russell (1952) constructed a list of 48 words consisting of 24 pairs selected on the basis of their Kent-Rosanoff norms (cf. Russell & Jenkins, 1954) to be strong associates, such as table-chair. The words were randomly presented for recall. Associative clustering was found in that the associated words, although separated during presentation, tended to be recalled together as clustered pairs. Such clustering is also predicted by associative overlap scores, that is, the degree to which pairs of words in a list share common associations that need not appear in the list (Marshall, as described by Cofer, 1965, pp. 267–269).

The possibility has been entertained that category clustering is simply a special case of associative clustering, but it now appears that conceptual categories can be effective bases for organization even when association strength is held constant. The Marshall study cited above included categorized and noncategorized pairs along with the (independent) variation in associative overlap. The findings showed greater clustering for the categorized pairs at each level of overlap. Cofer (1965, p. 271) concluded that a contrast between associational and categorical bases for clustering is not useful. Subjects will use either or both of these as bases for organizing their recall, and will find ways to organize even if the experimenter has not provided means in the list he presents.

The presence of conceptual categories and associative relations in a list presented for recall affect not only organization but the amount recalled as well. A few examples will serve to illustrate the effects of both types of relations. Underwood (1964, pp. 62–65) presented subjects with one of four lists of 16 words each for recall. Two lists contained words of low interitem (conceptual) similarity, for example, *daisy, wall, bee, second*; the other two contained four sets of words that were related in terms of their membership in a common conceptual category, such as countries, birds, or animals. The results for a single presentation and recall averaged about 11 items in the case of the unrelated lists, and over 14 in the case of the related lists. More dramatic results were obtained by Koeppel and Beecroft (1967) who repeated Underwood's experiment using a single 64-item list in which the two types of lists used by Underwood were mixed together, with the related words well-dispersed in the list. Six trials were given. The results are presented in Figure 7-10, where it can be seen that the facilitative effect of conceptual similarity was large. On the first trial, the ratio of recall of related to unrelated words was approximately four to one.

Associative relatedness was investigated by Deese (1959), who used his Index of Interitem Associative Strength to construct lists varying in the degree to which all the items of a list tend to elicit one another as free associates. He obtained a striking correlation of .88 between this index and the number of words recalled.

While it can be concluded from the above studies that conceptual and associative similarity among items are positively related to clustering and recall, a number of prominent researchers in the area (e.g., Cofer, 1965; Deese, 1968; G. Mandler, 1968; Tulving, 1968) have recently emphasized that such rela-

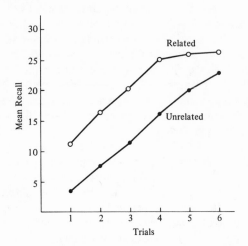

FIGURE 7-10.   Mean recall of related
and unrelated words as a function of trials. From
Koeppel and Beecroft (1967).

tionships do not constitute explanations of the phenomena. The relationships are correlational rather than causal. Deese (1968, p. 100), for example, has stated that associations are certainly not the cause of organization in recall, contrary to what he and others had implied earlier (e.g., Deese, 1959). The explanation is to be found in deeper structures of association, whose nature remains to be determined. Without attempting to propose such a theory, we shall examine some of the theoretical mechanisms that have been thought to be important in the interpretation of organization and memory.

G. A. Miller's (1956) concept of *chunking,* or unitization, occupies a central position in the interpretation of the relationship between organization and recall. Miller found that the immediate memory span was relatively constant at "seven plus or minus two" units over a wide range of materials and situations. What varies, however, is the size of the unit, lower-order elements becoming grouped into larger wholes, or "chunks," that can function as unitary memorial elements. Such chunking is particularly evident in language as a result of associative experiences, so that syllables are chunked into word units, words into higher-order phrase units, and so on (see Chapter 3). Tulving and Patkau (1962) took advantage of the notion of chunking and a procedure used by G. A. Miller and Selfridge (1950) in an analysis of free recall. Miller and Selfridge showed that the number of words recalled from long lists increased as the sequence of words presented increasingly approximated the statistical structure of English. In a similar experiment, Tulving and Patkau examined the recall protocols of their subjects in terms of "adopted chunks," which was defined as an uninterrupted sequence of words at recall corresponding to a similar sequence at presentation. They found that the number of words recalled varied with Thorndike-Lorge frequency and with order of approximation to English, but the number of adopted chunks that were recalled remained invariant at about six. The findings are consistent with the hypothesis that adopted chunks constitute the unit of recall, and that about six of these units (approximating the storage capacity of immediate memory, according to Miller) can be handled at one time. Similar results were also obtained by McNulty (1966). The relevance of these findings and the concept of chunking in the present context is that they can be applied to the interpretation of variables that affect organization and recall. For example, Cofer (1965, p. 270) suggested that highly associated words in a free recall list function as integrated units or structures.

Closely related to chunking is the concept of recoding (G. A. Miller, 1956). Recoding occurs when a group of items that are related in some way are given a new label. Thus, "apples, bananas, and oranges" can be recoded as "fruit." An important implication of the concept is that categorized lists of items might be recalled on the basis of such recoding (e.g., B. H. Cohen, 1963). More generally, such a view makes it possible to conceptualize memory structure in hierarchical terms.

G. Mandler (1967, 1968) has prepared such a structural model, which assumes that the organization of words in permanent storage follows a hierarchical schema in which the members of a category are subsumed under a superordinate category. For example, the superordinate category "acquaintances" includes family, social, and professional groups as subordinates, family subsumes blood relatives and others, and so on. The limit of the organized system is assumed to be about five units at each level of the hierarchy, with the same limit for the number of levels in any single organizational hierarchy. Retrieval from memory, as in a free recall experiment, presumably involves a search process within and between different levels of a hierarchy. Performance depends on the search time for units, which in turn depends upon how far apart the items are within the hierarchical structure. Such concepts as synonymity and meaning within such a system can be defined in terms of structural distances between words and a word's position within the hierarchy (cf. the discussion of structural meaning in Chapter 3), and measures of clustering and associative probabilities are indices of such parameters of the organizational structure.

Some information is available on relevant aspects of the model and its relation to free recall performance from G. Mandler's research (e.g., 1967), and Bower, Clark, Lesgold, and Winzenz (1969) recently demonstrated an impressive facilitating effect on recall when items are presented in a hierarchically organized pattern rather than randomly. Nevertheless, the model represents a preliminary statement. What is needed, according to Mandler, are rules about category formation and search patterns within the organization, as well as information on the mechanisms that enable one to get from the physical stimulus to the initial location within the system. The last point raises the general problem of retrieval cues in free recall.

Tulving (1968) in particular has emphasized the importance of retrieval systems as compared to storage of information in memory. The central problem is the identification of retrieval cues that provide access to and recovery of material from memory storage. Theoretically, such cues operate at every level of a hierarchical storage system such as Mandler proposes. One higher-order unit, such as a category label, could serve as a retrieval cue for other units, and one member of a higher-order unit serve as a retrieval cue for other members within the unit, and so on. Tulving and Pearlstone (1966) experimentally investigated the role of such retrieval cues in the recall of words from a categorized list. The list included category names, such as "vegetables" and "countries," each followed by words belonging to those categories. List length and number of words per category were varied. Subjects were tested only for their recall of the category instances, half the subjects within each condition being provided with the category names as cues during recall, and the other half being tested without the presence of such cues. The results showed cued recall to be higher than noncued recall for all combinations of the input variables. Moreover, the presentation of the category label as a cue affected only the number of accessible categories but not the number of words within a category, where accessibility was defined in terms of recall of at least one word from the category. Thus retrieval cues facilitated recall because they enabled subjects to recall more categories. Given access to a category, the words presumably were recalled as a unitary cluster. The finding and conclusions have been supported by other experiments using different procedures, including subject- rather than experimenter-organized word categories (e.g., Dong & Kintsch, 1968; G. Mandler, 1967) and analyses of inter-word response times as well amount recalled (e.g., Pollio, Richards, & Lucas, 1969).

The demonstrated effectiveness of retrieval cues has direct implications for the findings discussed thus far and for the later analysis of the possible role of imagery and other meaning attributes in free recall. Where items of a list are associatively related, recall of one member of such a group would provide the retrieval cue for other members of the cluster by associative arousal. In the case of lists containing conceptual or taxonomic categories, the category label presumably mediates the recall of the items within the category. Thus, Underwood (1964) suggested that the basic memory unit involved in the conceptual-similarity effect on recall is the category name as an implicit response. Its capacity as a retrieval cue is acquired during list presentation: An item such as "foxtrot" elicits the implicit category name "dance." When "waltz" is presented, it too should elicit the same implicit response, and so on. Thus the frequency of the implicit response "dance" is higher than that of any of the subordinate members of that category, and it tends to be remembered on the recall trial. In turn, it functions as an implicit retrieval cue for the members of the category. A similar analysis of mediation of recall by common cue-producing (implicit) responses has been presented by W. A. Bousfield, Steward, and Cowan (1964).

What factors control the occurrence of the initial retrieval cues? One possibility is suggested by the "spew" hypothesis (Underwood & Schulz, 1960, Chapter 6), according to which high-frequency words tend to be emitted first in free responding situations. This is implied in Underwood's (1964) analysis, described above, where the category label is assumed to be the most frequent (implicit) response during list presentation. Thus it is likely to be "emitted" to serve as a retrieval cue for a category word during the recall trial. The stimulus for emission remains unknown, however. Another interpretation (Tulving, 1968, p. 13) is based on the empirical finding of a recency effect in free recall (e.g., Murdock, 1962) and the idea of a rapidly decaying acoustic trace of recently presented items in immediate memory (Sperling, 1963): The items in the terminal serial position during input of a list are retrieved first from the "echo box" and then function as retrieval cues for other associatively or conceptually related responses. Deese (1959) proposed essentially the same idea, suggesting that recall consists of a small core of words directly available through immediate memory and of free associations to those words. The spew and echo box hypotheses obviously do not exhaust the possible hypothetical "mechanisms" that could be suggested as the basis for the initial retrieval of items in free recall, but they serve to identify the problem.

To summarize the organization hypothesis of free recall, it states that items are not retrieved as independent units but are interdependent, so that the recall of one item affects the recall of another. It assumes that immediate memory span imposes a basic limit on what can be recalled. The fact that recall for word units can exceed the span is explained in terms of the unitization or chunking of word units into higher-order structures, which in turn are recalled as units. It is the size of the functional units that varies in recall; the number of units that can be recalled presumably remains invariant. The formation of higher-order units is related to such factors as direct associative connections based on language habits, indirect associations, conceptual similarity, and so on. Clustering and subjective organization are the empirical manifestations of the underlying organizational structure, and the number of items recalled depends on the degree of organization that is possible under the conditions of a given experiment, and on the availability of effective retrieval cues.

The independence hypothesis   The independence hypothesis of storage in free recall has been expressed most uncompromisingly in terms of the concept of item availability by Asch and Ebenholtz (1962). They suggested that free recall does not depend upon interitem associations but instead depends solely upon availability of items in memory. They define availability as "accessibility to recall" and assume that it is a function of such variables as frequency and recency of exposure to the items of a list. These defining attributes of the concept have recently been made more explicit by Horowitz et al. (1966). They measure the concept in terms of the probability that an item can be recalled after a 15-second delay, and they demonstrated that availability grows fastest if the subject produces the item from memory. Availability also grows, but less rapidly, when the subject merely sees the items without producing it. Horowitz et al. did not apply the concept to free recall, but their defining operations accentuate a point made by Tulving (1968, p. 23) regarding Asch and Ebenholtz's use of the concept: It appears to be a redundant descriptive label for recall probability rather than an explanation of recall. Nevertheless, the suggestion that free recall is not dependent upon interitem associations is theoretically meaningful and testable.

Several studies bearing on the alternative hypotheses have been reported. Tulving (1966) conducted a transfer experiment in which subjects learned a "whole" list of 18 words after they had learned a "part" of the list, i.e., nine words. In another experiment (Tulving & Osler, 1967), subjects learned the nine-word list following the learning of the 18-word whole list. The reasoning behind the experiments was that, according to the independence hypothesis, transfer should be positive inasmuch as the traces of items, their availability, or their associations with the general experimental context (another version of the independence hypothesis) would be strengthened during memorization of items in the first list. The learning of the items in the second list should thus be facilitated. According to the interdependence hypothesis, on the other hand, there would be no reason to expect positive transfer in either case. The learning of a list that exceeds memory span requires the organization of items into higher-order units, and the higher-order units formed during the learning of the first list would be inappropriate in the second. Some of them would have to be modified or entirely new units would have to be formed, at least in the case of randomly selected words. The results were clear: Consistent with the organization hypothesis and contrary to the independence position, *negative* transfer was obtained in both experiments.

Slamecka (1968) tested the alternative theories in a series of experiments in which, following list presentation, one group of subjects was provided with some of the list items during recall, and its recall of the remainder was compared with that of a group that had no items provided. The rationale was that the presented items provide a context that, according to the interdependence hypothesis, should facilitate recall. Some of the context items would not have been recalled ordinarily, and their presentation should stimulate retrieval of those trace items with which they had been in contact in storage. If independent storage is the rule, however, there should be no difference in recall between the groups because functionally isolated traces should be immune to any changes in other traces. The results were fully consistent with the independence hypothesis: The provision of context even to the maximum degree possible did not facilitate recall performance. In discussing his results, Slamecka does not deny the importance of organization in free recall. While items may be stored independently, the output may be organized because of an orderly retrieval plan based, perhaps, on stored information concerning list structure.

The situation at present thus appears to be indeterminate regarding the alternative hypotheses of trace storage in free recall. While they have not been rigorously tested in the context of the meaning attributes under consideration in the present chapter, some results have been obtained that bear on the issue and therefore have implications for the theoretical interpretation of the effects of imagery-concreteness and the other attributes.

Imagery-concreteness and organization of recall   Item concreteness and imagery could be interpreted as having their effect through organizational factors, such as the facilitation of associative connections with other items, whether these operate during storage or retrieval. This seems particularly reasonable in the light of the finding that the image-evoking value of stimulus terms is a potent determinant of the formation of associations in paired-associate learning (see Chapter 8). In free recall, the initial retrieval of a few high-imagery items could provide effective retrieval cues for other items, perhaps via mediating images. If this is so, organization as measured by subjective organization or intertrial repetition indexes should be higher for concrete, high-imagery nouns than for abstract, low-imagery nouns, and for pictures than for words. Several studies provide evidence on the issue.

With respect to noun imagery, Tulving et al. (1965) found that their better-recalled vivid words were also subjectively organized to a greater extent than less vivid words, and accordingly suggested that "vividness or picturability is an important component of meaning of words that affects the ease with which words can be grouped into higher-order units" (p. 250). Such an interpretation of object superiority in free recall is similarly supported by Scott's (1967) finding of greater clustering of objects than of words even when the absolute amount of recall is statistically controlled. Paivio and Csapo (1969) showed the relationship over three levels of concreteness, with the degree of organization as measured by the A. K. Bousfield and W. A. Bousfield (1966) intertrial repetition index increasing from abstract words, to concrete words, to pictures. These findings are all consistent with the organization interpretation of the facilitative effect of concreteness-imagery in free recall.

Results inconsistent with the interpretation have been obtained in other studies. Paivio, Yuille, and Rogers (1969) did not find that organization was greater for high-I nouns, although they were recalled better than low-I nouns. Frincke (1968) found that words high in imagery-concreteness were more readily organized or clustered into groups than abstract, low-imagery words, but he also found that imagery remained significantly related to free recall when ease of clustering was held constant. Paivio, Rogers, and Smythe (1968) also failed to obtain higher intertrial organization for pictures than for the labels of the pictures, although the former were better recalled. Thus, while the organization hypothesis of the imagery-concreteness effect in free recall is supported by some studies, the relations expected on the basis of that interpretation have not been obtained in others.

It could be argued that some kind of organization occurred even in the case of the studies that yielded negative results but was not detected by the measures of organization or clustering employed in those studies. For example, effective organizational processes might involve what Tulving (1968) has termed "primary organization," which refers to consistent discrepancies between the order in which items are presented and the order in which they are recalled, independent of the subject's prior familiarity with the set of items involved. Primacy and recency effects in free recall are examples of such primary organization. Some suggestive evidence relevant to this interpretation will be discussed later in the context of short-term memory studies, but in general it must be concluded that the role of organizational factors in the concreteness effect remains in doubt.[2]

Word frequency effects and organization of recall   The effects of frequency on recall were found to be inconsistent, the relation varying from positive to negative in different studies. The evidence on interitem organization in relation to the effect is also ambiguous. Deese (1959) obtained positive relations between frequency and recall, which increased in magnitude as list length increased. Deese (1961) interpreted the finding in terms of interword associations. Such associations are more likely to occur among random collections of familiar words than of unfamiliar words because responses in association generally tend to be high-frequency words. The probability of associative clusters would thus be higher and recall would be differentially enhanced in the case of high-frequency words.

On the other hand Matthews (1966) found better recall for low- than for high-frequency words when the lists in each case consisted of associatively related words. These lists were comprised of a series of associatively related three-word groups, and clustering into the appropriate triplets was also greater during recall in the case of the less frequent words. Matthews interpreted the results in terms of associative interference (Underwood & Schulz, 1960). The number of associative groups to which high-frequency responses could be connected may be greater than those to which low-frequency words could be related. Since recall is a function of associative clustering, the greater number of alternatives that are possible to the high-frequency words may reduce the efficiency of clustering and introduce incorrect, although associatively related, words into the responses. This interpretation was supported by data that indicated that the high-frequency words were more loosely organized in the sense that they had relatively more connections outside of their particular associative triplets than did the low-frequency words. Matthews suggested that the superiority of the low-frequency words may thus be reducible to a process dependent on the frequency of experience of words occurring normally in few rather than varied contexts.

Matthews' interpretation can be viewed as a kind of distinctiveness hypothesis of free recall, in which distinctiveness applies to functional units or chunks rather than to individual words. According to such a view, interitem associations would facilitate recall to the extent that they enter into distinctive higher-order units,

---

[2] It should be noted that this conclusion applies specifically to imagery-concreteness as an item attribute and not to imagery as an experimentally-manipulated process, since it has been clearly shown that imagery instructions designed to promote clustering of items can have powerful effects on recall (e.g., Bower, Lesgold, & Tieman, 1969). Such studies are described in Chapter 10.

and to the extent that the number of such units is optimal for recall. Whether such an interpretation suffices to account for the variable effect of frequency in different experiments and its interaction with concreteness in the Paivio and Madigan (1970) experiment remains speculative, but it is at least plausible and testable.

Meaningfulness and organization of recall   The above analysis of frequency effects can be extended directly to the relation between associative meaningfulness and recall. In the study described earlier, Paivio, Yuille, and Rogers (1969) compared the relative effects of I and m when the two were varied over an equivalent range in different lists. They reasoned that the typical superiority of I as compared to m in paired-associate learning (see Chapter 8) might not be obtained in free recall. This was a deduction from the "interference paradox" of associative probability (Underwood & Schulz, 1960), according to which the effects of meaningfulness in associative learning can be either positive or negative, depending upon whether or not the implicit associative responses evoked by high m words mediate more correct associations than erroneous, interfering, ones in a given experimental situation. In the case of free recall, however, the implicit verbal associations should mediate greater clustering of high m than low m items and thereby enhance recall without creating the same possibility of associative interference. The postulated mediational mechanism is in principle the same as that proposed by Underwood as the explanation of conceptual similarity effects in free recall, the specific difference being that any mediation presumably would result from associative overlap in general rather than from common category names. The contrasting predictions for free recall and paired-associate learning were confirmed by Wallace and Underwood (1964), who found superior free recall with high-similarity lists than with low-similarity lists, whereas the reverse occurred in paired-associate learning, at least with normal subjects. (The design also included retarded subjects, a feature that will not be discussed here.) The results were attributed to facilitative and interfering effects of implicit associative responses.

As indicated earlier, the effect of m in the Paivio, Yuille, and Rogers (1969) study was smaller than that of I in two experiments. In the second of these, involving homogeneous lists of one or the other level of the attribute, the effect of m did not reach significance. Neither did intertrial organization scores differ for high m and low m lists. Thus, the prediction from associative probability theory was not supported. How are the negative effects to be explained? Matthews' analysis of frequency effects suggests one possibility: The associative overlap resulting from implicit associations might mean that some items enter into more than one mediationally defined cluster, thereby interfering with the formation of higher-order units. Increasing list m might result in a uniform increase in both facilitative and interfering associations, canceling out any differential effects that might have occurred. The hypothesis is speculative and somewhat cumbersome. Nevertheless, it is plausible and testable, e.g., by experimental manipulation of within-list associative overlap in such a manner as to create "cluster-confusion" as compared to an optimal number of mediationally differentiated clusters.

Summary and Theoretical Conclusions Concerning Free Recall and Meaning

The major empirical findings can be briefly summarized. At the level of meaningful verbal material and objects or their pictures, free recall is consistently related (positively) only to imagery-concreteness. The number of items recalled is highest in the case of objects or pictures, intermediate for their concrete-noun labels, and least for abstract, low-imagery words. The effects of word frequency and associative meaningfulness are weaker by comparison and inconsistent across experiments. The inconsistency in the case of frequency could be due to undetected interactions with item imagery, which have been demonstrated in studies involving manipulation of both variables in a factorial design. A number of other semantic and associative variables have failed to be significant predictors of recall.

The effect of concreteness is generally consistent with the dual-coding model, but alternative interpretations are possible within that framework. The effect could be related entirely to the increasing availability of imagery as concreteness increases, which implies that images are somehow qualitatively superior to words as memory codes. Alternatively, the effect could be interpreted in terms of coding redundancy, i.e., the increasing availability of two codes as concreteness increases. A definitive choice between the two cannot be made at this time, although the redundancy hypothesis tends to be favored. That the effect of concreteness may be mediated through organizational processes as opposed to independent storage of items has been supported by clustering data in some studies but not in others. The inconsistent and weaker effects of the other attributes are compatible with the view that direct or mediated interitem associations could either aid or interfere with the formation of higher-order functional units or chunks. There is a clear need, however, for further systematic evidence on the relations between meaning, organizational factors, and amount recalled before such views can be reasonably evaluated. More generally, the contributions of storage, retention, and retrieval mechanisms need to be differentiated in the various effects.

SERIAL LEARNING

Serial learning is distinguished from both recognition memory and free recall by the requirement that list items be retrieved sequentially, in their input order. Because of this feature of the task, serial learning was long regarded as the prototype of associative learning, each item being assumed to function in turn as stimulus and as response in an associative chain. That interpretation has recently become a matter of considerable controversy because predictions from it have failed to be confirmed in numerous experiments (see Underwood, 1963; Young, 1968). For example, strong positive transfer from serial to paired-associate learning would be expected but has generally not been obtained (e.g., Jensen & Rohwer, 1965b). Alternative interpretations have been proposed and supported, including the ordinal-position hypothesis (e.g., Young, 1962; Ebenholtz, 1963), which states that the functional stimulus is the position the item holds in the list; and response integration (e.g., Jensen & Rohwer, 1965b), according to which serial learning involves the formation of an integrated response unit. While the S-R chaining hypothesis has received renewed support from recent transfer experiments (e.g., Crowder, 1968; Postman & Stark, 1967; Saufley, 1967; Shuell & Keppel, 1967), it seems unlikely that it constitutes a sufficient explanation of serial learning.

It is unnecessary for our purposes to go into further detail regarding the above issues and the empirical evidence bearing on them, but they deserve mention because the basic processes underlying serial learning must be involved in the effects of relevant dimensions of meaning. In principle, therefore, such effects could shed some light on the theoretical mechanism involved, although the studies to date generally have not been designed for that purpose. An attempt will be made in any case to relate the findings to the issues wherever possible.

Imagery-Concreteness and Serial Learning

In one of the few studies that have been conducted on the effect of concreteness in serial learning, Paivio, Yuille, and Rogers (1969) speculated that, to the extent that mechanisms other than S-R association are involved in serial learning, associative imagery as indexed by noun I might be relatively less effective in serial recall than in free recall. Some support for this suggestion was provided by the finding that immediate memory span, a sequential recall task, does not differ for concrete and abstract nouns (Brener, 1940). The latter task does not involve repeated trials with the same item sequence, however, and it is unsafe to generalize from it to serial learning, as we shall see.

The same 12-item lists were used as in the free recall experiment described in the preceding section. One list consisted of high-I, and the other of low-I items, with m and frequency controlled. Two experiments (Experiments III and IV in the published report) were conducted with slight differences in procedure, each involving alternating study and serial recall trials. The results are shown in Figure 7-11, where it can be seen that noun imagery had a consistent positive effect from the first trial on in both experiments. Comparison with the free recall data from the same study indicated further that I was equally effective in the two tasks. It was suggested that the finding might support an interpretation of serial recall learning partly in terms of the facilitation of S-R chaining by associative imagery, although I might also have its effect through a nonassociative mechanism.

Pictures have also been found to be superior to words in serial learning (e.g.,

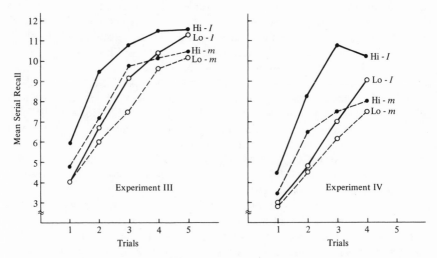

FIGURE 7-11.   Mean serial recall scores over trials as a function of high and low levels of list l and list m, in two experiments by Paivio, Yuille, and Rogers (1969).

Herman, Broussard, & Todd, 1951), although not without exception. Paivio and Csapo (1969) compared pictures, concrete nouns, and abstract nouns in serial recall learning and again found abstract nouns to be inferior to the other two stimulus types at the slower of two relatively fast rates of presentation. (The rationale for the rate manipulation and its effects will be discussed later.) However, pictures and concrete nouns did not differ, suggesting that pictures may not be as consistently superior to concrete nouns in that task as they are in both recognition memory and recall. These findings can perhaps be explained in terms of the dual-coding model. Serial learning requires the subject to retain item information, as in free recall, as well as sequential information. The superiority of concrete words and pictures over abstract words could be related to the availability of two codes and the facilitative effect of this on item retrieval. The less consistent result for picture-concrete noun comparisons could mean that the facilitating effect of increased imagery on item retrieval in the case of pictures is somewhat offset by the reduced availability of the verbal code, which is essential for the retrieval of order information. Whether pictures are superior to their names or not would thus be a function of other variables that affect the availability of the verbal code, such as rate of presentation, which was relatively fast (two items per second) even at the slower rate in the Paivio and Csapo experiment. We shall return to this issue later.

Frequency and Associative Meaningfulness in Serial Learning

Word frequency and m effects in serial learning are generally difficult to interpret because different dimensions of meaning have been confounded in the experiments. Postman (1961, 1962) compared high and low levels of Thorndike-Lorge frequency in two investigations involving serial learning. In one experiment, high-frequency words were found to exceed low-frequency words on m, and this can be assumed to be the case in the other experiment as well. Despite the confounding, the results are of interest because both variables have had inconsistent or weak effects in other memory tasks. Postman's results for both experiments showed the high-frequency lists to be learned faster, in terms of trials to criterion, than low-frequency lists. Since the other memory tasks have generally involved mean recall scores as the learning criterion, comparisons are somewhat uncertain, but the findings do suggest that frequency-m may have a more consistent positive effect in serial learning than in recognition memory or free recall.

Noble (1952b) found that high m lists were learned more easily than low m lists. Since the high m items consisted of meaningful words from his dissyllable list, whereas the low m items were nonsense words, the two levels undoubtedly differed on a number of meaning dimensions. Therefore, the m effect cannot be attributed to associative meaning per se. The same criticism also applies, although less strongly, to a study by Noble, Showell, and Jones (1966). They used consonant-vowel-consonant (CVC) trigrams scaled on meaningfulness according to Noble's (1961) m' index, which is based on group ratings of the number of associations a given CVC evokes. Association value (the relative frequency of subjects who reported at least one association to the CVC) was held constant at or near the upper limit of that scale. Thus the lists of CVCs included a large proportion of real words. It is likely nevertheless that m' was confounded with familiarity and imagery, since the upper end of the m' scale appears to include relatively more high-frequency concrete words than do the CVCs at lower values of the scale. The issue is of some consequence inasmuch as two independent experiments in the Noble et al. study showed serial learning to be a positive function of m'.

Clearer evidence of the effectiveness of m independent of frequency and I was obtained in the experiment by Paivio, Yuille, and Rogers (1969). Just as I had been varied with m constant, m was varied over high and low levels in two serial lists while I and frequency were held constant. The results for two experiments are presented in Figure 7-11 along with those for I, already discussed above. In both cases, serial recall learning was easier for high m than for low m lists. Although the effect of I appears to be greater than that of m in the second experiment, the Attribute by Attribute Level interaction does not reach significance. Thus it can be concluded that m and I have roughly equivalent effects in serial learning.

The pattern of relations differs from that obtained in recognition memory and free recall, where I consistently proved to be more effective than m, and it was in fact doubtful whether the latter had any effect at all. Too little research has yet been done to warrant strong conclusions, but the data suggest that the implicit verbal associations indexed by m somehow facilitate the formation of interitem sequential associations. Perhaps this occurs because the associative reactions evoked by a given list member do not mediate incorrect associations with items in remote serial positions. Until recently this would have seemed an illogical suggestion; it appears less so now in the light of Slamecka's (1964) evidence that remote associations may play little if any part in serial learning. To the extent that this is so, the effect of m could be explained in terms of the facilitation of sequential associations between items through verbal mediating processes.

MEANING AND SHORT-TERM MEMORY

Before considering the effect of stimulus meaning attributes on short-term memory (STM), we must dispose of the problem of how STM is to be defined. The definition can be in either theoretical or empirical terms, but the former is a matter of considerable controversy, while the latter involves rather arbitrary decisions about what is "short," etc. (cf. Melton, 1963; Postman, 1964). The problem is illustrated by single-trial free recall, which is often regarded as a STM task, yet both STM and long-term memory (LTM) processes have been invoked to explain certain features of the performance data (see below). The definitional problem cannot be resolved here, and STM will simply be defined in terms of the tasks that have generally been used to investigate STM and that involve a test of retention within seconds or at most a few minutes after presentation of the items. Relevant theoretical issues will be discussed in the context of the research findings.

Recent investigations of acoustic and semantic factors in STM provide an appropriate introduction to the issues because that research has raised the question of whether semantic factors are at all effective in STM. The subsequent sections on the effects of concreteness and other dimensions of meaning will show that the answer depends on the nature of the STM task, especially on whether it involves memory for items or memory for their order.

Acoustic-Motor versus Semantic Factors in STM

Conrad (1964) reported a study in which sequences of six letters of the alphabet were presented visually for immediate recall. The same letter vocabulary was used in a test in which the spoken letters had to be identified when heard in a background of white noise. The results showed a high correlation between letters confused in the listening test and letters confused in the recall test, despite the different input modalities in the two phases of the study. Subjects in both tasks confused letters that sounded alike, such as B, C, P, T and V. Conrad concluded from this that the memory trace in the immediate memory situation has an acoustic or verbal base. This finding has been repeatedly confirmed for short-term memory (STM) tasks (e.g., Wickelgren, 1965), although there has been some uncertainty about whether the crucial variable is the acoustic or motor component of the verbal trace. Hintzman (1965) presented evidence that the confusion errors in STM may be linked more to articulational similarities than to acoustic similarities, suggesting that storage and retrieval are based upon speech motor cues. Pinkus and Laughery (1967) investigated the role of both factors by varying the phonemic uniqueness and pronunciability of CVC strings in a standard memory span procedure. Both factors had significant effects, suggesting that the crucial memory code underlying STM is auditory-motor in nature, and either, or both, of the components could be functional, depending on which is made salient in the task. The findings from studies involving distinctive-feature analyses suggest even more generally that different combinations of acoustic and motor properties of sounds, as well as the ease with which the sounds can be labeled, can influence the overall accuracy and types of intrusion errors in immediate serial recall (e.g., Sales, Haber, & Cole, 1968, 1969). In a recent review, Wickelgren (1969) argued that the data on the issue are inconclusive—the STM trace may be auditory or articulatory, or it could be in an abstract verbal system that is neither purely auditory nor purely articulatory.

Whatever specific interpretation is adopted, it is clear that the above investigators have generally emphasized properties of the verbal representational system as being crucial in STM performance (cf. D. J. Murray, 1967, 1968). A related series of studies has explicitly contrasted such verbal acoustic (or motor) factors with semantic variables in STM. Baddeley (1964, 1966a) presented subjects with a series of five-word sequences for immediate sequential recall. In one condition, the sequences consisted of acoustically similar words such as *mad, man, mat, cad,* and *can.* In another condition, they consisted of words with similar meaning, such as *big, long, broad, great,* and *tall.* Control lists in each case consisted of comparable dissimilar words. The results of several experiments consistently showed large adverse effects of acoustic similarity. The effect of semantic similarity was also reliable but very small, being only about one-twelfth that of acoustic similarity. Formal similarity was also investigated, and it failed to have any effect. In other experiments (Baddeley, 1966b; Baddeley & Dale, 1966), the STM effect was confirmed, but long-term memory (LTM) was found to be impaired by semantic but not acoustic similarity. Baddeley (1966b, p. 308) summarized as follows: "It seems then that whereas STM relies very largely on acoustic coding and is relatively unaffected by the semantic content of the message to be stored, . . . LTM uses semantic coding extensively, . . . though not exclusively."

The above findings are important because they represent one kind of behavioral evidence that STM and LTM obey different laws, at least in regard to interference in memory (cf. Adams, 1967, pp. 40–41). The general implication is that semantic factors should not be effective in STM if interference is the major cause of forgetting. This is one implication that will be examined in the following sections. In terms of the present conceptualization of meaning, however, Baddeley's conclusion suggests that STM would not be affected by attributes that define visual imagery in particular, since these are not related to the motor-acoustic speech code. More generally, STM performance should be unaffected by referential or associative meaning. Let us examine the facts.

Imagery-Concreteness and STM

Brener's (1940) study has already been cited as showing no significant difference between concrete and abstract nouns in immediate memory span. This finding contrasts sharply with the effects of concreteness in the other memory tasks thus far considered, but it is consistent with Baddeley's conclusion that semantic factors are ineffective in STM.

The conclusion is not supported, however, by studies involving tasks other than memory span. Borkowski and Eisner (1968) investigated STM as a function of noun concreteness using the distractor technique introduced by J. Brown (1958) and L. R. Peterson and M. J. Peterson (1959). In three experiments, subjects were visually presented with a series of trials, each involving a set of four or five nouns, mixed with respect to the concreteness level of the words in the set. To prevent rehearsal, each set was followed by a counting task until the signal for recall was given. Retention intervals up to 20 seconds were tested. The results generally showed significantly better retention for the more concrete words, particularly in the second experiment.

Picture-word comparisons   Inferences concerning STM and LTM for pictures and concrete nouns are possible on the basis of serial position effects in free recall. A characteristic of free recall data from subjects who have had practice with the task is a serial position curve showing better recall for items occurring at the beginning and the end of the list during input (e.g., Murdock, 1962). These are referred to as primacy and recency effects. The primacy effect is not well understood, but the recency effect is generally attributed to early recall of terminal input items (Tulving, 1968). The recency effect has been shown to be affected by experimental variables that do not affect the rest of the serial position curve. For example, the effect is reduced or washed out when recall is delayed for 30 seconds (Glanzer & Cunitz, 1966; Postman & Phillips, 1965).

Such data have been taken as strong evidence for two kinds of mechanisms in free recall. Waugh and Norman (1965) follow William James (1890) in distinguishing between primary memory and secondary memory. The former has limited capacity, and items in it are displaced unless they are rehearsed. With rehearsal, they may be transferred into secondary memory, which has greater storage capacity. The recency effect in free recall is assumed to involve both primary and secondary memory, while the prior asymptotic level of the curve reflects storage in secondary memory. Waugh and Norman appropriately refer to the retrieval of recent items as the "echo box" phenomenon, mentioned earlier.

Glanzer and Cunitz (1966) similarly distinguished between short-term and long-term storage mechanisms in free recall. The former is assumed to be involved in the recency effect, whereas the latter applies to the material recalled from the beginning of the list. Thus the U-shaped serial position curve is assumed to be a composite of two output curves, one declining from the beginning to the end of the list, representing output from long-term storage; the other, rising from the beginning to the end, representing output from short-term storage.

The serial position effect and its interpretation in terms of STM and LTM processes are relevant to data from the experiment by Paivio, Rogers, and Smythe (1968), discussed earlier, in which free recall was found to be higher for pictures than for their labels. The data for each of four trials were analyzed in terms of input serial position. Significant differences were obtained on the first two trials. The mean recall for pictures and words are presented in Figure 7-12 as a function of input serial position, collapsed into five blocks of five items each. It can be seen that on the first trial the picture superiority involved a differential recency effect (significant for the last two serial position blocks). On the second trial, pictures were significantly superior in the first two blocks (primacy) and the final block of items (recency). For words, the shift from greater primacy on Trial 1 to greater recency on Trial 2 is analogous to Wing's (1967) finding for two successive one-trial free recall lists. Wing suggested that subjects initially adopt a forward recall strategy, then switch to backward recall to capitalize on recency and minimize proactive interserial interference.

An examination of item output order in the Paivio, Rogers, and Smythe

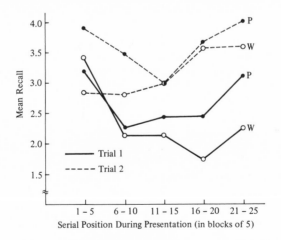

FIGURE 7-12. Recall scores for pictures (P) and words (W) on trials 1 and 2 as a function of input serial position. The higher recall for pictures from the end of the input list on trial 2 can be interpreted as a STM effect. From Paivio, Rogers, and Smythe (1968).

(1968) data indicated that such a shift occurred from Trial 1 to 2 in the case of both pictures and words, suggesting that the higher recall for pictures cannot be attributed to a different output strategy. The superiority of pictures in the case of terminal input items on Trial 1 and early input items on Trial 2 could mean that pictures are less susceptible to interserial interference or, more generally, that pictures are more easily retrieved from LTM according to the Glanzer and Cunitz (1966) type of model. In addition, pictures are apparently better retrieved from STM, as indicated by the higher recall for recent pictures than for recent words on Trial 2.

Further evidence on STM effects as a function of concreteness was recently obtained by Smythe and Paivio (unpublished). We used the L. R. Peterson and M. J. Peterson (1959) paradigm in a manner similar to Borkowski and Eisner (1968). Each trial involved presentation of a sequence of three items, these being homogeneous with respect to the type of item assigned to any given subjects. That is, one group received a series of trials with picture triplets, another with concrete nouns, and the third with abstract nouns. The results are shown in Figure 7-13 for the series of trials, where it can be seen that retention scores again were highest for pictures, next for concrete nouns, and least for abstract nouns. In addition, the typical proactive interference effect was obtained for all three stimulus types, with retention scores decreasing over the first three test triplets in particular (cf. Keppel & Underwood, 1962). The somewhat smaller proaction effect in the case of pictures is suggestive, but the Attribute by Trial

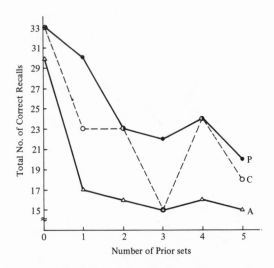

FIGURE 7-13. Short-term memory for sets of pictures (P), concrete nouns (C), and abstract nouns (A), showing proactive interference effect as a function of number of prior sets presented.

interaction was not significant. Thus the suggestion made above in relation to the Paivio, Rogers, and Smythe (1968) data, that pictures may be less susceptible than words to proactive interference, was not confirmed by these data. Nevertheless, retention once more proved to be directly related to imagery-concreteness.

A comparison of word imagery, *m*, and frequency in STM   In another experiment, Paivio and Smythe (1971) compared noun *I* with *m* and frequency in the L. R. Peterson and M. J. Peterson (1959) task. Subjects were presented with a series of items varying on one of the three attributes while the other two were held constant. Each subject received only one type of material (e.g., *I* varied with *m* and frequency constant), with four items per set. The results are presented in Figure 7-14. Noun *I* again had a highly significant positive effect, whereas the effect of *m* was nonsignificant (cf. Borkowski & Eisner, 1968); frequency had a significant and substantial negative effect. These striking results are in complete agreement with those obtained in the recognition memory and free recall experiments discussed earlier. The frequency effect may be restricted to the mixed-set condition (i.e., high- and low-frequency nouns occurring in each set of four), inasmuch as Loess (1967) failed to obtain any effect of word frequency in the Peterson and Peterson task using sets of items that were homogeneous with respect to frequency level. The concreteness effect is general, however, inasmuch as it appeared under homogeneous set conditions in the picture-word experiment described above and mixed-set conditions in the present experiment. It is clear from these findings that, if the Peterson and Peterson (1959) method qualifies as an STM task, certain semantic factors are strongly involved in such memory.

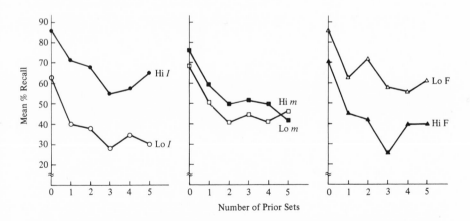

FIGURE 7-14.   Short-term memory for sets of nouns varied in imagery (*I*), meaningfulness (*m*), and frequency (*F*) as a function of trials. From Paivio and Smythe (1971).

Other Evidence of Semantic Factors in STM

Release from PI   In 1963, Wickens, Born, and Allen reported a study in which proactive interference was generated by repeated trials on an STM task involving consonants as items. They then shifted to digits and observed what they termed "release from PI" (proactive interference), where the new information was recalled at approximately the same level as was obtained on the first trial of the series. In a subsequent series of studies (see Wickens, 1970, for a summary), the release phenomenon was demonstrated with shifts on various semantic dimensions. These have involved the Peterson and Peterson (1959) experimental paradigm. Subsequent to the build-up of PI via a series of trials with a word triad, a critical triad is presented that differs on some semantic dimension from the preceding series. Wickens and Clark (1968), for example, investigated the three Osgood dimensions of connotative meaning in this fashion. A series of three-word sets from one end of a dimension, such as words that are evaluatively negative, was presented for four trials. On the fifth trial, a triad from the opposite end of the dimension (e.g., evaluatively positive words) was presented.

The results for the evaluative dimension are presented in Figure 7-15, where the release-from-PI phenomenon appears as an increase in percent correct on the fifth trial. Similar results were obtained with shifts from one extreme to the other on the potency and activity dimensions, as defined by the semantic differential. Wickens and Clark interpreted these results to mean that subjects encode verbal materials by some meaning characteristic associated with the

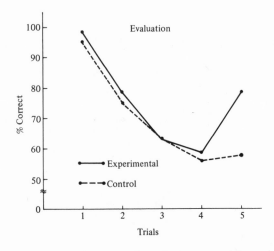

FIGURE 7-15.   STM effects for experimental and control groups on the Evaluation scale. From Wickens and Clark (1968).

extremes of Osgood's scales. Turvey (1968) questioned such an interpretation on the basis of his own data, which showed the release effect only when the preshift series was homogeneous with respect to the meaning dimension involved, although each series as a whole differed from the critical one in meaning. Nevertheless, the phenomenon does indicate a semantic influence on STM and is therefore consistent with conclusions from the studies of concreteness effects using the Peterson and Peterson procedure.

One curious finding deserves special mention. Wickens and Engle (1970) reported a study in which the shift effect was investigated using high- and low-imagery words from the Paivio, Yuille, and Madigan (1968) norms. Although the high-imagery items were better remembered, the shift effect was not significant. On the other hand, a shift in Thorndike-Lorge frequency resulted in a substantial release from PI in another study (see Wickens, 1970). The differential effects contrast with the consistent positive effects of word imagery and the inconsistent effects of frequency in various memory tasks, suggesting that memory performance and release from PI are sensitive to different properties of words. The absence of a shift effect for imagery led Wickens and Engle (1970) to conclude that concrete and abstract words are not encoded differently, and that the superiority of the former in STM performance may be due instead to greater semantic overlap and hence greater interitem interference among abstract than among high-imagery items. Paivio and Begg (1970a) tested that interpretation by systematically varying noun imagery and interitem relatedness (associative overlap) within and between noun triads in the Peterson and Peterson paradigm. Although average overlap did not differ for the two classes, high-imagery nouns were again recalled better than abstract nouns. The only effect of overlap was an interaction of within- and between-triad overlap: High within-triad overlap facilitated recall when between-triad overlap was low. Paivio aand Begg concluded that differential interference attributable to interitem semantic or associative relatedness cannot account for the superior recall of high-imagery nouns in STM, and that differential availability of imagery as an alternative memory code for concrete and abstract items remains the preferred interpretation. The paradoxical shift effects are not thereby explained, however, and a clear solution to the problem must await further evidence.

Acoustic versus associative factors   A number of studies have compared acoustic confusability and associative factors as predictors of STM. Since the latter involves the influence of the associative meaning of items in relation to other items, the comparisons are relevant to the general issue of meaning in STM. Baddeley, Conrad, and Hull (1965) found a highly significant correlation between the predictability of six-consonant sequences and STM. However, the study confounded sequential predictability with acoustic confusability. Conrad, Freeman, and Hull (1965) corrected this by independently varying each factor. They obtained a highly significant effect of acoustic confusability, whereas sequential predictability was much less important, although its effect was significant.

J. F. Marshall, Rouse, and Tarpy (1969) investigated the same problem using an STM recognition task similar to that used by Underwood (1965) to investigate associative interference (see above). They presented 230 commonly used words to subjects auditorily. Early in the sequence, 35 "pivot" words were presented interspersed with buffer items. The rest of the list included one repetition of each pivot word, its high associate, medium associate, synonym, and a rhyming word. The results showed that the mean frequencies of false recognitions were related to the nature of relationships to the pivot word in the order in which they are listed above: False positives were highest for the high associates of the pivot words and least for the rhymes. They concluded that associational coding plays a significantly greater role in STM than does acoustical coding. They agree with Conrad et al. (1965), however, that the coding method depends partly upon the material to be stored. An item is coded by arousing a cluster of both associatively similar items and acoustically similar items. The relative strength of the two types of code depend on the nature of the item, with associative coding dominating in the case of common words. Acoustical coding is presumably more important in the case of material such as consonant strings.

The above conclusion needs qualification. It will be recalled that Baddeley (e.g., 1966a) obtained a much greater interference effect from acoustic than from semantic similarity using highly familiar words. This effect is opposite to that obtained by Marshall et al., who found significantly more recognition errors for semantically similar words than for the acoustically similar words. Since Baddeley did not vary the associative relationships among the word sequences, the relative effect of this variable cannot be evaluated, but the reversal for acoustic and semantic similarity factors in the two studies suffices to indicate that the nature of the material used is not the only important variable determining the STM code.

The other important factor appears to be the nature of the task. Almost all of the studies that have showed the dominance of the acoustic confusability effect in STM have used immediate sequential memory as the task (cf. Adams, Thorsheim, & McIntyre, 1969). Those showing semantic or associative factors to be important have predominantly used the Peterson and Peterson task, and, in the case of J. F. Marshall et al., recognition memory. While the Peterson and Peterson task could be used in such a manner as to involve sequential memory, this has not always been the case in the studies cited above; in any case, the number of items per set have generally been below memory span. Thus it may be that acoustic (or motor) factors predominate in immediate sequential memory tasks, whereas higher-order meaning becomes dominant in nonsequential STM tasks.

Summary and Conclusions Concerning Meaning and STM

The empirical findings to date indicate that auditory-motor factors outweigh semantic variables in their effect on sequential STM tasks, whereas the reverse appears to be true in LTM. In other STM tasks, however, semantic factors assume greater importance. Thus retention in the Peterson and Peterson task is a positive function of imagery-concreteness, as it was shown to be in other tasks considered in previous sections. Other semantic factors, such as the Osgood dimensions of connotative meaning, have been shown to be important in STM using the release-from-PI phenomenon introduced by Wickens (1970) and his collaborators. Interitem associative and synonymity relations proved to have greater effects than rhyme relations in recognition memory.

These findings can be analyzed in terms of the levels-of-meaning approach we have been following. The immediate memory span task presumably depends particularly on factors related to the verbal representational level of meaning, i.e., auditory-motor factors. Their influence is reflected particularly in the acoustic and articulatory effects that have been observed, where confusions presumably are based on similarities at the level of representational meaning. Other evidence of the involvement of factors at this level appears in studies showing the importance in sequential memory of chunking letter or digit elements into higher-order pronounceable units (Pinkus & Laughery, 1967), or into frequently used digrams (Howe, 1967), or grouping them by rehearsal into optimal (three-digit) chunks (Wickelgren, 1964). All of these presumably involve factors affecting the availability of functional units of different sizes within the verbal representational system.

Higher-order meaning, such as referential imagery and verbal associative reactions, apparently become important in nonsequential tasks, and "picturability" appears to contribute to retrieval in its own right. That is, it facilitates retention beyond what can be explained on the basis of verbal codability alone, otherwise there is no reason why pictures should be remembered better than concrete words in the Peterson and Peterson task. This argument echoes what has already been stated in relation to recognition memory and free recall.

We turn now to a study that permits us to evaluate both sequential and nonsequential task performance in the context of the dual-coding model.

THE DUAL-CODING HYPOTHESIS AND MEMORY

Recall that the dual-coding hypothesis assumes that imaginal and verbal processes are differentially available as memory codes for abstract words, concrete words, and pictures. The image code increases in availability uniformly over the three levels, whereas the verbal code is highly available as a representational response to words but somewhat less available as a verbal referential (labeling) response to pictures. These assumptions have been supported by latency measures of the arousal of the two processes (Chapter 3), which are particularly relevant to the rate manipulation introduced as one of the experimental variables in the experiment to be considered. The other relevant feature of the hypothesis is the distinction between sequential and parallel processing—the verbal system is specialized for sequential processing; the image system, for parallel processing in the spatial sense but not for sequential processing.

Deductive Consequences and a Test of the Model

The implications of the theoretical analysis were tested by Paivio and Csapo (1969) by varying the availability, or accessibility, of the two memory codes along with the necessity of sequential processing in the memory task. Availability was manipulated by varying stimulus concreteness and rate of presentation. Since words can be read faster than objects can be named, the arousal of the verbal memory code can be prevented during input in the case of pictorial stimuli without eliminating it in the case of words by using a sufficiently fast rate of presentation. That is, at a fast rate the subject can read a word without having time to label a picture. The arousal of referential or associative images to concrete or abstract words would also be interfered with by the fast rate.

Given a discrete stimulus series without any intrinsic serial order, it follows from the hypothesis that memory should be poorest at a very fast rate for picture stimuli in memory span and serial learning, which require serial processing. Pictures should not suffer even at a fast rate in free recall and recognition memory tasks, however, since serial order information need not be retained and the appropriate verbal labels presumably can be retrieved from concrete memory images after the stimulus series has been presented. At a slower rate, where the subject can supply a verbal label, picture stimuli should not suffer relative to words even in the serial processing tasks, and they would be expected to surpass words in the free recall and recognition tasks, presumably because the high availability of both codes enhances the probability of their retrieval. No difference would be expected between concrete and abstract words on any task at the fast rate, since only the verbal code can be utilized. At the slower rate, however, the concrete should exceed the abstract in free recall, recognition, and serial learning because of the arousal of associative imagery, which can enhance unit retrieval or the formation of higher order units over trials, but not in memory span, which involves only immediate memory for serial order and is presumably affected only by the availability of the verbal code. A corollary prediction is that variation in rate should have the greatest effect generally on memory for pictorial stimuli and the least effect on abstract words.

The experimental test of the predictions involved the presentation of a nine-item list (cf. Figure 7-6, above) of familiar pictures, their concrete noun labels, or abstract words over a series of trials at either a fast rate (5.3 items/sec.) or a slow rate (2 items/sec.), in one of the four memory tasks. These particular rates were selected on the basis of pilot research and information concerning naming and reading response latencies (see Chapter 3) and temporal factors in perceptual and short-term memory tasks (Aaronson, 1967). The faster rate was such that subjects had insufficient time to label the pictures implicitly, but could easily recognize them as well as implicitly read the words. At the slower rate, the pictures could be implicitly labeled without difficulty.

The results were remarkably consistent with the predictions. The rate effect was significant overall, and a double interaction of rate by stimulus attribute indicated, as predicted, that the effect was clearly greatest for pictures and least for abstract words. The double interaction was further qualified by a triple interaction of rate, stimulus attribute, and task, which is presented in Figure 7-16. A series of comparisons revealed the following effects. Consistent with predictions, memory span and serial learning scores were significantly poorest for pictures at the fast rate. At the slow rate, pictures remained inferior in memory span, although none of the differences between stimulus types was significant. By contrast, pictures, along with concrete words, were superior to abstract words in serial learning, which is a complete crossover from the fast rate. The effects for free recall and recognition memory were similar to each other and differed from the patterns for the serial memory tasks: At the fast

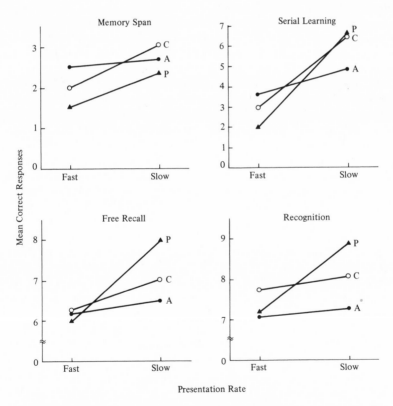

FIGURE 7-16.   Mean number of correct responses in 4 memory tasks for pictures (P), concrete words (C), and abstract words (A) at two presentation rates. From Paivio and Csapo (1969).

rate, none of the differences between stimulus types was significant within either task; at the slow rate, pictures were remembered best, abstract words most poorly, and concrete words were intermediate, as in other free recall and recognition experiments described earlier in this chapter. Finally, the effect of presentation rate was significant for pictures on all tasks; for concrete words in memory span, serial learning, and marginally in free recall; and, for abstract words, only in serial learning.

In summary, memory for pictures tended generally to suffer at the fast rate, but the effect was significant only in the sequential memory tasks, presumably because the verbal code essential to performance was least available. The slow rate benefited picture memory most, particularly in the learning tasks, presumably because both memory codes were increasingly available at that rate over trials. Memory for abstract words was least affected by rate, presumably because only (or mainly) the verbal code was involved.

The contrasting effects of pictures and words in nonsequential and sequential tasks is strikingly illustrated by further data. The number of new items correctly recognized as new in the test trial of the Paivio and Csapo recognition memory task were separately analyzed as a function of stimulus attributes and rate. The results are plotted in Figure 7-17, which shows that pictures were superior to words at both the fast and the slow rate. Since the verbal code was presumably not available during fast input in the case of pictures, the finding provides strong evidence that some aspects of stimulus information are better retained in the visual image code than in the verbal memory code alone. Although they did not include words in their experiment, Potter and Levy (1969) similarly found that new distractor items were rarely identified incorrectly as old

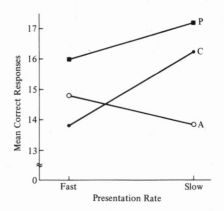

FIGURE 7-17. Mean number of items correctly recognized as "new" in the recognition memory task as a function of stimulus type and presentation rate. From Paivio and Csapo (1969).

in a test of recognition memory for pictures, even when the old items had been presented at rates as fast as 8 per second.

Sequential memory without verbal responding   The deficiency of imagery in memory for temporal order was confirmed in a further study (Paivio & Csapo, unpublished), which did not require the subjects to respond verbally. The items were again presented sequentially at fast or slower rates. Memory for temporal order was tested using a discrimination-of-recency task (cf. Fozard & Lapine, 1968; Yntema & Trask, 1963) in which two items from the list were presented and the subject was required to indicate which had occurred more recently in the input list. Different degrees of item separation were sampled, and discrimination generally improved as separation increased. The relevant finding in the present context, however, was that pictures were significantly inferior to words at the fast rate but not the slower rate (see Figure 7-18), paralleling the results for immediate memory span.

Precisely the same pattern of results emerged in another experiment that involved a serial reconstruction task, i.e., following list presentation, the subjects attempted to reconstruct the input order of items by placing blocks containing the stimuli in spatially ordered slots representative of their temporal sequence. The results for both rates are shown in Figure 7-18 along with those for the recency discrimination experiment.

Quite different results have been obtained with slower rates of presentation, at least in the recency discrimination task. Fozard and Lapine (1968), using a self-paced procedure, and Fozard (1970), using a rate of 1.6 items per second, found discrimination of recency to be better for pictures than for concrete

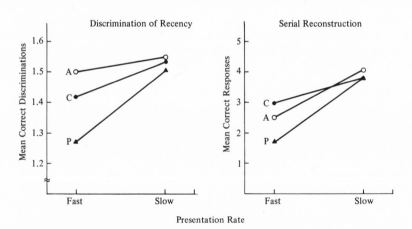

FIGURE 7-18.   Mean number of correct responses in discrimination of recency and serial reconstruction tasks for pictures (P), concrete nouns (C), and abstract nouns (A) at fast (5.3 items per sec.) and slower (2 items per sec.) rates of presentation.

nouns. Perhaps subjects can make effective use of both verbal and nonverbal information available in pictures at the slower rates, but how this might be done remains obscure at the moment.

The general conclusions from the foregoing data are that the concrete (visual) memory code can indeed function efficiently in the storage of nonsequential, nonverbal item information (which can be verbally retrieved), whereas the verbal code is efficient for storing sequentially ordered information. Given sufficient time for their evocation on a given trial, and repeated learning trials, the two codes apparently summate in their facilitative effect on information retrieval, as indicated by the picture, concrete word, abstract word ordering of memory scores in free recall, recognition memory, and serial learning. This may also be the case in recency discrimination at slow rates. These data therefore support the information (or code) redundancy interpretation of the facilitative effect of concreteness in those tasks, although the nonverbal code alone apparently contributes to the superiority of pictures in recognition memory, at least in regard to the occurrence of false positives.

Relevance to Current Theoretical Conceptions and Issues

As stated at the outset, the dual-coding model was not intended to be a complete theory of memory, and a more formal and detailed theoretical statement therefore remains to be developed. Even as it stands, however, the model has considerable scope and power. There appears to be no obvious alternative current model that provides a satisfactory account of the range of data discussed here, and certainly none that would have generated the predictions that were made and experimentally confirmed. The greatest deficiency of contemporary theoretical and empirical approaches to memory is that they have been concerned almost entirely with auditory-motor *verbal* memory. This is most apparent in the case of conceptions of short-term storage, or primary memory (e.g., see the summaries by Adams, 1967; Atkinson & Shiffrin, 1968; Murdock, 1967b), but it also applies to long-term or secondary memory storage. Atkinson and Shiffrin, for example, state that long-term memory clearly exists in other modalities, but the lack of data forced them to restrict their attention primarily to the "auditory-verbal-linguistic store" in their discussion of long-term storage. It may be that the dual-coding hypothesis and the data relevant to it can be encompassed by expanded versions of any of the contemporary models of memory (Norman, 1970), but this remains to be demonstrated.

It is possible to examine the adequacy of some of the assumptions of recent theoretical approaches to memory when applied to the Paivio and Csapo data. One generalization that has already been noted is that representation in STM is through an auditory or motor speech code. This conclusion is supported by the acoustic and articulatory confusion effects obtained in STM studies discussed earlier, as well as by sensory-modality effects. Retention in a variety of STM tasks is generally better with auditory than with visual presentation (e.g., Craik, 1970; Dornbush, 1968; Mackworth, 1964; Margrain, 1967; Murdock,

1967a, 1968; D. J. Murray & Roberts, 1968). This finding is consistent with the interpretation that the verbal representational system is more directly aroused by auditory input because the system itself involves the auditory receiving areas. The auditory superiority diminishes at slow rates of presentation and as a function of age, presumably because subjects in both cases are better able to read and rehearse items at the time of perception (cf. Murray & Roberts, 1968). These data can be readily incorporated into the dual-coding model presented here: The verbal code is more available, or accessible, when the verbal stimulus is auditory than when it is visual.

The modality effect obviously cannot account for the picture-word memory data in any explicit sense, inasmuch as input modality was always visual. Thus the effect is relevant here only in the same sense as the acoustic confusion data are relevant; both implicate the verbal symbolic system in STM. The inferiority of pictures in immediate memory span, discrimination of recency, and serial construction at the fast rate can be explained in terms of the availability of the verbal code, but none of the instances in which pictures are superior to concrete words and the latter to abstract words can be explained in terms of verbal memory (short- or long-term) alone. Another coding system must contribute its effect; and here it is insufficient to say merely that a *visual* code is involved, since the modality data tell us that visual memory is inferior to auditory memory when the stimuli are words. The visual code is superior only in the storage of concrete (object) information, as suggested relatively directly by pictures, or indirectly (associatively) by concrete words. Moreover, it is superior only when immediate memory for temporal or sequential information need not be retained.

The situation is analogous to what Brooks (1968) suggested in discussing the "boundaries" of the hypothetical symbolic systems associated with visual and speech monitoring in perceptual tasks (see Chapter 5); the two memory codes cannot be identified in a simple and direct manner with traditional sensory channels. The image code is visual in the studies considered, but it is specialized for nonverbal information, not visual word-images. Conversely, the verbal code cannot be functionally equated with the auditory modality, although that modality may be an important component of the verbal system. The point was emphasized in the context of research on acoustic confusability in STM tasks and it is reinforced by data from an experiment by Warren, Obusek, Farmer, and Warren (1969). They found that the temporal pattern of successively presented nonverbal sounds, such as hisses, buzzes, and tones, could not be recognized, although the individual stimuli were readily perceived. The result contrasts with the efficiency of the verbal system in sequential memory tasks and indicates that this efficiency cannot be attributed to "auditory memory" in general. Whatever the contribution of the auditory system to sequential memory, it appears to be specific to verbal stimuli. The nonverbal sounds investigated by Warren et al. behaved much like pictures presented at a fast rate in the Paivio and Csapo (1969) experiment in that order information was poorly retained in each case, apparently because of the unavailability of the verbal code. Thus we are led once more to emphasize the functional distinctions between verbal and nonverbal *symbolic* modalities rather than auditory and visual sensory modalities, while at the same time recognizing that symbolic and sensory modes are partially correlated.

Relation to Other Multimode Approaches to Memory

Although formal theoretical statements concerning the attributes of visual memory are lacking, others have presented views on multimodal or multicomponent memory systems that are relevant here. Wallach and Averbach (1955) proposed multiple-memory modalities corresponding to the sensory modalities, but they also recognized possible distinctions involving symbolic modes inasmuch as they contrast verbal and visual memory. They obtained evidence that such multiple traces enhance recall and recognition but also found that recognition depends on the similarity between the perceptual modality involved in the recognition test and the memory modality of the previous experience (cf. Murdock, 1967a). The experimental tests involved only verbal material, however, with backward reading of a visually presented word serving as the visual memory condition on the assumption that only visual traces would be functionally useful in that condition. Nevertheless, their general reasoning can be extended readily to picture-word comparisons.

Bower (1967) proposed a multicomponent model of the memory trace in which the trace is assumed to consist of different components that together can be expressed as a multicomponent vector. In that paper, Bower made no distinctions in terms of symbolic modalities, but imagery presumably could be incorporated into the model, particularly in view of his own recent interest in the phenomenon (Bower, 1969).

Underwood (1969) has recently presented a comprehensive multidimensional approach in which memory is viewed as a collection of attributes that serve to discriminate one memory from another and to act as retrieval mechanisms for a target memory. The attributes he identified are temporal, spatial, frequency, sensory modality, associative nonverbal (including visual imagery), and associative verbal. Underwood's conception of memory is generally compatible with the views presented in this book, although the present approach is less neutral theoretically in that many of the specific attributes discussed by Underwood are viewed here as functional components of more general verbal and nonverbal symbolic systems.

The following contributions are also directly relevant here. Koen (1966) elaborated on Bruner's (1964) theory of multiple modes of representation and obtained experimental evidence that enactive, iconic, and verbal coding all contributed to the recognition of pictorial stimuli. R. L. Taylor and Posner (1968) used a recognition memory procedure in which a set of three upper-case alphabetic letters was presented and subjects were subsequently required to indicate whether or not a single "probe" letter was the same as any of the three letters originally presented. The use of visual and verbal (name) codes was manipulated by presenting the probe letter in upper case or in lower case (forcing the use of a name code), as in the classification experiments discussed in Chapter 5. The results led Taylor and Posner to conclude that the visual memory code is organized to represent the environment spatially, whereas the verbal code is organized so that at any point in time items are retrieved in a fixed order. Their proposal is obviously consistent with the model presented here. Finally, Brook's (1968) distinction between visual and linguistic symbolic modalities, previously discussed in relation to perception, is equally pertinent in the context of memory phenomena.

All of the above views share common features with the present model, although they are individually narrower in scope. Thus none of them includes within a single testable model assumptions concerning different levels of imaginal and verbal meaning, and specified functional distinctions between two symbolic (memory) systems that are coordinated to the meaning dimension. The integrative and heuristic value of the model has been amply supported, although it obviously remains in need of further detailed elaboration with respect to the functional properties of the two postulated memory codes.

Relation to the Mnemonic Systems

It is appropriate also to note the relevance of the present findings to the ancient mnemonic systems. One assumption of those systems has been consistently supported: Concrete objects are particularly easy to remember. Other assumptions at the very least require qualification. Simonides assumed that the visual modality is superior to the auditory, and his early followers accepted this view even in regard to memory for words. It turns out empirically, however, that words are better remembered when presented auditorily rather than visually. Visual memory is superior only if we interpret it in the sense of visual memory for concrete objects, but this conclusion, too, must be qualified, since it does not hold for sequential tasks, especially at very fast rates. However, visual imagery appears to contribute even to serial learning when items are presented at a moderate rate (e.g., two items per second), suggesting that the ancient assumption concerning the efficiency of visual imagery in memory was generally correct.

Untested Implications of the Model

The need for factual information has been emphasized at various points throughout the chapter, but data are most notably lacking on the implications of the crucial distinction between the *spatial-* and *sequential-*processing capacities of the two coding systems. Spatial information was not a salient feature of the memory tasks considered in this chapter except in the sense that pictured objects are spatial entities. The functional uniqueness of the image system should be revealed most clearly by studies that permit such objects to be organized into spatial compounds. Such organization would be expected to enhance memory for objects more than for words, since the verbal representational system presumably integrates words into higher-order units temporally (sequentially) rather than spatially.

Comparisons of memory for words and objects under successive and simultaneous presentation conditions would be a straightforward approach to the problem, but relevant research is sparse and what there is provides only incomplete information because the experimental designs have not included all of the conditions that would be of interest here. For example, McGeoch and Whitely (1926) investigated immediate recall after a brief exposure to an array of pictured objects, but they did not compare this with successive presentation or similarly presented words. Recently, L. M. Horowitz, Lampel, and Takanishi (1969) found that nursery school children remembered sets of pictures or objects best if they were unitized into a "scene," next best if they were simultaneously presented in a row, and most poorly if they were presented successively on the same spot. The superiority of the unitized condition did not depend on naming in the case of objects (although it did in the case of pictures), suggesting that spatial integration particularly benefits memory for nonverbal stimuli. Uncertainty remains, however, since we do not know how memory for printed words would be affected by an appropriate spatial arrangement, as compared to the successive presentation, of such stimuli.

The significance of the distinction between spatial and sequential integration comes up more explicitly as an issue in theoretical approaches to associative learning, which has been investigated most often using the paired-associate learning design or extensions of it. The issues and the research will be considered in the next chapter and the ones that follow.

SUMMARY

Of the stimulus attributes considered in this chapter, imagery-concreteness is the best predictor of memory performance in tasks such as recognition memory and free recall, which require the retention of item information. The number of items correctly remembered in such tasks uniformly increases from abstract words, to concrete words, to pictures. This does not occur in tasks such as immediate memory span and discrimination of recency, which principally involve memory for the order of the items. These findings are generally consistent with the view that either images or words, or both, can serve as effective memory codes for the retrieval of item information. Nonverbal images may suffice in recognition memory, which does not require a verbal response, but the verbal code must be stored along with the image, or be retrievable from it, in the case of tasks such as free verbal recall, which require a verbal response. The hypothesized differential capacity of the two coding systems for sequential processing is implicated in the sequential memory tasks: The verbal code is essential to performance in such tasks because it is specialized for sequential processing, whereas the image code is not. This hypothesis was most strongly supported by the finding that sequential memory for pictures was inferior to that for words at a very fast rate of presentation, which presumably prevented implicit labeling of the pictures without preventing reading of the words.

Other dimensions of meaning generally showed weaker and less consistent relations to memory performance. Negative relations have been consistently obtained for word frequency in recognition memory: Rare words are easier to recognize than familiar ones. In free recall, the results for frequency are inconsistent and perhaps dependent upon the concreteness of the items; in one experiment, for example, frequency was positively related to recall when the items were concrete but negatively when they were abstract. Verbal referential meaning and associative meaningfulness are also inconsistent in their effects, sometimes showing positive relations, sometimes none, and sometimes negative relations to amount remembered. The variable effects are poorly understood, but verbal associative interference seems to be an important factor throughout. Especially in recognition tasks, strong pre-experimental associations between correct and incorrect items can result in incorrect responses (false positives). Similar processes may operate in free recall, perhaps through organizational mechanisms.

The theoretical interpretations require elaboration, particularly in regard to the role of memory mechanisms operating during storage, retention, and retrieval of information in memory. It remains to be determined whether the findings and the dual-coding hypothesis can be incorporated into contemporary memory models without severe modifications in the latter. The postulated capacity of the image system for processing and storing spatial information also needs systematic investigation in relation to the kinds of memory tasks that were the concern of this chapter.

8
Meaning and Associative Learning

This chapter is concerned with the effects of the various dimensions of stimulus meaning on associative learning and memory, and with the functions of imaginal and verbal processes in such learning, as inferred from the observed effects. Attention again centers on the imagery value or concreteness of items because that attribute provides the only semantic definition of imagery as a process. The major contrasting variable in the empirical-theoretical debate will be verbal associative meaningfulness, which defines the availability of implicit verbal reactions that could serve as mediators of associations between items, but comparisons will also be made with numerous other attributes in order to isolate the primary semantic correlates of associative learning. It can be said in anticipation of the data that imagery-concreteness turns out to be singularly effective as a stimulus attribute. The theoretical interpretation of that effect accordingly becomes the focal problem of the chapter.

Since the relevant research has involved the paired-associate learning paradigm almost exclusively, its essential features will be outlined briefly, along with some of the descriptive conventions associated with it (for more detailed information, see, e.g., Deese & Hulse, 1967; Goss & Nodine, 1965; Hall, 1966). The learner is presented with a series of stimulus-response (S-R) pairs, for example, *house-pencil*, and *ocean-tree*. His task is to learn the association so that, given the stimulus term alone (e.g., house), he will be able to respond with the appropriate response term (pencil). Two basic procedures have been used, the *anticipation* method and the *study-test*, or recall, method. In the anticipation method, the stimulus terms and S-R pairs alternate in the presented list and the subject is required to anticipate the response when the stimulus term appears. The correctness of his response is confirmed or disconfirmed by the subsequent appearance of the S-R pair. In the study-test or recall method, all of the S-R pairs are first presented, usually one pair at a time, followed by the recall or test trial, during which the stimulus terms alone are presented and the learner attempts to provide the correct response to each. Over a series of trials, the study and test phases are alternated, usually with the order of the S-R pairs and stimulus-terms varied from trial to trial. Comparisons of the two procedures (e.g., Cofer, Diamond, Olsen, Stein, & Walker, 1967; Goss & Nodine, 1965) have yielded no important differences that would affect the conclusions to be made here. Therefore, the distinctions will not be discussed except to point out that the recall method has the advantage of being easily adapted to group testing procedures.

What features of the paired-associate task distinguish it from those considered in the last chapter? The explicit emphasis on the formation of associations is not a strong distinguishing feature, inasmuch as interitem associations of some kind are required in serial learning and memory span, and appear to play an organizational role in free recall as well. A more important feature appears to be the clear functional distinction between stimulus and response members of the paired associates. One member is explicitly designated as the stimulus in the sense that it functions as a retrieval cue for the to-be-remembered response term during the anticipation or test trial. To the extent that a similar distinction is valid in serial learning (as noted in the last chapter, there is some question presently concerning the nature of the functional stimulus in that task), the stimulus and response functions of items are confounded, each item except the first and last serving in each capacity during learning. Other list items presumably can function as retrieval cues in free recall, but such cues are entirely implicit at least in the case of the initially recalled items. In recognition memory, the items may be said to serve as their own retrieval cues, but the stimulus-response distinction does not apply in the analytic sense. Thus, although associative processes and retrieval cues are presumably involved in all of these tasks, paired-associate learning is unique in the sense that each to-be-remembered item has associated with it another item whose sole function is to serve as a cue or reminder. This feature has certain analytic advantages that will become apparent in later theoretical discussions.

The theoretical interpretation of paired-associate learning is an interesting problem in its own right (see Battig, 1968), but the various views on the problem will be considered here only to the extent that they bear on specific issues that concern us. Generally this will be done in the context of relevant studies, but one analytic convention deserves mention at the outset. Underwood and Schulz (1960) presented a detailed analysis of paired-associate learning as a two-stage process, namely, response learning and association. The former involves learning to produce the response as an integrated unit, which is particularly important when the response term is unfamiliar or otherwise difficult to emit. The associative stage involves learning the appropriate S-R linkage. Because we will be mainly concerned with situations involving familiar words and pictures, much of the attention here will be on the associative stage, but response learning becomes an important consideration from time to time.

THEORETICAL ORIENTATION

The major theoretical framework for the analysis of the findings is an imagery hypothesis that combines aspects of the ancient views on mnemonic imagery with the imagery component of the two-process theory of meaning. This will be contrasted with a conventional verbal mediational interpretation of the effects of meaningfulness in paired-associate learning.

Item Imagery and the Conceptual-Peg Hypothesis

The classical mnemonic systems shared with associationism generally the fundamental assumption that the recall of one idea will prompt recall of another with which it has been associated. Moreover, it assumed that ease of association is related to the concreteness of the to-be-associated events, particularly that of the recall cue. This view was explicitly stated by Quintilian and accepted by later mnemonists such as Feinaigle (1813), who suggested that, "Sensible objects have a powerful effect in recalling to mind the ideas with which it was occupied when those ideas were presented" (cf. Chapter 6). This assumption was extended implicitly to the level of word meaning, since the names of objects were proposed as cues for the arousal of the images that were to serve as memory localities for to-be-remembered items of information. The assumption apparently persists also in the more contemporary rhyming mnemonic technique (Chapter 6) in which the items *one-bun, two-shoe,* and so forth, serve as associative aids or memory "pegs" for to-be-remembered items. The peg words, *bun, shoe, tree,* etc., are relatively concrete and high in their image-arousing value, and this feature may be important to the efficiency of the mnemonic technique independent of the instructions to make use of imagery.

The above reasoning can be extended directly to the analysis of the effects of concreteness and imagery in a standard paired-associate learning task. Consider the situation where both members of a pair are highly familiar concrete nouns, such as *house-pencil,* and the learner is told that he is to associate the two so that, given one member of the pair, it will remind him of the other. Because of their strong imaginal meaning, the nouns would tend to arouse images readily, and the subject may therefore attempt to associate the two by generating a compound image of a house and a pencil in some kind of spatial relationship. During recall, when "house" is presented alone, it may redintegrate the compound image from which the response "pencil" could be retrieved. If this analysis is valid, it follows that the ease of learning a stimulus-response association would depend on the image-arousing value of both members of the pair, but that of the stimulus member will be relatively more important. The imagery value of both stimulus and response would contribute to the formation of the compound image when the two are presented together on the study trial. On recall trials, however, when the stimulus is presented alone, its image-arousing value would be particularly crucial because the stimulus must serve as the cue that redintegrates the compound image from which the response component can be retrieved and recoded as a word. This theory has been metaphorically termed the conceptual-peg hypothesis of paired-associate learning (Paivio, 1963), according to which the stimulus term functions as a "peg" to which its associate is hooked during learning trials and from which it can be retrieved on recall trials. The more concrete the stimulus, the more "solid" it is as a conceptual peg and the better the recall.

The chief empirical implication of the hypothesis is that variation in the concreteness or imagery value of stimulus terms should have a greater effect on associative learning than the same degree of variation in the concreteness of response terms. Note carefully that this prediction applies to the standard paired-associate learning situation in which the stimulus and response functions of pair members are explicitly distinguished. The conceptual-peg hypothesis is essentially a retrieval theory—a high-imagery item is especially effective as a retrieval cue for the to-be-recalled associate. The concreteness of the nominal response is assumed to be relatively less important during the recall stage, but the formation and the storage of the compound-mediating image during the study trial presumably depend equally on the concreteness of both members of the pair. It will be seen later that this distinction has important implications when the standard paired-associate learning procedure is modified, e.g., when the "response" member is presented as the retrieval cue in a test of backward association, or when a recognition rather than a recall test is used to evaluate associative learning. Other implications of the imagery-mediation theory will be discussed later in the context of relevant research.

Meaningfulness and Verbal Processes in Associative Learning

The imagery hypothesis contrasts with an alternative approach to the role of meaning in associative learning, which has stressed measures of verbal associative meaningfulness (e.g., Noble's m; see Chapter 3) as the appropriate empirical variables, and verbal processes as the underlying mechanisms. Typically, studies using such measures have found that pairs are easier to learn when they are high in meaningfulness, and that the meaningfulness of the response term is more potent than that of the stimulus term (Goss & Nodine, 1965; Underwood & Schulz, 1960). Note that the differential response effect contrasts with the prediction from the conceptual-peg hypothesis, which assumes that concreteness has more weight on the stimulus side. The response effect has generally been attributed to the availability of verbal responses during the response learning stage. How the defining attribute itself, i.e., the number of implicit associations an item evokes, could influence response availability has not been stated (cf. Goss & Nodine, 1965, p. 119), and Underwood and Schulz (1960) in fact concluded that number of associations was not a relevant attribute at that stage. They preferred instead to emphasize emitted frequency (i.e., how often the response unit has been produced by the subject in the past) as the critical attribute, although their own experimental evidence was equivocal on the issue. From the present viewpoint, the question is whether the response effect can be attributed to verbal associative or representational meaning. To the extent that number of associations per se is relevant, associative meaning could be involved. To the extent that frequency or other measures of unit availability are effective, representational meaning would be implicated. Some evidence bearing on the problem will be reviewed presently, although the issue is not a central one here because the studies that concern us most have generally used highly available units such as real words, and response learning is therefore relatively unimportant. In contrast, the traditional research on meaningfulness has usually involved nonsense syllables, at least as low-meaningful units, and it is not surprising that response integration is critical to learning.

The effect of meaningfulness during the associative stage of learning has been discussed in terms of the availability of implicit verbal associations as potential mediators of stimulus-response connections. For example, the associative probability hypothesis, proposed by Underwood and Schulz (1960, p. 296), states that the greater the number of associates elicited by an item, the greater the probability that one of these will link up with another item. Underwood and Schulz assumed further that associates elicited by either the stimulus or the response member could contribute to the associative probability—they may, "in a manner of speaking, 'throw out' associates in an effort to find one that is common to both" (p. 296). This analysis emphasizes the facilitative effect of mediators that are common to the stimulus and response members of a given pair, but Underwood and Schulz (1960, p. 46) also recognize the interference paradox of associative probability, namely, that an increased number of implicit associations may lead to incorrect associations as well. We shall have occasion to say more about the paradox later.

The parallels and contrasts between the imagery-mediation and associative probability hypotheses are readily apparent. Both emphasize associative processes evoked by pair members as potential mediators of stimulus-response connections, but one emphasizes nonverbal imagery while the other stresses verbal processes. Both infer the processes from relevant item attributes, concreteness being the defining attribute in the case of imagery theory, and verbal associative meaningfulness in the case of associative probability. Both stress the importance of the availability of the potential mediators, but the image hypothesis assumes that the latency or ease of image arousal is the crucial factor, whereas associative probability puts the emphasis on the number of available associations. The image theory emphasizes the spatial characteristics of the compound-mediating image, whereas associative probability assumes that the verbal mediators function as verbal chains, i.e., sequentially. These similarities and contrasts are most noteworthy because of their relevance to the two-process theory of meaning and memory. In effect, the imagery hypothesis is a theory about the functional properties of one symbolic system, and associative probability, of the other. The hypotheses are not necessarily incompatible. They emphasize different operations and, to the extent that both are valid, they complement each other as theoretical approaches to the explanation of paired-associate learning. The research to be reviewed later will enable us to evaluate the validity and relative predictive power of each, and to compare them with alternative interpretations.

The research review and discussions that follow deal in turn with the following issues: (a) the effect of imagery-concreteness as an empirical variable and its implications for the imagery hypothesis; (b) comparisons of concreteness with other empirical attributes, including meaningfulness and frequency, with attempts to interpret the various effects; (c) conceptual difficulties encountered by the imagery hypothesis; (d) the implications of the two-process approach to meaning and mediation regarding the directionality of associations; (e) finally, some alternative interpretations of the effects of imagery-concreteness.

CONCRETENESS AND IMAGERY IN PAIRED-ASSOCIATE LEARNING

Initial Evidence and Theory

The effect of concreteness in paired-associate (PA) learning was first demonstrated in studies involving pairs in which both members were concrete or both were relatively abstract. An early study by Busemann (cited in Reed, 1918a, p. 141) involved school children learning eight-pair lists of concrete nouns, abstract nouns, adjectives, verbs, and meaningless words. The percentages of correct recalls for each of these were 80.5, 70, 51.7, 49.2, and 14, respectively. Leaving aside for the moment the question of whether adjectives, verbs, and nonsense words are part of an effective abstractness continuum, the finding at least indicated the superiority of concrete nouns over abstract nouns. More recently, Epstein, Rock, and Zuckerman (1960) tested several hypotheses concerning the role of familiarity and meaning in associative learning. One of a series of paired-associate learning experiments demonstrated that pictures of pairs of familiar objects are learned more easily than abstract noun or verb pairs. The effective dimension was extended further by Iscoe and Semler (1964), who found that both normal and retarded children learned object pairs more easily than picture pairs. The finding was essentially replicated by Semler and Iscoe (1965). Thus, different experiments show that PA learning increases systematically with increased concreteness of the pairs.

How were the findings explained? Iscoe and Semler (1964) interpreted the inferiority of pictures relative to objects in terms of reduced cues. Epstein et al. based their analysis on an organizational explanation of associative learning originally proposed by Köhler (1929). Köhler suggested that pairs of nouns such as lake-sugar, boot-plate, girl-kangaroo, and so on, are easier to learn than pairs of nonsense syllables because the nouns can be imagined as a series of pictures that constitute well-organized wholes. The lump of sugar might be seen as dissolving in a lake, the boot resting on a plate, and so forth. Epstein et al. expressed the same notion by saying that conceptualization of objects is facilitating because it encourages the formation of organized units. Although the authors do not discuss it in such terms, the hypothesis can be regarded as an explicit statement of the assumption underlying the use of imagery as a mnemonic aid, "conceptualization of objects" being translatable into the phrase "forming images of objects."

The experimental evidence does not demand the conclusion that the superior learning for pairs of discrete pictures over concrete noun pairs (or concrete noun over abstract noun pairs) involves conceptual organization of the pairs, or association for that matter. Instead, it could be argued that concreteness simply increases the availability of the response units. However, the results of further experiments by Epstein et al. provided more direct support for their hypothesis. Pictures of paired objects were learned either with each pair presented as a meaningful unit (e.g., a hand in a bowl) or with the members of pairs as separate units (a hand beside a bowl). Learning was highly superior under the former condition. Another experiment showed that learning of pairs of concrete nouns learned as parts of a three-word phrase in which the middle word was an intelligible connective (e.g., lamp in bottle) was easier than when the middle word did not reasonably connect the members of a pair (e.g., lamp how bottle). The former were also learned better than the same nouns without connectives (lamp-bottle) and better than the nouns in phrases that formed sound grammatical units but not good conceptual units (e.g., lamp or bottle). While highly relevant to the general issue of the nature of the mediation process in associative learning, these results involve the addition of contextual information, or contextual meaning, to the PA situation and they do not resolve issues related to the effects of concreteness in the *absence* of connectives. Further consideration of the Epstein et al. studies and other related research will accordingly be postponed to Chapter 11, which deals with the direct assessment and manipulation of such mediators. Here, we shall confine our attention to the attributes of stimulus and response units, and inferences concerning mediation or other processes from the effects of such attributes.

The functional distinction between stimulus and response units becomes crucial when we attempt to base inferences solely on the effects of item attributes. The distinction was not considered by Köhler or Epstein et al., nor were stimulus and response attributes independently manipulated in any of the studies considered thus far. An interpretation of the facilitating effect of concreteness in terms of organized conceptual units implies that concreteness of the stimulus term is crucial, since it is the stimulus that, on recall trials, must reinstate (conceptually, symbolically) the organized stimulus-response unit experienced during their paired presentation. This argument is a restatement of the conceptual-peg hypothesis presented earlier, and evidence relevant to it will now be considered.

Stimulus Attributes and the Conceptual-Peg Hypothesis

The conceptual-peg metaphor was introduced without reference to imagery by Lambert and Paivio (1956), who reported an experiment concerned with the effect of word order on the sequential learning of groups of nouns and relevant, modifying adjectives. Since adjectives usually precede nouns in ordinary English usage (e.g., the red, white, and blue flag), superior learning might have been expected for the adjective-noun order. The converse was in fact predicted from the hypothesis that nouns are better conceptual pegs for their adjectival modifiers than vice-versa. The hypothesis was tested using a serial learning task involving seven groups of words, each group consisting of a noun and three modifying adjectives. For one group of subjects, each noun preceded its adjectives; for the other, adjectives preceded nouns. The conceptual-peg hypothesis was supported by the finding that the noun-adjective order was significantly easier to learn than the adjective-noun order of presentation.

Imagery was explicitly incorporated into the metaphorical hypothesis in a subsequent study by Paivio (1963). Specifically, it was suggested that stimulus-evoked imagery is the mechanism responsible for the superior learning Lambert and Paivio found for the noun-adjective order, particularly since most of the nouns used in that study were relatively concrete. The extended hypothesis was tested in two experiments involving noun-adjective pairs, with noun-adjective order and abstractness-concreteness of nouns varied. It was predicted that learning would be superior with concrete nouns and that this effect would be greater on the stimulus side of pairs, where the noun's image-evoking capacity could have its effect on response retrieval. Stated another way, the noun-adjective order was expected to be particularly favored when nouns were concrete. Consider the pairs *valley-deep* and *place-deep*. The former should evoke a single compound image of a specific valley with the intrinsic property of depth. The stimulus cue, valley, presented during the recall trial, would suffice to re-evoke the particular image, which would in turn mediate the response, deep. The pair, place-deep, would not evoke imagery so readily because of the referential generality of the noun "place," and whatever imagery is evoked would not be so reliably elicited by the subsequent presentation of "place" as a cue. When the pairs are presented in the adjective-noun order, the effect of noun concreteness should be essentially the same as in the noun-adjective order during the study trial, when both members are presented. On recall trials, however, the stimulus cue "deep" would be less effective in reinstating a specific image than the noun "valley" and, since the latter is not explicitly present as a cue, its image-arousing capacity would be less important to recall performance than when it serves as the stimulus; at least, so it was assumed in the hypothesis.

Confirmation of the prediction called for an interaction of noun-concreteness and adjective-noun order, so that the superior recall with concrete nouns would be greater when the nouns serve as stimulus terms. The results of one experiment, involving elementary school children, showed the differential effect; a comparable experiment with university students as subjects did not. Both experiments did, however, show better recall with nouns in the stimulus rather than the response position, confirming the original Lambert and Paivio (1956) finding. The results for both children and adults are presented graphically in Figure 8-1. The adult pattern of results was replicated in a further experiment by Kusyszyn and Paivio (1966).

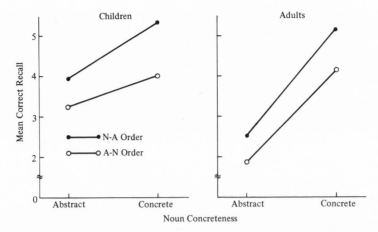

FIGURE 8-1.   Mean number of correct responses to stimuli during recall test as a function of adjective-noun word order and noun concreteness. The Concreteness X Word Order interaction is significant for children but not adults. Data from Paivio (1963).

The noun-adjective experiments thus yielded interesting results with respect to word order and main effects of concreteness but only weak support for the hypothesis that noun concreteness would be differentially effective on the stimulus side of pairs. We shall return later to a consideration of the possibility that the word-order effect might itself be attributable to the differential imagery value of nouns and adjectives. At this point, we turn to one feature of the adjective-noun situation that might limit the generalization and inferences that can be made from the data. The word sequences or pairs used in those experiments involved relatively strong direct associative connections to begin with, and these may have tended to obscure any mediational effects attributable to imagery. The conceptual-peg hypothesis was accordingly tested further in a series of experiments involving relatively unrelated noun-noun pairs, with abstractness-concreteness systematically varied among both stimulus and response members.

The theoretical argument differs in one respect from that involved in the adjective-noun situation, although the general mediating function attributed to imagery remains the same. An adjective-noun pair comprises a single conceptual unit in which the adjective specifies some attribute of the noun concept, whereas an unrelated noun pair comprises two conceptual units. If imagery is to function effectively as a mediator of the noun-noun association, it must consist of a compound image incorporating the representations evoked by each word individually. Such encoding of stimulus and response terms into a compound image presumably would occur during the study trial. To be effective in prompting response recall, the compound image must be rearoused by the stimulus member alone during the recall trial. The process could be conceptualized as involving an organized compound in which both elements are redintegrated by the stimulus, as Köhler apparently assumed, or it could be viewed as a two-stage affair in which the stimulus first elicits an appropriate referential or associative image and this in turn arouses the image corresponding to the response term, in an imaginal associative chain. In either case, the image-evoking capacity of the pair member that serves as the stimulus would be critical during the recall trial, since it would affect the reliability with which at least one component of the mediating image is reinstated. Specificity and reliability of the evoked imagery would also affect the ease with which the appropriate verbal response can be retrieved from the mediating image. The analysis thus assumed a complex sequence of encoding during both study and recall trials, and a further decoding process during recall in order to reproduce the response.

The hypothesis was first tested by Paivio (1965), using 16 pairs of nouns, four of each possible combination of stimulus and reponse abstractness-concreteness. The specific prediction was that the four types of pairs would rank in the order: concrete-concrete, concrete-abstract, abstract-concrete, and abstract-abstract, in increasing order of difficulty, thus reflecting the greater potency of concreteness on the stimulus side. The results of four study-test trials using college students were exactly as predicted, with abstractness-concreteness of stimulus members accounting for eight times the variance attributable to response concreteness. The means of the total recall scores over four trials are shown for each type of pair in Figure 8-2.

The reliability of the findings for noun pairs was confirmed and their generality extended in subsequent research. The experiments were designed to clarify problems of interpretation arising from the initial study, and they will

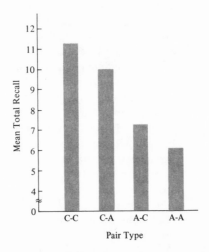

FIGURE 8-2. Mean total PA recall scores over four trials for noun pairs as a function of stimulus and response abstractness-concreteness. Data from Paivio (1965).

be considered in detail in the context of such problems later. A brief summary at this point will indicate the nature of some of the extensions. Paivio and Olver (1964) investigated the effects of denotative generality-specificity, rather than abstractness-concreteness. That is, all of the words were concrete, but some words, such as *furniture* and *money*, were relatively general, whereas others, such as *table* and *dollar*, were relatively specific. The four types of pairs involved in the experiment were general-general, general-specific, specific-general, and specific-specific. The results of four alternating learning trials and recall trials showed that stimulus specificity was positively related to recall, but response specificity was not. Imagery ratings also showed that specific nouns were superior to general nouns in their capacity to evoke images, and stimulus imagery was found to correlate positively with recall.

Yarmey and Paivio (1965) investigated the effect of noun-concreteness on stimulus and response sides when the other member of the pair was a nonsense syllable. That is, some subjects learned noun-nonsense syllable pairs, whereas others learned syllable-noun pairs. The results again showed superior learning with concrete nouns rather than with abstract nouns as stimuli, but the effect of noun concreteness was not significant on the response side. While consistent with the conceptual-peg hypothesis, this finding raises a problem for an interpretation in terms of mediating imagery. Specifically, how can a nonsense syllable response be transformed into a concrete image? The question will be considered later in detail.

In a further experiment, Paivio and Yarmey (1966) extended the analysis of concreteness effects to pictures and words, which were systematically paired into the four possible S-R combinations. It will be recalled that Epstein at al. (1960) compared only pairs in which both members were pictures or both were words. Thus it could not be ascertained whether pictures facilitated S-R linkage or simply enhanced response learning. Wimer and Lambert (1959) had reported that paired-associate learning with nonsense syllables as responses was easier when the stimulus members were objects than when they were the names of objects. However, they did not similarly vary concreteness on the response side and it could not be determined whether objects are more facilitative on the stimulus side, as the conceptual-peg hypothesis predicts. The Paivio and Yarmey study confirmed the prediction: Pictures were more facilitative as stimulus members than as response members. In fact, there was some suggestion that pictures might pose a decoding problem as responses, inasmuch as picture-word pairs were easier to learn than picture-picture pairs.[1] This suggestion, too, will be discussed further in subsequent sections.

---

[1] An unpublished Ph.D. dissertation by Lumsdaine (1949), which recently came to my attention, clearly has priority as showing the differential stimulus and response effects of picture-word variation. His study included the four possible combinations of pictures and words as stimulus and response items in PA lists. Like Paivio and Yarmey, Lumsdaine found that pictures were superior to printed words as stimulus terms. However, words were better than pictures as response terms, which is what Dilley and Paivio (1968) found with children as subjects. These findings will be discussed again in later contexts.

Interpretations aside, it should be noted that the above findings contrast sharply with a rather common empirical generalization in verbal learning literature (e.g., Goss & Nodine, 1965, pp. 219–220; Noble & McNeely, 1957), namely, that response factors are crucial in paired-associate learning, whereas stimulus factors are relatively unimportant. In the present instance, the stimulus attribute turned out to have much more weight than the response attribute, indicating at least the heuristic value of the hypothesis that generated the novel finding. However, it does not follow that the imagery hypothesis has been unequivocally confirmed, for the findings raise a number of empirical and theoretical issues that must be resolved before any particular interpretation can be confidently embraced.

The identification of the effective meaning dimension is a major problem. Is noun imagery, as indexed by ratings, or picturability in the case of object- or picture-word comparisons, "really" the effective empirical attribute or is it some correlated attribute such as meaningfulness? This is a general problem faced by all investigators concerned with interpretation of the effects of correlated attributes of items (cf. Underwood & Schulz, 1960). In this case, if the observed relations involving word imagery can be attributed to some other empirical variable, the theoretical argument for stimulus imagery as the effective underlying process is obviously weakened. The first task, therefore, is to compare imagery-concreteness with other potentially relevant item attributes and to consider the theoretical implications of the findings.

IMAGERY AND MEANINGFULNESS COMPARED

The most important alternative to imagery is verbal associative meaningfulness, especially as indexed by Noble's m, which has been empirically related to paired-associate learning in numerous studies and theoretically linked to verbal mediating processes in the manner specified by the associative probability hypothesis described earlier. As indicated in Chapter 3, concrete nouns generally surpass abstract nouns in m as well as rated imagery, or I (Paivio, Yuille, & Madigan, 1968); furthermore, m and I correlated about equally with paired-associate learning scores in the Paivio (1965) experiment, which first confirmed the predicted differential effect of imagery-concreteness on the stimulus side of pairs.

It seemed unlikely at the outset that meaningfulness could be the effective variable because its effect is usually greater when varied among response members than among stimuli, contrary to the effect of concreteness. However, as pointed out earlier, the studies that show a bigger response effect of meaningfulness typically have involved lists in which the high-m items are meaningful words whereas the low-m items consist of nonsense syllables or paralogs, which are devoid of meaning in the conventional sense. Response learning is accordingly a major problem in the latter case and it is not surprising that meaningfulness is then more influential on the response side. When only familiar words are used, response learning is relatively less important and m may not show its typical response-term potency. That this may be the case is suggested by several studies in which m appeared to be either more effective on the stimulus side or equally effective on both sides of pairs (Epstein & Streib, 1962; Goss, Nodine, Gregory, Taub, & Kennedy, 1962; G. Mandler & Campbell, 1957).

The problem was clarified by a series of experiments that showed unequivocally that the effects of imagery cannot be attributed to differences in associative meaningfulness and at the same time provided information on the relative potency of the two empirical attributes. In the first of these studies, Paivio, Yuille, and Smythe (1966) attempted to vary concreteness, imagery, and m individually in different lists in such a manner that one attribute was systematically varied among stimulus and response members while maintaining within-pair constancy on the other two variables. Because of the positive correlations among the three variables, only a restricted range of independent S-R variation was possible. Despite this limitation, the results showed the usual positive stimulus effect for imagery, but its response effect was not significant. Meaningfulness had a significant positive effect on both stimulus and response sides when the pairs consisted of nouns that were relatively abstract but not when m was varied within concrete pairs. Other studies (Paivio, 1967; Paivio & Olver, 1964) have shown that partialing out m statistically had little effect on the positive correlation between learning scores and noun imagery, but, with imagery similarly controlled, the relations between learning and m were reduced to zero.

More rigorous control over the range of variability in the contrasting variables was subsequently achieved using words from the normative sample of 925 nouns for which scores are available on rated concreteness, rated imagery, and 30-second production m (Paivio, Yuille, & Madigan, 1968). As already indicated in previous discussions (e.g., Chapters 3 and 7), concreteness and I correlate .83 in the sample, rendering it generally impractical to control concreteness while varying imagery, although this had been attempted in the Paivio, Yuille, and Smythe (1966) experiment described above. In that case, however, concreteness was treated as a dichotomous variable—that is, nouns were simply categorized as concrete or abstract rather than being measured on a more finely graded scale. In our subsequent paired-associate studies using the new norms, we have generally allowed concreteness and I to covary, although evidence to be considered in a later section has shown that imagery is somewhat superior to concreteness as a predictor of learning.

An experiment by Smythe and Paivio (1968) involved independent variation in imagery and m over three levels (high, medium, and low) on stimulus and response sides, so that the range of variation of the two variables was roughly equal in terms of standard score units based on the distribution of each variable in the normative sample. The results included complex interactions, but the relevant findings in the present context were that I again was positively effective, more so on the stimulus side, whereas the only effect of m was a slight *negative* one occurring on the response side of pairs when the pairs consisted of low-imagery items.

The above findings indicate clearly that m cannot explain the consistent positive effect of imagery and that any effect of m is at best inconsistent and weak. An established variable cannot be dismissed lightly, however, so the question was asked in one more way: Does m contribute at all to the observed effects when allowed to covary with imagery, as it did in the original Paivio (1965) experiment? To answer this, Paivio, Smythe, and Yuille (1968) constructed three 16-pair PA lists. In one list, imagery was held constant while stimulus and response m were varied in a factorial design, so that different pairs were high m-high m, high m-low m, low m-high m, and low m-low m. In another list, m was held constant while I was similarly varied, and in a third, I and m were covaried—that is, the nouns were either high or low on both imagery and meaningfulness. The range of variation of the independent variable in the three lists was again roughly equivalent in standard score units. The critical question was whether the covarying attributes would be more effective than imagery alone, thereby indicating that m added something in the former case. The means of the total recall scores over four trials are shown in Figure 8-3. Separate analyses of the data for each list indicated again that m had a negative effect, recall being better for low-low pairs than for other pair types. The effects of imagery were again highly significant on both stimulus and response sides, with the former having greater weight. The covarying attributes also had positive effects, attributable primarily to the high recall scores for high-high pairs. In contrast with the imagery-varied list, however, the list with the covarying attributes also showed a significant interaction of stimulus and response attributes, reflecting the relatively high recall of pairs in which both members are low in both imagery and m. Thus, even when allowed to covary with imagery, m apparently contributed a negative effect.

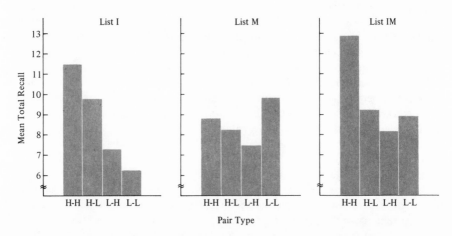

FIGURE 8-3. Paired-associate learning as a function of high (H) and low (L) levels of stimulus and response I (List I), m (List M), and I-m covaried (List IM). From Paivio, Smythe, and Yuille (1968).

The effects of noun imagery have been demonstrated with various procedures in the different experiments, including lists that are mixed with respect to stimulus and response variation in imagery, as well as homogeneous lists. The *m* effects always involved a mixed-list design. A further experiment was accordingly conducted by Paivio, Smythe, and Yuille (1968) using homogeneous lists of the four possible S-R combinations of high and low *m*, with imagery controlled. The results revealed no significant effects, although the trend again was for somewhat better recall of low *m*-low *m* pairs than of the other combinations.

The conclusion from these studies is clear. *The relations between noun imagery and paired-associate learning not only can not be interpreted in terms of meaningfulness, but imagery is the more potent of the two empirical variables.* The effects of *m* have, in fact, varied from slightly positive, to zero, to slightly negative in the different experiments. The variable effects of word *m* require explanation (this will be attempted below), but they do not appear to be directly relevant to the interpretation of the noun imagery effect. Moreover, it may be noted that differences in *m* cannot account for the effects of object or picture-word variation, inasmuch as Wimer and Lambert (1959) and Dominowski and Gadlin (1968) obtained superior learning with objects and pictures, respectively, as compared to words as stimuli, without the words used in the studies being inferior to the pictures in associative meaningfulness.

General Implications of the Findings

The relative effects of imagery and *m* as demonstrated by the above studies have general implications regarding the interpretation of the effects of meaningfulness as reported in recent literature. As we have frequently noted, such effects typically are interpreted almost exclusively in terms of verbal associative processes. This remains a plausible interpretation where meaningfulness has been varied over a range extending from real words to nonsense words, although even here the issue is plagued by the fact that many dimensions of meaning, including familiarity and imagery, undoubtedly covary in such studies (cf. the arguments regarding other memory tasks discussed in the preceding chapter) and any one may have contributed to the observed effects. The strictures regarding interpretations of *m* effects in terms of verbal associative meaningfulness are more severe in the case of studies involving only real words, and in which imagery-concreteness has not been controlled.

A description of two specific studies will serve to illustrate the above points. D. J. Mueller and Travers (1965) reported a paired-associate learning study involving a comparison of high *m*-low *m* pairs with low *m*-high *m* pairs. On the basis of the usual finding of a stronger positive effect of *m* on the response side than on the stimulus side of pairs, it would have been expected that the low *m*-high *m* pairs would be easier to learn. The reverse was in fact obtained. The result is not surprising when we examine the items used in the study: The low-meaningfulness items consisted of nonsense syllables such as DEJ, YIL, POB, etc., whereas the high-*m* items consisted entirely of familiar concrete nouns such as HAT, BAG, DAY, and BED. Thus the finding of a greater positive effect of the nominal meaning variable, *m*, on the stimulus side is interpretable in terms of imagery—indeed, the results are entirely consistent with the Yarmey and Paivio (1965) learning data for noun-nonsense syllable pairs when noun *m* was held constant and concreteness was varied.

The second illustrative study is one by Saltz (1967), in which the effects of *m* and Thorndike-Lorge frequency were compared as stimulus variables in paired-associate learning. The frequency effects will be considered fully in a later section and at this point attention is centered only on the effects of meaningfulness. Three different experiments agreed in showing that increased stimulus *m* facilitated learning. Saltz discussed the findings in terms of verbal associative mechanisms, but an examination of the experimental pairs again reveals that imagery-concreteness was not controlled and it covaried with *m*. This is most apparent in the case of relatively frequent words. For example, in Saltz's list of words occurring 100–2000 times per 4.5 million, the items at the high-*m* end consisted of highly concrete words such as COUNTRY, WINDOW, BUILD-ING, STREET, and GARDEN. Those at the low-*m* end include REPLY, JOURNAL, PROMISE, MATTER, QUESTION and RETURN. All but one of these (JOURNAL) are abstract. The point need not be labored—given the relative ineffectiveness of *m* when imagery was controlled in the studies described earlier, Saltz probably emphasized a relatively ineffective variable.

The caution regarding interpretations in terms of *m* obviously may apply to studies other than those of Mueller and Travers and of Saltz. It also extends to word classes other than nouns. Kanungo (1968) used function words such as ABOUT, ENOUGH, FROM, and HENCE, and their scrambled nonsense-word versions (BAUTO, HEUGON, MORF, EHNEC, etc.) as items in paired-associate learning. The 60-second production *m* (Noble, 1952a) scores were clearly higher for the function words (mean *m* = 4.14) than for the nonsense word (mean *m* = 2.97). The results showed that, after response learning had been equated by prior familiarization trials with the list items, the higher *m* of the function words did not facilitate associative learning. The finding again suggests that *m* is an ineffective variable unless it covaries with other attributes. The absence of any high imagery items in Kanungo's lists is particularly apparent, and his failure to obtain significant effects is therefore not surprising in the light of the present theoretical and empirical context.

A possible explanation of the meaningfulness data   The interference paradox of associative probability theory (Underwood & Schulz, 1960, pp. 46–47) provides a possible explanation of the variable effects of *m*. Recall that the associative probability theory suggests that an increase in the number of associations elicited by an item increases the probability that one or more of these will enter into mediated association with other items in the list. That is, two items may share an implicit associative response in common. Where the mediated association happens to be correct, facilitation would be expected.

The paradox, of course, is that the common implicit responses may mediate incorrect associations and hence interfere with learning. As applied to the variable effects of m, this analysis implies that correct mediated associations have been favored in those instances in which m has been observed to have a positive effect (for example, Paivio et al., 1966), and incorrect mediation has been favored where negative effects have occurred (e.g., Paivio, Symthe, & Yuille, 1968). In other cases, positive and negative mediated associations have simply canceled each other out.

Satisfactory direct evidence for the above interpretation is lacking, although L. D. Barnes and Schulz (1966) did obtain support for one deduction from the theory. They reasoned that a slow presentation rate would provide an opportunity for subjects somehow to select the correct association from interfering incorrect ones. To test this, they compared paired-associate learning for high m-high m and low m-high m pairs at test intervals of 2.5, 3.5, and 4.5 seconds, using a multiple-choice test procedure in which the correct response had to be selected from among four alternatives presented with each stimulus term. Consistent with their hypothesis, recall was superior for the low m-high m pairs at the two faster intervals, whereas high m-high m were superior at the 4.5 second interval. The finding is certainly suggestive, but once again our confidence in any interpretation is weakened by a confounding of item attributes. Barnes and Schulz used high-m and low-m dissyllables from Noble's (1952a) list, which certainly differ greatly in familiarity (and probably imagery) as well as m, thus making it impossible to conclude that implicit associations per se are crucial to the effects.

We turn now to studies concerned with the relative effects and interactions of word frequency and imagery. In seeking to interpret some of the findings, we shall have occasion once more to consider possible interfering effects attributable to implicit verbal associations.

Imagery and Frequency Compared

Word frequency was controlled in the studies reviewed above, so we can be certain that the effects of imagery in any given experiment are not due to frequency. It remains possible, however, that the two variables interact in such a manner that the effect of imagery as a stimulus or response attribute is qualified by the relative familiarity of the items. Conversely, frequency effects may be modified by item imagery, as they were shown to do in free recall when mixed lists are used (see Chapter 7). We shall see that such interactions do indeed occur and we are therefore faced with the problem of interpreting complex effects that implicate both imaginal and verbal processes.

An unpublished experiment conducted in the context of the Paivio et al. (1966) study described earlier in relation to imagery and m effects involved the same design in regard to frequency variation as that reported for imagery and m. Half the pairs of a 16-pair list were concrete and half were abstract nouns. Within each concreteness level, frequency was factorially varied on the stimulus and response sides so that two pairs each were high frequency-high frequency, high frequency-low frequency, and so on. The results of four study-test trials are shown in Figure 8-4, where it can be seen that, within concrete nouns only, response frequency had a slight positive relation to recall. Within abstract nouns, however, the effects of both stimulus frequency and response frequency were significantly negative, largely because of the relative ease of learning low-low pairs. In addition, it is obvious from Figure 8-4 that recall was again much better for concrete pairs than for abstract pairs.

In a subsequent study, Paivio and Madigan (1970) factorially varied frequency and imagery among stimulus and response members of 16-pair mixed lists. Two basic lists were constructed from 64 nouns, 16 of which were high on both variables, 16 were high imagery and low frequency, and so on. Two new lists were constructed by re-pairing the items from the original lists, and four additional lists resulted from reversing the S-R position of pairs in the four basic lists. Each subject was presented four study-test trials with two such lists. The strongest effect overall was that of stimulus imagery. The consistency of this effect was apparent from the fact that recall was better when stimulus *I* was high than when it was low regardless of the level of the other variables. Significant but smaller positive effects were also obtained for response imagery and response frequency. The main effect of stimulus frequency was negative in direction but not significant.

Several interaction effects were significant, but the strongest of these was the triple interaction of stimulus imagery, response imagery, and stimulus frequency, which is presented in Figure 8-5. No attempt will be made here to interpret all of the details of this complex pattern and attention is directed

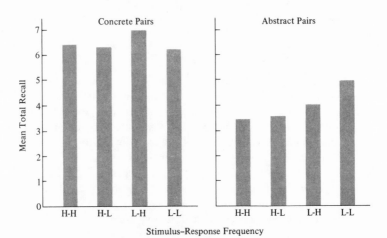

FIGURE 8-4.   Mean total recall scores over four trials as a function of high (H) and low (L) levels of stimulus and response frequency, within concrete and abstract noun pairs.

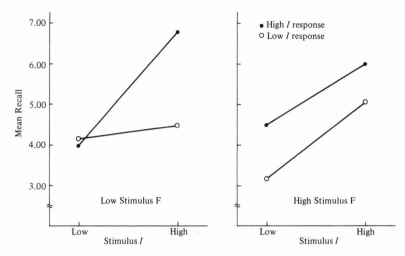

FIGURE 8-5. Mean total recall scores as a function of stimulus imagery, response imagery, and stimulus frequency. From Paivio and Madigan (1970).

instead to one specific comparison.[2] Note that recall was highest when both members of the pair were high imagery but stimulus frequency was low. Conversely, recall was poorest when both members were low imagery but stimulus frequency was high. Thus stimulus frequency apparently contributes negatively to the stimulus effect of imagery—high-imagery stimulus nouns are especially effective when the words are relatively infrequent and low-imagery stimuli are especially ineffective when the words are highly familiar.

The strong positive effect of stimulus imagery is consistent with the conceptual peg interpretation in which mediating imagery is assumed to be the crucial mechanism. Response imagery presumably contributes to this effect by facilitating the formation of a compound image incorporating the referents of both members of a pair during study trials. But why is *low* stimulus frequency additionally facilitative under these conditions, as shown by the triple interaction?

---

[2] Caution is required in the interpretation of this interaction because of the mixed-list design and the relatively small sampling of pairs representing each combination of stimulus and response variables, but several considerations suggest that on the whole it represents a reliable pattern. The mean value of each point in the interaction is based on the recall scores for four pairs and the effect is highly significant statistically. Moreover, some of its most notable features are consistent with data from the first experiments (Figure 8-4). Thus the highest recall in the latter was for concrete (high *I*) pairs with low-frequency stimuli and high-frequency responses. Precisely the same combination of attributes was associated with the highest recall in the Paivio and Madigan study, although the contribution of response frequency does not appear in the triple interaction. Conversely, the lowest scores in the first experiment were for abstract (low *I*) pairs in which the stimulus members were high frequency, again paralleling closely the Paivio and Madigan data. Given their apparent reliability, these interesting results merit theoretical consideration.

An obvious possibility is that low frequency somehow facilitates stimulus (or pair) differentiation. This could be interpreted in terms of either imaginal or verbal mediating processes. According to the imagery interpretation, low stimulus frequency might mean that the stimulus-evoked images are relatively unusual and therefore suffer little interference from images evoked by other stimuli in the list. This interpretation is consistent with the principle of novelty or bizarreness of images that was advocated in the ancient mnemonic systems. It is also attractive because a single type of mediator would suffice to account for both the strong positive effect of stimulus I and the additional contribution of low stimulus frequency to that effect. Unfortunately, this interpretation is weakened by the doubtful validity of the bizarre-image principle, according to other data to be considered in Chapter 10.

The alternative possibility is that pre-experimental verbal associative habits are for some reason less likely to compete and interfere with the learning of the new associative response when the stimuli are low frequency and concrete than when they are high frequency and abstract. One basis for such an effect is suggested by Underwood and Postman's (1960) analysis of the role of unit-sequence (i.e., word-word) habits. Such habits could have transfer effects in the experimental setting that are either positive or negative, depending on the relationship between the subject's pre-experimental associations and those to be acquired in the learning task. The amount of transfer (positive or negative) should increase with the frequency of prior usage of a word because the higher the frequency, the larger the number of different contexts in which the word is likely to appear and hence the larger the number of different associations which it acquires. Postman (1962) tested and found some support for this hypothesis in three experiments. One experiment, for example, involved high-, medium-, and low-frequency nouns paired in all possible combinations of stimulus and response frequency in different lists. The results showed that (a) speed of learning first increased then decreased as a function of stimulus frequency— that is, lists with medium-frequency stimuli were learned faster than those with stimuli of high or low frequency; (b) speed of learning varied directly with response frequency; and (c) the rate of overt errors was a positively accelerated function of the frequency level of both stimuli and responses—that is, errors were highest when either member of the pair was high frequency. Thus both facilitative and interfering effects were associated with frequency level.

Postman's results suggest that it might be reasonable to interpret the negative contribution of stimulus frequency in the Paivio and Madigan experiment in similar terms. Abstract and concrete nouns did not differ in associative meaningfulness, but it is possible nevertheless that high-frequency abstract nouns elicit a greater number of *different* words as associates than do low-frequency concrete nouns, and that associations interfere with the learning of the new associative response.

A somewhat similar proposal has been suggested by Saltz (1967) in the study described earlier in relation to the effects of m, in which Saltz also investigated the effects of stimulus-term frequency when m was held constant. The results of three different experiments showed that increased stimulus frequency was associated with slower learning. Saltz suggested that S-R systems involving more frequent stimuli are more resistant to disruption from new responses to be acquired in the learning task. More simply stated, new associations will be more difficult to learn because of the stronger pre-experimental language habits associated with high-frequency stimuli. This interpretation is similar to the Underwood-Postman unit-sequence interference hypothesis, except that the latter emphasizes the *number* of different S-R associations and their effect on the forgetting of newly acquired associations, whereas Saltz emphasizes the *strength* of the S-R habit and its resistance to disruption by new learning. As applied to the interaction of frequency and imagery in the Paivio and Madigan experiment, Saltz's analysis implies that low imagery-high frequency stimuli involve strong pre-experimental verbal S-R systems that are particularly resistant to disruption by the new responses to be acquired during the learning task.

Neither of the above versions of the associative-interference interpretation is incompatible with the imagery mediation hypothesis. The latter is not intended as a complete theory of associative learning, and verbal associative factors would supplement imagery in a manner that would be consistent with the more general two-process theory of meaning and mediation. Thus the analyses suggest generally that pre-experimental verbal associative habits may interfere with new learning when the words are abstract and imagery is not readily available as a potential mediator of the S-R connection. When the items are concrete, imagery is presumably the dominant mediator, but its effects may be modified to some extent by verbal associative factors, as suggested by the frequency effects. No independent evidence of the contributions of both processes are available in the data considered in this chapter, but subsequent chapters focus on precisely this problem. Unfortunately, even there we will not find much direct evidence bearing on the associative-interference interpretations of word frequency effects, and interference theory itself is generally plagued by uncertainties (e.g., Underwood & Ekstrand, 1966) that we cannot resolve here.

To summarize the findings for imagery and frequency vis-a-vis the issues with which we are concerned, the data indicate first of all that imagery and frequency are distinct variables. In general, imagery is much more potent than frequency and the two variables again show contrasting patterns of relations to paired-associate recall. The positive effect of imagery is consistently greater on the stimulus side of pairs, whereas frequency is generally facilitative only on the response side (cf. Postman, 1962; Shapiro, 1969), and its effect is negative on the stimulus side under some combinations of stimulus or response imagery. Frequency is also differentiated from *m* in that its effect is consistently positive as a response variable, whereas that of *m* is inconsistent when imagery is controlled. This positive effect of frequency seems generally interpretable in terms of verbal representational meaning and the effect this has on response availability. It is noteworthy, finally, that the stimulus effects of imagery and frequency in PA learning parallel their respective positive and negative effects in free recall, recognition memory, and the L. R. Peterson and M. J. Peterson (1959) STM task, as described in Chapter 7; the positive response effect of frequency, on the other hand, is comparable to the consistent positive effect this variable was seen to have on the speed of perceptual recognition.

Other Confounding Word Attributes

The findings considered thus far rule out m and frequency as variables that might provide an alternative basis for the explanation of the effects of imagery-concreteness, but they do not eliminate the possibility that some other unidentified correlate of I might be responsible for the effects. This issue was clarified by a factor-analytic study (Paivio, 1968a), described previously in connection with the measurement of meaning (Chapter 3). The study involved 96 nouns for which mean scores were obtained on ease of learning and various semantic and associative characteristics. The other noun attributes, 27 in all, included several measures of concreteness and imagery, and other potentially effective variables such as m, familiarity, impressiveness, associative reaction time, and so on. The correlations between each of these attributes and paired-associate learning scores when the items served as stimuli and when they served as responses are presented in Table 8-1. It can be seen that only nine of the individual attributes and a rating scale polarity variable (the average departure of ratings from the neutral point on 15 scales) correlated significantly with one or both of the PA learning scores and, of these, rated I was the best predictor of learning, especially when varied on the stimulus side. Closely following I as a predictor were the other indices of imagery and concreteness. The correlations between m and learning can be entirely accounted for in terms of imagery, since the predictive power of m is reduced to zero when I is controlled (see the earlier discussion of m).

The above study suggests that rated imagery defines the effective noun attribute even better than the closely related variable, rated concreteness. The conclusion has been further supported in a study by Yuille (1968). He constructed a 20-pair PA list comprised of equal numbers of concrete-concrete, concrete-abstract, abstract-concrete, and abstract-abstract pairs in which I (as well as m and frequency) were held relatively constant. This was achieved by selecting the abstract nouns from a group of 51 "unusual" nouns from the Paivio et al. (1968) norms, which have medium I scores but low concreteness ratings (see the description in Chapter 3), and matching these with 20 concrete nouns with comparable I but with high concreteness ratings. The results of four study-test trials showed that stimulus concreteness was positively related to recall, but several types of evidence suggested that concreteness alone has little effect on learning. First, the pattern of results was unlike that obtained in any previous study in which imagery-concreteness has been varied in that abstract-abstract pairs were relatively well recalled, particularly on the first trial. Second, variation in concreteness independent of imagery was made possible only by the selection of a particular class of abstract nouns, which are characterized by their emotional connotation according to rating data. A correlation of −.48 between

Table 8-1

Pearsonian Correlations between PA Learning and Word Attributes as Stimulus and as Response Variables (data from Paivio, 1968a)

	Side of Attribute Variation	
Attribute	*Stimulus*	*Response*
Rated imagery	.54	.31
Rated vividness of imagery	.49	.21
Imaginal RT	—.42	—.20
Rated concreteness	.39	.13
Meaningfulness (*m*)	.37	.21
Rated tangibility	.33	.07
Semantic differential polarity	.33	.14
Preciseness	.27	.10
Verbal RT	—.21	—.09
Rated emotionality	—.20	—.02
Associative variety (pooled groups)	—.14	—.22
Associative variety (RT group)	—.05	—.10
Associative variety (TC group)	—.08	—.19
Frequency	—.14	—.06
Rated familiarity	.04	.15
Goodness	.02	.05
Impressiveness	.02	.08
Complexity	—.07	—.04
Activity	—.10	—.02
Usualness	.10	.10
Specificity	.15	.13
Hardness	.14	.01
Interest	—.03	.04
Rated meaningfulness	—.07	.09
Smoothness	.08	—.02
Colorfulness	.09	.18
Width	—.13	—.08
Note: A correlation of .20 is significant at $p = .05$		

stimulus emotionality and recall indicated that relatively unemotional words were recalled better than those rated higher in emotionality, replicating a finding in the factor-analytic study (Paivio, 1968a) described above. This correlation was reduced to —.24 when concreteness was partialed out, but stimulus concreteness also turned out to be quite unrelated to recall ($r = -.06$) when emotionality was similarly controlled. To summarize the main conclusions, concreteness could be varied independent of *I* only when emotionality was allowed to covary, and rated emotionality accounted for the recall data at least as well as concreteness. These conclusions clearly do not apply to rated imagery, which was shown to be superior to emotionality and concreteness as a stimulus predictor of paired-associate learning in the factor-analytic study. To the extent that emotionality can be equated with the concept of arousal, these observations are relevant also to recent findings (Butter, 1970) in which imagery and arousal effects apparently were confounded.

Thus the empirical conclusion is secure: All of the available evidence is consistent with the generalization that imagery is the most potent meaning attribute yet identified among familiar words—or nouns at least—and that this effect is greatest when imagery is varied as a stimulus attribute in associative learning. We turn next to a consideration of the interaction of stimulus with response attributes, which bears on the interpretation of the empirical effects in terms of mediating imagery.

The Imagery Hypothesis and Response Attributes

The imagery hypothesis of associative learning is further challenged by problems raised by the characteristics of the response members of pairs. An analysis in terms of stimulus-elicited mediating imagery is relatively straightforward and intuitively plausible when both members of the pair can be assumed to evoke images readily. It is less straightforward when a concrete noun is paired with an abstract noun, but here too it can be seen how a concrete stimulus might "prime" imaginal encoding of an abstract response in accordance with the analysis of associative meaning discussed in Chapter 3. For example, "religion" as a response term might be encoded as a church, given a concrete stimulus as the cue. It is more difficult similarly to interpet the finding by Yarmey and Paivio (1965) that noun concreteness is relatively more effective on the stimulus side even when the other member of the pair is a nonsense syllable. A mediational interpretation of the effect apparently requires a theory of multiple stages of coding in which it is assumed that a high-imagery stimulus term somehow increases the probability that a nonsense-syllable response will be encoded into a meaningful word and then further translated into concrete imagery. This would involve an extension of the concept of associative meaning, again as discussed in Chapter 3, where it was suggested, for example, that the nonsense syllable JAQ may be first encoded as JACK and then as the image of a person named Jack. The additional assumption in the present context is that a high-imagery stimulus term would tend to encourage such encoding. It must be assumed further that decoding from the mediator back to the nonsense-syllable response is not difficult, otherwise decoding errors would occur. The assumed coding sequence seems unusually complex in comparison with most contemporary mediation theories, including ones in which multiple stages have been postulated (e.g., McGuire, 1961). Nevertheless, a number of studies of coding processes in learning and memory (e.g., Lindley, 1963; Underwood & Erlebacher, 1965), to be considered in the next chapter, have provided evidence of effective syllable-to-word coding. The additional assumption of a further transformation into a nonverbal code does not go beyond the complexity of the conceptual-peg hypothesis itself except in assuming that an implicit verbal response can also be an effective cue for image arousal.

The above analysis in any case has testable implications. It suggests that the probability that mediating imagery would be effectively involved in paired-associate learning when the response term is a nonsense syllable will be a function of both the image-evoking value of the noun stimulus and the ease with which the syllable response can be encoded as a word. Paivio and Madigan (1968) tested the hypothesis using high-imagery and low-imagery nouns as either stimulus or response members for nonsense syllable associates, which in turn were either high association value consonant-vowel-consonant (CVC) syllables or low association value consonant-consonant-consonant (CCC) trigrams. It was reasoned that the hypothesis would be supported if the differential superiority of high-imagery nouns on the stimulus side of pairs is greater when their nonsense syllable associates are high rather than low in association value, since the former more readily suggest meaningful words that could enter into image-mediated linkage with the high-imagery stimuli. In other words, the magnitude of the stimulus effect of noun I should be a function of the association value of the response term. No such interaction should emerge with the nouns as response members since the nonsense word would not act as an effective cue for the evocation of mediating imagery during recall trials.

The results of four alternating study-test trials for the different pair combinations are shown in Figure 8-6. The results (confirmed by statistical analyses) were clearly as predicted for the first two trials—that is, the imagery value of the stimulus noun had no effect on the first two trials when the response term was low association value, but stimulus I was effective on all trials when the response was high association value. However, stimulus I was effective by trial four even with the low association value trigrams as responses. Note also that noun imagery was positively effective on the response side regardless of stimulus association value.

The Paivio and Madigan results for both levels of association value were incidentally confirmed in a study by Yarmey and O'Neill (1969), which was mainly concerned with broader issues to be considered later. The findings that are pertinent here were obtained using a design that essentially duplicated that used

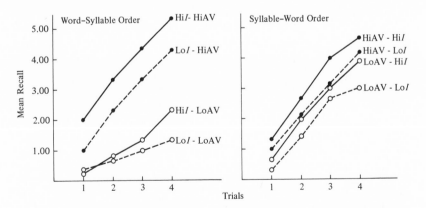

FIGURE 8-6. Mean paired-associate recall over four trials as a function of S-R order, noun imagery, and trigram association value. From Paivio and Madigan (1968).

by Paivio and Madigan. In one experiment, relatively high association value syllables served as stimuli or responses for concrete or abstract nouns; in another, the nonsense words were low association value CCC trigrams. Learning proceeded by the anticipation method to a criterion of two consecutive errorless trials. The mean total errors to criterion for each experimental group are shown in Table 8-2. These data indicate that, with high association value syllables as

Table 8-2

Mean Total Errors to Criterion as a Function of Noun Abstractness-Concreteness (CN versus AN), Nonsense Syllable Association Value (High versus Low AV), and S-R Order (Noun-Syllable versus Syllable-Noun). Data from Experiments II and III, Yarmey and O'Neill (1969)

	Noun-Syllable Order		Syllable-Noun Order	
	CN-NS	AN-NS	NS-CN	NS-AN
High AV	55.00	126.43	90.57	112.50
Low AV	212.83	242.25	113.08	183.25

associates, subjects made many more errors when the stimulus term was an abstract noun than when it was concrete, but no significant difference was obtained as a function of concreteness when the nouns served as responses. With the low association value trigrams as associates, on the other hand, pairs were found to be somewhat easier to learn when the noun member of the pairs was concrete than when it was abstract, but the interaction of concreteness by stimulus-response position was not significant, indicating that, in this case, noun concreteness was not more effective on the stimulus than on the response side of pairs. These findings are, therefore, in complete agreement with the Paivio-Madigan hypothesis.

The results just considered together with those previously described for noun-noun pairs support the following conclusion: To the extent that a *differential* effect of noun imagery-concreteness on the stimulus as compared to the response side is crucial to the imagery mediation theory of paired-associate learning, such mediation is most probable when the response term is a meaningful word, although it may also be involved to some degree when the response is a nonsense syllable provided that it readily suggests a word. In addition, the results show that noun *I* has some effect on both sides of pairs regardless of the nature of the associate, suggesting that some nonmediational process, such as differentiation based on semantic dissimilarity or distinctiveness, or response availability in the case of the response effect, may be involved. We shall return later to the question of the relative contributions of mediation and differentiation as alternative theoretical mechanisms.

It should be noted, finally, that the hypothesis that was examined in this section is amenable to a more refined test. A study by Imae (1968), previously mentioned in Chapter 3, involved Japanese two-letter syllables (corresponding to English CVCs), which were classified by a group of Japanese subjects into seven parts of speech (noun, verb, etc.). The noun-type syllables were further classified into concrete and abstract types when two-thirds of the subjects selected one alternative. The remainder were classified as indefinite. An incidental recall test after the rating task showed higher recall for the "concrete" than for the "abstract" syllables. These results are important for two reasons: First, they provide general support for the Paivio and Madigan hypothesis by showing that nonsense syllables reliably suggest words of particular types; second, they encourage further tests of the hypothesis using syllables that have been classified according to Imae's procedure into concrete and abstract noun types. Obvious predictions could be made for such items in paired-associate tasks of the kind under consideration, but the research remains to be done.

Pictures as response items   We have seen that nonsense-syllable responses pose an obvious problem for the imagery hypothesis of associative learning. A somewhat similar problem arises when pictures (or objects) serve as response members. It was noted earlier that, as a *stimulus* variable, concreteness appears to function as a single effective dimension that extends from abstract nouns, to concrete nouns, to objects or pictures, in increasing order of effectiveness. The stimulus superiority of objects or pictures over their concrete noun labels has been demonstrated in a number of experiments involving various procedures and with either adults or children as subjects (Dilley & Paivio, 1968; Lumsdaine, 1949; Paivo & Yarmey, 1966; Wimer & Lambert, 1959). The positive effect over the three levels of stimulus concreteness has been obtained within a single experiment by Csapo (1968) and Dominowski and Gadlin (1968).

The linear effect of concreteness does not obtain on the response side of pairs. Whereas learning has generally been easier when response nouns are concrete rather than abstract, pictures as response members are either not facilitative (Paivio & Yarmey, 1966) or are more difficult to learn than concrete nouns (Dilley & Paivio, 1968; Lumsdaine, 1949). The contrasting positive effect of pictures as stimulus members and their negative effect as response members are reflected most consistently in the fact that picture-word pairs are easier to learn than picture-picture pairs. This was true in the three studies just cited. Csapo's (1968) results are an exception to this generalization in that he found pictures to be superior to concrete words both as stimulus and as response terms, with picture-picture pairs being easier to learn than picture-word pairs. Why his results differed from those obtained in the previous three studies remains unanswered, but it is in any case safe to conclude that pictures are not consistently facilitative and may even have a negative effect as response members of pairs.

How is the paradoxical response effect of pictorial items to be explained? Paivio and Yarmey (1966) suggested that picture response terms may present a symbolic labeling or decoding problem. Thus, while the formation of a compound (mediating) image may be facilitated by pictures during the study trial, it may be more difficult during recall to decode the mediating image to yield the appropriate verbal response when the response component of that image was originally evoked by a picture rather than a word. On the basis of this hypothesis, Dilley and Paivio (1968) predicted that the negative effect of pictures as response terms would be particularly great with young children as subjects because they would be expected to experience greater difficulty than adults in transforming the concrete memory image of a pictorial response item into an overt verbal response. The results of an experiment with children were fully in accord with the prediction: Picture response items created much greater learning difficulty for them than Paivio and Yarmey (1966) had found with adults.

The decoding hypothesis could be expressed in terms of the relative availability of the verbal code in the case of the two kinds of response items, as discussed in the preceding chapter: The verbal code is simply less available (or less accessible) in the case of pictures. Since pictures presumably facilitate the formation of an imaginal mediator during paired presentation, the hypothesis implies that the advantage of pictures at that stage is more than offset by the decoding problem they present during recall. Unfortunately, the hypothesis is at odds with what was suggested in the earlier analysis of free recall. The consistent finding was that free verbal recall is higher for pictures than for their concrete noun labels, and this was interpreted in terms of the greater availability of the imaginal memory code in the case of pictures. The assumption was that the concrete memory image could be readily decoded to yield the verbal response provided that the pictures can be easily named. There seems to be no reason to assume that the situation would differ in the case of recall of the response term in paired-associate learning. Thus we are led to the conclusion that the difficulty lies, not in the decoding of the response component of an imaginal mediator, but elsewhere in the symbolic transition from stimulus to response.

Further consideration of the response problem will require taking account of findings from studies in which mediation has been experimentally manipulated. The relevant studies are reviewed in Chapter 11 and the present issue accordingly must be left in abeyance until then.

Adjective Imagery and the Conceptual-Peg Hypothesis

The discussions thus far have been concerned mainly with variation in the imagery value of nouns, although it was implied earlier that the lower recall for adjective and verb pairs, relative to noun pairs, found by Busemann (in Reed, 1918a, p. 141) might be attributable to differences in abstractness. The issue will be considered in more detail here, with reference specifically to adjectives. It is apparent that adjectives must be more abstract and therefore lower in imagery value than concrete nouns at least, inasmuch as adjectives refer to abstract properties that are not picturable except as part of some object that they qualify. To the extent that this is true, the superiority of the noun-adjective order of presentation in learning adjective-noun pairs (e.g., Paivio, 1963) could be interpreted simply as a special case of the differential facilitating effect of concreteness, or imagery value, on the stimulus side of pairs. This formulation differs from the conceptual-peg hypothesis as it was applied to noun-adjective pairs (Paivio, 1963) in that the emphasis is now placed explicitly on the differential imagery values of nouns and adjectives, rather than on some vague grammatical difference between the words. A similar interpretation of the noun-adjective order effect in terms of differential abstractness was in fact proposed by Lockhart (1969), who pointed out that such an explanation denies the importance of form class as such.

The proposed interpretation was not adequately tested in any of the studies considered earlier (Kusyszyn & Paivio, 1966; Paivio, 1963), and their findings left open the possibility that form class may have some effect independent of differential imagery values. This is true particularly of the studies with adults, which showed the superiority of noun-adjective over adjective-noun order to be as great when the noun member was abstract as when it was concrete. Lockhart (1969) found support for the abstractness interpretation in a study concerned with retrieval asymmetry, i.e., the relative effectiveness of stimulus and response members as retrieval cues in noun-adjective pairs (see further below). However, no evidence was directly provided on the possible role of adjective imagery in the order effect.

Such evidence was obtained in a study by Yuille, Paivio, and Lambert (1969) who also extended the experimental design to include French subjects learning adjective-noun pairs in their own language. Thus the experiment involved adjective-noun order, noun imagery, adjective imagery, and language (English and French) as variables. Noun imagery values were based on the Paivio, Yuille, and Madigan (1968) norms, and adjective imagery data were obtained specifically for the study. Subjects were presented three alternating study test trials with each of two 16-pair lists, one list having pairs in the noun-adjective order; the other, in the adjective-noun order. Each list was mixed with respect to noun and adjective imagery, so that there were four pairs of each possible combination of high and low imagery values. Examples of each type of pair are: *butter-pretty* (high *I*-high *I*), *skin-wise* (high *I*-low *I*), *method-cold* (low *I*-high *I*), and *amount-plain* (low *I*-low *I*).

The results showed the usual superior learning for pairs in the noun-adjective order, and for ones containing high imagery nouns. In addition, adjective imagery had a significant positive effect. These effects were qualified by significant interactions, of which only the most relevant ones will be discussed here. Interactions involving adjective-noun order and imagery showed that the imagery level of both adjectives and nouns had a greater effect with the words in the stimulus rather than the response position in the pairs, which is consistent with the conceptual-peg hypothesis. In addition, an interaction of noun and adjective imagery showed that the former had the greater effect.

The above interactions were to some extent qualified by a triple interaction of noun imagery, adjective imagery, and order, which is illustrated in Figure 8-7.

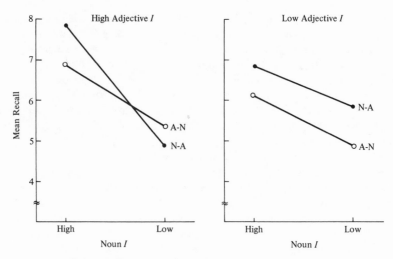

FIGURE 8-7. Mean total PA recall for adjective-noun pairs as a function of noun imagery, adjective imagery, and adjective-noun word order. From Yuille, Paivio, and Lambert (1969).

This interaction indicates in part that the largest effect of imagery was obtained for noun *I* when pairs were in the noun-adjective order and the response adjectives were high in imagery. This feature of the complex effect is consistent with the imagery hypothesis in that learning is easiest when both members are high imagery and when the stimulus member is a noun. Recall suffers particularly when the stimulus noun is low imagery. However, another feature of the interaction shows the effect of adjective imagery: While pairs in the noun-adjective order are generally easier to recall than those in the adjective-noun order, the reverse is true in the case of pairs in which the adjectival member is high imagery and the noun is low imagery.

The Yuille et al. experiment indicates that stimulus imagery is effective to some degree when varied among adjectives as well as nouns. The greater effect of noun imagery may be partly due to a relatively larger variation of imagery within that class, inasmuch as the mean rated *I* values for high and low levels, respectively, were 6.45 and 2.94 for nouns and 5.70 and 3.84 for adjectives. Absolute comparisons are unwarranted on the basis of these figures, however, since the *I* ratings were obtained from different groups of subjects, each group rating words of one class only. Since the rating of a word is likely to be influenced by the context in which it occurs, comparisons of adjectives and nouns on *I* obviously should be based on a mixed set of words rated by the same group of subjects. Such ratings have been obtained since the above study was completed. A group of subjects rated a sizable sample of words that included nouns, adjectives, verbs, adverbs, and function words. The data for nouns and adjectives generally confirm those obtained by Yuille et al. in that the range of variability (as measured by the standard deviation) of *I* values was considerably lower for adjectives than for nouns. Thus it seems reasonable to conclude that the smaller effect of adjective imagery, as compared to noun imagery, is partly due to a more restricted range of imagery variation in the case of the former.

A recent experiment by Philipchalk and Begg (1970) provided evidence that adjective imagery and noun imagery have similar effects when differences in the range of imagery variation are reduced. The study included nonassociative as well as associative tasks, but our interest in the present context is only in the latter. The to-be-learned items included high- and low-imagery nouns and adjectives associated with nonsense syllables embedded in sentence fragments. Thus one list contained such items as "The QOF blister," another "The rusty QOF," a third "The QOF explanation," and a fourth "The basic QOF," where blister and rusty are relatively concrete whereas explanation and basic are relatively abstract. The concrete and abstract nouns had mean rated imagery scores of 6.62 and 2.67, respectively; the concrete and abstract adjectives, 5.28 and 2.21.

A study-test procedure was used such that the sentence fragments were first shown successively; then the sentence frames were presented with the nonsense syllables missing, and the subjects attempted to fill in the blanks. Thus, the nouns and adjectives in effect functioned as stimuli for the recall of the associated syllable, much as in the noun-nonsense syllable paired-associate learning experiments described earlier. The results for four trials are presented in Figure 8-8, where it can be seen that concreteness (i.e., high imagery) of both nouns and adjectives strongly facilitated associative recall. Moreover, the effects of noun imagery and adjective imagery were approximately equal as evidenced by the

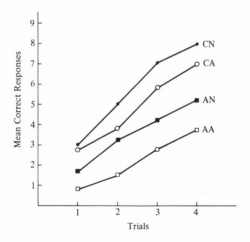

FIGURE 8-8. Mean recall scores over four trials for nonsense syllables as a function of the imagery-concreteness of associated nouns and adjectives. Based on data from Philipchalk and Begg (1970).

fact that the interaction of form class and concreteness was not significant. Nouns on the average were somewhat better cues than adjectives, although this effect also failed to reach significance.

Another experiment involved the same general procedure with the modification that associative learning was evaluated by a recognition test rather than a recall test. The subjects chose the appropriate CVCs from a list that contained all of the alternatives and inserted them into the blanks, as in the recall study. The results again showed a strong positive effect of concreteness but, in addition, the form class effect was significant, as was the concreteness by form class interaction. Thus, CVCs were better remembered when they were paired with nouns than when paired with adjectives, and the effect of concreteness-abstractness was greater for nouns than for adjectives.

Taken together, the results of these experiments suggest that stimulus imagery has a strong effect on associative recall whether varied within nouns or adjectives, and that any differential effect of imagery within the two form classes could be largely due to differences in the range of imagery variation. That form class may have some residual effect not attributable to imagery remains a possibility, however, as suggested by the recognition test results in the Philipchalk and Begg experiment, as well as by the Yuille et al. results for pairs in which adjective imagery is low (the right side of Figure 8-7). There is no evidence in that case of an interaction of noun imagery by adjective-noun order. More specifically, noun-adjective order was superior to adjective-noun order even when the nouns were abstract and at least as low in imagery as the associated adjectives. In this case, "nounness" per se seemed to be the important stimulus variable, as though nouns indeed were superior conceptual pegs.

These findings call for careful parametric research on the precise nature of the function relating word imagery to associative learning. Such research also needs to be extended to include word classes other than nouns and adjectives. Even as they stand, however, the results strengthen one conclusion: Words that are high in imagery-concreteness are extraordinarily effective as stimulus cues in associative learning. In this regard, the metaphorical conceptual-peg hypothesis has been supported without exception.

IMAGERY-CONCRETENESS AND ASSOCIATIVE DIRECTIONALITY

With the exception of the Philipchalk and Begg experiment, the studies that we have considered up to this point have generally involved the standard paired-associate learning procedure in which the first-presented or left-hand member of a pair is designated the stimulus in the sense that it serves as the retrieval cue on the recall trial. The alternative is to present the nominal "response" term as the retrieval cue at some point during learning. Such a procedure, combined with variation in item concreteness, provides us with an opportunity to evaluate one of the important theoretical distinctions between imaginal and verbal processes in relation to associative learning, namely, their differential functional capacity for spatially parallel and sequential information processing. A specific hypothesis relating the distinction to pair concreteness and directionality of mediated associations will be examined following a discussion of the general psychological problem to which the hypothesis and research evidence are related.

Is the associative process directionally asymmetrical or symmetrical? The central issue concerns the directionality of associations formed during associative learning. A major controversy has evolved around two opposing points of view (see Ekstrand, 1966). The traditional associationistic view has been that the associative process is directed, with the direction corresponding to the directionality of the original experience involving two events. Thus, if the order of experiencing events A and B is from A to B, recall also proceeds from A to B. Empirically, this viewpoint has been manifested in studies comparing the strength of "forward" and "backward" associations in paired-associate learning. Consistent with the directionality hypothesis, it has frequently been found that associative recall is better in the forward direction. Theoretically, these findings imply that separate "forward" and "backward" associations are simultaneously formed, and that forward associative "bonds" are stronger than backward bonds.

In opposition to the above viewpoint, Asch and Ebenholtz (1962) proposed the hypothesis of associative symmetry, which states that *"When an association is formed between two distinct terms, a and b, it is established simultaneously and with equal strength between b and a"* (p. 136). Unidirectional or asymmetrical associations are not possible under any conditions. Although Asch and Ebenholtz leave the question open, they also favor the view that the relation of symmetry refers to one association only, not separate associations from a to b and b to a. Why, then, have empirical studies yielded evidence of weaker backward than forward associations? The answer is that such differential effects are an artifact of *differential availability of items.* More specifically, when a subject learns pairs in the A-B direction, he has practice with producing B as a response, and hence it becomes more available than item A, which serves only as the recall cue and need not be produced as a response. Thus, while recall of A given B as the stimulus may be relatively weaker than recall in the reverse direction, this asymmetry is not a property of the association per se. Directionality may also occur because the subject has acquired knowledge of order in addition to the (symmetrical) association, but this knowledge and the association are distinct operations.

Asch and Ebenholtz (1962) obtained evidence for symmetry using stationary visual forms of approximately equal availability, although some asymmetry favoring forward recall was obtained in other experiments. Evidence has subsequently been obtained by other investigators supporting both the symmetry position and associative asymmetry (see Ekstrand, 1966). The issue remains unresolved, although the evidence does suggest that either symmetry or asymmetry may obtain, depending on experimental conditions that are yet to be identified. In the present section, we shall examine just such a hypothesis concerning associative directionality, relating it to semantic attributes of stimuli—most particularly, imagery-concreteness—and the inferred underlying imaginal and verbal symbolic processes.

The Associative Directionality Hypothesis

The hypothesis is straightforward: *To the extent that associations involve visual imagery, they will be symmetrical; to the extent that they involve the verbal symbolic system (or auditory-motor processes generally) they will tend to be directed, with the degree of directional asymmetry depending on the relative asymmetry of associative experience involving two or more events.* Thus, if the associated events A and B are directly represented or coded in memory as visual images, associative memory for the events will be symmetrical—either event will be remembered equally well, given the other as a cue. If the events are stored verbally (or in an auditory-motor system generally), the association will be stronger in one direction (e.g., A to B) unless associative experience occurs equally in both directions (A to B and B to A). Since the availability of imagery presumably varies directly with item concreteness, it follows that the more concrete the pair items, the more likely is it that they will be associated symmetrically. Conversely, the more abstract and devoid of imagery they are, the more likely is it that the association will be unidirectional.

The hypothesis is novel only in its explicitness; it is implicit in numerous statements that have been made in the preceding chapters and in the very nature of the two symbolic systems as postulated here. Theoretically, visual imagery is specialized for parallel processing in the spatial sense. This implies associative symmetry in the case of a compound image involving two events: The image is spatially parallel, and either component should be equally effective as a retrieval cue for the other component, and either should be equally available as a "response" (in the S-R analytic sense). On the other hand, the verbal symbolic system is specialized for sequential processing, which clearly implies directionality of associations formed between units unless the item sequences have been experienced in both directions. Such directionality is obvious in the case of sentences, letters of the alphabet, etc., which can be recalled in a backward direction only with difficulty. Auditory sequences, such as melodies, and motor sequences, such as tying one's shoelaces, are other examples of the directional bias characteristic of auditory and motor sequences. The stimulus and behavioral patterns in such instances are temporally organized and unidirectional.

The above distinction between spatial (stationary) and temporal organization of multiple units was not lost on Asch and Ebenholtz (1962), but they chose to interpret the differential directionality in the two cases in nonassociative terms. Associative symmetry applies to relations *between* units, although directionality is an essential characteristic of the *internal* organization of many units. Stationary visual units apparently show complete equidirectionality between their parts, whereas units that are extended in time (e.g., melodies and movements) are characterized by directionality. An ordinary sentence is a syntactical structure, i.e., a directionally organized unit, which accounts for the relative difficulty of backward recall of sentences. Similarly, the comparative difficulty of reciting the alphabet backward may derive from the fact that recitation has constituted the alphabet into an auditory-motor unit. A word is both a visual entity and an auditory-kinesthetic unit; in the latter aspect, but not necessarily the former, it is directional.

The Asch and Ebenholtz analysis is highly reminiscent of the analysis of serial learning discussed earlier (Chapter 7). The traditional analysis of serial learning was in terms of associative chaining. When transfer experiments raised difficulties for that interpretation, alternative explanations were suggested, including the ordinal position and response integration hypotheses. Asch and Ebenholtz in effect also deny the validity of the associative chaining interpretation of the formation of temporal sequence in behavior when they assert that associations per se are symmetrical and reversible. With respect to extended units, on the other hand, they favor something analogous to Jensen and Rohwer's (1965b) suggestion that serial learning involves the formation of an integrated response sequence.

There is complete agreement between the present hypothesis regarding associative directionality and the Asch-Ebenholtz position vis-à-vis within-unit organization in that both suggest that symmetry holds for visual-spatial representations, whereas directionality is characteristic of auditory-motor-verbal representations. The disagreement arises in connection with the distinction between intraunit and interunit relations. This may well be a semantic problem without important deductive consequences, as can be seen if we consider different stages in the formation of a higher-order integrated unit from two lower-order elements, A and B, which involve auditory-motor processes. It is implicit in the Asch-Ebenholtz position that when A and B are first experienced in close temporal contiguity, an associative relation develops, and this relation is characterized by directional symmetry. After some unspecified amount of associative experience, A and B presumably become integrated into a unit, AB, to which the concept of association is inapplicable and which may be characterized by a directional bias with respect to the processing of its components (e.g., AB is easier to reproduce than BA).

Serious logical and empirical difficulties are raised by such an argument. By what independent criteria are association and integration to be distinguished? Assuming that such criteria can be suggested, at what stage of associative experience or practice does an associative relation between A and B change to integration of the two elements into a compound unit? What is the basis for assuming that different principles regarding directionality of processing might hold at different stages? These questions may have answers, but no evidence bearing on them appears to be presently available. In any case, I prefer not to make a qualitative distinction between association and integration. As others (e.g., Tulving, 1968) have pointed out, association is a descriptive term that refers to the probability of one event given another. The reasoning applies equally to integration of elements into higher-order units. A possible distinction is that

association might be used to refer to an association between some environmental event and a response, whereas integration might be applied to events
entirely within the organism. For example, the latter might be used specifically
to mean response integration, i.e., R-R relations, but clearly this would be inappropriate where the reference is to integration of visual units into higher-order
visual images. Such distinctions in terminology appear, therefore, to be of limited usefulness. Be that as it may, the issue will not be pursued here inasmuch
as we shall be concerned primarily with studies involving associative learning
situations of the kind that have been generally used to investigate the question
of associative directionality.

Research Evidence Relevant to the Hypothesis

The Asch and Ebenholtz (1962) experiments provide evidence bearing
on the hypothesis that either symmetry or asymmetry may be obtained, depending on the symbolic processes involved in the task. The clearest support for
associative symmetry emerged from their Experiments II, III, and IV, which
involved visual (nonverbal) forms comprised of two components or "terms" in
various geometrical relationships to each other. In one case, the stimuli were
visual figures, the contours of which were made up of discontinuous smaller
forms in a constitutive relation to each other. Each pattern thus consisted of the
overall form and its constituents or modes, each of which previously had been
shown to be equally available to recall (Asch, Ceraso, & Heimer, 1960). An
example pattern is shown in Figure 8-9a. Ten such patterns were presented singly
for one trial. A recall test was then given in which either the form or the mode
of each figure served as the stimulus, and the subject was instructed to draw
the missing term. The results showed that there was no consistent directional
preference for either forms or modes—recall was equidirectional. The results
were essentially the same for the other two experiments, which involved inclu-
sion (one component enclosed a larger form; see Figure 8-9b) and part-whole
relations (Figure 8-9c). Thus associative symmetry was the rule in the case of

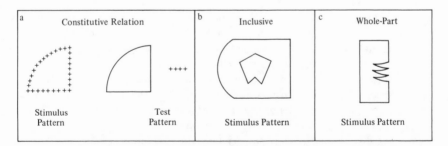

FIGURE 8-9. Examples of visual forms involving (a) constitutive, (b) in-
clusive, and (c) whole-part relations between the two connected components within
each pattern. From Asch and Ebenholtz (1962).

compound geometrical forms, which presumably are stored in memory as concrete spatial images with their components in parallel.

Forward associations were stronger than backward, however, when the items were nonsense syllables learned successively in a-b-c triplets (Experiment VI) or a-b pairs (Experiment VII). Asch and Ebenholtz argue that the asymmetry in these instances resulted from differential availability of one term produced by the anticipation learning procedure. However, the results are also consistent with the view that the asymmetry stemmed from the essential role played by the verbal system in the processing of such items.

Difficulties are raised for the hypothesis by the fact that associative symmetry has also been obtained with verbal items. Thus, according to Ekstrand (1966), the clearest evidence for symmetry comes from a study by Houston (1964). He used compound stimuli (colors and CVCs) and single-digit numbers as responses, and found that B-A recall to the colors (which presumably served as the functional stimuli during A-B learning) was equal to A-B recall to the digits. B-A recall to the color-CVC compounds was asymmetrical, however, presumably because the CVCs were not available as responses for the B-A test. If we assume that the color component was coded only verbally during learning, the data for B-A recall to the colors are inconsistent with the hypothesis that asymmetry obtains when the verbal system is involved. Note, however, that the colors might be stored visually rather than verbally. Moreover the associates were single-digit numbers, and evidence on tachistoscopic recognition of numbers by Dick and Mewhort (1967), summarized previously in Chapter 4, indicated that numbers are less influenced than alphabetic material by order-of-report and sequential-redundancy variables, suggesting that processing of numbers is not strictly "verbal." It could be argued, therefore, that the color-number combinations used by Houston were in fact stored as compound visual images and that such storage accounts for the associative symmetry he obtained. This explanation would not account for the finding of symmetry or near-symmetry in other instances in which at least one member of each pair was a nonsense word (e.g., Asch & Lindner, 1963; L. M. Horowitz, Brown, & Weissbluth, 1964; Merryman & Merryman, 1968). The prediction of asymmetry with purely verbal items, therefore, fails to be uniformly supported, although it has been obtained in some instances (e.g., Battig & Koppenaal, 1965). Because of the various procedures used in these studies, however, it is difficult to draw firm conclusions that are relevant to the particular hypothesis under examination here.

Word concreteness and associative symmetry-asymmetry   In considering the effects of imagery-concreteness on associative directionality, we must distinguish between effects attributable to the differential potency of concrete and abstract words as retrieval cues, and directional asymmetry or symmetry. The retrieval-cue effect introduces complexities analogous to those created by stimulus-response differences in availability. Two studies have been reported that revealed such retrieval asymmetries in forward and backward recall. The results are of interest in their own right in that they provide further evidence for the conceptual-peg hypothesis, as well as being relevant to the associative symmetry-asymmetry issue.

Lockhart (1969) carried out three experiments in which the subjects were given one study-test trial with adjective-noun pairs. The pairs were presented in either adjective-noun or noun-adjective order, and either member of a pair could serve as the cue for recall of the other. Lockhart reasoned that if associations are symmetrical, recall should be independent of the word given as the cue. Experiment I, involving concrete nouns and adjectives, showed recall to be independent of presentation order but superior when cued by the noun. Experiment II involved two lists, one comprised of adjective-concrete noun pairs (e.g., agreeable-pocket) and the other comprised of the adjectival equivalents of the abstract nouns paired with the same concrete nouns as in the other list (e.g., agreement-pocket). The only significant result was that recall was again superior when cued with the concrete noun. Thus the asymmetrical recall was attributable to the relative abstractness of adjectives. Consistent with this generalization, Experiment III showed no asymmetry effect with adjective-abstract noun pairs.

Lockhart concluded that adjective-concrete noun pairs are associatively linked in such a fashion that the concrete noun provides more cues for the retrieval of the adjective than vice versa. An examination of intrusion and omission errors led him to reject differentiation, or distinctiveness, as an explanation (this feature will be discussed further in a later section), and he suggested that mediating imagery could provide a plausible, if speculative account of both the asymmetry effect and the error data. This suggestion essentially supports the conceptual-peg hypothesis. However, Lockhart's findings do not support the present theory that associations would be directionally asymmetrical when processing is verbal. Adjective-abstract noun pairs presumably involved relatively less imagery and more verbal symbolic activity than did pairs involving concrete nouns, yet symmetry was obtained with the former. However, only one study-test trial was given, and subjects were told that recall might be cued with either member of a pair. These conditions may have favored rehearsal in both directions, resulting in *directional* symmetry despite the asymmetrical effects of concrete and abstract retrieval cues.

Yarmey and O'Neill (1969) investigated forward and backward association strength as a function of noun concreteness, using noun-noun and noun-nonsense syllable pairs in different experiments. Only the noun-noun experiment will be considered here. The study differed from Lockhart's in that multiple trials were given during both forward and backward learning, and subjects were not informed during the former that backward learning would later be tested. The explicit purpose of the study was to test predictions from the conceptual-peg hypothesis. Yarmey and O'Neill reasoned that both forward and backward learning would vary directly with the imagery-concreteness of the noun serving as the stimulus for recall. The crucial comparison is between concrete-abstract pairs and abstract-concrete pairs, for which predictions from item availability and conceptual-peg hypotheses differ. According to the former position, a test of backward association strength should yield superiority for concrete-abstract pairs, since the high I (concrete) noun serving as the response during backward recall should be more available than the low I (abstract) noun that must be recalled when abstract-concrete pairs are reversed. The conceptual-peg hypothesis, on the other hand, predicts that backward recall would be better for pairs originally in the abstract-concrete order, since the high I items would function as the stimulus "pegs" when the pairs are reversed. The results were fully consistent with the latter hypothesis: Concrete-abstract pairs were somewhat superior to abstract-concrete pairs during forward learning, and the turned-over abstract-concrete pairs (i.e., with the concrete nouns now serving as stimuli) were clearly superior in backward learning. Moreover, the transfer effect from forward to backward learning was greater from abstract-concrete pairs to their reversed versions than from concrete-abstract to their reversals when account was taken of the data from appropriate control groups.

The above findings from the Yarmey-O'Neill experiment, like those of Lockhart, essentially demonstrate retrieval asymmetries related to noun imagery-concreteness regardless of the direction of the test. They are relevant to the associative symmetry issue because they indicate that such factors must be taken into account in any test of the hypothesis, but they do not in themselves constitute a sensitive test of the relation of item concreteness to associative symmetry because the strong retrieval effects overshadow any directional differences that might occur during the formation of associations.

Restricting the analysis to concrete-concrete and abstract-abstract noun pairs would provide better evidence of any differences in associative directionality inasmuch as the imagery level of the retrieval cues would be held constant for forward and backward recall tests within any given type of pair. Such pairs were included in the Yarmey and O'Neill experiment, and a comparison of error scores during backward learning (taking into consideration appropriate control group data) showed that transfer from forward to backward association was stronger for concrete than for abstract noun pairs. That is, asymmetry was greater for the latter, as predicted from the associative directionality hypothesis, which relates symmetry-asymmetry differences to the relative availability of imagery as an associative mediator.

Similar results have been reported in a number of experiments. Epstein (1962b) reported backward recall scores as a percentage of forward recall: 84 percent for concrete words and 39 percent for abstract words. Wollen (1968) presented high- and low-imagery noun pairs for one study trial, then tested recall using both stimulus and response members as cues. He found that backward recall was actually somewhat higher than forward recall in the case of the high-imagery pairs, whereas forward recall was superior for low-imagery pairs. Thus associative directionality effects agreed with input order in the case of low-imagery pairs but not high-imagery pairs. Although the reversal in the latter case is not expected, the results of all of these experiments are generally consistent with the hypothesis that the more available the imagery code, the more likely is it that associative recall will be symmetrical.

Smythe (1970) conducted a series of experiments similar to the above, in which he exercised great care to ensure equal availability of both members of the pair during the recall test. He also extended the analysis to pictures in one experiment. In agreement with the hypothesis that generated the research, small but consistent differences in recall symmetry-asymmetry occurred as a function of pair type. Thus picture and concrete noun pairs resulted in symmetrical recall, whereas abstract noun pairs generally showed higher forward than backward recall. Symthe also measured the latency of the correct response and found this to be even more sensitive to differences in associative directionality in that it more consistently yielded statistically significant comparisons within experiments than occurred with number of items correctly recalled as the performance measure. The results for the experiment involving pictures as well as word pairs are shown in Figure 8-10. The data indicate that recall latency was significantly slower for backward recall than for forward recall in the case of abstract noun pairs but not picture pairs or concrete noun pairs. The same pattern of latency differences occurred for abstract and concrete nouns in other experiments that involved additional variables, including a comparison of auditory and visual presentation of the items.

The recall and latency data from these experiments agree in showing that associative recall is symmetrical, or nearly so, when the pairs are concrete but asymmetrical (recall being easier in the forward direction) when the pairs are abstract. The results provide strong inferential support for the hypothesis that imagery is involved in the learning of concrete pairs. Generated by both members of the pair, such images are spatially parallel compounds that can be redintegrated equally easily by either verbal item as the retrieval cue, and decoded to yield its

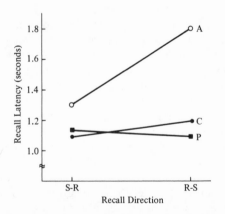

FIGURE 8-10. Mean latencies of forward (S-R) and backward (R-S) recall for picture (P), concrete noun (C), and abstract noun (A) pairs. Based on data in Smythe (1970).

associate during recall. Imagery is less probable in the case of abstract pairs, hence they are likely to be learned by rote, or mediated verbally by sentences or phrases, with the verbal associative connections being sequential and unidirectional in either case unless rehearsal is permitted in the backward direction as well.

The directionality effects considered here have involved item concreteness as the crucial variable. The hypothesis that such effects would vary according to the degree of involvement of imaginal and verbal processes is also testable using experimental procedures designed to affect the different mediation processes directly. Other aspects of Wollen's study involved such conditions, as have those of other investigators. These will be considered in the next chapter. In the meantime, we can conclude that any theoretical analysis of associative directionality needs to take into account the meaning attributes of individual items. Large differences in associative meaningfulness have been shown to have predictable effects (e.g., Harrigan & Modrick, 1967; J. Richardson, 1960), and the studies reviewed here indicate that imagery-concreteness is important even when differences in m are minimized. However, the relative effects of m and imagery have not been explored as systematically in relation to associative directionality as they have been in relation to standard paired-associate learning and, in the absence of firm data, comparisons of the two attributes will not be attempted in the present context.

ALTERNATIVE INTERPRETATIONS OF THE EFFECTS OF IMAGERY-CONCRETENESS

The empirical conclusion from the research on meaning and associative learning can be restated firmly: Imagery-concreteness is the most potent of any meaning attribute yet identified among relatively familiar and meaningful items (as opposed to meaning attributes varied among unfamiliar nonsense material). The effect of this variable is consistently greater when varied among stimulus members than when varied among response members of pairs, a fact that has been emphasized repeatedly as providing support for an interpretation of the effects in terms of an intrapair associative mechanism, i.e., stimulus-evoked mediating imagery. However, alternative explanations are possible, including ones based on stimulus differentiation, or direct rather than mediated associations. Such possibilities will now be examined in detail.

Stimulus Differentiation

Differentiation and the closely related concepts of distinctiveness and similarity (or dissimilarity) have already been discussed in relation to recognition memory in the preceding chapter. Theoretically, the function of differentiation or distinctiveness of items in associative learning is to protect particular interitem associations from interference by other possible associations involving the same items.[3] The basis of the interference is generally assumed to lie in the similarity relations among items: The greater the similarity among items in a list, the greater the probability of associative errors. The basis of such associative interference can be viewed in terms of gradients of generalization, direct associations between similar items, or common or similar implicit responses evoked by different items (Underwood, Ekstrand, & Keppel, 1965). A choice among these alternatives is not essential for our purposes. The critical issues have to do with the operational definition of similarity, its effect on paired-associate learning, and how these might be applicable to the concreteness effect.

Similarity has been variously measured in terms of relative distances between items along some physical dimension: common letters; similarity of meaning based, for example, on common verbal associations; judgments of similarity; and so on (for a review of scaling techniques, see Goss & Nodine, Chapter 5). The empirical generalizations regarding the relation between similarity and paired-associate learning appear to hold for the different measuring procedures. Goss and Nodine summarize the data as follows: "In general, acquisition rate and similarity of stimulus members and similarity of response members have been related inversely with similarity of stimulus members the more potent variable" (1965, p. 221). In other words, the greater the similarity among stimulus members in particular, the slower the learning. Conversely, the more dissimilar or distinctive the stimuli, the faster the learning. This generalization holds even for the special instance of the single item, as indicated by the finding that the isolation effect (the von Restorff phenomenon)—i.e., the facilitated learning of an item that "stands out" because of some distinctive characteristic—is relatively stronger on the stimulus side of pairs (Erickson, 1965).

Two recent studies will serve to illustrate some of the scaling procedures and relevant findings. The stimulus similarity effects have been demonstrated with various materials within a single study by Runquist (1968). In four separate experiments, he varied formal similarity of low-m CVCs, synonymity of adjectives, associative overlap (number of common associates) of Kent-Rosanoff stimuli, and semantic distance of words from the semantic atlas (J. J. Jenkins, Russell, & Suci, 1958). The last index was based on ratings of words on a number of 7-point semantic differential scales (e.g., good-bad). The similarity relationship between any pair of words was defined as the average difference between them on the evaluative, potency, and activity dimensions. The mean distance between all pairs of words in a given list defined the degree of stimulus similarity. Runquist found a strong inverse relation between acquisition performance and formal similarity, while the indices of meaningful similarity produced somewhat smaller but nevertheless significant effects. The effect of mean-

---

[3] The experimental research and theory in the general problem area have their origins in the work of E. J. Gibson (1940), who viewed associative verbal learning in terms of classical conditioning and the reciprocal mechanisms of stimulus generalization and differentiation. For a review of this background see, e.g., Underwood (1961).

ingful similarity is of particular interest here, since any differences in similarity relations among abstract words as compared to concrete words is likely to be based on meaning rather than on formal characteristics. However, formal similarity is also a relevant variable, since it might be the basis of the facilitating effect of pictures as compared to words.

Underwood et al. (1965) varied conceptual similarity in a series of experiments. Conceptual similarity among verbal units was defined in terms of common implicit associative responses. Thus the high-similarity lists consisted of items such as *dog, cat, horse,* and *cow,* which occur reliably as responses to the category name "four-footed animals." The low-similarity lists consisted of items such as *captain, cotton, leg,* and *cow,* which occur as responses to different category labels. The results of one set of experiments showed that similarity among stimulus terms was deleterious to learning, while similarity among response terms had no effect on learning. The results are pertinent here because the items were all concrete nouns and it is possible that the conceptual similarity, or dissimilarity, is founded on perceptual imagery as well as on the category labels.

The most crucial general feature of the above findings for the imagery data is the fact that the effect of similarity is greater when varied among stimulus members than when varied among response members of pairs. That is, dissimilarity or distinctiveness of stimulus members is particularly facilitative. Thus, it could be argued that high-imagery stimulus items benefit associative learning only because they are relatively more distinctive and suffer less associative interference from other items in a list than do low-imagery stimuli.

The above argument rests on the assumption that similarity relations based on associative processes underlie item discriminability. An alternative interpretation, which nonetheless has the same implications for the concreteness effect, is provided by E. Martin's (1968) encoding-variability hypothesis of stimulus meaningfulness effects in paired-associate learning tasks. Martin proposed that stimulus meaningfulness exerts its effect through stimulus recognition processes that necessarily precede association. Recognition is based on stimulus encoding, which refers to the elicitation of an (implicit) encoded version of the nominal stimulus. Since this encoded version is the functional stimulus for association formation, progress in associative learning depends on the stability of stimulus encoding from trial to trial. But nominal stimuli are variably encodable, hence they may be perceived differently on different occasions. This is the hypothesized basis of meaningfulness effects: The number of alternative encodings is greater for low- than for high-meaningful stimuli, and it accordingly takes longer for the selection of a particular encoding response that can serve as the functional stimulus for associative learning in the former case.

While originally applied to meaningfulness, the above analysis can be readily extended to concreteness: Perhaps encoding variability is greater for more abstract stimuli than for more concrete stimuli, and this is the basis of the strong positive effect of stimulus concreteness in paired-associate learning. This hypothesis differs from the interference interpretation described above in that Martin assumes that discrimination is based on encoding rather than on associative responses. The nature of the encoding processes is unclear, but in the present theoretical context, they might be conceptualized as being analogous to representational meaning reactions, as distinct from referential or associative meaning. In any case, the implication again is that stimulus concreteness may have its facilitative effect via stimulus recognition and discrimination rather than mediated association.

Let us now examine some research findings that bear on the alternative interpretations, keeping in mind that they are not necessarily incompatible alternatives; that is, it may turn out that imagery facilitates both differentiation and association. The discrimination hypothesis of imagery effects would be supported indirectly by evidence that item imagery and item discriminability are related, and directly by evidence that stimulus imagery influences paired-associate learning only when such correlated differences in discriminability are present. Evidence on the imagery-discriminability relation will be considered first.

Item imagery and discriminability   The finding that recognition memory scores increase from abstract words, to concrete words, to pictures (Chapter 7) suggests that imagery value is related to discriminability, inasmuch as it is also known that similarity-dissimilarity relations among test items and distractors is an important determinant of recognition scores. The discrimination learning paradigm provides a more direct approach to the investigation of the relation. In such learning, the subject is required to learn which member of each pair in a successively presented list of paired items has been arbitrarily designated as "correct" by the experimenter. Paivio and Rowe (1970) compared the effects of noun imagery-concreteness, m, and frequency on discrimination learning. One group of subjects was given eight study-test trials on a 16-pair list in which half the pairs were high imagery and half were low imagery, while frequency and m were held approximately constant at a medium value. Frequency and m were similarly varied for other groups. Figure 8-11 shows the mean errors over eight trials for each variable. It can be seen that high-imagery pairs were much easier to discriminate than low-imagery pairs. Conversely, fewer errors tended to be made in the case of low-frequency than high-frequency pairs, although the trend was not significant. Variation in m had no effect. The reliability of the imagery effect has been established in subsequent experiments, including one that involved homogeneous lists with respect to imagery level, rather than mixed lists. The finding is, of course, highly interesting in its own right, but in the present context, the major point is that imagery is indeed a powerful determinant of stimulus differentiation, and the plausibility of the differentiation hypothesis of imagery effects in paired-associate learning is thereby enhanced.[4] The associative function attributed to images in the imagery-mediation

----

[4] The findings are generally relevant to the theoretical interpretation of verbal discrimination learning. The results for noun frequency were discussed in Chapter 7 in relation to the frequency theory of such learning (Ekstrand et al., 1966) and its application

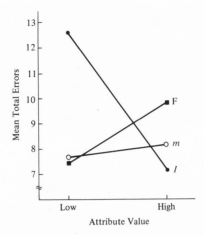

FIGURE 8-11. Mean number of errors over eight verbal discrimination learning trials as a function of level (high versus low) of pair imagery (*I*), meaningfulness (*m*), and frequency (F). Based on data in Paivio and Rowe (1970).

theory is not ruled out by this evidence, however, since there is no reason to assume that differentiation and association are mutually exclusive. The results, in any case, do not provide any direct evidence on the relation between imagery, stimulus discriminability, and associative learning. Such evidence is considered next.

Evidence from paired-associate learning studies   The recognition memory and discrimination learning data suggest that concrete, high-imagery nouns are in some sense more "distinct" than abstract, low-imagery nouns. Such distinctiveness would presumably be based on meaning and hence could be inter-

to recognition memory. Paivio and Rowe (1970) discussed the imagery effect in terms of the frequency theory, suggesting that verbally evoked images may be analogous to the implicit associative responses (IARs) considered by Ekstrand et al. to play a role in discrimination learning. Thus high-imagery words designated as correct may evoke images more often than the incorrect words, thereby contributing to the process of differential frequency discrimination. The explanation seems strained, but it is a possibility that must be given due consideration and compared with other possible interpretations of this striking effect of noun imagery. The problem has been investigated further in a series of studies (e.g., Rowe & Paivio, 1971a, 1971b), whose findings indicate that imagery and frequency mechanisms can function independently in discrimination learning, and that imagery can have simultaneous but distinct effects on discrimination and incidental associative learning.

preted as a form of acquired distinctiveness, or what Saltz (1963) has described as cognitive differentiation. Saltz's investigation of the effects of such a variable in paired-associate learning is therefore relevant here. He varied the availability of color cues accompanying each verbal stimulus by presenting them during learning but not recall trials, or vice versa. Color differentiation was found to facilitate learning even when the color was not presented during the recall trial and therefore could not be explicitly used as a cue. The pertinent feature of Saltz's study here is that his procedure provided an opportunity for color sensations to be conditioned to the verbal stimuli, which may thereby have acquired distinctive "concrete" meanings (cf. Phillips, 1958). The effect of imagery-concreteness of nouns could be similarly interpreted as cognitive differentiation resulting from prior association of concrete words, but not abstract words, with specific objective referents. Alternatively, one might argue that such differentiation is based on verbal associates rather than images evoked by the items without changing the basic principle. Indeed, given the theoretical view that abstract words are differentiated from concrete in terms of the relative unavailability of imaginal associative reactions in the former case, any comparison of similarity relations within the two classes of nouns should be based, not on imagery, but on some meaning attribute that they share. Verbal associative meaning is such an attribute and it is especially appropriate because similarity relations can be readily measured in terms of common verbal associates, i.e., associative overlap.

The above interpretation of the facilitating effect of stimulus concreteness was tested in the Paivio (1965) study using associative overlap as the index of distinctiveness. Recall that the experiment involved 16 concrete nouns and 16 abstract nouns paired in all possible stimulus-response combinations, and that a positive effect of concreteness was much greater on the stimulus side of the pairs. To the extent that distinctiveness was involved in the effect, greater overlap would be expected among the abstract nouns than among the concrete nouns that constituted the word lists. An associative overlap score, based on the total number of associates a given noun had in common with the other 15 members of the same (concrete or abstract) class, was derived for each noun from the associations of a sample of the subjects that had contributed m data in the study. The mean overlap scores of the two classes of nouns did not differ significantly. Furthermore, a product-moment correlation of $-.21$ between overlap scores of stimulus terms and mean recall scores, although appropriate in sign, was also insignificant. Thus distinctiveness, defined in terms of associative overlap, could not explain the very strong effect of stimulus concreteness on learning, and some kind of positive associative interpretation is accordingly favored over one based on stimulus differentiation.

The same conclusion emerges from Lockhart's (1969) experiment, in which he tested a differentiation interpretation of the superior recall he obtained for adjective-noun pairs when recall was cued by concrete nouns rather than adjectives. He argued that if the poorer recall obtained with adjectival cueing is attributable to their relative lack of differentiation or distinctiveness, then adjectives as stimuli should produce more intrusion errors than would result with noun stimuli. On the other hand, an interpretation in terms of the presence or absence of effective retrieval cues would predict a higher proportion of omission errors with adjective cueing. An analysis of errors provided no support for the differentiation hypothesis: Relatively more intrusion errors actually occurred with noun cueing, whereas omission errors were clearly higher with adjective cueing than with noun cueing. These data therefore are more consistent with an associative-retrieval than a differentiation interpretation.

Differentiation has also been proposed as a possible explanation of the facilitative effect of objects and pictures in comparison with words. Wimer and Lambert (1959) found better learning when objects rather than their noun labels served as stimuli for nonsense-syllable responses. Intralist stimulus similarity was determined for both objects and nouns using the average semantic differential distance between items within each class as the index. The results showed that there was significantly less meaningful similarity among the objects than among their names, which accords with an interpretation of the learning data in terms of stimulus differentiation based on meaning.

Dominowski and Gadlin (1968) reasoned that, if differentiation is a factor in the stimulus effect of concreteness, learning differences would be obtained only when lists are used. They tested this hypothesis using a short-term memory procedure in which they tested only one pair at a time. The pairs involved two-digit numbers as responses, and pictures, object names, or category names as stimuli. Each subject was tested with only one type of stimulus material using a modified L. R. Peterson and M. J. Peterson (1959) task that required the subject to recall both members of a briefly exposed pair following a variable delay interval involving a filler task to prevent rehearsal. In contrast with a standard paired-associate learning experiment, in which lists involving the three types of material were learned best with picture stimuli and most poorly with category names, the short-term memory task resulted in inferior recall for pictures. This finding influenced Dominowski and Gadlin to reject the imagery-mediation interpretation of the stimulus effect of item imagery and to suggest differentiation as a plausible (although untested) alternative.

Any generalizations from the Wimer and Lambert (1959) and Dominowski and Gadlin (1968) findings to other studies of stimulus imagery effects can be questioned on several grounds. In the first place, neither study involved response terms that would be likely to produce a strong differential effect of imagery on the stimulus as compared to the response side of pairs if such comparisons were made. Wimer and Lambert used nonsense syllables, and Dominowski and Gadlin used two-digit numbers. While numbers have not been systematically investigated as stimulus and response members for associates varying in imagery, it is possible that they would behave somewhat like nonsense syllables in that they may not readily suggest object-images that could be incorporated into compound mediators representing both members of pairs. If so, item imagery would still be expected to facilitate learning, just as Paivio and Madigan (1968) and Yarmey and O'Neill (1969) found even when low-association-value trigrams were paired with nouns, but this effect would probably be weaker than when nouns serve as associates and it might not reveal the contribution of imagery to associative mediation, as reflected in a differential effect of imagery on the stimulus side of pairs. Since neither Wimer and Lambert nor Dominowski and Gadlin varied concreteness on the response side of pairs, these suggestions remain speculative.

Other questions are raised by the procedures used by Dominowski and Gadlin. In their study, each pair was presented for only .3 seconds, followed immediately by the recall test or by a delay interval during which the subject named colors. Such a brief exposure is probably insufficient for associative processes to have their effect, and the filler task presumably interfered with any image arousal (in the case of words) or verbal coding (in the case of pictures) that might otherwise have occurred during the delay interval following the exposure. In brief, it is likely that the conditions of the task prevented the formation of effective imaginal or verbal mediators in much the same manner as the rapid presentation rate used by Paivio and Csapo (1969—see Chapter 7) was assumed to do in memory tasks other than paired associates. Further evidence relevant to this point is reviewed in Chapter 10, where it will be seen that a one-second presentation rate for pairs (without interfering activity) is probably the minimum at which mediation effects will be obtained.

Finally, Dominowski and Gadlin required their subjects to recall both members of each pair. Although they tested the effectiveness of the different stimuli as retrieval cues by considering only those instances in which both members were recalled, it is by no means certain that an implicit cue (even a high-imagery one) is as effective as one that is explicitly presented during the recall trial. Dominowski and Gadlin argue otherwise, but evidence to be presented in Chapter 10 suggests that item concreteness is not effective in associative learning when the items are not explicitly presented as retrieval cues during recall, although they presumably are available to the subject from memory.

The differentiation and imagery mediation (conceptual peg) interpretations of the effects of item imagery were recently investigated by Raser and Bartz (1968). Their subjects were presented a homogeneous list of word-word, word-picture, picture-word, or picture-picture pairs only once, and associative learning was tested by a recognition procedure in which the stimulus member was presented along with seven response alternatives, one of which was the correct one. Contrary to the usual finding, the results showed a significant facilitative effect of pictures as response terms but not as stimulus terms. This was taken as support for the differentiation hypothesis. However, as Raser and Bartz acknowledge, the recognition procedure places more emphasis on the response term than does the usual paired-associate learning procedure. Indeed, since both members of a pair are available to the subject during the test trial, there is no reason why either should be favored as a retrieval cue. Under these conditions, differentiation among the "response" alternatives may well be a major factor and one that is strongly affected by item imagery. The results, in any case, are not directly relevant to the conceptual-peg hypothesis, which was intended to be applicable to associative learning situations in which one item serves as a retrieval cue for another (absent) member.

None of the above studies involved a direct experimental comparison of discrimination and association. This was done by Wicker (1970a). He compared pictures and words as stimuli for numbers or letter responses in a paired-associate task. Following presentation of a 30-pair list, subjects were shown the stimuli one at a time interspersed with 30 other distractor items that had not been presented in study trials. The subjects were first tested for stimulus recognition and then associative recall on each item. Consistent with previous findings, both recognition and recall were superior when pictures rather than words served as study-trial stimuli. This difference dropped to nonsignificance, however, when stimulus recognition was held constant by considering associative recall only for those instances in which the stimulus was recognized with certainty. Wicker concluded that the picture-word stimulus effect is best described in terms of differences in discriminability or encoding of stimulus items (interpretable perhaps in terms of Martin's encoding variability hypothesis) rather than association.

Wicker's results indicate that stimulus recognition processes do indeed play a significant role in the facilitative effect of pictorial stimuli, but they do not constitute definitive evidence against an associative interpretation. Note that Wicker used numbers or letters as response items. As in the Dominowski and Gadlin (1968) study described above, such response items are not expected to be as conducive to the formation of compound mediating images as the picture or concrete-noun responses used in the studies in which the mediation hypothesis was proposed (e.g., Paivio & Yarmey, 1966).

In summary, the available empirical data do not permit a clear choice between differentiation and mediated-association interpretations of the stimulus imagery effect. A direct test involving associative overlap as the index of stimulus similarity within concrete and abstract words failed to provide support for differentiation as did an analysis of types of errors. Other experiments involving picture-word comparisons provide evidence consistent with the differentiation hypothesis, but in each case the alternative hypotheses failed to be adequately tested.

The present tentative conclusion is that both processes are probably involved. Such a conclusion is consistent with recent theoretical analyses of the subprocesses involved in paired-associate learning (e.g., McGuire, 1961; Polson, Restle, & Polson, 1965; Underwood et al., 1965). It is also consistent with the imagery mnemonic system of the ancients (see Chapter 6), in which the rules for the formation of images of places and things were designed to facilitate both association and differentiation. Probably the most effective "conceptual pegs" are those that evoke images that are well differentiated from each other and at the same time provide strong linkage to the appropriate response members of pairs.

The measurement of differentiation (dissimilarity) among images, and mediated associative bond strength independent of differentiation, are likely to be difficult problems, particularly in view of the difficulties encountered in recent attempts to distinguish empirically between the concepts of cognitive differentiation and mediated association (see Birnbaum, 1966; Greeno, 1968; Saltz & Ager, 1968; Saltz & Wickey, 1967). Direct comparisons of the two processes within the same experimental design will in any case be a necessary component of research directed at the problem. The above study by Wicker included this feature, as did an experiment by Bahrick (1969). It is particularly encouraging and relevant that Bahrick was able to demonstrate that discriminative and associative learning begin immediately and proceed independently throughout training with pairs of meaningful pictures. With meaningless drawings, on the other hand, associative performance did not improve until some discrimination had developed. The finding for pictures is consistent with the above suggestion that effective "pegs" promote differentiation as well as association, although Bahrick's study does not provide comparative data for different levels of concreteness nor direct evidence that mediation was involved.

Direct versus Mediated Association

Even if we assume that stimulus-term imagery facilitates S-R association, this does not in itself demand the further conclusion that the effect is a mediational one. It might be argued instead that the strength of the direct association between stimulus and response members is for some reason related to their imagery-concreteness. This seems unlikely in the case of the experiments involving only nouns, or pictures and nouns, inasmuch as the pairing has generally been random with the restriction that obvious pre-experimental associative relations between members of a pair have been avoided in the construction of the paired-associate lists. In the case of related adjective-noun pairs, direct association is potentially a more plausible explanation of the effects, but the empirical data discussed earlier appear to be directly contrary to what would be expected from such an approach in that the noun-adjective order is easier to learn despite the fact that English language habits favor the adjective-noun order of usage.

The available experimental evidence on the effect of intrapair associative strength on paired-associate learning also fails to provide a reasonable basis for a direct associative approach to the concreteness effect. Associative strength has been found to have a significant effect on children's learning (e.g., McCullers, 1967; for additional references, see the review by Goulet, 1968, p. 366). In the case of adults, however, Postman (1962) found that increased S-R associative probability facilitated learning when the word frequency of stimuli was low but not when it was high. Since many of the studies that demonstrated the stimulus imagery effect involved adult subjects and only high-frequency nouns, it seems unlikely that associative probability played a significant role in the finding, although the problem merits further investigation, particularly in view of Kamman's (1968) recent demonstration that direct associative connections are predictive of associative learning among adults.

Associative probability might operate in another way, which is particularly relevant to the adjective-noun order effect. Perhaps nouns elicit only a few alternative modifying adjectives while the same adjectives elicit (modify) many different nouns: The noun-adjective order might therefore be easier to learn than the reverse order because the transition probability from stimulus to response is higher in the former case. Kusyszyn and Paivio (1966) tested this hypothesis by obtaining the appropriate association data (adjectives to nouns and nouns to adjectives) and constructing paired-associate lists in which word order, noun concreteness, and transition probability (the stimulus members of particular pairs elicited few or many alternative responses) were the variables. The association data showed that nouns and adjectives did not differ on the average in the number of alternative associates they evoked. The learning data showed that transition probability had a significant effect, so that recall was higher with stimulus members that elicited few rather than many alternative responses. Regardless of transition probability, however, recall was better for the noun-adjective order and when nouns were concrete. Thus, while transition probability was effective, it could not account for the effects of concreteness and the superiority of nouns as retrieval cues.

The issue need not be labored further. The available evidence provides no support for an interpretation of the effects of stimulus imagery in terms of direct associative probability. We are compelled, therefore, to accept a mediational approach in general, although the precise mediating mechanism remains somewhat uncertain at the moment. Let us be very clear about what is meant by this conclusion. It is in no sense intended as a denial of direct, nonmediated S-R associations in the learning studies that have been considered here, just as an associative approach in general is not a denial of stimulus differentiation as a factor in the observed effects. It seems obvious on a priori grounds that two events can become associated in memory simply as a result of contiguous occurrence, without any mediational link based on other events, otherwise we cannot account for the "primitive" associations that occur in the absence of meaning. Furthermore, even in the case of meaningful units it is reasonable to assume that simple contiguity is a sufficient condition for associative learning, although not the only one and not necessarily the most effective one. In fact, we need not assume—the data from three experiments by Spear, Ekstrand, and Underwood (1964) supported the conclusion that the contiguous appearance of two verbal units will result in the development of an association between them even while the subject is learning other associations. What is being asserted here, however, is that the effect of mere contiguity should not differ for concrete and abstract units, and that the *differential* effects of such stimuli therefore must be attributed to differential coding processes or mediators, which subjects bring to the learning situation as a result of prior experiences involving those items. Imagery and verbal processes are two classes of such mediators, and their functional role will be directly explored in the next three chapters.

SUMMARY

Numerous paired-associate learning experiments support the conclusion that imagery-concreteness is the most potent item attribute affecting performance in that task as it was found to be in other memory tasks considered in the preceding chapter. Moreover, the positive effect of this dimension is consistently greater when varied among stimulus members than when varied among response members of pairs. The stimulus imagery effect has been demonstrated with picture-word experiments, as well as ones involving variation in the imagery level of nouns and adjectives. The response effect is less consistent than the stimulus effect, and there is some evidence that pictures may even hinder learning relative to words as response members, perhaps because the verbal code is less available or accessible in the former case. With adjective-noun pairs, recall is better when cued by the noun than when it is cued by the adjective, and there is some evidence to support the view that this effect is due at least in part to the greater average concreteness, or imagery-arousing capacity, of the nouns. The effectiveness of high-imagery items as retrieval cues extends also to backward associations, and there is suggestive evidence that high imagery of the pairs favors associative symmetry, whereas low imagery is more likely to result in directional asymmetry. The data are generally consistent with the theory that concrete items readily evoke images that can function as mediators of associative learning, and that the imagery value of the stimulus members is particularly important on recall trials because the stimulus must redintegrate the image that mediates response retrieval. Other evidence suggests that stimulus imagery may promote differentiation among stimulus terms as well as S-R association.

The effects of verbal associative meaningfulness (m) and of frequency contrast sharply with those of imagery-concreteness. When varied over a wide range extending from familiar words to nonsense material, m typically has a greater effect on the response side than on the stimulus side of pairs. When varied only within familiar words, with imagery and frequency held constant, m has either been ineffective or has had only slight effects, which have been negative as often as positive. Frequency has sometimes shown a negative effect when varied on the stimulus side of pairs and generally a small positive effect on the response side. Frequency and imagery have been shown to interact in a complex manner, suggesting a novelty effect based on imagery, or interference based on verbal association, or both.

The relative effects of the different meaning attributes in paired-associate learning are similar to their effects in recognition memory, free recall, and the Peterson and Peterson short-term memory task, suggesting that similar processes are involved in each. All of the data strongly implicate imagery as a potent underlying process, whose functioning facilitates item recognition and discrimination as well as interitem associations. The results suggest further that verbal processes may be a source of interference as well as associative facilitation. Although the problem has not been extensively investigated, the results of a factor-analytic study, which included free recall as well as paired-associate learning scores, suggest that imagery-concreteness may have its strongest effect as a stimulus variable in associative learning situations, as compared to its role in other memory tasks. In general, however, the evidence supports the view that imagery is highly effective both as a memory code and as an associative mediator, consistent with what was assumed in the ancient mnemonic techniques.

9
Verbal Mediation in Learning and Memory

This chapter and the two that follow deal with research and theory related directly to the mediating functions of the symbolic processes in learning and memory. Such functions will be inferred from evidence based on direct experimental manipulation of the mediation processes as well as questionnaire data concerning the types of learning strategies subjects report using in a given task. We begin with verbal mediation because it has received the lion's share of attention in verbal learning research until very recently. Since the methodological problems and effective variables related to mediation have been explored most fully in that context, verbal mediation provides a background against which the more recent studies of imagery mediation can be compared in Chapter 10. It will be seen, however, that a separate consideration of verbal and imaginal mediation does not satisfactorily reveal the *unique* functional characteristics of either postulated process. Accordingly, Chapter 11 will be devoted to studies in which imaginal and verbal mediators have been explicitly compared. Only then will we be in a position to consider a comprehensive theoretical analysis that incorporates both processes, although specific theoretical issues will be considered throughout the three chapters.

The discussion of verbal mediation is divided into two major sections. The first deals with "natural language mediators" as inferred from postlearning questionnaire reports; the second, with a variety of experimental procedures, all of which are designed to encourage the learner to use verbal mediators in the learning task. These manipulations include: (*a*) instructions to mediate, (*b*) presentation of sentence contexts for to-be-learned items, (*c*) associative priming of mediators, (*d*) presentation of cues that facilitate the transformation of meaningless units into more meaningful ones, and (*e*) mediation transfer paradigms. Many of these studies have also included measures of verbal associative meaningfulness in their research design, thereby providing a supplementary source of evidence on verbal mediation processes through the interaction of meaningfulness with the experimental variables.

The literature review summarizes some of the more important variables, effects, and methodological problems in this research area. The major goal, however, is to provide clues to the functional nature of the verbal symbolic system in relation to learning and memory. Thus we will be alert to evidence that bears on the definitive theoretical properties of that system, such as its sequentially operating characteristics. The problem is difficult because, as already noted above, the studies generally were not designed to differentiate verbal mediators from imagery—nor from any other process with different postulated properties for that matter. Nevertheless, the various approaches to verbal mediation provide important initial evidence and are interesting in their own right. Hence they will be considered in some detail. Much of the empirical work has involved paired-associate learning and it accordingly receives the major emphasis here, although other memory tasks are discussed as well.

NATURAL LANGUAGE MEDIATORS (NLMs)

It has long been known that human subjects routinely use their linguistic skills to facilitate learning and memory, but such "natural language mediators" (NLMs) have been systematically investigated only recently. Research on the problem is motivated by increasing experimental evidence that simple rote learning is largely a fiction. Even in tasks specifically designed to minimize the role of prior linguistic habits, subjects persistently (from the viewpoint of the rote learning tradition, one might almost say, perversely) find complex ways of coding items or mediating interitem associations, rather than learning by rote (e.g., see Adams, 1967; Battig, 1966; Bugelski, 1962; Underwood & Schulz, 1960). For the moment, we can leave open the question of how much of this mediational activity is truly verbal in nature and simply review the research in which the nominal emphasis has been on verbal processes. We shall be especially concerned with the generalizations that can be drawn from the data regarding the nature and conditions of effective mediation.

NLMs Inferred from Subjects' Reports Following Learning

Perhaps the earliest systematic investigation of the problem was a series of studies by Reed (1918a, 1918b, 1918c) on the use of associative aids (his term for the mediators that subjects reported) in paired-associate learning. In one experiment, for example, Latin-English word pairs with which mediators were reportedly used were learned much faster than without such aids. Reed (1918c) presented a penetrating analysis of such associative learning situations as simple problems to be solved by thought. His description of the effect of practice on the use of associative devices is particularly interesting. Thus:

. . . the learning of the associated pairs was accomplished by means of associative aids in most cases. . . . Later the response became fixed and mechanized
and the associative aids dropped away. The subjects reported that they
thought of nothing in these cases. The responses had become habits. Then
when the words were to be learned in new orders . . . we find associative aids
coming up again, and the responses indefinite and slow. A new problem had
occurred and again the associative aids were set into operation to solve it
(pp. 390–391).

Reed's interpretation of paired-associative learning as a problem solving situation and his analysis of the genesis of thought processes used to solve them,
with unconscious habit and reflex action as the final stages, is extraordinarily
relevant today, and we shall have occasion again to refer to aspects of his contribution.

Underwood and Schulz (1960, pp. 296–300) obtained reports from subjects
on how they "hooked up" trigram-word pairs. They found that subjects reported
some association for 73 percent of the pairs, and that learning scores were significantly higher for items for which associates were reported than for ones for
which no associations were reported. While fully aware that the reports do not
prove a causal relation, the authors concluded that subjects do make use of
such associations for learning at least some of the pairs. They observed further
that most of the associations involved single-step rather than multistep mediation, and that a subject may use several types of mediators in learning the list,
e.g., one based on letter identity, one on sound similarity, another on meaning.
These observations have important implications, to be considered later, concerning the complexity of useful mediators and the relation between type of mediator
and item attributes. The results of another study (J. M. Barnes & Underwood,
1959) suggested that mediators tend to drop out as learning progresses, which
accords with Reed's observations.

Bugelski (1962) described five categories of natural mediators used by subjects in learning nonsense-syllable pairs. These included the formation of one
meaningful word from the two syllables, two words, phrases, abstract analyses
of the syllables, and some vague association with one part of the combination.
Mediators were reported for 67 percent of the pairs, which is quite similar to
the percentage reported by Underwood and Schulz. An examination of Bugelski's data also suggests that, as trials to criterion increased, there was a concomitant increase in the number of cases in which no mediator was reported.

A more elaborate system for classifying associative strategies was proposed
by C. J. Martin, Boersma, and Cox (1965). The system was based on the examination of subjects' written reports of how they attempted to form associations
between the members of pairs of low meaningful paralogs from Noble's (1952a)
list. The following seven categories were identified: no reported associations,
repetition, single-letter cues, multiple-letter cues, word formation, superordinate
(i.e., a selection of elements from each of the two paralogs, that had some relationship to each other), and syntactical (i.e., the subject reported selecting ele-

ments from each of the two paralogs and embedding these elements into a sentence, phrase, or clause). The categories were described by the investigators as representing a continuum of cue complexity. The related experiments showed an increasing monotonic relationship between level of strategy employed and performance on the learning task. Further studies showed that the use of associative strategies is related to verbal associative meaningfulness (m), particularly of the stimulus member of a pair (C. J. Martin, Cox, & Boersma, 1965), and that subjects who were required to report the associative strategies they had used during acquisition showed higher retention scores than those not reporting strategies, the superiority of the former increasing with the length of the delay since the learning phase (Boersma, Conklin, & Carlson, 1966).

The most extensive series of studies on NLMs has been conducted by Montague and Adams, and their coworkers at the University of Illinois (e.g., Kiess & Montague, 1965; Montague, Adams, & Kiess, 1966; for a recent summary, see Adams, 1967). These studies have uniformly found a positive relation between reported use of mediators and performance in learning and recall situations. Montague and Wearing (1967) obtained results which agreed with those of Martin, Boersma, and Cox (1965) in showing that fewer errors in learning were associated with more complex mediators. In addition, however, they found that the Martin et al. scale categories 3, 4, and 5 (single-letter cues, multiple-letter cues, and word formation) were rarely used and they concluded that if the subject uses a NLM at all, it is a complex one, and that a dichotomous classification of NLM versus rote might accordingly be preferable to the more elaborate scheme. In any case, such a dichotomy has been used in most of the Illinois studies.

Montague et al. (1966) found that more NLMs were used during acquisition of the paired-associate list when the presentation time for pairs was longer and when the pairs were high rather than low in rated meaningfulness according to Noble's (1961) m' scale. The latter agrees with the Martin, Cox, and Boersma (1965) finding mentioned above. In a retention test 24 hours after acquisition, Montague et al. asked their subjects to recall the response member of each pair and the NLM he had used in acquisition. The results showed an overall retention score of 72.6 percent for items to which NLMs had been originally formed and later remembered correctly, whereas retention was negligible for pairs learned by rote (5.8 percent) and pairs for which the original NLMs had been forgotten or seriously changed (1.8 percent). A further experiment by Adams and Montague (1967) involved a retroactive interference paradigm, in which subjects first learned AB pairs, then AC pairs (i.e., pairs in which the stimuli from the AB list were paired with different responses); then they were asked to recall the AB pairs. The subjects were questioned about the use of NLMs after original (AB) and interpolated (AC) learning. The results showed a considerably higher proportion of correct recall of AB pairs for which NLMs had been reported during original learning than for those learned by rote. Whether the interpolated AC list was learned by rote or mediation was not similarly related to recall. Thus the pairs originally learned by mediation apparently were more resistent to retroactive inhibition than were unmediated pairs.

The above studies involved paired-associate learning. The role of NLMs has also been investigated in short-term memory, with comparable results. Groninger (1966) briefly instructed his subjects about NLMs but did not urge them to use such devices. Following each recall trial, the subject was asked whether he "made any association" (i.e., used any mediator) when he first saw the trigram to be recalled, and what type it was. The results showed that the reported use of mediators increased with trials, and that the percentage reported was much higher for high-association-value trigrams than for low-association-value trigrams. Furthermore, the use of mediators appeared to facilitate recall as a function of trials. That is, while all items showed high retention on the first trial, natural language mediation seemed to be necessary to maintain high retention on subsequent trials. The finding was interpreted to mean that the use of mediators deters proactive interference effects of prior items. These findings are striking, particularly considering the brief presentation time involved (i.e., 2 seconds). Presumably for this reason, the mediators were generally simple ones, such as imposing a word on the trigram or representing it by its initials.

Kiess (1968) investigated NLMs in two experiments involving a short-term memory task similar to that used by L. R. Peterson and M. J. Peterson (1959). He varied the association value of the consonant-vowel-consonant (CVC) items over high, medium, and low levels, and used item presentation times of 2, 3, and 4 seconds. Reports of NLMs were obtained during presentation of the CVC and again at the end of a retention interval that varied from 0 to 30 seconds. Thus it was possible to relate retention to NLMs that were actually available to the subject during learning rather than recall only, as was the case in Groninger's experiment. Figure 9-1 shows that items with NLMs were better retained

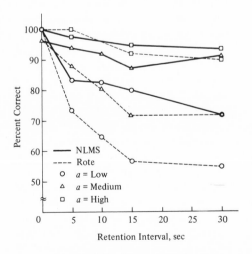

FIGURE 9-1. Percentage of correct recalls over retention intervals as a function of report category and item association value (a). From Kiess (1968).

than those without NLMs at all retention intervals except 0 seconds, and that recall increased with association value. The number of reported NLMs also increased, and the latency of the NLM response decreased, with an increase in association value. These findings are in general agreement with Groninger's and with the earlier paired-associate learning and retention data. Somewhat surprisingly, presentation time was only slightly related to the number of NLMs reported during learning, and had no effect on CVC recall.

The results of all of the above studies agree in suggesting that NLMs may facilitate learning and retention, but the relationships are correlational and it is impossible to say with certainty that NLMs actually played a causal role. The investigators have been fully aware of this. Adams and Montague (1967), for example, suggest three alternatives: NLMs may occur at the time the questionnaire is given and not during associative learning; NLMs are close correlates but not determinants of association; or, NLMs may actually play a causal role. The following studies were intended to reduce the ambiguity of interpretation.

Independent Manipulation of NLMs

The plausibility of a causal interpretation would be increased if the probability of a natural language mediator could be independently manipulated. Montague and Kiess (1968) set out to do this by obtaining NLM data for a large number of pairs from one group of subjects, and then using these norms to vary associability (i.e., as mediated by NLMs) in paired-associate learning studies with other groups. (Note that this procedure parallels other investigations of the effects of item attributes, such as meaningfulness, as discussed in the previous chapters.) The NLM data were obtained from 240 subjects, who wrote down any NLM they could think of that would link the stimulus and response members of each of several hundred pairs of CVCs. The association value of individual CVCs was also varied between pairs but was approximately equal for each member of a given pair. Several different associability indexes were derived from the data, but these will not be considered separately here. The important findings have to do with the relation of associability to learning performance. Associability (AS) and association value (AV) were varied in four different paired-associate experiments involving different designs. The results of the first three experiments were somewhat disappointing, as indicated by the authors' summary: "Taken together, the results of these three experiments show a consistent, but minor, effect of AS value when it is manipulated in lists composed of a mixture of various levels of AS and AV. The AS value does not have much predictive power over and above variation of AV" (Montague & Kiess, 1968, p. 20). As implied in that statement, association value (AV) was strongly related to learning.

In the fourth experiment, associability and association value were varied within a single long list of pairs presented for a single trial. The CVCs were either high or low association value and within each level of that variable there were two levels of associability. Because associability and association value were correlated, the two variables were not factorially varied, and four different levels of associability were represented over the two association value levels. The results showed that recall increased with associability, the recall means being .94, 1.77, 3.79, and 7.48 for increasing levels of the associability variable. The effect of associability was also significant within low association value (the first two means) and within high-association-value levels (the last two means). Moreover, the difference between associability means is significantly greater within high- than within low-association-value pairs. A similar interaction was also obtained in one of the other experiments in the study. Thus, NLMs, as inferred from associability values derived from an independent group, do predict paired-associate learning, the relation being stronger when the association value of paired items is high than when it is low. In general, however, association value appears to be a superior predictor of learning, even in the fourth experiment.

The most sophisticated interpretation of natural-language mediators to date appeared recently in a doctoral thesis by Prytulak (1969). He defined natural-language mediation as an encoding-decoding process—the subject encodes nominal stimuli (e.g., CVCs) that are not part of their natural language into functional stimuli that are, and then decodes the latter back into the nominal stimuli. Prytulak investigated the encoding and decoding processes by requiring subjects to write NLMs to CVC nonsense syllables and then to reconstruct the original CVCs from the written NLMs. On the basis of these data, Prytulak developed an objective classification system to describe the observed encoding and decoding strategies or transformations. These transformations involved various operations including substitution (e.g., the CVC "YAS" is changed to the NLM "YES" by letter substitution), internal or external addition (e.g., FEL changed to FEEL, LOC changed to LOCOMOTIVE); permutation (e.g., MIR changed to RIM), deletion (e.g., TEV changed to TV), semantic association (e.g., LIS changed to FLEUR), and phrasing (e.g., MEV encoded as MILLION ELECTRON VOLTS). Many transformations require more than one operation for their description. For example, a transformation of LOC to TRAIN involves external addition to form LOCOMOTIVE, which becomes TRAIN through semantic association.

Next, Prytulak ranked the various transformations according to their relative success in generating NLMs that were easy to decode. Ease of decoding was empirically calculated as the probability that the original CVC would be correctly reconstructed from a NLM generated by a particular transformation in the association-reconstruction study. The resulting hierarchy of transformations was referred to as a "T stack" in which transformations (Ts) producing easy-to-decode NLMs were placed higher in the stack than transformations producing difficult-to-decode NLMs. The particular T stack that Prytulak used in his study is shown in Table 9-1 together with examples of the transformations involved at each level. The stack represents an ordinal scale, so that for every CVC-word pair in Table 9-1, no T higher than the one used will generate a familiar word (i.e., one with a frequency of one or more per million in the Thorndike-Lorge word count). This ordinal property of a CVC (or T) is referred to as its "stack depth."

The T stack constitutes a model of NLM formation in which stack depth is the major predictive variable. When required to encode a CVC, the subject is assumed to work sequentially down the T stack, trying one T after another until one is found that succeeds in generating an English word. To the extent that this conceptualization is valid, stack depth should predict NLM latency and probability. The lower the CVC in the stack, the greater the number of unsuccessful Ts that must be worked through before a successful one is encountered, hence the longer the time required for NLM discovery and the lower its probability in a given time interval.

The predicted relation between number of unsuccessful Ts, as inferred from the T stack, and probability of NLM discovery was tested using CVC association values as the index of NLM probability, inasmuch as Prytulak found the latter two variables to be substantially correlated. In support of the prediction, correlations of $-.71$ and $-.60$ were obtained between number of unsuccessful Ts and Krueger (1934) and Glaze (1928) association values, respectively. The latency prediction was not tested directly by Prytulak, but the analysis implies a negative relation between NLM latency and NLM probability, which is sup-

Table 9-1

Transformations of the T stack with Illustrations and Probability Values for Correct Reconstruction of CVC from NLM. Adapted from Prytulak (1969)

Type of Operation*	Examples of Transformations	Probability of Correct Reconstruction
1 Identity	pin-pin	.88
2 External addition (S)	lov-love	.89
3 Internal addition (V)	wod-wood	.88
4 Internal (C) + external (S) addition	fex-flexible	.78
5 Internal (V) + external (S) addition	pym-payment	.71
6 Internal addition (C)	jek-jerk	.68
7 Internal addition (V)	zel-zeal	.59
8 Internal (C) + internal (V) + external (S) addition	foh-forehead	.57
9 Substitution	kut-cut	.52
10 Internal (C) + external (S) addition	vaq-vanquish	.44
11 Substitution + external (S) addition	koz-cozy	.40
12 Substitution	yit-yet	.36
13 Internal (V) addition + deletion	byf-bye	.36
14 Substitution + external addition (S)	wiq-wick	.29
15 Internal addition (C)	buh-bunch	.24
16 Substitution + internal (C) addition	zyt-zest	.20
17 Substitution + external (S) addition	jyz-jazz	.20

* Abbreviations: S = suffix, V = vowel, C = consonant; note also that the present description of types of operations is incomplete. Thus, apparently identical operations at different levels are further differentiated into sub-types (e.g., 14 and 17 involve different types of substitutions).

ported by the finding that NLM latencies are longer for low- than for high-association-value CVCs (Kiess, 1968; Schaub & Lindley, 1964). Thus the predictions were supported at least indirectly. The model was also predictive of NLM uncertainty: The greater the stack depth of a CVC, the more varied the NLMs generated by a group of subjects.

The T stack model was also extended to memory phenomena. Prytulak hypothesized that when the subject is asked to remember a CVC, he generates an NLM and stores the latter along with the T operations involved in its production. During recall, the subject attempts to retrieve the NLM and the T operations, then attempts to reconstruct the CVC by applying the reverse T operations to the NLM. The retention of T operations was found to be negatively related to the number of operations involved. Some operations were also found to be more memorable than others. Thus certain operations, such as external addition (changing LOC to LOCATION), are evident in the NLM itself and are well retained. At the other extreme are the substitution operations that do not "signal" themselves—that is, the NLM does not indicate what substitution was made, and the operation is easily forgotten.

The validity of the T stack as a predictor was tested in short-term memory and paired-associate learning tasks. Two short-term memory studies provided CVC memorability data, which were then related to various predictors, including the CVC's stack depth, the Thorndike-Lorge frequencies of the words generated by the transformations in the T stack, a combination of stack depth and frequency (called the "T model"), trigram frequency, meaningfulness (association value), pronounceability, and the like. The results showed that the T model was the best single predictor of memorability, its correlations with recall being .76 and .67 in the two experiments.

One paired-associate learning experiment employed CVC stimuli and word responses so that the stack depth of the transformation relating stimulus to response was varied. The prediction was that learning difficulty would increase with stack depth. The results were partially consistent with the prediction, two of three comparisons yielding the expected differences. A further analysis showed that the number of interfering Ts was a better predictor of error scores than was stack depth, where interfering Ts refers to Ts higher in the stack than the T relating a given CVC to the correct response, and which also can be applied to the CVC to generate a word that would be incorrect in the experiment. A second experiment, generally identical to the first except that the pairs were reversed so that the words served as stimuli for CVC responses, also failed to demonstrate the learning differences predicted by the T model.

The negative paired-associate findings notwithstanding, Prytulak's natural-language mediation model is an appealing approach to the problem of verbal mediation because of its rigor and generally impressive predictive power. It should be noted that his analysis of mediational processes in terms of transformations parallels psycholinguistic interpretations based on the linguistic theory of transformational generative grammar, to be discussed in detail in Chapter 12. In particular, Prytulak's view that a CVC may be remembered by transforming it into an NLM and then storing the NLM along with the transformational operations is precisely analogous to G. A. Miller's (1962) hypothesis that a complex sentence is stored as a simpler ("kernel") sentence along with a transformational "footnote" that indicates what syntactical operation must be performed in order to retrieve the original sentence. It will be seen, however, that the transformational hypothesis has been only inconsistently supported in sentence-memory experiments (Chapter 12), suggesting that Prytulak's model too should be viewed with caution.

Conclusions and Issues Arising from the Research on NLMs

A number of general empirical conclusions and questions of interpretation are suggested by the above research.

1. Positive relations have been consistently observed between reported mediators and learning and memory performance. Although the causal sequence is ambiguous in such correlational data, the consistency of the relation under varying conditions suggests that the reports are valid indicators of devices actually *used* by subjects to associate pairs or remember items. The causal interpretation is strengthened by successful predictions of paired-associate learning from independently obtained NLM associability data for pairs, although the predictive power of the latter is not particularly impressive in comparison with a traditional measure of associative meaningfulness. Prytulak's T-stack model of NLM generation also failed to be a strong predictor of associative learning, although it was highly successful in short-term memory. These findings raise questions about the role of *linguistic* mediators in paired-associate learning, but a detailed discussion of that issue must be postponed until later.

2. The reported natural language mediators vary greatly in complexity, and there is some disagreement concerning the relation of such complexity to learning and memory. C. J. Martin, Boersma, and Cox (1965) and Montague and Wearing (1967) found that the more complex the reported mediation strategy, the better the learning. However, Underwood and Schulz (1960, p. 300) stated that few of the associative aids their subjects reported were elaborate in the sense of requiring more than one step, and that this is reasonable inasmuch as it is difficult experimentally to get a positive effect in learning across mediators more than one step removed. Groninger (1966) also found the reported mediators in short-term memory to be relatively simple. In a sense, Prytulak's (1969) model and supporting memory data suggest that the efficiency of NLMs is related directly to their simplicity, but this conclusion depends on a particular definition of simplicity (i.e., the number of operations involved in encoding a CVC into a word) and is applicable primarily to CVC units. More generally, Prytulak suggested that short stimulus strings are encoded at the next highest level—CVCs as words, and word pairs as sentences. The number of steps would presumably increase further where both members of the pair are nonsense syllables. The complex strategies described by Martin et al. appear to be consistent

with such an interpretation, which is theoretically important here because it increases the plausibility of the complex mediational model that was proposed in the preceding chapter for associative learning involving concrete and abstract nouns paired with nonsense syllables. The issue of mediator complexity will come up repeatedly in this chapter, and at this point we may conclude that the differences in empirical findings are related to differences in experimental methodology, including such factors as the meaningfulness of learning materials, type of task (e.g., short-term memory versus paired associates), presentation rate, and the method of obtaining reports of natural language mediators.

3. The findings uniformly indicate that natural language mediators are reported more frequently as the associative meaningfulness of the pairs increases. Note that this can be interpreted simply as a corroboration of the meaningfulness values themselves: Association value, m, and NLMs all reflect the capacity of the individual items to evoke associative reactions. In the case of paired-associates, the NLMs presumably incorporate the contextual relation between members of a pair, but it is still not surprising that associability via NLMs should be related to the association values of the individual items. This interpretation of NLMs in no way reduces their theoretical importance to learning and memory. Rather, it suggests that common symbolic processes underlie the different associative measures and presumably mediate, in part at least, their relation to performance. The NLM data also suggest, however, that associative mediators may be effective even when one or both members of each pair is a nonsense word. *Indeed, such mediators presumably are all the more necessary if learning is to take place efficiently under these conditions* (cf. L. L. Clark, Lansford, & Dallenbach, 1960).

4. The importance of temporal factors is suggested by several findings. More natural language mediators are reported in paired-associate learning with longer presentation times for pairs (Montague et al., 1966), but a two-second rate seems sufficient for the effective utilization of NLMs with paired associates as well as items in short-term memory experiments (Groninger, 1966; Kiess, 1968). Kiess' experiment also showed no effects attributable to either NLMs or association value in STM at a 0-second retention interval, but such effects increased uniformly as the interval increased. Although a ceiling effect may contribute to the lack of differences at the 0-second interval, these data are also consistent with the analysis of associative meaning in earlier chapters: Associative processes take time to be aroused and to have their effect, and their effect is a function of the memory load involved in the task. The lack of any effect at zero seconds delay, for example, parallels the relative ineffectiveness of associative variables in tachistoscopic recognition (Chapter 4) and in immediate memory span (Chapter 7). The importance of temporal factors is corroborated and a more precise analysis of their effects made possible by other experimental studies of mediation considered later.

5. A general conclusion suggested by the findings of Reed (1918b) and J. M. Barnes and Underwood (1959) is that mediators tend to drop out as a function of practice. In apparent contradiction to this generalization, Run-

quist and Farley (1964) found that reported mediators increased with learning trials up to a point. However, they obtained such reports in a separate session after learning, in which the pairs were again presented and the subjects were asked to report any mediator and its latency was measured. Under such conditions, prior learning experience may indeed facilitate mediational reactions to the pairs, but it is possible that such devices were actually utilized less frequently in learning as pairs became better learned over trials. An alternative hypothesis, proposed by Prytulak (1969), is that an inverted U-shaped relation exists between use of NLMs and amount of practice. That is, NLMs first increase and then decrease as a function of trials, with the peak trial depending on such factors as item meaningfulness (cf. Adams & McIntyre, 1967, pp. 441–442).

6. A final issue concerns the nature of the mediation process that can be inferred from the studies of natural-language mediation. It is reasonable to assume that much of the symbolic activity is indeed verbal, particularly in studies that involved nonsense words as items. Nevertheless, nonverbal imagery may well have been involved to a greater or lesser degree in many experiments. Reed in fact reported the use of imagery as well as verbal devices as associative aids, and others have also made references to imagery in their studies (e.g., Bugelski, 1962; Runquist & Farley, 1964). However, no such category emerged in those studies in which attempts were made to classify NLMs according to complexity, and the very term "natural-*language* mediation" and its definition tends to preclude such a category. Adams (1967), for example, discusses NLMs exclusively in terms of implicit verbal response chains, simple or complex language habits, etc., and this emphasis is apparent in most of the investigations of natural-language mediation.

Is it reasonable to suppose that subjects might sometimes say that they used a nonverbal image to link the members of a pair if they were given the opportunity to do so? We have no direct evidence from the NLM research itself, although the examples of mediators reported in these studies certainly are suggestive. Thus, in his summary of the study of NLMs and retroactive inhibition, Adams (1967, p. 90) gave the phrase "I thought of troops landing on a shore" as a sample of a sentence association for the pair INSHORE-VICTOR. Where is the reference to *verbal* mediation here? Even the to-be-learned items are absent in the reported mediator, and it seems more reasonable to classify the mediating "thought" as a nonverbal process of some kind. Similarly, as a sample of word association for the pairs RETAIL-WEALTHY, the illustrative NLM is "money." It may well reflect a verbal process, but it appears to be the experimenter's rather than the subject's choice to classify it as such.

The above examples may be exceptions, but in the absence of more complete published descriptions of natural-language mediators, they are all we have to go on. It could be argued that these examples involve meaningful words only and the suggestion that imagery may play a mediational role is not applicable to studies involving nonsense material. Again, the available published evidence does not necessarily support such a conclusion. The illustrative example of a syntactical mediator presented by C. J. Martin, Boersma, and Cox (1965) for the pair RENNET-QUIPSON was: "Changed Rennet to Bennet and saw Quips in Quipson—thought: Bennet Cerf Quips on TV." Might the subject (or an experimenter for that matter) have classified such a mediator as involving non-verbal imagery if he were encouraged to do so? The answer to the question is important, for it would provide evidence relevant to the theory suggested in the last chapter, that imagery might be involved in noun-nonsense syllable learning via a complex encoding-decoding sequence, in which the nonsense word is first transformed into a meaningful one and then incorporated into an image involving both members of the pair, as Paivio and Madigan (1968) suggested. The RENNET-QUIPSON example certainly appears to exemplify the first part of such a coding sequence and the "thought" may well illustrate the image phase. The suggestion remains speculative, although increasingly plausible in the light of the NLM data. It should be emphasized, in any case, that the claim is not that such a process is the rule, but only that it can and does sometimes occur. The major portion of any mediation process involving nonsense words may well be verbal. Indeed, such a conclusion is inevitable given the theory that the availability of mediating imagery depends on the image-evoking capacity of items.

We turn now to a consideration of experimental studies of verbal coding devices and mediators, in which the above issues are examined further.

EXPERIMENTAL MANIPULATION OF VERBAL MEDIATION AND CODING

A variety of methods have been used to manipulate verbal coding devices and associative mediators in verbal learning, ranging from instructions to mediate to training or experience with specific verbal mediators. The different procedures are similar in many respects and a number can be regarded generally as variants of mediational "priming." For convenience, however, they will be considered under headings that identify the concepts emphasized by the investigators.

Instructions to Mediate and Sentence Contexts

The effects of verbal mediation instructions, sometimes accompanied by specific sentence contexts for the to-be-learned items, have been investigated most often in relation to paired-associate learning and occasionally in serial learning. The studies have been concerned with such issues as developmental factors in the effective utilization of mediators, the effects of varying the grammatical class of the contextual sentences, experimenter-provided mediators versus subject-generated mediators, and rate of presentation of the to-be-learned material. Different studies also provide some data on the relative effectiveness of the mediation procedures with meaningful as compared to nonsense material, although systematic comparisons have not been made. We shall first consider the research on paired-associate learning of meaningful material.

Paired-associate learning   One study by A. R. Jensen and Rohwer (1963) involved mentally retarded adults, who, the investigators reasoned, would be less likely than college students to use verbal mediators spontaneously. Because most of the subjects could not read, the stimulus material consisted of pictures of common objects. Paired-associate learning was investigated in two experiments. In the mediation condition of one, the subjects were simply asked on the first trial to make a sentence or phrase linking the two items of a pair. In the second, a standard set of mediating verbalizations (in addition to instructions) was provided by the experimenter on the initial presentation of pairs. For example, the phrase for SHOE-CLOCK was "I threw the shoe at the clock." In the nonmediation condition, the subjects were asked only to name the stimulus and response terms. Mediation instructions in both experiments had a dramatic facilitating effect on learning, suggesting that retardates do not spontaneously use verbal mediators in such a situation. This conclusion was strengthened by the finding that, on a retest 10 days later, the two groups did not differ significantly from each other, indicating that the instructed subjects had forgotten the technique. The findings were corroborated and extended in further research by A. R. Jensen (1965) and A. R. Jensen and Rohwer (1965a). The latter study involved subjects at seven age levels ranging from 5 to 17 years of age, matched on IQ and socioeconomic background. The results showed that paired-associate learning was markedly facilitated by sentence-mediation instructions, particularly in the age range from 7 to 13. Learning also correlated strikingly with age when subjects were given no mediation instructions, suggesting that the spontaneous use of mediators increased with age.

Rohwer (1966) subsequently confirmed the facilitative effect of sentence mediators with children and showed in addition that sentences containing verbs (e.g., the DOG closes the GATE) aided learning more than sentences with prepositions (the DOG on the GATE) or conjunctions (the DOG and the GATE). The superiority of verb connectives has been repeatedly demonstrated by Rohwer and his collaborators (see Rohwer, 1970), but the effect is not always large and has sometimes failed to occur (Yuille & Pritchard, 1969).

Another important finding regarding sentence mediators is that recall of the embedded noun pair is better when subjects generate their own linking sentence than when they simply read or listen to and repeat an equivalent linking sentence (Bobrow & Bower, 1969; Pelton, 1969). Bobrow and Bower attributed the effect to superior sentence comprehension when it is actively generated. Interesting in its own right, the finding may also help explain such empirical inconsistencies as the following. Olton (1969) found that sentence mediators significantly increased the rate of learning but had only a marginal effect on recall one week later when the degree of learning was equated for mediation and control groups. Olton's finding for retention contrasts with the conclusion from studies of natural-language mediation that NLMs facilitate retention as well as learning (e.g., Montague et al., 1966). Perhaps the difference results from the fact that Olton presented the sentence mediators, whereas NLMs are generated by the subject and are therefore more effective mnemonics.

Other studies have yielded negative as well as positive effects of verbal mediation instructions in paired-associate learning when the pairs included items that are not meaningful words. R. B. Martin and Dean (1966) failed to obtain a significant effect of such instructions on paired-associate learning of nonsense syllable-word pairs. However, Wind and Davidson (1969) found that the learning of such pairs was facilitated by providing a sentence context for the syllable, followed by the corresponding word in parentheses. For example, the context for BAP DINNER was "What time is BAP served? (DINNER)." Note that the relative effectiveness of the procedures in these two studies contrasts with the above finding that subject-generated mediators are more effective than ones provided by the experimenter when both members of the pair are meaningful words. Apparently the presence of a meaningless CVC in the pair makes it more difficult for subjects to discover a useful verbal mediator on their own.

Schwartz (1969a) reported two experiments comparing verbal mediation and standard instructions in one-trial paired-associate learning. Her list consisted of letter-word pairs, such as A-PIE and D-CAT, which were constructed on the basis of association norms in such a manner that a high-probability implicit associative response could serve as a mediator. Thus the primary associative responses to the letters A and D are the words *apple* and *dog,* respectively, which in turn evoke the words *pie* and *cat* as primary associates. Subjects in the instructed group were told that the strategy of changing the left-hand letter into a word beginning with that letter might make it easier to learn the pairs. The first experiment involved a 2-second rate of presentation on both study trials (pairs) and recall trials (stimulus items), whereas the recall trials were untimed in the second. The results showed that instructions to mediate greatly increased the number of reported mediators in both experiments, but learning was facilitated by the instructions only in the second.

Schwartz interpreted her findings in terms of a distinction made by Schulz and Lovelace (1964) between the *discovery* and *utilization* of mediators (to be discussed in more detail below, under mediation paradigms): the 2-second rate permitted the discovery of mediators during pair presentation but was too fast to permit their effective utilization. She tested this interpretation in a subsequent experiment (Schwartz, 1969b) by comparing the number of correct responses whose latencies were 2 seconds or less with those whose latencies exceeded 2 seconds during an 8-second recall interval. The results showed that instructions to mediate facilitated recall of both short- and long-latency responses, casting doubt on the interpretation of her earlier results in terms of the discovery-utilization distinction. This does not necessarily imply that the distinction is invalid, but may simply mean that 2 seconds was not the critical interval in her study. The particular time limitation for effective utilization of mediators presumably depends in part on the nature of the stimulus items involved—a point that may be relevant to Martin and Dean's failure to get significant instructional effects with nonsense syllable-word pairs, although it does not explain the one negative finding by Schwartz. In any case, we shall see later that mediation instructions can be effective at even faster rates than two seconds when both members of the pair are meaningful words.

Serial learning Mediation instructions have also had contrasting effects on serial learning. The A. R. Jensen and Rohwer (1963, 1965a) studies described earlier included serial-learning experiments using the same materials and general approach as the paired-associate experiments. The mediation condition in serial learning involved presentation of phrases similar to those used in paired-associate learning, linking each item to the one following. These were presented only on the initial trial. In contrast with the results for paired-associate learning, instructions to mediate had no effect on serial learning. The later study (A. R. Jensen & Rohwer, 1965a), which involved subjects ranging in age from 5 to 17 years, showed in addition that serial learning beyond the age of eight scarcely correlated with age under either standard or mediation instructions. These findings contrast sharply with the paired-associate learning results, which the authors interpreted to mean that paired-associate learning benefits much more than serial learning from transfer from past verbal experience. The subject's verbal experience enriches his "associative network" and increases the availability of relevant verbal mediators. Serial learning, however, appears to depend little on mediating associations (A. R. Jensen, 1962; A. R. Jensen & Rohwer, 1965b) and may reflect a more "primitive" ability that is relatively unaffected by the amount of previous verbal experience.

Jensen and Rohwer's conclusion does not agree fully with the fact that word imagery (I) and meaningfulness (m) are effective in serial learning (see Chapter 7), at least if such effects are interpreted in terms of mediation processes aroused by high-I or high-m items. Their results and conclusions are also inconsistent with strong positive effects of verbal mediation obtained by Bower and Clark (1969). These investigators had their subjects learn 12 serial lists of 10 nouns each either by a narrative-chaining method or a control condition. Each narrative-chaining subject was instructed to construct a meaningful story around the words to be remembered and was permitted as much time as was needed to do so (usually 1–2 minutes). Each control subject, yoked to an experimental subject, had the same amount of time but was told simply to study and learn each serial list. Recall was tested immediately after each list. In addition, after the 12th list had been studied and recalled, the subject was asked to recall all of the lists successively beginning with the first, the cue for recall of a list being the first word in that list. The immediate recall test following the study of a list showed almost perfect recall for both groups. However, the two groups differed enormously in their later recall of all 12 lists. Figure 9-2 shows that the narrative group recalled six to seven times as much as their yoked controls. Bower and Clark interpret the effect as probably being due to thematic organization, which increased learning, decreased interlist interference, and guided

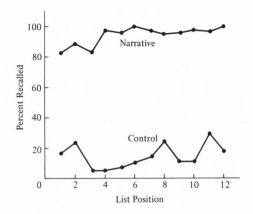

FIGURE 9-2. Median percentages re-
called over 12 serial lists by narrative and control subjects. From Bower and Clark (1969).

reconstructive recall. The first-word cue presumably prompted recall of the
theme, from which the person could reconstruct the sentences and retrieve the
critical words.

The contrasting results obtained by Jensen and Rohwer on the one hand and
Bower and Clark on the other are explainable in terms of the different procedures
that were employed. The sentence mediators used by Jensen and Rohwer linked
only a given word with the one following and were unrelated to each other,
whereas Bower and Clark permitted the subject to construct narratives that
provided thematic organization for the entire list. The different learning procedures (anticipation versus continuous study) and different materials (pictures
versus concrete nouns) may also have contributed to the discrepant findings.
In any event, the Bower and Clark finding makes it clear that verbal mediation
instructions can have powerful effects in serial learning, just as they can in
paired-associate learning under appropriate conditions.

As in the case of the research on natural-language mediators, the studies
considered in this section nominally involved verbal mediators, but the results
are open to an alternative interpretation in terms of nonverbal imagery, at least
as a supplementary mediating mechanism. Such a view is especially compelling
in those experiments in which pictures served as the to-be-learned items. In
addition, it can be argued that the meaning of such sentences as "I threw the
shoe at the clock" is experienced in terms of concrete imagery, which serves
as the associative mediator for the critical noun pair. Imagery may have been
similarly involved as a factor in the effect of narrative stories on serial learning,
as Bower and Clark suggested. Evidence bearing directly on the imagery hypothesis will be considered later when we compare imaginal and verbal mediation,
along with a re-examination of such findings as the effects of grammatical class.

Associative Priming of Verbal Mediators

Dallett (1964) investigated the associative-probability hypothesis of Underwood and Schulz (1960) by a method of associative priming of implicit mediators in paired-associate learning. On the first trial when the stimulus trigram (e.g., BAC) was presented, an attempt was made to alter the subject's associative response to the stimulus by presenting a word that was an associate of the trigram (e.g., back) according to free-association norms. For half the subjects, the mediator was relevant to the response (RETURN) that subsequently appeared; for the other half, it was irrelevant to the response (EGGS). Other conditions in the study were an unprimed control, an association to the stimulus term before the response appeared, and a practice group that was presented the response word itself instead of a mediator. Following learning, all subjects were questioned about any associative aids they had used in learning.

The results showed that the priming of a relevant mediator produced faster learning than irrelevant priming. However, the control group did not differ from the relevant group and, on the basis of the responses to the postexperimental questionnaire, this was interpreted to mean that the relevant mediators were readily available without priming. Priming with the response word itself led to performance similar to the control group's. The association group showed generally inferior learning to the control group, but items that happened to elicit relevant mediators were learned better than those that apparently elicited irrelevant mediators. The experiment corroborates findings from the NLM studies described earlier in which mediation has been assessed by postexperimental questioning of subjects and, like Schwartz's (1969a, 1969b) studies, also demonstrates some experimental control over the mediation process. However, the failure to find a difference between the performance of the control group and relevant mediation group suggests that the priming procedure is not potent enough to substantially increase the availability of relevant mediators. In this respect, relevant priming seems comparable to instructions to mediate in its effect, at least with college students as subjects, judging from some of the studies discussed above. On the other hand, irrelevant priming effectively interfered with learning and thereby provided support for a mediational interpretation of the findings generally.

Verbal Coding of Individual Units

Both facilitating and interfering effects attributable to mnemonic devices or coding strategies have been demonstrated by manipulating conditions that facilitate the transformation of items into more meaningful units. Lindley (1963) investigated the effect on short-term memory of the presence or absence of cues designed to control the coding performed by the subject. Three-letter items of high, medium, and low meaningfulness were the to-be-recalled stimuli. The recoding cues consisted of additional letters in appropriate positions to make a complete English word. For example, the items CQU and WAS became aCQUire and WASh with the recoding cues present. When such items were presented, the subject spelled and later recalled only the three crucial letters, which appeared in capital type. The results showed that recoding cues facilitated recall of low-meaningful items but interfered with recall of high-meaningful items. Lindley interpreted the finding as reflecting the joint influence of chunking and interference. The recoding cues permit the subject to recode items into larger chunks of information. This is useful with low-meaningful items that are not already organized into chunks. However, the extra letters also compete with the to-be-recalled letters tending to produce errors at recall, particularly in the case of high-meaningful items in which the letters are already coded as one chunk. Further experiments in the same study showed that presenting only the extra letters as decoding cues during recall trials also facilitated short-term memory with low-meaningful items. These findings were confirmed and extended by Schaub and Lindley (1964) and Lindley and Nedler (1965).

Underwood and Keppel (1963) studied free recall learning of lists of 10 trigrams, such as TFA and UTB, which could be transformed into three-letter words by rearrangement of the letters, e.g., UTB, becomes TUB or BUT. Parallel groups were either instructed or not instructed concerning the transformational possibilities. Each of the groups was further differentiated on the basis of the nature of the correct response allowed, one group being allowed to write the letters of each trigram in any order and the other group being required to write down the trigrams as presented. Whether or not subjects actually attempted to code was inferred from the responses they gave, i.e., whether they responded with words constructed from the trigram. The results showed that when subjects could respond with letters in any order, performance was facilitated if the trigrams were encoded into words. This facilitation was greater in the instructed group than in the noninstructed group, apparently because more subjects encoded in the former group. On the other hand, if the subject was required to write down the trigram as presented, encoding to words and decoding to trigrams inhibited performance.

Forrester and Spear (1967) extended Underwood and Keppel's study by varying the rated pronunciability of trigrams as well as coding instructions and recall restrictions. The important new finding was that allowing subjects to recall the letters of a trigram in any order did not facilitate recall of items of high pronunciability. Analyses of the responses suggested that this occurred because such items were not coded to words. The authors concluded that pronunciation itself is a type of code that is used whenever applicable. An alternative possibility, however, is that the subjects used a coding system other than the anagram code designated by the experimenter—for example, the easily pronounced trigrams TUC and SNU might be encoded as "truck" and "snow." The basis of the coding would be acoustic or articulatory in this case as well, but the effective mediator would be a meaningful unit that can be relatively easily decoded.

Underwood and Erlebacher (1965) considered further conditions and extended the study of coding to include paired-associate as well as free-recall learning. In one experiment, the number of coding rules was varied in free recall, such that one coding rule applied to all items, e.g., moving the last letter of each trigram to the second position formed a meaningful word (RTA would become RAT, for example). Other lists required either two or four different coding rules. The results showed that learning was faster when one decoding rule was applicable than when two or four rules were required (cf. M. R. Mueller, Edmonds, & Evans, 1967). Subsequent experiments showed, however, that the facilitation produced by a one-rule list was relatively small when comparisons were made with the learning of a list composed of actual words—i.e., one-rule lists were learned much slower than word lists. In the case of paired-associate learning, varying the number of decoding rules applicable to the response terms produced results closely paralleling those found in the first free learning experiment. Encoding of a stimulus term to a word also influenced learning positively, but such encoding did not occur unless the possibilities were easily perceived by the subject. Sound coding of limited usefulness was also demonstrated for response terms. Underwood and Erlebacher concluded that coding systems: (a) may influence learning positively if decoding is simple; (b) will produce only a small positive effect even under favorable conditions; (c) may have no positive effect even if used and may, under certain conditions, inhibit learning. It should be emphasized that these conclusions are based on one type of coding system only, viz., anagram coding of trigrams into words. Thus the conclusions need not be valid for other types of coding, especially ones involving the addition of letters or suffixes, which appear generally to be more effective according to Prytulak's (1969) analysis.

A study by Podd and Spear (1967) combined response codability, instructions to code, and what was essentially a priming condition designed to induce coding. Consonant trigrams that could be transformed into meaningful words by insertion of vowels (e.g., DLL becomes DULL) served as response terms in paired-associate learning. Stimuli were either related to the coded response (e.g., bright-DLL) or were high-meaningful CVC trigrams unrelated to the coded response. Instructions to code and relatedness were varied orthogonally. The results showed that both instructions and relatedness facilitated learning, the effect of the latter being considerably greater than that of the former. In a second experiment, relatedness and length of anticipation interval were varied orthogonally. It was expected that a longer anticipation interval would benefit the related group more than the unrelated group because if relatedness induced a set to code, then subjects in the related group would need the extra time to decode the responses. The expected relationships occurred during the early stages of learning. From these and other data, the authors concluded that relatedness not only provides the subject with a coding strategy, but also provides (perhaps simultaneously) a stable mnemonic device with which to implement this strategy.

The studies considered in this section indicate that coding of response items into more meaningful units is affected by the difficulty of the transformation involved, properties of the stimulus term or cues associated with it that might induce coding behavior, and instructional sets. Stated more briefly, a coding or mediating strategy can be induced by the characteristics of the stimulus and the response, as well as by instructions or other contextual conditions introduced by the experimenter. Whether the coding strategies indeed do facilitate learning depends on the ease of retrieving the required response from its encoded representation. The implications of these conclusions will be considered again later.

Mediation Transfer Paradigms

Verbal mediation has been studied most extensively using mediated transfer paradigms in which potential mediators are either inferred from association norms or are "built in" experimentally. These paradigms have their antecedent in the associative-chaining mnemonic introduced by Kothe (see Chapter 6), who had suggested that such pairs as "wine-Jacob," could be connected by the verbal chain, "wine-cellar-staircase-ladder-Jacob." The modern experimental methods, findings, and issues in the area have been thoroughly reviewed by a number of writers (e.g., Earhard & Mandler, 1965; Horton & Kjeldergaard, 1961; J. J. Jenkins, 1963; Kausler, 1966; Kjeldergaard, 1968). Because of the ready availability of those summaries, the present review of the area will be relatively brief, with an emphasis on the highlights and recent developments that are most relevant here.

Mediated transfer studies generally involve the learning of two or more lists in which the last list involves paired items that are unrelated except for a common implicit associate, which theoretically serves to link the pair members. Three different paradigms have been commonly investigated: (a) chaining, (b) acquired stimulus equivalence, and (c) acquired response equivalence. With the letters A, B, and C representing verbal items, a three-stage forward association chaining paradigm can be schematically represented as A-B, B-C, A-C, where item B serves as a response term for A during first stage (A-B) learning, as a stimulus term for C in the second stage (B-C), and presumably functions implicitly to mediate the A-C association during the third, test-stage learning. That is, A is assumed to arouse B as a covert response, which in turn evokes C. The second, B-C stage may be experimentally produced, i.e., the subject learns a B-C list, or it may be inferred from word association norms. Performance on the test list would be compared with the performance under a control condition, for example, A-B, X-C, A-C, where X refers to unrelated terms that substitute for the B terms in the experimental paradigm; or A-B, B-C, A-C$_R$, where the third stage involves re-pairing of A with C response items at random, such that no A-C$_R$ pair has a common B term; and so on.

The acquired stimulus equivalence paradigm, A-B, C-B, A-C, stems directly from the work of Hull (1939), who reasoned that two stimuli associated with a common response acquire equivalence in the sense that they implicitly evoke the common response that in turn produces a common proprioceptive stimulus. The events, implicit B-stimulus consequences of B, serve to link the otherwise unrelated items A and C. The acquired response equivalence model, B-A, B-C, A-C can be analyzed in an analogous fashion. Both paradigms assume that backward associations develop and are positively effective in one stage of the model (Horton & Kjeldergaard, 1961). For example, in the first stage (A-B) of the stimulus-equivalence paradigm, a B-A association develops and A is presumably elicited as an implicit response to C during the second stage in the chain, C-B-implicit A. Again assuming backward association, A-C should thus acquire some associative strength that would be reflected in the subject's performance during the third (test) stage.

Two examples will serve to illustrate the experimental and language-habit approaches to the investigation of mediation paradigms. Bugelski and Scharlock (1952) obtained positive evidence for mediated transfer using an experimental chaining paradigm. Twenty college students learned three paired-associate lists of nonsense syllables, in three sessions. Each subject learned the experimental A-B, B-C, A-C lists, as well as the control lists, A-B, B-C, A-D. Learning was found to be superior for pairs having a common implicit mediator than for control pairs. W. A. Russell and Storms (1955) investigated mediated transfer when the mediating association was inferred from pre-existing language habits as determined from the Kent-Rosanoff norms. The paradigm involved four stages, A-B, B-C, C-D, and A-D, where A-B and A-D were lists learned successively in the laboratory and the B-C and C-D stages (constituting a B-C-D chain) were inferred from the association data. For example, in the implicit chain, Soldier-Sailor-Navy, Soldier (the B term) frequently elicits Sailor (C) as an associate, which elicits Navy (D), but Soldier rarely elicits Navy. The results showed that subjects who learned nonsense syllable-word pairs such as ZUG-Soldier (A-B) showed facilitation when tested for learning of pairs such as ZUG-Navy (A-D), in comparison with a control group that learned A-X pairs. In the example, the assumed mediator was "Sailor."

Numerous studies have subsequently appeared in which various paradigms and variables have been investigated. Horton and Kjeldergaard (1961) tested the eight possible three-stage paradigms and found positive mediated transfer effects with all but one paradigm. Their findings have been generally confirmed in other studies. J. J. Jenkins (1963) tested 16 different four-stage paradigms, where all stages were experimentally acquired. His results were entirely negative, which was surprising because such mediation had been achieved in earlier studies involving nonverbal material (e.g., Shipley, 1935) and did appear to be implicitly involved in the W. A. Russell and Storms (1955) experiment. Subsequently, however, positive transfer has been demonstrated in four-stage verbal mediation paradigms (Grover, Horton, & Cunningham, 1967; C. T. James & Hakes, 1965; Williams & Levin, 1968).

An extensive methodological critique of mediation-paradigm research has been presented by Earhard and Mandler (1965). Their survey revealed that paradigm and control conditions differ with respect to nonmediational factors such as forgetting and interference, which tend to produce effects similar to those predicted from the mediation model. Thus they argued that what has been attributed to verbal mediation may be an artifact resulting from unlearning of the mediator as a function of negative transfer during the second-stage learning. G. Mandler and Earhard (1964) obtained evidence supporting their interference hypothesis, but subsequent studies (e.g., Goulet, 1966; Horton, Grover, & Wiley, 1968; J. J. Jenkins & Foss, 1965; Kausler & Deichmann, 1968; Schulz, Liston, & Weaver, 1968) have provided strong support for mediated associations while ruling out interference and pseudomediation interpretations. The overall evidence indicates that, although the confounding variables described by Earhard and Mandler certainly cannot be ignored (see Earhard & Earhard, 1968), verbal mediation is firmly entrenched as a reliable psychological phenomenon.

The early research on mediation paradigms was essentially concerned with demonstrating the phenomenon, but an increasing number of recent studies have been concerned with investigating variables that influence the magnitude of the mediation effect. The most relevant of these variables for our purposes are considered in the following sections.

Item meaningfulness and concreteness   M. J. Peterson and Blattner (1963) investigated mediation effects resulting from the presentation of a single A-B pair and a single B-C pair, the test of mediation involving selection of the "right" response from three alternative responses, C, D, and E, to the stimulus A in the third stage. In several experiments, the meaningfulness of the items varied from consonant-consonant-consonant trigrams to meaningful words. They found that mediational responding increased as the meaningfulness of the learning material increased. The conclusion was corroborated and extended to additional paradigms in a later study (Peterson, Colavita, Sheahan, & Blattner, 1964). Horton (1964) also investigated the effects of meaningfulness of the common (B) term in simple chaining and acquired response equivalence paradigms. The B terms were either high m or low m dissyllables from Noble's (1952a) list. Mediation effects were found to be greater with the high m mediators. These findings are consistent with those stemming from experiments described earlier (e.g., Boersma et al., 1966; Montague et al., 1966) on meaningfulness and the use of natural-language mediators. In both cases, high verbal associative meaningfulness presumably enhances the availability and effectiveness of verbal processes as mediators.

Paivio and Yarmey (1965) and Yarmey (1967) also investigated the effect of abstractness-concreteness of the common term in three-stage paradigms and found that mediation effects were only slightly greater when the noun mediator was concrete than when it was abstract. Christiansen (1969) failed to obtain any effect of mediator concreteness with adult subjects, although earlier Christiansen and Stone (1968) had found concrete high-imagery nouns to be better mediators than abstract, low-imagery nouns with seventh-grade students. The latter effect might be due to meaning attributes other than imagery-concreteness, however, inasmuch as m was not controlled. Furthermore, while the two classes of words were equated on Thorndike-Lorge (1944) frequency, it may be that the concrete words were more familiar than the abstract to the young subjects (cf. Paivio & Yuille, 1966). These data suggest that imagery as a word attribute plays only a minor role in mediated transfer involving words and nonsense syllables, and that implicit verbal processes are indeed the major associative factor in such designs. We shall see later, however, that nonverbal imagery is a plausible explanation of transfer effects in other studies.

Time factors   Schulz and Lovelace (1964) examined the effect of time factors using a four-stage chaining paradigm in which the second stage (B-C) was inferred from language norms. In one experiment, subjects were allowed either two or four seconds as the test-list study interval. No significant mediation effect was obtained, although some subjects reported awareness of the relationship between members of pairs. This led Schulz and Lovelace to distinguish between the *discovery* and the *utilization* of mediating associations, the former being a necessary but not sufficient condition if effective utilization is impossible. In a second experiment, they accordingly increased the anticipation interval during the test stage to four seconds, thus allowing more time for the utilization of mediators. Significant mediation effects were obtained under this condition, supporting their hypothesis.

A subsequent study (Schulz & Weaver, 1968) compared the effects of variation in the length of the study interval (presumably the mediator "discovery" phase) and the test interval ("utilization") in a three-stage mediation paradigm. The results showed greater mediated transfer effects with a 3-second than with a 1.5-second test interval during the test stage. Study interval variation (1 and 2.5 seconds) had no effect on mediating associations, however, and Schulz and Weaver concluded that the amount of time required for the elicitation and discovery of mediation may be very brief—perhaps less than one second. Indeed, under some circumstances, the mediator apparently can be discovered entirely during the test-stage test interval, without any study trials (Weaver, Hopkins, & Schulz, 1968). Their data leave the conceptualization of the discovery stage somewhat uncertain but clearly show the importance of time for the utilization of mediators. Note that these findings can be related to effects of temporal factors discussed earlier in connection with NLMs (e.g., Montague et al., 1966; Prytulak, 1969), mediation instructions (e.g., Schwartz, 1969a, 1969b), and response decoding (Podd & Spear, 1967). They are also consistent with J. Richardson's (1968) finding that the latencies of overt associative responses increased with the number of implicit associative responses that were assumed to occur as a result of prior training with an associative chain. Thus we have some suggestive evidence consistent with the view that verbal mediation processes function sequentially.

Awareness   Since we are concerned in general with the role of symbolic factors in verbal learning, it is relevant to consider the subject's verbally expressed awareness of relationships among conditions in mediation paradigms. In effect, this raises the question of whether conscious awareness is a necessary, defining feature of the mediational functioning of the verbal symbolic system. The most common assumption in the verbal learning literature appears to be that it is not. In agreement with this view, a number of investigators have reported mediated transfer effects when subjects were apparently unaware of the mediating associations (e.g., Bugelski & Scharlock, 1952; Horton & Kjeldergaard, 1961; M. J. Peterson, 1963; W. A. Russell & Storms, 1955). However, other studies have suggested that awareness is an important factor. R. B. Martin and Dean (1964) used the Russell and Storms (1955) procedure, in which the mediating B-C-D chain was constructed from word association norms. Several conditions were manipulated in order to encourage the explicit use of mediators (e.g., pronouncing the B term during the anticipation of D to the stimulus, A, in the test stage). In addition, subjects were asked to describe how they had learned each pair. The amount and kind of mediation reported was affected by the nature of the pair and the learning conditions, and superior learning was present only for those pairs for which subjects reported using mediators. Horton (1964) categorized subjects on the basis of postexperimental interviews into three groups according to level of awareness. He found that unaware subjects showed no facilitation on mediated pairs, whereas highly aware subjects showed clear evidence of mediated learning. Evidence of mediated learning among both aware and unaware subjects was obtained by Seidel (1962) and Yarmey (1967). In Yarmey's study, there was nevertheless a significant positive correlation between reported awareness of mediators and learning scores. Lee and Jensen (1968) similarly found that the magnitude of the facilitative effect of mediation paradigms is closely linked with the subject's degree of awareness of the relationships between A-B, B-C, and A-C lists.

The evidence leaves the role of awareness in some doubt, although it seems apparent that, whatever this variable is, it affects the level of mediated learning. A parallel may be noted between the findings in this area and research on operant conditioning of verbal behavior and classical conditioning of meaning. The early research on the former problem yielded evidence of conditioning in the absence of awareness, but later studies, in which awareness was defined more carefully, failed to find the conditioning effects without awareness (see the review by Spielberger & DeNike, 1966). Similarly, A. W. Staats and C. K. Staats (1957, 1958) reported the apparent transfer of the evaluative meaning of different (UCS) words to other (CS) words or nonsense syllables using a classical conditioning paradigm, the transfer occurring without reported awareness on the part of the subjects. However, subsequent studies (e.g., Hare, 1964; Paivio, 1964) have found little evidence of such an effect except when subjects were able to verbalize the relations among stimuli. As a consequence of such findings, cognitive interpretations of the conditioning effects have been suggested. Spielberger and his associates have argued that "what is learned" in verbal conditioning is awareness of a correct response-reinforcement contingency, and Hare (1964) concluded that subjects apparently regard the meaning conditioning experiment as a problem solving task in which they rate items as they thought they were expected to. The issue is certainly not closed inasmuch as recent studies have again demonstrated positive reinforcement effects in verbal conditioning despite little evidence of awareness, but cognitive factors nevertheless continue to be emphasized in a manner that was not typical of the early research (e.g., see Dixon & Moulton, 1970).

The emergence of cognitive interpretations is apparent in mediated transfer studies as well. Earhard and Mandler (1965) suggest that mediation paradigms can be viewed as concept learning tasks in which the subject is presented with the problem of finding a rule or plan that fits the structural arrangement of items and enables him to re-pair the terms of a test list. While they do not reject the conditioning model of mediation, they suggest that it may have limited applicability to the verbal behavior of adult subjects, who can and do use overlearned strategies and plans to mediate. Such a viewpoint applies equally to all the approaches to verbal mediation that have been considered in this chapter. Montague et al. (1966), for example, suggest that natural-language mediators represent the application of well-learned language habits to new verbal material. Where such mediators can be applied, verbal learning is a case of positive transfer. It should be remembered, finally, that this kind of analysis was anticipated long ago by Reed in his treatment of associative learning as a problem situation to be solved by thought.

Verbal associations versus meaning similarity in mediated transfer   The studies considered thus far ostensibly were concerned with the mediational function of verbal associative processes. The possibility that nonverbal factors, such as imagery, may be operative in some experiments involving natural-language mediators was suggested earlier, although the studies generally provided no specific evidence of such a process. In the case of mediated transfer studies, a relevant theoretical issue concerning the interpretation of the mediation process has generated some research. One view is that the process is verbal-associative in nature, while the other states that it involves a representational (meaning) process that is essentially nonverbal (cf. the parallel interpretations of meaning discussed in Chapter 3). The former has been supported particularly by Bousfield (1961), while the latter is obviously a statement of the theoretical position maintained by Osgood, who does not deny the effectiveness of verbal chaining but objects to the claim that it is the only mechanism contributing to mediated verbal transfer (Osgood, 1961, p. 95). Thus Osgood's theory predicts that mediation effects could be a function of similarity of meaning of the items in a transfer situation.

Early evidence relevant to the issue was reviewed by Wynne and Cofer (1958), who conclude that mediated transfer and other mediation phenomena are more accurately predicted from measures of verbal association or overlap than from measures of meaning relations. However, some support for the effectiveness of meaning similarity has been obtained subsequently. Bastian (1961) and Ryan (1960) compared transfer effects when either the stimulus or response words of the original list and transfer list had strong associative connections and low similarity of meaning, with transfer when associative connections were weak and similarity high. Both association and similarity produced positive transfer in comparison with control conditions. In both studies, however, the effect of verbal association was greater than that of meaning similarity (see also Sassenrath & Yonge, 1967), and Bastian suggested that similarity may have been effective only because of associative connections present in the subject's verbal behavior. Consistent with such a view, Smythe (1966) found no difference in transfer with synonymity (as compared to nonsynonymity) of meaning between the noun stimulus members of original and transfer lists when associative overlap was controlled. He also varied noun imagery in order to test the hypothesis that similarity of nonverbal images might mediate transfer when the stimuli in the two lists are high-imagery synonyms. Noun imagery, too, failed to affect transfer, although it had its usual strong effect on learning. Smythe suggested that the negative findings might be attributable to the difficulty of entirely eliminating associative overlap, which appears to be facilitative even when minimally present (J. J. Jenkins, 1963) and may have overridden the effects of other variables in his experiment.

In striking contrast with the above studies, however, Kasschau and Pollio (1967) found semantic similarity to be just as effective as associative relations in mediating transfer. They attributed the difference to their use of separate lists rather than the mixed-list design used, for example, by Ryan (1960), arguing that the latter permits selective utilization of the more easily detected associative relations. The demonstration of independent effects of semantic and verbal-associative relations is important, but we are left wondering about the mechanisms that differentiate semantic from associative effects. Common emotional reactions might constitute the nonverbal basis of semantic similarity and the transfer in some instances. In others, the semantic relation may be based on imagery, particularly in the case of concrete words such as *stem* and *trunk,* or *king* and *chief.* The possibility has not been systematically explored, but some relevant evidence will be presented later in the context of the theoretical analysis of mediation in Chapter 11.

SUMMARY

The research considered in this chapter generally involved no systematic comparisons that would reveal functional attributes unique to verbal mediation and distinct (theoretically) from other mediational processes. The comparisons of associative and semantic bases of mediation in the last section did suggest that subjects can make use of both kinds of information under certain conditions, but nothing was revealed that might indicate in what way, if any, associative and semantic mediation processes differ in their functions. Thus the best that we can do at this point is to summarize the most consistent empirical findings from the verbal mediation research so that later comparisons will be easier.

One striking feature of the research is the predominance of studies involving nonsense words as items, and the finding that their learning is generally enhanced by the use of verbal mediators, regardless of how the latter are defined or manipulated. Nevertheless, the effectiveness of mediators is a function of the verbal-associative meaningfulness of the to-be-learned syllables—generally, the more meaningful the units, the more effective the mediators—indicating that the availability of verbal-associative reactions to the items is an important factor. The exceptions to this generalization are the situations that involve coding strategies, such as anagram coding, which require a transformation of the unit itself into a more meaningful one. Here the coding strategy is helpful with low-meaningful units, provided that the decoding problem is not difficult, but it is not helpful and may even have a negative effect with more meaningful units. The reason may be that in the latter case the recoding strategy destroys an integrated unit, thereby hindering the retrieval of that unit. In the case of natural-language mediators and the manipulation of mediators in mediation paradigm studies, on the other hand, the to-be-learned units themselves remain intact but are somehow embellished or interconnected by the addition of the potential mediators as new verbal units. Thus mediators may be more effective with high-meaningful items in the latter case because such items are already integrated into units, and the function of the mediator is to act on the intact unit so as to facilitate its retrieval or its linkage to another integrated unit. The apparently contradictory effects of meaningfulness are thus resolved if we think of unit recoding and interunit mediation as techniques designed to facilitate the formation of still-higher-order meaningful units: Recoding does this in the case of unintegrated sequence of letters, and words or sentences as mediators accomplish it in the case of unrelated pairs of relatively meaningful CVCs or words. One (untested) implication of this analysis is that the addition of verbal mediators should have no facilitative effect on, and may even hinder, associative learning between words that are already strongly associated, e.g., window and pane.

This analysis points to a feature that has been emphasized throughout the preceding chapters as a characteristic of verbal symbolic processes: The recoding and mediating techniques involve symbolic transformations that are tied to sequential ordering of verbal elements. A more meaningful verbal string is created by the re-ordering of elements, as in anagram coding, or by the addition of letter elements (DLL becomes "dull") or word elements (two unrelated words are associated by the addition of linking words or phrases) resulting in a higher-order, sequentially organized (syntactic) unit. The process is apparently stepwise and linear, as evidenced for example by J. Richardson's (1968) data showing that response latency increases as a function of the number of links assumed to be involved in the implicit associative chain.

There is suggestive evidence here and there, however, of a symbolic shift into a nonverbal system, as when a NLM or instructional set involves a sentence whose meaning can be expressed as an image independent of the particular verbal units that are to be learned; or mediated transfer based on semantic (synonym) relations rather than common verbal associates. With the exception of the latter, the operations involved in the above research were not designed to be definitive of such nonverbal processes. We turn next to studies in which the operational emphasis has been specifically on nonverbal imagery.

10

Imagery Mediation in Learning and Memory

This chapter focuses on experimental evidence and conclusions from studies that have been concerned specifically with imagery as a mediator in learning and memory tasks. Some of the studies simply provide experimental confirmation that imagery mnemonic techniques can be extraordinarily effective, as the proponents of such systems have claimed over the centuries (see Chapter 6). Others provide evidence bearing on certain assumptions and precepts associated with those systems, such as the rule that mnemonic images should be novel or bizarre and the assumption that the same memory loci can be used over and over again without interfering effects. Certain findings also provide a hint that the memory information in mediating images is organized in a spatially parallel form, as distinguished from the sequential characteristic attributed to verbal mediators. Generally, however, the studies reviewed in this chapter were not designed to distinguish the two postulated systems. That task is reserved for the next chapter.

The discussion is organized into sections dealing with evidence derived from (*a*) subjective reports, (*b*) instructions to use imagery, (*c*) training on specific imagery mnemonic techniques, and (*d*) the use of pictures and objects as mediators. Specific empirical and theoretical issues are raised in the context of these general topics.

EVIDENCE BASED ON SUBJECTIVE REPORTS

In contrast to the many studies of natural-language mediation, in which verbal mediators have been inferred from postlearning subjective reports, none of the studies concerned explicitly with imagery mediation has based its theoretical inferences solely on this approach. However, some interesting and highly relevant evidence can be found in a series of studies by Richard A. Monty and his collaborators. The subjects in these studies were required to keep track of the number of occurrences of each of several different symbols (e.g., digits, tones varying in pitch) presented sequentially. The important finding from our viewpoint is that for both visual stimuli (e.g., Monty, Taub, & Laughery, 1965) and auditory stimuli (Monty & Karsh, 1969), *the majority of subjects report encoding the stimuli in a spatial form.* For example, in the case of auditory stimuli, Monty and Karsh (1969) found that 80–90 percent of their subjects reported mentally picturing a set of windows or columns corresponding to the stimulus array. Individual running tallies of the occurrences of the stimuli were kept in these columns, with rehearsal of the latest tallies after each stimulus presentation.

The "spatial window" model of encoding is especially interesting here because it appears to represent a specific form of mediating imagery theory. The mental windows in effect correspond to the memory places of the ancient mnemonists and the tallies that are somehow stored in those places are the to-be-remembered things. The windows or columns together with their tallies are, of course, more abstract mental entities than the concrete places and things envisaged in the imagery mnemonic system, but a similar mediating process appears to be involved. In any case, conceptualizing the spatial encoding model in such terms might suggest novel experiments that would reciprocally benefit our theoretical understanding of both the keeping-track phenomenon and the mediating function of mental images.

INSTRUCTIONS TO USE IMAGERY

The earliest experimental study of the effects of imagery instructions appears to have been a free recall experiment by Kirkpatrick (1894), previously described in Chapter 7 in the context of object-word comparisons. In another part of the study, 10-item lists of concrete nouns were presented to subjects with or without instructions to form a mental picture of the objects named. The result, replicated in two studies, was that recall was slightly but consistently better under the imagery instructions. In one experiment, the immediate mean recall scores for 379 subjects (ranging in age from elementary school to college level) were 6.85 and 7.48 for no imagery and imagery conditions, respectively; in another, the respective means for 180 students were 7.33 and 8.01. Recall after three days for the latter group was more markedly influenced by the imagery instructions, the means being 2.61 and 4.22 for no-imagery and imagery conditions.

Kirkpatrick's study is of special interest because it further supports the hypothesis proposed in Chapter 7 that imagery can function as an alternative or supplementary memory code, which enhances the probability of correct recall of concrete words. The problem has been neglected and it obviously needs further study using a variety of controls. A master's thesis study (Rogers, 1967) conducted at Western University failed to replicate the Kirkpatrick finding with concrete nouns, but did obtain facilitated recall for abstract nouns under imagery instructions. Conversely, Gupton and Frincke (1970) found that imagery instructions facilitated free recall for noun-verb pairs when the imagery value of the nouns was high but not when it was low. The empirical inconsistencies probably can be attributed to differences in the items and procedures used in these experiments. While the discrepancies remain to be resolved, the experiments nonetheless agree in showing positive effects of imagery instructions under certain conditions.

The above studies involved instructions to image to individual items. Alternatively, subjects could be asked to form mental pictures combining more than one item in a single image, thereby taking advantage of the capacity of the image system to organize items spatially. Although it did not involve comparisons with no-image controls or conditions in which subjects were told to image single items, a study by Bower, Lesgold and Tieman (1969) nevertheless indicates clearly that subjects can make very effective use of such a mnemonic strategy in free recall. This was indicated, for example, by the finding that recall suffered if subjects were forced to regroup items from trial to trial, and was facilitated by conditions that encouraged the formation of larger imagery groups over trials. An experiment by J. H. Mueller and Jablonski (1970) demonstrated directly that instructions to combine items in imagery results in higher recall than standard free recall or sentence mediation conditions. The comparison with verbal mediators is especially relevant to the next chapter and at this point we need only note generally that imagery mnemonics enhance free recall performance, particularly when they emphasize spatial organization of items.

Paired-associate learning   Imagery mediation instructions have been investigated more often in paired-associate learning situations. Although it did not include comparisons with control conditions, a study by W. H. Wallace, Turner, and Perkins (1957) is interesting because it demonstrated an extraordinary efficiency in the formation of associations with the apparent use of imagery. Six subjects were presented randomly selected but familiar noun-noun pairs, such as HAT-LION and HAM-WHISKEY, under instructions to form a mental picture connecting each pair. When a given list had been presented, the subject was given one word of each pair and told to recall the other. Except for occasional speed trials, subjects were allowed to set their own pace while forming the associations. The lists used varied in length from 25 to 700 pairs, and a given list was presented only once. The results were striking. At a self-paced rate subjects recalled up to 300 items perfectly and, even with 700 pairs, correct recall was in the order of 95 percent. The study has methodological shortcomings, such as the small number of subjects and lack of systematic investigation of such variables as the rate of presentation and the nature of the mediation instructions (the authors acknowledged that there was no evidence that the instructions to form mental pictures are useful or necessary). The reported results are nevertheless so extraordinary that the investigation merits replication to confirm and extend the findings. A direct attempt to do so by Seibel, Lock-hart, and Taschman (1967) resulted in weaker effects and then only under certain conditions that suggested to the investigators that the effect may be a motivational one. This possibility comes up repeatedly in subsequent discussions, but we will eventually reject it in favor of alternative explanatory principles in the theoretical analysis to be presented in the next chapter.

Spiker (1960) found that instructions to use "mildly humorous" associations or images to link members of pairs (e.g., for the pair "cake-boat," they were instructed to visualize a boat made of cake) greatly enhanced learning in children. McNulty (1966) compared groups receiving no instructions, motivating instructions, and instruction to mediate by forming "ridiculous, bizarre or ludicrous" associations between members of pairs. He also varied the letter sequences comprising the stimulus items in terms of the order of approximation to English. The results were not significant within any one of three· experiments, although mediating instructions were somewhat superior to the other conditions in all three when the stimulus terms were actual words. This superiority was greatest among subjects who appeared to be relatively unmotivated, again suggesting a possible motivational factor in the weak effect.

The separation of nonverbal imagery from verbal mediators is unclear in the above studies, although the instructions were generally intended to affect the use of imagery. McNulty's study is an exception in that it is uncertain from his description whether the "bizarre associations" were meant to be images or verbal mediators, or perhaps either. In any event, he appeared to favor a verbal-mediational interpretation of the effect. Another striking feature of the above studies is the variability of the magnitude of the effect of the mnemonic instructions, paralleling the observation made in relation to verbal mediation instructions. Perhaps the simplest interpretation is that college students tend to use mnemonics so readily that instructions add little to that "baseline." This explanation has been supported in other studies by mediation reports obtained from subjects after learning, as well as by comparisons of the effects of imagery mediation and rote learning instructions (e.g., Paivio & Yuille, 1967, 1969). These experiments generally involved comparisons with verbal mediation conditions as well, and their findings will be considered in detail in the next chapter.

One such experiment is relevant in the present context, however, since it involved only imagery and rote learning instructions, and showed powerful effects of imagery on both short-term and long-term retention of paired associates. Schnorr and Atkinson (1969) used a within-subjects design in which half of the items in a 32-pair list of concrete nouns were studied by rote repetition and the other half by imagery. Three such lists were presented for one study-test trial, and retention was tested again one week later. The results of the immediate recall test showed much higher recall for the pairs learned by imagery, the percentage correct for the three lists ranging from about 80 to 90 percent, as compared to 30 to 40 percent for those learned by repetition. In addition, imagery resulted in significantly better long-term retention when the measure of retention was the proportion of items correctly recalled on the initial test that were correctly recalled one week later. The study therefore demonstrated that noun pairs studied by imagery are better learned and remembered than items studied by rote. Note also that the long-term memory effect obtained by Schnorr and Atkinson contrasts with Olton's (1969) relative failure to demonstrate effects of sentence mediators on retention after one week (see Chapter 9), suggesting that imagery may be superior to verbal mediation as a mnemonic aid for concrete-noun pairs. Results related to knowledge of the study method at the recall test also suggested that different memory stores (imaginal and verbal?) are associated with the two study methods. These findings, nevertheless, bear only indirectly on the question of the relative potency of imaginal and verbal mediation techniques.

Winograd, Karchmer, and Russell (1971) studied the effect on recognition memory of the reinstatement of a cue word that had accompanied the to-be-remembered word during the study trial. Although the subjects were required only to recognize the to-be-remembered words (i.e., paired-associate learning was not explicitly required), the study is relevant here because imagery mediation and associative instructions were involved. They found that the presence of the cue words on the test trial facilitated recognition under instructions to link the two words by bizarre mental images but not under instructions simply to associate the two words. Consistent with the analysis presented in Chapter 8, Winograd et al. concluded that imagery mnemonics have their effect by unitizing pair elements in a compound image, which is redintegrated by the cue word on the test trial and can be decoded to yield correct recognition of the to-be-remembered word. This unitizing function of mediating images in associative learning will be examined more critically in later sections.

Serial learning   Delin (1969) investigated the effect of imagery-mnemonic instructions on serial learning of a list of 16 concrete nouns. He used an anticipation procedure with a slow (11-second) presentation rate and mnemonic subjects were instructed to "connect each item to the preceding one by making a vivid and active mental image containing the two items." They were to avoid connecting the images together in a string. The control subjects were given standard serial anticipation instructions. The mnemonic subjects learned the list in significantly fewer trials and with fewer errors than the control group. Here, too, it should be noted that the positive effect of imagery mnemonics contrasts with the absence of any effect of sentence mediators in the A. R. Jenson and Rohwer (1965b) study, discussed in the last chapter, which was somewhat comparable to Delin's in that subjects were asked to connect successive pairs of items and it involved a slow (self-paced) rate. Thus we have further indirect evidence that imagery may be superior to verbal mediation in serial learning. Moreover, the results indicate that an imagery interpretation of the facilitative effect of noun concreteness in serial learning (Chapter 7) is not unreasonable.

It can be concluded that simply instructing subjects to use imagery as a mnemonic technique can facilitate performance in free recall, serial learning, and paired-associate tasks. The interpretation of the effects remains uncertain, however, particularly in regard to the role of verbal processes.

TRAINING ON SPECIFIC IMAGERY MNEMONIC SYSTEMS

Although training on the use of imagery as an associative aid has long been advocated by mnemonists and commercial courses claiming to improve memory, until recently there has been an extraordinary lack of psychological research on the efficacy of such methods. A substantial empirical literature has emerged on the topic over the last few years, however, suggesting that the deficiency will be quickly overcome. Apart from confirming the efficacy of imagery mnemonics, experimenters have begun to explore variables that influence the magnitude of the effects and the relevance of such effects to more traditional theoretical problems in verbal learning and memory. We shall be concerned in this section with such contributions as well as with whatever the research reveals about the functional nature of imagery.

The Hook Method

A study by R. K. Smith and Noble (1965) was perhaps the earliest to provide some qualified positive evidence for the efficacy of mnemonic training. They investigated the effects of a mnemonic technique recommended by Furst (1957), a contemporary "memory expert." The method is essentially Feinaigle's (1813) technique as described in Chapter 6—a number-letter alphabet (1-t, 2-n, 3-m, 4-r, etc.) is translated into reference words (tea, Noah, May, ray, etc.) that, when clearly imagined as concrete objects, are supposed to provide stable "hooks" upon which the to-be-recalled items may be "hung." In the Smith and Noble study, an experimental group was given a one-hour lecture-demonstration on the method, including presentation of drawings of paired objects designated by key words and the to-be-learned items as an illustration of how they might be visualized (see Figure 10-1). In addition, the experimental subjects practiced the method for four days in private. They were then required to apply the technique to serial verbal learning of a 10-item list of low, medium, or high scaled meaningfulness (m'). Control subjects learned the lists without any formal experience with the technique and in fact were told not to use any special system in learning. The 20-trial learning phase was followed by a recall and relearning phase 24 hours later. The results showed significant effects of the method on recall and relearning but not on the initial learning phase. Method and item meaningfulness interacted in a complex manner, with no differences occurring for high m' lists, large differences for medium m' lists, and small differences for low m' lists. The authors concluded that Furst's technique has limited usefulness during the acquisition of a serial verbal list, and perhaps a significant facilitating effect on retention, provided the material to be recalled is

Tea-Cup   Noah-Wine   May-Cherry   Ray-Camera Film   Law-Firecracker

Jaw-Nut   Key-Champagne   Fee-Accordion   Bay-Coca Cola   Toes-Dance Record

FIGURE 10-1. Drawings used by Smith and Noble during the mnemonic training phase to illustrate how Furst's key reference words could be combined in imagery with a list of to-be-remembered words. From Smith and Noble (1965).

of medium or low meaningfulness, but no efficacy for remembering highly meaningful materials learned under the conditions of the experiment.

Smith and Noble discuss a number of methodological questions, including the complex set of operations involved in Furst's technique and the consequent difficulty of attributing any effects to "hooking" and "imaging" per se. Further aspects of the study will be considered here. The fact that the overall beneficial effect of training with the technique was significant only for recall and relearning trials appears consistent with the finding by Boersma et al. (1966) that the reporting of associative strategies after learning improved subsequent recall, the more so as the retention interval increased (see Chapter 9). It may also be related to Groninger's (1966) finding, also reported in the last chapter, that natural-language mediators benefited short-term retention increasingly over trials, presumably by increasing resistance to proactive inhibition. R. K. Smith and Noble's finding that the mnemonic technique did not facilitate learning or retention of highly meaningful items could again be attributed to the spontaneous use of mnemonic aids on the part of control subjects despite the instructions not to use any special techniques. The studies of natural-language mediators discussed earlier indicate that the reported use of such devices is related directly to the meaningfulness of the items. Furthermore, a study by Paivio and Yuille (1969) has shown that subjects found it difficult not to use such aids with meaningful material even when they have been instructed to learn by rote (see Chapter 11 for a detailed description).

The greater effect of the technique with medium m' lists than low m' lists might be attributable to greater difficulty of using imagery with low m' items. The situation is precisely analogous to that involved in the study by Paivio and

Madigan (1968) discussed in Chapter 8. Recall that in that experiment stimulus-term imagery value facilitated paired-associate learning more when the responses were high- rather than low-association-value syllables. This was attributed to the greater difficulty of translating the low-association-value syllables to meaningful words that could in turn be encoded as images. Smith and Noble do not present any theoretical rationale for expecting the imagery technique to be more effective with material of low or average meaningfulness than it is with material of high meaningfulness, but the complex model suggested by Paivio and Madigan appears applicable to their results for medium- and low-meaningful material.

Their experiment raises several further questions. As Smith and Noble recognize, use of the "hook" technique changes the serial learning task into one of invariant paired-associate learning with highly meaningful (that is, high-imagery) mediators functioning as stimuli. In view of these conditions, one wonders about the comparability of the tasks for control and experimental groups. A better control might have been to have the control subjects use "hooks" devoid of imagery, possibly a system involving verbal mediators only. A related problem concerns the control for motivational effects of the training on mnemonic aids, since it could again be argued that any superiority shown by their experimental groups is due to such a variable rather than to the coding technique per se. Despite such problems, the study was an important initial evaluation of the efficacy of training on the mnemonic use of imagery.

Senter and Hauser (1968) reported a study similar to Smith and Noble's in that experimental subjects were trained on the use of the "hook" mnemonic, which they applied to serial anticipation learning of a 20-item CVC list. The list contained 10 high-association-value (100 percent) and 10 low-association-value (0 percent) CVCs alternated within the list. In contrast with Smith and Noble's results, Senter and Hauser's trained subjects performed significantly better than their untrained ones, and the superiority occurred for items of both levels of association value. Another finding of interest, shown in Figure 10-2, was that the classical serial position curve was distorted in the case of high-association-value syllables under the mnemonic condition, with relatively high performance for items in the middle of the list (cf. Ross & Lawrence, 1968), suggesting that the mnemonic reduces interitem interference. This possibility will be discussed again later on.

There is no obvious explanation for the discrepancy between the Smith-Noble and Senter-Hauser results other than procedural variations, such as differences in list length, rate of presentation, and mixed-level versus homogeneous lists in regard to association value.

The "One-bun" Rhyming Mnemonic System

Impressive evidence of the efficiency of images as mediators of associative learning have been obtained in experiments using the one-bun, two-shoe rhyming mnemonic technique described in Chapter 6. It is similar to the Furst (or Feinaigle) technique described in the preceding section but makes explicit use

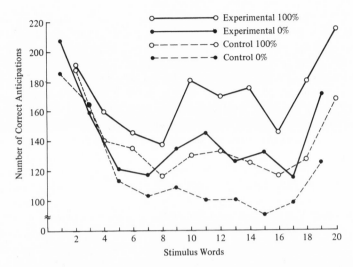

FIGURE 10-2. Frequency of correct anticipation of each trigram as a function of list position for experimental subjects who used the imagery mnemonic system and for control subjects. The trigrams were 100% or 0% association value, alternated in the list. Note that the classic bow-shaped serial position curve is distorted in the case of the 100% trigrams for the experimental group. From Senter and Hauser (1968).

of number-word rhyming to get from the numeral to the image. Furthermore, the one-bun studies to be described have explicitly used the paired-associate learning paradigm with numbers as stimuli, rather than serial anticipation learning. The difference is important because, although serial learning with the imagery mnemonic in a sense becomes invariant-position paired-associate learning, the stimulus cues (if used) are entirely implicit in the procedure used by Smith and Noble. In the one-bun procedure, however, the numerals at least are presented explicitly as cues, although the peg words and images remain implicit.

Bugelski, Kidd, and Segmen (1968) required their subjects to learn two lists of 10 common words each in such a manner that they would be able to recall the words by their ordinal position. The first list was a control list, identical for all subjects, in which the to-be-recalled items were read to them and immediately thereafter the numbers 1–10 were called out in random order and the subjects attempted to supply the appropriate words. Following this, the experimental group subjects were told that such learning would be aided by using the rhyming technique with each item. The first word in the list could be learned by "picturing" it inside a bun as a sandwich filler, etc. The subjects then learned the following number-word rhyme: ONE-BUN, TWO-SHOE, THREE-TREE, FOUR-DOOR, FIVE-HIVE, SIX-STICKS, SEVEN-HEAVEN, EIGHT-GATE, NINE-WINE, TEN-HEN. A rhyme control group was also taught the rhyme but was not told about its possible mnemonic use. A third group was a standard control group that simply learned two successive lists without being told about the rhyme. Rate of presentation was also varied, different groups being presented the list at 2, 4, or 8 seconds per word. During recall, the rate was 4 seconds for all groups.

The mean recall scores (subjects were credited with 2 points for recalling an item in its correct ordinal position, 1 point for recall of the item but not the correct number) are presented graphically in Figure 10-3. It can be seen that the imagery mnemonic technique clearly benefited recall relative to the control conditions at the 4- and 8-second presentation rates but not at the 2-second rate. The rate effect in general parallels what was described earlier for verbal mediation studies. We shall see later, however, that the specific rate at which imagery can be effective varies with the experimental design used.

Imagery and interference effects   In a subsequent experiment, Bugelski (1968) investigated the effect of the rhyme mnemonic on the one-trial learning of six successive lists of 10 items each, with a view to possible differences in interference effects across lists. Following successive list learning, subjects were asked to recall as many items as possible from all of the lists, in their correct ordinal positions (e.g., all the number 1 items, etc.). Figure 10-4 shows the number of items of each list that were recalled during the original successive-list learning phase and the one recalled from each list on the overall retention test. It can be seen that imagery-mnemonic subjects showed uniformly high recall for each list during original learning, without any evidence of negative transfer. Controls showed alternating high and low performance levels suggestive of interference on list 2 and again on lists 4 and 6, but not on lists 3, 5, and 7. Bugelski suggested that the rise and fall might be a function of the amount learned in a prior list, which could serve to interfere with successive list learning.

The total recall scores also show markedly superior retention by the experimental subjects, their average recall being 63.4 percent over all lists as compared

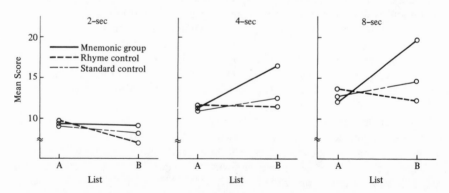

FIGURE 10-3.   Mean scores on first (A) and second (B) lists for three time groups and three treatment groups. The different treatments intervened between lists A and B. Based on data in Bugelski, Kidd, and Segmen (1968).

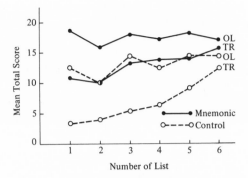

FIGURE 10-4.   Learning scores for original learning (OL) of each six lists and total recall (TR) scores for mnemonic and control groups. From Bugelski (1968).

to 22 percent for the controls. Moreover, the experimental subjects recalled almost equally well from all lists, whereas controls recalled mainly from the last two lists. Thus the evidence suggests that the mnemonic technique somehow reduced interitem interference. In agreement with this generalization, Ross and Lawrence (1968) also found proactive-inhibition (as well as serial-position) effects to be absent in paired-associate and serial learning tasks involving sequentially ordered memory places or *loci* as the mnemonic pegs (their interesting study is unfortunately weakened by the small number of subjects used and the absence of appropriate control conditions). Also suggestive is a study by Crovitz (1970), in which subjects were required to remember forty words in sequence using a 20-location map of a street and the imaginary walk technique of the ancients (see Chapter 6, above). The subjects were told to put the images of the items in the street addresses, so that the imaginary route had to be taken twice. The average sequential recall was a remarkable 34 out of 40 (most subjects scored over 35), indicating little interference from having placed two items in each memory locus. Similar results obtained by Bower, to be considered in the next section, also support the conclusion that imagery mnemonics reduce interitem interference. These findings provide experimental validation for the ancient assumption that imaged memory places, like wax tablets, can be used over and over again for remembering different things.

However, results inconsistent with that generalization have been obtained by others. Wood (1967) reported negative transfer when the same noun pegs were used as stimuli for successive word lists. Keppel and Zavortink (1969) found that the one-bun mnemonic facilitated learning of four sets of number-word pairs but, in contrast with Bugelski's finding, their mnemonic group as well as their control groups showed increasingly poor recall of the earlier lists when tested for recall of all lists following learning of the last list. Thus the conditions under which mnemonic pegs do and do not reduce interference obviously need clarification. The issue is important because the use of peg images apparently can reduce forgetting over long retention intervals. A recent study by Groninger (1971), for example, showed that subjects using the method of loci recalled more items after retention intervals of 1 week and 5 weeks, and forgot less between the two test periods, than did control subjects. Clearly, if differential interference cannot account for such effects we must seek other explanations, including the possibility that imagery memory traces are particularly resistant to decay.

Bower's Research on Imagery Mnemonics

Dramatic effects of imagery mnemonics have also been demonstrated by Gordon Bower (1969), who used a variety of techniques designed to create high memory load. One experiment involved concrete noun pairs learned either under standard paired-associate instructions or under instructions to learn each pair by visualizing some interaction involving the objects denoted by the two words. They were told, for example, that the words COW and SHOP could be learned by imagining a scene in which a COW is standing at a cash register, making a purchase in a SHOP. The novel feature of the study, however, was the manner in which the to-be-learned pairs were presented. A list of 20 pairs was presented at a rate of 5 seconds per pair, followed by a test trial in which the stimulus member was presented alone, and then a second study trial (but no test) with the same pairs. After that, a second list of 20 pairs was similarly presented, and so on, through five successive 20-pair lists, for a total of 100 pairs. At the end of this sequence, recall was tested for all five lists.

The results showed that the imagery subjects recalled about one and a half times more items than the control group in both the immediate and delayed test. The delayed recall was actually slightly better than the immediate, perhaps because the extra study trial more than compensated for any cumulative interference over successive lists. As Bower points out, these results probably underestimate the effect of imagery because interviews with the control subjects suggested that some of them spontaneously used imagery to learn the pairs, paralleling what we have already noted in the case of natural-language mediators.

Another experiment involved a novel application of the rhyming one-gun, two-shoe mnemonic. Bower reasoned that the technique provides a systematic retrieval scheme, the advantages of which could be reduced by degrading some of its essential features. This was done by reducing the number of imaginal hooks or pegs the subject was taught to use in learning a 20-item list. Thus different groups were required to use 10 hooks, with two words per hook; five hooks, with four words per hook; two hooks, with 10 words per hook; or one hook (one-gun) with all 20 words. Subjects were instructed and trained on the procedure with an emphasis on constructing a "grand imaginal scene" involving all the to-be-recalled words in a key image, although the items were presented serially one at a time at a 5-second rate.

Bower's expectation was that retrieval would become more disorganized with fewer hooks—the subject would fail to exhaust all words attached to a hook, lose track of what he had recalled, or unlearn earlier words as new ones were added to a hook. The results were completely contrary to these expectations: Recall immediately after presentation of a list of 20 items, or at the end of five lists of 20 words, was equally good regardless of the number of pegs used, averaging 86 percent for the immediate and 72 percent for the delayed tests, as compared to 52 percent and 28 percent, respectively, for control subjects given standard free recall instructions. Bower concluded that subjects can elaborate memory images containing a rather large number of objects without unlearning or interference.

The above conclusion was tested in another experiment by introducing a condition that made it more difficult for the subject to generate a single visual image involving all the items associated with a peg. The paired-associate learning paradigm was used, such that all subjects were required to recall 20 response words but the number of stimulus words was either 20, 10, or 4 for different groups. The subjects with 4 stimuli, for example, were required to associate five different response words with each stimulus word, this being done under imagery instructions. The difficulty of imagery elaboration was varied by using either a "massed" or "separate" presentation procedure for the S-R sets. Under the massed condition, all response words associated with a given stimulus were presented for simultaneous study. In the separate condition, each response appeared separately with its stimulus, with the different S-R pairings being spaced throughout the list of 20 pairs. Each subject had one such trial with four successive lists, followed by a delayed recall test of all four lists.

Figure 10-5 shows the results for the immediate recall test, for both massed and separate conditions (the delayed test yielded very similar data and is not shown). It can be seen that the massed procedure yielded essentially the same results as were obtained with the peg technique, i.e., one stimulus word was just as effective as a retrieval cue for two or five response words as it was for one. When the various S-R pairings involving a common stimulus were separated, however, recall fell off directly with the number of responses per stimulus. This suggests that unlearning may indeed have occurred under these conditions. If this were so, however, a recency effect should have been evident, so that later responses paired with each stimulus are better recalled than earlier ones. This was indeed true for the two-response list but not the five-response condition. Thus the effect of spacing could not be explained in terms of simple unlearning, and Bower concluded that the problem seems to be related instead to retrieval difficulties.

Another experiment by Bower demonstrated that mediation instructions are more effective when subjects are asked to imagine the objects suggested by the word pair in some kind of interaction rather than separated. This finding will be discussed in more detail later, along with similar results by others, inasmuch as interaction or relatedness is a pervasive feature of imagery that may account for differential effects of imagery and verbal mediation in some instances.

Bugelski's and Bower's experiments show remarkably strong effects of the

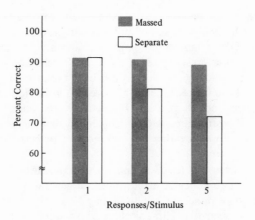

FIGURE 10-5.   Immediate recall as a function of the number of response words attached to each stimulus word. "Massed" refers to the simultaneous presentation of the several responses to each stimulus; "separate" refers to temporally distributed presentations of the several S-R pairs involving the same stimulus. Adapted from Figure 3 in Bower (1969).

imagery mnemonic devices on recall performance. Moreover, the magnitude of the effects is relatively comparable for the two despite differences in procedure. For example, Bugelski (1968) obtained an average of 85 percent correct recall during original learning over six lists of 10 items, using the same pegs with each list, whereas Bower obtained a score of 86 percent over five lists of 20 items even with the number of responses per peg varied. Control list performance was somewhat higher with Bugelski's procedure, 65 percent as compared to 52 percent with Bower's. Rough comparability also appears in connection with the effect of spacing on recall for multiple responses per stimulus. Bugelski's use of the one-bun technique with six successive lists is analogous to Bower's paired-associate spacing procedure involving five responses per stimulus, and the average percentages of correct recall under the two conditions are 63.4 and slightly under 70 percent, respectively, for delayed recall. Immediate recall was higher under Bugelski's procedure, however, perhaps because of such procedural variations as the shorter list used by Bugelski, the one-bun procedure as compared to the paired-associate paradigm, etc. The precise factors cannot be determined without further comparative research.

Imagery Instructions and Peg-Word Concreteness in the Mnemonic Systems

The imagery mnemonic experiments considered thus far raise several important questions. One concerns the effectiveness of the imagery component in the mnemonic instructions. Apart from the issue of separating the contribution of verbal mediators from imagery, which will be dealt with extensively later, the above studies generally did not include an adequate control for mnemonic instructions per se. Bugelski et al. (1968) came closest to doing so in that they had one control group learn the one-bun, two-shoe rhyme. However, these subjects were not informed of its possible mnemonic use independent of any reference to imagery, and the observed effects therefore cannot be attributed specifically to the imagery component of the instructions given to the experimental group.

Another question, which concerns the role of the mnemonic pegs as retrieval cues, brings us around full circle to a reconsideration of the conceptual-peg hypothesis discussed in the last chapter. Recall that the hypothesis originated as an extension of the one-bun mnemonic system, the critical assumption being that the concrete meaning of the peg words themselves is an important factor influencing the arousal of mediating images. The finding that concrete, high-imagery nouns are superior to abstract, low-imagery nouns as stimulus cues in paired-associate learning supported the hypothesis, but the effect of variation in concreteness was not tested directly in the context of the one-bun mnemonic system. While it is reasonable to expect that concrete nouns would indeed be superior pegs, a direct test of the proposition is far from trivial because the peg words are not explicitly presented as stimuli in the mnemonic system as they are in paired-associate learning. Instead, the retrieval cues in the technique are numerals, and the noun pegs together with any images they may arouse must be implicitly supplied by the subject.

Both of the above problems were investigated by Paivio (1968b). Subjects were presented one study and test trial with each of two 10-item lists of concrete nouns. The conditions for the first list excluded prior mnemonic instructions and were identical for all subjects. The items were read aloud at a 4-second rate, the to-be-recalled nouns being preceded by the numerals 1–10. Then the numerals alone were read in random order, and the subject attempted to recall the corresponding items. The second list was preceded by mnemonic instructions, with or without reference to the use of imagery, and training on either a concrete or an abstract rhyme. The concrete rhyme consisted of the familiar one-bun device in which the peg words, *bun*, *shoe*, etc., are concrete and relatively high imagery. The abstract rhyme—ONE-FUN, TWO-TRUE, THREE-FREE, FOUR-BORE, FIVE-LIVE, SIX-TRICKS, SEVEN-GIVEN, EIGHT-FATE, NINE-TIME, TEN-SIN—consisted of peg words of lower imagery than the corresponding concrete pegs. The subjects given the imagery set were instructed to use mental images along with the rhyme in order to recall the items. The subjects not given the imagery instructions were told to recall the list by saying to themselves the rhyming words along with the to-be-remembered item, for example, one-bun-pencil. Following the instructions, all subjects learned the appropriate rhyme, after which they were presented one study trial and one test trial with the second list of nouns. A further (standard) control group simply learned two successive lists without mnemonic instructions of any kind.

The results were very clear. Recall was generally better for the list learned under mnemonic instructions than for the control list, and under imagery instructions rather than no imagery instructions. These overall effects were completely qualified, however, by a highly significant interaction of the list and imagery variables. As can be seen in Figure 10-6, recall was comparable for all groups on the first no-mnemonic list, and that recall increased dramatically on the second list for subjects given the imagery set regardless of whether the mnemonic rhyme was concrete or abstract. The mnemonic instructions without imagery had no beneficial effect—if anything, recall tended to be lower under the mnemonic than under the control condition. The last finding is comparable to that obtained for the no-mnemonic control group, whose mean recall scores were 5.23 and 5.14 for first and second lists, respectively.

The above results confirm the findings of Bugelski et al. (1968) and Bower (1969), and extend them by demonstrating that the *imagery* instructions per se are indeed a most effective feature of the one-bun mnemonic technique. The unexpected outcome was that concreteness showed no effect approaching significance, although the trend was appropriate under the no-image mnemonic condition. This contrasts sharply with the findings for standard paired-associate learning, where noun imagery-concreteness has consistently had a strong positive effect when varied on the stimulus side of pairs. This applies whether or not imagery instructions are added to the design, as will be seen later when the relevant studies (e.g., Paivio & Yuille, 1967, 1969) are discussed in detail. In the latter studies item imagery in fact accounts for more of the variance in recall scores than does the instructional set to use imagery when both variables are

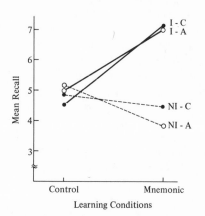

FIGURE 10-6. Mean number of items recalled in ordinal position under control conditions and under mnemonic conditions involving image (I) and no image (NI) instructions and concrete (C) and abstract (A) peg words. From Paivio (1968b).

included in the same design. The relative effects of the two variables are completely reversed, therefore, in the context of the mnemonic system.

How are the contrasting effects to be explained? One possibility is that the imagery mnemonic instructions in effect enable the subject to concretize the abstract pegs, i.e., he has time to generate stable images to them. While this may be correct as a partial explanation, it is insufficient to account for the failure to obtain a significant difference between concrete and abstract rhyme conditions in the absence of imagery instructions, nor does it explain the fact that item concreteness has relatively more effect than imagery instructions on the learning of noun-noun paired associates when both are included in the same experiment. The differences can be interpreted more reasonably in terms of the relative weights of the cues that determine the arousal of mediating imagery. In the case of the paired-associate studies, the stimulus nouns are explicitly presented on both study and recall trials, and their image-evoking capacity is a potent determinant of mediation strategies and response recall with or without the addition of imagery instructions, as indicated by mediation reports and performance data (e.g., Paivio & Yuille, 1969—see later). In the one-bun mnemonic system, however, the crucial peg words (*bun, shoe,* etc.) are not explicitly presented but must be implicitly supplied by the learner. Even concrete-noun pegs cannot function effectively as cues for the arousal of mediating images under these conditions unless primed by the instructional set. The contribution of concreteness as a variable is accordingly depressed while that of the imagery instructions is relatively enhanced.

Implications of the analysis for presentation rate effects   The above analysis has testable implications for issues discussed earlier. It suggests that the discovery and utilization of mediating images should be more efficient under the standard paired-associate procedure, when both the concrete stimuli and imagery instructions are explicitly presented. A comparison of the effects of presentation rate in different experiments provides some indirect support for the deduction. We saw earlier that Bugelski et al. (1968) found the one-bun procedure to be facilitative at exposure rates of 4 or more seconds per item, but not at 2 seconds. However, Wood (1967) found that imagery instructions facilitated recall with a paired-associate procedure at a 2-second and a 5-second rate, although the effects were stronger at the slower rate. Gruber, Kulkin, and Schwartz (1965) explored still finer gradations of the rate variable using a one-trial paired-associate procedure with a list of 30 concrete-noun pairs. The results presented in Figure 10-7 show that imagery mnemonic instructions facilitated response recall at rates of 1 second or slower for the presentation of each pair during the study trial but not at a 0.5-second rate. The explicit presentation of stimulus nouns as cues during the study trial, or recall trial, or both, in the Gruber et al. and Wood experiments apparently permitted faster mnemonic processing than did the one-bun technique in Bugelski's experiments, in which only numerals served as explicit cues. The problem obviously deserves more systematic study, so that rates are independently varied within the study trial

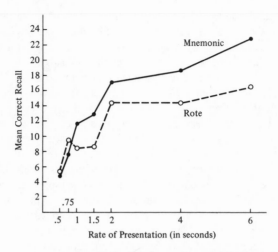

FIGURE 10-7. Mean number of paired-asso-
ciate response words correctly recalled on the test trial
as a function of rate of pair presentation on the study
trial. Adapted from Figure 2 in Gruber, Kulkin, and
Schwartz (1965).

and the test trial, along with the presence or absence of the stimulus nouns during each phase, and with simultaneous variation in the mnemonic instructions,
all within a single design. The problem is especially important because it is
related to the more general issue of the role of retrieval cues in memory, and the
conditions under which they are effective (see, e.g., Tulving & Osler, 1968, and
the discussion of retrieval cues in Chapter 7 of the present volume).

It should be noted that the Gruber et al. finding that subjects were able to
take advantage of the mnemonic instructions at a 1-second rate but not a
.5-second rate is generally consistent with data on the latency of image arousal,
as presented in Chapter 3. Several sources of information reviewed in that context suggested that subjects could generate images to stimulus words within a
period of .6 to .75 seconds. Since the Gruber et al. study involved pairs rather
than single words, 1 second may well represent the lower bound for the arousal
of effective mediating images, but we cannot be sure without further study.

PICTURES AND OBJECTS AS MEDIATORS

In earlier chapters we discussed numerous picture-memory experiments
in which the effects of picturability were interpreted in terms of imaginal processes. Imagery mediation can be inferred even more directly when pictures
explicitly serve as mediators rather than as the to-be-associated items in the
learning task. Wollen (1968) compared the effects of relevant and irrelevant
picture mediators on the learning of noun-noun pairs. The nouns were either

high or low in their imagery value according to the Paivio, Yuille, and Madigan (1968) norms. In the relevant picture mediation condition, pictures depicting the members of each pair were presented along with the pairs, and subjects were told to use the pictures to learn the pairs. The noun pairs and pictures are shown in Figure 10-8. These mediators and noun pairs were re-paired in the

FIGURE 10-8.   High- and low-imagery noun pairs and relevant picture mediators used by Wollen (1968).

irrelevant picture condition, and a third group was presented the pairs without the mediators. All subjects were tested for both forward (S-R) and backward (R-S) recall without the pictures. Figure 10-9 shows that subjects in the relevant condition recalled approximately twice as many responses as subjects shown irrelevant or no pictures. This was true for both low-imagery and high-imagery noun pairs, although recall was generally better for the latter. Finally, S-R and R-S recall were about equal. The facilitating effect with low-imagery pairs is particularly interesting because the picture mediators obviously involve concretization of the meaning of some of the more abstract low-imagery nouns (e.g., "strength" was represented by a dumbbell). Thus they might be expected to create a greater decoding problem during recall than when the pairs are concrete. Evidently this did not occur to a degree sufficient to counteract the beneficial effect of the mediating images.

Yarmey (1969) reported an interesting experiment patterned after an earlier one by Berger (1965) in which dolls were used as mediators in a three-stage paradigm. The nature of the effective mediator was uncertain in that study because the dolls were named by the experimenter, and the names rather than the dolls served as the stimuli during test trials. In Yarmey's study, unfamiliar and unnamed persons served as the common (mediating) B elements in a three-stage B-A, B-C, A-C paradigm. The A and C items were CVC nonsense syllables. In the first stage, experimental assistants held up flash cards, each of which contained a CVC; then recall of the CVC was tested with the person as the stimulus. This was repeated for four alternating study-test trials. The same procedure was followed in stage 2 with different CVCs. On test-stage 3, another

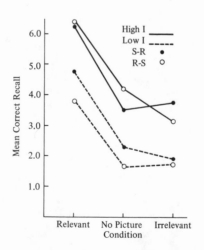

FIGURE 10-9. Mean correct S-R and R-S recall as a function of picture mediation condition and noun imagery level. Based on data from Wollen (1968).

assistant, not previously exposed to the subjects, held up the flash cards. These contained stimulus and response (A and C) CVCs, half involving pairs in which the members had previously been associated with the same person in stages 1 and 2, and half being interference (A-Cr) controls in which no A-C pair had a common associate. Only two study-test trials were used in the third stage. The results showed that the mediated paired associates were much better recalled than the interference paired associates, the respective means being 5.63 and 2.02 (a highly significant difference).

The results of a postlearning questionnaire completed by the subjects indicated that they had used mediators rather than direct association to learn most of the pairs. Person images were reported more often with mediated pairs, whereas other mediation strategies predominated in the case of the interference pairs. An example of a report that reveals person (image) mediation was: "JEP and QAB were the same boy and I saw the boy in my mind." Yarmey concluded that imagery indeed functioned as the mediator.

EFFECTIVE ATTRIBUTES OF MEDIATING IMAGES

Overall, the imagery mediation experiments leave no doubt that instructional sets and other procedures designed to encourage the use of imagery as a mnemonic aid can have dramatic effects on recall. But why, precisely, are the imagery mnemonics so effective? The question will be considered in more depth in the next chapter, where imaginal and verbal mediators are compared, but we can begin here by considering attributes of the experimentally defined images that might influence their mnemonic effectiveness. Vividness, bizarreness, and the nature of the figural organization of the image have received most attention.

Vividness

The major emphasis in the early research on the relationship between imagery and memory was on the vividness of the experienced image: The more vivid the image, the more effective it should be as a memory representation. The problem was investigated primarily in relation to individual differences in imagery, a topic to be discussed in detail in Chapter 14. The relevant point here is that measures of individual differences in the reported vividness of imagery generally have not been very successful as predictors of memory performance, although a recent series of studies by Sheehan (e.g., 1966a) has yielded some positive evidence that reported vividness is related to accuracy of visual memory.

Outside of the individual difference context, few studies have attempted to investigate vividness systematically. Bower (1969) found that the rated vividness of imaginal scenes suggested by noun pairs was predictive of the later recall of the pair: More vivid "scenes" were better remembered. This occurred even under incidental-learning conditions, suggesting that the relationship was not simply an artifact of some kind of relative learning set that influenced both vivdness and recall. Nevertheless, image vividness needs to be operationally distinguished from other possible correlates before such relations can be interpreted with confidence, particularly in view of Paivio's (1968a) finding that rated vividness of imagery correlated highly with imaginal latency and its analogue, rated ease of image arousal. In any case, we cannot be sure of the role of vividness in the imagery mediation effects nor of the conceptual status of the vividness concept itself until further systematic experimental research is done on the problem.

Bizarreness of Imagery

One of the cardinal principles of the ancient art of memory was that mnemonic images should be novel or bizarre in order to be effective (see Chapter 6). This feature was incorporated into the procedures used in a number of the investigations of imagery mnemonics discussed above, but so far it has been manipulated systematically as an independent variable only occasionally. A study by Delin (1968) did yield evidence suggesting that bizarreness indeed facilitates memory. He instructed his subjects to form images connecting three pairs of words and to write descriptions of the images. These images were to be as bizarre and active as possible. The descriptions were then rated by two judges on the degree to which they corresponded to the instructions. The subjects were unexpectedly tested 15 weeks later for recall of the response members, given the stimulus members as cues. The results showed that the image descriptions originally given by the subjects who correctly recalled the items had been rated significantly better in terms of fulfilling the criteria of activity and bizarreness than were the descriptions of those who did not recall the items.

The results from another series of studies have been entirely negative. A group of subjects in one experiment by Wood (1967) was instructed (along with a descriptive example) to use bizarre mental pictures to link pairs of words. Another group was given the same instructions except that they were told to use common rather than bizarre images. Recall scores for the two groups did not differ significantly—if anything, the common image group performed somewhat better than the bizarre image group. Atwood (1969) similarly found no evidence that mnemonic images in the classical place-system need to be bizarre and unusual in order to be effective. Wollen (1969) used a picture-mediation procedure patterned after the one described above to investigate bizarreness. His results showed that varying the bizarreness of the mediating pictures had no effect. Thus several experiments, using different procedures, have failed to support the mnemonic rule that has received uncritical acceptance over the centuries. The contrast between their results and Delin's leaves the role of bizarreness in some doubt. Since Delin used a much longer retention interval than the other investigators, it is possible that bizarreness is especially important for long-term retention. Further research is needed to resolve the issue, but the evidence to date does not indicate that bizarreness is a potent determinant of the effectiveness of mediating images.

Figural Organization

The capacity of the imagery system for achieving integrated spatial organization of item information has been repeatedly emphasized as one of its dominant functional characteristics. This was discussed in relation to the imagery-mediation (conceptual-peg) hypothesis of concreteness effects in associative learning (Chapter 8), where the emphasis was on the arousal of compound images by both members of a noun pair during the study trial, and the redintegration of the compound by the stimulus member on the recall trial. Such a conceptualization implies that the degree of figural unity or integration of the mediating image would be an important determinant of its effectiveness. The finding that paired-associate learning of picture pairs is facilitated by the presentation of the pictorial items in such a way that a pair forms a good conceptual unit (Epstein et al., 1960) is positive evidence that this is indeed the case. More direct evidence has been obtained recently that such organization is a critical feature of effective mediating images.

Bower (1969) reported an experiment in which one group was given standard instructions in which they were asked to image a scene of two objects interacting in some way. The second group was given "separation" instructions in which they were asked to image the two objects one at a time separated in their imaginal space, like two pictures being seen on opposite walls of a room, with one object-picture not being influenced in any way by the contents of the other object-picture. The cues for the images were concrete-noun pairs. A cued recall test showed that the interactive imagery subjects recalled 71 percent, whereas the separated imagery subjects recalled only 46 percent of the response terms, a highly significant difference. Bower concluded that instructions to image the objects per se have little effect on associative learning and that the important component instead is the interactive relation between the imaged objects. Bower (1970a) showed further that the advantage of interactive imagery remains substantial even when only recognized stimulus items are considered, indicating that interactive imagery indeed has its effect through associative mediation rather than stimulus differentiation (cf. Chapter 8).

Results leading to the same conclusion have been obtained by others. Atwood (1969) presented his subjects with a series of 12 phrases, each linking three concrete nouns and describing an imaginary scene. The subjects were instructed to visualize the 12 scenes without elaboration of any kind. In half the phrases, the three objects were represented in spatial proximity but with a minimum of interdependence (e.g., "*mouse* walking by *soap* toward a *chain*"). The other six phrases described imaginary scenes in which the objects were arranged into unified wholes (e.g., *Dog* wearing a *helmet* and chewing a *watch*"). Following presentation of a complete list, each subject was given the first noun in each phrase and asked to supply the other two, e.g., given "mouse" the subject must supply "soap" and "chain." The results showed that an average of 4.8 out of 6 unified images were recalled as compared to only 3.2 out of 6 of the images in which the parts were merely juxtaposed. The difference was significant and again supported the conclusion that figural unity is a significant determinant of the recall of compound visual images. Eiles (1970) similarly found that mediation instructions designed to encourage interactive images produced better learning of concrete noun pairs than did instructions that simply emphasized object imagery.

A. M. Taylor, Josberger, and Prentice (1970) extended the analysis to "4-tuples." Their subjects, sixth-grade children, were required to associate a concrete stimulus noun with three response nouns (e.g., *boy* with *lion, banana, cup*). A unitized-imagery group was trained to imagine one picture containing the imaginal referents of all four nouns doing something together. A paired-imagery group imagined three separate pictures, one interacting picture for each pairing of the stimulus noun with the three response nouns. Control groups engaged in rote repetition of the entire 4-tuple or of the three separate pairings. The results showed that imagery subjects recalled approximately three times as many words as the repetition controls and, consistent with the results of the above studies, recall tended to be best under the unitized-imagery condition, although its superiority to paired imagery was not statistically significant.

Wollen (1969) demonstrated the importance of imagery organization using his picture-mediation procedure. Subjects were presented concrete noun pairs accompanied on the study trial by drawings depicting the referent objects either in some kind of interaction (e.g., a cigar on a piano) or side by side without interaction (a cigar beside a piano). On recall trials, only the stimulus noun was presented. The results showed that recall under the interacting picture condition was more than double the recall under the noninteracting condition! Subjects in the latter group in fact performed more poorly than those who learned the noun pairs without any picture mediators, which is unexpected inasmuch as others have simply found no difference between somewhat comparable picture mediation and control conditions (e.g., Morelli, 1970). The superiority of the interacting picture-mediation condition is clear in any case, and fully consistent with the findings of the studies that used instructional sets to manipulate the same variable.

The studies reviewed in this section indicate that, among the variables that have been considered meaningful, spatial organization is perhaps the most important feature of effective mediating images. However, it does not necessarily follow that noninteractive images are entirely devoid of mediational value. While such images may be no more effective than the mediating images aroused spontaneously by concrete noun pairs alone under standard control conditions, both conditions may nonetheless produce effects that surpass a rote learning base-line, or one involving a relative absence of imagery, as is assumed to be the case with abstract noun pairs. Be that as it may, the effectiveness of imagery-mediation conditions is clearly enhanced by the addition of cues that suggest some kind of relational organization or unitization of the imaged objects. This is consistent with what would be expected if the mediating mechanism indeed involves a symbolic system that is specialized for organizing and processing spatially parallel information. Verbal processes obviously must be involved as well, however, especially when the imagery set is verbally induced and the to-be-associated items are words.

SUMMARY AND IMPLICATIONS

The results of numerous studies involving imagery instructions, training on imagery-mnemonic systems, and use of pictures as mediators completely validate the basic assumption behind the classical memory techniques: They can be extraordinarily powerful as memory aids. Occasional studies yielded only weak effects, perhaps because their procedures did not adequately prevent control subjects from using images spontaneously. The findings are somewhat comparable in this regard to those derived from verbal-mediation studies, and there are other points of similarity as well. Both verbal- and imagery-mediation studies have shown rate of presentation to be an important variable, in keeping with the view that the discovery and utilization of mediators take some minimal amount of time. Both have produced some data suggesting that mediators reduce interference effects. These and other possible similarities are interesting and important.

At least as important from our viewpoint, however, are the unique characteristics of imaginal mediation that would enable us to distinguish it theoretically from verbal mediation. On this point, the above data are silent, for they involve no direct comparisons of the contributions of the two systems. Some observations strongly suggest that a spatially parallel image system is indeed involved, such as Bower's finding that, when accompanied by imagery instructions, a single peg word can serve as a retrieval cue for several response words just as effectively as for one. Unfortunately, we cannot be sure that verbal mediation instructions would not produce the same results, particularly in view of Bower and Clark's (1969) finding that subjects can recall a long series of words with extraordinary accuracy by weaving them into a narrative. (Conversely, of course, we cannot be sure that the latter involves only verbal processes, as we noted in Chapter 9.) The demonstration that spatial organization is an important feature of mnemonic imagery suggests even more strongly that a spatially parallel information-processing system plays a crucial role in the observed effects, but the absence of comparisons with comparable verbal mediation conditions leaves the relative contribution of imaginal and verbal systems indeterminate.

The only direct evidence that the effective process is visual imagery comes from subjective reports. Both Bugelski and Bower obtained imagery descriptions or vividness ratings that are quite persuasive in suggesting that the mental activity associated with subsequent memory performance is subjectively distinguished from verbal thought. The questionnaire data in Yarmey's study also pointed to imagery as the effective mediator. Nevertheless, we need more convincing evidence that imaginal and verbal mediators are distinct and, more important, that the difference has *theoretical* significance. This calls for a clear demonstration that the two postulated processes are functionally different, rather than merely being different names for a single process or for two processes that nonetheless are behaviorally indistinguishable in mediating learning tasks. We turn next to a consideration of that problem.

11
Distinguishing Imaginal and Verbal Mediators

The evidence reviewed in the last two chapters demonstrated clearly that imaginal- and verbal-mediation procedures can influence learning and memory, but the inferred mediating processes were not theoretically distinguished. The many similarities in the effects of the different procedures in fact lead us to question the necessity of postulating two classes of mediators. It becomes compelling to do so only if differential effects can be demonstrated as a function of variation in the empirical operations that define the two theoretical concepts. Toward that end, the present chapter focuses on evidence derived from studies in which imaginal and verbal mediators have been directly compared.

The first section provides an initial theoretical orientation in terms of variables that may influence the availability and effectiveness of imaginal and verbal mediators in associative-learning tasks. This is followed in turn by discussions of evidence derived from mediation questionnaires, mediation instructions, and comparisons of pictorial and verbal material as associative mediators. The final section returns to the theoretical issues and attempts an integrative analysis of the most consistent findings reviewed in the present chapter as well as the two preceding ones, basing the analysis on the three functional distinctions that were introduced in Chapter 2.

INITIAL THEORETICAL ORIENTATION

Any differences in the observed effects of imaginal- and verbal-mediation procedures are potentially attributable either to the relative availability or relative effectiveness of the underlying processes, or both, depending on the nature of the stimulus situation and demands of the task. We have already encountered this distinction in the theoretical analysis of tasks in which the functioning of the two processes was indirectly inferred from the relation between item attributes and performance. Thus the analysis of sequential and nonsequential memory tasks (Chapter 7) was based partly on the assumption that images and verbal processes are differentially available as memory codes for concrete and abstract items, and partly on the hypothesis that they are differentially effective in the storage of sequential as compared to nonsequential item information. Similarly, the imagery theory of concreteness effects in paired-associate learning (Chapter 8) implies that images are effective mediators and that their availability depends on the concreteness of the to-be-associated items, especially the stimulus member. The learning data were entirely consistent with the latter hypothesis, and comparisons with other item attributes indicated that the effects cannot be readily explained in terms of verbal processes alone. The evidence on mediator availability was indirect, however, and no conclusions could be drawn concerning the relative effectiveness of imaginal and verbal mediators when their availability is equated. The reasoning involved in the above hypotheses will now be extended to situations in which the availability and effectiveness of the two classes of mediators can be determined and compared more directly.

Concreteness and Mediator Availability

The imagery hypothesis together with its retrieval-cue (conceptual-peg) corollary can be restated to refer explicitly to the availability of images as potential mediators and extended to incorporate verbal processes, in accordance with the two-process theory of meaning and mediation. The hypothesis states that the availability of imaginal, but not verbal, mediators is related directly to concreteness of the to-be-associated pair. Thus images are assumed to be most available in the case of object- or picture-pairs, somewhat less available with concrete noun pairs, and least available when the pairs are abstract. Because the stimulus item must serve as a retrieval cue during recall trials involving a paired-associate procedure, the concreteness of the nominal stimulus term will have greater importance overall than that of the response term in determining the availability of imaginal mediators. The availability of verbal mediators, on the other hand, should not be affected by item concreteness per se, although it could depend on verbal-associative meaningfulness and, in the case of objects or pictures, verbal-referential meaning or codability. It should be noted that the analysis subsumes the conceptual-peg hypothesis (Chapter 8) in that any *differential* effects associated with concrete stimuli are still attributed to the greater image-arousing capacity of such stimuli. In addition, the mediational role of verbal associative processes is now made explicit, whereas it was not stated in the earlier conceptual-peg analysis.

Relative Effectiveness of Imaginal and Verbal Mediators

The above analysis provides no theoretically motivated basis for expecting one type of mediator to be more effective than the other when they are equally available. However, alternative hypotheses follow from the proposal that the mediational functioning of images and verbal processes is related to their spatial and sequential characteristics, respectively. This functional distinction could favor imagery in at least two ways. The information in imagery mediators might be more effectively chunked or unitized and therefore better retained than the sequentially organized information in verbal mediators because there would be less to remember in the case of images. If chunking is equally efficient, however, images might still have the advantage during retrieval because parallel processing of multifaceted information, which associative mediators must contain, apparently proceeds more quickly than sequential processing of the same amount of information (Neisser, 1967). This implies that images might be "searched" faster than verbal mediators for the relevant associative information. On the other hand, the mediator must also be decoded correctly, and it could be argued that fewer decoding errors will occur with verbal mediators because transformations to and from another (nonverbal) symbolic code are not required in order to retrieve the verbal response. The precise predictions that might follow from the above hypotheses would depend on particular task characteristics, such as rate of presentation and whether or not a verbal response is involved in the retention test. I will return to a more detailed consideration of these and other possibilities following an examination of the relevant empirical findings.

The empirical implications of the availability hypothesis and the effectiveness issue will now be examined, initially with reference to research involving verbal items only and later in relation to studies involving pictorial material. We shall first consider evidence from postlearning questionnaire reports and then evidence from studies in which the mediation processes have been experimentally manipulated. It will be seen that the emphasis throughout is on interactions between item attributes and the operations that define the type of mediator involved in the task and that both positive and negative effects are predicted for imaginal and verbal mediators, depending on item concreteness in particular.

EVIDENCE FROM MEDIATION REPORTS

Mediator Availability

The differential-availability hypothesis derived from the two-process theory of meaning and mediation implies that subjects will report frequent use of both images and verbal mediators to learn noun pairs in which at least the stimulus member is concrete, whereas verbal mediators should predominate in the case of abstract nouns. The results of a series of experiments are partly consistent with these expectations. A study by Paivio, Yuille, and Smythe (1966), previously cited in Chapter 8, involved a postlearning questionnaire that described mental images and verbal mediators as well as a no-mediation category. The instructions explained that various "tricks" or devices are sometimes used to remember items, that these might be verbal (e.g., a phrase or rhyme connecting two words) or mental images (e.g., a mental "picture" that includes the items), or that one might learn an association without such devices, possibly by just repeating pairs over and over. Examples of verbal and imaginal mediation were included. The 16 pairs of the list were presented on a page and beside each pair were the response categories VERBAL, IMAGE, and NONE. The subjects were asked to check the appropriate category and describe in a few words the device used to associate each pair. An analysis of these data using judges to categorize the descriptions indicated highly significant agreement between the categories subjects checked and the independently classified descriptions. Accordingly, subsequent statistical analyses of the relations between item attributes and mediation strategies were based only on the checked categories.

A striking pattern of relations emerged in which images were predominantly reported as mediators for pairs in which both stimulus and response members were concrete and high in rated imagery, whereas verbal mediators predominated in the case of pairs in which both members were abstract. Verbal-associative meaningfulness (m) had also been varied in the experiment, and the results showed that imagery-mediation reports did not differ as a function of m, but more verbal mediators were reported for high-m than for low-m pairs. These results were clearly as predicted from the hypothesis, but comparisons of stimulus and response variation revealed that reports of imagery mediation were affected as much by stimulus as by response imagery-concreteness despite the fact that actual learning scores were more strongly related to concreteness of the stimulus member (see Chapter 8). A possible explanation is that both members of each pair appeared on the mediation questionnaire sheet, and the concreteness of either member may have influenced the mediation report. This suggestion also raises the possibility, to be discussed again later, that the reports were entirely determined by the attributes of the items on that sheet, rather than by what actually occurred during learning.

The study is obviously open to various criticisms. One is that only three learning strategies (imagery, verbal, and no mediation) were assessed, and it is possible that this artificially increased the negative correlation between the reports of imagery and verbal mediation for pairs—that is, checking one category obviously results in a zero-score for the other. To reduce the probability of one mediation category's being selectively favored, the associative strategies specified in the questionnaire were extended in subsequent research to include rote repetition and a general "other" category. The "other" category has been generally used infrequently by subjects and will not be considered here. The "no mediation" reports are also relatively uninteresting theoretically, since they simply show a negative relation to learning scores and factors (such as item concreteness) which influence learning. Accordingly, the discussion will be restricted to the imaginal, verbal, and repetition strategies.

The results of the subsequent studies are generally consistent with the two-process theory of associative mediation, with the modification that images and verbal mediators are not used equally often with concrete items. Instead, images apparently are more available than verbal mediators, or subjects have a preference for using (or reporting) imagery, in the case of pairs in which at least the stimulus member is concrete and high-imagery. On the other hand, verbal mediators have generally shown smaller relations to item attributes than in the initial study. These points are illustrated by the Paivio, Smythe, and Yuille (1968) experiment described earlier (Chapter 8). Subjects in that experiment learned one of three lists: In one, noun imagery (I) was varied on stimulus and response sides while m was held constant; in another, m was similarly varied while I was controlled; and in the third, imagery and m covaried. Figure 11-1 shows the mean number of times that imagery, verbal, and repetition strategies were reported for the four types of pairs in each list. Note that imagery was reported most often for pairs in which both members are high in imagery, next for high I-low I pairs, and so on, indicating a stronger relation (confirmed by the statistical analysis) with stimulus I than with response I. This pattern parallels the relation of noun imagery to learning scores and is fully consistent with the imagery-mediation hypothesis. The pattern is similar for the list in which I and m covaried. Verbal mediators and repetition showed no such pattern in either list and, in the case of the list in which only m was varied, none of the reported strategies was significantly related to meaningfulness.

Mediator Effectiveness

The relations between the reported use of mediators and learning scores were also considered in the above studies and the results suggest that imagery was generally the most effective mediator. Thus Paivio et al. (1966) found that, when item attributes were ignored, the overall mean number of correct recalls per item for pairs that subjects reported learning by imaginal, verbal, and no mediators, respectively, were 3.03, 2.69, and 1.85, which differ significantly from each other. Further comparisons indicated that imaginally mediated pairs were learned better than verbally mediated pairs when the noun pairs were concrete but not when they were abstract.

The Paivio, Smythe, and Yuille (1968) study similarly revealed that imagery mediation was superior to verbal when each of the pairs contained at least one member that is high in imagery-concreteness. A correlational analysis involving item attributes, learning scores, and frequency of reported mediators for individual items over all three lists also confirmed the imagery-mediation interpretation of the differential effect of noun imagery-concreteness on the stimulus side of pairs (i.e., the conceptual-peg hypothesis). Since the S-R position of pairs had been counterbalanced for different subgroups of subjects, mean frequencies of reported learning strategies and mean learning scores could be determined for each item when it served as a stimulus member and when it served as a response. The intercorrelations among the data revealed that reported use of imagery correlated substantially with learning when the items were stimuli ($r = .56$) and less strongly ($r = .39$) when they were responses. The corresponding relations for reported verbal mediators and reported use of repetition were clearly nonsignificant. Note that the correlations involving reported imagery are

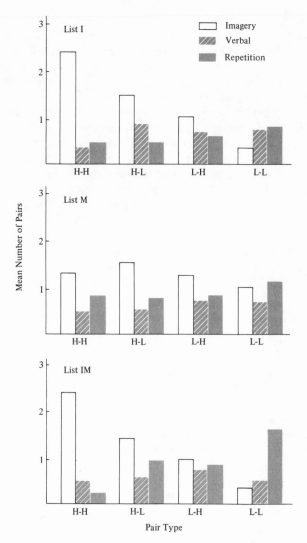

FIGURE 11-1.   Mean number of pairs for which imagery, verbal, and repetition strategies were reported as a function of high (H) and low (L) values of stimulus and response imagery (List I), *m* (List M), and imagery and *m* covaried (List IM). From Paivio, Smythe, and Yuille (1968).

slightly higher than the correlations of .50 and .22 between rated imagery (*I*) and learning scores when the items served as stimuli and as responses, respectively. Moreover, even when the effect of stimulus *I* was partialed out statistically, the frequency of reported imagery mediation for items serving as stimuli still correlated significantly (.36) with paired-associate learning.

To summarize thus far, the availability hypothesis has been supported by the finding that the frequency of reported use of imagery increases with concreteness, especially of the stimulus member of pairs, whereas verbal mediation reports do not vary as a function of item concreteness. Reported imagery also correlates positively with learning scores, supporting the mediational interpretation of item imagery effects, whereas reported verbal mediators failed to show any significant relation to learning. Finally, learning scores are higher for pairs reportedly learned by imagery than they are for pairs learned by verbal mediators, at least when the pairs are concrete. Thus imagery mediators apparently are highly effective, perhaps more so than verbal mediators.

The above data are of course entirely correlational, and the causal sequence therefore remains uncertain, just as we noted earlier in the discussion of natural-language mediators (Chapter 9). In the present instance, the relations could be a joint function of the instructions accompanying the mediation report sheet, the learning experience, and the nature of the items constituting the pairs. For example, the instructions for the questionnaire may have suggested to the subjects that they must have used some type of associative aid, and the image-arousing value of the items appearing on the questionnaire may then have influenced their choice of the imagery category just as it influenced their learning. However, such interpretations do not easily explain the *differential* patterns of relations, especially if one takes the traditional behavioristic view that the mediational processes involved must be entirely verbal. If this were so, why should verbal mediators *fail* to show strong relations to item attributes and learning when subjects have as much opportunity to report such mediators as they do imagery? The plausibility of the view that associations were in fact mediated by imagery is further enhanced by the fact that, in the Paivio, Smythe, and Yuille (1968) study, the correlation between reported imagery and learning scores, although reduced, remained significant even when the contribution of stimulus I was partialed out.

Despite the remarkable relations and their consistency with theory, introspective reports alone are unlikely to settle matters conclusively, and we turn to another approach that combines experimental manipulations with item attributes and subjective reports.

EXPERIMENTS INVOLVING MEDIATION INSTRUCTIONS

Instructional sets have been used in a series of studies to test deductions from the two-process theory. In general, the expectations were that imagery instructions would interact with item concreteness in such a manner as to enhance imaginal associations to concrete stimuli more than to abstract, with a consequent facilitating effect on learning when the items (or at least the stimulus members) are concrete but not when they are abstract. Indeed, an imagery set might be expected to interfere with performance in a learning situation involving abstract items because of the difficulty of discovering images for such pairs. No such interaction would be expected with verbal instructional sets, inasmuch as the availability of verbal mediators is theoretically independent of concreteness.

Latency of Mediator Discovery

One prediction from the theory, already considered in Chapter 3, is that associative reaction time will be longer to abstract than to concrete stimulus words when the subject is asked to indicate when an image occurs to the word, whereas the difference (if any) will be smaller under verbal-associative instructions. The experimental test (Paivio, 1966) strongly supported the prediction (see Figure 3-1). Yuille and Paivio (1967) extended the analysis to noun pairs in which imagery-concreteness was varied on stimulus and response sides, and subjects were asked to press a key either when they discovered an image that would link the members of pairs or when they discovered an appropriate verbal mediator (i.e., a connecting word, phrase, or sentence). The straightforward prediction was that the latency of mediator discovery would vary with concreteness, especially of the stimulus noun, under imagery but not under verbal mediation instructions. The results, shown in Figure 11-2, were precisely in accord with the prediction: Subjects took much longer to discover imaginal mediators for pairs with abstract stimuli than for ones with concrete stimuli, but this difference did not occur under a verbal-mediation set. The interaction has been confirmed in later studies (Colman & Paivio, 1970; Yuille & Paivio, 1968).

Once more the important theoretical question is whether it is necessary or even compelling to invoke both images and verbal mediators to explain the latency data. One might argue that the slow associative reactions observed under imagery instructions when stimuli are abstract occur simply because such instructions interfere with verbal processes, resulting in a longer covert verbal chain. Such a view would be consistent, for example, with Glanzer and Clark's (1963a) verbal-loop hypothesis. However the verbal hypothesis would be strained to account for the interaction of stimulus concreteness and set. Thus, in the case

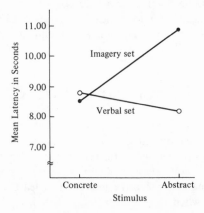

FIGURE 11-2. Mediation latency as a function of stimulus concreteness and mediation set. From Yuille and Paivio (1967).

of mediator discovery (as in the case of associative reactions to single words; Chapter 3), imagery instructions did not result in longer latencies than verbal mediation instructions when stimuli were concrete, and abstract stimuli created no associative difficulty under the verbal set. Difficulty was experienced only under the imagery set when the stimulus member, or both, were abstract. It seems reasonable to conclude, therefore, that the data reflect the operation of two processes in the manner specified by the theory.

Mediation Sets and Learning

The preceding studies provided data relevant only to the discovery of potential mediators and not their effectiveness in learning. The two-process hypothesis was extended to learning studies in which subjects were given instructional sets to use verbal or imaginal mediators to learn lists of noun pairs varying in their semantic attributes. The straightforward predictions were that a set to use imagery would facilitate the learning of pairs in which at least the stimulus member is concrete and would hinder (or at least not facilitate) learning of pairs with abstract stimuli, whereas a verbal-mediation set should be equally effective with concrete or abstract stimuli. Moreover, the conceptual-peg hypothesis and its supporting data, together with the finding from the mediation report studies showing that associative learning was better for pairs reportedly learned by imagery than for those learned using verbal mediators, suggest that the imagery set should prompt better learning than the verbal set in the case of concrete pairs.

Paivio and Yuille (1967) investigated the problem using a mixed list of noun pairs, half of which were concrete and high *I*, while the other half were abstract and low *I*. One group of subjects was instructed to associate the pairs using nonverbal images ("mental pictures"), another group was told to use verbal mediators (words or phrases), and a third group was told to learn the pairs by repeating them over and over to themselves. The rote repetition condition was introduced in an attempt to control for the spontaneous use of mediators, so prevalent in these studies. Subjects under each condition were presented four alternating study and recall trials. The recall scores for each condition are plotted in Figure 11-3. The statistical analysis of these data revealed that both mediation groups performed considerably better than the rote repetition control, and that concrete pairs were learned better than abstract pairs. Both of these results simply confirm previous findings. The facilitating effect of the mediation instructions also tended to be greater with the concrete pairs, but the overall interaction was not significant. More important theoretically, there was no indication whatever that imagery instructions were any *less* effective than verbal-mediation instructions in the case of abstract pairs, nor more effective with concrete pairs, so the critical predictions were not supported.

From these results, it appeared that the theory behind the differential predictions might be wrong, but an alternative explanation that could save it was suggested by mediation report data obtained from subjects in the experiment.

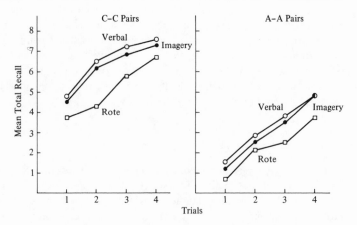

FIGURE 11-3. Paired-associate learning over four trials for concrete-concrete and abstract-abstract noun pairs, under instructions to use imagery, verbal mediators, or rote repetition. Based on data from Paivio and Yuille (1967).

Subjects given the imagery set reported using imagery to learn most of the concrete pairs, but relatively few of the abstract pairs. For the latter, they reported relatively more use of verbal devices or rote repetition than they did in the case of the concrete pairs. Conversely, images were reported relatively frequently even by the verbal and repetition set groups for concrete pairs. *The generalization suggested by these reports is that associative strategies are only partly controlled by experimental sets and that, over trials, subjects increasingly revert to associative habits aroused by the semantic characteristics of the to-be-learned items.* They may abandon the use of rote repetition generally, resorting to imagery in the case of concrete pairs and verbal mediators in the case of abstract pairs; imagery may be dropped, despite instructions to use it, when the pairs are abstract and do not readily arouse images; and so on.

We investigated certain implications of the above analysis in two subsequent experiments. Yuille and Paivio (1968) reasoned that the tendency to change strategies would be reduced by inducing a stronger set to use a particular associative strategy. They attempted to do so utilizing a transfer paradigm. In the first of two stages the subject was given practice on the discovery of either verbal or imaginal mediators with a list of concrete noun pairs or a list of abstract noun pairs. A control group had practice with rote repetition. The subjects were told that they would later use the device to learn another list, and that the initial task was to provide practice at discovering mediators. Thus a pair was presented visually and the subject pressed a key when he had "discovered" an appropriate mediator, at the same time describing it. This phase duplicated the conditions of the earlier mediation reaction time experiment (Yuille & Paivio, 1967), and was used because it involved practice on mediation without an explicit set to learn. The second task involved paired-associate learning of one of four lists of noun pairs, each consisting of a particular combination of stimulus and response concreteness. In one list the pairs were concrete-concrete, in another concrete-abstract, and so on. Independent groups were used in a factorial design, so that one group practiced associative imagery on the first list and were required to use it subsequently to learn concrete pairs; another group transferred to abstract pairs on the learning task, etc. It can be seen that the tasks were designed to produce facilitation under some conditions and interference under others. In particular, it was expected that subjects who practiced imagery with concrete pairs and then were required to learn abstract pairs would show the greatest interference, while those transferring to concrete pairs would show the greatest positive transfer. Subjects who practiced on verbal mediation were expected to show positive transfer regardless of item attributes, inasmuch as such devices should be effective even with abstract pairs.

The major findings were that both imaginal and verbal sets again produced better learning than the repetition condition, and imagery-concreteness had its usual potent effect, more so on the stimulus side of pairs. Set, concreteness, and trials interacted in such a manner that the superior recall with the mediation sets was clearly greater on the first trial (but not thereafter) when either the stimulus or response was concrete than when it was abstract. Figure 11-4 shows the interaction effect on the first trial for stimulus concreteness and set. The mediation sets clearly produced much higher recall during the initial trial than did rote repetition, particularly when at least one member of each pair was concrete and high I, but the *differential* effects predicted for imaginal and verbal sets again failed to appear.

Once again it seemed possible that, despite the use of a procedure that was

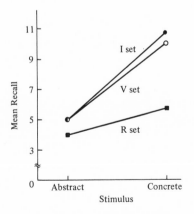

FIGURE 11-4.   Mean recall for Trial 1 as a function of imagery (I), verbal (V), and repetition (R) learning sets and stimulus abstractness-concreteness. From Yuille and Paivio (1968).

intended to induce persistent learning strategies, these learning sets were over-ridden by the demands of the to-be-learned items themselves. This was suggested by the fact that the effect of the mediation sets had disappeared by trial 3, whereas stimulus concreteness remained significantly effective over all four trials. We decided, therefore, to test directly the hypothesis that subjects change their learning strategies over trials in such a manner as to take advantage of the meaning of the items (Paivio & Yuille, 1969). We did so using a trial-by-trial probe of associative strategies as a function of instructional set and noun con-creteness. Different groups were given imagery, verbal, repetition, or standard paired-associate learning instructions, and subgroups within each were ques-tioned after one, two, or three trials concerning the method they had used to learn each pair.

The results confirmed the previous findings and extended them in that the verbal- and imaginal-mediation sets facilitated learning in comparison with the standard (no set) as well as the repetition condition. Some of the expected changes in the pattern of reported mediators over trials also occurred. Figure 11-5 shows that subjects given the imagery and verbal sets most often reported having used the corresponding type of mediator to learn the pairs, and this was true for all trials. In the case of the repetition set, on the other hand, rote repetition was frequently reported after one learning trial and then dropped sharply despite the fact that the two- and three-trial groups had been reminded after each trial to use repetition. The pattern of reports suggested that verbal mediators to some extent replaced repetition on the second trial, whereas imagery was generally favored by trial 3.

The effects were also qualified by the item attributes. As in the Paivio, Smythe, and Yuille (1968) study described earlier, repetition and verbal-media-

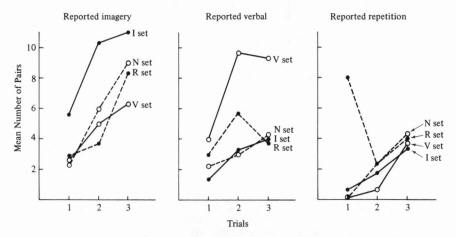

FIGURE 11-5. Mean number of pairs for which imagery, verbal mediators, and repetition were reported by subjects given Imagery (I), Verbal (V), Repetition (R), or No (N) set, and as a function of trials. From Paivio and Yuille (1969).

tion reports were relatively little affected by concreteness, although verbal mediators tended to show a greater increase over trials for pairs in which both members were abstract than for other pair types. By contrast, imagery reports were strongly affected by concreteness in a manner closely resembling its effect on learning. Figure 11-6 shows the parallel effects on reported imagery and recall scores as a function of concreteness and trials. In addition to the identical ranking of the four types of pairs on both response measures, it can be seen that concrete-abstract pairs show the most striking increase over trials on each dependent variable.

To summarize the mediation-set results thus far, they consistently point to imagery as a preferred and an effective mediation strategy in the case of pairs in which at least the stimulus is concrete and high in rated imagery, whereas verbal mediation is less affected by concreteness. In these respects the data accord with the two-process theory of associative meaning and mediation, but the results provide only weak support for the suggestion that subjects given an imagery set actually resort to verbal mediators in the case of abstract pairs. Such changes could actually have occurred but were not detected by the mediation questionnaire. Alternatively, it may be that some individuals can make effective use of imagery even in the case of abstract pairs. Support for such an interpretation was obtained by MacDonald (1967) in a study of the retention of imaginal and verbal mediators and recall of paired associates. Subjects instructed to use images frequently reported the use of a concrete image to symbolize one or both members of abstract pairs (e.g., "boy scout" for the pair *chance-deed*), and the mnemonic effectiveness of such mediators was evidenced by high recall of the pair only when the mediator was correctly recalled. The suggestion also has some

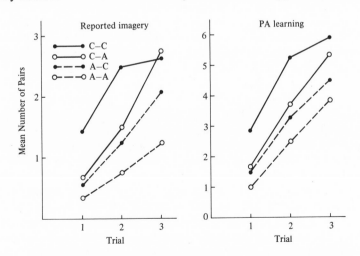

FIGURE 11-6. Mean number of pairs for which imaginal mediators were reported and mean number recalled as a function of stimulus-response concreteness and trials. Adapted from Paivio and Yuille (1969).

support from Wollen's (1968) finding, described earlier, that relevant picture mediators were as beneficial with relatively low-imagery pairs as with high-imagery pairs. Still, subjects did not have to generate appropriate mediating images in Wollen's experiment, and the fact remains that subjects find it more difficult to do so (according to the mediation latency data) when the pairs are abstract than when they are concrete, whereas the ease of discovering verbal mediators is not similarly affected by concreteness.

A further alternative is that verbal mediators, although easily discovered, are relatively ineffective unless accompanied by imagery (Yuille & Paivio, 1968). This view is not likely to find many supporters, but it is a logical alternative that should not be lightly dismissed, particularly since verbal mechanisms were also found to be deficient as the basis of effective meaningfulness in the studies reviewed in Chapter 8. I will have occasion to raise the possibility again in later discussions.

The Elusive Interaction Confirmed

That learning might be better under an imagery- than a verbal-mediation set when the pairs are concrete was proposed as a possible prediction from the two-process theory. It was strengthened by the earlier observation that recall scores were higher for pairs reportedly learned by imagery than for those learned by verbal mediation, but the mediation-set data provided no additional support. The reverse prediction for abstract pairs was such an obvious deduction from the differential mediator-availability hypothesis that it originally seemed almost trivial. Any triviality ended, however, with the repeated failures to confirm the notion. Apart from the increasing possibility that the theoretical views themselves are far off target, the most probable explanation of failure remained the difficulty of establishing strong and persistent sets to use mediating devices that are incongruent with the associative processes most readily aroused by the nouns themselves. The problem was finally solved by a procedure that literally forced subjects to generate a particular kind of mediator for a given pair (Paivio & Foth, 1970). When instructed to use an imaginal mediator, the subjects were required to generate (mentally) an image incorporating both members of a pair and then to draw the "image" on paper, with the understanding that the quality of the drawing was unimportant. Under verbal-mediation instructions, they were similarly required to think of a mediating phrase or sentence, then write it down. Different groups of subjects were presented a list of 30 concrete or 30 abstract noun pairs, but each subject used both types of mediators, generating images to 15 (randomly assigned) pairs and verbal mediators to the other 15 in a given list. This was achieved by placing a card containing the to-be-associated noun pair beside one of two cue cards on which appeared the words *imaginal* and *verbal*. Each pair was exposed for 15 seconds, and the time from the card exposure to the initiation of the drawing or written response was recorded. Following exposure to all 30 pairs, the stimuli were presented one at a time, and the subjects attempted to recall the responses. Because the facilitative effects of both sets had been repeatedly demonstrated and interest centered on the comparison of the two instructional sets, a nonmediation control group was not included in the study.

Figure 11-7 shows a highly significant interaction precisely in accord with expectations for both concrete and abstract pairs: Imagery produced significantly higher recall than verbal mediation when the pairs were concrete and significantly inferior recall when the pairs were abstract. In addition, concrete pairs were generally recalled much better than abstract pairs—the usual finding for this variable. Two further experiments established the reliability of the relations and the importance of the mediator production procedures for demonstrating imagery-set inferiority with abstract pairs.

Latency data were also obtained in the first experiment for mediator production and response recall. Figure 11-8 shows that the pattern of mediator latencies is highly similar to that obtained by Yuille and Paivio (1967), who used keypress latency as the criterion of mediator discovery (cf. Figure 11-2, above). The recall latencies for correct responses are longer on the average for abstract pairs than for concrete pairs. Note also that latencies are faster under the imagery set than under the verbal set for concrete pairs. As we shall see next, these data have important implications for the interpretation of the learning results.

Differential mediator-availability as an explanation of the abstract-pair results   The inferiority of images with abstract pairs can be attributed to the greater difficulty of discovering such mediators, as evidenced by significantly longer latencies of images than of verbal mediators (Figure 11-8), as well as relatively more failures to produce images, in the case of abstract pairs. Moreover, the mean latencies of image generation correlated significantly at —.47

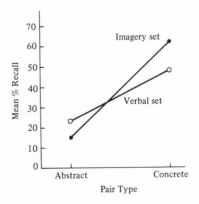

FIGURE 11-7.   Percentage of response nouns correctly recalled as a function of pair concreteness and imaginal versus verbal mediation conditions. From Paivio and Foth (1970).

with mean recall scores for the pairs whether or not failures to produce an image were included in the computation of mean latency scores. Thus the longer it took to generate an image for a pair, the poorer the subsequent recall. A comparison of mean percent recall scores for only those abstract pairs for which mediators were formed showed that the verbal mediation condition still tended to be superior to imagery, but the difference was no longer statistically significant. These data suggest strongly that the poorer learning of abstract pairs under imagery sets than verbal sets can be explained entirely in terms of differential availability of the two classes of mediators.

Differential mediator-effectiveness as an explanation of the concrete pair results The superiority of images with concrete pairs cannot be readily explained in terms of differential availability, however, inasmuch as the two types of mediators were produced equally quickly on the average (see Figure 11-8) and failures of mediator discovery were rare. Note, however, that concrete pairs are recalled more quickly in the imagery than in the verbal-mediation condition (Figure 11-8). Thus images indeed appear to be more effective than verbal mediators for response retrieval despite their equal availability on the study trial. These findings are consistent with an analysis in terms of another functional distinction, briefly proposed in the beginning of this chapter. To recapitulate in the present context, images may be superior because the associative information is stored as a spatially parallel representational unit—that is, words are transformed into object images. The formation of such images is facilitated by concreteness and by experimental procedures such as the one just described. If the compound image is reliably reinstated by the stimulus cue on recall trials, it can be quickly "inspected" and decoded to yield the verbal response. On the other hand, verbal mediators together with the to-be-associated words must be stored sequentially as a string of "mental words," resulting in a relatively greater

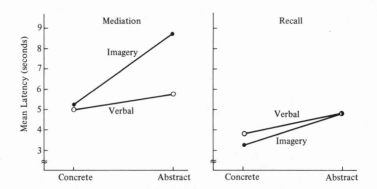

FIGURE 11-8. Mean latencies of images and verbal mediators on the study trial and of responses recalled on the test trial as a function of pair concreteness and mediation set. Based on data in Paivio and Foth (1970).

memory load during storage, or longer search time and less efficient retrieval of the relevant response from the mediator during recall, or both. An alternative or additional possibility (a variant of the coding redundancy hypothesis) is that the imagery mnemonic increases the availability of *both* imaginal and verbal mediators during recall, whereas the verbal mediation condition primarily affects the availability of verbal mediators. These speculations will be elaborated further and compared with other possible interpretations in a theoretical section at the end of this chapter.

Why did this experiment yield results consistent with the theoretical analysis whereas our earlier efforts failed to differentiate imaginal and verbal mediators clearly? The rationale behind the experiment suggests that it did so because the procedure effectively insured that subjects actually followed the instructional sets. This procedure apparently was crucial in the case of abstract pairs because the difference failed to occur when mediator production was not required, although the conditions were otherwise identical. On the other hand, image superiority occurred in a phase of the Paivio and Foth experiment even without mediator production. Other experiments, to be described below, have confirmed the latter finding.

Further Complementary Evidence

We can now turn to the results of other studies that provide evidence consistent with aspects of the two-process hypothesis, particularly when considered in the light of the complete confirmation provided by the Paivio and Foth study. Wood (1967) conducted a series of experiments in which he investigated various factors related to the use of mnemonics, some of which have already been considered. Only those findings that are most relevant in the present context will be discussed here. As in most of the studies reviewed above, Wood found that the effects of imaginal- and verbal-mediation instructions did not differ, although both were markedly superior to a no-mnemonic control group. He also tested the prediction that type of set and noun concreteness would interact. Each subject was presented one study and recall trial with four paired-associate lists, comprised of the four possible stimulus-response combinations of concrete and abstract nouns. Half the subjects were given instructions to use bizarre imagery to associate the members of each pair, and half were given verbal-mediation instructions. From the conceptual-peg analysis (Paivio, 1965), Wood predicted that the difference between concrete and abstract lists should be greater under imagery- than under a verbal-mediation condition, the difference being specifically manifested in superior performance on concrete (stimulus) lists under the imagery condition. Although Wood did not suggest this, we would also expect that the verbal-mediation condition would be superior to imagery with abstract pairs.

The interaction of list type and mediation instructions failed to reach significance, although some crucial comparisons were in the expected direction. The mean recall scores for concrete-concrete, concrete-abstract, abstract-concrete, and abstract-abstract pairs, respectively, were 19.92, 18.25, 16.46, and 8.62 for the imagery condition, and 20.58, 17.33, 17.04, and 10.42 for the verbal condition. As Wood points out, the imagery condition was superior (although not significantly so) to the verbal condition only for concrete-abstract pairs. Moreover, the difference between concrete-abstract and abstract-concrete pairs was relatively greater for the imagery group. Both of these comparisons are consistent with the imagery hypothesis. In addition, note that the largest difference favoring the verbal condition occurred with abstract-abstract pairs, which accords with the Paivio and Foth results and the hypothesis that verbal mediators are more available than images for such pairs. In themselves, however, these nonsignificant trends in the Wood experiment are only suggestive and comparable generally to the results of most of the studies discussed above, in which mediation sets were induced solely through instructions.

Yarmey and Csapo (1968) also tested the two-process theory of meaning and mediation using instructional sets. Different groups were given imagery, verbal, verbal-imaginal combined, or standard (no set) instructions prior to learning a list of concrete- or abstract-noun pairs. In addition to the instructions, however, the imagery set subjects were given two examples that were illustrated by a comical drawing showing an interaction of the objects designated by the nouns. The verbal-set group were shown cards with sentences containing the to-be-learned pairs, and the imaginal-verbal group were shown both drawings and sentences. The important findings were that concreteness and the mediation sets again facilitated recall, and that concreteness and set interacted in a manner partly consistent with theoretical expectations. While there were essentially no differences between set conditions for concrete pairs, the verbal set produced better recall than the imagery or control conditions with abstract pairs.

The absence of set effects in the case of concrete pairs is perhaps explained by the fact that only 10 pairs were used and the task was easy for all groups. But why did the Yarmey and Csapo procedure produce results consistent with the two-process hypothesis in the case of abstract pairs while the majority of other studies involving instructional sets failed to do so? Perhaps the presentation of pictorial examples under the imagery condition was especially effective in inducing an imagery set, much as subject-produced drawings were in the Paivio and Foth experiment. Yarmey and Csapo also pointed out that the rate for presenting pairs (5 seconds per pair) was slower than that generally used by Paivio and his associates, and this might have been the important factor. However, Yuille and Paivio (1968) and Wood (1967) used a 5-second rate without getting the same results as Yarmey and Csapo. It might be noted, finally, that Yarmey and Csapo ran single, intact groups in each of their experimental conditions, and the possibility of group sampling error cannot be ruled out as a contributing factor. Despite these uncertainties, the fact remains that their results for abstract pairs were consistent with predictions from the theory, and further supportive evidence was provided by postlearning interviews in which the subjects generally reported using verbal mediators for learning abstract pairs and imaginal mediators for concrete pairs.

An experiment by Hulicka and Grossman (1967) involved only concrete nouns, but it included other features that make their results interesting and relevant here. They compared old (mean age 74.1) and young (mean age 16.1) subjects on paired-associate learning of common nouns under one of three sets of mediational instructions, following the learning of a trial list. A control group was given standard instructions. One mediation group was given self-image instructions, in which they were asked to attempt to form an image that included both items of the pair. Subjects in an experimenter-image instructions group were provided with a word or phrase that linked the words of the pair and were instructed to form an image of the scene suggested by the phrase. Subjects in a verbal instructions group were given the same connecting words or phrases but were not instructed to form images. The mediation groups were told explicitly that the instructions were intended to facilitate learning. The learning task consisted of a single learning and recall trial with each òf three experimental lists. Following the task, each subject was questioned about the technique he had used during learning.

The results showed that the performance of both old and young subjects improved under mediation instructions, both with the technique alone and with the technique plus specific mediators. In both age groups the best performance was by subjects who supplied their own mediating images, confirming the superiority of imagery over verbal mediation and the importance of generating the mediators rather than having them supplied (cf. Bobrow & Bower, 1969). When no instructions were given on the use of mediators, the young subjects reported much more frequent use of mediation techniques than did the old subjects (cf. Canestrari, 1968). Instructions to make use of mediators increased their reported use by both groups, and under such instructions the old subjects showed relatively more improvement than the young subjects.

An interesting contrast appeared in the relative use of verbal devices and imagery by the two groups. The older subjects reported use of verbal devices more frequently than did the young ones (for 26 percent as compared to 6 percent of the pairs). This finding is consistent with the developmental view of symbolic processes, discussed in Chapter 2, in which verbal processes were assumed to become increasingly dominant over iconic with increasing age. However, the data also indicated that, although the old subjects reported imagery less frequently than the young (34 percent versus 77 percent of the pairs), both groups made more overall use of imaginal than verbal devices. Since the nouns used in the experiment apparently were relatively concrete, that finding is consistent with the view that imagery is the "preferred" symbolic mediator in the case of concrete items.

A number of other experiments have also found imagery instructions to be superior to verbal mediation conditions with concrete items. Raser and Bartz (1968) compared imagery, verbal mediation (i.e., a word or letter cue), and standard instructions in a one-trial paired-associate task involving a 40-pair list comprised of pictures and concrete nouns in all possible pair combinations. A recognition procedure was used in the test trial. The results for the instructional conditions showed that performance was best for all pair types under imagery, next under standard, and poorest under the verbal instructions. Bower (1969) reported several experiments that showed that if subjects are given linking sentences to read, their subsequent recall of concrete noun pairs is higher if they were told to image a visual scene compatible with the sentence than if they were not told to image. Although the difference was reduced, imagery subjects were superior even when the verbal subjects were instructed to generate their own linking sentences for the noun pairs (see also Bower & Winzenz, 1970). A. M. Taylor and Black (1969) studied the effects of imagery instructional sets and four conditions of grammatical connectives on children's learning of noun pairs. The results showed that recall increased when imagery instructions were added to the sentence mediators. Rimm, Alexander, and Eiles (1969) found that visual imagery mediation instructions greatly facilitated learning of concrete noun pairs in comparison with verbal mediation (a sentence or phrase) as well as standard paired-associate and rote rehearsal instructions. Thus we have reliable evidence that images are superior to verbal mediators with concrete pairs, or at least enhance learning beyond a level that can be readily explained on the basis of verbal processes alone.

In an experiment concerned with pupillary dilation during the learning of noun paired associates, Colman and Paivio (1970) found that imagery-mediation instructions produced significantly higher recall than either verbal mediation or standard control conditions when at least the stimulus members of the to-be-learned pairs were concrete. Colman has subsequently replicated the finding under comparable conditions. One unique feature of the Colman experiments deserves mention: Subjects fixated on a plus ($+$) sign on a ground glass screen in the pupillary recording apparatus while the noun pairs or stimuli were being presented auditorily. Perhaps the subjects were especially efficient in generating mediating images in this situation because it was relatively free from visual distractions. While completely speculative with respect to these findings, evidence supporting the general point has been obtained in the following study.

Selective perceptual interference with mnemonic processing   The above research on mediation instructions has demonstrated convincingly that imaginal and verbal mediation processes are functionally distinct. It would be desirable also to show that mnemonic imagery does indeed involve visual processes, whereas verbal mediation involves an auditory-motor system, as it is theoretically assumed. Atwood (1969) recently obtained evidence in support of such a distinction using Brooks' (1967) method of selective interference, which was described previously in Chapter 5. Recall that Brooks demonstrated a conflict between reading verbal messages and imagining the spatial relations described by the messages but not between listening to the same messages and visualization. Atwood adapted the method to image-mediation learning, reasoning that if genuine visual imagery is involved, the use of such a mnemonic system should be disrupted by concurrent visual perception, whereas auditory perception should be less interfering. Conversely, a more abstract verbal learning task, which involves the verbal system but presumably not imagery, should not be affected by visualization but might be interfered with instead by auditory perception because the verbal conceptual processes are more closely tied to the auditory system.

Atwood tested the above hypotheses by presenting some subjects (auditory) with 35 phrases designating visual scenes, such as "nudist devouring a bird" and "pistol hanging on a chain," which they were instructed to visualize. One group of these subjects was presented with the visual stimulus "1" or "2" one second after each phrase. Those presented with "1" were required to give the vocal response "2," and vice versa. Another group received no interfering signals during the interphrase intervals. Immediately after presentation of the 35 phrases, all subjects were given the first word of each phrase (e.g., "nudist") and were asked to respond with the last word ("bird").

Other groups of subjects had the same three interference conditions, but the learning task consisted of 21 phrases designating abstract but meaningful relations, such as "the intellect of Einstein was a miracle" and "the theory of Freud is nonsense." Prior to the task, subjects were told to "contemplate the meaning of each phrase as a whole" during the interval that followed. The subjects were then tested for associative recall in the same manner as the imagery group. While this task did not explicitly require subjects to mediate verbally, it can be interpreted as involving verbal mediation because of the abstractness of the to-be-associated words (e.g., "intellect" and "miracle") and of the contemplation task.

Atwood's critical predictions were that, in the imagery mediation conditions, subjects presented with visual interference should have lower recall scores than those presented with auditory interference. The reverse would be expected for subjects in the abstract mediation condition. Figure 11-9 shows a significant

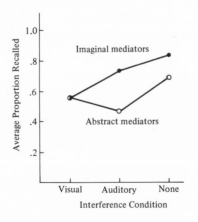

FIGURE 11-9. Average proportion of words correctly recalled as a function of type of interference and mediation conditions. Based on data in Atwood (1969).

interaction that exactly confirmed both predictions. These results justify the conclusion that mnemonic imagery is indeed a process that involves the visual system whereas abstract verbal mediation implicates the auditory system. The generalizations made about the two symbolic systems in relation to perceptual and memory phenomena thus extend to associative learning tasks involving mediation instructions.[1]

To summarize the major findings from studies that have compared imaginal- and verbal-mediation instructions, the results have shown that images are much less available for abstract than for concrete noun pairs, but no such difference occurs in the case of verbal mediators. Despite the differential availability of the two codes as a function of concreteness, it has been unusually difficult to confirm the hypothesis that they are differentially effective in paired-associate learning as a function of variation in concreteness, apparently because subjects sometimes can use images effectively with abstract pairs and because they tend to switch to strategies that are optimally effective for particular types of items, rather than follow the instructional sets passively. When subjects were forced to use a particular strategy by having them explicitly generate imaginal mediators (drawings) or verbal mediators (sentences) for pairs, the expected interaction was strongly confirmed: Imagery mediation instructions produced better recall than verbal mediation with concrete noun pairs and inferior recall with abstract pairs. The latter difference appeared to be related directly to the difficulty of image production. The generalization that images are superior to verbal mediators with concrete pairs has been supported in many other experiments, and further suggestive support for the general inferiority of image instructions with abstract pairs has also been obtained. Finally, Atwood's selective interference experiment yielded evidence consistent with the assumption that mnemonic imagery involves visual processes, whereas more abstract verbal-conceptual mediation "ties up" the auditory system.

PICTORIAL AND VERBAL MEDIATORS

In the last chapter we considered experiments involving pictures or objects as associative mediators of to-be-learned verbal items. Recall, for example, that Wollen (1968) showed that relevant pictures enhanced recall of both concrete and relatively abstract noun pairs. Such findings strongly imply imagery mediation but, since the studies involved no comparisons of pictures and verbal mediators, it is impossible to determine the relative contributions of the two

---

[1] It should be noted that Brooks (personal communication) has been unable to replicate Atwood's findings in a series of attempts to do so. This does not deny the validity of the original hypothesis but it does suggest that the operation used by Atwood to manipulate concurrent activity may be too minimal to produce reliable effects. This important problem obviously needs further study.

symbolic systems to the effects. The problem is not entirely eliminated simply by comparing pictures and words as mediators, inasmuch as pictorial cues might be verbalized and the referents of verbal cues visualized, but such a comparison is at least a necessary, if not sufficient, feature of any experiment that uses this approach to differentiate the inferred processes. The experiments to be considered in this section involved such comparisons.

Pictures versus Words as Mediators for Abstract Pairs

G. R. Marshall (1965) experimentally compared pictures and their concrete noun labels as mediators for abstract noun pairs. His procedure is of particular interest here because the mediators in effect represented concretization of the to-be-learned pairs, much as in the case of the relevant picture mediators that Wollen (1968) used with abstract nouns. However, in addition to comparing verbal and pictorial mediators, Marshall employed single relevant items rather than pairs as mediators. Thus the picture or concrete noun mediator in each case bore a symbolic associative relation to the abstract pair items. For example, the mediator for the pair FORMULA-INNOCENCE was the word *baby* or a picture depicting a baby; for DEPTH-MYSTERY, the mediator was *sea*; for WELFARE-SUCCESS, *money*, and so on.

Subjects in the picture-mediation condition of Marshall's experiment were shown the word pairs, 16 in all, printed on cards with a drawing of the mediating item between the nouns, as in the example shown in Figure 11-10. The concrete-noun mediation group saw the same pairs with the nouns corresponding to the pictures printed between the abstract nouns in lower-case letters. Two additional groups were controls, one receiving the pairs without mediators, the other with the stimulus and response words randomly paired. On test trials, only the abstract stimulus noun was presented in all conditions. The results over five trials are depicted in Figure 11-11, which shows an interaction of learning conditions and trials, so that the picture-mediation condition was superior to the others after a few trials. These recall data suggest that the more concrete (pictorial) mediators led to greater facilitation. More intrusion errors occurred in the concrete-noun than in the picture-mediation condition, however, suggesting that the picture-concrete noun difference may have been due to an associative interference effect in the case of the concrete nouns. Nevertheless, the concrete nouns also generally facilitated learning relative to the no-mediator control group, so that the intrusion errors do not reflect absolute interference. The results also suggest that subjects may have been able to discover mediators more readily for the experimental word pairs alone than for the re-paired controls, since learning was superior for the former. The study merits systematic replication in order to clarify the source of the differential effects and also to extend the design to include variation in the concreteness of the to-be-learned items. As it stands, Marshall's study (like Wollen's) indicates that concrete images can serve as effective mediators even for abstract noun pairs when the mediators are provided by the experimenter and the discovery problem is thereby circumvented.

JUSTICE   WIND

SHAPE   TEMPO

INNOCENCE   FORMULA

FIGURE 11-10. Examples of abstract pairs and picture meditators used in the experiment by Marshall (1965).

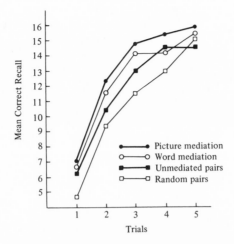

FIGURE 11-11. Mean correct recall for the four classes of pairs used in
Marshall's (1965) experiment.

Pictorial and Verbal Compounds as Contextual Cues

Other studies have varied the nature and complexity of pictorial and verbal compounds, which incorporate the to-be-learned pair units along with contextual cues that bring the pair into a meaningful relationship. The important question again is to determine the extent to which the effects of such visual and verbal elaboration are mediated by visual imagery as compared to verbal processes. Evidence on aspects of the problem appeared in a study by Epstein, Rock, and Zuckerman (1960), already discussed in Chapter 8. Recall that pictorially represented object pairs, such as those shown in Figure 11-12, in which each pair formed a meaningful unit (e.g., a hand in a bowl), were easier to learn than pairs in which the members are presented as separate units (a hand beside a bowl). The meaningful units apparently contained additional relational information that served somehow to link the components together in memory more effectively than did the separate presentation of the components. This feature of the experiment has its analogue in the comparisons of interactive and noninteractive images in the last chapter. Another aspect of the Epstein et al. study showed that pairs of nouns were learned more readily as parts of a three-word phrase in which the middle word was an intelligible connective (e.g., lamp in bottle) than when the middle word did not reasonably connect the members of a pair (e.g., lamp how bottle). The former was also learned better than the same pairs without connectives (lamp-bottle) and better than grammatical phrases that did not form good "conceptual units" (e.g., lamp or bottle). The verbal conditions included three different "verbal compounds," and the findings indicated that learning was facilitated most when the compound depicts an interaction that would be

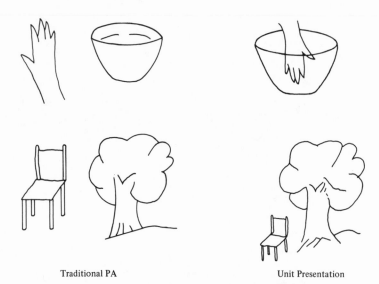

Traditional PA   Unit Presentation

FIGURE 11-12. Examples of picture pairs presented according to traditional paired-associate and unit presentation methods. From Epstein, Rock, and Zuckerman (1960).

meaningful at a concrete (object) level, suggesting that the effect could be interpreted in terms of verbally evoked imagery, although the separate contributions of imagery and of verbal symbolic processes cannot be teased apart on the basis of these data. It can be concluded generally, however, that representations that suggest organization or interaction of the units, whether the organization is suggested verbally or pictorially, are better learned than unorganized units.

Other investigators have compared the effects of sentences and pictorial representations as contextual cues in paired-associate learning, using procedures similar to those used by Epstein et al. but in which the mediational function of the cues is more apparent. Thus Davidson (1964) investigated children's paired-associate learning using picture pairs as the to-be-learned items and a recognition procedure for test trials. He compared five conditions, including (a) the pictured pairs alone; (b) the pairs plus their spoken names; (c) the pairs plus preposition phrases (e.g., chair under shoe); (d) the pairs plus nine-word sentences (e.g., the chair doesn't look large under the shoe); and (e) the sentence together with the pair pictured as described by the sentence, e.g., a large shoe was shown resting across the arms of a chair. The results showed that learning was much better under the last three mediational conditions than for picture pairs alone or the naming condition. Moreover, the prepositional link was as effective a mediator as the interactive pictures together with the descriptive sentence. In a similar study, Davidson and Adams (in press) found that associative learning was facilitated by both pictorial interaction and prepositional connectives, but the latter appeared to be somewhat more effective than the former. They concluded that verbalization is the preferred symbolic process in young children—a conclusion that is supported by some studies described below but not by others.

Reese (1965) investigated the effects of visualization and verbalization of interactions between pictorially represented stimulus and response items, also using children as subjects. The pictures were on cards. The stimulus cards depicted familiar animals (Cat, Rabbit, etc.). The response cards were either "unit-response" cards, depicting everyday objects (Umbrella, Scissors, etc.), or "compound-response" cards, which depicted interactions between the stimulus and response items (e.g., a cat carrying an umbrella). In the learning task, the response items were presented verbally as well as pictorially. Two groups of subjects, one presented the unit-response cards and the other the compound-response cards, were given verbal descriptions of the interactions between items ("verbal compounds"), e.g., "cat carrying an umbrella." Another two groups were given only the names of the response items. The results showed that verbal compounds and visual compounds were equally effective, and both facilitated associative learning. Reese considered three possible interpretations: that verbal context and visual imagery are equally effective, that the subjects visualized the heard descriptions, or that they verbalized descriptions of the seen interactions. Although Reese recognized that the available data did not permit a clear choice among the alternatives, he tended to favor a verbal explanation. More recently, however, he has proposed an explanation in terms of integrated imagery and contextual meaning (Reese, 1970), which will be discussed in more detail later.

Milgram (1967) conducted a study similar to Reese's in design and purpose, but with certain modifications, such as an increase in the number of subjects, an extension of the age range to include younger and older children, increasing the list length with age, etc. Experimental subjects learned a list of picture pairs under either a verbal context or a visual-compound condition. The verbal-context groups repeated a sentence presented by the experimenter that described an interaction between the members of pairs. Thus "The *cap* was on the *book*" accompanied the picture pair *book-cap*. The visual-compound subjects were shown a series of special cards in which the stimulus and response members were depicted as interacting in a manner corresponding to the equivalent verbal description. Control groups learned without the additional cues. The results again showed that both verbal and visual contexts produced faster learning than the control condition. In addition, however, the verbal condition tended to be consistently superior to the visual, the difference being significant with four-year-old children. From these results and postexperimental interview data, Milgram concluded that children are more likely to give covert verbal descriptions to visual (pictorial) presentations than covert visualizing responses to verbal presentations.

Milgram's generalization can be questioned on several grounds. The postexperimental interviews were interpreted by judges who based their inferences concerning the use of verbal or imaginal mediators on what the children said. As we have repeatedly noted, it is not clear whether such verbalizations reflect verbal thought or imagery even when the verbal description corresponds to a "sentence." Additional reasons for questioning an exclusively verbal interpretation are suggested by a consideration of the procedures used by both Reese and Milgram, as well as by Davidson. All subjects in their experiments were presented the to-be-learned pairs pictorially; what was varied was the nature of the contextual cues that accompanied the pictures. Thus no condition was included in which the pairs themselves were presented only verbally. This is an important omission, since we know from studies described in the last chapter that picture pairs are easier to learn than word pairs, even for children (e.g., Dilley & Paivio, 1968). The latter finding in itself seems to preclude an interpretation solely in terms of verbal mechanisms, but it would be interesting to know in addition how the effect is influenced by verbal and visual elaboration.

A further point concerns the distinction between the stimulus (retrieval cue) and response functions of items in a paired-associates task, and the encoding and decoding stages presumed to be involved in learning the pairs in the Reese and Milgram experiments. Milgram's verbal interpretation may indeed apply to the response decoding involved in recall but not necessarily to the encoding (mediator-formation) stage. The children in Milgram's study may have found pairs easier to learn when a sentence context was used during their presentation for the same reason that children in the Dilley and Paivio (1968) study found picture-word pairs easier to learn than picture-picture pairs. In each case, verbal presentation of the response term facilitated subsequent retrieval of the verbal response, but imagery may have been involved as a major factor during storage. Alternative interpretations are possible, however, and these will be considered later.

Some of the above problems were taken into account by William Rohwer and his collaborators at the University of California, Berkeley, in an interesting series of experiments in which the nature of the verbal contexts and visual compounds was systematically varied (for a recent summary, see Rohwer, 1970). The studies grew out of the observation, mentioned earlier in connection with verbal mediation, that children found it easier to learn pairs of nouns in the context of a short sentence in which they are connected by a verb (e.g., the DOG closes the GATE) than when presented in the context of a phrase in which they are connected by a preposition (the DOG on the GATE) or a conjunction (the DOG and the GATE) or when presented alone (DOG-GATE). Although some recent studies have failed to obtain the effect (Levin, in press; Davidson, Schwenn, & Adams, 1970; Yuille & Pritchard, 1969), it has occurred so consistently in Rohwer's studies that it needs explaining. Possible explanations that were considered included: less intralist similarity (hence less interference) among sets of verb strings; greater response predictability in the case of verb strings; superior recallability of verb strings as units; and the fact that the verbs used in Rohwer's experiments generally implied some kind of overt action. Each of these hypotheses could be rejected on the basis of experiments designed to test them (e.g., Rohwer & Lynch, 1966, 1967). A more recent interpretation (Suzuki & Rohwer, 1968), based on the theory of transformational generative grammar, is that verb strings link the nouns more closely in the underlying deep structures of the respective sentences than do other types of connectives (see Chapter 12 for explanation of the deep-structure concept).

Particularly interesting here is the further hypothesis that verb strings produce most rapid learning because they arouse the most effective visual images of the objects by the nouns. To assess the contributions of verbal and visual components of the mediating process, Rohwer and his collaborators combined verbal and pictorial modes of pair presentation along with variation in the type of contextual sentence that accompanied each pair. In one experiment (Rohwer, Lynch, Levin, & Suzuki, 1967), third- and sixth-grade children learned a list of 24 pairs by the study-test method. The pairs were presented either as pictures of objects or as the printed names of the objects. As each pair was presented, the experimenter uttered the names of the objects or the names connected by one of the three types of connecting phrases, i.e., conjunction, preposition, or verb. The results showed that learning was much more efficient with picture pairs than with word pairs, confirming the findings from other studies that we have considered earlier. In addition, verb connectives facilitated learning of both word pairs and picture pairs. As stated above, the superiority of pictures over words is sufficient to rule out a purely verbal explanation of the learning of picture pairs, but the additional contribution of the verb connective is not thereby explained.

Another experiment by Rohwer, Lynch, Suzuki, and Levin (1967) extended the pictorial depiction mode to include motion picture analogues of the different types of phrases. Thus, in a "coincidental" depiction condition, the two objects in each pair simply appeared side by side, corresponding to the conjunction phrase; in a "locational" condition, the two objects were oriented spatially in a manner consistent with the corresponding prepositional phrase; and in an "actional" condition, the objects were depicted in an actional sequence corresponding to the verb phrase (e.g., for the sentence "The DOG closes the GATE," the film sequence depicted a toy dog walking to a gate and closing it). The experiment involved the learning of 24 paired associates by children from grades one, three, and six. The learning was by the study-test method, with the to-be-learned items being presented only pictorially. During the study trial, the pairs appeared in one of the three depiction modes described above, accompanied by one of four types of verbal description (naming, conjunction string, preposition string, or verb string). On test trials, the experimenter named each stimulus object as it appeared on the screen, and the subject attempted to recall the name of the missing associate.

The results indicated that both the pictorial and the verbal factors affected performance. In the case of the depiction variable, learning was best with action pictures, next best with locational pictures, and poorest with coincidental pictures. The verbalization main effect was such that only verb phrases facilitated learning; conjunction, preposition, and control conditions did not differ. Moreover, the superiority of the verb phrase over the control condition occurred mainly within the coincidental picture condition. The results for the control (naming) condition alone showed that locational and action pictures produced equivalent learning and both were superior to the coincidental condition. The latter result, it may be noted, parallels and extends the Epstein et al. (1960) finding that a picture pair that makes a "good conceptual unit" is easier to learn than a pair in which the members simply appear side by side, and the finding that interactive images are better mediators than noninteractive ones (Chapter 10).

When considered together, Rohwer's experiments show an orderly increase in associative learning as the paired items progressed from nouns to stationary (object) pictures to motion pictures. This aspect of the findings can also be viewed as an extension of the effect of the abstract-concrete dimension. That is, motion pictures of objects can be interpreted as more representative of objective reality than still pictures and they are apparently most effective in promoting associative learning of the depicted items. The fact that this was generally true even in the absence of verbalization other than naming is particularly indicative of the potency of visual imagery. Verb phrases also improved recall, although only in the coincidental depiction condition. As Rohwer et al. point out, these data do not indicate that verbal processes are primary, otherwise more facilitation should have been produced by the verbalization than the pictorial depiction factor, which was not the case. They also suggest that an explanation in terms of "covert pictorial processes," i.e., imagery, is insufficient to account for all of the data. Both processes must be involved, and alternative interpretations of their mode of operation have been proposed in relation to age trends in the data.

Age Trends in the Effects of Picture Depiction and Verbal Contexts

Evidence from the studies discussed above suggest a developmental trend, so that pictures showing interactions of the pair members are as facilitative as sentences for older children. With younger children, however, verbalization tends to be superior to the picture compounds. The superiority was significant in Milgram's (1967) experiment for children aged four, but not seven or nine. It appeared as a nonsignificant trend in Reese's (1965) study and was significant in post hoc comparisons in Rohwer's experiments (see Reese, 1970; Rohwer, 1970). Recall, too, that Dilley and Paivio (1968) found that young children experienced difficulty with pictures as response items, although they were beneficial as stimuli.

The age trends have been interpreted in somewhat different ways. Dilley and Paivio (1968; see also Paivio, 1970b) suggested that young children may be able to encode pictures in terms of visual imagery, but they have difficulty in decoding such images to yield the appropriate verbal response on the test trial. The hypothesized difficulty is in the transformation from visual imagery to a verbal mediating process during retrieval. This interpretation is supported to some extent by the finding that preschool children remember pictures better than words in a recognition memory task that does not require a verbal response (Corsini, Jacobus, & Leonard, 1969). However, a similar study involving paired-associate learning would provide a more direct test of the hypothesis (cf. Davidson & Adams, in press).

Rohwer's (1970) preferred interpretation similarly emphasizes developmental changes in both processes, but with a subtle difference: He suggests that the capacity for deriving full benefit from action imagery develops later than the capacity to benefit from analogous verbal elaboration. This change may involve growth in the child's ability to store an appropriate verbal tag along with the action imagery. Thus the emphasis in Rohwer's analysis is on *what is stored during input* (cf. Tulving & Osler, 1968). Note that both Dilley and Paivio's and Rohwer's explanations imply that the availability of both symbolic codes at some stage during the storage-retrieval sequence is important to performance. In this respect, both are consistent with a two-process approach to meaning and mediation, but they add a developmental dimension to the analysis: The availability of the symbolic memory codes is related to the age of the subject.

After considering a number of alternative hypotheses, Reese (1970) proposed a view based on an analysis of reading recently presented by Bugelski (1969; see Chapter 13 for a more complete discussion of Bugelski's views). Reese's argument essentially is that imagery was not effectively aroused at the younger ages in the above studies because the pictures used were devoid of details. The young child in effect fails to "read" the materials in the sense that, although the stimulus and response items may arouse images, they arouse no *imagery*. The child may notice the pair elements, but the picture as a whole arouses no meaning, whereas sentences do arouse the requisite imagery because the salient elements and their interactions are explicitly named. The sentence has contextual meaning given by imagery.

One implication of Reese's analysis is that detailed pictures should be easier to learn than less detailed ones. In apparent disagreement with this view, Wicker (1970b) found no difference in the effectiveness of color photographs and simple line drawings as stimuli in paired-associate learning, nor did Paivio, Rogers, and Smythe (1968) find any facilitation in free recall from adding color to line drawings. However, both of these experiments involved university students as subjects, so the findings are not directly applicable to children of the age that Reese considered. The Iscoe and Semler (1964) finding that children (particularly retarded children) whose mental age averaged about 6½ years learned object pairs more easily than picture pairs (see Chapter 8) is consistent with Reese's theory. However, the problem obviously requires more decisive research of a basic nature, beginning, perhaps, with studies designed to reveal how people of different ages actually do interpret or decode pictorial information, and how their understanding is affected by such characteristics as the amount of detail in the pictures (for a relevant discussion, see Kolers, 1969).

The theoretical views discussed in this section are not necessarily incompatible alternatives, although they differ in their specific emphasis. The common feature in each interpretation is the assumption that relevant associative processes are less likely to be aroused in younger children than in older ones by pictorial material. This can be rephrased, as above, to state that the processes are less available in the case of the younger subjects. The reference is to the differential availability of verbal processes (during storage or retrieval) in Rohwer's and Paivio's analyses, and effective visual imagery in Reese's. Interestingly, Reese's suggestion is that sentences more effectively arouse action imagery in young children than do drawings depicting the same interactions. This means, in a sense, that, for them, the sentences are more concrete than the drawings! The precise implications of these views remain to be investigated.

THEORETICAL ANALYSIS OF IMAGINAL AND VERBAL MEDIATION

Although factual information is lacking on many specific issues regarding the effects of the two types of mediators, we can conclude from the available evidence not only that both images and verbal mediators greatly enhance learning relative to appropriate control conditions but that they are sometimes differentially effective. Some tentative interpretations will now be considered in which the emphasis is on various principles and features of the dual coding theory that have been discussed throughout this and the preceding chapters. Interest centers on the differential effects of the two mediating systems, but it will be helpful first to review general principles relevant to both.

Motivation

It has sometimes been suggested that mnemonic instructions in particular might be effective simply because they increase the subject's motivation to learn. This suggestion can be disposed of quickly. It is difficult on the face of it to see how the addition of an imagery component to the already elaborate one-bun, two-shoe instructions, for example, can enhance motivation enough to account for the dramatic effect that this feature has on recall (Paivio, 1968b). A second objection is that motivation or interest simply cannot explain the differential effects of imaginal and verbal mediators in some tasks. In the Paivio and Foth (1970) study, for example, one would have to argue that imagery instructions were more motivating than verbal in the case of concrete pairs but less so with abstract pairs. Finally, the interpretation cannot easily handle incidental-intentional task comparisons. In a study mentioned earlier, Bower (1969) had one group of subjects rate the vividness of imaginal scenes suggested by concrete noun pairs. Intentional subjects did so as well but were also told that they had to remember the pairs. Subsequent cued recall did not differ for the two groups, and both were greatly superior to comparable control subjects in another experiment. These considerations suffice to rule out motivation as a sufficient explanation of mediator effectiveness and it will not be discussed further.

Transfer and the Assimilation of Items into Higher-Order Cognitive Structures

The most common general interpretation of mediator effectiveness, expressed in various ways since Reed's (1918a, 1918b, 1918c) analysis, is in terms of transfer: The use of mediators essentially involves the application of information in long-term memory storage to the learning of new response units or new associations. Unmediated rote learning may be relevant primarily to the original development of these long-term memories, which correspond theoretically to the symbolic representations and associations that define representational, referential, and associative meaning (see Chapter 3). The establishment of such meaning presumably is a slow process in which frequency is the key variable (cf. Hebb's analysis of early learning and the growth of cell assemblies, 1949). In a later memory task involving familiar units, rote rehearsal would contribute little to the availability of a representational process that is already well established. It would contribute to the growth of an association between two familiar units, as in chunking or unitization, but this would also be a relatively slow process if restricted to rote rehearsal because the integrative process is gradual. In addition, rote rehearsal keeps the subject in a verbal mode related only to the to-be-remembered items, possibly resulting in interference from already established associations between the individual units and other (extraexperimental) items. These suggestions might explain why rote learning may be slow but not why mediators speed up the process.

When a subject uses mediators, he is taking advantage of the pre-established representations or associative habits to construct a more meaningful (and therefore more available) unit or relationship between units. The process of generating or discovering such higher-order mediating structures corresponds to the "effort after meaning" emphasized by Bartlett (1932). In the case of paired-associate learning, the mediated relation may involve associative chaining, so that, on recall trials, the stimulus term evokes the mediator, which in turn serves as the retrieval cue for associative arousal of the response. Alternatively, the relation can be viewed as a single integrated structure. This structure might be a sequentially organized pattern in which unrelated verbal items are incorporated into the meaningful context of a phrase or a sentence, or the items might be transformed into a spatially integrated visual image. In the case of a verbal pattern, recall could be redintegrative (cf. L. M. Horowitz & Prytulak, 1969), so that the stimulus redintegrates the entire mediating structure, including the stimulus member itself, as well as the nominal response unit. Since images would ordinarily be nonverbal, associatively aroused by the stimulus and requiring decoding to produce the response (the exception would be an image that incorporates visual representatives of the words themselves), the process would be redintegrative only in the sense that the compound image may be re-evoked as a unit by the stimulus word, rather than as two successive images.

The problem of response selection   Redintegration in a strict sense implies only that a minimum of selection may be required in order to produce the response because the mediator itself specifies the response. Even in the case of verbal mediation, however, redintegration may be incomplete—the sentence frame may be evoked by the stimulus, but the response may be missing, in which case response selection is a problem because the mediator might generate alternative responses, only one of which is correct. This would also be true in the case of imagery mediation, as when concrete noun responses have synonyms that could be mediated by the same response-term image. For example, the image of an adult female may generate "lady" or "woman" as a response (for evidence that such confusions occur, see Chapter 13). How does the individual select a particular response on the basis of the verbal or nonverbal mediator? One possibility is that a recoding rule is stored along with the mediator, as Prytulak (1969) suggested, in which case the difficulty of response retrieval would depend on the extent to which the redintegrated portion of the mediator provides cues to the appropriate rule. Alternatively, decoding might involve a "search" process in which the subject associatively generates implicit verbal responses to the image or the verbal context and then selects one response on the basis of a recognition memory process, perhaps taking advantage of temporal information, or "time-tags," to discriminate between the correct (recent) alternative and others in long-term storage (cf. Yntema & Trask, 1963). *An effective mediator would be one that minimizes the number of response alternatives.* Thus, if the original pair was *house-woman*, a mediating image of a house with an adult female in the doorway would effectively restrict the number of alternative responses to the retrieval cue *house*, as would the analogous sentence mediator. The probability of recognizing the correct implicit response would thus be enhanced, just as reducing the number of alternatives in an explicit recognition memory task increases recognition scores.

Nonassociative tasks   In the case of such tasks as free recall and the Peterson and Peterson short-term memory task, mediators might facilitate recall simply by providing a more meaningful and memorable contextual unit that, if recalled, could function as an implicit retrieval cue for the to-be-remembered unit much as in mediator-to-response decoding in the paired-associate learning task. Alternatively, mediators might enhance recall by increasing redundancy, i.e., by providing an additional memory code for a given item. The latter suggestion involves the same general principle as the dual coding interpretation of picture and concrete word superiority over abstract words in free recall and other nonsequential memory tasks (Chapter 7), with the addition that allowance is made for the arousal of the second code by instructional sets or other priming techniques. Thirdly, mediators may enhance the organization of the to-be-remembered items into higher-order units or chunks, thereby facilitating recall.

Functional Distinctions and the Differential Effects of Images and Verbal Mediators

The differential effects of the two classes of mediators can be analyzed in terms of the concrete-abstract, parallel-sequential, and static-dynamic functional distinctions between the two systems (see Chapter 2).

Concreteness-abstractness and the functional availability of the two symbolic systems   It was concluded earlier that the inferiority of imagery with abstract noun pairs in the Paivio and Foth (1970) experiment can be adequately explained in terms of the concrete-abstract functional distinction: It is simply more difficult for the subject to discover, or generate, images (as compared to verbal mediators) for such pairs. This interpretation was supported by the finding that the recall difference was essentially eliminated when we considered only those pairs for which subjects had been able to generate a mediator during the study trial. Other studies in which image mediators (i.e., pictures) were provided by the experimenter showed that such mediators were effective even with abstract pairs. Thus the difficulty appears to be in the discovery and not the utilization of images for such pairs. On the other hand, numerous experiments have shown that imagery is more effective than verbal mediation with concrete noun pairs, and this difference cannot be explained in terms of any differential availability of the two types of mediators. Image instructions have also produced better learning than verbal instructions in the case of picture pairs. What especially requires interpretation, then, is the general superiority of imaginal over verbal mediators in learning when both are equally available.

Parallel versus sequential processing   This functional distinction provides a partial explanation of the apparent superiority of imagery. It has been repeatedly suggested that spatial integration is what makes imagery uniquely effective as a mnemonic aid. This was discussed in some detail at the end of the last chapter in relation to Köhler's organizational interpretation of associative learning, the conceptual-peg hypothesis, and in particular the consistent finding that relational organization or figural unity is an important determinant of the effectiveness of imagery mediators. The point came up again in this chapter when we compared the effects of different kinds of pictorial and syntactical contextual cues in associative learning.

Such studies demonstrate the importance of meaningful spatial organization in mnemonic imagery, but they do not in themselves explain why such images should lead to better recall than analogous verbal mediators, which also provide an integrated context. The answer may be that the difference in the type of organization provided by the two systems is correlated with differences in ease of information processing. In the case of integrated images, the associative information is stored in parallel. Assuming that the stimulus term functions as an effective retrieval cue for the entire compound on recall trials, the image can be quickly scanned and decoded to yield the verbal response. On the other hand, verbal mediators, together with the to-be-associated words, must be stored sequentially, which could mean that memory load during storage is greater than in the case of imagery, or that redintegration of the sequential verbal mediator takes longer and is more subject to error than image redintegration during recall. Some support for the latter interpretation was obtained by Paivio and Foth (1970), who found that the latency of recall of the response word in concrete pairs was longer under verbal mediation than imagery conditions, although the latency of mediator discovery during the study trial did not differ under the two sets.

The visual-spatial characteristics of imagery may also contribute more than verbal mediators to the distinctiveness or discriminability of the stimulus word and hence to response recall. This possibility was discussed in Chapter 8 in relation to the effects of stimulus abstractness-concreteness, but no evidence on the relative contributions of imaginal and verbal mediators to stimulus distinctiveness appears to be available at present. Another version of this hypothesis is that imagery contributes more than verbal mediation to differentiation between pairs rather than between stimulus members alone, but again no direct evidence is available.

Static versus dynamic functioning   Finally, the superiority of imagery may depend not only on its capacity to represent information spatially but also on its transformability, as discussed in Chapter 2 in relation to the static-dynamic functional distinction. Imagery provides an efficient mechanism for the symbolic transformations and "flights" of thought involved in mediation, presumably because of the motor component of imagery. The property may explain the effectiveness in paired-associate learning of action pictures relative to static representations as contextual cues, of sentences with verb connectives rather than conjunctions, and of instructions to generate interactive images. In each case, the mediation technique primes the generation of dynamic images that effectively bring the to-be-associated units into a meaningful integrated relationship.

Interaction of Imaginal and Verbal Systems

The intent of the preceding discussion must not be misunderstood. Although the emphasis is on the differential properties of imaginal and verbal processes and their contributions to memory, it is likely that the two systems interact continually in tasks that are assumed to involve imagery. Where the learning task involves concrete nouns, for example, any use of mediating imagery obviously requires word-to-image coding during input and vice versa during recall. Moreover, it is likely that in many instances the generation of an imaginal mediator might be on the basis of a sentence or phrase first aroused by the to-be-learned items. This is most apparent in studies (e.g., Hulicka & Grossman, 1967) in which a connecting sentence is presented to both verbal- and imagery-mediation groups, but only the latter are asked to image the interaction suggested by the sentence. The differential effects obtained under such conditions are still attributable to the imagery component, but this does not necessarily mean that imagery mediation *alone* is more effective than verbal mediation alone. What the evidence does permit us to infer is that imagery enhances memory even for verbal units beyond a level that can be explained on the basis of verbal process alone. The effect might indeed be attributable to the functional differences between the two systems, but it is equally likely that it reflects their interaction. The image system may contribute flexibility and speed to the transformations involved in mediated learning, whereas the logical verbal system keeps the transformations on track, i.e., relevant to the learning task and the items involved in it. A further implication is that any superiority observed under imagery mnemonic conditions may result from the addition of imagery to a verbal baseline laid down during the subject's initial representational or associative reactions to the to-be-learned items, i.e., two mediational systems are potentially available rather than one. Verbal mediation conditions may be more likely to restrict the subject to the verbal system alone. Such an interpretation is analogous to the information redundancy explanation of concreteness effects, as discussed in Chapter 7. These suggestions are consistent with the two-process theory and with much of the data reviewed in this chapter, although at the moment they remain speculative and in need of more adequate empirical investigation.

SUMMARY

The following summarizes the more important general conclusions, interpretations, and the theoretical issues arising from the mediation research reported in this chapter and the last two.

1. Associative strategies, coding or transformation of items, and so on, are the rule rather than the exception in verbal learning situations, at least for normal adult subjects. In fact, special procedures are necessary to override strong associative habits in order to study "unmediated" learning. An obvious implication is that rote learning is a misnomer for much of the research that has been conducted under that name. This does not mean, of course, that such research is without value, but it does mean that an important source of variability has often been uncontrolled and that the theoretical interpretations arising from such studies are gross oversimplifications at best.

2. The relation of mediation processes to task difficulty arising from the nature of the to-be-learned material is a complex one. Reed's (1918b) analysis, supported by his own findings and by occasional ones since then, is that associative aids are used during the initial stages of associative learning, when the task is difficult. As training progresses, mediators drop out. On the other hand, a number of studies show that mediators are more often reported when meaningfulness (in the general sense) is high rather than low. The apparent paradox is easily resolved by differentiating between availability and usefulness of mediators: They are readily available when task meaningfulness is high, but they are particularly useful or necessary for learning and recall when meaningfulness is low or the task difficult. Such a conception is in agreement with Reed's analysis of verbal learning tasks as problems requiring thought for their solution. In Bartlett's terms, the cognitive processes involved represent an "effort after meaning," that is, an "attempt to connect something that is given with something other than itself" (1932, p. 227).

3. The degree of difficulty of the task may be related to meaningfulness in the sense of familiarity, abstractness-concreteness, or associative meaningfulness (m). In many investigations, a combination of unfamiliarity, abstract-

ness, and low m may contribute to learning difficulty. This is particularly likely in studies that have used nonsense material as items. The emphasis on verbal mediation in much of that research may be directly attributable to the use of such material. That is, although subjects may find even verbal mediation difficult with nonsense syllables, it is at least possible to encode by transforming the items into meaningful words—the "effort after meaning" is a verbal process. Imagery would be ruled out as an effective mnemonic aid unless the subject first encodes items into meaningful words. Furthermore, those words would have to be highly concrete according to the theory presented here. In view of the complexity of such a process, imaginal coding and mediation would be expected to be inefficient and infrequently used as a strategy with unfamiliar verbal material. Some research nevertheless suggests that imagery can be effectively used with nonsense words under special circumstances, and perhaps more often if the stimulus member is a meaningful word (Paivio & Madigan, 1968).

4. With meaningful words, instructional sets to use imaginal or verbal mediators can greatly facilitate learning. In some studies involving imagery mnemonics, for example, the subjects using such a technique may remember several times the number of items recalled by a control group. The differences are especially impressive when the control group is instructed to use rote repetition, thereby controlling for the spontaneous use of mediators. These findings are important not only in showing the positive effect of the mediation instructions but also in demonstrating that rote rehearsal is a much less efficient way of learning such material.

5. It has been difficult empirically to separate the contributions of imaginal and verbal mediators in learning and memory. Theoretically, it was expected that imagery would be particularly effective for learning concrete noun pairs and relatively ineffective with abstract nouns, whereas verbal mediators were expected to be less affected by variation in concreteness. This prediction received only mild and inconsistent support from an initial series of paired-associate learning studies, suggesting that it may be superfluous to postulate two processes rather than only one. Such a uniprocess theory could be rejected for several reasons: (a) When questioned about the learning strategies they used, subjects apparently had no difficulty in distinguishing between images and verbal mediators, and the frequencies of the two categories consistently bore a strong relation to item attributes—reported images were related directly to item (especially stimulus) concreteness-imagery, verbal mediators were not; moreover, reported imagery was the better predictor of learning performance; (b) the latency of discovery of the two classes of mediators always conformed to the predictions—images are discovered much more slowly for abstract- than for concrete-stimulus pairs, but verbal mediators are not similarly affected by concreteness; (c) finally, when subjects were forced to follow the different instructional sets by drawing the mediating images and writing the sentences, images indeed proved to be superior with concrete pairs but inferior with abstract pairs, as the theory predicted. Several additional experiments have confirmed the superiority of imagery with concrete pairs.

The difficulty of differentiating imaginal and verbal symbolic processes empirically in associative learning is an interesting puzzle in its own right, and several contributing factors are suggested by the data. One is that adult subjects tend to abandon mediational strategies they have been asked to use if those strategies are inappropriate for the to-be-learned items, and to substitute more appropriate strategies instead; according to these data, moreover, imagery is a preferred strategy when at least one member of a pair is concrete and high in its image-arousing value. A second possibility is that subjects can make surprisingly effective use of imaginal mediators even with abstract pairs. This possibility has been supported by subjective reports, correlations between mediation latencies and recall scores for abstract pairs, and experiments involving pictorial mediators for such pairs. And third, instructions to use verbal mediators may, in fact, generate images rather than "purely" verbal processes, perhaps because the "contextual meaning" aroused by concrete sentences is experienced as imagery.

6.   Accepting the functional usefulness of imaginal and verbal mediators does not thereby explain their *modus operandi*. Why precisely do mental images or mental words aid in remembering associations or individual items? General motivational or attentional factors may contribute, but it seems most unlikely that they play a major role in the effects. A theoretical approach based on item attributes and functional distinctions between the two symbolic systems, which constitutes a theory of meaning and code availability, relates the memory effects to the number of available codes and the functional significance of the two codes for different memory tasks. The superiority of imaginal and verbal mediators over rote repetition presumably can be attributed generally to the "discovery," under the mediation instructions, of higher-order visual-spatial or verbal-sequential units that incorporate to-be-associated items as components and from which the response can be decoded by a process of implicit labeling or associative responding. The decoding may involve a search process in which appropriate responding is dependent upon recognition memory once the mediator has permitted the generation of possible alternatives. Visual imagery, when readily generated, may be more effective than verbal mediation because the information in the image is spatially organized, permitting a rapid read-out of the relevant components, whereas the information in verbal storage is sequentially organized as a string of "mental words" that may take up more space in memory, or require longer search time with less efficient retrieval of the relevant response during recall, or both. In addition, a symbolic motor component may contribute to the transformational efficiency of mediating imagery. Where both systems are relevant to the task, however, they presumably interact continually in their mediational functioning, and imagery mnemonics may be especially effective because they enhance the probability that both symbolic systems will be brought into play in the learning task.

12
Language and the Symbolic Processes: Linguistic Models and Associationism

In this chapter and the next, we extend our consideration of the functional significance of the symbolic processes to grammatical variables and units larger than the single word. We have discussed such factors from time to time in various contexts but not in a systematic and unified way, as will be the case here. Our concern generally is with the classical problem of the relationship between language and thought. More specifically, attention will focus on the role of the symbolic processes in the understanding, retention, and production of language. Because this entails an emphasis on extended segments of verbal behavior, we are obviously faced with phenomena of greater complexity than heretofore, but we also encounter a problem that appears to differ qualitatively from those previously considered. Linguists and psychologists interested in language behavior are agreed that the crucial psycholinguistic problem is the creativity or productivity of language (e.g., Chomsky, 1966; Hebb & Thompson, 1954). We can combine and readily recombine familiar units to make up new utterances, which can be understood equally easily by others. The nub of the theoretical issue is found in grammar and the sentence. G. A. Miller (1962) stated it plainly: "I do not see how we are going to describe language as a skill unless we find some satisfactory way to deal with grammar and with the combinatorial processes that grammar entails" (p. 748). Osgood posed the problem as a challenge: "Can our psychological theories incorporate and render comprehensible the way human beings understand and create sentences?" (1963, p. 735).

An essential feature of the psychological issue is the old problem of meaning, related in this case to syntax as well as to word units. Thus Garrett and Fodor (1968) assume "that understanding a sentence entails pairing it with an appropriate semantic interpretation and that the interpretation is uniquely determined by relevant lexical and syntactic data (p. 451)." Since the fluent speaker is able to provide an interpretation for an indefinitely large set of sentences, it is necessary to assume further that he is equipped with the ability to provide both "structural descriptions" and "semantic readings" for sentences. These inseparable components of syntacticity and semanticity of language behavior constitute the puzzle that psycholinguistic theories and empirical studies have attempted to solve.

Our ultimate aim is to apply the two-process model of meaning and mediation to the relevant psycholinguistic problems with special emphasis on the mediational role of imagery. This will be done in the next chapter. Inasmuch as the imagery approach is novel, however, its value can be fully appreciated only in comparison with contemporary theoretical approaches that have inspired most of the psycholinguistic research in recent years and that have themselves been the focus of a major theoretical debate. I am referring here to varieties of S-R behavior theory on the one hand and contemporary linguistic theory on the other. The psycholinguistic contributions of these approaches will be reviewed in this chapter. Since the alternatives have been discussed in detail by their protagonists (see Dixon & Horton, 1968), our treatment of the theories can be relatively brief, with an emphasis on those features that are most relevant to later discussions. The presentation is organized into three sections covering S-R theoretical approaches, linguistic theory (including a critical evaluation of that approach), and empirical evidence arising from research related to these conceptual models.

STIMULUS-RESPONSE ASSOCIATIONISM

Stimulus-response associationism has been the basis of two general approaches to the study of verbal behavior, both of which have been discussed earlier in relation to the problem of meaning (Chapter 3). One is the verbal-associative approach espoused, at least at one time, by Bousfield, Jenkins, and Deese, among others. The other is the representational mediation process approach identified particularly with Osgood. These two general approaches have certain features in common, including an emphasis on habit as a theoretical construct, and mechanisms such as reinforcement, generalization, and transfer, which presumably determine the nature and the strength of the linguistic habits acquired by the individual and the conditions of their effective arousal. In addition, both make use of the concept of mediation, although they differ in their interpretation of the mediation process. Inasmuch as Osgood (1968) has questioned the sufficiency of both S-R associationism and linguistic theory, his views will be considered later in the context of the evaluation of those approaches.

The S-R associationistic model provides an adequate explanation of simple verbal associative habits in terms of prior word-word associative experience. Such habits can be viewed simply as verbal response chains that are part of the individual's linguistic repertoire as a result of appropriate shaping by the reinforcing community (cf. Skinner, 1957). The model requires elaboration, however, in order to be applicable to more general grammatical habits that are independent of specific interword associations. Such elaboration has taken the form of higher-order conceptual habits and verbal mediating mechanisms.

Underwood (1965), discussing the psycholinguistic relevance of concepts derived from verbal learning research, indicated how the concept of second-order habits can be applied to problems of sentence comprehension and sentence learning. Grammatical habits, according to Underwood, are second-order habits whose major role is that of ordering verbal output. For example, studies that vary the degree to which a sequence of words approximates formal linguistic ordering are varying the degree to which the subject's grammatical ordering habits are appropriate in that situation. The more closely the sequence approaches grammatical ordering, the greater the facilitating effect of grammatical habits in reproducing the order.

Underwood defines a second-order habit as one that determines the class of responses at any moment but not the specific instance of the class. Such habits are conceptual in that they supersede any particular instance. This is precisely the nature of grammatical habits—words of a given class, such as nouns, are appropriately placed in the context of other words in a sentence. Underwood raised two critical questions in this connection: What communalities among the instances provide the basis for the concept learning, and what is the nature of the stimulus needed to elicit the second-order (grammatical) habits? At least two serious attempts have been made to answer essentially these questions within the framework of the S-R model.

J. J. Jenkins and Palermo (1964; Jenkins, 1965) identified the central problem in the acquisition of grammar as that of class formation. That is, what is learned in the acquisition of grammar is a set of classes of words such as nouns, adjectives, and verbs on both the stimulus and the response sides in grammatical behavior. The theoretical mechanism they proposed for such acquisition is the general verbal mediation model previously discussed in relation to mediation paradigms (Chapter 9). According to that model, two words acquire class equivalence by being associated in the same sentence frame. Thus, experience with two different words, X and Y, in the same contexts, ABCXD and ABCYD, should result in a relation such that C elicits X and Y, and both X and Y elicit D. Eventually, with repeated experience in these and other common contexts, X and Y come to be members of the same class and have the capacity to elicit each other as associates. Various predictions based on this approach have been supported by word association and experimental data (e.g., J. J. Jenkins, 1965).

M. D. S. Braine (1963) proposed a similar mechanism, which he termed *contextual generalization*, for the acquisition of grammatical structure. Braine defines contextual generalization as follows: "When a subject who has experienced sentences in which a segment (morpheme, word, or phrase) occurs in a certain position and context, later tends to place this segment in the same position in other contexts, the context of the segment will be said to have generalized and the subject to have shown contextual generalization" (1963, p. 323). From a number of experiments, in which this type of generalization was investigated by having subjects learn miniature artificial languages, Braine formulated a theory about how grammatical structure is developed. The theory includes three propositions. First, "what is learned" are the locations of units or expressions in utterances. Second, such units can form a hierarchy in which longer units contain shorter units as parts, the location that is learned being the location of a unit within the next-larger containing unit, up to the sentence. Thus, one learns the location of letters and syllables within words, words within phrases, and phrases within sentences. Finally, Braine assumes that the learning is a case of perceptual learning: The learner becomes familiar with the sounds or expressions in the positions in which they occur.

Braine acknowledged that some aspects of the structure of a natural language such as English raise problems for the theory. For example, it is not relevant to the learning of contrasts between word orders (e.g., GEORGE HIT JOHN versus JOHN HIT GEORGE) and at present it has difficulty explaining how the child learns to produce and understand grammatical transformations. In view of these difficulties, Braine suggested that the scope of the theory should be limited to the "kernel" of the language, i.e., the grammatical structure of simple declarative statements like THE LIGHT IS ON. Despite this stricture, however, Braine's theory has been subjected to the criticisms that have been directed at S-R behavior theories in general by contemporary linguists and linguistically oriented psycholinguists.

The Linguists' Critique of S-R Theories

The criticisms of S-R approaches began with Chomsky's (1959) review of Skinner's (1957) book, *Verbal Behavior*. Chomsky examined the ways in which Skinner applied such behavioristic concepts as stimulus, response, reinforcement, shaping, and generalization to the "functional analysis" of language and its acquisition. In each case, he found the extended notions to be wanting as descriptive or explanatory concepts. Thus he noted that some of the terms ("stimulus," "control," etc.) are "mere paraphrases" for vocabularly commonly used to describe behavior. The term "reinforcement" purportedly has lost whatever objectivity it has had in the laboratory setting. Data are lacking for such doctrinal claims as the necessity of slow and careful shaping of verbal behavior through differential reinforcement. Skinner's view of sentence structure as a set of lexical items in grammatical frames is said to be inadequate, for it fails to account for the fact that different sentence structures can underlie expressions that have the same frame (a point that anticipates the crucial distinction between deep structure and surface structure, to be discussed more fully below). On the basis of such observations, Chomsky concluded that Skinner's formulation provides no advantage over traditional mentalistic descriptions of verbal behavior.

Others have recently extended such criticisms to all varieties of associationism and S-R learning theory. These criticisms have centered principally on the asserted inadequacy of S-R theories to handle certain crucial characteristics of a language such as English. Chomsky (1957) demonstrated that English cannot be conceptualized in terms of a finite state Markov process, according to which a speaker produces a sentence from "left to right" (i.e., sequentially) in such a manner that the choice of each successive word in the sequence is progressively limited by the preceding words already produced. Such sequential dependencies obviously exist in English, but there are also many constructions in which they are absent, such as recursions in which a phrase is embedded within another. Thus, in the sentence *The boy who hurt his leg walked to the store*, the phrase *who hurt his leg* is embedded within the sentence *The boy walked to the store*. The latter involves a dependency between the noun phrase *The boy* and the verb phrase *walked to the store* that extends across the embedded portion. Such recursions provide unlimited possibilities that cannot be handled within a finite state model. Another critical linguistic feature that challenges S-R theories is the possibility of grammatical transformations (passives, negatives, etc.). Both of these features, recursion and transformation, exemplify the creativity already stressed as characterizing language.

The mediational S-R learning models proposed by J. J. Jenkins and Palermo (1964) and M. D. S. Braine (1963) have been rejected on the grounds that they are incapable of explaining the above features of grammatical behavior (for a summary, see, e.g., McNeill, 1968, pp. 408–412). The mediation-paradigm approach of Jenkins and Palermo would generate a network of associations comprising a finite-state grammar, creating the difficulty that the learner must acquire all the transitions among grammatical classes that are allowable in the language. Because of the large number of these, it is in principle not possible for mediation paradigms to account for the speed at which the child acquires the skill to produce a large number of transitions. Braine's theory, according to McNeill, does provide a basis for explaining productivity or creativity. However, it too has the shortcoming that it cannot formulate transformations because the contextual generalization mechanism applies only to the surface features of the speech presented to a child, and not to the base structures in terms of which transformations are defined (see below). Moreover, contextual generalization purportedly cannot account for recursions, especially of the self-embedding kind.

TRANSFORMATIONAL GENERATIVE GRAMMAR

The positive contribution of the linguistic approach to psycholinguistics stems from the development of the theory of transformational generative grammar, chiefly by Noam Chomsky (e.g., 1957, 1965). The features of the theory that are most important for our purposes will be briefly reviewed, followed by a discussion of their psychological significance. In regard to the latter, we should note that the model is primarily intended to be a model of linguistic competence, not performance. Thus it is concerned with an *ideal* speaker-listener with perfect knowledge of his language and without the psychological limitations of distractibility, shifts of attention, finite memory, etc., that would affect performance. The theory is in effect a description of what the speaker-hearer needs to know in order to use the language. A performance model presumably would incorporate such a description as a basic component, but it would have to consider other factors as well.

The theory retains the essential characteristics of traditional and structural linguistics, which were concerned mainly with the description of language at different levels of its hierarchial structure extending from the sound units to the sentence as a whole. The structural description of a sentence, for example, involves a *constituent analysis* whereby the sentence is divided into its constituent units in successive binary divisions by means of a branching tree diagram or a system of bracketing. Thus a simple active sentence would be first divided into subject and predicate, the subject into article plus noun, and so on. One of the characteristics of a generative grammar is that the descriptive analysis is done according to a system of *phrase-structure rules* that specify how to rewrite the symbols that are used to label each level of the hierarchical structure in such a manner as to derive or generate grammatical sentences. In effect, such a grammar assigns an abstract structural description that can be represented as a branching tree diagram with the nodes labeled by symbols. An example of such a phrase-structure analysis is presented in Figure 12-1. The example shows that the sentence symbolized by S is first rewritten as noun phrase (NP) and verb phrase (VP), the noun phrase is rewritten as article (T) plus noun (N), and so on. Such a labeled diagram is known as a Phrase-marker, or P-marker.

Chomsky's transformational generative grammar includes such phrase-structure rules as one component and in addition includes transformational rules (adjunctions, deletions, permutations) that operate on the output of the phrase-structure rules, i.e., on the P-marker, to transform the sentence into one with a different form, such as a passive into an active sentence. The advantage of the transformational grammar over other models such as a phrase-structure grammar is that it is less restricted in the kinds of operations that are possible and has

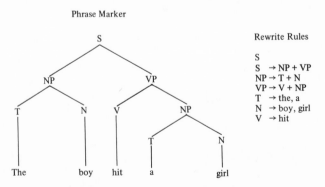

FIGURE 12-1. An illustration of the derivation of a sentence by the application of the rewriting rules of a generative grammar, and the corresponding structural description of that sentence in terms of a labeled tree diagram, or phrase marker.

greater explanatory power. For example, transformational grammars can resolve the semantic ambiguity of certain kinds of sentences that cannot be done by phrase-structure grammars or the finite-state grammars described earlier. This leads to the central idea of transformational grammar, which is also the most important one for us to understand from a psychological point of view, for it brings meaning into the linguistic picture, viz., the distinction between surface and deep structure.

Surface Structure and Deep Structure

The basic notion behind this distinction has a long history in linguistics (see Chomsky, 1966) although the particular terms are recent. Surface structure is related to the physical form, or sound pattern, of the sentence, which can be described in terms of the phonology and phrase-structure analysis of descriptive linguistics. Surface structure thus determines the phonetic interpretation of the sentence. Deep structure refers to the underlying abstract structure, which determines the semantic interpretation of the sentence and which can be described in terms of more elementary phrase-markers from which the surface structure is derived on the basis of the transformational rules. The important point is that deep structures and surface structures need not be the same: Different deep structures can underlie identical surface structures; conversely, identical deep structures may underlie different surface structures. The semantic implications of such distinctions can be clearly seen in the case of ambiguous sentences such as *They are cooking apples*, the underlying sense of which is either to the effect that "some people are cooking apples" or that "the apples are for cooking." In this instance, a phrase-structure analysis will reveal the ambiguity by assigning alternative constituent divisions to the original sentence, i.e., (*They*) ((*are cooking*) (*apples*)) and (*They*) ((*are*) (*cooking apples*)). In other instances (e.g., *the shooting of hunters is terrible*) it will not, since the immediate constituent structure is identical for the two possible interpretations. A transformational analysis will, however, specify different derivations for the alternatives, just as it will reveal similarities and differences among sentences generally by revealing the deeper structures that underlie their manifest form. For our purposes, it is unnecessary to know how this might be done in detail (the theory of transformational grammar itself is undergoing change and many of its features are most tentative; see Chomsky, 1965), but a general understanding of the approach is important for later discussions.

Surface structure can be described in terms of an immediate constituent or phrase-structure analysis of an actual sentence. Deep structure, however, refers to a more abstract structure that is conceptualized as the basis of the sentence and described in terms of an *underlying*, or *base*, *phrase-marker* associated with a *basic string*. These base phrase-markers are generated by a system of rules called the *base* of the syntactic component of the generative grammar. To illustrate with a simplified example, the underlying structure of the sentence *John hurt himself* might be described as follows:

John hurt John may be regarded as the basic string and the entire sequence of symbols in the tree diagram as its base phrase-marker. The significant feature here is that the equivalence of the subject and object of the original sentence is explicitly revealed in the deep structure, i.e., as described by the base phrase-marker. A full descriptive account would contain more symbols. Moreover, sentences are usually more complex, and their deep structures accordingly might consist of more than one phrase-marker as constituents. For example, the basis of the sentence *The boy and girl went to the store* may be loosely said to consist of base phrase-markers associated with the underlying sentences "the boy went to the store" and "the girl went to the store," according to Chomsky's (1957) version of transformational grammar. (Recent alternative conceptions would simplify the analysis of such sentences, but this need not concern us here.)

While the rules of the base of the syntactic component of the grammar generate the abstract deep structure, which determines the meaning of the sentence, the major function of the transformational rules is to convert the deep structure into the more concrete surface structure that describes the form of the sentence. The basis of the sentence is said to be "mapped into" the sentence by such rules. More specifically, the transformational rules derive phrase-markers from phrase-markers, thereby ultimately assigning to a sentence a *final derived phrase-marker* that represents its surface structure.

The preceding discussion has been concerned mainly with the syntactic component of generative grammar. The other two essential components of such a theory are the *phonological* and *semantic* components. The rules of the phonological component operate on the surface structures or, more specifically, on the final derived phrase-markers, indicating their phonetic character. That is, they specify how the sentence is to be pronounced. The function of the semantic component, on the other hand, is to provide a semantic interpretation of each sentence. Thus it is of the greatest interest here, although it is also the least developed aspect of the theory. Nevertheless, advances have been made in describing the form it might take. Katz and Fodor (1963) pioneered in the development of such a semantic theory, and Katz and Postal (1964) subsequently combined their conception with Chomsky's theory of generative grammar in an attempt to provide one integrated description of natural language. Important modifications have been proposed by others (e.g., McCawley, 1968), but the Katz-Fodor-Postal version exemplifies the general nature of the linguistic approach to semantic theory, and we shall confine our attention to it for the present.

A Semantic Theory

The problem for a semantic theory, according to Katz and Fodor, is to describe and explain a fluent speaker's ability to interpret novel sentences at the point where grammar leaves off. A grammar provides only an incomplete account, for it does not specify the meanings of the lexical units individually or in combination within a sentence. That this is so is obvious from the fact that grammar assigns identical structural descriptions to sentences with different meanings (cf. *The boy hit the girl* and *The girl hit the boy*) and different descriptions to sentences with identical meaning (*The boy hit the girl* and *The girl was hit by the boy*). The features of the ability of the speaker that must be accounted for by a semantic theory of language include the detection of nonsyntactic ambiguity (for example, the meaning contributed by the word *bill* in the sentence *The bill is large*), specification of the number of interpretations or readings such sentences can be assigned, detection of semantic anomalies (e.g., *The paint is silent*), and decisions about paraphrasing (is a particular sentence, S_1, a paraphrase of another sentence, S_2?). On the other hand, the effect of the setting on how a sentence is understood, which depends on all the knowledge of the world shared by speakers, is beyond the scope of such a theory. As we shall see later, this is an important limitation from the psychological viewpoint, since it excludes just those semantic features (e.g., reference) that are essential for the understanding of verbal behavior.

Semantic markers   A central problem of the semantic theory is the characterization of the alternative meanings of lexical units in such a manner that a particular interpretation can be assigned to the combination of lexical items within the sentence as a whole. This is done within the theory by *semantic markers*, which are close analogues of grammatical markers. Thus semantic markers are the elements in terms of which semantic relations are expressed, just as grammatical markers are elements in terms of which syntactic relations are expressed. For example, the semantic marker Male represents an aspect of the conceptual similarity between such words as *man, boy, father, uncle*, etc. Such markers express the systematic relations between lexical units, as opposed to distinguishers, which are introduced into the theory to express whatever is idiosyncratic about the meaning of an item. The lexical information contained in the different classes of markers is expressed in the form of a tree diagram. Figure 12-2 shows such a diagram for the word *bachelor*. The representation includes a grammatical marker (noun), semantic markers (human, animal, male) in parentheses, and distinguisher (who has never married, etc.) in brackets. Such a semantic representation obviously depends on a dictionary of the language —indeed, it *is* a dictionary. It differs from conventional dictionaries, however, in its capacity to characterize semantic relations between items in a way not done by conventional dictionaries. In addition, it provides a formalization of the dictionary entry, thereby permitting a formal statement of another essential component of the theory, the projection rules.

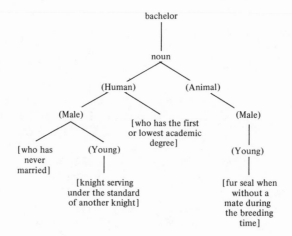

FIGURE 12-2. Dictionary entries for the word *bachelor* in terms of grammatical marker, semantic markers, and distinguishers. From Katz and Fodor (1963, p. 190).

Projection rules   While the dictionary associates sequences of semantic markers with the lexical items, i.e., it associates "readings" with the items, the *projection rules* specify how to apply the information in the dictionary in order to arrive at the correct semantic interpretation of a given sentence. In effect, the projection rules *select* the appropriate sense of each lexical item on the distinct basis of grammatical information provided by the phrase-structure analysis of the sentence. More specifically, the projection rules operate on the underlying phrase-markers of a sentence, i.e., its deep structure rather than its surface structure (Chomsky, 1965; Katz & Postal, 1964), since the syntactic information relevant to a semantic interpretation is uniquely characterized only in deep structures. The semantic information from the dictionary is therefore assigned to lexical items in base phrase-markers, and the projection rules then proceed up the phrase-structure tree, amalgamating readings of the lexical items in order to derive appropriate semantic interpretations for higher-order constituents, ultimately the sentence itself. As a miniature example, consider the words *colorful* and *ball* in the sentence *The man hits the colorful ball.* Both words have several dictionary meanings, i.e., are associated with different semantic markers. Thus, two possible readings for *ball* are as follows:

(1)   Ball ⟶ Noun concrete ⟶ (Social activity) ⟶ (large) (Assembly) ⟶ [For the purpose of social dancing]

(2)   Ball ⟶ Noun concrete ⟶ (Physical object) ⟶ [Having globular shape]

The word *colorful* similarly has alternative meanings as a color adjective and as an evaluative adjective corresponding roughly to picturesqueness. The task of the projection rules is to effect an amalgamation of semantic markers on the basis of syntactic as well as other semantic information in the sentence in order to arrive at an appropriate characterization of "colorful ball" as Noun Concrete ⟶ (physical object) ⟶ (color), etc., corresponding to the meaning that the skilled speaker would unambiguously assign to the two words in that sentence.

The above is a very brief sketch of the syntactic and semantic components associated with the linguistic theory of transformational generative grammar, as viewed by Chomsky and his followers, but it will suffice for our purposes. Chomsky's summary of the "form" of such a theory provides a concise review of its main features:

> A grammar contains a syntactic component, a semantic component, and a phonological component. The latter two are purely interpretive; they play no part in the recursive generation of sentence structures. The syntactic component consists of a base and a transformational component. The base, in turn, consists of a categorial subcomponent and a lexicon. The base generates deep structures. A deep structure enters the semantic component and receives a semantic interpretation; it is mapped by the transformational rules into a surface structure, which is then given a phonetic interpretation by the rules of the phonological component. Thus the grammar assigns semantic interpretations to signals, this association being mediated by the recursive rules of the syntactic component (1965, p. 141).

Psychological Relevance of the Linguistic Model

We noted at the outset that the linguistic model is intended to be a theory of linguistic competence, not performance. Even with that stricture, however, it represents a kind of psychological theory in that it characterizes what the language user needs to know about a language in order to use it in a grammatically and semantically acceptable way. The stricture is in any case only loosely adhered to, since there is an increasing tendency among proponents of the theory to treat it as a performance model, in that it is used to explain the understanding and production of sentences, and predictions from it have been compared empirically with predictions from other models. For example, G. A. Miller (1962) at one time proposed the hypothesis that people remember a nonkernel sentence, such as a passive, by first transforming it into its underlying kernel (simple, active, declarative) sentence, and then storing the kernel along with a footnote about the syntactical structure. The transformational footnote, if remembered, enables the subject to make the necessary grammatical transformation during recall (see later). The hypothesis generates the prediction, among others, that nonkernel sentences would be more difficult to recall than kernel sentences. The specific assumption that complex sentences represent transforms of kernel sentences is now outdated, and the hypothesis might be rephrased in terms of transformations of deep structures (recently the hypothesis has been expressed in terms of memory for the semantic interpretation plus syntactic markers by G. A. Miller & McNeill, 1969, p. 705). The essential point however, is that the hypothesis relates memory for sentences to transformational grammar in such a manner that predictions about performance can be generated and tested.

Although the validity and usefulness of the linguistic model do not seem to depend on such a stand, the model has also been rendered psychologically relevant by linking it to a nativistic theory of language acquisition. Thus Chomsky (1965) postulates a "language-acquisition device" (LAD), which is defined as an innately determined mechanism responsible for the development of linguistic skill as described by transformational generative grammar. While the model refers to competence, it is also taken by McNeill (1968) as a performance model in that he contrasts LAD with an empiricist approach to speech acquisition in young children. These and other psychological extensions of the linguistic theory will be examined in more detail later in the context of relevant research.

The linguistic model is also psychological in the sense that it is derived from observation of language behavior; that is, it represents generalizations from such behavior with respect to all three components of the model. Moreover, the adequacy of the model is tested behaviorally if only in the sense that the sentences generated or readings provided by the model must correspond to what is intuitively felt to be appropriate by a skilled language user. Psychological data are thus the ultimate criteria of the adequacy of the theory. At the present stage they also provide elements that the theory takes as given. Thus, in the semantic theory of Katz, Fodor, and Postal, the atomic elements in terms of which meaning is described—the semantic markers—are left undefined, and the problem of accounting for their meaning rests with psychology. These considerations serve to illustrate the psychological relevance of the linguistic theory and also point to some of its shortcomings.

Evaluation of the Linguistic Approach

The transformationists' critique of S-R models has been challenged by MacCorquodale, Osgood, and Staats. MacCorquodale (1970) presented a systematic and telling rejoinder to the original source of the linguists' criticisms, namely, Chomsky's (1959) review of Skinner's (1957) *Verbal Behavior*. Following a detailed examination of Chomsky's arguments, MacCorquodale concluded that the review did not constitute a critical analysis of Skinner's book. Instead, Chomsky criticized an "amalgam of some rather outdated behavioristic lore" that had nothing to do with Skinner's account; he misunderstood Skinner's purpose, which was to present a hypothesis about the causes of verbal behavior rather than an accomplished explanation; and Chomsky's review ignored much that was central to an understanding, application, and assessment of Skinner's position, especially his repeated emphasis on interactions among controlling variables acting concurrently rather than one at a time. MacCorquodale suggested, finally, that it might be more profitable for psycholinguists to spend their time developing the positive aspects of their point of view rather than attempting to destroy behaviorism but, if they are determined to do the latter, they should first understand what the behaviorists really said, and how behaviorisms differ from one another.

Osgood (1968, 1969) also has taken strong exception to the uncritical lumping together of "S-R theories" in the transformationists' claim that such theories are not capable in principle of accounting for language behavior. He emphasized the distinctions between single-stage and multiple-stage S-R theories on the one hand, and nonrepresentational and representational mediation theories on the other, arguing that single-stage and nonrepresentational (e.g., verbal-mediation) models are indeed quite inadequate, but multiple-stage representational mediation theories such as his own have not been ruled out of the running, even on the basis of the criteria used by the linguistically oriented psycholinguists.

A. W. Staats (1968, in press) has noted similarly that the criticisms of S-R models are based on an oversimplified view of learning theory and that linguists have not explored the power of the full range of psychological concepts and principles currently available. While such principles have been fractionated even within the psychology of learning, an integrated approach is possible and can serve as an adequate foundation for a learning analysis of language. Staats has himself attempted such an integration of the principles of classical and instrumental conditioning and their interrelationships. Moreover, he has attempted to show how the resulting complex S-R mechanisms can be used to account *in principle* for the learning of language, including the complex skills involved in grammatical behavior, and to provide an account of the behavior of the language user in actual situations.

Osgood and Staats also turn the tables on the linguistic critics by pointing to the shortcomings of the linguistic approach as an explanatory theory of language behavior. The counterattack is not directed at linguistics in its own proper domain as an abstract descriptive theory of the structure of language, but rather at its adequacy as an explanatory (psychological) theory of language behavior. While Chomsky and other proponents of transformational grammars have acknowledged the limitations of their model with respect to linguistic performance, the line between competence and performance is not clearly drawn. Performance does depend on competence as well as on such factors as the linguistic setting and the limitations imposed by psychological factors of memory, attention, and so forth; thus a theory of competence is part of a theory of performance. In any case, as noted above, the transformationists have not restricted their claims in a manner consistent with their disclaimers regarding performance, but have in fact extended their competence model to the language user. Accordingly, they are open to whatever criticisms emerge from an examination of their approach from the psychological point of view.

Osgood finds the linguistic approach wanting on a number of counts. However much the innate factors emphasized, for example, by McNeill (1968) and Lenneberg (1967) influence language development, there is much about language that is learned, and transformational grammars have nothing to say about the nature of such learning. Thus they can say nothing about sign learning and hence nothing about reference or other fundamental aspects of meaning. Furthermore, while sequential dependencies are insufficient as characterizations of grammatical behavior, they are not irrelevant. The evidence is overwhelming that such dependencies play an important role in language, and again linguistic theory per se can say nothing about how they are acquired. In regard to the occurrence of language behavior, the grammatical rules fail to account for selection among alternatives in such a manner as to produce a particular meaningful sentence. Contrary to what the transformationists assume when they assert that the syntactic component is central and the semantic and phonological components operate on its output (e.g., Garrett & Fodor, 1968), one does not first generate an empty grammar and then decide what to say. Instead, one first decides what to say, then how to say it. Thus, the semantic component is central and the syntactic component operates on its output.

A. W. Staats' (in press) criticisms are more general, being directed at the transformational generative model as an explanatory theory. He notes that the controversy between linguistic and learning theories is yet another occurrence of an old issue in psychology, viz., nativism versus empiricism. The linguistic approach is a nativistic theory, as Chomsky and others have acknowledged, and like earlier nativistic approaches (e.g., in developmental psychology) it has attempted to show the inadequacy of environmental factors in general and learning theory in particular as explanations of certain facts of behavior, in this case language. However, a discreditation of learning theory does not constitute support for a nativistic theory. What is needed is the positive identification of relevant independent variables—causal factors—that are responsible for the linguistic competence and that permit the prediction and control that characterize scientific theories. Such factors presumably would be of the nature of biological (anatomical and physiological) events, but the relevant ones have not been identified by the transformationists. Instead, they point to the regularities, complexities, universal features, and creativity of language and argue that they must reflect innate mental structures. But linguistic observations alone cannot serve as a basis for making statements about the determinants of the linguistic events themselves. This state of affairs limits the very nature of linguistic theory as an explanatory theory of language behavior: It cannot *in principle* provide an explanation of language acquisition or language behavior. The theory represents generalizations from observations of language responses in some subjects and can generate predictions concerning the language responses of other subjects in the linguistic community. It is therefore what is known in psychology as an R-R (response-response) type of theory, and such theories are not explanatory—they say nothing about the independent variables that control behavior. Thus, such response-inferred concepts as "deep" versus "surface" structure, language universals, grammatical rules, "competence" as an innately given mental process, etc., are completely circular and nonexplanatory, contrary to the claims of the Chomskian psycholinguists.

Similar rejoinders have been presented by others (e.g., Esper, 1968, pp. 207–233; Hebb, Lambert, & Tucker, 1970), but the point has been made and it need not be labored. I am persuaded by the above arguments and my own examination of the relevant empirical evidence (see Chapter 13) that the theory of transformational generative grammar is presently insufficient and unsatisfactory in type as a psychological theory of language. In regard to the latter point, the arguments in favor of a nativistic approach to language have been presented in greatest detail and with the most thorough documentation by Lenneberg (1967). Here is to be found a compilation of data showing remarkable regularities in the time of speech acquisition, anatomical and physiological correlates of linguistic skills, and other evidence on the "biological foundations" of language that might justify a nativistic position. The book is important and it ought to be read by every student of psycholinguistics, but I am not convinced that the evidence it presents compels one to favor a nativistic theory over a learning theory approach, even in terms of relative emphasis. There can be no argument with the assertion that innate structures are vital for language acquisition, but such a view and the evidence consistent with it do not constitute a *positive* theory of language acquisition that does much more than predict that an organism will speak because it is human. It is true that the data on the aphasias indicate that certain anatomical regions of the brain are crucial to language function. Such information is theoretically relevant and of great practical importance, but it does not explain language in any sense that is theoretically satisfying. The finer structures remain unidentified; and even when they have been mapped out, the fact will remain that the structures can produce no speech without exposure to the appropriate environmental conditions. The learning theories presently available may be inadequate for the job, but language behavior will remain most inadequately explained without reliance on *some* kind of learning theory.

Critique of the semantic approach   In a review of Katz and Fodor's (1963) semantic theory, Bolinger (1965) questioned their approach on a number of points, two of which are especially relevant to the theoretical viewpoint adopted in this book. One concerns the problem of the linguistic unit. Katz and Fodor assume that morphemes are the minimal familiar lexical units of sentences and that the understanding of sentences is a compositional process involving such units. Knowledge of the meanings of the morphemes and the grammar of a language enables the speaker to determine the meaning of a novel sentence on the basis of how the morphemes are arranged in the sentence. This approach involves an emphasis on the "striking originality" of sentences, whose understanding is to be explained by the compositional process. Bolinger suggests, however, that what is considered novel depends on one's orientation. He is "more inclined to be surprised at the deadly repetitiousness of language ... and even more surprised at the conformity of linguists to the view that what is 95% old not only in its elements but in much of its internal structure, is to be regarded as 100% new" (1965, p. 571).

Bolinger pushes familiarity upward from the morpheme to "concatenations of morphemes" that repeat themselves. There are countless numbers of these, and they are the sources of the sense characterization we carry in our heads. Bolinger is referring here to what we have previously discussed as higher-order linguistic units. The point is obviously relevant to the question of sequential dependencies, which are omnipresent in language in the form of such "concatenations of morphemes" or higher-order units whose meaning is grasped as a whole rather than through a compositional process operating on the lower-order lexical units. This has specific relevance in regard to the function of semantic markers and projection rules in the Katz-Fodor theory. Among other things, the markers are intended to disambiguate lexical units with more than one meaning—*of weather*, for example, disambiguates the word *spell* in the phrase "spell of weather." But, Bolinger argues, if the latter was previously learned as a unit, there was no ambiguity to begin with. The psychological problem that arises here is the point at which integration takes place: When are A and B grasped as an integrated whole as compared to separate units that operate on each other?

The above question has come up in several earlier contexts, notably in the discussions of meaning (Chapter 3) and associative symmetry (Chapter 8). In relation to meaning, the question bears on the size of the unit to which the concept of verbal representational meaning can be applied. Earlier it was suggested that the representational symbolic unit can vary in size, depending on the frequency with which the constituent elements have been experienced contiguously. Such experience presumably determines the availability or familiarity of a given verbal string as a unit. In the case of associative symmetry, Asch and Ebenholtz (1962) distinguished between integration and association, but it was argued here that these might be better viewed simply as labeling different stages in the development of interitem associations.

The above discussion relates to what Bolinger termed the problem of the speaker's knowledge of the language, i.e., his familiarity with linguistic units of varying size. The second related problem concerns the speaker's knowledge of the world, which Katz and Fodor explicitly rule out of their semantic theory because it involves too much, although they recognize its role in resolving linguistic ambiguities. As Bolinger points out, there is no ambiguity in the sentence *Our store sells alligator shoes* because our knowledge of the world tells us that alligators do not wear shoes, so it cannot mean "shoes for alligators." There are no semantic markers in the theory for such information. But why, asks Bolinger, should this be so? Where do markers like (Animal), (Physical object), and (Female) come from if not from knowledge of the world? What is wrong, then, with (Shoe-wearing) as a semantic marker? In any event, it is clear that the failure explicitly to include knowledge of the world in the semantic theory greatly limits its power as an explanation of the fluent speaker's ability to produce and understand the sentences of his language, both because such knowledge is part of the speaker's linguistic skill and because the interpretation of the very elements of the theory, the semantic markers, also depends on such knowledge.

Closely related to the role of knowledge of the world is the effect of the situational context on the understanding and production of language. This, too, is intentionally left out of the semantic theory and the linguistic theory generally, contributing greatly to their incompleteness as models of either competence or performance. Many utterances that may be linguistically ambiguous or anomalous are not so in the context of the setting in which they occur. Such grammatical complexities as recursions can often be explained on the basis of the situational context. Staats (in press) suggests, for example, how embedded phrases might occur under the influence of environmental stimuli, as when a football announcer, who began to say "The end is running downfield," changes this to "The end with the torn shirt runs downfield" upon noticing the player's ripped jersey. This is in agreement with Osgood's (1968) general point that in ordinary language use the semantic component is central and the syntactic component operates on its output, rather than the other way around, as the transformationists' competence model asserts. The views expressed in this section also accord with Olson's (1970) recent cognitive theory of semantics, which attributes semantic and syntactic decisions to the speaker's knowledge of the intended referent, rather than to deep syntactic structures.

On the status of deep structure in the linguistic model   The preceding comments lead to a reconsideration of the relationship between deep structure and semantics as viewed by Chomsky. The notion that deep structure is an essential level of linguistic description, distinct from the semantic level, has been widely accepted by students of transformational grammar, but there are indications that this attitude may be changing. McCawley (1968) recently analyzed various difficulties associated with Chomsky's conceptions, questioning particularly the value of postulating syntactic "selectional features," which are assigned to the base component of a grammar and which determine the semantic interpretation of a sentence. McCawley's analysis led him to conclude that, while there is a need to posit the existence of semantic and surface syntactic representation, the concept of an intermediate deep structure level may be unnecessary. It is in any case necessary to justify such a level, for

> . . . there is no a priori reason why a grammar could not instead consist of, say, a "formation-rule component," which specifies the membership of a class of well-formed semantic representations, and a "transformational component," which consists of rules correlating semantic representations with surface syntactic representations in much the same fashion in which Chomsky's "transformational component" correlates deep structures with surface syntactic representations. Moreover, the burden of proof in choosing between these two conceptions of linguistic competence rests with those who posit the existence of the extra level . . . (1968, p. 165).

McCawley goes on to suggest further that "the syntactic and semantic components of the earlier theory will have to be replaced by a single system of rules which convert semantic representation through various intermediate stages into surface syntactic representation" (p. 167). The semantic representations might be regarded as trees labeled with syntactic category labels, and the rules that convert semantic representation to surface structure therefore would "map ordered labeled trees onto ordered labeled trees" (p. 168), diminishing the traditional formal distinction between semantic and syntactic representations.

McCawley's proposals have far-reaching implications not only for linguistic theory but for psycholinguistic theory as well. Numerous psychological studies of language behavior to be reviewed below have tested theories based on the deep structure concept. If the latter is abandoned in favor of a more direct emphasis on semantic representation, the corresponding psycholinguistic theories would also have to be drastically modified. If the modifications followed McCawley's conception of grammar, they would likely involve an emphasis on the centrality of meaning quite in keeping with Osgood's general views on the issue, although not necessarily his particular interpretation of meaning. Be that as it may, much of the psycholinguistic research generated by transformational grammar has been based on the assumption that the deep structure concept is an essential part of linguistic theory at least, and our review of the research will necessarily reflect the emphasis it has been given to date.

Except for Bolinger's and McCawley's critiques, in which they view the semantic model in its own domain as a linguistic theory, this brief evaluation of the transformationist approach is not intended as a commentary on the adequacy of that model as a descriptive generalization about language as a formal system, in which regard it is generally acknowledged to be a revolutionary achievement, even by its critics (e.g., Uhlenbeck, 1967). Rather, it is a critique of the approach to the extent that psychological relevance is claimed for it. We have found it to be deficient from that viewpoint, but its fate as a psychological theory ultimately depends upon specific empirical data rather than argument alone.

EXPERIMENTAL EVIDENCE

The balance of the chapter deals with the research evidence bearing on the linguistic and associative approaches to psycholinguistic phenomena. Investigators in this area, as in others that we have considered in previous chapters, face the important problem of distinguishing operationally between relevant variables in such a manner that a clear test of the alternative conceptual models is possible. Linguistically oriented psycholinguists, being especially concerned with the psychological relevance of theories of grammar, typically have sought to differentiate the effects of grammatical variables from those of associative and nonsyntactical semantic factors. This has been difficult enough, but transformational grammar creates the further complication that surface structure and deep structure also must be operationally distinguished. Thus variables related to the former include, for example, grammaticality and phrase-structure analyses of strings of words, whereas those related to deep structure include manipulations of such factors as the complexity of the transformational history or of the deep structure of sentences as defined in the theory of transformational grammar. Associative approaches have been faced with the converse problem of controlling grammatical and semantic factors while attempting to manipulate intraverbal associative habits. These attempts have met with varying degrees of success, but we shall see later that any conclusions arising from linguistically or associatively based studies must be interpreted cautiously because the studies have uniformly ignored variables that, when manipulated, reveal the separate contributions of imaginal and verbal symbolic systems in language behavior.

The research review is organized into four major sections, dealing with perception and comprehension on the decoding side and production and memory on the encoding side of language behavior. Each section seeks to differentiate between the effects of grammatical, associative, and semantic factors, but the major emphasis is on the first of these because they have received most attention in the recent literature.

Perception

Psycholinguistic studies of perception have been guided primarily by linguistic approaches aimed at demonstrating the effectiveness of grammatical variables and the operation of implicit rules or structural analyses in the perception of sentences. However, systematic comparisons with associative and semantic variables have been rare in this area and only the most tentative generalizations are possible on the basis of the data.

G. A. Miller and Isard (1963) attempted to differentiate the effects of syntactic and semantic features of spoken sentences on their intelligibility. The basic material consisted of a series of five-word, normal grammatical sentences, such as *Colorless cellophane packages crackle loudly.* A second set consisted of word sequences with the same syntactical structure as the normal grammatical sentences, constructed by selecting the first word from the first sentence of the normal set, the second from the second sentence, and so on. The resulting sentences therefore were "grammatical" but semantically anomalous, e.g., *Colorless yellow ideas sleep furiously.* A third set consisted of ungrammatical strings constructed by haphazardly scrambling the words from different sentences (e.g., *Sleep roses dangerously young colorless*). Subjects listened to the recorded sentences spoken in the presence of masking noise and attempted to repeat what they heard. The results of three experiments showed that the normal grammatical sentences were easiest to hear, the semantically anomalous sequences were intermediate, and the ungrammatical strings were the most difficult to perceive. Figure 12-3 shows the data for one of the experiments. Miller and Isard interpreted these findings in terms of the use of nonphonological linguistic rules—both syntactic and semantic—as opposed to simple stimulus probabilities in the perception of sentences. However, the nature of such rules and just how they are used in perception remained unspecified. It is by no means certain, moreover, that grammatical and semantic factors were effectively teased apart by the procedure, inasmuch as the grammatical but semantically anomalous sentences may have been more meaningful (in some bizarre sense) than the ungrammatical strings.

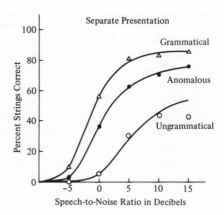

FIGURE 12-3.   Percent strings heard correctly as a function of speech-to-noise ratio when each type of test material is presented separately. From Miller and Isard (1963, Figure 3, p. 223).

A series of studies designed to reveal perceptual effects of phrase structure was initiated by Fodor and Bever (1965). Their subjects listened to tape-recorded sentences, each of which had an auditory "click" superimposed at some point. The clicks in different sentences were oriented around the major constituent break, as determined by a phrase-structure analysis. For example, in the sentence *That he was happy was evident from the way he smiled,* the major break is between *happy* and *was.* For one copy of this sentence, the click was located at this major break; in other copies the clicks were placed progressively farther from the break. The subjects were required to write down a sentence immediately after it was presented and then indicate by a slash where they thought the click had occurred. Fodor and Bever hypothesized that errors in click locations would be systematically related to the structural descriptions of the sentences. Consistent with this hypothesis, the majority of errors were in the direction of the major constituent break, as though the clicks were "attracted" toward such boundaries. Subsequent experiments (see Garrett & Fodor, 1968, pp. 465–466) controlled for such variables as memory and acoustic features that might mark the constituent boundaries. The effect was not modified by these controls, apparently justifying the conclusion that perception of sentences is an active process involving a structural analysis rather than a passive response to acoustic cues.

A recent experiment by Feldmar (1969) raises important questions about the click phenomenon and its interpretation. Feldmar presented each stimulus sentence twice in succession with one click superimposed on each presentation. The location of the clicks was systematically varied around the major syntactic break. In one condition, subjects gave an immediate judgment of the order of occurrence of the two clicks and then recalled the sentence and marked the location of the clicks. In the other condition, they first recalled the sentence and marked the location of the clicks. The major findings of relevance to the present context was that click location errors were significantly related to variation in the constituent boundaries when sentences were recalled prior to the click judgments, which essentially confirms what Fodor and Garrett found, but when the order of clicks was judged immediately after stimulus presentation, no tendency for clicks to migrate toward constituent boundaries was observed. The "click migration" phenomenon thus appears to be related to memory and response factors rather than to perceptual (input) factors, although Feldmar concluded that the issue remains to be definitively resolved, particularly in view of the complexity of the phenomenon.

The preceding experiments were concerned with the effect of surface structure on perception. A study by Mehler and Carey (1967) investigated perceptual effects of both surface and base (deep) structure. Their subjects listened to a series of eleven sentences embedded in white noise. Following each sentence, they recorded what they had heard. Each series was so constructed that the first 10 sentences were identical in either surface or base structure and the 11th was a syntactically different test sentence. Thus the intention was to induce a set for a particular grammatical structure in the hope that this might impede the perception of sentences with different structures. Consistent with this hypothesis, perception scores for the test sentences showed that changes in both surface and base structure disrupted perception, with surface structure having the stronger effect.

In general, then, the perception studies provide some evidence of the psychological relevance of grammar, but the effects of grammatical, associative, and semantic variables are yet to be systematically compared in perceptual tasks.

Comprehension

The central question to be considered in this section is the extent to which syntactic theory alone can account for a subject's ability to understand connected discourse. A number of investigators have extended G. A. Miller's (1962) psychological interpretation of transformational grammar to the study of sentence comprehension. The basic assumption is that subjects understand complex sentences by decoding them to their underlying kernels, according to an early version of the hypothesis (e.g., Gough, 1965), or to their underlying deep structures, according to a later version (Gough, 1966). It follows that the ease of understanding of sentences is a function of their *transformational complexity*, i.e., the number and nature of the transformations that separate a sentence from its underlying kernel or structure. Predictions from this hypothesis hinge on how grammatical theory defines the various transformational operations and on the psychological relevance of such operations (Garrett & Fodor, 1968). It has been inferred from the grammar that the order of complexity of sentence types is from kernel (simple, active, affirmative, declarative), to negative, to passive, to passive-negative in increasing order of difficulty. Initial support for such an ordering was provided by the results of a sentence-matching test of the time required to perform grammatical transformations (G. A. Miller, 1962). The experiments under consideration here extended the above reasoning to the problem of comprehension of sentences as measured by the time required to make the decision that a sentence is true or false with respect to a referent situation.

Gough (1965) used stimulus sentences such as "The boy hit the girl" or "The boy kicked the girl," and the negative, passive, and negative-passive transformations of these kernels. The "events" that confirmed or falsified the sentences were ink drawings depicting the possible permutations of a boy or a girl hitting or kicking a boy or a girl. Each sentence was read to the subject, followed immediately by the exposure of a picture. His task was to depress one of two buttons indicating his judgment of whether the sentence was true or false with respect to the picture.

Gough's results showed considerable agreement with the transformational decoding hypothesis in that verification time increased from kernel, to passive, to negative, to negative-passive. However, the ordering of the passive and negative sentences departs from expectations, inasmuch as the passive is assumed to be grammatically more complex than the negative—an assumption that G. A. Miller's (1962) data on transformational complexity supported. Gough's data also revealed that truth value interacted with the affirmative-negative variable in such a manner that true judgments were faster than false in the case of affirmative (kernel and passive) but not negative sentences. These findings were interpreted to mean that the difference between affirmative and negative sentences must include a semantic component as well as a syntactic transformation, for the difference between true and false sentences is semantic.

Experiments by McMahon (1963) and Slobin (1966) involved the same general procedure as Gough's and in general yielded the same ordering of verification speed for the four types of sentences. In the case of Slobin's study, the ordering was obtained with children as well as adults, and the differences were particularly strong when the sentences and referent situations were ones in which the subject and the object are reversible (e.g., The dog is chasing the cat). With nonreversible sentences (e.g., The girl is watering the flowers), the difference between active (affirmative or negative) sentences and their passive counterparts was largely washed out. Slobin interpreted the latter finding to mean that nonreversibility presents fewer opportunities for confusion, since there is only one probable subject and one probable object of action. Nonreversibility therefore facilitates comprehension of passive sentences because the logical subject and object are easily distinguished despite a reversal of grammatical subject and object. While some features of Slobin's results were discrepant from those of McMahon and Gough, they lead to the same general conclusion that syntactic theory alone cannot account for the data—semantic factors are important as well and can sometimes override the effect of syntax.

Gough (1966) tested the transformational decoding hypothesis further by introducing a 3-second delay between the end of the sentence and the picture that verified it. He reasoned that if the sentence has to be reduced to its underlying structure before it can be understood, as the hypothesis implies, then the delay interval would permit such a transformation to be completed, and subsequent verification time would reflect only the verification process and not the transformation. Any differences attributable to transformational complexity should therefore be eliminated or reduced under the delay condition as compared to the conditions of the earlier experiment, in which the verifying picture immediately followed the sentence. The results of the experiment failed to confirm the prediction, for active sentences were still verified faster than passive, and negative faster than affirmative. Gough concluded that while a transformational description of sentence complexity remains plausible, the transformational decoding hypothesis of the process of comprehension is weakened. He considered sentence length as an alternative explanation, since length had been confounded with transformational complexity in the earlier studies. A second experiment showed, however, that the active-passive difference is not an artifact of sentence length.

V. A. Morris, Rankine, and Reber (1968) essentially replicated Gough's (1966) study, with the modification that their subjects reconstructed the Noun-Verb-Noun relations in input sentences by pressing a set of labeled keys in the proper sequence (e.g., "girl-kick-boy" for the sentence "The boy was kicked by the girl") instead of verifying the sentences with respect to pictures. The results replicated Gough's when the subjects responded immediately, but when their response was delayed by 3 seconds, the differences between sentence types were washed out, contrary to Gough's results but consistent with the transformational decoding hypothesis. Morris et al. concluded that response availability is crucial in finding support for the hypothesis. They also stressed the importance of semantic factors in the effects and the possibility that many of the results might be alternatively explained in terms of a surface structure model (Yngve, 1960; see later discussions).

The above findings strongly suggest that verification time in studies such as those of Gough, McMahon, and Slobin is not a function of understanding but of the verification process. Gough speculated that this process may involve a comparison of sentence and verifying event in terms of habitual ways of describing such events. Normally the active voice is used in such descriptions, and the difficulty of the comparison process may be a function of the discrepancy between the order of events in a given sentence (e.g., a passive) and those in the implicit (active) description, or it may involve a habitual order of scanning pictured events, where the scanning habits themselves derive from descriptive habits. As already noted, Slobin (1966) considers similar interpretations of the "mismatch" between sentence and event. These suggestions raise important questions concerning the nature of the mediating process in sentence comprehension, to which we shall return after considering one more illustrative experiment.

Stolz (1967) asked whether native speakers of English can behave as if they have direct access to the highly abstract grammatical rules and constructs in-

cluded in theories such as Chomsky's. If they can, they should be able to understand readily any novel sentence as long as its structural description conforms to
the rules of their language. In short, their comprehension should reflect the productivity of the grammatical rules. To answer this question, Stolz presented to
his subjects self-embedded relative clause sentences such as *The vase that the
maid that the agency hired dropped broke on the floor.* A subject was required
to decode the sentence into its component clauses and to write each clause as
a simple sentence. Stolz reasoned that, if a subject is able immediately to decode
the sentence correctly, he is displaying productivity in its strong sense as predicted by linguists. If he is able to process them only after encountering several
examples of the same structure, he might be described as having learned the
structure during the experiment and as displaying productivity in a weaker
sense. Finally, if he performs only at a chance level, he would not be displaying
productivity at all.

On the assumption that some subjects would not display strong productivity,
Stolz introduced two types of clues that might help subjects to learn the relevant
grammatical rule. One was a feedback condition in which subjects were given a
paraphrase of the sentence, revealing its meaning, after their decoding attempt.
Another clue was to have the semantic structure of the sentence support the
syntax, so that, if all possible Noun-Verb-Noun sequences were considered, only
the correct ones would be semantically sensible. The above example (The vase
that the maid . . . etc.) is an illustration of such semantic constraint. By contrast, *The dog that the cat that the bird fought scolded approached the colt*
exemplifies a semantically neutral sentence in which all possible Noun-Verb-
Noun sequences would be meaningful.

The semantic constraint variable and the presence or absence of feedback
were factorially varied among independent groups of subjects, who were presented a block of sentences of one combination of the two variables, e.g., a
semantically supported sentence followed by feedback. All subjects were then
presented, without feedback, a second block of sentences that were semantically
neutral. The results showed generally that only about half the subjects displayed
strong productivity, i.e., they could decode the structures without the aid of
semantic clues or feedback. The results for the second block of sentences showed
that the only condition under which the structures were effectively learned was
when feedback was coupled with an absence of semantic constraints in the first
block. Stolz concluded that subjects may rely heavily on semantic information—
word meanings—in decoding a sentence. Thus when such information was present in the first block of sentences in the experimental situation, syntactic processing may have been largely bypassed, and subjects failed to learn the structural
rule necessary for decoding the semantically neutral sentences in the second half
of the experiment. When semantically neutral sentences were presented in the
first half, however, the subjects were unable to interpret them semantically and
were accordingly forced to attend to feedback information in order to learn the
syntax. The learning then generalized to the second block of sentences.

The comprehension studies reviewed above support the psychological relevance of grammar in that transformational complexity correlates reasonably well with ease of comprehension, and that a grammatical rule (recursive self-embedding) can be used readily by some subjects and learned by others in an experimental session. *But the studies do not uniformly support the more specific hypothesis that the cognitive processes involved in comprehension parallel the steps involved in the derivation of a sentence according to transformational rules. What they do show consistently is that word meaning plays a crucial role in comprehension and verification—a role that overrides syntactical information unless care is taken to suppress relevant semantic cues.* The nature of the effective meaning process and of the more general symbolic activity that mediates the behavioral indices of comprehension remains obscure in these studies, however. The verification latency experiments are potentially important in this regard because they permit one to incorporate features of the referent situation into one's theoretical account. The suggested interpretations (e.g., Gough, 1966; Slobin, 1966) have tended to emphasize implicit verbal descriptions of those situations as containing the relevant syntactic or semantic information, but this is not the only possibility. The sentences, when concrete, may be decoded instead into nonverbal imagery and the information in the image compared with the information in the referent picture or sentence. Such information could also be involved in the mediation of other reactions such as the button-pressing sequence in the task used by V. A. Morris et al. (1968). The experiments under consideration were not designed to test such a possibility, but we shall see that an interpretation of comprehension and verification partly in terms of imagery is supported by the results of a number of recent experiments, to be considered in detail in the next chapter.

Verbal Production

Information on factors that affect verbal production can be found in the literature on word associations (e.g., Woodworth, 1938; Laffal, 1965). Some of the relevant findings have been mentioned in this book from time to time, and no further systematic review of such data will be attempted here. Rather, the major emphasis will again be on larger linguistic units on the response side and on grammatical structure (along with semantic and associative factors) on the input side.

A body of research has dealt with the relation between linguistic variables and speech hesitations (silent pauses, filled pauses such as "ahs," and various other nonfluencies of speech). The findings are relevant here because they could throw light on factors that influence creative productivity in natural language. Goldman-Eisler (1958) showed that hesitation pauses preceded a sudden increase of information, estimated in terms of transition probabilities as determined by the accuracy with which judges could guess successive words in a sentence that had been produced by another speaker, given a preceding (or subsequent) part of the sentence as a context. That is, hesitations were associated with points of uncertainty in the message. These points did not coincide consistently with linguistic structure, however, although structure appeared to be one factor. Maclay and Osgood (1959) similarly found that hesitations coincided with points of uncertainty, and that these were related to both phrase boundaries and lexical choices within boundaries. Filled pauses such as "ahs" tended to coincide with phrase boundaries, whereas unfilled pauses fell within phrase boundaries. Maclay and Osgood viewed the data as supporting the notion of two levels of organization in encoding, viz., lexical (or semantic) and grammatical (or structural). Boomer (1965) found that the number of hesitations were much higher in the position following the first word of a phrase unit than in other locations, where the phrase unit was defined in terms of stress patterns in speech. These studies show that hesitations in speech are related to both structural and semantic variables, but the prediction of such phenomena is as yet quite uncertain, perhaps because their occurrence is determined by emotional-motivational as well as cognitive factors (see, e.g., Lay & Paivio, 1969; A. Reynolds & Paivio, 1968). It will be seen later (Chapter 13) that one semantic variable (abstractness-concreteness) is particularly important, implicating imagery in the phenomenon.

Other investigations using various dependent variables have presented both positive and negative evidence for the role of grammatical structure in the generation of sentences. Consistent with the transformational view that kernel sentences are less complex than their transformations, Singh, Brokaw, and Black (1967) found that oral reading of kernels was less disrupted by interfering sidetone or noise than were the transformations. On the other hand, H. H. Clark (1965), using measures of diversity and covariation of words used by subjects to generate sentences, found evidence that subjects did not generate passive sentences simply by transforming active sentences. Instead, subjects apparently generated the sentences sequentially from left to right. The different studies are not comparable because of the many differences in design and procedure, but they serve to reinforce the conclusion from the research on sentence comprehension that the transformational model does not generate predictions about grammatical behavior that are consistently supported, and to this extent at least it must be regarded as insufficient.

Some interesting support for the operation of grammatical category as a mediator of sentence generation was obtained by Pylyshyn and Feldmar (1968). Words such as *cross*, which are grammatically ambiguous (they can be used either as a noun or a verb) were paired with nonsense words rendered unambiguous as to part of speech by appending suitable noun endings (e.g., -INESS, -ILITY) or verb endings (e.g., -IVATE, -ILIZE). A posttest following paired-associate learning of such pairs showed that the ambiguous words were disambiguated by the associative experience inasmuch as they were used in sentences predominantly as words of the same part of speech as the associated nonsense word. Although the effect was restricted to individual words in their experiment, Pylyshyn and Feldmar suggested that the conceptualization might be applicable to larger grammatical units such as phrases. Thus the abstract symbols of generative grammars (NP, VP, and the like) might be viewed as functioning psychologically as mediators. This is an explicit statement of what transformational approaches to sentence processing imply, and we shall see later that it is also implicit in surface-structure models of memory (e.g., N. F. Johnson, 1965; Yngve, 1960).

Effects of verbal associative relationships on sentence production have also been demonstrated in a number of studies. J. L. Prentice (1968) found that, in a sentence-completion task, word-associates were put into the same sentence more often than nonassociates. Rosenberg (1967) asked subjects to write stories that included groups of associatively related or associatively unrelated nouns. Complex sentences produced by the subjects were analyzed into basic underlying sentences. For example, the sentence *A needle, thread, and pin are helpful if you want to do some sewing* would be reduced to four sentences: *A needle is helpful. A thread is helpful. A pin is helpful. You want to do some sewing.* The results showed that associatively related nouns that occurred in the same complex sentence were more likely than unrelated nouns to appear as identical constituents in the same underlying sentences, whereas the unrelated nouns more often occurred in different underlying sentences. These studies indicated a relationship between association and syntax that cannot be ignored in any theoretical analysis of the psychology of linguistic structure.

Memory and Learning

The bulk of the systematic evidence on the psychological relevance of grammar and on the role of associative and semantic factors in sentence processing comes from studies of memory and learning. The psychological construct of unitization, or chunking, runs as an explicit or implicit orienting theme through much of this research, for the evidence indicates that subjects remember sentences or passages in which the number of elementary units (e.g., words) exceeds memory span by somehow chunking them into higher-order units. This concept has already been discussed at some length in Chapter 7 and elsewhere. The central issue in the present instance is the identification of the language variables that are used as the basis for chunking, and the psychological nature of the processes through which the variables operate.

Order of approximation to English   Evidence on the effects of linguistic variables on chunking and recall has been obtained using the G. A. Miller and Selfridge (1950) procedure for varying the degree to which a sequence of words approximates the statistical structure of English. Miller and Selfridge varied sequential dependencies in terms of the number of items that determine the next one in the sequence. Thus a zero-order approximation consisted of words drawn at random from Thorndike and Lorge (1944); the first-order approximation took into account the relative frequencies of words in the language (achieved by scrambling the words from higher-order lists); the second-order of approximation was developed by presenting a common word such as *he, it,* or *the* to a subject with instructions to use it in a sentence. The word he used directly after the given word was then given to another subject, who similarly used it in a sentence; and so on, until a sequence of the desired length was achieved. For higher-order approximations, the length of the determining context was increased, up to six adjacent words for a seventh order of approximation to English. A final set of words was taken directly from literary passages. Miller and Selfridge found that, when such lists were presented to subjects for recall, the number of words recalled increased with approximation to English up to the fifth order, with no further increase for seventh order and text material. This relation was particularly strong with relatively long lists.

That chunking is involved in the order-of-approximation effect was clearly demonstrated in the Tulving and Patkau (1962) experiment, previously summarized in Chapter 7. They found that the number of words recalled as an uninterrupted sequence ("adopted chunks") increased with approximation to English—that is, the closer the approximation to English, the more words in the chunk—but the number of chunks recalled remained invariant at about six. Their findings suggest that the facilitating effect of approximation to English can be accounted for in terms of the length of the sequence that functions as a unit during recall. However, the nature of the effective linguistic variable is not revealed by such data. Miller and Selfridge (1950) had originally interpreted their finding in terms of sequential constraints—"short range associations that are familiar to the *Ss*"—as opposed to meaning. In the context of the chunking hypothesis, their interpretation implies that unitization is dependent upon word-to-word associative habits. However, such associations are confounded with grammaticality and with semanticity when order of approximation is varied. Coleman (1965) found that, when strings were ranked by subjects for grammaticalness, order of approximation correlated highly with grammaticalness. Thus chunking (hence recall) also could be based on grammatical cues rather than associations. Similarly, meaningfulness or semanticity in general appears to increase with degree of approximation. The different variables have been investigated in subsequent research.

Salzinger, Portnoy, and Feldman (1962) applied the "cloze" procedure, in which subjects are required to guess words that have been deleted from a passage, to 50-word passages from Miller and Selfridge (1950). They found that the proportion of words correctly guessed increased from zero order to seventh order. In addition, the proportion of words in the same grammatical category as the deleted words increased from zero to third order, while the number of exact correct words continued to increase for higher-order approximations. From these findings Salzinger et al. inferred that the improvement in memory observed by other investigators must be attributed primarily to increased syntactic structure between orders 1 and 2, about equally to syntax and meaning between orders 2 and 3, and primarily to meaning beyond order 3.

Results consistent with the Salzinger et al. hypothesis have been reported by Tejirian (1968). He tested recall for standard passages varying from first to sixth order of approximation, and for comparable passages in which the words in particular grammatical categories were randomly altered in such a manner that their semantic structure varied while syntactic structure remained constant. He found that the number of words correctly recalled could be accounted for entirely by syntactic structure up to third order, whereas differences in semantic structure alone accounted for increases beyond the third order. On the basis of further analysis, Tejirian concluded that syntactic and semantic structure facilitated recall primarily by enabling subjects to group words into chunks of varying lengths, while the number of chunks recalled remained relatively constant. The findings are thus consistent with the Tulving and Patkau (1962) hypothesis and also show that both grammaticalness and meaning contribute somehow to chunking and recall proficiency. However, they do not reveal the nature of the specific grammatical or semantic variables that are involved in the effects, nor do they throw light on the nature of the symbolic processes through which the variables operate.

Surface structure and transition error probability Studies designed to identify the effective grammatical variables in chunking and recall and to test psychological interpretations of such effects have taken either surface structure or deep structure as their point of departure. Focusing on surface structure, N. F. Johnson (1965) hypothesized that subjects may chunk to-be-recalled material into phrase units on the basis of their knowledge of grammar. To test this hypothesis, he had subjects learn sentences as responses to digits in a paired-associate learning task. Their responses were scored for the conditional probability that the words in the sentences were wrong, given that the immediately preceding word was correct. Johnson assumed that the pattern of these transition error probabilities (TEPs) for a sentence would reveal functional subunits in that the TEP would be relatively high at the boundaries of phrase units and low within units. For example, in the sentence *The tall boy saved the dying woman*, there should be a higher probability of an error on the transition between *boy* and *saved* than on any other. The results were consistent with this expectation. In addition, TEPs varied within phrases, with the pattern of variation seeming to reflect the phrase structure of the entire sentence as determined by an immediate constituent analysis. The findings have been confirmed and extended in subsequent studies (see N. F. Johnson, 1968).

While the TEP data relate chunking to grammatical units, they do not in themselves indicate that grammatical structure per se, rather than association or meaning, is the basis of the grouping. N. F. Johnson (1966) argued that subjects do in fact use the structure in a manner predictable from his theory of sentence generation. According to the theory, which is similar to one proposed by Yngve (1960; see below), subjects generate sentences by decoding higher-order encoding units into their constituents. Thus a stimulus first elicits a recoding device that represents the entire sentence. The speaker then applies a decoding rule that translates the sentence into Subject and Predicate; he stores Predicate in his short-term memory while he further decodes Subject into Article plus Modified Noun; and so on. One implication of the model is that any associations involved are probably between the hypothetical decoding operations rather than the responses themselves. The operations involved in producing a phrase are adjacent; those involved in going from one phrase to the next are not. Consider the sentence *The tall boy saved the dying woman.* The model assumes that when the subject produces *tall,* he then recovers "Noun" from memory and decodes it into *boy.* Thus there should be a direct association between *tall* and *boy.* However, after *boy* is produced the next step is to recover "Predicate" from memory and decode it into "Verb" plus "Noun Phrase." Only then is the Verb decoded into *saved,* and there should accordingly be no direct association between *boy* and *saved* when the subject learns the sentence.

Johnson tested the hypothesis by having subjects learn sentences as paired-associate responses. Prior to the task, the subjects were given another paired-associate task to establish adjective-noun (within phrase) or noun-verb (between phrase) associations between items to be subsequently used in the sentence learning task. On the basis of the theoretical model, it was expected that the adjective-noun association would transfer to sentence learning, thereby reducing the probability of errors on that transition, whereas the noun-verb association would not show such transfer because the direct association presumably is not used to integrate the noun-verb transition. The results were entirely consistent with the hypothesis.

Rosenberg (1968) argued that Johnson's failure to find a significant effect of associative habit upon transition errors at the phrase boundary could be attributed to the weakness of laboratory-established, as compared to natural-language, associations. Rosenberg investigated this possibility by having subjects learn sentences containing strong between- and within-phrase interword associations (e.g., *The old king ruled wisely*) or ones containing weak associations (e.g., *The poor king dined gravely*) throughout. The TEP patterns for the two experiments were consistent in suggesting that the words in the low-association sentences are indeed recoded into phrase units but that the words in the high-association sentences are recoded into units that transcend the phrase boundary. Moreover, the probability of transition errors at the phrase boundary decreased as associative strength across the boundary increased. Rosenberg concluded that, in learning the sentence, the subjects recode the words into the largest chunks possible, the recoding being based upon the syntactic and associative-semantic structure of the sentence. Furthermore, the associative-semantic relations revealed by association norms appear to be more important than phrase structure in recall, as indicated by the fact that high-association sentences were easier to recall than low-association sentences.

Grammatical nonsense material and recall   Other investigators have used nonsense strings containing grammatical morphemes in an attempt to determine the "pure" effect of syntactical (surface) structure on learning independent of meaningfulness, familiarity, and transitional dependency. Epstein (1961, 1962a) achieved such structure in one series of sentences by the use of nonsense syllables along with two function words without referential meaning (e.g., articles) and by adding grammatical tags, such as *ed,* to syllable stems. This procedure generated such Alice-in-Wonderland sentences as, *A vapy koobs* *desaked the citar molently um glox nerfs.* In other sentences, the grammatical tags were omitted or items were randomized. Two further categories involved meaningful words that were sententially meaningless (like the anomalous strings used by G. A. Miller & Isard, 1963; see above) and were either syntactically or randomly structured. Subjects learned each sentence by the method of serial recall. The results showed that the syntactically structured material was easier to learn than the unstructured material. Epstein (1963) attributed the effect to a "temporal schema," which refers to syntactical constraints placed on the temporal ordering of items within a structured series, as distinguished from rhythmical patterning and left-to-right transition dependencies. Although the data did not indicate how such a schema operates to facilitate recall, Epstein suggested that it might do so because it is congruent with the forward recall strategy adopted by most of his subjects.

Positive effects of syntactic structure using nonsense items were also obtained by Forster (1966), but other studies have yielded negative results. In an unpublished study, Rosenberg (cited in Dunne, 1968) used strings of four consonant-vowel-consonant syllables (CVCs) of low and approximately equal association value, controlling for letter similarity. The CVCs in different strings contained grammatical, ungrammatical, or no endings. No differences in recall were found for the various strings. Dunne (1968) reasoned that grammatical structure may be facilitative only when subjects perceive the structure and are therefore able to take advantage of it to organize recall. To test this, subjects were required to learn unstructured, grammatically structured, or scrambled-structured strings of CVCs under instructions which either cued or did not cue for structure. The results showed no effect of the instructional set and, contrary to Epstein's and Forster's findings, performance on the unstructured sequences was superior to the structured and scrambled-structured strings combined. Dunne suggested that structure may impede learning by increasing the amount of material to be learned. After examining previous studies, she concluded that a syntactic facilitation effect may depend upon the meaningfulness of the material, occurring only when the nonsense items are more "wordlike" than the CVCs used in her study, or when real words are used, as in the following study.

Marks and Miller (1964) tested free recall for meaningful grammatical and semantically anomalous sentences, anagram strings formed by scrambling the word order of normal sentences so that the semantic components remained intact but the syntactic structure was destroyed, and word lists formed by scrambling the anomalous sentences. The results showed that normal sentences were easiest and word lists most difficult to recall, while anagram strings and anomalous sentences were intermediate in difficulty. An analysis of types of errors revealed, in addition, that semantic errors (intrusions of words from one string to another) occurred most frequently in anomalous sentences and word lists, whereas syntactic errors (bound-morpheme errors—viz., omission or incorrect addition of prefixes and suffixes—and inversions of words within strings) occurred most often in anagram strings and word lists. Thus the error scores differentiated between semantic and syntactic factors, and showed that both facilitated learning.

Slamecka (1969) obtained similar results using a recognition rather than a recall test of memory, indicating that the differences in the Marks-Miller study indeed reflected a memory effect rather than response reconstruction.

The above studies involved essentially dichotomous scaling of degree of grammaticalness. Coleman (1965) used a form of generative grammar to generate a four-level scale of grammaticalness. Level I was generated by randomly drawing words from English prose. Level II was generated by drawing words according to restrictions imposed by several rules of the generative grammar. Levels III and IV involved progressively greater numbers of such rules. The psychological meaningfulness of grammatical level was demonstrated by the findings that naive subjects ranked the word sets of the different levels in the predicted order of grammaticalness, and that the ease of learning the sets was a function of grammatical level. Inspection of the scales also shows that grammaticalness correlates with meaning, with word strings of Level IV being "almost meaningful" (e.g., *They pushed back the homes first*). Note that the last observation again points to the difficulty of teasing apart grammaticalness and semanticity at the real-word level.

A similar problem has been encountered in attempts to differentiate interword associations and grammaticality, although their separation apparently is easier than the separation of meaning from either. Thus Rosenberg (1966) compared the effects of syntactic and associative relationships on sentence recall in a factorial design involving grammatical versus ungrammatical word order as one variable and high, moderate, and low free-association strength between words as the other. Subjects were given four study and recall trials with a list of sentences. The results showed that recall was facilitated by grammatical order and by high (as compared to moderate or low) associative strength. The variables did not interact, indicating that their effects were independent. An analysis of errors revealed that more syntactic errors occurred in the recall of ungrammatical than grammatical sentences, and intrusion errors were more frequent in the recall of sentences of low or moderate interword associative strength than ones of high strength, paralleling the distributions of syntactic and semantic errors obtained by Marks and Miller (1964).

The above findings justify the empirical generalization that grammaticality can facilitate learning and recall, to some extent independent of associative habits and semanticity, with the possible qualification that grammaticality and meaning interact in such a manner that the former is effective when varied using real words but relatively ineffective when varied by adding grammatical endings to nonsense syllable stems. It is also possible, as N. F. Johnson (1968, pp. 433–435) concluded, that the facilitating effect of grammar is small in absolute terms and in comparison with the effect of variation in meaningfulness when grammaticality is held constant. The latter suggestion should be viewed cautiously, however, because inferences concerning the relative effectiveness of grammatical and semantic factors must be based on studies in which the two are varied not only independently but over a comparable range of values as well. This type of control has not been achieved in the research to date, although in principle the problem is identical to that encountered in studies concerned with the relative effects of different word attributes in verbal learning (cf. Chapter 8) and presumably could be similarly investigated using appropriate scaling techniques.

With the exception of Coleman's (1965) attempt to scale grammaticalness on the basis of the rules of a generative grammar, the above studies were generally concerned with surface-structure variables rather than deep structure. We turn now to research on the latter and to studies that have compared transformational grammar and surface structure models as predictors of memory.

Surface structure versus transformational complexity in sentence memory

Extending his transformational decoding hypothesis to memory, G. A. Miller (1962) proposed that a subject remembers a nonkernel sentence by first transforming it to its underlying kernel sentence and then storing the kernel along with the appropriate transformational rule as a footnote or tag. Thus *The girl was hit by the boy* presumably would be stored as some kind of representation corresponding to *The boy hit the girl* plus a tag indicating that a passive transformation is required for recall. One implication of this notion is that kernel sentences should be easier to remember than nonkernels because there is less to store in the former case.

The initial experimental tests yielded impressive support for Miller's hypothesis. Mehler (1963) found that prompted recall was higher for kernel (simple, active, affirmative, declarative) sentences than for any of seven transformations of the kernels. Also consistent with the hypothesis, the majority of syntactical errors involved responses nearer to the kernel than was the correct response, as though the subjects tended to simplify their responses grammatically. Savin and Perchonock (1965) reasoned ingeniously that the amount of memory space required for storing a sentence in immediate memory could be estimated from the amount of material that could be recalled in addition to the sentence. If kernels take up less of the capacity of immediate memory than do transformations, as the hypothesis implies, more additional material should be correctly recalled along with kernel sentences than with their transformations. Their experiment required subjects to recall a sentence and as many additional words as possible from a list of eight unrelated words that were presented immediately after the sentence. The results were consistent with the hypothesis: More words were recalled after kernels than after nonkernels, suggesting that transformational tags do indeed take up storage space.

Despite this early promise, subsequent studies have consistently failed to support the hypothesis. One series of these pitted transformational complexity against an alternative surface-structure model based on an index of the *structural complexity* of a sentence initially proposed by Yngve (1960). This measure assigns a number to each word in a sentence in such a manner that the more embedded the word in the sentence, the higher is the number assigned to it. This is formally done by drawing up a phrase-marker tree for the sentence and counting the number of left branches leading to each word. The mean of this set constitutes an index of the structural complexity, or "depth," of the sentence as a whole.

The psychological rationale behind the use of the depth measure as a predictor of recall was explicated and tested by E. Martin and Roberts (1966). The essence of the theory is that listening to and reproducing sentences involves sequential encoding responses to individual words, such responses including an anticipatory component or expectation of what is coming next. The particular encoding responses elicited by words, in the case of listening, depends upon the stimulus situation (word classes, pitch, stress, etc.) for the listener and the listener's linguistic habit structures (knowledge of word-word and class-class transition probabilities, etc.). In the case of sentence production (as in recall), a parallel analysis assumes that the encoding responses are a major component of what is stored in memory, and that these stored expectations function as commitments to reproduce a sentence in certain ways. The number of these expectations or commitments reflects the structural complexity of the sentence and determines the memory load imposed by the sentence.

Martin and Roberts illustrate the theoretical rationale and its relation to Yngve's depth index using the sentence *The new club member came early.* When the listener hears *The*, he expects to hear the rest of the noun phrase and a predicate of some kind. Corresponding commitments are incurred by the speaker in uttering the same sentence. Thus two expectations or commitments are aroused by the word *The*, which is said to be structurally embedded to a depth of 2. The words *new* and *club* similarly arouse expectations of the rest of the noun phrase and a predicate, and each is accordingly assigned to a depth of 2. The noun member has depth 1 because only the predicate is expected. The intonation of the verb *came* indicates something more to come and it is assigned a 1. Finally, the pitch and stress of the adverb *early* indicate that it is the terminal word and it is assigned depth 0. The sentence can thus be characterized by the numbers, 2, 2, 2, 1, 1, 0. The mean of these numbers represents the average depth of the sentence. According to the psychological model, the likelihood of recall of the sentence is inversely related to this depth index.

To compare the power of the surface structure and transformational models, Martin and Roberts varied sentence complexity, as defined by the Yngve depth index, and sentence kind (kernel and five transformations) in an orthogonal design, so that each sentence type included representatives of high and of low depth value. A set of six sentences was read aloud to the subjects for a series of six free recall trials. Consistent with the depth hypothesis, sentences of low mean depth were generally easier to remember, the differences being highly significant for all but two of the sentence types. Sentence kind, on the other hand, showed only one consistent effect: Kernels were uniformly *inferior* to nonkernels in recall, which is directly contrary to the prediction from the transformational model.

Roberts (1968) subsequently investigated the effects of mean depth, syntactic type (active versus passive), and associative direction between the subject and object of a sentence. All three variables had significant effects on free recall learning. Mean depth appeared to have the strongest and most consistent effect, while syntactic type and association had weaker effects that were qualified by interactions. Moreover, where syntactic type was effective, passive sentences were recalled better than actives, which again is consistent with E. Martin and Roberts (1966) but contrary to the transformation hypothesis.

The theoretical issue is further complicated by the results of other studies. Inexplicably, E. Martin and Roberts (1967) failed to replicate the depth effect obtained in their earlier studies. Perfetti (1969) tested the depth hypothesis in two experiments, one of which also included two transformational dimensions. Neither experiment supported the depth hypothesis—in fact, contrary to that hypothesis, certain sentence types in one experiment were easier to recall when their depth (i.e., structural complexity) was high rather than low. The transformational variables also proved to be ineffective except in interaction with mean depth. These negative findings indicate that the Yngve-type surface-structure model does not represent the psychological processes underlying memory for connected discourse any more adequately than does the transformational decoding hypothesis.

Other investigations have similarly failed to support the transformational model, while at the same time revealing the importance of nonsyntactic semantic variables. Slobin (1968) read brief stories in the passive voice to subjects ranging in age from 5 to 20 years, who were asked to retell the story as accurately as possible. One series of stories consisted of full passives in which the actor was mentioned. The following is a sentence from one such story: "On the first day of school Bob was introduced to his new teacher by the principal, and was given a reading book by the teacher." Another series consisted of truncated passives, without mention of the actor, e.g., "On the first day of school in September Bob was introduced to his new teacher, and was given an interesting reading book." The crucial question was whether there would be a tendency for truncated passives to be recalled in the active voice with a generalized actor, plus footnotes indicating passive voice and deletion of the underlying subject, as the transformational decoding hypothesis would suggest. The results showed that there was a significantly greater tendency for full passives than for truncated passives to be retold in the active voice (62 percent as compared to 39 percent), indicating that truncated passives are stored in a manner that facilitates retrieval of their original syntactical form. Slobin concluded that the underlying semantic content may influence the selection of a particular grammatical form in encoding a sentence, and that there is no uniform relationship between syntactic complexity and psychological complexity of sentences.

Bregman and Strasberg (1968) interpreted the transformational hypothesis to mean that the syntactical footnote is stored as an independent component in the retention of nonkernel sentences and is therefore independently forgettable. They tested this notion by a recognition test in which subjects attempted to identify the grammatical form in which each of a series of sentences had been presented. If wrong, they were given a second choice. It was found that the second guesses were correct more often than expected by chance, which was taken to discredit the original hypothesis because, if the syntactic symbol were the only representation of the grammatical form of the sentence, it should have been retained in an all-or-none manner. The fact that it was not, indicated that subjects reconstructed the syntactical form of the sentence from other aspects of their memories. The subjects' answers to a postexperimental questionnaire suggested that these other aspects included a number of semantic features such as truth value, salience of the surface subject, and action imagery. Bregman and Strasberg concluded that *the findings require a theory of sentence recall that distinguishes between the transmission code (the sentence form) and the semantic message (the idea or meaning). The former is generally forgotten once it has done its job and the semantic message has been decoded.* Essentially the same point has been made by others (e.g., Brent, 1969; Fillenbaum, 1966; Sachs, 1967a). Later, we will examine the relevance of these views to the two-process model of meaning and mediation as applied to memory for sentences.

The experimental evidence thus appears to be overwhelmingly against the transformational decoding hypothesis, but it should be noted that the positive findings obtained by Savin and Perchonock (1965) were not directly challenged by the above studies, none of which replicated the Savin and Perchonock design. Recent replications by Matthews (1968) and Glucksberg and Danks (1969) suggest, however, that Savin and Perchonock's results can be attributed to differential word-recall delays rather than to space taken up by grammatical markers in immediate memory—the more complex the sentence, the longer the delay between word presentation and word recall. Error data also failed to support the transformational model in the Glucksberg and Danks experiments. *The conclusion is compelling that the transformational interpretation of memory for sentences is entirely without support,* and we must look for an alternative predictive model.

Complexity of deep structure in memory   Still within the framework of transformational grammar, a final theoretical possibility is that deep structure itself plays a role in sentence processing independent of transformational complexity. Evidence favoring such an interpretation has emerged from a series of experiments by Rohrman (1968), who contrasted his approach with the surface-structure model presented by Martin and Roberts (1966). Rohrman questioned their theory and evidence on several grounds but, since we have already seen that the model lacks firm support, we need consider only his most serious objection: In trying to vary the Yngve depth index and transformational complexity orthogonally, Martin and Roberts introduced uncontrolled but systematic changes in deep structure that entirely confounded their manipulations of surface structure.

Rohrman controlled for such shortcomings and tested the predictive power of deep structure by comparing memory for English subject nominalizations, such as *growling lions*, and object nominalizations, such as *raising flowers*, which are identical in surface structure but differ in the complexity of their underlying structures. The deep structures from which they are derived are shown in Figure 12-4, where it can be seen that the object nominalization has an extra node. Moreover, while both deep structures undergo one transformation to reach the surface form, they differ in the type of transformation involved: Subject nominalizations involve a permutation transformation to reverse the order of elements (from *lions growl* to *growling lions*), whereas the object nominalizations involve a deletion transformation to eliminate the indefinite nominal (PRO) functioning as the subject of the underlying string (*PRO raise flowers* becomes *raising flowers*). Stated simply, an element essential to the meaning of the object nominalizations is missing from their surface structure—*raising flowers* implies that *someone* raises flowers. The dummy element is explicit only in the deep structure. The subject nominalizations involve no such element—that "lions growl" is clear in the surface structure of *growling lions*. Thus the object nominalizations are more complex than the subject nominalizations in their deep structure but not in their surface structure, and they differ in their transformational two kinds of speeches also differed in vocabulary level and sentence length, so the finding is only suggestive, though consistent with what would be expected.

The experimental test of the hypothesis involved presentations of 10 nominalizations, five of each type, for a single free recall trial. Consistent with expectations, significantly more subject than object nominalizations were recalled. Two further experiments, in which the procedure was modified to control for certain factors, yielded the same result. A final experiment involved nominalizations that differed in their transformational histories but were equivalent in the complexity of their deep structures. No difference in recall was obtained in this case, indicating that the effect in the three prior experiments could be attributed to complexity of deep structure rather than to differences in the type of transformation involved in the derivation of subject and object nominalizations from their deep structures.

Rohrman concluded that the deep structure interpretation of memory is

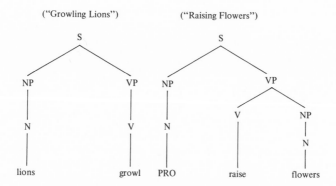

FIGURE 12-4.   Deep structures of subject nominalizations (e.g., growling lions) and object nominalizations (e.g., raising flowers).

"compatible with virtually all other current work in the area and the long traditional literature. A problem plaguing earlier work has been the vagueness resulting from using 'meaning' as the memory representation which Ss store, and this was obviously what took place. Using the notion of deep structure . . . provides a great deal more precision and is theoretically and practically more . . . useful than the older semantic terminology" (1968, p. 912).

Precisely what "older semantic terminology" is being referred to in the statement is unclear, but we may assume that the asserted conceptual superiority of deep structure is intended to apply generally to previous semantic approaches to psycholinguistic problems. One relevant psychological dimension was considered in a study by Rohrman and Polzella (1968). As before, they found that nominalizations with less complex deep structures were easier to recall than those with more complex ones and, in addition, association data showed that the two types of nominalizations did not differ in the number of associations they elicited, i.e., their verbal-associative meaningfulness (m). These data were taken as further support for the notion that the underlying structure of a sentence adequately serves as a conceptualization of the memory representation of that sentence. It should be noted, however, that *the alternative index of meaning they considered has been found to be relatively ineffective in memory studies at the real-word level* (Chapters 7 and 8), and it comes as no surprise that here, too, m bore no relation to recall. In the light of what we do know about the effective word attributes in memory tasks, Rohrman's linguistic interpretation remains uncompelling precisely because he failed to control for *imaginal* meaning in his experiments. We shall see in the next chapter that, when such a control is introduced, deep structure complexity fails as a predictor of recall; conversely, when deep structure is controlled but imagery is varied, the latter once more emerges as a potent factor in memory for language. In anticipation of the later discussion, we can conclude that deep structure models in general, whether based on structural complexity or transformational complexity, have thus far been unable to account satisfactorily for the way people remember sentences when alternative interpretations have been adequately tested.

One important set of positive findings leaves the issue open. Blumenthal (1967) found that the final nouns in passive sentences were more effective cues for the recall of the entire sentence when the noun functioned as the logical subject (e.g., *tailors* in the sentence *Gloves were made by tailors*) than when it functioned as an adverbial modifier (e.g., *hand* in the sentence *Gloves were made by hand*). Blumenthal hypothesized that the logical subjects are more effective prompts because they are more inclusively involved in the sentence as a whole at the deep structure level than are adverbials. Blumenthal and Boakes (1967) obtained further support for the hypothesis using improved procedures and sentence materials. Their results are particularly challenging to alternative hypotheses because surface structure and various noun features, including concreteness-abstractness, apparently were carefully controlled. It remains to be seen whether the deep-structure interpretation will hold up under further testing.

The general implications for psycholinguistic theory of the results that have been considered in this chapter will be discussed at the end of the next chapter, where they can be compared and contrasted with conclusions based on research generated by the two-process theory of meaning and mediation.

SUMMARY

This chapter has been concerned in general with the identification of effective linguistic variables and with the formulation of a theoretical psycholinguistic model that could explain the effects. The unique emphasis was on grammatical variables, as distinguished from associative and semantic variables, and on linguistically based models, especially ones based on Chomsky's theory of transformational generative grammar. The research in the area has shown that linguistic variables in general are effective, and that grammatical, associative, and semantic variables all contribute to the effect, but it has proven difficult to tease them apart. This is particularly so with respect to the contribution of semantic factors to the effect of syntax. Chunking or unitization seems to be one important psychological process through which these variables have their effect on memory in particular.

The theoretical models derived from linguistics have emphasized either surface structure or deep structure. Initial studies testing the different approaches yielded positive evidence for their validity, but subsequent experiments with more adequate designs and controls have generally produced contradictory findings. This is especially true of research concerned with memory for sentences or phrases. The conclusion is that none of the linguistic models provides a satisfactory account of language from a psychological viewpoint. What does emerge repeatedly from the research is evidence of the centrality of meaning in effects related to linguistic structure, although an overall conceptualization of the nature of effective meaning and its relation to syntax is wanting.

13
Imagery and Language

This chapter extends the dual-coding model to psycholinguistic phenomena. The central question is whether such an approach provides a viable alternative, or the foundation of an eventual alternative, to the associationistic and linguistic conceptions discussed in the last chapter. The first of three sections devoted to the issue reviews the dual-coding theory with specific reference to its relevance to psycholinguistic problems. The second reviews the available empirical evidence on the role of imaginal and verbal symbolic processes in language comprehension, production, and memory. The final section presents some speculative views concerning the implications of the model for such linguistic phenomena as poetry and metaphor. In view of its novelty as a theoretical construct in contemporary psycholinguistics, imagery will receive most of the attention throughout, but always with due regard for its conceptual status in the two-process model.

THEORETICAL ORIENTATION

The following analysis of the role of the symbolic systems in language behavior emphasizes the functional distinctions between verbal processes and imagery and their relations to meaning, as previously discussed in various contexts. As a theoretical approach to language, it differs from both S-R learning and linguistic theories in a number of respects but particularly in its explicit recognition of nonverbal processes in verbal behavior. By contrast, the verbal-associationistic approach to meaning and mediation and the transformational-linguistic model are exclusively intraverbal in their emphasis. Together they might form the basis for a comprehensive model of the organizational structure and functional properties of the "ideal" verbal symbolic system, but such a model would not constitute a general psycholinguistic theory because it would be incapable of dealing with nonverbal factors in verbal behavior. The more general S-R approaches of Skinner, Staats, and Osgood do take account of nonverbal factors, but they do not explicitly consider the functions of nonverbal symbolic processes as mediators of language behavior in a way that would distinguish them from verbal processes. That is, there is no emphasis on the possible functional distinctions between verbal and nonverbal processes that would have any differential predictive consequences vis-à-vis verbal behavior. *Here precisely lies the strength of the two-process approach: It specifies a distinct functional role for nonverbal imagery in the understanding and production of language.* This feature of the approach is most directly relevant to the problem of "knowledge of the world" in that such knowledge is assumed to be coded partly in the form of representational images of objects and events, and the mediational effects of these images are considered as being analogous to the effects of concrete settings themselves. It can be seen that this view represents an extension of the analogy drawn earlier between pictures and mental images. While not extensively researched, the above is certainly not a strange conception in common-sense approaches to language. What is new in the approach is the theoretical and operational specification of functional distinctions between imagery and the verbal symbolic system with respect to language, thereby rendering the theory testable.

The Functional Distinctions Reviewed

The two symbolic systems were theoretically characterized in Chapter 2 in terms of their relative efficiency for concrete as compared to abstract, static as compared to dynamic, and parallel versus sequential information processing functions. Thus imagery is assumed to be specialized for the symbolic representation of concrete situations and events, speed and flexibility of transformational thinking (the "flights" as compared to the "perchings" of the stream of thought), and parallel processing in the visual-spatial sense. The verbal system, on the other hand, is presumably characterized by its capacity to deal with abstract problems, concepts, and relationships, and for processing sequential information. These distinctions are, of course, relative rather than absolute, and the systems presumably overlap, particularly in regard to parallel processing in the operational sense. Moreover, rather than function autonomously, they are assumed generally to interact in their symbolic capacity.

The specific psycholinguistic implications of the functional distinctions will be discussed later as testable hypotheses in the context of relevant research. However, certain general implications may be noted here. An obvious one is that verbal descriptions of concrete situations and events from memory and verbal expressions of the manipulation of spatial concepts are likely to be mediated efficiently by nonverbal imagery, whereas abstract discourse and verbal expressions of abstract reasoning are more likely to be mediated entirely by the verbal system. A second (less obvious) implication is that the verbal behavior mediated by imagery is likely to be more flexible and creative than that mediated by the verbal symbolic system. This follows from the theoretical assumption that the spatially and operationally parallel image system is not characterized by logical and sequential constraints to the same degree as the verbal symbolic system. This implies further, and more specifically, that the understanding and the production of concrete language (presumably mediated partly by the image system) are more likely to reflect the creative aspects of the grammar of a language than are the understanding and the production of relatively abstract language (which is presumably linked more exclusively to the sequentially operating verbal symbolic system). The processing of abstract language is also likely to be slower and generally more difficult because of its dependence on the verbal system.

Imagery and Linguistic Meaning

The above propositions hinge on the assumption that linguistic meaning *is* (in part) imagery, or at least is closely linked to imagery. This assumption was discussed in detail in Chapter 3, particularly with reference to words as the linguistic units. Since we are concerned here with extended segments of language up to and beyond the sentence, a re-examination of that assumption is in order.

Bugelski's (1969) discussion of the reading process provides a relevant point of departure. Bugelski based his theoretical views on a classical analysis of the psychology of reading by Huey (1908). Huey argued essentially that reading for sense, or meaning, involves the arousal of images and feelings by sentences. However, he (like Titchener and others) was unable to resolve the apparent impasse created for the image theory by the difficulty of imaging relational words like *under* and *upon*, and he abandoned the problem. Bugelski asserted that Huey gave up too soon. There is no problem about imaging such words if one recognizes that they cannot be imaged alone. One cannot generate an image to *in*, but one can image relationships between objects that are brought together by such a word. In brief, Bugelski postulated the arousal of images by phrases or sentences rather than by individual words. This is in full agreement with our analysis of meaning presented in Chapter 3, where it was argued that the meaning of such words as verbs, adjectives, and prepositions depends upon the context created by the sentence. The present position differs from Bugelski's, however, in the explicit differentiation between imaginal and intraverbal meaning: Abstract phrases may be meaningful more or less exclusively in the intraverbal (contextual) sense without involving any arousal of nonverbal images or feelings. One might argue that such meaning would be rather impoverished, but it must be recognized as a limited instance at least.

As evidence for the image theory of reading for meaning, Bugelski cites his own research on the role of mnemonic imagery in verbal learning (e.g., Bugelski et al., 1968). The experiments by Reese (1970), Rohwer (1970), and others on the effects of pictorial compounds and sentence contexts on memory for verbal units, as described in the preceding chapter, are also relevant. Rohwer's studies, for example, indicated that sentence contexts involving verb connectives and action pictures are particularly facilitative in associative learning, possibly because both conditions involve the arousal of visual imagery that serves to mediate recall of the appropriate verbal response.

Further evidence for the image interpretation of sentential meaning is provided by a series of experiments on the role of spatial images in syllogistic reasoning by Huttenlocher (1968), who based her theory partly on a similar analysis of the role of spatial representations in reasoning presented earlier by DeSoto, London, and Handel (1965). A subject in these experiments is presented a three-term series problem such as "Tom is taller than Sam and John is shorter than Sam—who is tallest?" Huttenlocher's findings suggested that subjects invoked spatial images to solve such problems, with the imagery corresponding to the operations involved in making actual spatial arrangements of real objects according to analogous types of verbal description. Thus, the subject apparently first arranges the items described in the first premise, starting at a particular position (e.g., left) of his imaginary space. If the relational term in the problem describes a dimension to which he assigns a particular orientation, this determines which item he places first. In other cases, he starts with the item mentioned first, i.e., the grammatical subject. And so on. The obvious relevance of Huttenlocher's findings in the present context is the evidence they provide for imagery as the mental representative of the meaning of sentences that describe spatial relations. Her studies will be discussed in more detail later along with an alternative approach to such problems in terms of linguistic concepts.

Werner and Kaplan (1963) reported studies that demonstrate the arousal of images representing abstract dimensions such as time. Earlier we discussed this research as illustrating the process of "concretizing the abstract" (Chapter 2). In one series of studies, subjects were presented sentences such as *He runs, He is running, He ran, He will run.* His task was to transform these into images representing the agent ("he"), the action ("running"), and the temporal locus of the action. Subjects apparently represented temporality in terms of relatively personal and idiosyncratic images that concretized the time dimension by such means as specific characteristics of the agent, agent posture, and situational context of the action. In another study by R. Erle (cited by Werner & Kaplan, 1963, pp. 454–466), subjects were asked to represent in imagery the context of sentences involving the conjunctions *because, if,* and *but* (e.g., He paces a great deal because he works hard). Again, content was expressed in the form of images of concrete instances, typically condensed so that the two contents of the compound statement were, for example, represented as a single concrete event. Other means of imaginal representation included indicatory depiction and implicatory reference, where the agent's action or attribute was alluded to through some object in the total situation, such as an image of tools for "He works hard," an image of a traffic light to imply "intelligence and caution," and so on. These means are similar to those described in Chapter 11 in reference to the imaginal mediation of associations between abstract words. For example, an image of "boy scout," reported by one subject as a mediator for the pair *chance-*

deed, involves both condensation and implicatory reference. These examples illustrate the general point that even abstract meanings in sentences can be represented in the form of specific images of concrete objects and events. This is not to argue that they necessarily will be so represented, however, since it has already been proposed that the arousal of verbal processes might in itself be the mental correlate of abstract meaning.

The Two-Process Model and Language Acquisition

Contemporary learning theories that incorporate mediational concepts provide a reasonable account of many features of language learning but, as noted earlier, they have difficulty handling grammar and the creativity that it implies. On the other hand, the nativistic interpretation of linguistic competence ignores learning processes and is therefore quite incapable of dealing with language as a learned skill. Does the two-process model provide a reasonable alternative or supplement to either or both of the above? It is premature to propose a comprehensive analysis of language acquisition along those lines, and the present section does not profess to do so, but the direction such an analysis might take can be suggested.

What is proposed represents essentially an extension of the developmental analysis of the symbolic processes and of meaning as presented in Chapters 2 and 3. Recall that the symbolic processes were assumed to develop in a concrete-abstract sequence between and within the two major modes. Thus it was argued that imagery precedes verbal processes in its developmental onset, although the two modes continue to develop concurrently (and interactively) once verbal skills have begun; and that both processes become increasingly capable of representing and manipulating information not present in the here-and-now as the individual matures.

Conceptually, the analysis of meaning into three levels of associative complexity is assumed to parallel the developmental sequence of the symbolic modes, the major differences being the emphasis on stimulus characteristics (as well as the symbolic reactions to them) in the case of meaning. The first level, representational meaning, implies that mental representations corresponding to nonverbal and verbal stimuli have become available. The second hypothetical level, referential meaning, presumably involves the development of associations between the two classes of representation, i.e., between names and their referent images. Associative meaning is a further stage involving the development of complex associations between words, images, or both. The analysis presupposes the operation of learning mechanisms whose theoretical nature can be left unspecified here (see Chapters 2 and 3 for the relevant discussions).

The major implication of the above analysis for language acquisition is that linguistic competence and linguistic performance are dependent initially upon a substrate of imagery. Through exposure to concrete objects and events, the infant develops a storehouse of images that represent his knowledge of the world. Language builds upon this foundation and remains interlocked with it, although it also develops a partly autonomous structure of its own. Although speculative, these general assumptions would probably arouse little controversy if limited only to discrete objects and their names. An infant indicates by his behavior that he recognizes objects before he responds to their names, thereby showing that he has stored some kind of representation against which the perceptual information is matched. Later he can respond appropriately to the name of an object even in its absence (e.g., he may begin to look for it), indicating the emergence of a word-image relationship. Serious objections might be raised, however, if such an analysis were to be extended to grammatical word sequences, for surely it is too much to suggest that syntax is in any sense built upon a foundation of imagery. Yet this is precisely what is suggested.

The argument is as follows. The developing infant is not exposed merely to static objects but to objects in relation to other objects, and action sequences involving such objects. The events and relations are lawful, i.e., they tend to repeat themselves in certain essential respects—people enter a room through the same door in the same way repeatedly, a bottle is picked up in a predictable way, and so on. In brief, there is a kind of syntax to the observed events, which becomes incorporated into the representational imagery as well. This syntax is elaborated and enriched by the addition of an action component derived from the child's own actions, which have their own patterning or grammar. The child also learns names for the events and relations as well as the objects involved in them, which we interpret theoretically to mean that associations have developed between the mental representations of the objects, actions, etc., and their descriptive names. This basic stage becomes greatly elaborated as function words are acquired and as intraverbal associative networks expand through usage. Eventually, abstract verbal skills are attained whereby verbal behavior and verbal understanding are possible at a *relatively* autonomous intraverbal level, i.e., free of dependence not only upon a concrete situational context but to some extent from imagery as well.

Although systematic research remains to be undertaken on the acquisition model, it has testable implications that can be examined in the light of developmental information presently available. In particular, the theory suggests that the grammars first learned by children will be "tied to" the syntax of concrete objects and events, presumably via the medium of imagery, and only later will more abstract grammars emerge. The explanatory potential of such an approach will be compared later with that of the nativistic Language Acquisition Device as interpreted and applied by McNeill (1968) to children's acquisition of basic grammatical relations.

The Two-Process Model Compared with Associationistic and Linguistic Approaches

In certain respects, the two-process approach overlaps both S-R associationistic and linguistic views on the psychology of language. The emphasis on sequentially organized verbal mechanisms as the primary substrate of abstract language is consistent with the S-R theorist's stress on verbal associative experiences and the resultant sequential dependencies in language as important controlling variables in psycholinguistic phenomena. The present view, therefore, is that the associationistic model is essentially correct with respect to the intraverbal contextual aspects of abstract language in particular. Conversely, and somewhat paradoxically, the proposition that imagery plays an important psycholinguistic role in the case of referentially concrete aspects of language fits the transformationist's emphasis on the creative aspects and flexibility of language. This is paradoxical because the theory of transformational generative grammar is clearly intraverbal in its emphasis. This is particularly evident in the exclusion of situational factors and knowledge of the world from the semantic theory proposed by Katz, Fodor, and Postal, but the intraverbal emphasis extends similarly to all components of the transformationist's linguistic theory. Nonetheless, in the present approach, imagery in particular is attributed with freedom from sequential restraints, paralleling the linguist's stress on the recursiveness and novelty of sentences. Moreover, as a symbolic mode, imagery (theoretically) takes a form that differs markedly from the manifest, verbal form of language much as deep structure may differ from surface structure according to Chomsky's theory. While the concepts are drawn from qualitatively different theories and cannot be directly equated, it can be argued that imagery is the major *psychological correlate* of the deep structure of relatively concrete sentences. This follows from a joint consideration of the proposition that imagery is the primary basis of the meaning of such sentences and the transformationist's view that deep structure determines the semantic interpretation of a sentence. In the case of referentially concrete sentences, therefore, the semantic interpretation attributed to deep structures may be experienced as imagery, or at least may be behaviorally expressed in a manner reflecting the operation of the image system. The semantic interpretation of abstract material, on the other hand, presumably remains dependent upon the verbal system and may be experienced as implicit speech, which parallels the surface structure of sentences or corresponds to verbal transformations of them, possibly in the form of kernel sentences (cf. G. A. Miller, 1962). The value of such comparisons is questionable, however, particularly in view of the doubtful validity of the deep-structure concept in relation to the psychology of language, and perhaps even in relation to conceptions of grammar, if McCawley's (1968) analysis is correct (see Chapter 12). However we must reserve judgment on such matters for the moment.

The suggested theoretical distinctions must again be understood as relative rather than absolute: As in the case of the two-process theory of the meaning of individual words, concrete sentences presumably are meaningful at an intraverbal (contextual and associative) level as well as at an imaginal level. That is, their meaning is partly determined by the verbal contextual relations in themselves or by verbal associative processes evoked by the words. Conversely, abstract sentences may involve nonverbal imagery as well as verbal symbolic processes as the mental correlates of their meaning. The relative emphasis nevertheless implies that imagery is likely to be more prominent in the case of concrete sentences, and intraverbal processes in the case of abstract sentences. The relevance of the distinctions for S-R associative and linguistic interpretations ultimately depends, of course, on the kinds of psychological mechanisms particular theorists are willing to invoke in their explanations. As already noted, imagery has been generally neglected in both classes of theory, with certain exceptions such as A. W. Staats' (1968) treatment of imagery as a linguistically evoked mediating process possessing both response and stimulus properties, and Bugelski's (1969) learning approach to reading. This state of affairs will change only to the extent that the imagery concept can be shown to have predictive and explanatory power in psycholinguistic research. Its potential in that regard will be examined in the remainder of the chapter.

EMPIRICAL EVIDENCE

The functions of imaginal and verbal symbolic processes in language behavior presumably can be investigated using any of the operational approaches described in the earlier chapters, e.g., by manipulating instructional sets, item attributes, and so on. While different approaches have indeed been used, the major emphasis in this section will be on stimulus attributes, particularly the concreteness or image-arousing value of the linguistic material. In regard to the latter variable, it should be noted that the theoretical neglect of imagery referred to at the end of the last section has its counterpart in a most extraordinary absence of any systematic treatment of abstractness-concreteness as a dimension of linguistic meaning—extraordinary in retrospect because we now know how potent the variable is in verbal learning and memory tasks generally, but extraordinary also on a priori grounds, given the emphasis that linguists and psycholinguists have traditionally placed on the abstractness or generic nature of language as compared to other symbolic systems (see Chapter 3). Despite such an emphasis, there have been virtually no systematic attempts to explore the dimension empirically nor to consider its theoretical implications by contemporary students of psycholinguistics. General semanticists such as Hayakawa (1949) are notable exceptions, but they have had little impact on psycholinguistics and they have not explored the implications of their views empirically. Other psycholinguistic scientists have restricted their attention in the main to relatively concrete sentences (i.e., ones with direct reference to concrete objects and events) in the material chosen for research studies, as well as in the illustrative examples that so frequently crop up in discussions of linguistic issues. The theoretical and empirical consequences of this one-sided approach will become apparent in the following discussions of the effects of abstractness-concreteness and imagery as stimulus dimensions, as well as other experimental manipulations of the postulated underlying processes.

Concreteness and Imagery in Linguistic Comprehension

Students of communication have given some attention to the role of abstraction in comprehension of speech and writing, and there has been at least one attempt to scale the level of abstraction in written material. Flesch (1950) devised a formula based on a count of the percentage of "definite" words in a passage. Definite words included names of people, common nouns with natural gender, nouns referring to clock or calendar time, finite verbs, etc. The smaller the percentage of such words, the more abstract the passage as a whole. Although Flesch argued that the understandability of text material is related to abstractness, there appears to be no solid validation of his measure from that point of view. Clearly there is good reason to assume that the index or some variant of it would be predictive of performance on some measure of comprehension, but this needs to be empirically established.

The predicted relation has some factual support. Bloomer (1961) found that both frequency of occurrence and judged concreteness of words were negatively related to difficulty of reading the words, as determined by the accuracy of selecting synonyms for the word from another printed list. The superior performance for concrete words held up even with frequency partialed out. This finding provides some indirect support for Bugelski's (1969) view of the role of imagery in reading for meaning. A similar effect on listener comprehension was obtained by Beighley (1952), who found that speeches with a high ratio of concrete facts to abstract ideas were better comprehended than ones with the reverse ratio. How such concreteness was assessed is not stated, and the two kinds of speeches also differed in vocabulary level and sentence length, so the finding is only suggestive, though consistent with what would be expected.

More direct studies of the role of imagery in comprehension have been initiated by Paivio and Begg (1970b). The central problem is this: If imagery contributes to reading comprehension, as the present view of imagery-as-meaning and Bugelski's approach to reading suggest, we would expect indices of comprehension and image arousal to be substantially correlated. Indeed, imagery should precede understanding in time. The latter expectation was not supported, however, by Moore's (1915) early research on meaning and imagery reaction times, which showed that meaning generally preceded imagery, although the evidence is somewhat equivocal, since Tolman (1917) did find that individuals differed in which came first (see Chapter 3). However, the negative finding is not damaging to the imagery position, since the latter does not require images to be consciously experienced to be effective any more than associationistic or transformationist theories call for conscious correlates of associative habits or transformational rules. Nevertheless, in view of Moore's results, we did not expect to find imagery preceding comprehension in our laboratory tests. Instead, we expected strong correlations between the two kinds of reactions, and interactions between the conditions designed to arouse them and abstractness-concreteness of the stimulus material.

One of two experiments involved presentations of a series of typed sentences, which varied in syntactical type, under one of four instructional sets, namely, reading, imaging, comprehending, or paraphrasing. A sentence was presented, and the subject pressed a key when he had completed the required task. Correlations were computed between the mean latencies for individual sentences under each instructional set—that is, the sentences were the "subjects." The highest correlation (.83) was between imagery and comprehension latencies, followed by comprehension with paraphrasing (.79), then imagery and paraphrasing (.76). The correlations between reading and the other tasks were lower, ranging from .44 to .66. With reading latency partialed out, imagery, comprehension, and paraphrasing remained highly correlated (.69 to .77).

The correlational data suggest a common process but provide no basis for any particular causal interpretation. Unexpectedly, however, the mean latencies showed an orderly progression for all sentence types, with reading being fastest, followed by imagery, then comprehension, and finally paraphrasing. The interesting result is that imaging was consistently faster than comprehension or paraphrasing, the mean latencies being 4.87, 5.93, and 6.10 seconds, respectively. Considered together, the correlations and mean differences in latencies suggest that imagery makes it easier to understand and paraphrase sentences. The faster latency for imagery than comprehension is directly contrary to the earlier data for imagery and meaning, but the latter research was with individual words, and the reversal may have occurred because of the greater complexity of sentences. We shall return to this point later.

The above experiment involved sentences that were relatively concrete. The other experiment in the Paivio and Begg study investigated image and comprehension latencies using both abstract and concrete sentences. The study involved 50 concrete and 50 abstract sentences taken from an earlier memory experiment (Begg & Paivio, 1969), to be described later in this chapter. Each sentence was of the type "The (adjective) (noun) (past tense verb) a (adjective) (noun)." Examples of sentences categorized as relatively concrete and relatively abstract, respectively, are *The spirited leader slapped a mournful hostage* and *The arbitrary regulation provoked a civil complaint*. The sentences were presented one at a time using a tachistoscope. The subject pressed a button to expose the sentence, and released it as soon as he "had" an image or understood the sentence. Ten subjects were given the image set, and 10 the comprehension set.

On the basis of the dual-coding model and previous empirical findings, we expected an interaction between concreteness and the image-versus-comprehension instructional variable. The meaning of abstract sentences, like that of abstract nouns or noun pairs, is presumably tied more closely to the intraverbal context and verbal associative reactions than to imagery. Abstract sentences therefore should arouse images only with difficulty and yet be readily understood on the basis of their intraverbal meaning. This distinction would be reflected in much longer latencies for imagery than for comprehension. On the other hand, the meaning of concrete sentences is closely tied to concrete referents and their psychological representations in the form of imagery; this close relationship should be reflected in relatively small differences between image and comprehension latencies.

Figure 13-1 shows a significant interaction entirely in accord with our predictions. Subjects required much more time to generate images than to understand abstract sentences. The difference was in the same direction but much smaller for concrete sentences. Moreover, image latencies were longer for abstract sentences than for concrete sentences, but comprehension latencies did not differ significantly for the two kinds of material. The interaction indicates that imagery and comprehension cannot be equated, but it also suggests that they are much more closely related when the material is concrete than when it is abstract. This is confirmed by a correlational analysis involving mean comprehension and imagery latencies for each sentence. The correlation between comprehension and imagery was .71 for concrete sentences and significantly lower, .60, for abstract sentences. Nevertheless, when concrete and abstract sentences were pooled, the correlation was .81, highly comparable to the correlation of .83 obtained in the earlier experiment, suggesting that imagery and comprehension are closely related generally.

The absolute latencies of imagery and comprehension also have specific theoretical relevance in regard to the role imagery could play in comprehension behavior. On the basis of latencies reported by Moore (1915) for image arousal, Wickens and Engle (1970) argued that it takes too long to conjure up an image to words for imagery to be useful as an encoding dimension in language behavior. Specifically, they state that "Ordinary speech . . . flows too rapidly to permit one to dawdle over an item while awaiting its image" (p. 271). However, raw image latencies clearly cannot be taken as an estimate of the speed of the mental process itself, otherwise the logic must be extended to other hypothetical processes as well. In the present instance, for example, subjects took con-

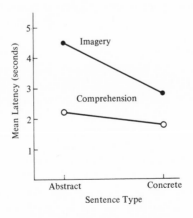

FIGURE 13-1. Mean comprehension and imagery latencies for abstract and concrete sentences.

siderable time to comprehend the sentences, according to their average comprehension reaction times. The values in the first experiment described above approximated 5 seconds, which is not only long in an absolute sense but exceeded the latency of image arousal. Clearly such latency data cannot be taken as representative of the average speed of the comprehension process in ordinary language behavior, although in some instances it might take 5 seconds or even longer to understand a complicated sentence. In any event, the general point is that the absolute latency of imagery, as that of comprehension, depends on a variety of stimulus factors such as the length, complexity, and abstractness of the stimulus material, as well as the precise experimental instructions and contextual cues that are involved in the experiment. While Moore reported an average value of about 1.5 seconds for image arousal, Tolman (1917) obtained values under 1 second for many subjects using a somewhat different procedure. Paivio (1966) obtained a mean latency of about 2.5 seconds for image arousal to concrete words, whereas Simpson (1970) obtained raw image latencies of about .9 second using well-practiced subjects. Such reports indicate that imagery can indeed occur quickly enough to verbal material to be functional in language behavior, including the complex process called comprehension. This conclusion is reinforced by the observation that the imagery latencies obtained by Paivio and Begg with concrete sentences as stimuli (see Figure 13-1, for example) are not inordinately longer than the latencies obtained to single word stimuli. The implication of this is that the subject presumably generates an image while the sentence is being read, not when reading is completed. Something of this kind may be the explanation of the finding that imagery latencies were faster than comprehension in one of the above experiments: Subjects may have generated an image to only part of the sentence, but understood it only after the entire sentence had been processed. The suggestion remains to be empirically tested, however.

The role of imagery in sentence comprehension has been further supported by other experiments involving a variety of tasks. Skehan (1970) investigated the effect of the imagery level of sentences (as defined by ratings) on their comprehensibility. Comprehension was indexed by the time required to make a true-false judgment of the sentence in relation to a referent sentence. Certain expected interactions between the transformational complexity of the sentences and their imagery value were not obtained, but comprehension was significantly faster for high- and medium-imagery sentences than for low-imagery sentences. The finding is consistent with an imagery interpretation, but alternative explanations based solely on verbal processes cannot be dismissed on the basis of these data. The core issue is the one raised in the last chapter in the discussion of studies by Gough (1965, 1966), McMahon (1963), and Slobin (1966): *Does the verification process involve a comparison of implicit verbal descriptions aroused by the target sentence and referent, or is one or both transformed into a nonverbal representation?*

An experiment by Rosenfeld (1967) provided strong support for a nonverbal interpretation of the symbolic transformations involved in such tasks. The experiment involved a same-different comparison between successive stimuli, presented either as nonverbal objects (figures) or verbal descriptions of the objects. The objects varied in number (two or three), color (red or blue), and form (circle or triangle). Thus a particular stimulus might consist of two red triangles, or three blue circles, and so on. The verbal stimuli were descriptions of the figural stimuli, e.g., "2 red triangles," "3 blue circles." The conditions of the experiment involved all possible combinations of objects and descriptions as first and second stimuli. Thus subjects compared objects with objects, words with words, words with objects, or objects with words. The interstimulus interval was also varied, so that the second stimulus was presented without delay or 2.5 seconds after the first. The subjects were presented only one type of second stimulus in any one session, thereby permitting them to anticipate the nature of the second stimulus. (Note that the latter feature and the experiment in general resembles the procedure used independently by Posner et al., 1969, to investigate the generation of visual information; see Chapter 5.) The dependent variable was the time required to judge the two stimuli as same or different.

Rosenfeld's experimental conditions were designed to investigate three hypotheses regarding the coding process involved in comparison. The *abstract entity* hypothesis (cf. Osgood's account of meaning as r_m-s_m) states essentially that both words and objects are translated into a third common entity. The *encoding* hypothesis states that objects are translated into words. The *decoding* hypothesis states that words are translated into figures. A combination of encoding and decoding is, of course, a further possibility. These hypotheses generated differential predictions regarding the latency of the matching response as a function of stimulus mode and delay. The results did not conform to predictions from the abstract entity and encoding (or encoding plus decoding) hypotheses, but they were fully consistent with a form of the decoding hypothesis. A strong form of that hypothesis, according to Rosenfeld, states that any instance of a word will increase comparison latency unless a delay permits the first stimulus to be decoded into a figural form before the onset of the second stimulus. The specific prediction from this hypothesis is that object-object, object-object (delayed), and word-object (delayed) conditions will have faster latencies than the other conditions involving words as at least one of the to-be-compared stimuli. This prediction was exactly borne out by the data. The strong decoding hypothesis also predicts, however, that the word-word condition would result in the greatest latency of the remaining conditions because both stimuli must be decoded before they can be compared. The latter prediction was not confirmed. Instead, the word-word latency was faster than that for the word-object, object-word, or object-word (delayed) conditions. This was taken to be consistent with a weaker form of the decoding hypothesis according to which the words were simply compared as visual word-forms rather than being decoded into their figural representation. Where the two stimuli are discrepant in mode, however, the hypothesis assumes that the word is translated into a nonverbal code, not object into word, and this is what the latency data suggest.

Rosenfeld's theoretical analysis and results clearly justify an image interpretation of sentence comprehension in studies involving a verification task with pictures serving as referent stimuli. The subjects in such instances presumably decode the sentence into a unified image and compare this with the referent picture in order to determine whether the meaning of the sentence is true or false. However, Rosenfeld's results for the word-word comparisons and his suggested interpretation cannot be extended in an equally straightforward way to a verification task in which sentences serve as referent stimuli, despite the superficial similarity of the two tasks. While the same-different judgment in the word-word comparison can be made on the basis of a physical stimulus match, a true-false judgment regarding one of two successively presented sentences differing in syntactical form must be based on meaning. Thus a strong form of the decoding hypothesis seems quite tenable as an interpretation of verification of sentences even where the referent stimulus is also a sentence: Both sentences, when they are concrete, may be decoded into nonverbal images before the truth value of one is determined. The important factors affecting the speed of the decision would presumably be the ease of image arousal to each sentence and the degree to which the relevant features of the two images are congruent.

If the above analysis is correct, such features as the syntactical form of the sentences might have their effect on comprehension because they determine either the ease of imagery or the arrangement of objects in the aroused images, or both. Huttenlocher and her associates have obtained evidence consistent with such an interpretation. In one experiment Huttenlocher, Eisenberg, and Strauss (1968) investigated children's comprehension of such statements as "The red truck is pushing the green truck" by requiring the children to place one toy truck relative to the second, which was fixed in place. The statements were presented either in the active form, as in the above example, or in the passive form (e.g., "The green truck is pushed by the red truck"). Ease of comprehension was measured by the time taken to place the mobile truck appropriately. In all cases it took longer to place the mobile truck when the statement was passive, which is in agreement with studies reviewed earlier (e.g., Gough, 1965; Slobin, 1966) in showing that passive statements are more difficult to understand than active ones. The results also showed that, for active statements, it was easier to place the truck described as grammatical subject whereas, for passive statements, it was easier to place the truck when it was logical subject but grammatical object. It was most difficult to place the truck when it was logical object but grammatical subject. Thus comprehension appears to be easiest when there is a correspondence between the perceived actor in the situation and the logical subject of the statement. When correspondence is lacking (in this case, when the mobile truck was logical object-grammatical subject), subjects apparently must carry out mental operations to achieve such a correspondence before they can understand the statement. Huttenlocher et al. suggest that the subject performs a preliminary grammatical analysis to identify the logical subject in the statement, which is generally more difficult in the case of passives. Then he brings the extralinguistic situation and the statement into correspondence by means of transformational imagery: When the mobile truck is described as logical object, the subjects coordinate logical subject and perceived actor by imagining that the fixed truck is actually mobile.

Huttenlocher (1968) obtained further support for the imagery interpretation of comprehension entirely at a verbal level using three-term syllogistic reasoning problems. The problems in one experiment were analogues of the truck problem in the above study in that they involved descriptions of races with three runners (A_1, A_2, and B) where one runner may "lead" or "be led by" another, or may "trail" or "be trailed by" another. The two premises were stated in either active or passive form. Thus the first premise might be "A_1 is leading A_2" or "A_2 is led by A_1"; the second might be "B is leading A_1" or "B is trailed by A_1"; and so on. After the second premise, the subject was asked either "Who is first?" or "Who is last?" The results showed that both errors and time taken to respond were greatest when B was grammatical subject-logical object in passive premises, i.e., B is led by (trailed by) $A_{(1,2)}$. This is precisely the condition found to be most difficult in the truck experiment, and Huttenlocher interpreted this as support for the view that the subject imagines A_1, A_2, and B as real objects to be arranged in space. As in the truck experiment, he must create a correspondence between perceived actor and logical subject in order to understand where B goes. This interpretation was further supported by the subjects' introspective reports in which they claimed that they do construct such imaginary spatial arrays in solving the problem.

Since we are particularly interested in comparing the imagery approach with other conceptual models, it should be pointed out that H. H. Clark (1969) has recently proposed an alternative analysis of deductive reasoning in terms of linguistic processes, which presumably operate at the deep structure level. The theory includes three principles from which predictions arise in regard to the processing of comparative sentences such as those found in the deductive reasoning problems. One principle states that functional relations, like the subject-predicate relation that underlies sentences, are more available from memory than other less basic kinds of information. Consider the sentence *John is worse than Pete,* which contains information in regard to functional relations (i.e., it implies that John is *bad*) and a comparison (*more than*). According to this first principle, the listener realizes that John and Pete are bad more readily than he grasps that John is relatively more extreme in badness. The second principle asserts that certain "positive" adjectives, like *long,* are stored in memory in a less complex and more accessible form than their opposites, like *short.* This principle predicts that *better* and *isn't as good as,* which have "good" in their deep structures, will be more easily understood and retrieved than *worse* and *isn't as bad as* propositions, both of which have "bad" in their underlying structures. Finally, the third proposition states that listeners can retrieve from memory only information that is congruent at a deep level to the information they are searching for. This implies that an answer will be retrieved more quickly when propositions and questions are congruent in their base strings (e.g., *If John is better than Pete, then who is best?*) than when they are incongruent (e.g., *If John is better than Pete, then who is worst?*).

The theory proved to be remarkably successful in predicting the principal differences in the time required to solve 2-term and 3-term series problems. Clark also compared his theory with the "spatial paralogic" theory of DeSoto et al.

(1965) and Huttenlocher's spatial image theory of deductive reasoning. In certain critical instances, Clark's theory correctly predicted the experimental results, whereas the imagery theories did not. Clark nonetheless found that some subjects reported having used spatial imagery, and he concluded conservatively that it has not been demonstrated that the use of spatial imagery differentially affects the solution of 3-term series problems.

The issue is not closed. Huttenlocher, Higgins, Milligan, and Kaufman (1970) denied that Clark's findings constituted a counterexample, and they reported further experimental evidence that supported their spatial imagery interpretation. Systematic research should also be conducted testing the possibility that some of the differences in experimental results resulted from uncontrolled variation in abstractness-concreteness of the reasoning problems. Thus Clark's problems dealt with "better than" and "worse than" comparisons, which appear to be more abstract and less picturable than the "leading" or "trailing" problems used by Huttenlocher. From the viewpoint of the dual-coding theory, it clearly follows that imagery should be relatively more available and effective the more concrete the deductive reasoning problem, whereas linguistic processes may be prepotent in the case of the more abstract ones.

To summarize, the experiments reviewed in this section strongly support the view that nonverbal imagery is involved in the comprehension of *concrete* sentences. When the sentence includes an actor and an acted-upon entity, the actor is imaged first, and the logical subject of the sentence is the "preferred" cue for such arousal. The ease of comprehension depends on the ease with which the sentence is decoded into such an image. Active sentences presumably generate images more readily than passives because the subject processes the sentence sequentially, from "left to right," and the actor-image is appropriately generated first by the grammatical subject in the active case but not the passive. Extending the conceptual-peg metaphor to sentences, we might say that the logical subject is the conceptual peg upon which the ease of image arousal and comprehension depends, and this peg is more difficult to locate in passive than in active sentences. While speculative, this analysis appears to be consistent with evidence that is presently available. The interpretation must be limited in any case to relatively concrete sentences. Highly abstract sentences presumably arouse images only with difficulty, but they can be understood. According to the two-process theory, comprehension in this case would depend relatively more on the intraverbal context itself and the linguistic and other associations evoked by that context, but the problem remains to be investigated.

Imagery and Concreteness in Language Generation

Common-sense observations suggest that spontaneous descriptive speech is often mediated by nonverbal memories of the concrete objects and events being described. The general point has been made repeatedly in this book and we need not labor it, but as a reminder of what is meant, the reader might try describing the inside of his house—rooms, doorways, windows, furniture—to someone and noting the nature of his ongoing thoughts while doing so. It is very likely that imagery will be observed to play a prominent role in the generation of the description. This obviously need not be the case with all language generation, especially when the topic is highly abstract. The problem has rarely been researched systematically in the psycholinguistic context, however, and we can do no more than review a few studies that touch on some relevant aspects of the general problem.

Goldman-Eisler (1961) reported an experiment in which subjects were shown humorous *New Yorker* cartoons, which are characterized by their subtle point or moral. When the subject had "got the point," he was required to describe the content of the story depicted by the cartoons and then formulate concisely the general point, meaning, or moral of the story. The relevant feature of this procedure is that it involves variation in abstractness of the verbal task, namely, descriptions of concrete events and generalizations abstracted from them. The former is stimulus-bound, the latter is not. The major finding was that subjects paused much more during the generalizations than during the descriptions. In other words, concrete speech was less hesitant, more fluent, than abstract speech. Goldman-Eisler interpreted the data in terms of two related factors, (a) freedom of choice among lexical items and (b) level of abstraction in generating content.

Goldman-Eisler's findings were essentially replicated and extended by Lay and Paivio (1969). They used three levels of task difficulty, including self-descriptions (name, sex, age, etc.), cartoon descriptions, and interpretation and evaluation of pairs of proverbs, such as "You cannot make a silk purse out of a sow's ear" and "Where there is a will, there is a way." These can be regarded as increasing in generality and abstractness from self-descriptions to the proverb task. The results showed that hesitations in speech (silent pauses, ahs, repetitions, false starts) were least frequent in the self-description task, intermediate in cartoon descriptions, and highest in the proverb task. Thus, speech generation becomes increasingly hesitant as the verbal task becomes more abstract. Unfortunately, abstractness was confounded with other variables that makes precise interpretation difficult. For one thing, the self-description task presumably involves more automatic speech, i.e., overlearned intraverbal sequences, which implicates associative habits; for another, the cartoon task differs qualitatively from the others in that the speech stimuli are nonverbal only in the former case.

A. Reynolds and Paivio (1968) investigated the effects of abstractness-concreteness, among other variables, on speech generation using only words as stimuli. Five concrete nouns and five abstract nouns, controlled for frequency and m, were shown to subjects one at a time. The subject's task was to define each word orally. These definitions were analyzed for the latency of their initiation, productivity (number of words), and for various types of nonfluencies and hesitations. The results showed that the concrete words, relative to abstract, elicited more speech (longer definitions), faster latencies of definitions, fewer unfilled and filled (ah) pauses, and fewer nonfluencies of other types. In brief, the concrete stimulus words generated more fluent defining speech than did the abstract words. Note that these results are congruent with an earlier finding

(Paivio, 1966) that concrete words evoke faster associative reactions that do abstract words. However, the latter difference is particularly great under imagery rather than verbal associative instructions—indeed, unpublished replications in our laboratory have shown no difference in verbal-associative latencies to concrete and abstract stimuli when *m* is controlled. Thus *the differences observed in the definition task are more analogous to those obtained in the associative reaction time task under imagery rather than verbal-associative instructions.* Again, this does not constitute a direct test of the role of imagery in speech generation but, considered together, the data from the different studies are consistent with the interpretation that concrete words generated more fluent definitions because they evoked nonverbal images that mediated the verbal output. The results parallel those obtained for the cartoon description task as compared to the more abstract interpretation and proverb tasks in the Goldman-Eisler and the Lay and Paivio experiments.

The problem is amenable to more direct approaches. In the absence of such studies, we turn to memory research, which implicates both understanding and generation of language, and provides support for the theoretical validity of the two-process approach.

Imagery and Verbal Processes in Memory for Language

Let us begin once again with a reminder of our theoretical position. Extended to connected discourse, the two-process model implies that concrete phrases or sentences, like concrete words, can be coded and stored in memory not only verbally but also in the form of nonverbal imagery. Thus if I say to you, "The boy is peeling a green orange," your understanding of the sentence is likely to include some kind of mental picture together with other implicit activities related to peeling oranges, not merely silent rehearsal of the words themselves. The input language code has "flipped over" into a nonverbal one and, if I now ask you to remember the sentence, you might do so by remembering the objects and actions involved in the image and then reconstructing the sentence from it. Such a transformation would be more difficult in the case of abstract sentences, such as *The theory has predictive power*, and they are likely to be stored in their verbal form.

The above analysis has interesting implications regarding memory for connected verbal material. Note especially that, in apparent contradiction to what was predicted from the model for lists of unrelated words, the model does *not* imply that high-imagery (concrete) sentences will necessarily be remembered better than low-imagery sentences. If concrete material indeed tends to be coded in a nonverbal form, then it must be decoded back in order to generate the correct verbal output. Decoding errors are therefore possible, especially in regard to such features of language as its grammatical form and precise wording. Of course, there is no real contradiction between these statements and earlier ones regarding individual words or word pairs. Imagery was regarded as potentially facilitative primarily in the retrieval of items from memory and not in the retrieval of their sequential order. In the latter case, availability of the verbal system was shown to be of crucial importance (see Chapter 7). Moreover, the possibility of decoding errors was recognized in the context of imagery mediation in paired-associate learning (Chapter 11). Common to all of these situations is the hypothesis that imagery may either facilitate or hinder memory for language, depending on such factors as the length of the to-be-remembered verbal units and what features of the message are to be recalled. Imagery may enable one to retrieve the general theme of the message and perhaps even some of its word units, but not necessarily its grammatical form.

These and other features of the theory will be considered in more detail in the context of specific research problems.

Imagery and thematic organization in recall   In the last chapter we discussed chunking or unitization as an important process in memory for connected discourse. The research reviewed in that context appeared to be dominated by the view that such chunking is based entirely on verbal-linguistic factors. Thus N. F. Johnson (1968) suggested that the sequential coding involved in sentence production follows the abstract (verbal) categories of constituent analysis—sentence is coded into subject and predicate, subject to article plus modified noun, and so on. This analysis implies that the units stored in memory correspond either to abstract linguistic units (recoding) or to integrated sequences of verbal responses. Similarly, Rosenberg (e.g., 1966) apparently assumed that chunking is intraverbal, although based on associative as well as grammatical habits. Other investigators (e.g., Tejirian, 1968) underscored the importance of semantic factors in chunking and memory, but they generally did not consider the ultimate (verbal or nonverbal) nature of the underlying semantic structure.

There are notable departures from such a verbal bias. Brent (1969) proposed the view that chunking is on the basis of linguistic units rather than isolated words and that a subject will tend to utilize the largest linguistic unit that he can. Despite the emphasis on linguistic units, however, we shall see that Brent's analysis implies that the ultimate unit of memory is essentially nonverbal. In his experiment, he compared serial learning for lists varying in length and in their level of linguistic unity. The four hierarchical levels were the paragraph, the natural sentence, the anomalous sentence, and the isolated word. At the paragraph level, words were arranged to form a series of sentences that, in the order presented, constituted a paragraph that told a simple story. At the natural sentence level, the same sentences were rearranged so as to destroy the integrative function of the paragraph while leaving the individual sentences unchanged. At the anomalous sentence level, the nouns within the natural sentences were scrambled, leaving the syntactic structure of the sentences unchanged while degrading their semantic structure. Finally, at the word level, the words were further rearranged so as to disrupt as much as possible any linguistic grouping of successive items in the list. The lists were learned by the serial anticipation method.

If the linguistic unit (rather than isolated word) is the basic unit of verbal learning, as Brent's theoretical analysis suggests, then errors should increase as a function of the number of linguistic units in the list when the number of words is held constant, whereas errors should be relatively independent of the number of words when the number of linguistic units is held constant. The results were totally consistent with the hypothesis. The most effective variable by far was the level of linguistic unity. List length alone had relatively little effect except in the case of the word lists.

Brent also hypothesized that the sequence of items within each unit is learned virtually immediately, while relations between units are learned slowly. If so, this should be revealed in the serial position error curves: The curve would be "scalloped" in appearance, with a relatively large number of errors on the first item of each linguistic unit and relatively few errors on the remaining items of each unit. In addition, Brent's suggestion that a subject will tend to organize a list at the highest level of linguistic unity available to him in the situation implies that the scalloping effect should be manifested most clearly between those linguistic units that are at the highest level of unity. The serial position error curves were consistent with these hypotheses in that an index of scalloping showed the natural sentence level of unity to result in two or three times more scalloping than the paragraph or anomalous sentence levels. Note that the scalloping index and the related hypotheses parallel N. F. Johnson's (1965) analysis in terms of probability of transition errors (see Chapter 12), with the difference that Johnson emphasized phrase boundaries, whereas Brent's analysis took into account linguistic units of varying size in a hierarchical model.

A second experiment tested the hypothesis that the integration of lower-order units is a process that unfolds in time. This was done by varying rate of presentation with the paragraph material, following the reasoning that increasing the rate should make it more difficult to integrate the lower-order units. This would be revealed in changes in the serial position curve as a function of rate. The data supported the hypothesis with paragraphs: A shift from a 3-second to a 1-second rate resulted in increased scalloping in the serial position curve analogous to that produced by a shift from the paragraph to the natural sentence level in the first experiment. Apparently the subjects were able, at the 1-second rate, to understand the meanings of the individual sentences in the paragraph as functional units, without being able to grasp the integrating story as a whole.

Brent's findings and his analysis of hierarchical linguistic structuring are clearly consistent with the general organization approach to memory storage as proposed, for example, by G. Mandler (1968) and others reviewed in Chapter 7. His discussion is also highly relevant to the present theoretical approach in that he suggests a distinction between verbal and nonverbal processes in unitization. Thus Brent suggested that the unit of memory is the unitary "idea" or "meaning" aroused by the discrete verbal elements in a sentence, and not the verbal elements themselves. A sentence is in effect a set of instructions telling the listener how to combine the "conceptual referents" of each verbal element in the sentence into this unitary idea. The psychological problem posed by such a formulation is the specification of the nature of the memory-storage structures, the manner in which stimulus sentences are transformed from a linear string of elements into a unitary structure during learning, and the manner in which these units are retransformed into a linear string of verbal elements during recall. *If we substitute "image" for the terms "idea," "meaning," "conceptual referent," and "unitary structure," Brent's theoretical assumptions and the questions arising from them correspond closely to the image theory of linguistic meaning that is proposed here in regard to concrete sentences.*

A similar emphasis on a possible nonverbal basis for the unitization of linguistic material in memory has appeared recently in a series of studies by Lachman and his associates (e.g., Lachman & Dooling, 1968; Pompi & Lachman, 1967). Pompi and Lachman proposed that the theme in connected discourse generates "surrogate processes" reflecting the essential idea of a passage, and that such processes can be used in the regeneration of the passage. They found support for this view in that thematically associated passages were retained better than the same material randomly presented, where retention was measured in terms of the number of words correctly recognized or recalled. Moreover, subjects made more thematically related errors in the case of memory for the connected discourse.

Pompi and Lachman suggested visual imagery as one form in which the discourse theme might be stored. Yuille and Paivio (1969) tested this hypothesis by varying concreteness as well as level of organization of the to-be-recalled passages. From the previous research on effects of word concreteness, it was expected that concreteness would enhance word recall. In addition, however, concreteness was expected to interact with level of organization on the basis of the reasoning that, if the basic idea of a passage is stored as visual images that can be scanned during recall to generate the verbal content, then thematic organization should be more facilitative with concrete (high-imagery) than with abstract (low-imagery) material. The subjects in the experiment were accordingly presented passages of high, medium, or low imagery-concreteness, as determined by the concreteness of words used to construct the passages. The overall concreteness level of the passages was also confirmed by subjects' ratings. The most concrete passages were taken from Pompi and Lachman (1967). For example, one described a medical scene in highly specific terms, beginning with "Chief Resident Jones adjusted his face mask while anxiously surveying a pale figure secured to the long gleaming table before him. . . ." The passages of medium and low imagery-concreteness were constructed to be thematically similar to the highly concrete passage but more abstract and general. Thus the medium-imagery passage began as follows: "Details concerning torturous disease are seldom discussed by the general public; medical personnel however cannot shelter themselves from such unpleasant malignancies. . . ." The generality and abstractness increased further in the most abstract passage.

Within each concreteness level, half of the subjects were presented the material in syntactical order and the other half, in random order for two learning and recall trials. The results were consistent with the predictions. More words were recalled as concreteness increased and, as shown in Figure 13-2, concreteness,

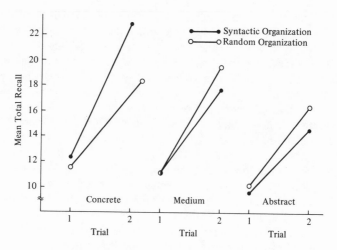

FIGURE 13-2.   Mean total recall scores for each trial as a function of abstractness and level of organization of the passage. Based on data from Yuille and Paivio (1969).

organization, and trials interacted in such a manner that recall was facilitated by syntactic order on the second trial, *but only when the content of the passage was highly concrete.*

The above findings suggest that imagery played an important role in the retrieval of verbal material, but the manner in which imagery might have such an effect is open to different interpretations. One possibility is that concrete, connected discourse evoked continuous action imagery during input, and some representative portion of this, perhaps the setting of the story, is retained and mediates reconstruction of the word units during recall. This view is somewhat analogous to the notion of abstract or generic images (Chapter 2) that presumably result from perceptual experience with specific instances of stimulus information (cf. Edmonds & Evans, 1966; Posner & Keele, 1968). The present situation differs, however, in that the necessary perceptual information must be generated from verbal input. Such imagery and its function in recall would correspond to what Bartlett referred to as getting "a general impression of the whole" on the basis of which one "constructs the probable detail" (1932, p. 206). Alternatively, what might be remembered are isolated details in the form of specific images aroused during verbal input, from which other details are constructed on the basis of relevant past experience functioning as an organizing "schema" (Bartlett, 1932, p. 209).

Parallel explanations based entirely on verbal processes could also be suggested. The syntactically organized concrete passages used by Yuille and Paivio (1969) may have aroused an implicit verbal summary or title, much as related contextual stimulus words can prime associative responses (see Cofer, 1967). Such a title would be expected to enhance recall perhaps in the manner of a verbal mediator (cf. Dooling, 1968); or, thematic order might simply facilitate organization of specific words from the passages into semantically or associatively related chunks, thereby enhancing recall (cf. Lachman & Dooling, 1968). An exclusive verbal interpretation cannot readily account for Yuille and Paivio's failure to obtain any effect of thematic organization in the case of abstract material, however, and it is preferable therefore to assume that imagery contributed to the effect.

That imagery might do so by providing an organizing schema rather than simply enhancing recall of individual words is suggested by two interesting experiments by J. H. Reynolds (1966, 1968). He found in the earlier study that prefamiliarization of verbal stimuli embedded in an integrated and meaningful map facilitated subsequent learning of sentences containing factual information related to the map. The transfer effect in that case was greater than that obtained through prefamiliarization with the verbal stimuli, the pictorial map, or nonintegrated combinations of each. Reynolds' explanation was that the integration of verbal and pictorial stimuli into a single meaningful whole permitted the formation of a mental organization akin to Tolman's (1948) concept of a cognitive map. However, the experiment did not show that "wholeness" of the verbal-perceptual configuration was critical—the important factor may simply have been the pairing of verbal labels with discrete components of the picture during prefamiliarization.

J. H. Reynolds (1968) tested the alternatives by comparing prefamiliarization conditions in which subjects saw either an integrated map structure, or the same verbal-pictorial stimulus combinations fragmented into separate units. Figure 13-3 shows each mode of presentation for one of the stimulus configurations used in the experiment. The prefamiliarization trials involved learning nonsense-syllable (CVC) names associated with each position on the map. A third group learned the CVC's in comparable locations on a sheet, without the accompanying pictorial material. Following the prefamiliarization phase, the subjects learned sentences beginning with the CVC's and ending with a word indicating an occupation, for example, KOT is a pilot, NEB is a gas station attendant, etc. The results showed no differences between conditions in learning the stimuli during the prefamiliarization stage. In subsequent sentence learning, however, the subjects prefamiliarized with the organized map structures showed better learning overall than either the discrete-picture or verbal groups. The difference was significant with a 2-second but not a 3-second rate of presentation, possibly because all groups performed at a near-ceiling level at the slower rate.

Reynolds' findings suggest that the "schema" interpretation of the effect of thematic organization in the Yuille and Paivio experiment may be correct: Thematic presentation of concrete (descriptive) verbal material enhances the generation of integrated, meaningful imagery that can mediate retrieval of the original verbal information. Note that this interpretation is simply an extension of the theoretical role attributed to imagery in the earlier discussions of paired-associate learning (e.g., Chapters 8 and 11). Imagery was assumed to facilitate learning of concrete noun pairs in particular by providing a compound spatial

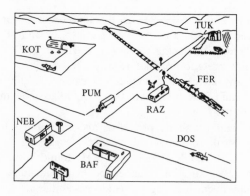

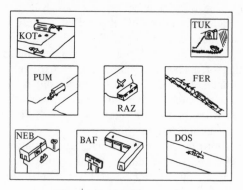

FIGURE 13-3. Example of integrated
and fragmented maps used by Reynolds as
familiarization material prior to sentence learning. From Reynolds (1968).

representation from which either member can be retrieved, given the other
member as a retrieval cue. Verb connectives and action pictures were similarly
assumed to have their effect by facilitating the formation of such organized
compounds.

Note that the above studies demonstrated facilitating effects attributable to
imagery. In the Yuille and Paivio experiment such facilitation presumably
occurred because subjects were required to recall only words from the passages
and not their syntactical order. Prefamiliarization with pictures in Reynolds'
study may have aided sentence learning because the sentences had a common
structure, and memory for syntax was not a problem. We turn next to research
that demonstrated negative as well as positive effects attributable to imagery.

Memory for meaning versus memory for wording   The preceding discussion implies that what we remember from connected discourse is largely the
general idea or meaning (expressed perhaps as imagery) from which the
wording may be generated or constructed. This was essentially Bartlett's view
of remembering. Is there no place in one's memory, then, for the specific

syntactically ordered wording of the sentence and not only the gist of it? The answer surely is yes, at least for immediate memory of short sentences, and the issue therefore revolves around quantitative and qualitative differences in memory for meaning and for wording, the factors that determine such differences, and the role (if any) of concreteness and imagery in the effects.

The referent experiment here is one by Jacqueline Sachs (1967a). Her study was concerned with recognition memory for syntactic and semantic information shortly after comprehension of connected discourse. The subjects in the study listened to recorded passages of connected discourse and, immediately after each passage, one of the sentences from it was repeated. The repeated test sentence was either identical to the one in the passage or changed in some slight way, and the subjects were asked to state whether it was "changed" or "identical." When changes occurred, they were either semantic or syntactical. The semantic changes were achieved by changing the subject and object in the sentence or phrase, by negation, or by substitution of a word that occurred elsewhere in the passage. Syntactic changes involved changes in wording that did not alter the meaning of the sentence, such as a change from active to passive voice or vice versa, or a change in the form of the base sentence. A further variable in the study was the amount of interpolated material (0, 80, or 160 syllables) that occurred between the original and the test sentence. The results are shown in Figure 13-4. It can be seen that, immediately after the original sentence, the accuracy of the judgments of identity and change were high for all test sentences. However, after 80 or 160 syllables of interpolated discourse, recognition

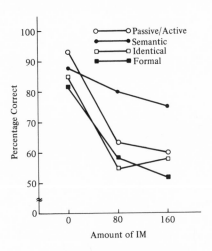

FIGURE 13-4. Percentage of "changed" judgments that were correct for semantic, passive/active, and formal changes in test sentences; and correct "identical" judgments for identical test sentences. From Sachs (1967a).

for syntactic changes dropped sharply to a near-chance level while remaining high for semantic changes.

Sachs (1967b) repeated the study with additional conditions that increased its rigor. For example, synonym changes were introduced into test sentences, thereby altering the specific wording without changing the meaning. The findings were as before: Changes in grammar or wording that did not affect the meaning were poorly detected after a few seconds, and synonym substitutions were particularly difficult to detect. On the other hand, recognition of semantic changes were again high at all retention intervals.

Sachs concluded that *the original form of the sentence is stored only for the short time necessary for comprehension to occur. Thereafter, the specific wording fades rapidly from memory. When a semantic interpretation has been made, the meaning is stored, and memory for the meaning is not dependent on memory of the original form of the sentence. Later "recall" of the sentence is a reconstruction from the remembered meaning.* These conclusions are generally consistent with our earlier discussion of the effects of thematic organization, and they are very strongly supported by Sachs' data.

A recent study indicates, however, that the above conclusions need to be qualified. Begg and Paivio (1969) investigated the implications of the two-process theory of meaning and mediation for the Sachs phenomenon. The main point has been repeatedly expressed here in various ways, but let me restate it specifically as it applies to the present problem. A concrete sentence, such as *The fat boy kicked a girl*, can be imaginally represented as an action picture in which the meaning of the entire sentence is summarized as one organized unit, or complex image. The information contained in abstract material, on the other hand, remains more closely linked to the sequentially organized verbal units themselves and can be summarized as an imaginal unit only with difficulty, e.g., by concretizing the abstract content so that it can be represented symbolically by a specific image. It follows that the most effectively coded, stored, and retrieved aspects of a concrete sentence will be those related to the sentence as a whole unit, such as its meaning. In abstract sentences, however, the specific words will be relatively better retained. The material used by Sachs was relatively concrete, and her results are consistent with the hypothesis as it pertains to such sentences. The converse prediction for abstract material was not tested by Sachs or by other investigators concerned with memory for wording and meaning.

Begg and Paivio evaluated the hypothesis using essentially the same design as Sachs (1967b), with the addition that relatively abstract as well as concrete sentences were included in the design. Also the amount of interpolated material was not varied (the test sentences occurred relatively early in the original passage). The following are examples of the concrete test sentences used in the study:

The loving mother served an excellent family.
The vicious hound chased a wild animal.
The cheerful artist entertained a lovely damsel.
The rolling hillside surrounded a muddy valley.

Examples of abstract sentences are:
> *The absolute faith aroused an enduring interest.*
> *The dull description constituted a boring chapter.*
> *The passive majority defeated a listless opposition.*
> *The final decision nullified a prior commitment.*

Semantic changes involved reversals of the subject and object of each sentence. Thus the first of the above examples became *The loving family served an excellent mother.* Lexical changes involved a synonym substitution that preserved the essential meaning of the sentence, e.g., *The loving mother served an excellent household.*

It was expected specifically that semantic changes would be recognized better than lexical changes that do not affect meaning in the case of concrete material, replicating the Sachs findings. Conversely, lexical changes should be better recognized than semantic in the case of abstract material. The results are plotted in Figure 13-5, which shows a striking interaction that precisely confirms both predictions.

The generalization that sentence meaning is better retained than its syntax or wording accordingly must be qualified by the nature of the verbal material involved. It is correct in a sense for concrete sentences but not for abstract sentences, but such a contrast between meaning and syntax can also be misleading, for it may be the assumptions concerning the nature of meaning that need qualification. In the case of concrete material, the meaning is not tied to the specific words but to the world of objects and events to which the words refer; such meaning, according to the present theory, is mentally represented in the form of nonverbal imagery. Comprehension of that meaning therefore depends

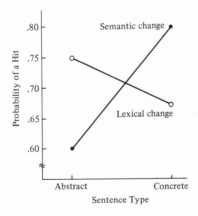

FIGURE 13-5. Correct recognition of semantic and lexical changes as a function of the abstractness-concreteness of sentences. From Begg and Paivio (1969).

upon the arousal of such imagery, and it is the imagery that is retained—that is, the nonverbal referential meaning of the sentence. When the sentence is abstract, however, its meaning is primarily intraverbal, tied to the verbal sequences themselves. To retain the meaning in this case *is* to retain the wording. This illustrates what was meant in the earlier theoretical discussion when it was suggested that processing of concrete sentences is more flexible and creative than the processing of abstract sentences. The latter is more closely tied to the sequence of words and the verbal symbolic system alone.

This theoretical analysis and the data again are consistent with the analysis and findings for associative learning and memory tasks as discussed in earlier chapters. Recall, for example, that sequential memory for pictures suffered relative to words when implicit naming was prevented by presenting the pictures at a fast rate, presumably because such memory is dependent upon the verbal symbolic system, whereas nonsequential memory was better for pictures than for words (especially abstract words) at slower rates, when imagery presumably could be functional (Paivio & Csapo, 1969; see Chapter 7). Similarly imagery mediation instructions produced better paired-associate recall than did verbal mediation instructions in the case of concrete pairs, but the reverse was true in the case of abstract pairs (Paivio & Foth, 1970; see Chapter 11).

If the above analysis is correct, it should be possible to manipulate the processes and their effects on memory for the meaning as compared to the wording of sentences by including mediation instructions, or rate of presentation, along with abstractness-concreteness as variables. This has not been done systematically as yet, but some suggestive information is available on the effect of procedures that would draw the subject's attention to the wording of sentences.

Wanner (1968) replicated Sachs' study with certain modifications. When he instructed his subjects to attend to the individual words as well as to the meaning, presumably forcing subjects to rely more on the verbal code than on nonverbal processes such as imagery, recognition for changes in meaning decreased, whereas recognition for changes in wording increased. Bregman and Strasberg (1968), whose study was discussed in the last chapter, found no evidence to support the view that sentences are remembered in terms of their syntactic form (e.g., a kernel sentence plus a transformational tag). What appeared to be stored instead was a semantic code (including imagery) from which the sentence form was constructed during recall. Earlier, however, Mehler (1963) and Savin and Perchonock (1965) had obtained evidence supporting the view that syntax is represented in the memory code. Bregman and Strasberg suggest that the contrasting results might be attributable to differences in retention intervals and sets. Savin and Perchonock used a 6- to 10-second recall interval, whereas Bregman and Strasberg's was in the order of a few minutes. Syntactic information may have been retained over the shorter interval but not the longer one. In addition, Savin and Perchonock instructed their subjects to recall verbatim. Mehler (1963) did not report such an instruction, but his procedure of repeated written recalls may have fostered a rote learning set. Both procedures thus constitute "verbal" sets that call attention to wording. On the other hand,

Bregman and Strasberg instructed their subjects to understand the meaning of the sentences, as did Sachs (1967a). The different findings can thus be reinterpreted in terms of procedures that differentially arouse verbal and nonverbal symbolic systems in sentence recall.

The implications of the analysis presented in this section have been further supported in several recent experiments. Begg (1971) investigated recognition memory for both meaning and wording of concrete sentences using a continuous recognition paradigm. Consistent with the findings discussed above, recognition memory was much better for meaning than for wording. The data showed in addition that the accuracy of meaning and wording judgments were uncorrelated, and that meaning judgments were as accurate when the test sentence was a paraphrase as when it was identical to the original. These and other analyses justified the important conclusion that memory for the meaning of concrete sentences is independent of memory for their wording and, more specifically, that the meaning is remembered as an image from which words are reconstructed at retrieval.

Prompted by the Begg and Paivio (1969) study described earlier, Wirtz and Anisfeld (1970) investigated false recognitions for adjective-noun phrases as a function of concreteness-abstractness and synonymity relations between old and new items. They found that more recognition errors were made to concrete synonyms than to concrete antonyms but there was no difference between the two kinds of phrases when they were abstract. The finding is completely in accord with the theory that the concrete phrases were coded as images and that similar images were evoked by synonymous but not antonymous phrases. Such confusions did not occur in the case of abstract phrases because they were encoded in their verbal form.

Finally, Anderson and Hidde (1970) had their subjects rate either the pronunciability or the image evoking value of 30 sentences, then unexpectedly asked them to recall the verb and object of each sentence given the subject as a retrieval cue. The subjects who rated imagery recalled over three times as many words as those who rated pronunciability. The errors that did occur tended to be predominantly synonym intrusions in the case of the imagery group but not the pronunciation group. These data suggest clearly that imagery facilitated recall through a reconstructive process, which sometimes resulted in decoding errors, whereas pronunciation subjects recalled verbatim and therefore avoided synonym errors but made more omission errors because they had not stored sentence meaning during input.

To summarize thus far, relative memory for the wording and meaning of sentences depends upon the retention interval, abstractness-concreteness of the sentence, and sets to attend to meaning or wording. Verbatim recall is favored by short retention intervals, which is consistent with the acoustic or motor-acoustic theory of sequential short-term memory discussed in Chapter 7. With concrete sentences, meaning is well retained over longer intervals whereas memory for wording fades rapidly. This is consistent with an image interpretation of sentence meaning and of memory mechanisms. With abstract sentences, wording is sometimes well-retained, perhaps because the wording itself is essential to the meaning. Finally, sets to attend to meaning and imagery on the one hand, and wording on the other, can modify the effect in the direction of better recall for meaning or wording, respectively.

Imagery versus deep structure in memory   We saw in the preceding chapter that the research literature generally has not provided support for deep structure interpretations of memory for sentences, especially ones based on transformational history. Sachs (1967a, 1967b), whose experiments were inspired partly by Chomsky's (1965) theory, also failed to obtain support for deductions from such a theory. In particular, the view that information derived from a sentence is stored as a kernel sentence was not supported, inasmuch as subjects did not seem to store passive originals in the active voice. Such changes should have been manifested as an asymmetry in recognition scores, depending on whether the change was from active to passive or vice versa. This asymmetry did not appear. Other differences expected from differences in deep structures (as this is currently conceptualized) also failed to occur. As a result, we were left with only one set of uncontradicted findings to consider in that context, namely, Rohrman's (1968) observation that memory for English nominalizations depends upon the complexity of their underlying structure.

Recall that Rohrman found nominalizations of the *growling lions* type to be easier than ones of the *digging holes* type. This was attributed to the greater complexity of the latter's deep structure. Whereas the base string of *growling lions* can be represented by "lions growl," the base of *digging holes* contains an element that is only implicit in the surface structure—some agent, PRO, digs holes. An examination of Rohrman's (1968) examples suggested, however, that the object nominalizations with the more complex base structures also may have been generally lower in imagery, less picturable, than the less complex subject nominalizations. Could the effective variable have been the availability of imagery rather than complexity of deep structure? To evaluate this question, Paivio (1971) first obtained imagery ratings for Rohrman's pool of nominalizations[1], following the procedure previously used for scaling nouns for imagery (Paivio, Yuille, & Madigan, 1968; see Chapter 3). The ratings showed that the subject nominalizations significantly exceeded the object nominalizations in their average imagery, indicating that an imagery interpretation of Rohrman's data was at least plausible. However, the two nominalization categories also overlapped considerably in imagery scores for individual items, and a more rigorous test of the hypothesis was called for. Items were selected from Rohrman's pool so that imagery and nominalization type varied factorially—half of the nouns of each type were high-imagery, and the other half were relatively low in rated imagery. The high-imagery subject nominalizations were items like *falling stars, dancing girls,* and *reigning kings*; low imagery subject nominalizations in-

---

[1] I am indebted to Rohrman for making his material available.

cluded *existing situations, clamoring masses,* and *persisting doubts.* Examples of high-imagery object nominalizations are *mopping floors, ironing clothes,* and *painting pictures;* low imagery object nominalizations included *hearing rumors, yielding points,* and *keeping secrets.*

Mixed lists of such items were presented to subjects for one free recall trial, following Rohrman's (1968) method of auditory presentation. The results, presented graphically in Figure 13-6, showed that nominalizations of high imagery were much better recalled than those of low imagery. Nominalization type had no main effect but did interact with imagery level in such a manner that more subject than object nominalizations were recalled when their imagery level was low, but this was reversed when imagery was high. The interaction is weak relative to the main effect of imagery, however, and provides no support for a general interpretation of the data in terms of deep structure.

To extend the generality of the findings, two further experiments were conducted using items from a new pool of nominalizations. This pool was generated by having subjects supply an appropriate participle to fill the blanks in base sentences corresponding to the two types of nominalizations, e.g., someone is _____ing holes (object): the tigers are _____ing (subject). Both high-imagery concrete and low-imagery abstract nouns were used in the frames, and the same nouns appeared in subject and object nominalization frames for different groups. From the normative data, nominalizations were selected so that word frequency and associative probability were matched for corresponding subject and object types. Imagery ratings were also obtained for the nominalizations. Items were selected from this pool for one experiment so that imagery varied over high, medium, and low levels for both nominalization types, and with the same nouns appearing as subject and as object nominalizations for

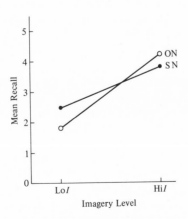

FIGURE 13-6. Mean recall scores for low- and high-imagery subject (SN) and object (ON) nominalizations. From Paivio (1971).

different groups. Another experiment involved high and low levels of imagery, crossed with nominalization type in such a manner that in some cases the same noun appeared in a subject nominalization of relatively high imagery (e.g., *lecturing teachers*) and an object nominalization of relatively low imagery (e.g., *replacing teachers*), and in other cases this was reversed (e.g., *vanishing butterflies* is low-imagery whereas *capturing butterflies* is relatively high imagery). Lists of such items were presented visually to subjects for a single free recall trial.

The results of both experiments confirmed the general conclusions from the first experiment: Nominalization imagery had a highly significant positive effect overall, but there was no main effect of nominalization type. Imagery and nominalization type interacted in both experiments, but the pattern was completely reversed in the two. Thus the imagery value of English nominalizations was positively related to recall in all three experiments. Nominalization type was never effective alone and its interactions with imagery showed an inconsistent pattern over experiments, indicating that some variable other than nominalization type was modifying the effect of imagery level. Further analysis suggested that one of the "noisy" variables may have been the imagery value of the noun member. Correlations were computed between mean recall scores for the nominalizations and the rated imagery values of the participles alone, the nouns alone, and the two combined (i.e., the intact nominalizations). The results were similar for the three experiments and the correlations were averaged. The average correlations are shown in Table 13-1, where it can be seen that noun imagery

Table 13-1

Correlations Between Attributes of English Nominalizations and Free Recall Scores (Average r Over Three Experiments)

Attribute	r with Recall
Nominalization type	.06
Nominalization imagery	.39
Participle imagery	.23
Noun imagery	.53
Note: $r_{.05} = .20$	

was the best predictor of recall, and nominalization type was the poorest. Thus complexity of deep structure is clearly inadequate as an explanation of the effects, whereas one based on imagery is consistently supported.

The failure of nominalization imagery to be superior to noun imagery as a predictor of recall is somewhat paradoxical from the viewpoint of imagery theory. However, the effect of noun imagery in this task seems comparable to its effect on the associative learning of noun-adjective pairs (see Chapter 8) and may be analogously interpretable in terms of the conceptual-peg hypothesis. While the nominalization study involved free recall of participle-noun compounds, subjects may have focused attention on the more salient noun members (cf. Turner & Rommetveit, 1968); if so, high noun *I* would be expected to facilitate recall of the noun together with its mediating image, which could then function as an implicit cue (conceptual peg) for the retrieval or reconstruction of the appropriate participle. Participle imagery, which presumably contributes to the overall imagery value of the compound, may be relatively unimportant, just as the imagery value of the response term is generally less effective than that of the stimulus member in associative learning. This would be especially true when the range of variation is relatively small, as it is in the case of participle imagery (cf. Yuille et al., 1969). This interpretation is speculative, however, and we must await further data before the apparent paradox can be resolved. Whatever the eventual outcome, it is clear that imagery predicts nominalization recall but deep structure does not.[2]

General Implications for Psycholinguistic Theory

The data on imagery and concreteness can now be considered in the context of the theoretical issues and findings considered in the last chapter as well as the present one. We have seen that grammatical factors in general influence learning and memory. For example, phrase structure and sentence boundaries influence chunking during recall. However, it has been difficult empirically to separate the effects of grammatical structure per se from associative and semantic factors, and specific theoretical interpretations that emphasize grammatical structure alone have proven inadequate as explanations and predictors of memory for sentences. The conclusion holds for surface-structure models, such as Yngve's, as well as deep-structure approaches, such as Miller's and Rohrman's. Repeatedly, investigators have been led to the conclusion that semantic factors override the effects of grammar. The semantic interpretations have generally been vague in regard to the effective underlying mechanisms, however, and it is by no means clear what specific predictions might be deduced from them. By contrast, the two-process theory, which emphasizes functionally distinct nonverbal imagery and verbal processes as the bases of linguistic meaning and memory coding, has generated specific predictions that have been uniformly supported in research to date. The model obviously requires a great deal of further testing to establish its scope and generality on the one hand, and its limitations on the other, but the variables it emphasizes and the findings it has already generated must be taken into account by any alternative psycholinguistic model that aims at comprehensiveness.

Wherein lies the strength of the two-process model in comparison with the linguistic approaches that have received such excited attention in recent years? I believe it is most particularly in its emphasis on "knowledge of the world" as a crucial substrate of language performance. We have seen earlier that transforma-

---

[2] This conclusion is further strengthened by the results of a recent study by Wearing (1971).

tional generative grammar, as a theory of mental structure, is an intraverbal theory in the sense that it encompasses only linguistic elements and their inter-relations. While its proponents recognize the importance of nonverbal situational factors and knowledge of the world as determinants of verbal behavior, such factors have been deliberately excluded from the theories (e.g., Katz & Fodor, 1963). This is a fatal omission from the psychological viewpoint, for it now seems clear that meaning is primary and syntax secondary in language behavior, and meaning *is* largely knowledge of the world as represented in nonverbal memory structures. Nor is the deficiency corrected by the transformationists' emphasis on linguistic competence (as opposed to performance) as their proper domain, for, if nonverbal processes are important determinants of linguistic performance, they should be somehow represented in the competence model of the the ideal speaker-hearer.

Heretofore, the psycholinguistic interpreters of that model have focused on the deep-structure concept as the basis of their performance theories—the behavioral manifestations of sentence comprehension and memory, for example, are assumed to be mediated by deep structures or transformational rules. But we have seen that deep-structure variables are poor predictors of memory performance in particular, whereas other (semantic) variables have been successful. It follows that either (*a*) the linguistic model has been misinterpreted by Chomsky's psycholinguistic followers, or (*b*) the theory is psychologically irrelevant, or (*c*) it needs to be modified. The first alternative seems unlikely, inasmuch as Chomsky (1968) himself has recently commented favorably on psycholinguistic interpretations of transformational grammar. The second is possible, but again proponents of the model have not operated on that assumption. The most likely outcome, therefore, is that the linguistic model will be modified, perhaps along the drastic lines suggested by McCawley (1968), wherein deep structure is eliminated and semantic features are given focal attention. If such modifications are to be psychologically relevant, however, they must take into account what is known about meaning from psychological research and, in doing so, psycholinguists (if not linguists) must find ways of articulating the linguistic concepts with knowledge of the world as represented in imagery or some other symbolic form. Moreover, research on this important problem will require new techniques for assessing knowledge of the world independent of the language used to describe it. The use of pictorial material, as in some of the experiments reported in this chapter, provides an obvious basis for such research, and recent techniques for studying the structure of internal representations (e.g., Michon, 1968; Shepard & Chipman, 1970) could be readily extended to the problem area.

The transformational psycholinguists have also slighted associative habits as determinants of language behavior. While such habits are not a sufficient explanation of understanding and production of sentences, there is ample evidence that they are important and should be included in any psycholinguistic model. Verbal-associative approaches to language provide an important corrective to the linguistic approach in this regard, but they have shared the latter's intraverbal emphasis and have generally neglected nonverbal processes. Mediational approaches such as Osgood's and Staats' provide a general framework for taking account of both classes of knowledge, nonverbal and verbal, as determinants of language behavior. The present two-process model shares that feature but, in addition, it specifies functional distinctions between the two systems that are not specified in the other models. We have seen that the behavioral implications of the distinctions have thus far been supported by psycholinguistic data, just as they have been supported by the findings from research on verbal learning and memory, indicating its theoretical validity at least within the range of phenomena encompassed by the investigations.

IMPLICATIONS FOR MISCELLANEOUS LANGUAGE PHENOMENA

Several linguistic phenomena to which the two-process approach is relevant will be discussed here briefly with the primary intention of identifying some researchable problems and indicating how the model might bear on them.

Language Acquisition

The potential relevance of the two-process theory for the problem of language acquisition was discussed earlier in the chapter. That general account will now be made more explicit by comparing it to McNeill's (1968) nativistic account of language acquisition, which is based on Chomsky's (1965) concept of the abstract Language Acquisition Device (LAD). LAD is a hypothetical device that develops a grammatical system by receiving a corpus of speech and passing it through an internal structure, part of which can be described by Chomsky's theory of grammar. McNeill extends LAD to the acquisition of language by children who, like LAD, are exposed to a corpus of speech and develop grammatical competence on the basis of this corpus. Children presumably have the same internal structure as LAD. Accordingly, the theory of grammar, being a hypothesis about LAD, is also a hypothesis about children's inborn capacity. An aspect of this capacity is reflected in the base structures, which contain the most universal features of language. What is learned in the acquisition of grammar are the linguistically unique transformations of the language, not these base structures.

The base structures include the subject and predicate of a sentence, the main verb and object of a verb phrase, and the modifier and head of the noun phrase, as these are defined in linguistics. If McNeill's theory is correct, evidence of such structures should be found in children's speech prior to the appearance of any transformations. McNeill interprets evidence from the speech of two children to be consistent with the theory. One was an English-speaking boy with three grammatical classes in his vocabulary. A sample of sentences from his speech included examples of every possible combination of those three classes that would correspond to basic (untransformed) grammatical relations but no examples representing transformations of base structures, although such combinations were possible. Thus *change Adam diaper* (corresponding to verb-object and modifier-head relations) occurred, but an inadmissable but possible combination such as *come eat food* (verb + verb + noun) did not. This is remarkable, says McNeill, because the surface structure of adult sentences contains many examples of such transformations. He concludes that the boy could express the basic relations but had not acquired English surface structure dependent upon knowledge of transformations.

The second example is from the speech of a 27-month old Japanese girl. It involves her use of two Japanese postpositions, *wa* and *ga*, which follow the surface subject of the sentence. Usage involving *wa* often can be translated into English with the expression *as for* (e.g., *As for cats, they eat fish*); thus *wa* is used whenever the predicate of a sentence attributes something to the surface-subject. The Japanese equivalent of *The cat-ga is eating the fish* illustrates a sentence taking *ga*. Such sentences are descriptive rather than attributive.

Wa and *ga* have nearly identical distribution in sentences, but they are distinguished by two theoretically interesting characteristics. One is that the girl's mother used *wa* twice as often as *ga*. The other is that, linguistically, only *ga* is derived from the underlying subject of a sentence; *wa* is derived from a completely different aspect of the base structure. The two distinctions lead to opposite predictions. Frequency of exposure to parental speech should favor the acquisition of *wa*, whereas the linguistic model suggests that *ga* will be used more often because it derives directly from a related aspect of the base structure— that is, *ga* is linked to the subject of the sentence in both its surface and deep structures, whereas *wa* is not. An examination of a sample of recorded speech revealed that the child in fact used *ga* 75 times and *wa* only six times, supporting the prediction from linguistic theory. Like the English boy, the Japanese girl apparently knew the basic grammatical relation of the subject.

McNeill concluded that these data not only support the nativistic interpretation but also go against the theory that grammar arises from names. According to such a view, children first learn names of objects, etc., then the names of two or more objects appearing together, and finally, two or three old names are combined into a single new name for the stable relation. The result is sentences like *doggie bite* and *baby sleep*. If this theory were correct, the Japanese girl would have favored *wa* rather than *ga*, since all such stable relations receive *wa* in Japanese parental speech. Inasmuch as she favored *ga* instead, the reference theory of the origins of grammar must be wrong. Indeed, reference and grammar must be acquired separately for, like all children, the Japanese girl frequently named objects and events.

McNeill's analysis is interesting and persuasive but nevertheless unsatisfactory, for it largely overlooks concrete situational factors and the concrete-abstract developmental sequence in the child's acquisition of language. Consider the Japanese *ga-wa* distinction: *Ga* is the post-position for description and *wa* for attribution. The former occurs in the context of specific concrete situations and descriptive sentences appropriate to such situations; the latter occurs in sentences that are more general in their reference. This distinction is clear from McNeill's general discussion and his illustrative sentences. The significance of the distinction is that ga-sentences, being more concrete and specific, will be more meaningful to the young child than the more general or abstract wa-sentences, despite the greater frequency of the latter in the adult language. The ga sentences are more meaningful in the referential sense, i.e., they correspond relatively directly to concrete objects and events the child has encountered and for which he has a representational substrate in the form of imagery. The same argument applies to the English-speaking boy's use of basic grammar. Both children speak in base sentences because such sentences parallel the syntax of concrete events (e.g., the sequence of events relating actor and acted upon) and concrete imagery. Transformation of such sentences are a later acquisition because they are more abstract, more removed from specific situations and images, and more dependent upon intraverbal skills.

The preceding account does not explain the acquisition of the more abstract verbal skills involved in transformed surface structure but, then, neither does McNeill's LAD. The analysis is intended only to show generally that it is not necessary to invoke an inborn LAD to account for basic grammatical relations in children's speech. The basic grammar derives from the nature of concrete events and can be conceptualized as built upon a substrate of imagery. It might be argued that this simply pushes the problem back to cognition generally, that LAD is responsible also for the prelinguistic cognitive skills, including images. As long as such an argument rests on a nativistic interpretation of LAD, however, it does not eliminate a basic difference in the approaches, for the present view is that the imagery derives from experience and parallels the syntax of external events in its form.

There is as yet no systematic evidence that tests the imagery interpretation of base grammar in young children, but the problem is researchable using such procedures as Rosenfeld's (1967) picture-description matching. Some relevant observations have in fact been reported by Klima and Bellugi-Klima (1969) in the course of elaborating on data obtained in an earlier experiment (Fraser, Bellugi, & Brown, 1963). An aspect of that study involved a test of comprehension of passive constructions using pairs of pictures with three-year old children whose speech did not contain passives. One picture showed a cat being chased by a dog, and another a dog being chased by a cat. When the children were asked to show *The cat being chased by the dog*, a number of them pointed erroneously to the picture of the cat chasing the dog, suggesting that they processed the passive sentences as though they were actives, i.e., in terms of subject-verb-object relations. Note, however, that if this interpretation is correct, the active "sentence" must be coded in a nonverbal form corresponding to objects and relations depicted in the picture if the children decode descriptive sentences in the same way as Rosenfeld's adult subjects decoded descriptions of figures. Thus the Fraser et al. data are consistent with the present hypothesis that the basic grammatical relations may be initially founded on imagery.

A final logical point may be noted regarding the relationship between McNeill's interpretation of LAD and the transformationists' critique of learning theories. According to McNeill, LAD is a native endowment that purportedly accounts for the child's acquisition of basic grammatical relations but not of transformations, which are learned. On the other hand, S-R learning theories have been criticized particularly for their inability to handle complex transformations, but it has not been shown that they are unable to explain the acquisition of basic grammatical relations. Thus the nativistic approach is offered as an alternative "explanation" of the simplest grammars, which learning theory may be able to handle as well, but not of the more complex grammatical phenomena that give the latter most difficulty. This logical paradox is further justification for an attempt to explain language acquisition in terms of an experientially based theory, even one as speculative as the two-process model presently is in regard to that issue.

The Symbolic Processes and Poetry

Simonides the mnemonist was first and foremost a poet. It is historically fitting, therefore, that we consider the relationships between poetry and the symbolic processes. The more general justification, however, is that such an examination potentially can add to our understanding of both literary and psychological issues. An obvious problem of mutual interest is the relationship between poetic imagery and imagery as a psychological process; another is the relation between poetry and memory.

The poetic image   Imagery has long existed in poetry but it became the central concept in the poetic movement known as "Imagism," which had its origin around 1910 in England and America (see, e.g., Pratt, 1963). Apparently the imagist poets sometimes used the term *image* in essentially the same sense as it has been used here when the reference is to word imagery, i.e., a verbally evoked visual representation of objects and events. T. E. Hulme, for example, viewed language and communication in terms of word images. Thus, the art of literature, from the writer's viewpoint, involves a "visual signification" or image that precedes the writing. There is a *"passage from the Eye to the Voice. From the wealth of nature to that thin shadow of words, that gramaphone."* The readers, on the other hand, "are the people who *see* things and want them expressed" (1955, p. 86). At other times the concept is used more generally, as when Ezra Pound refers to an image as "that which presents an intellectual and emotional complex in an instant of time" (Pound, 1954, p. 4).

The conceptual relation between poetic imagery and psychological imagery is a researchable question. Poems could be scaled on poetic imagery using ratings by sophisticated critics or teachers; and imagery in the psychological sense, using such procedures as ratings or latency measures of ease of image arousal. How highly will the two measures correlate? More detailed analysis could be made of the linguistic variables that contribute to such relationships. Is the vividness or latency of the poetic image—that "intellectual and emotional complex"—determined by the average imagery level of the words in the poem? By key words such as nouns and verbs? By certain syntactical arrangements such as high imagery words occurring early in the poem and functioning as "conceptual pegs" on which the rest of the "complex" hangs? Poets themselves have presented insights concerning such issues, but their views require interpretation and translation into relevant operations in order to be psychologically testable. What, for example, did the imagists mean by their prescriptive principle that imagist poetry should be "hard and clear, never blurred nor indefinite" (Pratt, 1963, p. 22)? Does it imply only the use of words that are concrete and specific in their reference, or something more? The psycholinguist could make his own assumptions and then seek to answer the questions in that context, but a collaborative effort between poet and psycholinguist might prove to be a mutually profitable approach to such questions.

Poetry and memory   The intimate nature of the relation between poetry and memory is evidenced by the long educational tradition in which "memory work" has been identified with poetic recitation. Perhaps poetry itself evolved as a mnemonic system for preserving and transmitting the valued traditions of early societies before writing was invented. To the extent that this is true, we might expect the useful mnemonic features of the speech sounds to be more characteristic of early rather than recent poetic forms. The latter, having developed in the context of writing, might have been freed to some extent from the need to preserve auditory mnemonics. It is interesting, for example, that one of the oldest epic poems in Europe, the Finnish *Kalevala* (its poetic form is imitated by Longfellow's *Hiawatha*), combines rhythmical and alliterative patterns with regular tonal cadence in a manner that may contribute summatively to ease of chunking, and hence, memorability. At the other extreme is contemporary "free verse," which, although by no means formless, is characterized by its freedom from the regular metre of earlier poetic forms.

Be that as it may, rhyming verse has been used for centuries as a mnemonic device (see Chapter 6) and persists as a feature in the "one-bun, two-shoe" technique that has been the subject of recent experimentation (Chapter 10). Independent of formal mnemonics, it has been shown that poetry is easier to learn than prose (McGeoch & Irion, 1952). This demonstrates only a global effect, however, without isolating the specific factors that are effective. At least three general "poetic variables" may be involved, including (*a*) rhythmical organization, based either on stress patterns and pitch changes generally, or syntax and pause patterns, or both; (*b*) acoustic similarity, including rhyming structure and alliteration; and (*c*) imagery. Visual structure is a fourth possibility in the case of printed poetry. Evidence is available on the effects of some of these individually but not in combination nor in the context of poetry. That the rhythm contributed by regular pausing contributes to memory is evidenced by the finding that short-term memory for sequences of digits is facilitated by rehearsing the items in nonoverlapping groups, with rehearsal in groups of three being optimal (Wickelgren, 1964). Visual grouping also affects the pattern of transition errors during recall of letter sequences (N. F. Johnson, 1968). The relation between rhythmic patterning and verbal memory has been extensively discussed by Neisser, who suggested that such a pattern "is a structure, which serves as a support, an integrator, and a series of cues for the words to be remembered" (1967, p. 235). Lenneberg (1967, pp. 107–119) has also discussed rhythm as an organizing principle in the production and understanding of language. In summary, these observations suggest that rhythm contributes to the memorability of poetry by providing organizational cues.

How does rhyming aid memory? Bower and Bolton (1969) investigated the problem using rhyming and unrelated paired-associate lists. They proposed that a rhyming relation such as *cat-mat* restricts the range of response alternatives to the stimulus, thereby changing recall essentially into a recognition test. The hypothesis was supported by the results of several experiments. One finding was that an assonance rule, in which the last phoneme is changed (e.g., hat-ham, bin-bit) and which restricts alternatives as much as a rhyming rule, facilitated performance as much as a rhyming rule. Another finding was that, when response alternatives were equated by multiple-choice tests for memory, the advantage of rhyming pairs vanished.

The Bower-Bolton hypothesis is a reasonable psychological explanation of the facilitating effect of rhyming in poetry. However, poems are usually more complex than paired associates and the interpretations may need elaboration. For example, rhyming is generally coordinated with rhythmical patterning, which varies according to the metre of the poem. How important for memory is regularity in the interval between the rhyming words? What interval is optimal? Do rhythm and rhyme interact in such a manner that the optimal rhyming interval differs for different rhythmical patterns? Essentially the same questions can be raised in regard to alliteration, which, like rhyming, is based on the patterning of acoustic similarity.

Rhythm, alliteration, and rhyming pertain to the phonology and syntax of the poem, that is, its surface structure. Psychologically, they reflect attributes of the verbal symbolic system that, in principle at least, can be varied independently of the content or meaning of the poem. Turning to poetic imagery, we are concerned directly with meaning and with a different (potential) contribution to the memorability of poetry. Whereas rhythm, alliteration, and rhyme can affect memory for the specific wording, imagery presumably can preserve the general theme or meaning but not the wording itself. This argument and evidence (e.g., Begg & Paivio, 1969) for it were discussed earlier independent of poetry, but it is particularly relevant in the present context. To the extent that the imagist poem, for example, presents "an intellectual and emotional complex in an instant of time," we would expect its meaning and theme to be particularly memorable, but its wording may be forgotten. Nevertheless, the image may facilitate memory for the poem by preserving its general theme or context in some kind of symbolic image or some specific aspects of the concrete information it conveys from which key words could be reconstructed. The mnemonic contribution of poetic imagery independent of phonology, or its possible interaction with phonological features, could be investigated in the laboratory, perhaps by writing miniature poems in which concreteness and thematic organization are varied while the poetic metre is held constant—or in which both kinds of variables are factorially varied. Of course, "natural" poems could also be used, although with an inevitable loss in experimental rigor.

Visual imagery could also be facilitative in the sense of visual memory for the pattern of the printed poem. Such visual memory would be ineffective for the retention of the entire poem, inasmuch as verbal sequences apparently are stored as auditory-motor patterns (see Chapters 2 and 7), but the locations of a few individual words may be retained, and these could provide a basis for the reconstruction of larger aspects of the overall pattern. Finally, imagery in the symbolic sense and imagery as a spatial patterning of words are combined in concrete poetry. In such a poem, "the visual form is often a metaphor, a spatial realization of what the poem as a whole is about" (F. Dunn, 1968). A poem about snails, for example, may be visually presented in a form that is somehow analogous to the action of a snail. Aside from whatever aesthetic value it may have, does such a pattern add anything to the memorability of a poem? If it does, is the symbolic significance of the pattern crucial to the effect? In what way does it interact or combine with the imagery aroused by the words themselves? With the acoustic pattern of the spoken poem? Answers to such questions may contribute generally to our understanding of the relationship between imaginal and verbal symbolic processes and language as a physical (visual and auditory) transmission code.

The Symbolic Processes and Metaphor

The creativity or productivity of language was identified at the outset as the crucial psycholinguistic problem. The reference was to syntactical creativity—the combinatorial processes of grammar. But equally important and interesting is the *semantic* creativity found in metaphor. An advertisement that urges you to "put a tiger in your tank" is semantically anomalous in its literal sense but not in what it symbolizes for the automobile driver who likes to take off with a roar. Of course, most metaphors are not newly created by their users. When we refer to a "warm personality," a "bright child," a "play on words," a "run of luck," and so on, we are using metaphorical expressions in a completely habitual way. They are "faded metaphors," whose meanings for the contemporary speaker are essentially literal. Nevertheless, all metaphors were once novel, and creativity must be regarded as one of their defining characteristics, just as it is of syntax, despite the repetitiousness of grammatical forms in everyday speech and writing.

Metaphor is unusually interesting for us because it throws into relief the intimate relationship between the symbolic modes, meaning, and language. It is often discussed in terms of images, but images with general rather than specific meaning. Thus Susanne Langer states that "Metaphor is our most striking evidence of *abstractive seeing*, of the power of human minds to use presentational symbols" (1948 reprint, p. 14). Conversely, the symbolic function of images is revealed in "their tendency to become metaphorical . . . [they are] . . . our readiest instruments for abstracting concepts from the tumbling stream of impressions" (p. 117). As general symbols, the images are not merely comprised of visual ingredients but are complex elements more appropriately described as "fantasies." Such fantasies are derived from specific experience, but the original perception of the experience is "promptly and spontaneously abstracted, and used symbolically to represent a whole kind of actual happening" (p. 118). Further abstraction of this literal generality under appropriate circumstances results in a metaphorical fantasy, a figurative meaning.

A number of psychologists also have emphasized the perceptual basis of metaphor, without necessarily referring to imagery. Thus R. W. Brown suggested that metaphorical extension involving the vocabulary of sensations (as when words like *warm, cold, heavy*, and *dull* are applied to personality, social manners, etc.) may be based on "correlations of sense data in the non-linguistic world" (1958, p. 154). Asch (1958) referred to functional similarities between the referents of the metaphor and the literal term. Osgood (1953) related metaphor to the intersensory experience of synesthesia. Werner and Kaplan (1963) observed that subjects who were required to express relational statements in terms of lines or images often did so in an abstract, metaphorical way. Such interpretations, although stressing perceptual processes and images, do not deny an intraverbal contribution to the similarity relation between the literal and figurative use of metaphorical terms. In discussing the metaphorical extension of the names of sense qualities, for example, Brown states that "Such a name will be applied to phenomena to which it has no real application because the name usually implies some other name which does have application" (1958, p. 154). That is, a verbal associative process is assumed in addition to sensory correlations.

A purely verbal interpretation is also possible, according to which literal term and metaphor are connected by common verbal associations. Koen (1965) obtained experimental support for such an interpretation in a situation in which subjects selected either a metaphor or a literal word to complete a sentence such as "The sandpiper ran along the beach leaving a row of tiny STITCHES/MARKS in the sand." They were instructed to choose the word most closely related to the group of ideas suggested by four cue words, which in normal usage were more often associated with either the metaphorical word or the literal word, or equally often with each. Consistent with the verbal associative interpretation, the metaphor was preferred when cued by its frequent associates but not otherwise. The finding does not necessarily rule out an image interpretation, however, since it could be argued that the cue words simply aroused images that were somehow "appropriate" to the image aroused by the sentence when completed by one rather than the other critical word.

The contrast between imagery and associative interpretations of metaphor can be viewed as a particular instance of the general controversy involving semantic and verbal associative (mediational) explanations of similarity relations (Chapter 3). A full treatment of the issue would require a discussion of common emotional reactions along with perceptual imagery under a (nonverbal) semantic category, and linguistic as well as verbal-associative approaches to metaphor under the verbal category. This will not be done here inasmuch as the purpose is simply to show that the interpretation of metaphor is not a unique psycholinguistic problem. Instead, it requires a joint consideration of the mediational function of both verbal and imaginal symbolic processes, particularly in relation to meaning similarity, paralleling the approach taken in this book in regard to various other phenomena.

A comparison with paired-associate learning is especially pertinent. We noted that imagery-mediated associations between abstract-abstract or concrete-abstract noun pairs is understandable only in terms of concretization of the abstract. Ocassionally this seemed to occur in the form of an image that symbolized both members of a pair, as when "boy scout" was reported as the imaginal mediator for the pair *chance-deed*. The image in this case is clearly metaphoric in nature, symbolizing in a single representation a complex idea that incorporates the meaning of both verbal items, that is, a boy scout is someone who takes a *chance* (opportunity) to do a good *deed*. The pictures used by G. R. Marshall (1965) as mediators for abstract noun pairs (e.g., a flag as the mediator for the pair *justice-wind*) were similarly chosen on the basis of their symbolic relationship to both members of the respective pairs. Both examples illustrate the creative use of imagery as a mediator of verbal associations—the generation of such a mediator in the one case, and the understanding of its relation to the word pair in the other. As in the case of metaphor, a new semantic relationship emerges. Such a conceptual parallel between the creation of new metaphors and mediated paired-associate learning has implications for both. On the one hand, image-mediated learning suggests an approach to the experimental study of the development of metaphoric meaning; on the other, the ubiquity of metaphor in natural language suggests that the discovery of images as effective mediators of associative learning, even with abstract words, may not be so strange or exceptional as was initially assumed in research concerned with the problem. Both phenomena may simply reflect a highly creative and productive function of images in language behavior. Moreover, both illustrate the point expressed in Chapter 3, that meaning is not a fixed attribute of words but is instead a variable reaction whose precise form depends on the verbal and nonverbal context in which the word appears.

SUMMARY

We have examined implications of the view that two coding systems mediate language behavior. One of these, the verbal representational system, presumably corresponds more or less directly to linguistic events themselves, that is, to properties of language as an auditory-motor or a visual-motor system.

The other code is nonverbal, corresponding to visual-spatial images representative of concrete objects and events, and capable of being associatively aroused by verbal stimuli and of mediating verbal behavior. The verbal system obviously must be involved in all psycholinguistic phenomena, but we assumed in addition that imagery plays an important role in the comprehension, retention, and production of concrete (descriptive) language in particular, whereas the processing of abstract language is assumed to be tied more closely to the linguistic representational system alone.

The theoretical value of the dual-coding model was supported by research findings related to language comprehension, production, and memory. In the case of memory, the model predicted both positive and negative effects attributable to imagery, depending on whether the subject was required to remember meaning, words independent of their syntactical order, or the exact wording and grammar of connected discourse. Imagery was also shown to be superior to a deep-structure model as a predictor of memory for English nominalizations. The model generally and its imagery component specifically were also shown to have interesting, testable implications in relation to language acquisition and the psychology of poetry and metaphor.

14
Individual Differences in Symbolic Habits and Skills

This chapter deals with individual differences in the efficiency of and "preference" for particular modes of symbolic representation. Such variations may be regarded as symbolic habits resulting from different patterns of experience during the development of the modes of representation, and their consideration here is simply an extension of the task of the preceding chapters, which has been to understand generally the functional significance of the symbolic modes. More specifically, individual differences can be measured and they accordingly constitute one class of defining operation that can be used to evaluate the functions of imaginal and verbal processes in perception, association, memory, and language. The historical and conceptual background of the problem will first be reviewed, followed by sections on the measurement of individual differences and research evidence on the functional significance of such differences in symbolic habits.

HISTORICAL AND CONCEPTUAL BACKGROUND

Imagery Types

The scientific study of symbolic habits began with attempts to classify individuals into types on the basis of the clarity or vividness of images experienced in different modalities. Such differences in imagery were first described by Fechner (1860, as reported by Woodworth, 1938), but their systematic empirical investigation began with Galton (1883). In what was the first questionnaire designed to investigate individual differences, he asked his subjects to imagine some definite object, such as their breakfast table, and then to answer a series of questions concerning the illumination, definition, and coloring of the image.

The questionnaire was sent initially to his friends in the scientific world and thereafter to persons in other occupations. He was astonished to find that many individuals reported little or no use of visual imagery. This was especially true of scientists, whose thinking tended to be predominately abstract and verbal— a finding that Binet compared with his own observation of the shift toward abstract thought among the more skillful chess players, as described in Chapter 2. Furthermore, Galton found little evidence for the existence of imagery types. Despite his conclusion concerning types, however, subsequent investigators became preoccupied with the search for "pure types" in terms of the habitual use of visual, auditory, or kinesthetic imagery.

The type approach was largely abandoned around 1910 when it became clear that pure types did not exist—that most people experience all kinds of images to some degree, and that distribution curves from studies of imagery were not multimodal as would be expected from a type theory, but approximately normal (Thorndike, 1914, pp. 272ff). It was still possible, of course, to accept the existence of individual differences conceptualized as extremes on a frequency distribution, and even the type notion persisted in modified form.

Thus Fernald (1912), whose study represents one of the most exhaustive investigations into the problem, classified her subjects into four groups, each group having more than one kind of imagery but showing a predominance of one type. Shaw (1919) followed Fernald's general approach and described her subjects as more or less verbal or visual, and so on. Attempts were also made to relate differences in imagery to performance on various tasks, i.e., to determine the functional significance of type of imagery. Although positive relations were obtained, the negative results were more striking. For example, Fernald found that individuals with high visual imagery were not superior on memory tasks that should have been particularly facilitated by the use of imagery, a finding that apparently influenced Watson's (1913) conclusion that imagery has no functional significance. We shall see later that this extreme conclusion is no longer justified even when directed specifically at the individual difference approach, although memory correlates of imagery "ability" continue to be more elusive than relations between memory and stimulus or experimental manipulations of imagery.

Visual and verbal imagery   The early typologies included verbal processes under the general term *imagery*, with finer distinctions being made in terms of visual, auditory, or kinesthetic verbal types. Woodworth (1938, p. 40) cites Stricker's descriptions in 1880 and 1882 of himself as an example of one whose word images are almost entirely motor in nature and who believed himself to be typical of most people. This observation is interesting because it indicates how readily verbal thought can be identified with motor processes on the basis of introspection. Auditory word-images were also commonly reported.

One of the most detailed attempts to assess individual differences in imagery was conducted by Griffitts (1927), who distinguished between verbal imagery and concrete imagery, the latter being specified in his testing procedure as referring to nonverbal content. In addition, however, he subdivided each type on the basis of sensory content. Thus even verbal imagery included visual-verbal, auditory-verbal, and kinesthetic-verbal components, and the term *inner speech* was equated with a combination or fusion of auditory and kinesthetic imagery. He tested for the dominance of the different types of imagery and found that, within concrete imagery, visual imagery dominated for most people; whereas, in the case of verbal imagery, the visual modality was subordinated to inner speech for the same subjects. He concluded (p. 72) that the majority of individuals who are said to be of the "visual type" probably are "concrete" thinkers, and those classed as "auditory-motor" are "verbal" thinkers. Griffitts' approach and results are particularly relevant because they are consistent with the conceptual distinction maintained here between concrete (visual) imagery and verbal (auditory-motor) symbolic processes.

A dichotomy between visual imagery and verbal *types* has been emphasized in a series of investigations beginning in 1929 on physiological correlates of mental imagery. Golla and Antonovitch (1929) reported a correlation between respiratory rhythm during mental tasks and imagery type as determined from answers to questions concerning thinking habits. Regularity of rhythm and amplitude, persisting during task performance, was associated predominately with visual imagery, whereas irregular respiration occurred among subjects characterized as having mainly auditory imagery.

Subsequently, in 1943, Golla, Hutton, and Walter related differences in electrical activity of the brain, as measured by the electroencephalogram (EEG), to different modes of thought, and this line of investigation has continued sporadically up to the present (e.g., Short, 1953; Slatter, 1960; B. B. Brown, 1966). The central issue in that research has been the relationship between EEG patterns and modes of thought, involving the hope that individuals could be classified into types on the basis of a purely objective, physiological measure. For example, at one extreme, habitual visualizers should show an absence of alpha rhythm, while at the other extreme, habitual verbalizers should show unusually persistent alpha. The underlying assumptions, of course, are that visual imagery, like visual perception, involves activity in the occipital cortex with resultant attenuation of the occipital alpha rhythm among those whose habitual mode of thought is visual-imaginal, whereas verbal thinking is mainly auditory-kinesthetic in nature. Results purporting to support such distinctions have been obtained in a number of studies (e.g., Golla et al., 1943; Short, 1953; Slatter, 1960), whereas others have failed to find evidence of such types (e.g., Drever, 1955; Oswald, 1957; Simpson, Paivio & Rogers, 1967; Walter & Yeager, 1956). Barratt (1956) reports, further, that suppression of the alpha rhythm is an unreliable index of visual imagery as defined by the demands of the task subjects are required to perform. The issue is unclear not only because of the conflicting empirical results but also because many of the studies involved methodological weakness, such as the classification of subjects into types on the basis of their verbal reports and the scoring of EEG records being conducted by the same person (see Simpson et al., 1967). The possibility that a relation may exist between physiological reactions and task-specific or habitual modes of symbolic activity is nevertheless intriguing and merits further careful study.

Some developmental implications of Galton's original work on imagery were pursued by Roe (1951). Noting Galton's finding that the majority of scientists he studied lacked mental imagery, whereas persons "in the general society" possessed such imagery, Roe suggested that the scientist's particular field may be important. Her study included 64 scientists from various fields, from whom she obtained interview data on life history and working habits (including modes of thought), as well as several kinds of test data. A significant pattern of relations was obtained between habitual type of symbolic activity and scientific field, with biologists and experimental physicists predominantly falling into the visual imagery group, whereas theoretical physicists, psychologists, and anthropologists were heavily concentrated in the group that reported habitual use of verbal symbolization. She also investigated the relation between habitual imagery of the scientist and the profession of their fathers, classified according to whether the profession was predominantly verbal (e.g., lawyer, clergyman) or less dependent on verbal manipulations (e.g., physician, engineer). The obtained relations, of borderline significance statistically, indicated that the fathers of most of the verbalizers were in "verbal" professions, whereas the fathers of visualizers were primarily in nonverbal professions. Roe speculated on whether the relations reflect heredity or training and experience. The preference here is for the latter interpretation, the different modes being viewed as acquired symbolic habits (cf. Bartlett, 1932, p. 304), but obviously the role of either factor cannot be determined from Roe's data or any existing evidence for that matter. In summary, Roe's findings supplement and extend the observations made long ago by Galton and Binet in showing that individual differences in symbolic habits are related to differences in occupation and experience. In general, these findings, too, are consistent with the view that nonverbal imagery is functional in concrete tasks (e.g., experimental physics), whereas verbal thinking is demanded by more abstract tasks (e.g., theoretical physics), and differences in conceptual habits develop accordingly or influence the individual's vocational choice, or both.

Extremes in Symbolic Habits and Skills

The general conclusion from the early research on individual differences in symbolic habits and abilities was that discrete types do not exist in the sense that they would be reflected in a multimodal distribution. However, individuals can of course fall at the extremes of the distribution with respect to the tendency and ability to engage in a particular form of symbolic activity, and occasionally these extremes depart sufficiently from the norm to constitute discrete (if rare) types. In this section we shall consider such types, with particular attention to eidetic imagery, number forms, and some mental characteristics of so-called idiot savants. No attempt will be made to present a detailed review of the literature of these phenomena. The emphasis instead will be on aspects that are especially relevant to our ultimate concern with functional distinctions between imaginal and verbal modes of representation.

Eidetic imagery   This kind of imagery has been characterized as an extremely vivid kind of visual imagery, the images having the quality of real perceptions, being projected "out there" rather than located "in the head," and apparently being more characteristic of children than of adults. Instances of imagery that might be classified as eidetic were described by Galton, and the conceptual distinction between such perceptlike images and ordinary memory images was made in 1907 by Urbantschitsch (cited in Woodworth, 1938). In subsequent decades, a flood of studies on the phenomenon appeared, culminating in the systematic investigations of Jaensch (1930). This extensive early literature has been thoroughly reviewed by Klüver (1928, 1931, 1932). Interest in eidetic imagery thereafter declined sharply, with only occasional reports appearing until recently, when interest was revived by Haber and Haber (1964). The reasons for the period of disinterest are obscure but probably included those that were responsible for the general neglect of imagery and other subjective phenomena following the behavioristic revolution. The unusual nature of the imagery, which apparently combines incompatible characteristics of the afterimage and the memory image (Hebb, 1968), may also have contributed to skepticism among psychologists and certainly made it difficult to formulate a reasonable theoretical interpretation of the phenomenon.

There has been a tendency to view such images as qualitatively distinct, but it has also been argued that "ordinary" memory images and eidetic images are part of a continuum (G. W. Allport, 1928; Klüver, 1932). More recently, Barber (1959b) concluded that different phenomena have been subsumed under the label, including negative and positive afterimages, hallucinatory behavior, and behaviors that may not reflect imagery at all. The belief that eidetic images are photographic in quality, that is, accurate copies of the stimulus situation, capable of being scanned for detail, is probably unwarranted, and Oswald (1960, pp. 80–81) in fact concluded that eidetic subjects are not unusually accurate in recall (see also Doob, 1964). On the other hand, some evidence suggesting higher accuracy of recall for visual details among eidetic than among noneidetic children has been obtained by others (Haber & Haber, 1964; Siipola & Hayden, 1965) when eidetic imagery is strictly defined to differentiate it from afterimages and memory. Leask, Haber, and Haber (1969) failed to confirm the finding with another sample of eidetic children, although these children appeared to be more confident and less hesitant in their memory reports than were noneidetic children. Despite the uncertainty of the group data, however, some individuals have been found to have eidetic images of astounding accuracy and duration when tested by careful objective procedures (Stromeyer & Psotka, 1970).

Some of the recent findings have important implications concerning the development of imaginal as compared to verbal processes. Siipola and Hayden (1965) found that the percentage of "eidetikers" was three times higher in their sample of retarded children than in the normal sample investigated by Haber and Haber (1964) and Leask et al. (1969). Siipola and Hayden expected such a difference from the hypothesis that eidetic imagery represents the prolonged retention of a primitive form of cognition. Since almost all of the eidetikers in their sample were from a brain-injured group rather than a familial-retardate group, yet only 50 percent of the former were eidetikers, they suggest that eidetic imagery may be related to damage in a specific area of the brain. Doob (1964, 1965, 1966), on the other hand, found a high frequency of eidetikers among some nonliterate African societies, and Siipola and Hayden were led to speculate whether early brain damage or illiteracy, or both, are sufficient conditions to produce eidetikers. The general implication of their analysis is that this unusual form of imagery is a functional development encouraged by any factor that restricts the ontogenetic development of abstract (verbal) modes of representation. As Doob concludes, such images "being concrete rather than abstract, may represent a survival from an earlier stage in the development of man and that normally they may be but need not be activated when the individual is experiencing some special kind of difficulty in coping with the environment (1966, p. 33)." It should be noted, however, that Leask et al. (1969) have not found any systematic differences in intellectual or other abilities between the eidetic sample and noneidetic children, and the probability of finding some kind of neurological correlate of eidetic imagery seems particularly remote at this time. Thus any particular theoretical interpretation of the phenomenon must be regarded as highly speculative.

Number forms and related phenomena   As part of his general concern with individual differences in imagery, Galton (1907) described, with striking examples, the phenomenon of "number forms." The term refers to the representation of numerals in some form of visual imagery, which Galton found to be a characteristic mode of thinking about numbers among some individuals. The figure "does not sound in their mental ear, but [its] written or printed form rises before their mental eye (p. 79)" and a series of numerals assumes a definite spatial pattern. The precise nature of the "form" varies among those who report the experience. It may consist of a line of any shape, a peculiarly arranged row of figures, or of a shaded space. Galton noted certain characteristics in common, however: They occur spontaneously, "independently of the will," their shape and position in the mental field of view is nearly invariable; and they have occurred as far back in childhood as the subjects could recollect. Related phenomena include spatial representations experienced by the individual in reference to days of the week, the year, their families, and so on.

Oswald (1960) questioned 300 persons concerning such imagery and concluded that at least one in four persons "possess" one or more of these images. They tended to occur, not whenever the numeral is thought of, as Galton had suggested, but only if a *series* is under consideration. Galton had also supposed that number forms function as memory aids, which "first came into existence when the child was learning to count, and was used by him as a natural mnemonic diagram . . . (1883, p. 87)." Oswald questioned their mnemonic usefulness, however, and suggested instead that they allow a semiconcrete, sensory comprehension of abstract concepts, particularly the concept of sequence. By the use of familiar concrete objects, such as a clock-face or a calendar, units with no inherent order can be arranged sequentially. Oswald's interpretation is particularly interesting because it supports the view suggested in Chapter 2, that images can have an abstract function for the individual. More specifically, number forms appear to exemplify what Werner and Kaplan (1963) referred to as concretization of an abstract referent, and also illustrate the manner in which spatially parallel imagery can function as a sequential processing system. Imagery presumably can serve these functions for all or most individuals, but they apparently do so in this consistent fashion only for some.

Symbolic habits among idiot savants and other "mental prodigies"   Eidetic images and number forms represent unusual symbolic abilities or habits that may remain restricted in scope, without any apparent general significance for behavior of the persons experiencing them. Examples of more general exaggerated symbolic habits occur among calculating prodigies, mnemonists, and other varieties of persons possessing unusual ability for particular mental tasks, often while remaining otherwise average or even below average intellectually. Such instances are of extraordinary interest here because the manifestations of modes of thought are thrown into relief, providing an unusual opportunity for the examination of their nature and functions. Unfortunately, while much has been written about such individuals, the descriptions often have been based on anecdote and uncontrolled observations, and hence do not provide useful scientific information. Some do, however, and we shall consider these with particular attention to evidence concerning the habitual use of imaginal or verbal modes of thought in the relevant activities.

The best known of these individuals are the calculating prodigies, particularly the *idiot savants*, who are capable of performing extraordinary feats of mental arithmetic while being generally dull, even in mathematics. An interesting summary of descriptive information (some of it by psychologists) on such individuals up to 1892 was provided by Ball (1956 reprint; for more detailed psychological descriptions of two of these individuals, see Binet, 1894). The following are some of the pertinent observations.

The calculators apparently differed in the extent to which they relied on auditory-motor representation or on visualization of numbers. Thus one calculator, Inaudi, trusted "mainly to the ear and to articulation." He could reproduce mentally the sound of the repetition of the digits of a number in his own voice and was confused if the numbers were shown to him in writing. Articulation of the digits seemed necessary for him to perform at his best and he generally repeated numbers aloud before beginning to work on them, the sequence of sounds being important. About 100 digits could thus be memorized in 12 minutes so that the sequence could be repeated forward or backward. Another prodigy, Bidder, also relied on the auditory sense and reported experiencing much greater difficulty in memorizing numbers when they were presented in writing than when they were "enumerated verbally." In direct contrast, Bidder's eldest son, somewhat of a calculating prodigy as well, worked with mental pictures of the figures and could "conceive no other way possible of doing mental arithmetic." Rückle, another calculator of note, also relied mainly on visualizing the numbers. These reports suggest that either mode of symbolic representation can function effectively in such mental tasks. However, the relative efficacy of the two modes would also be expected to vary as a function of such task characteristics as the degree to which it involves sequential or spatial processing. Consistent with such expectations, Binet (1894, Chapter 10) found that the auditory calculator, Inaudi, learned a sequence of 25 digits much more quickly then did a visual type, Diamandi; conversely, Diamandi excelled when the digits were presented as a number square and performance depended on visual memory for their spatial arrangement.

Such contrasts can also be found among more recent instances of "lightning calculators" and other varieties of uneven genius. One of the best known of these is the case of Salo Finkelstein, described by Bousfield and Barry (1933). Finkelstein was an extraordinary calculating genius whose mental computations were carried out in the form of vivid visual imagery. The numbers appeared as if written in Finkelstein's own handwriting on a blackboard, and were experienced in a relatively constant size and at a constant distance from the eyes. The span of imagery included about six digits, preferably in a horizontal arrangement. (These characteristics, it may be noted, resemble those described above for number forms.) Bousfield and Barry state that the imaginal process in this case is an integral part of the processes of memorization and calculation, apparently serving a reference (storage) function in that the imagery permits storage of numbers for subsequent reference while further calculations are carried out. The authors asserted, too, that "the involved manipulation of figures would undoubtedly be impossible" without such imagery, a suggestion not in accord with the earlier reports, noted above, of prodigies who preferred the auditory symbolic mode. Anastasi and Levee (1959) also describe an idiot savant, who, although poor in visual memory, could recite two and a half pages of prose after reading it once, and was proficient at remembering dates and reciting lists of digits backward. He did not specialize in mental calculations, however, and comparisons with prodigies such as Finkelstein may therefore be unwarranted.

The developmental origin of these unusual skills and habitual symbolic modes would obviously be of great interest, but systematic psychological research on the problem is lacking. Common features apparently occur in the life histories of calculating geniuses, however, which permit some general inferences to be made. Ball, in his early review, apparently assumed a specific hereditary component, stating that in common the prodigies were "blessed with excellent memories," but in addition he gave full weight to experiential factors revealed by the histories of these individuals. Prominent among these factors were incessant practice and social reinforcement, as indicated clearly in the following passage:

Blessed with excellent memories for numbers, self-confident, stimulated by the astonishment their performances excited, the odd coppers thus put in their pockets and the praise of their neighbours, they pondered incessantly on numbers and their properties; discovered (or in a few cases were taught) the fundamental arithmetical processes, applied them to problems of ever increasing difficulty, and soon acquired a stock of information which shortened their work. Probably *constant practice and undivided devotion to mental calculation* are essential to the maintenance of the power, and this may explain why a general education has so often proved destructive to it. The performances of these calculators are remarkable, but . . . are not more than might be expected occasionally from lads of exceptional abilities (1956, p. 487).

Another category of special genius characterized by an extraordinary emphasis on particular habits of thought is the mnemonics expert. An unusually detailed longitudinal study of such an individual has recently been reported by Luria (1968 translation). The mental life of his subject, S, was dominated by visual imagery so vivid that Luria suggested that his recall of events could more appropriately be described in terms of factors governing perception and attention than in terms applicable to memory. It resembled eidetic imagery in that S claimed literally to "see" the images, but according to Luria, the images were also differentiated from eideticism by such features as "greater mobility" and an amazing degree of synesthesia. With respect to the latter, his images were accompanied by a complex of sensations including tactual, kinesthetic, and taste experiences. The visual modality was dominant, however, in that sounds were transformed into or accompanied by visual images of "lines," "blurs," and "splashes" of color. Particularly interesting to us is the report that this translation into visual imagery was characteristic of his recall and his understanding of the meaning of words. Each word of a series summoned up a graphic image, distinguished from those of "the general run of people" by their extraordinary vividness, stability, and synesthetic quality.

These vivid images apparently enabled him to perform the remarkable feats of memory for which he was noted. After three minutes of study, a table of 50 numbers could be reproduced by "reading off" the numbers in the vertical columns, the rows, the diagonals, or in any designated square. Similar results were obtained with tables of letters. In these instances, S claimed that he continued to see the table and merely had to "read it off." Sequences of words were generally memorized by converting them into concrete visual images and putting these images into a concrete setting, for example, by distributing them along some roadway or street that he visualized. Although, as a professional mnemonist, S had been presented hundreds of such series, he was able to reproduce a particular series accurately as long as sixteen years after the session in which the words had been originally presented and recalled. Luria concluded that there appeared to be no limit to the capacity or durability of S's memory.

Coupled with whatever advantages resulted from such a capacity for vivid recall were the disadvantages of S's style of thought. Images dominated his awareness, appearing, often uncontrollably, in the form of associative chains. Their occurrence to words made reading difficult and chaotic because the irrelevant details were obstacles to a more general understanding of verbal passages as a whole. Abstract concepts were particularly confusing for they, too, had to be translated into graphic images to be grasped. The word *eternity*, for example, would evoke an image of some ancient figure. These persistent and agonizing attempts to concretize everything made the transition to "higher levels of thought" arduous and slow.

Like the other extremes (eidetic imagery, number forms, idiot savant) that have been considered in this chapter, Luria's mnemonist manifested, in an exaggerated form, processes that operate more subtly in most individuals. Concretization of abstract referents appeared to be characteristic of S's mode of thought and, in general, it may be said that he remained at a highly concrete functional level in terms of the developmental sequence discussed in Chapter 2. Images, not verbal associations, constituted for him the dominant associative meaning of words, as though words generally were concrete rather than abstract (cf. Chapter 3). The mnemonic techniques he developed as a professional mnemonist are strikingly like those taught long ago by students of the art of memory (Chapter 6). Finally, it is relevant that the S's production of language was not hindered by his dominant symbolic habit, for, however digressive the content of his speech, he was verbose. Thus imagery not only played a prominent role in his understanding of language but apparently served to mediate (in interaction with the verbal symbolic system) his linguistic production as well— problems that were part of the general topic of Chapter 13.

Other types of individual experiences occur and are relevant to the understanding of the nature of thought in general. However, they are only indirectly pertinent to the central problems of this book and will not be considered in detail. These include hallucinations, hypnogogic and hypnopompic imagery, body schema experiences, phantom limbs (following amputations), and so on. Many of these are described in detail by McKellar (1957), who also presents a more extensive account of those phenomena that have been discussed here briefly (e.g., synesthesia, diagram forms).

THE MEASUREMENT OF INDIVIDUAL DIFFERENCES

The concept of individual differences in imaginal and verbal symbolic habits is obviously of little scientific value unless the differences can be reliably measured. A theoretical consequence of such quantification, if it can be realized, is that the postulated symbolic processes would be operationally distinguished. Although the degree of success that has been achieved in such quantification and differentiation of the symbolic modes is far from satisfactory, some progress has been made since Galton's introduction of the "breakfast table" questionnaire. The major methods will be described briefly here in anticipation of later sections that deal with studies in which subjects have been selected on the basis of one or another specific measure.

Individual Differences in Imagery

Subjective ratings   Attempts to measure differences in imagery "ability" have included questionnaires and rating scales that have generally evolved from Galton's (1883) original method, in which he asked subjects to imagine some definite object, such as their breakfast table, and then answer questions concerning such characteristics as the brightness, definition, and coloring of the image. Betts (1909) developed a 150-item Questionnaire upon Mental Imagery, which represented a quantifiable expansion of Galton's questionnaire. Seven major sensory modalities were considered—the visual, auditory, cutaneous, kinesthetic, gustatory, olfactory, and organic. Subjects were asked to think of such experiences as the size and the shape of trees in a familiar landscape, the beating of rain against the window, the feel of velvet, lifting a heavy weight, the taste of oranges, the smell of roses, and the sensation of fatigue. They rated their images on a 7-point scale of *clearness* and *vividness*, ranging from "Perfectly clear and as vivid as the actual experience" to "No image present at all, you only *knowing* that you are thinking of the object." A major finding was a positive correlation between the reported vividness of imagery for the different modalities, without any support for the theory of imagery types.

Although comprehensive, Betts' original questionnaire was prohibitively long. Sheehan (1967a) recently developed a shortened form (35 items, 5 from each modality) on the basis of a factor analysis of the 150-item version and, in the course of the study, he confirmed and extended Betts' findings. Individuals differed considerably in their reported imagery, females reported somewhat more vivid imagery than males in all modalities except the kinesthetic, and no evidence of types emerged. A single factor accounted for 39 percent of the total variance on the test, with all 35 items from the short version loading highly on the factor, indicating a general ability to image. Correlations of .92 and .98 were obtained for two samples between the total scores for the shorter version and the long one, indicating the reliability of the former as a measure of this general ability. The questionnaire has been used by Sheehan to predict imagery in a number of experimental studies to be considered later.

Other modifications of Galton's method have been used by Griffitts (1927), Brower (1947), and Schmeidler (1965). Griffitts' study has already been described in the earlier discussion of the type theory. He used rating scales along with performance tasks to investigate individual differences in clearness of, and dominance relations among, visual, auditory and kinesthetic imagery. The most notable feature of his study from our point of view was his attempt to differentiate between verbal and nonverbal (concrete) imagery, with some suggestion of a correspondence between visual and concrete imagery on the one hand, and auditory-motor and verbal thought on the other. Schmeidler (1965), using a quantifiable version of the original breakfast table questionnaire, found a low positive correlation between imagery scores and a measure of creativity. Rejecting an acquiescence response set as an explanation of the relation, Schmeidler suggested instead that it tends to support the psychoanalytic thesis that creative individuals accept the products (i.e., images) of primary process thinking. A slightly modified version of Schmeidler's questionnaire has been used recently (e.g., Ernest & Paivio, 1969; Hyman, 1966; Paivio & Simpson, 1968; Simpson, Paivio, & Rogers, 1967) as part of an imagery test battery, with some success in the prediction of reactions presumed to be mediated by imagery, as we shall see.

Brower (1947) used a self-rating test of imagery in which subjects were presented a series of stimulus words or phrases relevant to eight imagery modalities (e.g., visual: yellow ribbon; auditory: drone of airplane; tactual: feel of velvet, etc.). For each stimulus, the subject rated his imagery experience on a 5-point scale. Brower found no significant relations between imagery scores and intelligence as measured by the Otis. A somewhat similar procedure in which words were rated for their imagery value was included in a factor-analytic study (Paivio & Rogers, unpublished) along with other measures of imagery as well as a number of indices of verbal-associative skills. The measures will be considered in more detail in a later section, which deals with the factorial structure of the symbolic habits.

Another dimension that has been measured by questionnaire is the controllability of voluntary concrete imagery. Originally developed by Rosemary Gordon, the test is described in detail by Richardson (1969, pp. 50–59) in the context of studies in which Gordon's test and Betts' vividness questionnaire were used with some success in the prediction of such behaviors as image-mediated motor learning.

Performance tests   Performance tests involving tasks presumably requiring the manipulation of images have been used by numerous investigators. The early studies, summarized by Woodworth (1938), were concerned with differentiating among types, and the tasks were based on the assumption that visual tasks require visual imagery, while auditory work requires auditory imagery. Some of the ones that are most relevant to later discussions will be considered here. Fernald (1912) used a spelling task in which words were pronounced to the subject, who was required to spell them backward. Presumably, if the subject had a photographic image of the word, he could simply read off the letters backward. Fernald found, however, that no subject was able to do so, although she did find that subjects reporting visual imagery performed somewhat better than did others. The task was discussed in Chapter 2 in connection with spatial characteristics of visual imagery, where it was pointed out that a strong directional component may be built into the task because of the sequential nature of spelling.

A similar task is the letter or number square, introduced by Binet (1894), in which the subject is presented with a square matrix of letters or numbers. He is required to read the letters from left to right while learning the pattern, but in the subsequent test may be required to recall them in vertical columns or diagonally. The assumption again was that the visualist should be able to read off the letters equally easily in any direction. However, as in the spelling task, even subjects reporting high visual imagery were able to recall the items much more rapidly in the left-to-right sequence than otherwise. (Here we might recall the exceptional performance of Luria's mnemonist, on similar tasks. It should also be noted, however, that S was permitted to scan the pattern freely in any sequence, rather than in the left-to-right direction only. This might account for his ability to recall the pattern in any sequence but would not explain the extraordinary capacity and persistence of S's memory.)

Another early approach, discussed by Woodworth (1938), was the method of distraction, which was based on the assumption that a visual process will be most readily disturbed by extraneous visual stimuli, an auditory process by auditory distraction, and so on. Thus, if the subject is most hampered by visual distraction, it could be inferred that he is learning visually. Although the test did not serve its intended purpose well, it is of interest because the general approach of attempting to interfere with the functioning of one or another symbolic mode has been frequently adopted in studies of perception and memory. Recall, for example, that Brooks (1967) used a method that essentially involves interfering with the visual or verbal thinking required for task performance by introducing other, incompatible visual or verbal components into the task (see Chapter 5).

Other objective tests discussed by Woodworth included ones based on the relative frequency of visual or auditory words occurring in association tests or in written works, relative proficiency in learning by visual or auditory presentation of material, and the picture description (testimony) test. These are of some interest here because the essential elements of the tasks have appeared independently in more recent experimental studies concerned with imagery, indicating common underlying assumptions to the effect that imaginal processes are reflected in the semantic content of language, perceptual selectivity, and coping with concrete (e.g., pictorial) tasks.

Most of the early studies involving the tasks described above combined such performance criteria with subjective reports of the type of imagery "used" by the subject. Some support for the predicted correspondence between the type of imagery required by the task and that reportedly used by the subject was occasionally obtained. Davis (1932) systematically repeated some of the earlier work, comparing subjective reports of imagery with performance scores for memory tasks involving different sense modalities. His results showed substantial relations between type of imagery and corresponding memory scores, so that subjects reporting use of auditory imagery, for example, displayed more accurate memory for tones than did those who reported other images or none.

Davis' study provided encouraging support for the functional significance of imagery as inferred from the individual difference approach, but the results are open to alternative interpretations that will be considered in a later context.

Standardized tests and the factorial structure of imagery   Many performance tests have been developed that can be interpreted as measures of imagery ability. The most prominent among these have been those concerned with visual-spatial ability. The space factor found by Thurstone (1938) was in fact defined as facility with spatial and visual imagery. It was measured by tests such as Flags (Thurstone & Jeffrey, 1956) in which the items are pairs of flags with the two members shown in different positions and the subject is to indicate whether or not one has been turned over to show the reverse side. Among the many tests of this kind, those that have been used in research on imagery include the Flags Test, the Minnesota Paper Form Board, the Kuhlmann-Finch Space Test, and Thurstone's Spatial Relations Test. Guilford's (1967) factor-analytic work suggests, however, that more than one factor may be represented by some of these tests. Furthermore, his definition of imagery identifies it with a factor other than spatial.

Within Guilford's structure-of-the-intellect model, the relevant abilities fall into the content category of *figural information*. Figural information is defined as being in concrete form, as perceived or as recalled in the form of images (1967, p. 227). The spatial ability tests are perceptual in nature and are grouped with the cognitive abilities, whereas Guilford interprets images as revivals of perceptual experience and accordingly places them in the category of memory abilities. For several reasons we shall adopt a more general viewpoint and consider imagery as appropriately falling within the cognitive category as well. One reason is that imagery has been empirically investigated using spatial ability tests; second, it has been difficult to differentiate among the relevant factors; and, third, imagery conceptually overlaps several of the factors in Guilford's model.

The most relevant cognitive figural ability factors identified by Guilford appear to be those labeled *cognition of visual-figural systems* (CFS-V) and *cognition of figural transformations* (CFT). The former is defined as an ability to apprehend visually the spatial arrangement of things in one's psychological field. Among the representative tests of CFS-V mentioned by Guilford are Thurstone's space tests, Aerial Orientation (used in Army Air Forces research by Guilford and his associates), and Spatial Orientation from the Guilford-Zimmerman Aptitude Survey (1948). CFT refers to transformations in visual information, including changes in sensory qualities and quantities, in location (movement), and in arrangement of parts. Guilford points out that CFT was difficult to differentiate from its "near neighbour CFS-V" because many space tests include both factors. Among the defining tests for CFT, he described Spatial Visualization I, which is a multiple-choice paper-folding-and-cutting test. Line drawings show how a sheet of paper is folded, with one, two, or three folds in succession, and how one or two holes are cut at certain places. The subject is to choose the correct one of five alternative drawings that depict how the paper might look when unfolded. Another, Spatial Visualization II, consists of a series of problems involving verbal descriptions of a block of wood of certain dimensions, say 3 by 3 by 3 inches, which is of a certain color and painted on the outside with another color. The subject is to imagine the block cut into 1-inch cubes, and is asked how many cubes have one color only or how many have one or more sides of the outside color.

The CFT factor obviously can be conceptualized in terms of transformational images, as described in Chapter 2. Thus, in their experimental study of imagery in children, Piaget and Inhelder (1966) used paper-folding problems analogous to those included in Guilford's Spatial Visualization I. The cube problem in Spatial Visualization II is also familiar to us from Chapter 2 as an example of transformational imagery, and Guilford himself emphasizes that, since the problem is presented verbally, the subject "must operate with visual imagery or some other surrogate for visual perception" (p. 101). The CFS-V tests, on the other hand, involve problems in which the perceptual information is more directly given. To the extent that this is the case, it may be inappropriate to regard such tests as measures of imagery ability. Thus the spatial ability tests, such as Flags and the Minnesota Paper Form Board, may be appropriate as measures of imagery primarily or only because they include a transformational component along with any visual-spatial component, as indicated by their loadings on both the CFT and the CFS-V factors. This interpretation of the MPFB has some experimental support. Gavurin (1966) investigated the relation between MPFB scores and anagram solving under two conditions, one permitting overt manipulation of anagram letters, and the other not permitting overt letter rearrangement. A significant correlation ($r=.54$) between the MPFB and anagram solving was obtained only under the latter (implicit or symbolic manipulation) condition. Thus the MPFB test can be appropriately interpreted as a measure of individual differences in the ability to manipulate visual images, or (in Guilford's terms) cognition of figural transformations.

The most relevant of Guilford's memory-ability factors appears to be *memory for visual-figural systems* (MFS-V), which is most clearly defined by tests used by Christal (1958) in a study of visual memory. As described by Guilford (1967, pp. 125–126), these include Position Memory, in which the subject is required to recall the position on a page at which he had, 4 hours earlier, studied number-word pairs in connection with another test. Position Recall I is similar, involving four study pages on each of which 12 figures are scattered, and the subject later is to recall the positions. Space Memory presents five squares, each divided into five sections, with an object in each section. The subject later reports in which section each object appeared. Guilford points out that these tests parallel the cognitive tests for factor CFS-V. It should also be noted that Christal's tests are basically similar to the figure- or letter-matrix tests used earlier by Binet (1894), Fernald (1912), and others as performance tests of visual imagery.

The conceptualization of imagery as a process that is involved in separate (cognitive and memory) factors can be readily appreciated. Despite the fact that cognition and memory can be theoretically and factorially distinguished, as in Guilford's work, they are interdependent phenomena that must involve common processes. As Guilford put it, there can be memory only if there has been cognition (1967, p. 211) and, conversely, memory storage is an essential condition or determiner of cognitions (p. 203). Imagery can be regarded as a manifestation of the figural information that is in memory storage, and this is how Guilford chooses to define the term. In addition, however, imagery as a symbolic process is one class of determinant of cognitions—a cognitive tool that can be used in an anticipatory and creative fashion in such cognitive problems as figural transformations. In the latter sense, imagery is a construction based on stored information, and it is understandable that the storage and the constructive utilization of imagery might constitute different abilities, which emerge empirically on different factors in the study of individual differences. Imagery is conceptually broader, therefore, than the ability concept. This is implicitly recognized by Guilford as indicated, for example, by his reference to the necessity for using imagery to solve the cube problems that constitute the Spatial Visualization II test.

It follows from the above that imagery may be involved to a greater or lesser degree in numerous categories of abilities and functions distinguished by Guilford. In particular, it should be reflected in tests of figural information other than the ones mentioned here, as well as in some tests of symbolic and semantic content categories. This is an empirical problem, however, and further speculation about it is unnecessary here.

It was indicated earlier that spatial ability tests had been used in several studies of imagery. Some of those will be briefly noted here. Barratt (1953) combined performance scores on the Minnesota Paper Form Board with a multiple-choice questionnaire concerning the subject's use of imagery on the test, subjects being classified as high or low in imagery on the basis of the combined data. Ray-Chowdhury (1957) adapted Barratt's questionnaire technique for use in conjunction with performance tests of intelligence (Koh's Block Design, Alexander's Passalong, and the Dearborn Form Board), and found substantial correlations between the questionnaire imagery scores and performance test scores. Kuhlman (1960) and Stewart (1965) found strong relations between individual differences on spatial ability tests and differential performance on learning tasks involving pictorial and verbal material. The substantive content of these and other studies will be reviewed in more detail later.

Behaviorial criteria for eidetic imagery   The classification of subjects on imagery could be based on objective behavioral criteria other than those already discussed. This has been done by Haber and Haber (1964), Doob (1964), and Siipola and Hayden (1965) in connection with the research on eidetic imagery described earlier. Four colored pictures were used as stimuli, and a number of scoring categories were used, including the presence of imagery, its color (positive color reports distinguishing eidetic images from afterimages), location (projected or internal), tense (the use of present tense indicating eidetic rather than memory images), eye movements, duration of images, and accuracy of report. Leask et al. (1969) examined each of the criteria critically in terms of such factors as the demand characteristics of the situation and concluded that the child's report that he *sees* an image should be the major criterion, with the others added primarily to delineate the nature of the imagery.

Individual Differences in Verbal Processes

Verbal processes were conceptualized as verbal images in the early research on imagery, the criterion generally being the subject's introspective report. Griffitts' (1927) study is representative of the methods used. Subjects were given a series of tasks and were required to give introspections at the close and sometimes at the middle of each. The tasks included such problems as backward repetition of a series of letters and numerals that were read to the subject, recall of letter squares and poems, and mental multiplication problems. The introspections involved ratings of the degree of dominance of verbal as compared to concrete imagery and, within each, the relative dominance of different sensory modalities. Thus, as in the earlier type approaches generally, Griffitts was concerned with differentiating between verbal and nonverbal processes as symbolic habits. Little attention was given to verbal abilities in the context of that early research, but it is appropriate to do so, and we shall consider potentially relevant tests of both verbal-symbolic habits and abilities in the following discussion.

The problem of finding appropriate tests of verbal processes is at least as difficult as the measurement of individual differences in imagery, and for the same reason: Verbal processes are pervasively involved in ability and other tests that are likely to be relevant. The pervasiveness is demonstrated, for example, by the large number of verbal factors that have emerged in factor-analytic studies (e.g., Guilford, 1967). A further problem is the requirement that the verbal tests be relatively uninfluenced by nonverbal imagery. Since factor-analytic methods are particularly suited to such problems, it may be instructive again to consider what pertinent information might emerge from Guilford's (1967) approach to the structure of the intellect.

Inasmuch as imagery is most specifically coordinated to the tests of figural information, it might be expected that verbal processes would be manifested in other ability factors. The most obvious candidates appear to be those involving symbolic and semantic content, and it is in such factors that most of the verbal ability tests are to be found. Such a division of abilities is in fact suggested by Guilford in relation to concrete and abstract information. Given an interpretation of "concrete" as that which is immediately given, it follows that "the concrete can be defined as figural information, and other kinds, particularly symbolic and semantic, can be considered abstract" (p. 206). He noted, however, that there are figural conceptions as well as other more generalizable varieties of figural information, which is analogous to the earlier argument here (Chapter 2) that images can serve abstract functions. Furthermore, it cannot be assumed that the responses to symbolic and semantic ability tests are mediated by verbal mechanisms alone nor, conversely, that figural information involves only imagery. Despite such difficulties, Guilford's factorial model provides a possible initial basis for selecting tests of verbal abilities that are factorially distinct from the most obvious imagery abilities. Although it has not been used explicitly as a basis for the investigation of individual differences in the two symbolic modes, and for that reason no systematic attempt will be made here to relate the discussion to the model, it provides a useful frame of reference.

Overt associative responses are generally assumed to reflect internal (verbal) mediating processes (Deese, 1965), and measures of associative fluency and verbal productivity would accordingly serve as indices of such processes. One of the simplest techniques is to apply Noble's (1952a) production method of measuring meaningfulness (m) to people rather than words, averaging the number of associates a subject produces to a series of stimulus words in some constant time interval (cf. Greeno, 1965; A. Reynolds & Paivio, 1968). Use of the same operation for the assessment of individual differences in symbolic habits and associative meaningfulness of words has obvious theoretical advantages, and both have been attempted. However, it was noted earlier in connection with the measurement of meaning (Chapter 3) that verbal associations and imagery are confounded in the semantic approach at least. Its fate as an individual difference measure will be considered presently. Other word-fluency and associational-fluency tests would presumably be relevant as well.

Another approach is to determine a subject's ability to produce words that "link" other words. Guilford's Association IV Test (French, Ekstrom, & Price, 1963), which requires the subject to find a word associated with two words, and Mednick's (1962) Remote Associates Tests, which requires the subject to find a common associate to three words, are examples of such tests.

All of the above would fall within one or another of Guilford's *divergent* (and possibly *convergent*) *production ability* categories. They appear potentially relevant to the prediction of performance in verbal-memory and associative-learning tasks and have been used for that purpose, as we shall see later, but their ultimate value in this regard remains uncertain at the present time. Numerous other tests listed by Guilford appear to be highly relevant on logical grounds, but they have not been empirically explored within the context of a theoretical approach to verbal learning and behavior.

Appropriate standardized tests of verbal symbolic habits are much more difficult to find than tests of verbal abilities. Nunnally and Flaugher (1963) have developed a number of associational methods to assess "semantic habits," which include tendencies to make positive or negative evaluations, to respond in terms of denotative attributes of objects, and to categorize things. The method is interesting and undoubtedly relevant to cognitive functioning, but it is difficult to determine to what extent scores on the test reflect associative reactions mediated by concrete images rather than verbal-associative habits. An inventory concerned with verbal thinking habits (or styles, or strategies) appears to be the most direct and obvious approach to the problem, and was attempted in the following study.

A Factor-Analytic Study of Imaginal and Verbal-Symbolic Habits and Skills

A factor-analytic study conducted by Paivio in collaboration with T. B. Rogers sought to determine the relations among measures of individual differences in imaginal and verbal processes. The study included items designed to measure symbolic habits as well as abilities. Several scores from verbal learning and memory tasks were also included, but the consideration of that portion of the study will be postponed to a later section.

The tests regarded as possible indices of imagery ability included Space Relations, Flags, and a portion of the Minnesota Paper Form Board (MPFB), Barratt's (1953) questionnaire on the MPFB, Sheehan's (1966a) shortened form of Betts' imagery questionnaire, a version of Galton's imagery questionnaire (Hyman, 1966), and mean word imagery (based on the subject's rating of 10 concrete and 10 abstract nouns on a 7-point scale). Note that the first three are perceptual or figural ability tests, whereas the remainder are verbal tests of vividness or ease of imagery.

The verbal ability tests included Advanced Vocabulary (French et al., 1963), associational fluency (based on the mean number of verbal associations to four concrete and four abstract words; A. Reynolds & Paivio, 1968), the Remote Associates Test (Mednick, 1962), Object Naming (French et al., 1963), and Alternate Uses (a test of divergent thinking in which the subject generates unusual uses for common objects; Christensen, Guilford, Merrifield, & Wilson, 1960). A rating scale measure was also provided by mean ratings of the 20 nouns on verbal-associative meaningfulness (i.e., rated m).

The degree to which the subjects habitually used imaginal and verbal modes of thinking was assessed by an 86-item true-false questionnaire developed specifically for the study. The items were selected on intuitive grounds, working from the assumption that individuals vary in their typical cognitive approach to different tasks. The following are examples of items designed to measure imagery habits: I often use mental pictures to solve problems; I can easily picture moving objects in my mind; I can add numbers by imagining them to be written on the board; I find it difficult to form a mental picture of anything (scored for "False" response). Examples of items intended to measure verbal thinking habits are: I enjoy doing work that requires the use of words; most of my thinking is verbal, as though talking to myself; I have difficulty producing associations for words (scored "False"); I enjoy solving crossword puzzles and other word games. A 7-point scale ("never" to "all the time") was also included to assess the habitual use of imaginal and verbal devices.

Finally, the subjects' grade-13 marks in geometry, geography, and English, and their overall grade averages were included to provide a basis for evaluating the predictive validity of the tests. We assumed that geometry and geography would be most likely to reflect spatial and imaginal ability, whereas English (and perhaps history) would reflect verbal skills. The overall average provided an index of general intelligence.

The tests were completed by 96 university students. The intercorrelations of the test scores were factor-analyzed, and the analysis subjected to a Varimax rotation. The results showed a loose factor structure comprised of 10 factors, including no less than four that could be regarded as imagery factors and two identifiable as verbal factors.

Factor I was obviously spatial (or figural transformational) ability, loading highest on Space Relations (.79) and the MPFB (.64), with moderate loadings also on Flags (.46) and Object Naming (.59). Geography and overall grade averages had the highest loadings (.34 and .27) of the grade 13 marks on this factor. Factor II was also an imagery dimension as defined by subjective reports. Thus its highest loadings were on the MPFB questionnaire (.71), the inventory items concerned with the habitual use of imagery (.65), Sheehan's imagery test (.55), and the Galton questionnaire (.46). However, the factor also loaded substantially (.48) on one spatial ability test, the MPFB. A third imagery factor was defined by the 7-point imagery-use scale (a loading of .73), the imagery habits questionnaire (.43), and Flags (.40). The Galton questionnaire had a factor loading of .32, and associative fluency to concrete noun stimuli, .27. The questionnaire items concerned with verbal thinking habits loaded negatively (−.68) on this factor. The fourth imagery factor had high loadings on geometry (.76) and the Galton questionnaire (.62). It also loaded slightly on imagery ratings of words (.28), and the imagery habits questionnaire (.25).

One of the two verbal factors was clearly associative fluency as defined by verbal associations to abstract stimulus nouns (a loading of .91), associations to concrete nouns (.81), and the Alternate Uses test (.70). It also loaded to some degree on Object Naming (.34), Vocabulary (.25), and rated m (.25). The other verbal factor was defined by the verbal habits questionnaire and Advanced Vocabulary, with factor loadings of .87 and .71 respectively.

The remaining factors are either difficult to define or represent method factors. In either case, they need not be considered here.

The results were generally interpretable and interesting despite the looseness of the overall factor structure. While the imagery factors obviously could be regarded as reflecting method variance, they were not defined only by method. Thus Factor I was defined by spatial ability tests, but it also included Object Naming, which involves verbal responses. A reasonable interpretation is that the naming of objects from memory, like the performance on the spatial tests, is mediated partly by nonverbal images. Moreover, test performance in each case seems to require flexible (transformational) rather than static imagery. Again Factor II was imagery, primarily as defined by subjective reports or ratings, but it also loaded substantially on the MPFB. Of the two verbal ability factors, associative fluency was rather specifically defined by the associational method, but it would be inappropriate to conclude on that basis alone that it is "nothing but" a method factor, since the method and content are inseparable. Be that as it may, the most encouraging implication of the factor structure is that imaginal and verbal processes emerged as different cognitive dimensions, just as they had in Thurstone's original work and in Guilford's recent research on the structure of the intellect. Neither symbolic mode is a unitary dimension, however, and the functional significance of the different components remains to be determined. The following is a review of some attempts to deal with the complex problem.

RESEARCH EVIDENCE ON THE FUNCTIONAL SIGNIFICANCE OF INDIVIDUAL DIFFERENCES

The evidence on the functional significance of imaginal and verbal symbolic abilities and habits will be reviewed under the following headings: (a) perception, (b) associative reactions, (c) memory and learning, and (d) language.

Perception

Imagery and perceptual illusions   Perceptual effects attributable to verbally evoked images and individual differences in the susceptibility to such effects have been described by Uznadze (1966). The research represented extensions of work on perceptual illusions aroused by experimental sets. The following experiment illustrates the basic phenomenon. A subject is repeatedly presented with two balls, one obviously larger than the other. He holds one in each hand and is asked to compare them and say which is larger. This is repeated 10 to 15 times with the larger ball always in the same hand, then the subject is presented with two balls that are identical in volume. In the majority of cases the subject reports an illusion of contrast: The ball held in the hand that previously held the smaller ball seems larger to him. A comparable visual illusion is found after the subject has viewed two circles differing in size, and analogous illusions occur in other sense modalities as well, although the effects are not always ones of contrast.

The experimental extensions to imagery were carried out by Natadze (as described by Uznadze, 1966, p. 117ff.). Instead of the subject's being given two balls, he is asked to imagine that in one hand he holds a larger ball and in the other a smaller one. This verbal set is repeated 15 times, after which the subject is actually presented two balls of equal size for comparison. The same type of experiment was carried out in the visual mode: The subject is first shown (once) what type of stimulus was to be imagined, then he is repeatedly asked to imagine on the screen two circles differing in size. Two equal circles are then presented, and the subject is asked to compare them. The usual illusion of contrast was obtained in both experiments, although it occurred less frequently than did illusions aroused directly by objects. The fact that subjects differed in their susceptibility to the illusion prompted an investigation of individual differences.

In one study Natadze tested professional actors, capable drama students, and persons with no connection with the stage. Illusions attributable to verbally aroused images were experienced by the professional actors in 87.8 percent of the instances; by drama students, 80 percent; and by nonactors, 31.1 percent. Thus the incidence of illusions aroused by imagination was highly correlated with dramatic talent. On the basis of remarks made by subjects during these experiments, the investigators concluded that the differences are attributable to imagery ability. In the conditions of the experiment, the actors experience vivid images of "scenes," whereas ordinary subjects experience more generalized or abstract mental activity presumably because they lack the degree of "figurative imagination" possessed by the actors (Uznadze, 1966, p. 131).

It might be argued that the reported effects are somehow an artifact of the demand characteristics of the experimental situation, although it seems unlikely that the subjects would have been aware of the nature of the illusion they were expected to experience. The results are in any case extremely interesting theoretically and they merit systematic replication, perhaps using objective tests to differentiate subjects on imagery ability.

Imagery and perceptual recognition   Some direct evidence on the relation between perceptual performance and imagery ability was obtained recently by Ernest and Paivio (1971). High-imagery and low-imagery subjects were selected on the basis of combined scores on Space Relations, the MPFB, and Barratt's (1953) questionnaire on the MPFB. As part of an experiment on incidental memory (to be discussed later), subjects were required simply to identify (verbally) pictures of objects, their concrete noun labels, and abstract nouns exposed individually for a duration of $\frac{1}{16}$ sec. The results showed that high-imagery subjects made fewer recognition errors than low imagers, particularly in the case of pictures. Analogous results were obtained in another unpublished experiment involving tachistoscopic presentation of verbal and nonverbal stimuli to the right or the left visual field at exposure durations of 10 to 20 msec. The study was particularly concerned with possible interactions involving visual field, type of stimulus, and visual imagery ability. The interactions were not significant, but high imagers were again superior to low imagers in their overall accuracy. These findings can be interpreted as further support for the continuity of visual imagery and visual perception, although it is yet to be established that the perceptual superiority of high imagers is restricted to the visual modality. This is necessary particularly in view of the fact that spatial scanning ability has been found to be associated with ease of both auditory and visual recognition under certain conditions (Frederiksen, 1967).

Verbal ability and perceptual recognition   Spielberger and Denny (1963) investigated the relation between visual recognition thresholds for words and verbal ability as measured by the College Board SAT Verbal Scale. The stimulus words varied in their Thorndike-Lorge frequencies. A significant interaction was obtained: Subjects with high verbal ability were superior to those with low ability in their recognition of infrequent words but not of frequent words. The findings can be interpreted most simply in terms of differences in frequency of experience with printed words: Subjects with high verbal ability may read more than those with low verbal ability, and the experiential difference shows up particularly in the case of infrequent words. This interpretation is consistent with Solomon and Howes' (1951) explanation of the finding that the correlation between personal values and thresholds for value-related words was higher for infrequent than for frequent words. For example, a person with strong religious interests probably reads religious material more often than a person less interested in religion, and the experiential difference presumably affects the ease with which unusual religious words are recognized. In terms of the analysis of levels of meaning (Chapter 3), verbal ability and personal values reflect the extent to which words in general or words in particular interest areas have acquired representational meaning (familiarity) as a function of individual experience. Individual differences in verbal abilities and the representational meaning of words are two faces of the same coin. We shall see next that this is true also in regard to higher-order associative meaning.

Individual Differences and Associative Reactions

Individual differences in the nature of associations has been a subject for research since Galton, but little in the way of systematic theory has emerged and much of the work that has been done is not directly relevant here. Just as we have been primarily interested in general dimensions of word meaning rather than the specific meanings of particular words, so too are we more interested here in individual differences that may yield clues to the nature of associative mechanisms in general than we are in idiosyncratic variations in the specific content of associations. Nevertheless, qualitative differences in associations are suggestive of differences in relevant cognitive styles. Such findings will be considered prior to data on quantitative dimensions, such as associative reaction time.

Qualitative differences in associations   The finding that children's associations tend to "stay by" the thing mentioned, whereas adults react more often with coordinates and opposites (Woodworth, 1938) could mean that stimulus-evoked imagery plays a more important role in children's than in adults' verbal-associative responses. This would be consistent with Bruner's (1964) emphasis on the predominance of iconic representation as a mode of thought prior to age seven or so. On the other hand, a shift from syntagmatic (sequentially related) to paradigmatic (same part of speech) word associations also tends to occur around the age seven or eight years (Brown & Berko, 1960; Ervin, 1961), suggesting increasing freedom from the influence of sequential-associative habits.

Such linguistic flexibility may be related to the development of effective mediational imagery or the formation of connections between the verbal and imaginal symbolic systems (cf. Chapter 11), rather than to the development of verbal skills alone. Such an interpretation is supported by Piaget and Inhelder's (1966) conclusion that the capacity for anticipatory and transformational images takes a developmental leap at age seven or eight. We shall return to this point later in the section on individual differences in learning and memory.

Early evidence on the relation between symbolic habits and associations was presented by Shaw (1919), who gave a word association test to subjects described as more or less verbal, or visual, etc. She found that associative reaction time (RT) tended to be faster for the verbal subjects than for the concrete-imaginal type and suggested that the occurrence of concrete imagery retarded RT more in the case of the latter type. Evidence consistent with such a view was also obtained by Davis (1932). In response to the stimulus word *childhood* in a free association test, subjects who reported their associations as exclusively or dominantly "visual" responded with a high proposition of nouns relative to other parts of speech, whereas those not high in visual imagery showed the reverse associative pattern. The visual imagers tended to respond with the names of the particular scenes or persons "appearing" to them in their visual images.

More recently, Siipola, Walker, and Kolb (1955) distinguished between "stimulus-bound" and "subject-bound" associative processes. The stimulus-bound associative pattern is tied to a set for speed, which limits the associations to the type that come most quickly, i.e., contrast associates. As a further consequence, the subject has no complex intervening processes to report. A subject-bound pattern is tied to a set to find a personally meaningful association, which involves a time-consuming intervening process, typified by concrete visual images of objects or events. Since the latter type of intervening process features concrete objects, the eventual verbal response is likely to be a concrete noun. Dunn, Bliss, and Siipola (1958) tested the theory, using personality variables that they assumed to be related to the differing associative patterns. In one study they predicted that impulsive or extraverted individuals would show the stimulus-bound pattern of association to stimulus words, whereas inhibited or introverted individuals would show the subject-bound pattern. These variables were measured using the Guilford Inventory of Factors STDCR (1940). The results confirmed the predictions for impulsivity-inhibition but not for introversion-extraversion. The data also indicated that concrete visual imagery is the intervening process most frequently reported under free conditions.

Similiar predictions were made in a second study for individuals differing on the six Spranger values, as measured by the Allport-Vernon-Lindzey Study of Values (1951). On the basis of a characterization developed by H. A. Murray (1938), economic, theoretical, and political values were classified as *extraceptive,* and aesthetic, religious, and social values as *intraceptive.* According to Murray, the extraceptive individual is objective, tough-minded, impersonal, practical, etc., whereas the intraceptive person is subjective, tender-minded, personal, etc. Dunn et al. reasoned that persons with high scores on the extra-ceptive values would show the stimulus-bound associative pattern, while persons with intraceptive values would show the subject-bound pattern. The predictions were generally confirmed: The extraceptive group had faster reaction times, gave more contrast associates, and reported that responses tended to come directly without mediating processes. In contrast, the intraceptive subjects had longer reaction times, gave more adjective-noun associates, and generally re-ported complex mediating processes, especially visual imagery. The general value of these results is that they contribute information concerning the per-sonality correlates of differences in associative patterns and reveal the prevalence of imagery as a mediator of associative reactions for certain individuals. That is, *complex* visual imagery appeared to be more characteristic of the intraceptive group. It cannot be concluded, however, that extraceptive subjects are therefore more verbal in their symbolic habits. Either they simply react more directly to stimuli, as Dunn et al. suggested, or their mediating processes are less complex and faster than those of the intraceptive group.

Individual differences in noun imagery and meaningfulness   The theo-retical analysis suggested earlier in relation to the acquisition of word meaning is relevant also to the problem of individual differences in associative habits. Such word attributes as imagery (or concreteness) and meaningfulness are defined in terms of the average associative reactions of groups of subjects to stimulus words, and variation around these averages presumably reflects differ-ential experiences involving word-object and word-word associations. Individual differences in the reactions that define the word attributes may be indicative, therefore, of differences in antecedent conditions related to word acquisition. Similarly, individual differences in general interests or values should reflect differential experience involving value-related objects and words. One would accordingly expect correlations between personal values or interests and the imagery value or associative meaningfulness of words, the magnitude of the relation depending on the extent to which the words have been experienced in concrete or intraverbal contexts related to the values. Some correlational evidence is consistent with such an interpretation. Bousfield and Samborski (1955) found positive correlations between religious and theoretical value scores and word *m*, i.e., the number of associations elicited by words related to those values. Paivio and Steeves (1967) only partially replicated those results (possibly because they used a briefer association period) finding significant but low correlations in the case of religious, political, and aesthetic areas. Higher correlations were obtained, however, between religious and theoretical values and the imagery ratings of value-related words, and these relations were also significant in the case of aesthetic and economic areas. The Bousfield and Samborski finding may reflect mainly intraverbal experience (hence verbal-associative meaning), whereas the Paivio and Steeves finding may result more from experiences involving associations of words with concrete objects and events (hence imaginal-referen-tial meaning). The findings are open to various interpretations, however, and

developmental and experimental studies are obviously required to test the speculative analysis.

Imagery ability and associative reaction time   In Chapter 3, we reviewed experimental evidence that showed that images occur much less readily
as associative reactions to abstract nouns than to concrete nouns, whereas the
latency of verbal associations was much less affected by variation in stimulus
concreteness (Paivio, 1966). The task can be extended readily to include
individual differences in relevant symbolic habits as a further variable. An
initial study on the problem was conducted by Miss Carole Ernest and the
writer. On the basis of a battery of spatial ability and questionnaire tests
similar to those used in previous studies (e.g., Ernest & Paivio, 1969), we
selected subjects who were either high or low in imagery ability. They were
presented concrete and abstract nouns individually under instructions to press
a key either when an image was aroused or when a verbal association occurred.
Thus the design included three classes of relevant variables: stimulus concreteness, imaginal and verbal instructional sets, and individual differences in imagery.

What results would be theoretically expected? Clearly, imagery ability and
instructional set should interact in such a manner that high-imagery subjects
would react faster than low-imagery subjects under the imagery set, but the
difference (if any) should be smaller under the verbal set. This was the direction
of the result obtained in the experiment, although the difference fell short of
significance.

All three variables would also be expected to interact, but alternative predictions are possible regarding the specific form of the interaction. To the extent
that the variables are additive, the imaginal superiority of high-imagery subjects might be expected to show up particularly in the case of concrete (high-
imagery) words. On the other hand, images should be readily available as
associative reactions to concrete words regardless of imagery ability, whereas
their occurrence to abstract words might be particularly dependent upon high
imagery. The latter alternative is in fact suggested by the rating data that define
noun imagery: Highly concrete words are rated as high in imagery by most
subjects—that is, the variance in the ratings for individual words is low (Paivio,
Yuille, & Madigan, 1968). Conversely, imagery ratings are generally lower in the
case of abstract words, but individuals vary more in their ratings—some subjects assign relatively high imagery values to them. The reaction time data were
consistent with the second alternative and the rating data: High-imagery subjects
were faster than low imagers under both imaginal- and verbal-associative instructions when the nouns were abstract but not when they were concrete. To
be fully consistent with theory, this associative superiority of high imagers should
be restricted to imaginal reactions to abstract words. The critical difference
tended to be appropriately greater under the imaginal than the verbal set, but
the required triple interaction did not approach significance.

In summary, some theoretical validation has thus been obtained for measures
of imagery ability in both perceptual and associative tasks. High-imagery

subjects are generally superior to low imagers in perceptual recognition and are also faster in their associative reactions, particularly their imaginal associations to abstract words. Note that the latter result is analogous to the Spielberger and Denny (1963) finding that the perceptual superiority of subjects who are high in verbal ability occurred only in the case of infrequent words. The common generalization from these findings is that individual differences in symbolic abilities are manifested in performance differences when cues for the relevant reactions are not readily available in the stimulus situation but must be supplied by the subject. Thus high verbal ability shows its effect under the impoverished stimulus conditions involved in tachistoscopic recognition and when the stimulus words are relatively unfamiliar. Similarly, the superiority of high-imagery subjects shows up in perceptual recognition of flashed stimuli, especially ones that are specifically relevant to their ability (i.e., pictures), and in their imaginal-associative reactions to abstract words, which are not ordinarily effective stimuli for image arousal. These tentative suggestions obviously require further testing and they also need to be evaluated in relation to the findings for learning and memory, to be considered next.

Learning and Memory

Early evidence   The research conducted during the early part of the century on imagery types and on the function of such differences in memory tasks typically relied on introspective methods to determine an individual's dominant symbolic mode, although some use also was made of objective tests, the performance of which presumably depended on particular modes of imagery (see Angell, 1910). The investigations of the function of imagery generally involved a comparison of individuals differing in their imagery ability in task performance. The results were generally contradictory or negative. Thus some investigators (e.g., Fracker, 1908; Kuhlmann, 1907) reported that imagery ability enhanced memory for visual forms or colors, whereas others failed to find such relations (e.g., Carey, 1915; Thorndike, 1907). In 1935, Annie Jenkin compared the performance of adults and children on learning associations between a series of verbal labels and pictures of familiar objects, or between nonsense words and nonsense figures. She reasoned that the adults are likely to be verbalizers and the children visualizers, and that the task was such as to favor visualization as a symbolic mode. The subjects were asked to report on how they learned the names, and from such reports Jenkin concluded that the verbal mode was superior to visual imagery. Like many of the earlier studies, however, her experiment was methodologically weak in regard to design, criteria for "types," and the assessment of mediation processes. It cannot therefore be regarded as a definitive test of the functions of imaginal and verbal symbolic habits.

Davis (1932) presented subjects tests designed to involve the use of different imagery modalities and had them report the dominant type "used" on each test. He found positive correlations on a number of tests—for example, between tonal memory and auditory imagery, and between memory for geometrical figures and visual imagery. From these data, he concluded that imagery does have "functional reality." The relations reported by Davis are correlational and open to the criticism that the subjective assessment of type of imagery was linked to the task from which performance scores were determined. However, the evidence is generally of the same kind as that presented in the recent studies of natural language mediators (see Chapter 9), which also are based on postexperimental reports by subjects and are accepted as suggestive of the mediation processes involved in learning. Thus, despite the many negative reports in the early literature, occasional findings suggest that individual differences in imagery may be predictive of performance on memory tasks.

Learning and individual differences in verbal processes   Considering the traditional emphasis on verbal associative processes in the conceptualization of meaningfulness and more recently in relation to associative verbal learning, there is an extraordinary dearth of research evidence on individual differences in relevant verbal symbolic processes. Indeed, individual differences have been generally neglected in verbal learning research, although the importance of the problem is recognized (cf. Noble, 1961; Gagné, 1967; J. J. Jenkins, 1967). Of course, such general factors as age, sex, and intelligence have received attention (e.g., McGeoch & Irion, 1952), and relevant recent findings involving differences of this kind were noted in preceding chapters. Thus Jensen and Rohwer (1963) obtained evidence indicating that mentally retarded adults do not spontaneously use verbal mediators, although they profited greatly from instructions to mediate. Hulicka and Grossman (1967; see also Canestrari, 1968) reported that young subjects reported more use of mediational techniques than old subjects when no instructions were given on the use of mediators. Under mediation instructions, the reported use of mediators increased, and old subjects showed relatively more improvement in paired-associate learning. A further finding was that the older subjects reported use of verbal mediators more often than did the young subjects. Such data are interesting and suggestive, but they do not reveal the nature of the effective processes associated with age and intelligence.

Two recent investigations have been concerned more directly with individual difference variables that appear to be conceptually related to the verbal symbolic processes under consideration here. G. Mandler and Huttenlocher (1956) obtained association data to 20 nonsense syllables from subjects who also learned a paired-associate list of different nonsense syllables. They found a positive but nonsignificant correlation between speed of learning and the number of associations given by the subjects on the association task. They further obtained the subject's number of associations to the 10 syllables that elicited the most, and the 10 eliciting the least, associations by the group as a whole. With the subject's associations to the 10 low syllables partialed out, a significant correlation was obtained between learning scores and number of associations given to the high syllables. Their study accordingly provided some evidence that individual differences in associative fluency are predictive of paired-associate learning.

Greeno (1965) obtained written associations to 10 words and 10 CVCVC nonsense words. Verbal fluency scores from this test were compared with scores from paired-associate learning of a list of 12 word-syllable pairs and free recall of a 30-word list. The results showed that paired-associate learning, but not free recall, correlated significantly with verbal fluency. The fluency scores based on words were somewhat better predictors of learning than scores based on the nonsense words. The finding that free recall performance was not predicted by the association test suggests that it is tapping individual differences in verbal fluency that are relevant particularly to situations involving associative verbal behavior. This adaptation of Noble's *m* measure thus seems a promising method for investigating the role of individual differences in verbal-associative processes in learning tasks.

Learning and memory and individual differences in imagery   The findings of some recent studies stand out in marked contrast to the relative failure of the early research to demonstrate relations between individual differences in imagery and learning and memory. The first two to be considered (Kuhlman, 1960; Stewart, 1965) are highly relevant theoretically but generally available at this time only as doctoral dissertations,[1] hence they will be discussed in some detail.

Kuhlman (1960) investigated the function of individual differences in visual imagery in young children in the context of a developmental view of thinking that in several respects is like the analysis of modes of representation presented in Chapter 2. She regarded imagery as a mode of thought that is necessary for the preverbal child and that becomes habitual because its use is reinforced. With the development of language and exposure to adult categories and concepts, which are based on language rather than perceptual properties of a visual stimulus, the use of imagery is normally relinquished. The degree to which this change occurs depends upon the permissiveness of parents and teachers with regard to the continued use of imagery and language appropriate to imagery, as compared to their insistence on the use of adult (verbal) categories and concepts. This analysis parallels that presented in Chapter 2 in terms of the ontogenetic development of thought and language from concrete to abstract as a function of increasing abstractness of tasks to which the children are exposed. Task abstractness in this context refers to the degree to which coping with the task demands use of attributes that are not available immediately in the perceptual situation and are most effectively represented as words rather than as nonverbal images.

From her theoretical analysis, Kuhlman hypothesized that subjects who are differentiated on the degree to which they retain the imagery habit—high and low imagers—would perform differently on two kinds of tasks. Visual imagery should facilitate reproduction of visual stimuli as well as the rehearsal of an

---

[1] Both were done under the direction of G. Mandler.

association between an object and its label in the absence of the object. High imagers should accordingly reproduce geometric designs more accurately and learn the names of a series of objects more readily than low imagers. On the other hand, grouping of objects into nonperceptual categories should depend more on verbal processes than on visual imagery, and high imagers should therefore be inferior to low imagers in assigning a series of objects to nonperceptual categories. In our terms, Kuhlman predicted a clear interaction between the subject's habitual tendency to use imagery and task concreteness, with imagery being facilitative on the more concrete memory and labeling tasks, and interfering on the more abstract categorization (concept-formation) task.

Kuhlman's subjects were children from kindergarten through grade four, divided into high- and low-imagery groups matched on intelligence. The subject's imagery category was based on the combined scores from four tests of spatial ability—Thurstone's Space Test, the Kuhlman-Finch Space Test, The Minnesota Paper Form Board, and the Flags Test. One of Kuhlman's experiments involved a test of memory for geometric forms, as determined from accuracy of reproductions. Another required subjects to learn the nonsense-syllable names of each of four objects that were representatives of four class concepts. This was repeated over ten series, each series of four containing one representative of each class.

The results of these investigations confirmed Kuhlman's hypotheses. High-imagery children were more accurate in their reproductions of geometric forms, particularly in the lower school grades, and such children required fewer trials than low imagers to learn the names of the objects. On the other hand, low imagers were superior to highs in correct anticipation of the nonsense names of the objects before they were actually shown the names. That is, the low imagers were better able to apply the labels already associated with specific represetatives of four classes to new specific instances, indicating more rapid acquisition of the general concept categories underlying the series. Stated briefly, the low imagers showed a high ability to abstract. Kuhlman's results also suggested that the inferior concept attainment of the high-imagery children was not a failure to generalize labels but rather a tendency to categorize objects on the basis of their sensory aspects instead of on more abstract features such as function.

Kuhlman observed that the difference between high and low imagers in concept formation decreased with age. From this she inferred that the habitual use of imagery was being replaced by more abstract language skills and that high imagers would be rare among adults. However, Stewart (1965), who accepted Kuhlman's views as a point of departure for her own research, reasoned that imagery differences would continue to adulthood and be detectable as performance differences on tasks appropriate for adults. In addition, she argued that imagery may remain the preferred method for storing, sorting, and retrieving concrete memory material. She accordingly investigated the interacting effects of the imagery of the individual and the image-evoking characteristics of the material to be remembered, with the expectation that concrete or "picturable" material would be remembered better by all subjects and that high imagers would benefit more than low imagers from concreteness. Conversely, low imagers were expected to show relatively less decrement in performance as a function of abstractness of the material.

Stewart tested these hypotheses in three experiments. The first involved paired-associate learning comparing pictures and words as stimulus terms for digit responses; the second investigated recognition memory for pictures and words; and the third varied the rated vividness (i.e., imagery) of words in a free recall experiment. The subjects were female university students categorized as high or low imagers on the basis of combined scores on the Flags and Spatial Relations tests. The two groups were matched on intelligence as measured by the vocabulary test from the Wechsler Adult Intelligence Scale and final-year high school marks.

The results of the paired-associate learning experiment showed that picture-stimulus lists were learned more quickly than word-stimulus lists (cf. Chapter 8). Furthermore, as shown in Figure 14-1, the picture lists were learned faster by high than by low imagers whereas the reverse was true for the word lists. Similarly, in the recognition experiment, both groups made fewer errors in the recognition of pictures than of words, but the high imagers were superior to low imagers in picture recognition, while low imagers were better than high imagers on word recognition. Thus both experiments confirmed the expected interaction of imagery type and stimulus concreteness, high imagers excelling when the stimuli are pictures and low imagers, when they are words. Interesting evidence was also obtained concerning the coding processes employed by the two types of subjects. An analysis of recognition errors suggested that high imagers were more

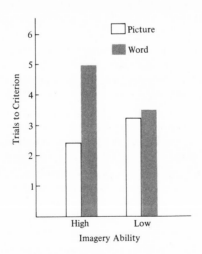

FIGURE 14-1.   Mean number of trials required by high-imagery and low-imagery subjects to learn a paired-associate list with pictures or words as stimulus members. Based on data from Stewart (1965).

likely to code a word as a picture than were low imagers, whereas low imagers were more likely to code a picture into a word than were high imagers. These findings appear to be remarkably in accord with the two-process theory in which imaginal and verbal symbolic processes are functionally coordinated to concrete and abstract task performance.

The results of Stewart's third experiment also were consistent with some of the expectations. In free recall of three lists of words varying in vividness, recall by both groups of subjects was best for the high-vivid list, next best for the medium-vivid list, and poorest for the low-vivid list. This finding is consistent with results obtained by others for such variables as word imagery and concreteness (see Chapter 7). Low imagers were superior to high imagers in their total recall of the word lists. However, imagery ability did not interact significantly with word vividness in the way it had with the picture-word variable, although there was an appropriate trend such that the general superiority of low imagers was not significant for the high-vivid list. Recall data were also analyzed for degree of subjective organization (Tulving, 1962). The results showed that subjective organization scores were greater for the high imagers on the high-vivid list, and greater for low imagers on the low-vivid list. Together with other evidence, the last finding suggested that high imagers depended upon imaging as a method of coding, but low imagers did not. Nevertheless, the differential coding and organization was not reflected in better recall of the high-vivid list by high imagers.

The positive results obtained by Kuhlman and Stewart are in marked contrast with the negative or weak findings generally obtained in earlier research relating performance to individual differences in imagery, but they are consistent in most respects with the theoretical model developed in earlier chapters of this monograph. However, the studies raise a number of questions that require consideration. The first concerns the inferences made by both investigators concerning modes of representation. The spatial ability tests provided empirical criteria for imagery differences but no independent criteria for differences in verbal symbolic habits, yet both authors interpret the performance of low imagers in terms of verbal processes. This is a plausible inference from the effects that were obtained, but the general implication of the classification procedure and analysis is that imaginal- and verbal-symbolic skills are bipolar. It is clearly preferable, however, to conceptualize the two processes as being independent (or partly independent) ability dimensions, particularly in view of the factor-analytic evidence discussed earlier. Recall that the spatial-ability or figural-transformational ability tests (including those used by Kuhlman and Stewart) were factorially independent of verbal skills. Thus an interpretation of the performance of low imagers in Kuhlman's and Stewart's studies in terms of differential verbal *abilities* does not appear justified, although it is still possible to argue that low imagers and high imagers differ in their habitual use of verbal processes—low imagers may have a greater preference for verbal thinking without being superior to high imagers in verbal ability.

A further problem is the theoretical relationship between Stewart's findings in particular and the effects of stimulus attributes and experimentally induced mediation sets described in Chapter 11. Specifically, are the effects of stimulus concreteness, instructions to use imagery, and individual differences in imagery all attributable to a common intervening process? With respect to picture-word variation and imagery ability, the answer is positive inasmuch as these variables interacted as expected theoretically in Stewart's recognition and paired-associate learning experiments. The results of the noun vividness experiment, however, appear inconsistent with theoretical expectations unless we assume that noun vividness is a more important determinant of aroused imagery than is imagery ability—an assumption not supported by the finding that even greater variation in stimulus concreteness (pictures as compared to words) did not override the contribution of individual differences in imagery in the paired-associates task. *These findings suggest that the imagery factor involved in the spatial ability tests and differential memory for pictures and words is not the same imagery variable that mediates the effect of noun imagery.*

A consistent imagery interpretation of the various findings could be preserved by assuming two kinds of imagery ability, one tied closely to perception and short-term memory for concrete events, the other to words as conditioned stimuli for long-term nonverbal memory images. The former presumably is the ability measured by the spatial tests used by Kuhlman and Stewart as well as other tests related to the processing of figural information, and is functional in situations involving memory for objects or pictures. The latter is conceptually linked to word meaning and could be described as an acquired disposition of the individual to react to words (especially concrete words) with nonverbal images. Such a disposition might be measured by the various imagery questionnaires or rating-scale procedures described earlier and is perhaps functional in memory tasks involving image-arousing verbal stimuli. The conceptual distinction is supported by the factor-analytic study (Paivio & Rogers, unpublished), also discussed in the earlier context, in which the spatial ability and verbal tests of imagery defined different factors. This argument is similar to one made recently by Neisser (1968), who distinguished between imagery as a process that represents spatial information effectively and imagery as a subjective (verbally reported) experience whose vividness may be unrelated to its usefulness or accuracy.

Neither of the above variants of a duoprocess approach to imagery is fully consistent with empirical data that are presently available. The factor-analytic study referred to above included a paired-associate learning task involving concrete and abstract nouns as stimuli and responses, and a similar task with an imagery mnemonic set added. If these variables and individual differences in imagery as measured by either verbal reports or spatial ability tests involve a common underlying process, learning scores associated with some combination of noun imagery and instructions (e.g., concrete pairs under an imagery set) should have correlated with at least one of the individual difference measures. In fact, all of the relevant correlations were nonsignificant. Thus imagery ability, whether measured verbally or by perceptual-type tests, appears to be unrelated to performance in learning tasks involving only verbal material varying in imagery even when imagery mnemonic instructions are added.

The above results suggest that imagery ability may predict learning and memory only in tasks involving nonverbal (pictorial) material, and only when imagery is defined by performance tests of spatial ability, as in Kuhlman's and Stewart's experiments. However, even this generalization must be qualified. We noted earlier that Davis (1932) found positive relations between recall and individual differences in imagery as measured by subjective reports. More recently, Sheehan (1966a, 1966b, 1967b) has found accuracy of visual memory to be related to individual differences in imagery as measured by his shortened version of the Betts questionnaire on imagery or by subjects' ratings of the vividness of imagery in the experimental setting. Thus in one experiment (Sheehan, 1967b), subjects were required to reconstruct from memory stimulus arrays comprised of elements varying in color, shape, and size. The arrays varied in overall complexity and regularity of pattern. One prediction was that poor imagers would show a greater difference in accuracy of recall for patterned and relatively unpatterned arrays than would vivid imagers because the poor imagers are more dependent upon being able to code the arrays symbolically (verbally?) in order to remember them, and such coding is difficult with unpatterned arrays. A similar prediction was made in regard to the effect of complexity. Although some discrepancies occurred, the results were generally consistent with the predictions. Sheehan concluded that differences in styles of perception lead to differences in retention: Vivid imagers perceive literally while poor imagers use coding devices to organize their perceptions.

Inasmuch as Sheehan, like Kuhlman and Stewart, used nonverbal stimuli in his experiments, it might be concluded alternatively that imagery ability as measured by either subjective reports or spatial ability tests is predictive of memory for nonverbal stimuli. Offsetting this, however, is a negative finding by Paivio, Rogers, and Smythe (1968). Subjects categorized as high or low in imagery according to combined scores on the Minnesota Paper Form Board and questionnaire measures were presented either pictures or words for free recall. Pictures were recalled better than words, but high and low imagers did not differ significantly in their recall of either stimulus type. Thus the presence of nonverbal stimuli in the memory task is no guarantee that imagery ability will be functionally relevant. Thus far, then, no single interpretation seems consistent with all of the data on imagery ability and learning.

Imagery ability and incidental learning   Some recent evidence suggests that imagery ability may be particularly relevant in incidental learning. Ernest and Paivio (1969) selected high- and low-imagery subjects on the basis of combined scores on Space Relations, the Minnesota Paper Form Board, and the MPFB questionnaire. In one experiment, such subjects learned a paired-associate list in which certain stimulus members were Stroop (1935) items, i.e., color names printed in incongruent colors, such as the word RED printed in green ink, whereas other stimuli were congruent in regard to name and color. For some subjects the functional stimulus for learning was the color and for others it was the color word. The responses were concrete nouns. The results showed no significant relation between imagery ability and intentional paired-associate learning, but high imagers were superior to low imagers in their incidental recall of the irrelevant component of the compound stimulus, particularly under certain combinations of color-word congruency and functional stimulus. The experiment was repeated with the modification that the color-word compounds served as response members and only the color was used as the functional (intentional) component of the response. Imagery was again unrelated to intentional learning, but high imagers were much superior in incidental learning, their recall of incidental components of the compound responses being more than twice that of the low imagers (i.e., 64 percent as compared to 30 percent correct recall). Apparently the general relation is not restricted to the imagery tests we used, for Sheehan and Neisser (1969) also found a substantial correlation between ratings of the vividness of imagery and accuracy of recall for incidentally presented material.

The simplest explanation of these findings seems to be that high imagers perceive and store visual information literally, as Sheehan has suggested. Low imagers may have lesser ability in this regard, or they may habitually code information verbally. In either case, high imagers would be more likely to perceive and retain incidental visual cues because these are unlikely to be coded verbally during the task, but they may not be superior with intentional cues, which low imagers can code and store verbally. Notice that this argument is analogous to that presented in Chapter 7 in relation to effects of verbal coding on recognition memory. To account for the inconsistent findings in that area, it was suggested that verbal coding may be used when readily available or when nonverbal storage is difficult because of stimulus complexity or because the subject has poor nonverbal visual memory. Verbal coding may not be essential, however, when labels are not readily available or when stimuli can be stored in an uncoded form because of their simplicity, or because the subject has good visual memory. The reference to visual memory (essentially an imagery variable) relates to an investigation by Klapp (1969), who found in one study that codability of colors correlated significantly with recognition memory for colors in the case of subjects with poor visual memory but not subjects with good visual memory. The latter apparently were able to store uncoded color information, much as high-imagery subjects retained incidentally presented visual information in the Ernest and Paivio experiments, i.e., literally. We cannot be confident about the generalization, however, since Klapp failed to confirm his original finding in a subsequent study.

This picture is blurred further by the results of still another study by Ernest and Paivio (1971). High- and low-imagery subjects were run in two incidental memory experiments. In one, pictures and words varying in color were presented for two free recall study and test trials, after which all of the items were presented in black and white outline and the subjects were required to recall the color of each item as originally presented. Free recall, as usual, was better for pictures than for words, and incidental recall for the colors was greatly superior in the case of pictures (independent of the difference in intentional recall for pictures and words). However, the only significant effect involving imagery level was an interaction which showed that high-imagery males surpassed low-imagery males, particularly in the free recall of words, whereas the reverse was true for female subjects. No imagery effect occurred in incidental recall.

A second experiment involved incidental free recall of a 72-item homogeneous list of pictures, their concrete noun labels, or abstract nouns. The orienting task in this case was identification of each item when it was flashed on a screen briefly ($\frac{1}{16}$ sec.). Following this, subjects were asked to write down all the items they could recall. As mentioned earlier in the context of perceptual studies, high-imagery subjects correctly identified more items than did low imagers, the difference being greatest in the case of pictures. No main effect of imagery level was obtained in incidental recall, but imagery and sex interacted in the manner shown in Figure 14-2. High-imagery females were superior to their low-imagery counterparts and to males generally. High- and low-imagery males did not differ significantly.

Thus any generalization regarding incidental memory and imagery needs to be qualified in terms of the sex of the subject and the nature of the task. A positive relation seems more probable when the intentional (orienting) task involves an explicit associative component, as in paired-associate learning (Ernest & Paivio, 1969) and item labeling (the second experiment by Ernest & Paivio, 1971), than when it does not (e.g., free recall); and a positive relation is more likely for females than for males. If we add the earlier conclusion that the presence of a nonverbal stimulus component (e.g., pictures, colors) is important, a pattern emerges that is consistent with many of the other findings discussed earlier. Thus both Kuhlman and Stewart found positive relations between

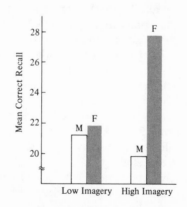

FIGURE 14-2. Incidental recall as a function of imagery level and sex. Data from Ernest and Paivio (1971).

imagery ability and paired-associate learning involving pictorial and verbal items in pairs; in addition, Stewart's sample consisted entirely of female university students. The relations have generally not been obtained with *verbal* free recall tasks, although it has been with simple reproduction of nonverbal stimuli (e.g., Kuhlman, 1960; Sheehan, 1966a, 1966b, 1967b). There are exceptions to all of these empirical generalizations, however, and at the present time no consistent interpretation can be suggested. Still, it is clear that individual differences in imagery are now predicting learning and memory with much greater success than in the early heyday of imagery research.

From the viewpoint of the two-process theory, there is an obvious need for research in which both verbal and imaginal abilities are systematically varied. Given the relative factorial independence of the two classes of abilities, such research would be quite feasible, but investigators must be prepared to cope with the additional complexities that it would create. Beyond this lies needed research of even greater complexity, incorporating relevant item attributes, instructional sets, and individual differences in a single design. The following experiment combined some of those features.

Imaginal and verbal factors in tactual form discrimination and retention
Hyman (1966) investigated the interactive effects of individual differences in imagery, verbal and imaginal pretraining, and type of task (concrete versus symbolic) on tactual form discrimination. Earlier investigations had indicated that visual imagery plays an important role in tactual form perception (see Chapter 5), and Hyman sought to clarify its role as well as that of verbal processes in a more complex task.

High- and low-imagery subjects were selected according to combined scores on the Minnesota Paper Form Board, the MPFB questionnaire, and a version of the Galton questionnaire. Verbal and imaginal pretraining, following Ranken (1963), consisted of training designed to induce the formation of either verbal or imaginal representations of a set of novel shapes. Moreover, the verbal labels encoded stimulus information that was either relevant or irrelevant to the subsequent problem. Following the pretraining phase, the subjects were required to combine two shapes mentally to form a new shape that was then tactually recognized (recognition test) or drawn (reproduction test). Subjects in the concrete condition could feel the blocks while mentally combining them, whereas those in the symbolic condition had to remember the shapes without handling them.

The results indicated more accurate and faster performance on the concrete than the symbolic task on both recognition and reproduction measures. Verbal pretraining facilitated subsequent performance when the labels encoded information relevant to successful performance, whereas irrelevant labels had essentially no effect. Pretraining on the use of imagery facilitated concrete but not symbolic task performance for subjects who were low in imagery ability but not for those who were high in imagery. In general, however, high imagers performed better than low imagers, the difference being greatest on the recognition task.

These rather complex results provide further evidence of the differential functions of verbal and imaginal mediators, although the two processes are not clearly separated. Relevant verbal pretraining was generally the most effective experimental condition, but it could be argued that this was so because the pretraining established a conditioned linkage between a verbal label and a nonverbal image of a shape, and that task performance in fact involved both processes. The overall superior performance of the high imagers is generally consistent with the findings of other studies reviewed above and is similarly interpretable in terms of the positive contribution of imagery ability in a task involving retention of figural information. The task differs from the others in a number of respects, however, most notably in that it was tactual rather than visual. The superiority of high imagers therefore suggests that the tactual information was transformed into visual information during the task, for the spatial tests that define imagery ability are visual tests. However, as argued earlier (Chapters 2 and 4), visual imagery itself presumably includes a motor component, and this may be partly why imagery ability was effective in Hyman's experiment.

Conclusions and issues arising from the memory research   The learning and memory studies permit us to conclude that individual differences in spatial or figural transformational ability, and sometimes verbal measures of imagery ability, are most consistently related to performance in learning and memory tasks involving nonverbal visual material and, in the case of incidental memory at least, visually presented words. In two experiments, individual differences in verbal associative fluency were related significantly to performance in verbal learning studies involving verbal material. These generalizations are consistent with theoretical expectations, but their limitations must be recognized. Imagery ability has not been uniformly successful in predicting memory for nonverbal material (e.g., free recall of pictures), and sometimes the relations were limited to female subjects. Imagery ability has also failed to interact with noun imagery and imagery-mnemonic instructions in verbal learning. These exceptions contrast sharply with the highly consistent effects of the imagery value or concreteness of items (pictures, concrete nouns, abstract nouns) and of imagery instructions. Moreover, from the limited empirical information thus far available, the failure to obtain interactions of word imagery and imagery ability in learning tasks contrasts with the significant interactions obtained for these variables in the associative reaction time studies discussed earlier. These and other inconsistencies indicate that some important theoretical insight is lacking in regard to individual differences.

A number of issues should be considered in future research. There is an obvious need for a more penetrating and comprehensive examination of the factorial structure of tests relevant to both nonverbal imagery and verbal associative processes. Also needed is research in which both imagery and verbal abilities are systematically varied. Such studies might help to clarify some of the inconsistencies that have been observed in research to date. It will be necessary, moreover, to investigate the ability variables in a variety of tasks. This has been done to some extent in the studies reviewed above, but not systematically enough and not always under the guidance of theoretically motivated considerations.

The significance of the task variable is indicated by several kinds of information. One is the large number of different semantic and figural memory factors that have been isolated (for example, see Brown, Guilford, & Hoepfner, 1968; Christal, 1958; Guilford, 1967). Another is the discovery by Fleishman and his associates that different abilities may be effective at different stages of practice on a complex learning task (see Fleishman 1966a, 1966b, for reviews). This discovery is specifically relevant here because their studies have shown that individual differences in perceptual-spatial and verbal abilities are most important early in perceptual-motor learning, whereas motor and task-specific variables become progressively more important as practice continues. An especially pertinent example is a study by Fleishman and Rich (1963). Two ability measures were obtained from their subjects, one a test of spatial ability (Aerial Orientation) and the other a measure of kinesthetic sensitivity based on difference thresholds for judgments of lifted weights. All subjects then received 40 one-minute trials on a two-hand coordination task in which they attempted to keep a target-follower on an irregularly-moving target disc. The results showed that overall performance on the coordination task correlated substantially with both spatial ability and kinesthetic sensitivity measures (the correlations were .49 and .58, respectively). The two abilities themselves were essentially uncorrelated. Correlations with performance on successive blocks of 10 trials decreased systematically over trials for the spatial ability measure, being significant only for the first three trial blocks; those involving kinesthetic sensitivity increased over trials, reaching significance in the last four blocks. Fleishman and Rich concluded that spatial ability is advantageous only in early stages of learning. The finer motor-adjustments required to reach high levels of proficiency presumably depend more on the ability to make use of proprioceptive cues.

A certain analogy may be noted between the Fleishman-Rich result and the observation made in Chapter 9 that the use of mediators or associative aids in paired-associate learning (as indicated by subjective reports) tends to decrease over trials. The associations become increasingly "automatic." Does this mean that different abilities play a critical role at different stages of verbal learning? To my knowledge, the question is unexplored in the context of the kinds of problems that we have been considering here, although Fleishman (1966b) discussed similar possibilities in relation to verbal learning generally.

A third source of evidence that theoretically-motivated considerations are important in relation to the task problem is the Paivio and Csapo (1969) study and subsequent related ones reviewed in Chapter 7, which showed that verbal processes are crucial in sequential tasks involving pictorial items but not in nonsequential tasks. Perhaps the functional significance of imaginal and verbal abilities would also be revealed by similar task manipulations.

Finally, it will be important to investigate individual differences variables and learning in the context of developmental studies. The need for this is indicated by developmental hypotheses such as Bruner's, in which a developmental shift from iconic dominance to verbal-symbolic modes of representation is assumed generally, but individuals may also be viewed as differing in the extent to which they continue to depend on imagery, as in Kuhlman's (1960) study. Related to this are the alternative interpretations of developmental changes in learning performance when pictorial materials serve as items (see Chapter 11). The precise ages of transition are uncertain, but young children experience difficulty in learning when pictures serve as response items in paired-associate learning and sometimes in free recall, but not in recognition memory nor when the items serve as stimulus members in associative learning. Do these age trends have their parallels in individual differences in learning abilities at later ages? If so, common interpretations should be possible—perhaps one of the alternatives suggested in Chapter 11 in relation to the developmental question would account for individual differences as well. A more general rationale for a joint consideration of individual differences and developmental factors is provided by Ferguson's (1954, 1956) theory of human abilities. Abilities, according to Ferguson, are general habits that have reached stability through overlearning in a variety of stimulus-response situations. Their development is attributed to transfer from one learning situation to another, and individuals presumably can differ in the generality of the ability (i.e., the number of situations to which it has transferred), its habit strength with respect to any specific stimulus-response situation, and so on. Individual differences in imaginal and verbal symbolic abilities can be viewed developmentally in precisely this fashion.

Language and Individual Differences in Symbolic Habits

The symbolic habits and abilities that we are concerned with have been infrequently investigated in relation to language, and our discussion can be brief. We have already noted Shaw's (1919) observations regarding differences in the verbal-associative reactions of imaginal and verbal types. She also investigated differences in vocabularies and concluded that her highly imaginal subjects generally had the largest proportion of words that might be expected to call up concrete imagery or sensations, whereas highly verbal types used the largest proportion of abstract terms. These observations suggest that differences in imaginal and verbal symbolic habits may be associated with differences in habitual vocabularies, but the problem obviously needs more study before firm generalizations are warranted.

A study by Stumberg (1928) revealed some interesting verbal and imaginal symbolic correlates of poetic talent. The subjects consisted of 28 individuals judged to have poetic talent according to various criteria, and 28 control subjects with little interest in reading or writing poetry. The two groups were matched approximately on intelligence, age, and education. The subjects were given a series of ten tests thought to be relevant to poetic talent, such as rhyming associations, controlled associations of adjectives to nouns, self-ratings of the vividness of imagery aroused by verbal cues (a bird, a moonlight scene, the face of a good friend, etc.), finding similes, and so on. The poetically talented group obtained substantially higher scores on all but one of the tests (Stumberg concluded that the two groups were differentiated on seven tests, but recomputation of the data in Table 1 of the report indicates that the differences were statistically significant in nine instances).

Stumberg stressed particularly the superiority of the poets in the number of figurative words given as associations in the controlled associations test and the number of similes and metaphors given in a similes completion test: ". . . the most striking and significant fact of all lies in the difference between the two groups with respect to figures of speech. . . . The ability to see a likeness in two otherwise dissimilar things and likewise the tendency to use phrases involving such an apprehension are especially characteristic of the poetically talented group" (p. 233). The difference can be interpreted in terms of a combination of imaginal and verbal symbolic abilities. The contribution of imagery is suggested by the traditional emphasis on its role in poetic metaphor (see Chapter 13) as well as by the superiority of poets on the imagery test in Stumberg's study. In terms of the critical ratio, the difference in the number of images reported by the two groups was actually the largest one obtained in the study. The role of verbal processes is suggested by the superiority of the poets on a rhymes test and a test requiring completion of poetic quotations, although these differences could also be interpreted simply as highly specific results of practice. In any case, the results certainly invite further study with more objective contemporary approaches.

An aspect of a study by A. Reynolds and Paivio (1968) serves as a final example of an approach that can provide relevant information in this problem area. Subjects were differentiated as high or low on associative productivity according to the average number of written associations they gave to stimulus words in a preliminary test. A subsequent experiment required them to define (orally) a series of concrete and abstract nouns. The results showed that the definitions given by high associative productivity subjects contained more words, had faster starting latencies, and were more fluent (contained fewer silent pauses) than those of the low productivity subjects. The definitions of the high associative productivity subjects were also judged to be qualitatively superior, on the average, in terms of how adequately they defined the concepts. These differences are particularly interesting because the groups were originally distinguished on the basis of a written association test, whereas the experimental task required oral production of natural (i.e., grammatical) speech. Thus the results apparently reflect the influence of individual differences in a rather general verbal associative ability.

Individual Differences in Symbolic Abilities Associated with Sensory Defects and Brain Lesions

Sensory deficits and brain damage have long been regarded as unique sources of information on man's symbolic capacities. A few of the most relevant implications will be considered here briefly without any attempt at a comprehensive coverage of the literature. Relative to normal subjects, the congenitally blind are deficient in visual imagery but not in imagery related to other sense modalities nor in their verbal symbolic functioning. Conversely, the deaf are deficient in language development and presumably the capacity for verbal thinking, but not in visual imagery. Brain lesions are relevant because they have provided neuroanatomical evidence supporting the functional distinction between verbal and nonverbal symbolic systems.

Implications of blindness   The imagery deficit associated with congenital or early blindness (Schlaegel, 1953) implies that language should have no meaning in terms of a capacity to arouse visual images. Linguistic concreteness should thus be related only to other sense experiences. Purely visual words would be effectively abstract, whereas words with referents that can be heard or felt or otherwise experienced would be the concrete words of the blind. A number of years ago Dr. Robert C. Gardner and Paivio (unpublished) investigated this hypothesis with a sample of blind students who were participating in a study concerned with language aptitude tests for the blind. We chose the paired-associate learning task in which noun imagery-concreteness had been shown to be so effective with sighted subjects. A 24-pair list was constructed from twenty-four nouns that we assumed to be primarily visual in reference (e.g., painting, sky, sunset, prince) and 24 that were primarily auditory (singer, laughter, prayer, echo, etc.). The visual words were assumed to be low and the auditory words high in imagery and concreteness for the blind. Equal numbers of pairs were auditory-auditory, visual-visual, auditory-visual, and visual-auditory. The subjects were auditorily presented the pairs for one study trial followed by a recognition test requiring the selection of the correct response from four alternatives presented after each stimulus. The results were consistent with expectations in that the visual-visual ("abstract") pairs were most poorly recalled on the average, and auditory-auditory ("concrete") pairs were recalled best. However, the differences were not statistically significant, perhaps because the task was unusually easy for the subjects and the scores for all pair types were high.

Recently, Paivio and Okovita (1971) repeated the study with some modifications. One experiment included 13 congenitally blind subjects ranging in age from 14 to 18 years and a matched group of 13 sighted subjects. Each subject was auditorily presented five paired-associate learning and recall trials with a list of 20 noun-noun pairs. The pair items were selected from a list of nouns from the Paivio, Yuille, and Madigan (1968) normative sample, for which ratings of visual and auditory imagery are also available (Yuille & Barnsley, 1969). The nouns were equated for their overall imagery and concreteness, but varied in their imagery modality. Thus 10 of the pairs consisted of nouns that were relatively high in visual imagery but low in auditory imagery, while the members of the other 10 pairs were high in both visual and auditory imagery. Examples of noun pairs rated high on both visual and auditory imagery are *orchestra-speaker*, *city-whistle*, and *trumpet-rattle*; pairs rated high on visual and low on auditory imagery are *star-tower*, *headlight-acrobat*, *sunset-rainbow*, and the like.

Our predictions were that the blind subjects would find the "purely" visual pairs more difficult than the pairs that also were high in auditory imagery. On the assumption that visual imagery is dominant for the sighted subjects, they should find both types of pairs equally easy and they should be superior to the blind subjects on the purely visual pairs. Figure 14-3 shows a significant interaction of pair-imagery type and sightedness, which confirmed the predictions. Both groups performed more poorly on the visual pairs than on the pairs in which both visual and auditory imagery was high, but the difference was statistically significant only for the blind subjects. Moreover, the latter were inferior to sighted subjects only on the purely visual pairs. A second experiment confirmed and extended the findings using contrasting word pairs that were either purely auditory or purely visual in their imagery value. These results are especially important because they provide theoretical validation for the imagery hypothesis on the basis of yet another operational definition of image availability.

Research on the above problem is also of interest because it raises questions regarding the nature of meaning and its relation to information processing capacities among the blind. We were alerted to such issues partly because of the difficulty of selecting "purely" visual words that had not been associated with concrete experience involving other modalities. Thus the list used in the first experiment included visual words such as *arrow*, *garden*, and *magazine*, which have referents that could have been experienced by touch or smell. Moreover, such words as *cloud*, *mountain*, *moon*, and *shadow*, while purely

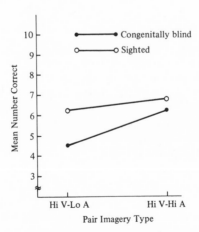

FIGURE 14-3.   Mean number of correct responses as a function of modality of pair imagery and subject type (blind versus sighted). Data from Paivio and Okovita (1971).

visual in a narrow sense, could have acquired concrete meaning metaphorically. Clouds are often likened to cotton wool, and *shadow* can refer to sound shadows or be experienced as temperature change by the blind. The sensory world of the blind in fact appears to be very rich in meaning. Observations by Brodey (1969), for example, indicate that their perception is based not only on direct tactual contact with objects but also on air currents, temperature changes, and distortions of sound patterns created by the objects and their interrelations. Their world is full of sound images that convey detailed information—a person is known from the sound of his breathing, a pretty girl, by the way her heels click when she walks. They know how light behaves by using radiant heat as an analogue. Kitchens and flowers and bugs are known by their smell. Such knowledge goes far beyond the ability merely to avoid objects on the basis of echos, remarkable as that ability is (e.g., Supa, Cotzin, & Dallenbach, 1944). How is this sensory experience reflected in the language of the blind? What, specifically, are the word attributes that define effective concrete meaning for them? We do not know the answers to such questions in detail, but the necessary word information could be obtained and the problem is generally researchable, as indicated by the studies reviewed here.

Implications of deafness It is generally accepted that the majority of persons who are born deaf do not acquire normal language competence (see Furth, 1966). It follows that they will be inferior to persons with normal hearing on tasks that depend directly on the development of the verbal symbolic system but not necessarily on tasks that are independent of language. Both implications have empirical support. In a series of experiments involving nonverbal procedures, Furth (1966) found deaf adolescents or adults to be generally comparable and sometimes superior to hearing subjects. One of few tasks on which the deaf were consistently inferior was memory span for digits, which presumably benefits from the availability of the verbal code in the case of hearing subjects, much as memory span for pictures benefits from the availability of a verbal label (Chapter 7). The two groups were comparable, however, on reconstruction memory span for forms, perhaps because the verbal code was unavailable even for the hearing subjects.

When Furth's subjects were children, however, those who were deaf generally performed more poorly than their hearing counterparts. The age change together with other evidence led Furth to suggest that the deficient performance of the deaf on some tasks is a result of experiential rather than linguistic deficiency specifically. He concluded that intelligent thinking is not dependent upon language.

Pettifor (1968) recently obtained evidence not entirely consistent with Furth's conclusions. The subjects consisted of 59 hard-of-hearing children of normal intelligence ranging in age from 5 to 14 years, and a hearing control group matched to the experimental group on age, sex, socioeconomic level, and approximately on intelligence. They were given a picture-sorting test designed to measure levels of conceptual thinking without requiring speech. One set of concepts was primarily visual-perceptual-concrete, involving a sorting of picture cards according to size, presence or absence of a blue border, and figure position on the right or left side of the card. Another set of concepts was primarily verbal-ideational-abstract (male-female, adult-child, and summer-winter). Each subject received visual, verbal, and total scores on the test. The major conclusions supported by various analyses are illustrated by Figure 14-4, which shows the mean visual and verbal scores for three age groups. The normal-hearing children were superior to the hard-of-hearing on both kinds of conceptual thinking, but the superiority was greater on the verbal-abstract concepts than on the visual-concrete concepts. The normal children performed equally well on both conceptual levels, but the hard-of-hearing children were better on visual than on verbal conceptualization. There was no interaction with age for accuracy scores (an analysis of errors showed a reduction for the hard-of-hearing subjects but not for the normal subjects; nevertheless the former remained inferior at all ages even by this analysis). Pettifor concluded that these facts do not accord with Furth's experiential-deficiency hypothesis and that more abstract levels of conceptualization are indeed dependent on language.

The relation of language ability to cognitive performance in general remains controversial. Vernon (1967) surveyed 33 studies, involving a total of more than 8,000 subjects, which compared the performance of hearing-impaired and normal control subjects on a variety of different performance tests of intelligence. In effect, the comparison involved a systematic manipulation of verbal language

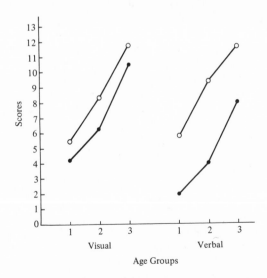

FIGURE 14-4. Rate of increase in visual and verbal scores with age on Pettifor Picture Sorting Test in normal (○) and in hard-of-hearing (●) subjects. From Pettifor (1968).

level while other relevant variables were held constant or randomized. The results indicated that the impaired and the normal subjects generally performed equally well on the tests, and Vernon concluded that there is no functional relation between verbal language and cognition or thought process. This conclusion agrees with Furth's generalization from his own data (see above) and with Rosenstein's (1961) earlier analysis of the literature on cognition in deaf children. On the other hand, Pettifor's findings suggest that the performance of language-impaired deaf subjects suffers when the task gets more abstract, but this does not occur in the case of hearing subjects. Regardless of their implications in regard to conceptual thinking in general, such findings at least corroborate the functional distinctions between verbal and nonverbal symbolic processes that have been emphasized here.

Since deaf children are deficient in language development, they should be particularly appropriate as subjects for the investigation of functions of imagery independent of language. Bugelski (1970) reported evidence on the problem using a paired-associate learning task. Deaf children were shown cards with cartoon drawings of animals as the stimuli and objects as responses. The "response" cards showed either the response object alone or the stimulus and the response interacting (e.g., a dog with scissors balanced on its nose), as in Reese's (1965) experiment previously described in Chapter 11. A recognition procedure was used on test trials. The results showed that deaf children could learn to associate one picture with another and that they performed almost as well as the hearing children Reese had tested. Similar results were obtained in two further memory experiments involving nonverbal stimuli. Bugelski concluded that the deaf children were probably making effective use of imagery in these tasks.

It should be feasible to extend such research to encompass imagery instructions and word imagery using older subjects. For example, in contrast to the blind study described above, deaf subjects should experience no auditory imagery to words with only auditory referents, and such words should therefore be relatively abstract and difficult to learn; conversely, words with visual referents should be high in imagery value and readily learned. Such possibilities remain to be investigated.

Brain lesions   Studies of aphasia provide the classical evidence that verbal functions are in some important sense "located" in one cerebral hemisphere, usually the left (for a summary of the evidence, see Lenneberg, 1967). Other investigations, mentioned briefly in Chapter 4, indicate that the right hemisphere may be specialized for certain nonverbal functions. Some of the clearest evidence for the verbal-nonverbal functional distinction comes from an impressive series of investigations conducted at the Montreal Neurological Institute by Dr. Brenda Milner and her associates (see Milner & Teuber, 1968). These investigations have shown that individuals with lesions of the left temporal lobe manifest disorders of memory and learning on verbal tasks, whereas those with right temporal-lobe lesions more often show the deficit on nonverbal tasks.

Thus patients with lesions of the left temporal lobe show selective impairment in verbal free recall, recognition memory, and paired-associate learning, but not in a variety of memory tasks involving nonverbal stimuli and responses. Conversely, right temporal-lobe patients show selective deficits, for example, in delayed reproduction of geometric designs and complex figures, and recognition memory for faces as well as for nonsense figures but not in analogous verbal memory tasks.

In addition to the obvious neuropsychological significance of the above findings, they are pertinent here because they are generally consistent with the two-process theory of symbolic functioning. Left hemisphere lesions are associated with behavioral deficits that can be conceptualized as a loss in verbal symbolic abilities, whereas right hemisphere lesions produce selective deficits in the individual's ability to process concrete (nonverbal) information from memory. Thus brain lesions apparently can produce individuals whose abilities correspond roughly to the verbal and nonverbal imagery types of the post-Galton era.

SUMMARY

Psychological research on imagery and verbal symbolic processes began with the study of individual differences. With few exceptions, the early research was notable for its lack of success in demonstrating that imagery has any functional significance as a mediator of behavior. Perhaps this relative failure was due to the emphasis on subjective reports of vividness of imagery as the operational definition of the underlying process. More recent investigations have used objective measures of spatial or figural transformational abilities, sometimes along with questionnaires and rating scales concerned with imagery, and measures of verbal abilities to differentiate individuals on the two postulated dimensions. The measurement problem remains acute, especially since factor-analytic studies have revealed many imagery and verbal ability dimensions, and it is uncertain which ones are the appropriate indices to use. Nevertheless, investigations involving such measures have produced considerable evidence for the functional significance of both processes.

The evidence has generally taken the form of an interaction between ability levels and relevant stimulus dimensions or instructional conditions. For example, high-imagery subjects have been found to be superior to lows in perceptual recognition, especially for pictorial material; in the speed of their imagery associations to abstract words in particular, as though high ability compensates for impoverished stimulus cues for image arousal; in associative learning and recognition memory involving pictorial items, whereas low imagers have been superior when only words are used in these tasks; and in incidental memory for visual material under certain conditions. Although fewer systematic investigations have been conducted on verbal abilities, analogous findings have occasionally been obtained with such measures. However, the studies have also produced negative and ambiguous findings. Imagery ability has not interacted with imagery-concrete-ness of words in the manner expected from the theory, and positive findings involving nonverbal stimuli such as pictures have not been obtained in all tasks. Thus, effects of imagery are less predictable when this process is defined by individual difference measures than when it is defined by stimulus character-istics or instructional sets.

Neurological deficits associated with sensory loss and certain brain lesions have produced individual differences in abilities that appear to reflect selective disturbances in verbal or nonverbal symbolic processes. These neuropsychological findings agree remarkably well with those derived from behavioral studies re-viewed earlier in their support for the two-process theory that attributes distinct functions to the two postulated symbolic systems. Of course, ambiguities and uncertainties remain to be investigated in this problem area, as in the case of individual differences generally, but the findings to date have been most en-couraging theoretically.

15

Extensions and Speculations

The main business of this book has been completed. We have reviewed the functional significance of imaginal and verbal symbolic processes in relation to problems of meaning, perception, learning, memory, and language. We have found that each of these overlapping areas could be conceptualized reasonably consistently within the framework of a model based on the postulated functional characteristics of the two symbolic systems. The empirical gaps and theoretical uncertainties nevertheless remain substantial even in the most thoroughly investigated of the above areas, so the broader enterprise that the book represents has only begun. Specific lacunae and the direction that research might take to fill them have been identified throughout the book, and it is unnecessary to re-emphasize them here. However, other relevant topics were treated only briefly if at all, usually because the factual evidence presently available is insufficient to warrant a detailed discussion of the area in terms of the variables and concepts on which our attention centered. I am referring particularly to such topics as physiological correlates and theories of imagery; the traditional cognitive research areas of concept formation, problem solving, and creativity; and the practical implications of the two-process approach for education. In this final chapter I will briefly discuss each of these topics, pointing to relevant findings where available, and suggesting possible directions that research might take in order to further our understanding of the theoretical or practical problems in those areas, and at the same time improve and extend the two-process theory itself.

PHYSIOLOGICAL CORRELATES AND THEORIES

Considerable research has been done on possible physiological correlates of imaginal and verbal symbolic activity, and relevant findings have been mentioned from time to time in this book. Such evidence was not accorded a more systematic coverage because my main purpose was to deal with evidence on the functional characteristics of the symbolic systems, and psychophysiological discoveries, interesting as they unquestionably are in their own right, have not yet revealed those characteristics as clearly as have behavioral indicators. Physiological measures might do so in the future, however, which is one reason for commenting on the matter here. The other reason is more immediate: Physiological correlates, together with behavioral data, provide useful convergent evidence regarding the validity of the kinds of theoretical constructs that we have stressed.

The contribution of physiological measures to the problem of defining mental events has been pointed out recently in relation to the use of eye-movement recordings to investigate dreaming. Specifically, rapid eye movements (REMs) have been found to correlate with dream reports (see Dement, 1965). In that connection, Stoyva and Kamiya (1968) have argued that the combined use of physiological measures and verbal report in the dream research represents a new strategy in the study of private events. The two measures are viewed as converging operations that serve to validate the concept of dreaming. Obviously the approach can be extended to other mental constructs, such as imagery in general. The suggestion is particularly appropriate because it accords with the general empirical-theoretical approach that has been emphasized throughout this book. At the same time, however, the eye-movement research thus far does not seem to have yielded specific information that contributes significantly to the solution of some of the issues that have been discussed in regard to imagery. This was noted earlier in connection with eye-movement correlates of waking visual imagery (Chapter 4). Recall that Deckert (1964) reported that imagining a moving pendulum was associated with eye-movement patterns similar to the smooth pursuit movements typically associated with visual perception of such a stimulus. However, the finding has not been replicated in subsequent research (Graham, 1970), so this evidence must be regarded as inconclusive in regard to the problem of similarities or differences in the processes underlying perception and imagery.

Pupillary activity is another physiological indicator that has recently enjoyed considerable popularity because the pupil appears to be a sensitive correlate of cognitive activity. H. M. Simpson and I have investigated this variable with some intensity in a series of studies (e.g., Simpson & Paivio, 1966, 1968) in the hope that it might be a fruitful approach to the study of imagery. These studies have indeed provided useful supplementary evidence in regard to the definition of imagery as an aspect of word meaning. We found repeatedly that the pupil dilates when a subject attempts to generate images to verbal stimuli, and that the magnitude of the dilation is greater and reaches a maximum later when the stimulus words are abstract than when they are concrete. This reaction is attenuated but not eliminated when control is exercised over such confounding variables as the motor response used by the subject to indicate task fulfillment. Colman and Paivio (1970) have also related such effects to paired-associate learning. Such results seem interpretable in terms of the concept of cognitive arousal or activation associated with task difficulty: It is simply more difficult (cognitively effortful) to generate images to abstract words than to concrete words, and this is reflected in the pupillary-dilation response just as it is reflected in reaction time and learning data. Thus, although it is gratifying to find the imagery construct validated by a variety of different operations, the pupil itself did not yield any unique information.

To indicate the kind of specific pupillary evidence that might be singularly valuable if it could be obtained, I will mention one more experiment (Paivio & Simpson, 1967). Subjects attempted to generate memory images of pictures of black or white objects to which they had been previously exposed a number of times. It would have been uncommonly interesting if we could have demonstrated that the pupil dilated more during recall of black pictures than of white pictures, since this would have constituted independent evidence of correlated differences in the *content* of imagery. As it turned out, such a difference did appear in the first experiment on the problem, but other interpretations could not be ruled out because of possible artifacts arising from the experimental procedure and, when these were subsequently controlled, the differential effect disappeared. Other unpublished attempts to find specific evidence have also been unsuccessful in our laboratory, hence the conclusion that the pupillary response can supplement behavioral evidence concerning cognitive activity, but it has not yet thrown any new light on the problem.

Numerous attempts have also been made to correlate electroencephalographic wave patterns with visual imagery. Some of these attempts were summarized in the last chapter, where it was noted that the results of such studies are generally inconclusive in that there seems to be no firm evidence that imagery could be differentiated from verbal thought in terms of alpha blocking. However, some recent work by Kamiya (cited in Stoyva & Kamiya, 1968, pp. 201-203) on the operant control of the EEG alpha rhythm promises to be a fruitful approach to the general problem. The first phase of these experiments involved a training procedure in which the subjects learned to discriminate the presence or absence of EEG alpha. The next phase demonstrated that subjects could acquire control over their alpha rhythm. This was achieved by a procedure in which a tone would sound whenever the subject was generating alpha frequencies within a desired range of 9–11 cycles per second. The tone started whenever alpha appeared and went off as soon as alpha vanished. Subjects became quite adept at turning alpha on and off. What is particularly relevant here, is that postexperimental interviews indicated that when alpha was "on" the subjects felt relaxed and were not experiencing any visual imagery. During periods of alpha suppression, on the other hand, the subjects reported "seeing" things. However, alpha was also suppressed if they reported exerting mental effort of some kind, suggesting that the physiological correlates may not be specific to imagery. They may be related instead to verbal processes, general cognitive arousal, or simply to asymmetry of lateral eye movements, which has been shown to correlate negatively with EEG alpha activity when a subject is engaged in a reflective mental task (Bakan & Svorad, 1969). It will probably be some time before the various contributing factors are teased apart.

Perhaps the most promising approach to the study of physiological correlates of the symbolic processes to date appears in John's (1967) discussion of the relation between meaning and evoked potentials recorded from the brain by means of scalp electrodes. One relevant finding is that different geometrical patterns such as a square and a circle elicit evoked-potentials differing in shape. John describes unpublished work (pp. 410–411) showing that wave shapes resembling those normally evoked by a particular geometric form can be obtained in response to illumination of an empty visual field if the subject merely imagines that the same form is present in the field. Different reactions were also obtained to the printed words *square* and *circle*, which were equated for area. John (p. 411) raises the interesting question of whether subsequent research can demonstrate an invariant aspect to the wave shape of responses evoked in the same region by presentation of a geometric form and the name of the form. Such demonstrations would obviously be of extraordinary interest here, specifically in regard to the validation of the construct of referential meaning.

The above discussion represents only a sampling of empirical data in the problem area and their implications for the conceptualization of the symbolic processes that have been posited here. The treatment in no way substitutes for the more thorough review that must be undertaken eventually by someone.

Attempts to explain imagery in neuropsychological terms, like psychophysiological studies of such processes, are interesting and important in their own right, but the contribution of such models to the problems we have dealt with in this book is similarly questionable. For that reason, I have not considered such theories to any extent and I will only mention them now to indicate the forms they take. The best known undoubtedly is Hebb's (1968) general theory, referred to in several places in the early chapters of this book (e.g., Chapter 3), in which imagery is conceptualized in terms of the activity of lower-order and higher-order assemblies in a hierarchial structure. These loop circuits are assumed to be set up primarily in the cortex, although some of them might be subcortical as well. Magda Arnold (1960) views the structures that mediate memory and imagination as being more localized than is the case in Hebb's theory. Specifically, she proposes that the relevant structures are located in parts of the limbic system, the recall of memory images in every sense modality presumably being mediated by the hippocampal circuit, and the rearrangement of memory images, that is, imagination, being mediated by the amygdaloid complex. Beritoff's (1965) conceptualization is closer to Hebb's. He proposes that the "neural substrate responsible for the generation of images of different objects seems to be located in the cerebral cortex, and its principal elements are believed to be the stellate cells . . . in the third and fourth layers of the primary areas of each [sensory] analyzer" (p. 342). A certain number of such cells are presumably integrated into a functional system with the help of internuncial and associational neurons during perception of an object. Still another model has been presented by Pribram (1969), who uses the concept of the hologram as the basis of his physiological conception of the memory image. The very diversity of these proposals suggests that we are probably not very close to achieving a neuropsychological model that satisfactorily describes the nature of imagery as we know it from behavioral evidence, let alone one that encompasses both imaginal and verbal processes and accounts for the functional similarities and distinctions between them. The development of such a theory remains one of the exciting neuropsychological frontiers from our standpoint.

CONCEPT FORMATION AND PROBLEM SOLVING

Much of the research reviewed in this book is indirectly relevant to the traditional cognitive research areas of concept formation and problem solving, and occasional instances are directly relevant to such problems. For example, in Chapter 14 we discussed Kuhlman's (1960) hypothesis that high-imagery children would be less efficient than low imagers in generalizing the label of a picture to new instances of the concept; another example from the same chapter is the effect of the verbal symbolic abilities of deaf subjects on concept learning. However, as is the case in numerous other problem areas that have been discussed at greater length in this book, cognitive research has generally ignored the contribution of nonverbal symbolic processes and has given almost exclusive attention to verbal mediation in the theorizing and empirical research. Thus verbal mediating responses have been given theoretical prominence in concept formation and problem solving by such people as Goss (1961) and Kendler and Kendler (1962), and this kind of orientation runs as a theme through a recent book devoted to human conceptual behavior (Bourne, 1966). Such approaches undoubtedly have been fruitful, but are also one-sided and incomplete because they do not give weight to the possible contribution of nonverbal imagery in mediating the behavioral effects with which they are concerned.

The relevance of nonverbal processes to concept formation can be seen in studies that have included variables that are operationally related to imagery. An early example is the research by Heidbreder (1946) on abstractness as an important variable in concept learning. She found that the ease of forming concepts was related to the concreteness of the stimuli that were to be grouped into conceptual categories. While the interpretation of her findings is a controversial matter (see Bourne, 1966, p. 62 ff.), an interpretation in terms of imagery, or the joint function of imagery and verbal processes, is plausible and amenable to further systematic research along the lines followed in the other research areas reviewed here. Predictions can be made, for example, about the kinds of concepts for which verbal and imaginal systems might be most relevant, and the information-processing stages during which they might be differentially operative. The latter point is illustrated by a recent qualifying-year thesis study completed by Mr. Albert Katz at Western University. The study extended an earlier one by Reed and Dick (1968), who investigated concept learning using words as the names of the concepts and of the instances. They found that concrete concepts were more easily learned than abstract concepts, in general agreement with Heidbreder's original findings. Katz reasoned that the Reed and Dick results, as well as the earlier ones by Heidbreder and others, were due to high-memory load conditions in the tasks used by those experimenters, and the differential ease of remembering concrete as compared to abstract information, as demonstrated by the studies reviewed in this book, rather than to differences in concept identification. Katz accordingly replicated the Reed and Dick study with the modification that subjects were tested under conditions of low memory load, in which previously presented concept instances remained in view as new ones were presented, as well as high memory load, in which past presentations were covered. Katz found that concrete concepts were learned faster than abstract ones under high memory load, which agrees with Reed and Dick, but he found no difference as a function of concreteness under low memory load. This finding suggests that all of the earlier findings on concreteness-abstractness effects in concept formation could be attributed to the facilitative effect of imagery on memory for concrete information relevant to the concept. More generally, however, the study illustrates the potential value of the concepts and findings presented in this book when they are extended to concept formation.

The Underwood and Richardson (1956) approach to verbal concept-learning tasks, in which the dominance level of verbal associative responses to stimulus items is varied, might also profit by taking imagery into account. These investigators provided a set of associative norms for the sense impressions aroused by stimulus items, so that it is possible to identify the most frequently given descriptive association to a particular word. Different stimulus words can then be grouped into a conceptual category on the basis of a strongly associated common label. Thus the words *snow, tooth, chalk,* and *milk* all elicit *white* as a common response. This approach implies that the speed at which a verbal concept can be discovered should be related to the strength or dominance of the common associate. Results supporting this prediction have been obtained in a number of studies (for a summary see Bourne, 1966, p. 109 ff.). Here again it can be seen, however, that it is possible to analyze the problem situation in terms of the contribution of nonverbal imagery to the information processing involved in it. The concrete nouns that are used as stimuli and the descriptive associative responses, although verbal in nature, presumably could reflect nonverbal imagery as a component of the underlying process. This suggestion is entirely speculative as things stand at present, but the problem is researchable.

CREATIVITY

The study of creativity is another enterprise to which the present approach might be particularly appropriate, and relevant concepts and findings have in fact been discussed in relation to associative learning, novelty or creativity of language, and so on. For example, the processes underlying the discovery of new metaphors was seen as common to such phenomena. The creative processes involved in science and art presumably involve more complex elaboration of similar processes. In contrast with the verbal-associative emphasis in such contemporary approaches as those proposed by Maltzman (1960) and Mednick (1962), imagery has been traditionally emphasized as an important element in the creative process by the creative individuals themselves, as well as by non-psychologists writing on the topic. It also finds a place in some contemporary psychological works. Rugg (1963) was cited in Chapter 2 as attributing associative flexibility to imagery, whereas the logical direction involved in creativity was attributed to verbal processes. Similarly, Berlyne (1965) discusses situational and transformational thinking, both involved in creativity, in terms of imagery and verbal mediation processes, with the former being attributed the major transformational function. The role of imagery in literary creativity has been recently discussed by Havelka (1968). A brief discussion of the relation between imagery and creativity appears also in A. Richardson's (1969) recent book on mental imagery, in which he points out the paucity of research on the problem.

The role of imagery in scientific creativity is highlighted by the models of science. The history of science is replete with examples of such models, which are transparent in their conceptual relation to imagery. This relation is also evidenced by the introspective reports of creative scientists themselves. Beveridge (1957) gives many examples of the important part that pictorial analogy can play in scientific thinking. Perhaps the best known of these is Kekulé's invention of the benzene ring, a revolutionary conception in organic chemistry that apparently first occurred to him as a dream in which long rows of atoms appeared to him as snakes, one of which seized its own tail. This became the basis of the hypothesis that he elaborated when he awoke. The most recent dramatic example of the role of visual models in chemistry is the double helix model of the DNA molecule (e.g., J. D. Watson, 1968). Arnheim (1969) has recently discussed at some length the role of imagery in the thought models of science generally (see also, Walkup, 1965). Examples of visual models in psychology include such diverse conceptions as Broadbent's (1957) mechanical model of attention and memory and Hebb's (1949) conception of the cell assembly as a three-dimensional neural latticework. The significance of such models is that the discovery phase of the creative process appears frequently to be mediated by concrete imagery, perhaps suggested as an analogy by an existing model from some other area of visual experience. The later formalization and verification of the model presumably brings in the more logical and directed verbal symbolic system, including ultimately the abstract symbolic system of mathematics. Scientific creativity thus appears to be one of the most dramatic examples of the interplay of imagery and verbal symbolic systems, but the systematic investigation of that interplay has scarcely begun.

EDUCATIONAL IMPLICATIONS

Probably the most important practical outcome of research on imagery and verbal processes will be in relation to problems of education. The information we already have on effects of concreteness and of mnemonic techniques, for example, has immediate practical implications for the problem of learning new subject matter. The idea is hardly new, inasmuch as it apparently was the chief motivation behind the development of mnemonic techniques in the eighteenth and nineteenth centuries (see Chapter 6). Since then, such methods have been almost totally ignored, and indeed downgraded, by educators and educational psychologists, but their potential value can be seen again in such work as Rohwer's (see Chapter 11) on the role of visual and sentence elaboration in children's learning. Bower (1970b) has recently made some explicit recommendations to educators from this point of view. He suggested, for example, that the best results from the use of a mnemonic aid arise when it is specifically tailored for particular memory performance with particular materials. According to Bower, this requires the construction of a mnemonic that, like problem solving, involves finding some way to sensibly relate the new, to-be-learned material to some familiar part of the student's prior knowledge.

Elsewhere (Paivio, 1970a), I have also pointed to educational implications of some of the specific findings that have been reviewed in this book. For example, the fact that concrete noun-abstract noun pairs are easier to learn than abstract-concrete pairs has implications in regard to an old question in communication and pedagogy, namely, is it more effective in communicating ideas to move from the relatively abstract and general to the more concrete and specific, or is it better to begin with the concrete and specific? The research I have described suggests that it may be more effective to begin with concrete, picturable examples and then move to the abstract or general ideas suggested by them, than to proceed the other way around. However, the hypothesis requires direct testing since the paired-associate situation is hardly representative of what goes on when individuals read or listen to more extended passages.

Finally, educational implications arise in regard to problems of language learning. One important problem is the identification of factors responsible for the development of effective linguistic meaning, such as concreteness. Chapter 3 referred to recent findings that suggested what kind of associative experience involving linguistic signs and their referents may be necessary for such learning to occur, but the problem requires more extensive research with young children before the major factors can be identified. A related problem is the role of nonverbal experience in the development of grammatical skills. I suggested earlier (Chapter 13) that the child first develops a repertoire of nonverbal imagery that has its own syntax or grammar because nonverbal objects behave in an orderly fashion, and that language builds upon this substrate of imagery. The problem is researchable, although there is very little specific evidence available at the moment. As I see it, these are among the most important applied research problems for the developmental psycholinguist and the educational researcher.

These brief comments on the implications of the present conceptual approach for such topics as creativity and the practical problems of education have been particularly speculative. Nonetheless, researchers in these areas are profoundly concerned with precisely those psychological processes that have been the focus of our attention, namely, memory and thought. The educational researcher seeks more interesting and effective ways of promoting learning and memory for new material, and combining stored information into the imaginative creations of the arts and sciences. The student of creativity seeks to understand the fundamental nature of the same processes. It would indeed be paradoxical if the theoretical and empirical variables that we have found to be such effective predictors of learning, memory, and association in a wide variety of laboratory tasks would prove to be otherwise in relation to the problems of creativity and education, but that remains to be determined.

References

Aaronson, D. Temporal factors in perception and short-term memory. *Psychological Bulletin,* 1967, **67,** 130–144.

Adams, J. A. *Human memory.* New York: McGraw-Hill, 1967.

Adams, J. A., & McIntyre, J. S. Natural language mediation and all-or-none learning. *Canadian Journal of Psychology,* 1967, **21,** 436–449.

Adams, J. A., & Montague, W. E. Retroactive inhibition and natural language mediation. *Journal of Verbal Learning and Verbal Behavior,* 1967, **6,** 528–535.

Adams, J. A., Thorsheim, H. I., & McIntyre, J. S. Item length, acoustic similarity, and natural language mediation as variables in short-term memory. *Journal of Experimental Psychology,* 1969, **80,** 39–46.

Allport, D. A. The rate of assimilation of visual information. *Psychonomic Science,* 1968, **12,** 231–232.

Allport, F. H. *Social psychology.* Boston: Houghton Mifflin, 1924.

Allport, F. H. *Theories of perception and the concept of structure.* New York: Wiley, 1955.

Allport, G. W. The eidetic image and the after image. *American Journal of Psychology,* 1928, **40,** 418–425.

Allport, G. W., Vernon, P. E., & Lindzey, G. *Study of values.* (2nd ed.) Boston: Houghton Mifflin, 1951.

Anastasi, A., & Levee, R. F. Intellectual defect and musical talent: A case report. *American Journal of Mental Deficiency,* 1959, **64,** 695–703.

Anderson, R. C. & Hidde, J. L. Imagery and sentence learning. Unpublished manuscript, University of Illinois, 1970.

Angell, J. R. Methods for the determination of mental imagery. *Psychological Monographs,* 1910, **13** (53), 61–107.

Anisfeld, M., & Knapp, M. Association, synonymity, and directionality in false recognition. *Journal of Experimental Psychology,* 1968, **77,** 171–179.

Antrobus, J. S., Antrobus, J. S., & Singer, J. L. Eye movements accompanying daydreaming, visual imagery, and thought suppression. *Journal of Abnormal and Social Psychology,* 1964, **69,** 244–252.

Antrobus, J. S., & Singer, J. L. Visual signal detection as a function of sequential variability of simultaneous speech. *Journal of Experimental Psychology,* 1964, **68,** 603–610.

Antrobus, J. S., Singer, J. L., & Greenberg, S. Studies in the stream of consciousness: Experimental enhancement and suppression of spontaneous cognitive processes. *Perceptual and Motor Skills,* 1966, **23,** 399–417.

Archer, E. J. A re-evaluation of the meaningfulness of all possible CVC trigrams. *Psychological Monographs,* 1960, **74** (10, Whole No. 497).

Arnheim, R. *Visual thinking.* Berkeley and Los Angeles: University of California Press, 1969.

Arnold, M. B. *Emotion and personality, Volume II: Neurological and physiological aspects.* New York: Columbia University Press, 1960.

Arnoult, M. D. Familiarity and recognition of nonsense shapes. *Journal of Experimental Psychology,* 1956, **51,** 269–276.

Asch, S. E. The metaphor: A psychological inquiry. In R. Tagiuri and L. Petrullo (Eds.), *Person perception and interpersonal behavior.* Stanford: Stanford University Press, 1958.

Asch, S. E., Ceraso, J., & Heimer, W. Perceptual conditions of association. *Psychological Monographs,* 1960, **57** (3).

Asch, S. E., & Ebenholtz, S. M. The principle of associative symmetry. *Proceedings of the American Philosophical Society,* 1962, **106,** 135–163.

Asch, S. E., & Lindner, M. A note on "strength of association." *Journal of Psychology,* 1963, **55,** 199–209.

Aserinsky, E., & Kleitman, N. Regularly occurring periods of eye motility and concomitant phenomena during sleep. *Science,* 1953, **18,** 274–284.

Atkinson, R. C., & Shiffrin, R. M. Human memory: A proposed system and its control processes. In K. W. Spence and J. T. Spence (Eds.), *The psychology of learning and motivation: Advances in research and theory,* Vol. II. New York: Academic Press, 1968.

Attneave, F. Some informational aspects of visual perception. *Psychological Review,* 1954, **61,** 183–193.

Attneave, F. Physical determinants of the judged complexity of shapes. *Journal of Experimental Psychology,* 1957, **53,** 221–227.

Attneave, F., & Benson, B. Spatial coding of tactual stimulation. *Journal of Experimental Psychology,* 1969, **81,** 216–222.

Atwood, G. E. Experimental studies of mnemonic visualization. Unpublished doctoral dissertation, University of Oregon, 1969.

Ausubel, D. P. A cognitive structure view of word and concept meaning. In R. C. Anderson and D. P. Ausubel (Eds.), *Readings in the psychology of cognition.* New York: Holt, 1965.

Ayres, J. J. Some artifactual causes of perceptual primacy. *Journal of Experimental Psychology,* 1966, **71,** 896–901.

Baddeley, A. D. Semantic and acoustic similarity in short-term memory. *Nature,* 1964, **204,** 1116–1117.

Baddeley, A. D. Short-term memory for word sequences as a function of acoustic, semantic and formal similarity. *Quarterly Journal of Experimental Psychology,* 1966, **18,** 362–365. (a)

Baddeley, A. D. The influence of acoustic and semantic similarity of long-term memory for word sequences. *Quarterly Journal of Experimental Psychology,* 1966, **18,** 302–309. (b)

Baddeley, A. D., Conrad, R., & Hull, A. J. Predictability and immediate memory for consonant sequences. *Quarterly Journal of Experimental Psychology,* 1965, **17,** 175–177.

Baddeley, A. D., & Dale, H. C. A. The effect of semantic similarity on retroactive interference in long- and short-term memory. *Journal of Verbal Learning and Verbal Behavior,* 1966, **5,** 417–420.

Bahrick, H. P. Discriminative and associative aspects of pictorial paired-associate learning: Acquisition and retention. *Journal of Experimental Psychology,* 1969, **80,** 113–119.

Bahrick, H. P., & Boucher, B. Retention of visual and verbal codes of the same stimuli. *Journal of Experimental Psychology,* 1968, **78,** 417–422.

Bakan, P., & Svorad, D. Resting EEG alpha and asymmetry of reflective lateral eye movements. *Nature,* 1969, **223,** 975–976.

Ball, W. W. R. Calculating prodigies. From *Mathematical recreations and essays,* 1892. Reprinted in J. R. Newman (Ed.), *The world of mathematics,* Vol. I. New York: Simon and Shuster, 1956, 467–487.

Barber, T. X. The afterimages of "hallucinated" and "imagined" colors. *Journal of Abnormal and Social Psychology,* 1959, **59,** 136–139. (a)

Barber, T. X. The "eidetic image" and "hallucinatory" behavior: A suggestion for further research. *Psychological Bulletin,* 1959, **56,** 236–239.(b)

Barnes, J. M., & Underwood, B. J. "Fate" of first-list associations in transfer theory. *Journal of Experimental Psychology,* 1959, **58,** 97–105.

Barnes, L. D., & Schulz, R. W. Meaningfulness and the associative phase of paired-associate learning. Paper presented at the meetings of the Midwestern Psychological Association, Chicago, Ill., 1966.

Barratt, P. E. Imagery and thinking. *Australian Journal of Psychology,* 1953, **5,** 154–164.

Barratt, P. E. Use of EEG in the study of imagery. *British Journal of Psychology,* 1956, **47,** 101–114.

Bartlett, F. C. *Remembering.* Cambridge (England): Cambridge University Press, 1932.

Barton, M. I., Goodglass, H., & Shai, A. Differential recognition of tachistoscopically presented English and Hebrew words in right and left visual fields. *Perceptual and Motor Skills,* 1965, **21,** 431–437.

Bastian, J. Associative factors in verbal transfer. *Journal of Experimental Psychology,* 1961, **62,** 70–79.

Battig, W. F. Evidence for coding processes in "rote" paired-associate learning. *Journal of Verbal Learning and Verbal Behavior,* 1966, **5,** 177–181.

Battig, W. F. Paired-associate learning. In T. R. Dixon & D. L. Horton (Eds.), *Verbal behaviour and general behaviour theory.* Englewood Cliffs, New Jersey: Prentice-Hall, 1968.

Battig, W. F., & Koppenaal, R. J. Associative asymmetry in S-R vs. R-S recall of double-function lists. *Psychological Reports,* 1965, **16,** 287–293.

Begg, I. Recognition memory for sentence meaning and wording. *Journal of Verbal Learning and Verbal Behavior,* 1971, **10,** 114–119.

Begg, 1., & Paivio, A. Concreteness and imagery in sentence meaning. *Journal of Verbal Learning and Verbal Behavior,* 1969, **8,** 821–827.

Beighley, K. C. An experimental study of the effect of four speech variables on listener comprehension. *Speech Monographs,* 1952, **19,** 249–258.

Bennet-Clark, H. C., & Evans, C. R. Fragmentation of patterned targets when viewed as prolonged after-images. *Nature,* 1963, **199,** 1215–1216.

Berger, S. M. Persons as mediators: A three-stage paradigm. *Psychonomic Science,* 1965, **3,** 53–54.

Beritoff, J. S. *Neural mechanisms of higher vertebrate behavior.* (Translated and edited by W. T. Liberson.) Boston: Little, Brown, and Co., 1965.

Berlyne, D. E. *Structure and direction in thinking.* New York: Wiley, 1965.

Berlyne, D. E. Mediating responses: A note on Fodor's criticisms. *Journal of Verbal Learning and Verbal Behavior,* 1966, **5,** 408–411.

Betts, G. H. *The distribution and functions of mental imagery.* New York: Teachers College, Columbia University, 1909.

Bevan, W., Dukes, W. F., & Avant, L. L. The effect of variation in specific stimuli on memory for their superordinates. *The American Journal of Psychology,* 1966, **79,** 250–257.

Beveridge, W. I. B. *The art of scientific investigation.* New York: Random House, 1957.

Binet, A. *Psychologie des grand calculateurs et joueurs d'échec.* Paris: Hachette, 1894.

Binet, A. (Translated by M. L. Simmel and S. B. Barron.) Mnemonic virtuosity: A study of chess players. *Genetic Psychology Monographs,* 1966, **74,** 127–162.

Birnbaum, I. M. Context stimuli in verbal learning and the persistence of associative factors. *Journal of Experimental Psychology,* 1966, **71,** 483–489.

Bloomer, R. H. Concepts of meaning and the reading and spelling difficulty of words. *Journal of Educational Research,* 1961, **54,** 178–182.

Blumenthal, A. Prompted recall of sentences. *Journal of Verbal Learning and Verbal Behavior,* 1967, **6,** 203–206.

Blumenthal, A. & Boakes, R. Prompted recall of sentences. *Journal of Verbal Learning and Verbal Behavior,* 1967, **6,** 674–676.

Bobrow, S. A., & Bower, G. H. Comprehension and recall of sentences. *Journal of Experimental Psychology,* 1969, **80,** 455–461.

Boersma, F. J., Conklin, R. C., & Carlson, J. E. Effects of reporting associative strategies on the retention of paired-associates. *Psychonomic Science,* 1966, **5,** 463–464.

Bolinger, D. The atomization of meaning. *Language,* 1965, **41,** 555–573.

Boomer, D. Hesitation and grammatical encoding. *Language and Speech,* 1965, **8,** 148–158.

Boring, E. G. *A history of experimental psychology.* New York: Appleton-Century-Crofts, 1950.

Borkowski, J. G., & Eisner, H. C. Meaningfulness and abstractness in short-term memory. *Journal of Experimental Psychology,* 1968, **76,** 57–61.

Borkowski, J. G., Spreen, O., & Stutz, J. Z. Ear preference and abstractness in dichotic listening. *Psychonomic Science,* 1965, **3,** 547–548.

Bourne, L. E., Jr. *Human conceptual behavior.* Boston: Allyn and Bacon, 1966.

Bousfield, A. K., & Bousfield, W. A. Measurement of clustering and of sequential constancies in repeated free recall. *Psychological Reports,* 1966, **19,** 935–942.

Bousfield, W. A. The occurrence of clustering in recall of randomly arranged associates. *Journal of General Psychology*, 1953, **49**, 229–240.

Bousfield, W. A. The problem of meaning in verbal behavior. In C. N. Cofer (Ed.), *Verbal learning and verbal behavior*. New York: McGraw-Hill, 1961.

Bousfield, W. A., & Barry, H. The visual imagery of a lightning calculator. *American Journal of Psychology*, 1933, **45**, 353–358.

Bousfield, W. A., & Cohen, B. H. The occurrence of clustering in the recall of randomly arranged words of different frequencies of usage. *Journal of General Psychology*, 1955, **52**, 83–95.

Bousfield, W. A., Esterson, J., & Whitmarsh, G. A. The effects of concomitant colored and uncolored pictorial representations on the learning of stimulus words. *Journal of Applied Psychology*, 1957, **41**, 165–168.

Bousfield, W. A., Puff, C. R., & Cowan, T. M., The development of constancies in sequential organization during repeated free recall. *Journal of Verbal Learning and Verbal Behavior*, 1964, **3**, 489–495.

Bousfield, W. A., & Samborski, G. The relationship between strength of values and the meaningfulness of value words. *Journal of Personality*, 1955, **23**, 375–380.

Bousfield, W. A., Steward, J. R., & Cowan, T. M. The use of free associational norms for the prediction of clustering. *Journal of General Psychology*, 1964, **70**, 205–214.

Bower, G. H. A multicomponent theory of the memory trace. In K. W. Spence & J. T. Spence (Eds.), *The psychology of learning and motivation*, Vol. I. New York: Academic Press, 1967.

Bower, G. H. Mental imagery and associative learning. Fifth annual symposium on cognition. Carnegie-Mellon University, Pittsburgh, Penn., 1969. To be published in Lee Gregg (Ed.), *Cognition in learning and memory*, New York: Wiley.

Bower, G. H. Imagery as a relational organizer in associative learning. *Journal of Verbal Learning and Verbal Behavior*, 1970, **9**, 529–533. (a)

Bower, G. H. Mnemonics. Symposium address, American Educational Research Association meeting, Minneapolis, March, 1970. (b)

Bower, G. H., & Bolton, L. S. Why are rhymes easy to learn? *Journal of Experimental Psychology*, 1969, **82**, 453–461.

Bower, G. H., & Clark, M. C. Narrative stories as mediators for serial learning. *Psychonomic Science*, 1969, **14**, 181–182.

Bower, G. H., Clark, M. C., Lesgold, A. M., & Winzenz, D. Hierarchical retrieval schemes in recall of categorized word lists. *Journal of Verbal Learning and Verbal Behavior*, 1969, **8**, 323–343.

Bower, G. H., Lesgold, A. M., & Tieman, D. Grouping operations in free recall. *Journal of Verbal Learning and Verbal Behavior*, 1969, **8**, 481–493.

Bower, G. H., & Winzenz, D. Comparison of associative learning strategies. *Psychonomic Science*, 1970, **20**, 119–120.

Bowers, H. Memory and mental imagery. An experimental study. *British Journal of Psychology*, 1931, **21**, 271–282.

Bowers, H. Visual imagery and retention. *British Journal of Psychology*, 1932, **23**, 180–195.

Bowra, C. M. *Greek lyric poetry*. London: Oxford University Press, 1961.

Braine, L. G. Asymmetries of pattern perception observed in Israelis. *Neuropsychologia*, 1968, **6**, 73–88.

Braine, M. D. S. On learning the grammatical order of words. *Psychological Review*, 1963, **70**, 323–348.

Bregman, A. S., & Strasberg, R. Memory for the syntactic form of sentences. *Journal of Verbal Learning and Verbal Behavior*, 1968, **7**, 396–403.

Brener, L. R. An experimental investigation of memory span. *Journal of Experimental Psychology*, 1940, **26**, 467–482.

Brent, S. B. Linguistic unity, list length, and rate of presentation in serial anticipation learning. *Journal of Verbal Learning and Verbal Behavior*, 1969, **8**, 70–79.

Broadbent, D. E. A mechanical model for human attention and immediate memory. *Psychological Review*, 1957, **64**, 205–215.

Brodey, W. The other-than-visual world of the blind. *Ekistics*, 1969, **28**, 100–103.

Brogden, W. J. Sensory pre-conditioning of human subjects. *Journal of Experimental Psychology*, 1947, **37**, 527–539.

Brooks, L. R. The suppression of visualization in reading. *Quarterly Journal of Experimental Psychology*, 1967, **19**, 289–299.

Brooks, L. R. Spatial and verbal components of the act of recall. *Canadian Journal of Psychology*, 1968, **22**, 349–368.

Brosgole, L., & Whalen, P. M. The effect of meaning on the allocation of visually induced movement. *Perception and Psychophysics*, 1967, **2**, 275–277.

Brower, D. The experimental study of imagery. I. The relation of imagery to intelligence. *Journal of General Psychology*, 1947, **36**, 229–231.

Brown, B. B. Specificity of EEG photic flicker responses to color as related to visual imagery ability. *Psychophysiology*, 1966, **2**, 197–207.

Brown, J. Some tests of the decay theory of immediate memory. *Quarterly Journal of Experimental Psychology*, 1958, **10**, 12–21.

Brown, R. W. Linguistic determinism and the part of speech. *Journal of Abnormal and Social Psychology*, 1957, **55**, 1–5.

Brown, R. W. *Words and things*. Glencoe, Ill.: Free Press, 1958.

Brown, R. W., & Berko, J. Word association and the acquisition of grammar. *Child Development*, 1960, **31**, 1–14.

Brown, R. W., & Lenneberg, E. H. A study in language and cognition. *Journal of Abnormal and Social Psychology*, 1954, **49**, 454–462.

Brown, S. W., Guilford, J. P., & Hoepfner, R. Six semantic-memory abilities. *Educational and Psychological Measurement*, 1968, **28**, 691–718.

Brown, W. P., & Ure, D. M. J. Five rated characteristics of 650 word association stimuli. *British Journal of Psychology*, 1969, **60**, 233–249.

Bruner, J. S. Neural mechanisms in perception. *Psychological Review*, 1957, **64**, 340–358.

Bruner, J. S. The course of cognitive growth. *American Psychologist*, 1964, **19**, 1–15.

Bruner, J. S., Olver, R. R., & Greenfield, P. M. *Studies in cognitive growth*. New York: Wiley, 1966.

Bruner, J. S., & Postman, L. On the perception of incongruity: A paradigm. *Journal of Personality*, 1949, **18**, 206–223.

Bruner, J. S., & Potter, M. C. Interference in visual recognition. *Science*, 1964, **144**, 424–425.

Bryden, M. P. Tachistoscopic recognition of non-alphabetic material. *Canadian Journal of Psychology*, 1960, **14**, 78–86.

Bryden, M. P. The role of post-exposural eye movements in tachistoscopic perception. *Canadian Journal of Psychology*, 1961, **15**, 220–225.

Bryden, M. P. Left-right differences in tachistoscopic recognition: Directional scanning or cerebral dominance? *Perceptual and Motor Skills,* 1966, **23,** 1127–1134.

Bryden, M. P. A model for the sequential organization of behaviour. *Canadian Journal of Psychology,* 1967, **21,** 37–56.

Bryden, M. P., Dick, A. O., & Mewhort, D. J. K. Tachistoscopic recognition of number sequences. *Canadian Journal of Psychology,* 1968, **22,** 52–59.

Bryden, M. P., & Rainey, C. A. Left-right differences in tachistoscopic recognition. *Journal of Experimental Psychology,* 1963, **66,** 568–571.

Bugelski, B. R. *An introduction to the principles of psychology.* New York: Rinehart, 1960.

Bugelski, B. R. Presentation time, total time, and mediation in paired-associate learning. *Journal of Experimental Psychology,* 1962, **63,** 409–412.

Bugelski, B. R. Images as mediators in one-trial paired-associate learning. II: Self-timing in successive lists. *Journal of Experimental Psychology,* 1968, **77,** 328–334.

Bugelski, B. R. Learning theory and the reading process. In *The 23rd annual reading conference.* Pittsburgh: University of Pittsburgh Press, 1969, in press.

Bugelski, B. R. Words and things and images. *American Psychologist,* 1970, **25,** 1002–1012.

Bugelski, B. R., Kidd, E., & Segmen, J. Image as a mediator in one-trial paired-associate learning. *Journal of Experimental Psychology,* 1968, **76,** 69–73.

Bugelski, B. R., & Scharlock, D. P. An experimental demonstration of unconscious mediated generalization. *Journal of Experimental Psychology,* 1952, **44,** 334–338.

Butter, M. J. Differential recall of paired associates as a function of arousal and concreteness-imagery levels. *Journal of Experimental Psychology,* 1970, **84,** 252–256.

Calkins, M. W. Short studies in memory and in association from the Wellesley College psychological laboratory. *Psychological Review,* 1898, **5,** 451–462.

Canestrari, R. E., Jr. Age changes in acquisition. *Human aging and behavior,* New York: Academic Press, 1968, 169–188.

Carey, N. Factors in the mental processes of school children. I. Visual and auditory imagery. *British Journal of Psychology,* 1915, **7,** 452–490.

Carmichael, L., Hogan, H. P., & Walter, A. A. An experimental study of the effect of language on the reproduction of visually perceived form. *Journal of Experimental Psychology,* 1932, **15,** 73–86.

Carnegie, D. *Public speaking and influencing men in business.* New York: Association Press, 1937.

Cartwright, D. Lewinian theory as a contemporary systematic framework. In S. Koch (Ed.), *Psychology: A study of a science,* Vol. 2. New York: McGraw-Hill, 1959.

Chomsky, N. *Syntactic structures.* The Hague: Mouton, 1957.

Chomsky, N. Review of *Verbal behaviour* by B. F. Skinner. *Language,* 1959, **35,** 26–58.

Chomsky, N. Aspects of the theory of syntax. Cambridge, Mass.: M.I.T. Press, 1965.

Chomsky, N. *Cartesian linguistics.* New York: Harper & Row, 1966.

Chomsky, N. Language and the mind. *Psychology Today,* 1968, **1** (9), 48–51; 66–68.

Christal, R. E. Factor analytic study of visual memory. *Psychological Monographs,* 1958, 72, (13, Whole No. 466).

Christensen, P. R., Guilford, J. P., Merrifield, P. R., & Wilson, R. C. *Alternate uses, Form A.* Sheridan Supply Company, Beverly Hills, California, 1960.

Christiansen, T. Sex and level of mediator abstractness as variables in mediate association. *Psychonomic Science,* 1969, **14,** 160–162.

Christiansen, T., & Stone, D. R. Visual imagery and level of mediator abstractness in induced mediation paradigms. *Perceptual and Motor Skills,* 1968, **26,** 775–779.

Clark, H. H. Some structural properties of simple active and passive sentences. *Journal of Verbal Learning and Verbal Behavior,* 1965, **4,** 365–370.

Clark, H. H. Linguistic processes in deductive reasoning. *Psychological Review,* 1969, **76,** 387–403.

Clark, H. J. Recognition memory for random shapes as a function of complexity, association value, and delay. *Journal of Experimental Psychology,* 1965, **69,** 590–595.

Clark, H. J. Random shape recognition at brief exposure durations. *Psychonomic Science,* 1968, **12,** 245–246.

Clark, L. L., Lansford, T. G., & Dallenbach, K. M. Repetition and associative learning. *American Journal of Psychology,* 1960, **73,** 22–40.

Clarke, F. J. J., & Evans, C. R. Comments on reports: Luminous-design phenomena. *Science,* 1964, **144,** 1359–1360.

Cofer, C. N. On some factors in the organizational characteristics of free recall. *American Psychologist,* 1965, **20,** 261–272.

Cofer, C. N. Conditions for the use of verbal associations. *Psychological Bulletin,* 1967, **68** (1), 1–12.

Cofer, C. N., Diamond, F., Olsen, R. A., Stein, J. S., & Walker, H. Comparison of anticipation and recall methods in paired-associate learning. *Journal of Experimental Psychology,* 1967, **75,** 545–558.

Cohen, B. H. An investigation of recoding in free recall. *Journal of Experimental Psychology,* 1963, **65,** 368–376.

Cohen, R. L. & Granström, K. Reproduction and recognition in short-term visual memory. *Quarterly Journal of Experimental Psychology,* 1970, **22,** 450–457.

Cole, M., Frankel, F., & Sharp, D. The development of free recall learning in children. Unpublished paper, Department of Psychology, University of California, Irvine, 1969.

Coleman, E. B. Approximations to English: Some comments on the method. *American Journal of Psychology,* 1963, **76,** 239–247.

Coleman, E. B. Responses to a scale of grammaticalness. *Journal of Verbal Learning and Verbal Behavior,* 1965, **4,** 521–527.

Colman, F., & Paivio, A. Pupillary dilation and mediation processes during paired-associate learning. *Canadian Journal of Psychology,* 1970, **24,** 261–270.

Conrad, R. Acoustic confusions in immediate memory. *British Journal of Psychology,* 1964, **55,** 75–84.

Conrad, R., Freeman, P. R., & Hull, A. J. Acoustic factors versus language factors in short-term memory. *Psychonomic Science,* 1965, **3,** 57–58.

Corsini, D. A., Jacobus, K. A., & Leonard, S. D. Recognition memory of preschool children for pictures and words. *Psychonomic Science,* 1969, **16,** 192–193.

Craik, F. I. M. The fate of primary memory items in free recall. *Journal of Verbal Learning and Verbal Behavior,* 1970, **9,** 143–148.

Creelman, M. B. *The experimental investigation of meaning.* New York: Springer, 1966.

Crovitz, H. F. *Galton's Walk.* New York: Harper and Row, 1970.

Crovitz, H. F., & Daves, W. Tendency to eye movement and perceptual accuracy. *Journal of Experimental Psychology,* 1962, **63,** 495–498.

Crowder, R. G. Evidence for the chaining hypothesis of serial verbal learning. *Journal of Experimental Psychology,* 1968, **76,** 497–500.

Crowder, R. G., & Morton, J. Precategorical acoustic storage (PAS). *Perception and Psychophysics,* 1969, **5,** 365–373.

Csapo, K. The effects of presentation rate and item attribute in paired-associate learning. Unpublished master's thesis, University of Western Ontario, 1968.

Dainoff, M., & Haber, R. N. How much help do repeated presentations give to recognition processes? *Perception and Psychophysics,* 1967, **2,** 131–136.

Dallett, K. M. Implicit mediators in paired-associate learning. *Journal of Verbal Learning and Verbal Behavior,* 1964, **3,** 209–214.

Darley, F. L., Sherman, D., & Siegel, G. M. Scaling of abstraction level of single words. *Journal of Speech and Hearing Research,* 1959, **2,** 161–167.

Daves, W. F., & Adkins, M. Stimulus variation and free recall: A confirmation. *American Journal of Psychology,* 1969, **82,** 122–124.

Davidson, R. E. Mediation and ability in paired-associate learning. *Journal of Educational Psychology,* 1964, **55,** 352–356.

Davidson, R. E., & Adams, J. F. Verbal and imagery processes in children's paired-associate learning. *Journal of Experimental Child Psychology,* in press.

Davidson, R. E., Schwenn, E. A., & Adams, J. F. Semantic effects in transfer. *Journal of Verbal Learning and Verbal Behavior,* 1970, **9,** 212–217.

Davis, F. C. The functional significance of imagery differences. *Journal of Experimental Psychology,* 1932, **15,** 630–661.

Deckert, G. H. Pursuit eye movements in the absence of a moving visual stimulus. *Science,* 1964, **143,** 1192–1193.

Deese, J. Influence of inter-item associative strength upon immediate free recall. *Psychological Reports,* 1959, **5,** 305–312.

Deese, J. Frequency of usage and number of words in free recall: The role of association. *Psychological Reports,* 1960, **7,** 337–344.

Deese, J. From the isolated verbal unit to connected discourse. In C. N. Cofer (Ed.), *Verbal learning and verbal behavior.* New York: McGraw-Hill, 1961.

Deese, J. *The structure of associations in language and thought.* Baltimore: The Johns Hopkins Press, 1965.

Deese, J. Association and memory. In T. R. Dixon and D. L. Horton (Eds.), *Verbal behavior and general behavior theory.* Englewood Cliffs, New Jersey: Prentice-Hall, 1968.

Deese, J., & Hulse, S. H. *The psychology of learning.* (3rd ed.) New York: McGraw-Hill, 1967.

Delin, P. S. Success in recall as a function of success in implementation of mnemonic instructions. *Psychonomic Science,* 1968, **12,** 153–154.

Delin, P. S. The learning to criterion of a serial list with and without mnemonic instructions. *Psychonomic Science,* 1969, **16,** 169–170.

Dember, W. N. *Psychology of perception.* New York: Holt, 1960.

Dement, W. C. An essay on dreams: The role of physiology in understanding their nature. In *New directions in psychology II.* New York: Holt, 1965.

DeSoto, C., London, M., & Handel, S. Social reasoning and spatial paralogic. *Journal of Personality and Social Psychology,* 1965, **2,** 513–521.

Dick, A. O., & Mewhort, J. K. Order of report and processing in tachistoscopic recognition. *Perception and Psychophysics,* 1967, **2,** 573–576.

Dilley, M. G., & Paivio, A. Pictures and words as stimulus and response items in paired-associate learning of young children. *Journal of Experimental Child Psychology,* 1968, **6,** 231–240.

DiVesta, F. J., & Walls, R. T. Factor analysis of the semantic attributes of 487 words and some relationships to the conceptual behavior of fifth-grade children. *Journal of Educational Psychology Monograph,* 1970, **61** (6, Pt. 2).

Dixon, T. R., & Horton, D. L. (Eds.) *Verbal behavior and general behavior theory.* Englewood Cliffs, New Jersey: Prentice-Hall, 1968.

Dixon, T. R., & Moulton, A. E. Effects of questioning unaware problem solvers in a "verbal conditioning" task. *Journal of Experimental Psychology,* 1970, **83,** 431–434.

Dominowski, R. L., & Gadlin, H. Imagery and paired-associate learning. *Canadian Journal of Psychology,* 1968, **22,** 336–348.

Donderi, D. C., & Kane, E. Perceptual learning produced by common responses to different stimuli. *Canadian Journal of Psychology,* 1965, **19,** 15–30.

Dong, T., & Kintsch, W. Subjective retrieval cues in free recall. *Journal of Verbal Learning and Verbal Behavior,* 1968, **7,** 813–816.

Doob, L. W. Eidetic images among the Ibo. *Ethnology,* 1964, **3,** 357–363.

Doob, L. W. Exploring eidetic imagery among the Kamba of Central Kenya. *Journal of Social Psychology,* 1965, **67,** 3–22.

Doob, L. W. Eidetic imagery: A cross-cultural will-o'-the-wisp? *Journal of Psychology,* 1966, **63,** 13–34.

Dooling, D. J. Effects of surrogate processes and syntactic constraint on the retention of connected discourse. Paper read at the meeting of the Eastern Psychological Association, Washington, 1968.

Dornbush, R. L. Shadowing in bisensory memory. *Quarterly Journal of Experimental Psychology,* 1968, **20,** 225–231.

Drever, J. Some observations on the occipital alpha rhythm. *Quarterly Journal of Experimental Psychology,* 1955, **7,** 91–97.

Ducharme, R., & Fraisse, P. Etude génétique de la mémorisation de mots et d'images. *Canadian Journal of Psychology,* 1965, **19,** 253–261.

Dukes, W. F., & Bastian, J. Recall of abstract and concrete words equated on meaningfulness. *Journal of Verbal Learnings and Verbal Behavior,* 1966, **5,** 455–458.

Dunn, F. Poetic space. *Scottish International,* January, 1968, 56–58.

Dunn, S., Bliss, J., & Siipola, E. Effects of impulsivity, introversion and individual values upon association under free conditions. *Journal of Personality,* 1958, **26,** 61–76.

Dunne, M. M. The effect of syntactic structure on learning. *Journal of Verbal Learning and Verbal Behavior,* 1968, **7,** 458–463.

Eagle, M., Wolitzky, D. L., & Klein, G. S. Imagery: Effect of a concealed figure in a stimulus. *Science,* 1966, **151,** 837–839.

Earhard, B., & Earhard, M. Mediation and pseudomediation: A reply to Horton. *Canadian Journal of Psychology,* 1968, **22,** 308–322.

Earhard, B., & Mandler, G. Mediated associations: Paradigms, controls, and mechanisms. *Canadian Journal of Psychology,* 1965, **19,** 346–378.

Eastman, R. The relative crossmodal transfer of a form discrimination. *Psychonomic Science*, 1967, **9**, 197–198.

Ebbinghaus, H. *Memory: A contribution to experimental psychology.* New York: Dover, 1964. (Originally published: Leipzig: Duncker & Humblot, 1885.)

Ebenholtz, S. M. Serial learning: Position learning and sequential associations. *Journal of Experimental Psychology*, 1963, **66**, 353–362.

Edmonds, E. M., & Evans, S. H. Schema learning without a prototype. *Psychonomic Science*, 1966, **5**, 247–248.

Eiles, R. R. Effects of mediational and motivational instructions on forward and backward recall of concrete paired-associate nouns. Unpublished doctoral dissertation, Arizona State University, 1970.

Ekstrand, B. R. Backward associations. *Psychological Bulletin*, 1966, **65**, 50–64.

Ekstrand, B. R., Wallace, W. P., & Underwood, B. J. A frequency theory of verbal-discrimination learning. *Psychological Review*, 1966, **73**, 556–578.

Eliava, N. L. A contribution to the problem of the role of set and attitude in perceptual processes. Voprosy psikhologii, 1961, No. 1. English translation: *Soviet psychology and psychiatry*, 1962, **1**, 16–20.

Ellis, H. C., & Muller, D. G. Transfer in perceptual learning following stimulus predifferentiation. *Journal of Experimental Psychology*, 1964, **68**, 388–395.

Ellis, H. C., Muller, D. G., & Tosti, D. T. Stimulus meaning and complexity as factors in the transfer of stimulus predifferentiation. *Journal of Experimental Psychology*, 1966, **71**, 629–633.

Ellson, D. G. Hallucinations produced by sensory conditioning. *Journal of Experimental Psychology*, 1941, **28**, 1–20. (a)

Ellson, D. G. Experimental extinction of an hallucination produced by sensory conditioning. *Journal of Experimental Psychology*, 1941, **28**, 350–361. (b)

Epstein, W. The influence of syntactical structure on learning. *American Journal of Psychology*, 1961, **74**, 80–85.

Epstein, W. A further study of the influence of syntactical structure on learning. *American Journal of Psychology*, 1962, **75**, 121–126. (a)

Epstein, W. Backward association as a function of meaningfulness. *Journal of General Psychology*, 1962, **67**, 11–20. (b)

Epstein, W. Temporal schemata in syntactically structured material. *Journal of General Psychology*, 1963, **68**, 157–164.

Epstein, W. *Varieties of perceptual learning.* New York: McGraw-Hill, 1967.

Epstein, W., Rock, I., & Zuckerman, C. B. Meaning and familiarity in associative learning. *Psychological Monographs*, 1960, **74**, (4, Whole No. 491).

Epstein, W., & Streib, R. The effect of stimulus meaningfulness and response meaningfulness in the absence of response learning. *Journal of Verbal Learning and Verbal Behavior*, 1962, **1**, 105–108.

Erickson, R. L. Differential effects of stimulus and response isolation in paired-associate learning. *Journal of Experimental Psychology*, 1965, **69**, 317–323.

Eriksen, C. W. Unconscious processes. In M. R. Jones (Ed.), *Nebraska symposium on motivation.* Lincoln: University of Nebraska Press, 1958.

Eriksen, C. W. Temporal luminance summation effects in forward and backward masking. *Perception and Psychophysics*, 1966, **1**, 87–92.

Ernest, C. H., & Paivio, A. Imagery ability in paired-associate and incidental learning. *Psychonomic Science*, 1969, **15**, 181–182.

Ernest, C. H., & Paivio, A. Imagery and sex differences in incidental recall. *British Journal of Psychology*, 1971, **62**, 67–72.

Ervin, S. M. Changes with age in the verbal determinants of word association. *American Journal of Psychology*, 1961, **74**, 361–372.

Esper, E. A. *Mentalism and objectivism in linguistics.* New York: American Elsevier, 1968.

Evans, C. R. Further studies of pattern perception and a stabilized retinal image: The use of prolonged after-images to achieve perfect stabilization. *British Journal of Psychology*, 1967, **58**, 315–327.

Feinaigle, G. von. *The new art of memory.* (3rd ed.) London: Sherwood, Neely and Jones, 1813.

Feldmar, A. Syntactic structure and speech decoding: The judgment of sequence in auditory events. Unpublished master's thesis, University of Western Ontario, 1969.

Ferguson, G. A. On learning and human ability. *Canadian Journal of Psychology*, 1954, **8**, 95–112.

Ferguson, G. A. On transfer and the abilities of man. *Canadian Journal of Psychology*, 1956, **10**, 121–131.

Fernald, M. R. The diagnosis of mental imagery. *Psychological Monographs*, 1912, No. 58.

Feuge, R. L., & Ellis, H. C. Generalization gradients in recognition memory of visual form: The role of stimulus meaning. *Journal of Experimental Psychology*, 1969, **79**, 288–294.

Fillenbaum, S. Memory for gist: Some relevant variables. *Language and Speech*, 1966, **9**, 217–227.

Fiss, H., Goldberg, F. H., & Klein, G. S. Effects of subliminal stimulation on imagery and discrimination. *Perceptual and Motor Skills*, 1963, **17**, 31–44.

Flavell, J. H., Beach, D. R., & Chinsky, J. M. Spontaneous verbal rehearsal in a memory task as a function of age. *Child Development*, 1966, **37**, 283–299.

Fleishman, E. A. Human abilities and the acquisition of skill. In E. A. Bilodeau (Ed.), *Acquisition of skill.* New York: Academic Press, 1966. (a)

Fleishman, E. A. Human abilities and verbal learning. In R. Gagné (Ed.), *Learning and individual differences.* Columbus: Merrill, 1966. (b)

Fleishman, E. A., & Rich, S. Role of kinesthetic and spatial-visual abilities in perceptual-motor learning. *Journal of Experimental Psychology*, 1963, **66**, 6–11.

Flesch, R. Measuring the level of abstraction. *Journal of Applied Psychology*, 1950, **34**, 384–390.

Fodor, J. A. Could meaning be an r_m? *Journal of Verbal Learning and Verbal Behavior*, 1965, **4**, 73–81. (a)

Fodor, J. A. A review of *Language and thought,* by J. B. Carroll. *The Modern Language Journal*, 1965, **49** (6), 384–386. (b)

Fodor, J. A., & Bever, T. G. The psychological reality of linguistic segments. *Journal of Verbal Learning and Verbal Behavior*, 1965, **4**, 414–420.

Forgays, D. G. The development of a differential word recognition. *Journal of Experimental Psychology*, 1953, **45**, 165–168.

Forrester, W. E., & Spear, N. E. Coding processes in verbal learning as a function of response pronounciability. *Journal of Experimental Psychology*, 1967, **74**, 586–588.

Forster, K. I. Left-to-right processes in the construction of sentences. *Journal of Verbal Learning and Verbal Behavior*, 1966, **5**, 285–291.

Fozard, J. L. Apparent recency of unrelated pictures and nouns presented in the same sequence. *Journal of Experimental Psychology*, 1970, **86**, 137–143.

Fozard, J. L., & Lapine, R. Comparison of discrimination of recency of pictures and names of common objects. Paper presented at Eastern Psychological Association meetings, Washington, D. C., 1968.

Fracker, G. C. On the transference of training in memory. *Psychological Monographs*, 1908, **9** (38), 56–102.

Fraisse, P. Recognition time measured by verbal reaction to figures and words. *Perceptual and Motor Skills*, 1960, **11**, 204.

Fraisse, P. Le temps de réaction verbale. *Année Psychologique*, 1964, **64**, 21–46.

Fraisse, P. Motor and verbal reaction times to words and drawings. *Psychonomic Science*, 1968, **12**, 235–236.

Fraser, C., Bellugi, U., & Brown, R. Control of grammar in imitation, comprehension, and production. *Journal of Verbal Learning and Verbal Behavior*, 1963, **2**, 121–135.

Frederiksen, J. R. Cognitive factors in the recognition of ambiguous auditory and visual stimuli. *Journal of Personality and Social Psychology*, 1967, **7**, Monograph No. 639.

French, J., Ekstrom, R., & Price, L. Kit of reference tests for cognitive factors. Princeton, N.J.: Educational Testing Service, 1963.

Frincke, G. Word characteristics, associative-relatedness, and the free-recall of nouns. *Journal of Verbal Learning and Verbal Behavior*, 1968, **7**, 366–372.

Furst, B. *Stop forgetting*. New York: Garden City, 1948.

Furst, B. *The practical way to a better memory*. New York: Fawcett World Library, 1957.

Furth, H. G. *Thinking without language*. New York: Free Press, 1966.

Gagné, R. M. (Ed.). *Learning and individual differences*. Columbus, Ohio: Merrill, 1967.

Galton, F. *Inquiries into human faculty and its development*. (1st ed.) London: MacMillan, 1883. (2nd ed.) London: J. M. Dent & Sons, 1907.

Garrett, M., & Fodor, J. A. Psychological theories and linguistic constructs. In T. R. Dixon and D. L. Horton (Eds.), *Verbal behavior and general behavior theory*. Englewood Cliffs, New Jersey: Prentice-Hall, 1968.

Gavurin, E. I. The relationship between spatial aptitude and verbal problem solving. Paper read at the annual meeting of the American Psychological Association, New York, 1966.

Gibson, E. J. A systematic application of the concepts of generalization and differentiation to verbal learning. *Psychological Review*, 1940, **47**, 196–229.

Gibson, E. J. *Principles of perceptual learning and development*. New York: Appleton-Century-Crofts, 1969.

Gibson, E. J., Bishop, C. H., Schiff, W., & Smith, J. Comparison of meaningfulness and pronunciability as grouping principles in the perception and retention of verbal material. *Journal of Experimental Psychology*, 1964, **67**, 173–182.

Gibson, J. J. Observations on active touch. *Psychological Review*, 1962, **69**, 477–491.

Gibson, J. J. *The senses considered as perceptual systems*. Boston: Houghton Mifflin, 1966.

Glanzer, M. Grammatical category: A rote learning and word association analysis. *Journal of Verbal Learning and Verbal Behavior*, 1962, **1**, 31–41.

Glanzer, M., & Clark, W. H. Accuracy of perceptual recall: An analysis of organization. *Journal of Verbal Learning and Verbal Behavior,* 1963, **1,** 289–299. (a)

Glanzer, M., & Clark, W. H. The verbal loop hypothesis: Binary numbers. *Journal of Verbal Learning and Verbal Behavior,* 1963, **2,** 301–309. (b)

Glanzer, M., & Clark, W. H. The verbal-loop hypothesis: Conventional figures. *American Journal of Psychology,* 1964, **77,** 621–626.

Glanzer, M., & Cunitz, A. R. Two storage mechanisms in free recall. *Journal of Verbal Learning and Verbal Behavior,* 1966, **5,** 351–360.

Glanzer, M., & Fleishman, J. The effect of encoding training on perceptual recall. *Perception and Psychophysics,* 1967, **2,** 561–564.

Glaze, J. A. The association value of nonsense syllables. *Journal of Genetic Psychology,* 1928, **35,** 255–267.

Glucksberg, S., & Danks, J. H. Grammatical structure and recall: A function of the space in immediate memory or of recall delay? *Perception and Psychophysics,* 1969, **6,** 113–117.

Goldman-Eisler, F. Speech production and the predictability of words in context. *Quarterly Journal of Experimental Psychology,* 1958, **10,** 96–106.

Goldman-Eisler, F. Hesitation and information in speech. In C. Cherry (Ed.), *Information theory.* London: Butterworths, 1961.

Goldstein, K., & Scheerer, M. Abstract and concrete behavior: An experimental study with special tests. *Psychological Monographs,* 1941, **53,** No. 2.

Golla, F. L., & Antonovitch, S. The respiratory rhythm in its relation to the mechanism of thought. *Brain,* 1929, **52,** 491–510.

Golla, F. L., Hutton, E. L., & Walter, W. G. The objective study of mental imagery. *Journal of Mental Science,* 1943, **89,** 216–223.

Gomulicki, B. R. The development and the present status of the trace theory of memory. *British Journal of Psychology Monograph Supplement,* 1953, No. 29.

Goodglass, H., & Barton, M. Handedness and differential perception of verbal stimuli in left and right visual fields. *Perceptual and Motor Skills,* 1963, **17,** 851–854.

Gorman, A. M. Recognition memory for nouns as a function of abstractness and frequency. *Journal of Experimental Psychology,* 1961, **61,** 23–29.

Goss, A. E. Early behaviorism and verbal mediating responses. *American Psychologist,* 1961, **16,** 285–298.

Goss, A. E., & Nodine, C. F. *Paired-associate learning: The role of meaningfulness, similarity, and familiarization.* New York: Academic Press, 1965.

Goss, A. E., Nodine, C. F., Gregory, B. N., Taub, H. A., & Kennedy, K. E. Stimulus characteristics and percentage of occurrence of response members in paired-associates learning. *Psychological Monographs,* 1962, **76** (12, Whole No. 531).

Gough, P. B. Grammatical transformations and speed of understanding. *Journal of Verbal Learning and Verbal Behavior,* 1965, **4,** 107–111.

Gough, P. B. The verification of sentences: The effects of delay of evidence and sentence length. *Journal of Verbal Learning and Verbal Behavior,* 1966, **5,** 492–496.

Goulet, L. R. Retroaction and the "fate" of the mediator in three stage mediation paradigms. *Journal of Verbal Learning and Verbal Behavior,* 1966, **5,** 172–176.

Goulet, L. R. Verbal learning in children: Implications for developmental research. *Psychological Bulletin,* 1968, **69,** 359–376.

Graham, K. R. Eye movements during visual mental imagery. Paper presented to the Eastern Psychological Association, Atlantic City, April, 1970.

Greeno, J. G. Verbal fluency, free recall and paired-associate learning speed. *Psychological Reports,* 1965, **16,** 659–660.

Greeno, J. G. Associative effects vs. differentiation: Comment on Saltz and Wickey's reply to Birnbaum. *Psychological Reports,* 1968, **22,** 347–350.

Greenwald, A. G. Sensory feedback mechanisms in performance control: With special reference to the ideo-motor mechanism. *Psychological Review,* 1970, **77,** 73–99.

Griffitts, C. W. Individual differences in imagery. *Psychological Monographs,* 1927, No. 172.

Groninger, L. D. Natural language mediation and covert rehearsal in short-term memory. *Psychonomic Science,* 1966, **5,** 135–136.

Groninger, L. D. Mnemonic imagery and forgetting. *Psychonomic Science,* 1971, in press.

Grover, D. E., Horton, D. L., & Cunningham, M. Mediated facilitation and interference in a four-stage paradigm. *Journal of Verbal Learning and Verbal Behavior,* 1967, **6,** 42–46.

Gruber, H. E., Kulkin, A., & Schwartz, P. The effect of exposure time on mnemonic processing in paired associate learning. Paper presented at the Eastern Psychological Association meeting, Atlantic City, 1965.

Guilford, J. P. *An inventory of factors STDCR.* Beverly Hills, California: Sheridan Supply Co., 1940.

Guilford, J. P. *The nature of human intelligence.* New York: McGraw-Hill, 1967.

Guilford, J. P., & Zimmerman, W. S. *The Guilford-Zimmerman aptitude survey.* Beverly Hills, California: Sheridan Psychological Services, 1948.

Gupton, T., & Frincke, G. Imagery, mediational instructions, and noun position in free recall of noun-verb pairs. *Journal of Experimental Psychology,* 1970, **86,** 461–462.

Haber, R. N. A replication of selective attention and coding in visual perception. *Journal of Experimental Psychology,* 1964, **67,** 402–404. (a)

Haber, R. N. Effects of coding strategy on perceptual memory. *Journal of Experimental Psychology,* 1964, **68,** 357–362. (b)

Haber, R. N. The effect of prior knowledge of the stimulus on word recognition processes. *Journal of Experimental Psychology,* 1965, **69,** 282–286.

Haber, R. N. Nature of the effect of set on perception. *Psychological Review,* 1966, **73,** 335–351.

Haber, R. N. Repetition as a determinant of perceptual recognition processes. In W. Watken-Dunn (Ed.), *Symposium on models for the perception of speech and visual form.* Cambridge: M.I.T. Press, 1967, 202–212.

Haber, R. N. Temporal integration of suprathreshold perceptual processes. Paper presented at the American Psychological Association meeting, San Francisco, 1968.

Haber, R. N., & Haber, R. B. Eidetic imagery: I. Frequency. *Perceptual and Motor Skills,* 1964, **19,** 131–138.

Haber, R. N., & Nathanson, L. S. Processing of sequentially presented letters. *Perception and Psychophysics,* 1969, **5,** 359–361.

Haber, R. N., & Standing, L. G. Direct measures of short-term visual storage. *Quarterly Journal of Experimental Psychology,* 1969, **21,** 43–54.

Hake, H. W., & Eriksen, C. W. Role of response variables in recognition and identification of complex visual forms. *Journal of Experimental Psychology,* 1956, **52,** 235–243.

Hall, J. F. Learning as a function of word-frequency. *American Journal of Psychology,* 1954, **67,** 138–140.

Hall, J. F. *The psychology of learning.* New York: J. B. Lippincott, 1966.

Hall, J. F., & Ugelow, A. Free association time as a function of word frequency. *Canadian Journal of Psychology,* 1957, **11,** 29–32.

Handel, S., & Garner, W. R. The structure of visual pattern associates and pattern goodness. *Perception and Psychophysics,* 1966, **1,** 33–88.

Harcum, E. R. Visual hemifield differences as conflicts in direction of reading. *Journal of Experimental Psychology,* 1966, **72,** 479–480.

Harcum, E. R., & Dyer, D. W. Monocular and binocular reproduction of binary stimuli appearing right and left of fixation. *American Journal of Psychology,* 1962, **75,** 56–65.

Harcum, E. R., & Finkel, M. E. Explanation of Mishkin and Forgay's results as a directional-reading conflict. *Canadian Journal of Psychology,* 1963, **17,** 224–234.

Harcum, E. R., & Friedman, S. M. Reversal reading by Israeli observers of visual patterns without intrinsic directionality. *Canadian Journal of Psychology,* 1963, **17,** 361–369.

Hare, R. D. Cognitive factors in transfer of meaning. *Psychological Reports,* 1964, **15,** 199–206.

Harrigan, J. E., & Modrick, J. A. S-R and R-S acquisition as a function of meaningfulness. *Psychonomic Science,* 1967, **9,** 199–200.

Harris, C. S., & Haber, R. N. Selective attention and coding in visual perception. *Journal of Experimental Psychology,* 1963, **65,** 328–333.

Hart, J. T. Luminous figures: Influence of point of fixation on their disappearances. *Science,* 1964, **143,** 1193–1194.

Havelka, J. *The nature of the creative process in art.* The Hague, Netherlands: Martinus Nijhoff, 1968.

Hayakawa, S. I. *Language in thought and action.* New York: Harcourt, Brace, 1949.

Hebb, D. O. *The organization of behavior.* New York: Wiley, 1949.

Hebb, D. O. The semiautonomous process: Its nature and nurture. *American Psychologist,* 1963, **18,** 16–27.

Hebb, D. O. *A textbook of psychology.* Philadelphia: Saunders, 1966.

Hebb, D. O. Concerning imagery. *Psychological Review,* 1968, **75,** 466–477.

Hebb, D. O., Lambert, W. E., & Tucker, G. R. Language, thought and experience. Unpublished manuscript, McGill University, 1970.

Hebb, D. O., & Thompson, W. R. The social significance of animal studies. In G. Lindzey (Ed.), *Handbook of social psychology.* Cambridge, Mass.: Addison-Wesley, 1954, **1,** 532–561.

Hefferline, R. F., & Perera, T. B. Proprioceptive discrimination of a covert operant without its observation by the subject. *Science,* 1963, **139,** 834–835.

Heidbreder, E. The attainment of concepts: I. Terminology and methodology. *Journal of General Psychology,* 1946, **35,** 173–189.

Herman, T., Broussard, I. G., & Todd, H. R. Intertrial interval and the rate of learning serial order picture stimuli. *Journal of General Psychology,* 1951, **45,** 245–254.

Heron, W. Perception as a function of retinal locus and attention. *American Journal of Psychology*, 1957, **70**, 38–48.

Herring, B. S., & Bryden, M. P. Memory colour effects as a function of viewing time. *Canadian Journal of Psychology*, 1970, **24**, 127–132.

Hershenson, M. Stimulus structure, cognitive structure, and the perception of letter arrays. *Journal of Experimental Psychology*, 1969, **79**, 327–335.

Hershenson, M., & Haber, R. N. The role of meaning in the perception of briefly presented words. *Canadian Journal of Psychology*, 1965, **19**, 42–46.

Hintzman, D. L. Classification and aural coding in short-term memory. *Psychonomic Science*, 1965, **3**, 161–162.

Hochberg, J. E. *Perception*. Englewood Cliffs, New Jersey: Prentice-Hall, 1964.

Hochberg, J. E. In the mind's eye. In R. N. Haber (Ed.), *Contemporary theory and research in visual perception*. New York: Holt, Rinehart, and Winston, 1968.

Hochberg, J., & Galper, R. E. Recognition of faces: I. An exploratory study. *Psychonomic Science*, 1967, **9**, 619–620.

Hockett, C. D. The origin of speech. *Scientific American*, 1960, **203** (3), 88–96.

Holt, R. R. Imagery: The return of the ostracized. *American Psychologist*, 1964, **19**, 254–264.

Horowitz, L. M., Brown, Z. M., & Weissbluth, S. Availability and the direction of associations. *Journal of Experimental Psychology*, 1964, **68**, 541–549.

Horowitz, L. M., Lampel, A. K., & Takanishi, R. N. The child's memory for unitized scenes. *Journal of Experimental Child Psychology*, 1969, **8**, 375–388.

Horowitz, L. M., Norman, S. A., & Day, R. S. Availability and associative symmetry. *Psychological Review*, 1966, **73**, 1–15.

Horowitz, L. M., & Prytulak, L. S. Redintegrative memory. *Psychological Review*, 1969, **76**, 519–531.

Horowitz, M. J. Visual imagery and cognitive organization. *American Journal of Psychiatry*, 1967, **123**, 938–946.

Horton, D. L. The effects of meaningfulness, awareness, and type of design in verbal mediation. *Journal of Verbal Learning and Verbal Behavior*, 1964, **3**, 187–194.

Horton, D. L., & Kjeldergaard, P. M. An experimental analysis of associative factors in mediated generalizations. *Psychological Monographs*, 1961, **75** (11, Whole No. 515).

Horton, D. L., Grover, D. E., & Wiley, R. E. Mediation, recall and instructional effects. *Journal of Verbal Learning and Verbal Behavior*, 1968, **7**, 539–542.

Houston, J. P. Ease of verbal S-R learning as a function of the number of mediating associations. *Journal of Verbal Learning and Verbal Behavior*, 1964, **3**, 326–329.

Howe, M. J. A. Digram-frequency and immediate memory. *British Journal of Psychology*, 1967, **58**, 57–62.

Huey, E. B. *The psychology and pedagogy of reading*. New York: MacMillan, 1908. (Reprinted, Cambridge, Mass. by M.I.T. Press, 1968).

Hulicka, I. M., & Grossman, J. L. Age-group comparisons for the use of mediators in paired-associate learning. *Journal of Gerontology*, 1967, **21**, 46–51.

Hull, C. L. Goal attraction and directing ideas conceived as habit phenomena. *Psychological Review*, 1931, **38**, 487–506.

Hull, C. L. The meaningfulness of 320 selected nonsense syllables. *American Journal of Psychology*, 1933, **45**, 730–734.

Hull, C. L. The problem of stimulus equivalence in behavior theory. *Psychological Review*, 1939, **46**, 9–30.

Hull, C. L. *Principles of behavior*. New York: Appleton-Century-Crofts, 1943.

Hulme, T. E. *Further speculations* (S. Hynes, Ed.). Minneapolis: University of Minnesota Press, 1955.

Humphrey, G. *Thinking*. London: Methuen, 1951.

Hunter, I. M. L. *Memory*. Harmondsworth: Penguin, 1964.

Hunter, W. S. The delayed reaction in animals and children. *Behavior Science Monographs*, 1913, **2**, No. 6.

Huttenlocher, J. Constructing spatial images: A strategy in reasoning. *Psychological Review*, 1968, **75**, 550–560.

Huttenlocher, J., Eisenberg, K., & Strauss, S. Comprehension: Relation between perceived actor and logical subject. *Journal of Verbal Learning and Verbal Behavior*, 1968, **7**, 527–530.

Huttenlocher, J., Higgins, E. T., Milligan, C., & Kaufman, B. The mystery of the "negative equative" construction. *Journal of Verbal Learning and Verbal Behavior*, 1970, **9**, 334–341.

Hyman, J. A. Performance of high and low imagers on two complex tactual discrimination tasks following imagery and verbal pretraining. Unpublished doctoral thesis, University of Western Ontario, 1966.

Imae, K. Wordness and abstractness of the so-called nonsense verbal materials. *Japanese Journal of Psychology*, 1968, **39**, 200–211.

Imai, S., & Garner, W. R. Structure in perceptual classification. *Psychonomic Monograph Supplements*, 1968, **2**, 153–172.

Irion, A. L. Rote learning. In S. Koch (Ed.), *Psychology: A study of a science*. New York: McGraw-Hill, 1959.

Iscoe, I., & Semler, I. J. Paired-associate learning in normal and mentally retarded children as a function of four experimental conditions. *Journal of Comparative and Physiological Psychology*, 1964, **57**, 387–392.

Jaensch, E. R. *Eidetic imagery and typological methods of investigation*. New York: Harcourt Brace, 1930.

Jakobovits, L. A. Mediation theory and the single-stage S-R model: Different? *Psychological Review*, 1966, **73**, 376–381.

Jakobovits, L. A., & Lambert, W. E. Stimulus-characteristics as determinants of semantic changes with repeated presentation. *American Journal of Psychology*, 1964, **77**, 84–92.

Jakobson, R., & Halle, M. *Fundamentals of language*. Pt. 2, Two aspects of language and two types of aphasic disorders. 's Gravenhage: Mouton, 1956.

James, C. T., & Hakes, D. T. Mediated transfer in a four-stage stimulus equivalence paradigm. *Journal of Verbal Learning and Verbal Behavior*, 1965, **4**, 89–93.

James, W. *Principles of psychology*. New York: Holt, 1890. (Reprinted by Dover, 1950.)

Jampolsky, M. Étude de quelques épreuves de reconnaissance. *Année Psychologique*, 1950, **49**, 63–97.

Jenkin, A. M. Imagery and learning. *British Journal of Psychology*, 1935, **26**, 149–164.

Jenkins, J. J. Mediated associations: Paradigms and situations. In C. N. Cofer and B. S. Musgrave (Eds.), *Verbal behavior and learning*. New York: McGraw-Hill, 1963.

Jenkins, J. J. Mediation theory and grammatical behavior. In S. Rosenberg (Ed.), *Directions in psycholinguistics*. New York: MacMillan, 1965.

Jenkins, J. J. Individual differences in verbal learning. In R. M. Gagné (Ed.), *Learning and individual differences*. Columbus, Ohio: Merrill, 1967.

Jenkins, J. J., & Foss, D. J. An experimental analysis of pseudomediation. *Psychonomic Science*, 1965, **2**, 99–100.

Jenkins, J. J., & Palermo, D. S. Mediation processes and the acquisition of linguistic structure. In U. Bellugi and R. W. Brown (Eds.), *The acquisition of language. Monographs of the Society for Research in Child Development*, 1964, **29** (1), 141–169.

Jenkins, J. J., & Russell, W. A. Associative clustering during recall. *Journal of Abnormal and Social Psychology*, 1952, **47**, 818–821.

Jenkins, J. J., Russell, W. A., & Suci, G. J. An atlas of semantic profiles for 360 words. *American Journal of Psychology*, 1958, **71**, 688–699.

Jenkins, J. R., Neale, D. C., & Deno, S. L. Differential memory for picture and word stimuli. *Journal of Educational Psychology*, 1967, **58**, 303–307.

Jensen, A. R. Transfer between paired-associate and serial learning. *Journal of Verbal Learning and Verbal Behavior*, 1962, **1**, 269–280.

Jensen, A. R. Rote learning in retarded adults and normal children. *American Journal of Mental Deficiency*, 1965, **69**, 828–834.

Jensen, A. R., & Rohwer, W. D. Verbal mediation in paired-associate and serial learning. *Journal of Verbal Learning and Verbal Behavior*, 1963, **1**, 346–352.

Jensen, A. R., & Rohwer, W. D. Syntactical mediation of serial and paired-associate learning as a function of age. *Child Development*, 1965, **36**, 601–608. (a)

Jensen, A. R., & Rohwer, W. D. What is learned in serial learning? *Journal of Verbal Behavior*, 1965, **4**, 62–72. (b)

Jensen, G. D. Effect of past experience upon induced movement. *Perceptual and Motor Skills*, 1960, **11**, 281–288.

John, E. R. *Mechanisms of memory*. New York: Academic Press, 1967.

Johnson, N. F. The psychological reality of phrase-structure rules. *Journal of Verbal Learning and Verbal Behavior*, 1965, **4**, 469–475.

Johnson, N. F. On the relationship between sentence structure and the latency in generating the sentence. *Journal of Verbal Learning and Verbal Behavior*, 1966, **5**, 375–380.

Johnson, N. F. Sequential verbal behavior. In T. R. Dixon and D. L. Horton (Eds.), *Verbal behavior and general behavior theory*. Englewood Cliffs, New Jersey: Prentice-Hall, 1968.

Johnson, R. C. Latency and association value as predictors of rate of verbal learning. *Journal of Verbal Learning and Verbal Behavior*, 1964, **3**, 77–78.

Johnson, R. C., Frincke, G., & Martin, L. Meaningfulness, frequency, and affective character of words as related to visual duration thresholds. *Canadian Journal of Psychology*, 1961, **15**, 199–204.

Johnson, R. C., Thomson, C. W., & Frincke, G. Word values, word frequency, and visual duration thresholds. *Psychological Review*, 1960, **67**, 332–342.

Jones, D., & Spreen, O. Dichotic listening by retarded children: The effects of ear order and abstractness. *Child Development*, 1967, **38** (1), 101–105.

Kahneman D. Method, findings and theory in studies of visual masking. *Psychological Bulletin*, 1968, **70**, (6, Pt. 1), 404–425.

Kamman, R. Associability: A study of the properties of associative ratings and the role of association in word-word learning. *Journal of Experimental Psychology Monograph*, 1968, **78**, (4, Pt. 2).

Kanungo, R. Paired-associate learning of function words. *Psychonomic Science*, 1968, **10**, 47–48.

Kaplan, S., Kaplan, R., & Sampson, J. R. Encoding and arousal factors in free recall of verbal and visual material. *Psychonomic Science*, 1968, **12**, 73–74.

Karwoski, T. R., Gramlich, F. W., & Arnott, P. Psychological studies in semantics. I. Free association reactions to words, drawings and objects. *Journal of Social Psychology*, 1944, **20**, 233–247.

Kasschau, R. A., & Pollio, H. R. Response transfer mediated by meaningfully similar and associated stimuli using a separate-lists design. *Journal of Experimental Psychology*, 1967, **74**, 146–148.

Katz, J. J., & Fodor, J. A. The structure of a semantic theory. *Language*, 1963, **39**, 170–210.

Katz, J. J., & Postal, P. M. *An integrated theory of linguistic description*. Cambridge, Mass.: The M.I.T. Press, 1964.

Kausler, D. H. (Ed.) *Readings in verbal learning*. New York: Wiley, 1966.

Kausler, D. H., & Deichmann, J. W. Mediation vs. pseudomediation in kindergarten children. *Psychonomic Science*, 1968, **13**, 119–120.

Kendler, H. H., & Kendler, T. S. Vertical and horizontal processes in problem solving. *Psychological Review*, 1962, **69**, 1–16.

Keppel, G., & Underwood, B. J. Proactive inhibition in short-term retention of single items. *Journal of Verbal Learning and Verbal Behavior*, 1962, **1**, 153–161.

Keppel, G., & Zavortink, B. Further test of the use of images as mediators. *Journal of Experimental Psychology*, 1969, **82**, 190–192.

Kiess, H. O. Effects of natural language mediators on short-term memory. *Journal of Experimental Psychology*, 1968, **77**, 7–13.

Kiess, H. O., & Montague, W. E. Natural language mediators in paired-associate learning. *Psychonomic Science*, 1965, **3**, 549–550.

Kimble, G. A. *Hilgard and Marquis' "conditioning and learning."* New York: Appleton, 1961.

Kimura, D. Cerebral dominance and the perception of verbal stimuli. *Canadian Journal of Psychology*, 1961, **15**, 166–171.

Kimura, D. Right temporal-lobe damage: Perception of unfamiliar stimuli after damage. *Archives of Neurology*, 1963, **8**, 264–271.

Kimura, D. Left-right differences in the perception of melodies. *Quarterly Journal of Experimental Psychology*, 1964, **14**, 355–358.

Kimura, D. Dual functional asymmetry of the brain in visual perception. *Neuropsychologia*, 1966, **4**, 275–285.

Kimura, D. Functional asymmetry of the brain in dichotic listening. *Cortex*, 1967, **3**, 163–178.

Kimura, D. Asymmetries in perception related to hemispheric differentiation of function. In M. Kinsbourne (Ed.), *Hemispheric asymmetry of function*. London: Tavistock, in press.

Kimura, D., & Folb, S. Neural processing of backwards-speech sounds. *Science*, 1968, **161**, 395–396.

Kirkpatrick, E. A. An experimental study of memory. *Psychological Review*, 1894, **1**, 602–609.

Kjeldergaard, P. M. Transfer and mediation in verbal learning. In T. R. Dixon and D. L. Horton (Eds.), *Verbal behavior and general behavior theory.* Englewood Cliffs, N. J.: Prentice-Hall, 1968.

Klapp, S. T. Individual differences in nonverbal memory for visually presented material. Unpublished doctoral dissertation, University of California, Berkeley, 1969.

Klima, E. S., & Bellugi-Klima, U. Syntactic regularities in the speech of children. In D. A. Reibel and S. A. Schane (Eds.), *Modern studies in English: Readings in transformational grammar.* Englewood Cliffs: Prentice-Hall, 1969.

Klüver, H. Studies on the eidetic type and eidetic imagery. *Psychological Bulletin,* 1928, **25,** 69–104.

Klüver, H. The eidetic child. In C. Murchison (Ed.), *A handbook of child psychology.* Worcester, Mass.: Clark University Press, 1931.

Klüver, H. Eidetic phenomena. *Psychological Bulletin,* 1932, **29,** 181–203.

Koen, F. An intra-verbal explication of the nature of metaphor. *Journal of Verbal Learning and Verbal Behavior,* 1965, **4,** 129–133.

Koen, F. Codability of complex stimuli: Three modes of representation. *Journal of Personality and Social Psychology,* 1966, **3,** 435–441.

Koeppel, J. C., & Beecroft, R. S. The conceptual similarity effect in free recall. *Psychonomic Science,* 1967, **9,** 213–214.

Kohler, I. (Translated by H. Fiss.) The formation and transformation of the perceptual world. *Psychological Issues,* 1964, **3** (12, Whole No. 4).

Köhler, W. *Gestalt psychology,* New York: Liveright, 1929.

Kolers, P. A. Some formal characteristics of pictograms. *American Scientist,* 1969, **57,** 348–363.

Kristofferson, A. B. Word recognition, meaningfulness, and familiarity. *Perceptual and Motor Skills,* 1957, **7,** 219–220.

Krueger, W. C. F. The relative difficulty of nonsense syllables. *Journal of Experimental Psychology,* 1934, **17,** 145–153.

Kuhlman, C. K. Visual imagery in children. Unpublished doctoral thesis, Radcliffe College, 1960.

Kuhlmann, F. On the analysis of the memory consciousness for pictures of familiar objects. *American Journal of Psychology,* 1907, **18,** 389–420.

Kurtz, K. H., & Hovland, C. I. The effect of verbalization during observation of stimulus objects upon accuracy of recognition and recall. *Journal of Experimental Psychology,* 1953, **45,** 157–164.

Kusyszyn, I., & Paivio, A. Transition probability, word order, and noun abstractness in the learning of adjective-noun paired associates. *Journal of Experimental Psychology,* 1966, **71,** 800–805.

Lachman, R., & Dooling, D. J. Connected discourse and random strings: Effects of number of inputs on recognition and recall. *Journal of Experimental Psychology,* 1968, **77,** 517–522.

Laffal, J. Response faults in word association as a function of response entropy. *Journal of Abnormal and Social Psychology,* 1955, **50,** 265–270.

Laffal, J. *Pathological and normal language.* New York: Atherton Press, 1965.

Lambert, W. E. Associational fluency as a function of stimulus abstractness. *Canadian Journal of Psychology,* 1955, **9,** 103–106.

Lambert, W. E., & Paivio, A. The influence of noun-adjective order on learning. *Canadian Journal of Psychology,* 1956, **10,** 9–12.

Landauer, T. K. Rate of implicit speech. *Perceptual and Motor Skills*, 1962, **15**, 646.

Langer, S. K. *Philosophy in a new key*. Cambridge, Mass.: Harvard University Press, 1942. (Reprinted by Mentor Books, New York, 1948)

Lantz, D., & Stefflre, V. Language and cognition revisited. *Journal of Abnormal and Social Psychology*, 1964, **69**, 472–481.

Lashley, K. S. The problem of serial order in behavior. In L. A. Jeffress (Ed.), *Cerebral mechanisms in behavior: The Hixon symposium*. New York: Wiley, 1951.

Lawrence, D. H., & LaBerge, D. L. Relationship between recognition accuracy and order of reporting stimulus dimensions. *Journal of Experimental Psychology*, 1956, **51**, 12–18.

Lay, C. H., & Paivio, A. The effects of task difficulty and anxiety on hesitations in speech. *Canadian Journal of Behavioral Science*, 1969, **1**, 25–37.

Leask, J., Haber, R. N., & Haber, R. B. Eidetic imagery in children: II. Longitudinal and experimental results. *Psychonomic Monograph Supplements*, 1969, **3** (3, Whole No. 35), 25–48.

Lee, S. S., & Jensen, A. R. The effect of awareness on three-stage mediated association. *Journal of Verbal Learning and Verbal Behavior*, 1968, **7**, 1005–1009.

Leeper, R. A study of a neglected portion of the field of learning—the development of sensory organization. *Journal of Genetic Psychology*, 1935, **46**, 41–75.

Lenneberg, E. H. Color naming, color recognition, color discrimination: A reappraisal. *Perceptual and Motor Skills*, 1961, **12**, 375–382.

Lenneberg, E. H. *Biological foundations of language*. New York: Wiley, 1967.

Leuba, C. Images as conditioned sensations. *Journal of Experimental Psychology*, 1940, **26**, 345–351.

Leuba, C., & Dunlap, R. Conditioning imagery. *Journal of Experimental Psychology*, 1951, **41**, 352–355.

Levin, J. R. Factors related to the sentence facilitation of paired-associate learning: Some characteristics of verbs. *Journal of Educational Psychology*, in press.

Liberman, A. M., Cooper, F. S., Shankweiler, D. P., & Studdert-Kennedy, M. Perception of the speech code. *Psychological Review*, 1967, **74**, 431–461.

Lieberman, L. R., & Culpepper, J. T. Words versus objects: Comparison of free verbal recall. *Psychological Reports*, 1965, **17**, 983–988.

Lindley, R. H. Effects of controlled coding cues in short-term memory. *Journal of Experimental Psychology*, 1963, **66**, 580–587.

Lindley, R. H., & Nedler, S. E. Supplementary report: Further effects of subject-generated recoding cues on short-term memory. *Journal of Experimental Psychology*, 1965, **69**, 324–325.

Lobb, H. Vision *versus* touch in form discrimination. *Canadian Journal of Psychology*, 1965, **19**, 175–187.

Lobb, H. Cross-modal transfer of training in form discrimination. Address to the Annual Meeting, Canadian Psychological Association, 1968.

Lobb, H. Asymmetrical transfer of form discrimination across sensory modalities in human adults. *Journal of Experimental Psychology*, 1970, **86**, 350–354.

Lockhart, R. S. Retrieval asymmetry in the recall of adjectives and nouns. *Journal of Experimental Psychology*, 1969, **79**, 12–17.

Loess, H. Short-term memory, word class, and sequence of items. *Journal of Experimental Psychology*, 1967, **74**, 556–561.

Long, E. R., Reid, L. S., & Henneman, R. H. An experimental analysis of set: Variables influencing the identification of ambiguous, visual stimulus-objects. *The American Journal of Psychology*, 1960, **73**, 553–562.

Lumsdaine, A. A. Effectiveness of pictures versus printed words in learning simple verbal associations. Unpublished doctoral dissertation, Stanford University, 1949.

Luria, A. R. (Translated by L. Solotaroff.) *The mind of a mnemonist*. New York: Basic Books, 1968.

MacCorquodale, K. On Chomsky's review of Skinner's *Verbal behavior*. *Journal of the Experimental Analysis of Behavior*, 1970, **13**, 83–99.

MacCorquodale, K., & Meehl, P. E. Edward C. Tolman. In *Modern learning theory*. New York: Appleton-Century-Crofts, 1954.

MacDonald, V. N. Effects of word concreteness, mediation set, and retention interval on reported mediators and recall of noun paired associates. Unpublished master's thesis, University of Western Ontario, 1967.

Mackworth, J. F. Auditory short-term memory. *Canadian Journal of Psychology*, 1964, **18**, 292–303.

Maclay, H., & Osgood, C. E. Hesitation phenomena in spontaneous English speech. *Word*, 1959, **15**, 19–44.

Maltzman, I. On the training of originality. *Psychological Review*, 1960, **67**, 229–242.

Mandler, G. Associative frequency and associative prepotency as measures of response to nonsense syllables. *American Journal of Psychology*, 1956, **68**, 662–665.

Mandler, G. Organization and memory. In K. W. Spence and J. T. Spence (Eds.), *The psychology of learning and motivation: Advances in research and theory*. New York: Academic Press, 1967.

Mandler, G. Association and organization: Facts, fancies, and theories. In T. R. Dixon and D. L. Horton (Eds.), *Verbal behavior and general behavior theory*. Englewood Cliffs, New Jersey: Prentice-Hall, 1968.

Mandler, G., & Campbell, E. H. Effect of variation in associative frequency of stimulus and response members on paired-associate learning. *Journal of Experimental Psychology*, 1957, **54**, 269–273.

Mandler, G., & Earhard, B. Pseudomediation: Is chaining an artifact? *Psychonomic Science*, 1964, **1**, 247–248.

Mandler, G., & Huttenlocher, J. The relationship between associative frequency, associative ability, and paired-associate learning. *American Journal of Psychology*, 1956, **69**, 424–428.

Mandler, J., & Mandler, G. *Thinking: From association to gestalt*. New York: Wiley, 1964.

Margrain, S. A. Short-term memory as a function of input modality. *Quarterly Journal of Experimental Psychology*, 1967, **19**, 109–114.

Marks, L. E., & Miller, G. A. The role of semantic and syntactic constraints in the memorization of English sentences. *Journal of Verbal Learning and Verbal Behavior*, 1964, **3**, 1–5.

Marshall, G. R. The effect of concrete noun and picture mediation on the paired associate learning of abstract nouns. Paper presented at the meeting of the Eastern Psychological Association, Atlantic City, 1965.

Marshall, G. R., & Cofer, C. N. Associative indices as measures of word relatedness: A summary and comparison of ten methods. *Journal of Verbal Learning and Verbal Behavior*, 1963, **1**, 408–421.

Marshall, J. F., Rouse, R. O., Jr., & Tarpy, R. M. Acoustic versus associative models of short-term memory coding. *Psychonomic Science,* 1969, **14,** 54–55.

Martin, C. J., Boersma, F. J., & Cox, D. L. A classification of associative strategies in paired-associate learning. *Psychonomic Science,* 1965, **3,** 455–456.

Martin, C. J., Cox, D. L., & Boersma, F. J. The role of associative strategies in the acquisition of P-A material: An alternate approach to meaningfulness. *Psychonomic Science,* 1965, **3,** 463–464.

Martin, E. Stimulus meaningfulness and paired-associate transfer. *Psychological Review,* 1968, **75,** 421–441.

Martin, E., & Roberts, K. H. Grammatical factors in sentence retention. *Journal of Verbal Learning and Verbal Behavior,* 1966, **5,** 211–218.

Martin, E., & Roberts, K. H. Sentence length and sentence retention in the free learning situation. *Psychonomic Science,* 1967, **8,** 535–536.

Martin, R. B., & Dean, S. J. Implicit and explicit mediation in paired-associate learning. *Journal of Experimental Psychology,* 1964, **68,** 21–27.

Martin, R. B., & Dean, S. J. Reported mediation in paired-associate learning. *Journal of Verbal Learning and Verbal Behavior,* 1966, **5,** 23–27.

Matthews, W. A. The relation between association norms and word frequency. *British Journal of Psychology,* 1965, **56,** 391–399.

Matthews, W. A. Continued word associations and free recall. *Quarterly Journal of Experimental Psychology,* 1966, **18,** 31–38.

Matthews, W. A. A frequency analysis of controlled, continuous word association. *British Journal of Psychology,* 1967, **58,** 227–236.

Matthews, W. A. Transformational complexity and short-term recall. *Language and Speech,* 1968, **11,** 120–128.

McCawley, J. D. The role of semantics in a grammar. In E. Bach and R. T. Harms (Eds.), *Universals in linguistic theory.* New York: Holt, Rinehart and Winston, 1968.

McCullers, J. C. Associative strength and degree of interference in children's verbal paired-associate learning. *Journal of Experimental Child Psychology,* 1967, **5,** 58–68.

McGeoch, J. A., & Irion, A. L. *The psychology of human learning.* New York: Longmans, 1952.

McGeoch, J. A., & Whitely, P. L. The recall of observed material. *Journal of Educational Psychology,* 1926, **17,** 419–425.

McGuigan, F. J. (Ed.). *Thinking: Studies of covert language processes.* New York: Appleton-Century-Crofts, 1966.

McGuire, W. J. A multiprocess model for paired-associate learning. *Journal of Experimental Psychology,* 1961, **62,** 335–347.

McKellar, P. *Imagination and thinking.* New York: Basic Books, 1957.

McKinney, J. P. Disappearance of luminous designs. *Science,* 1963, **140,** 403–404.

McKinney, J. P. Lateral asymmetry in the stability of the visual field. *Psychonomic Science,* 1966, **5,** 175–176. (a)

McKinney, J. P. Verbal meaning and perceptual stability. *Canadian Journal of Psychology,* 1966, **20,** 237–242. (b)

McKinney, J. P. Handedness, eyedness, and perceptual stability of the left and right visual fields. *Neuropsychologia,* 1967, **5,** 339–344.

McMahon, L. Grammatical analysis as part of understanding a sentence. Unpublished doctoral dissertation, Harvard University, 1963.

McNeill, D. On theories of language acquisition. In T. R. Dixon and D. L. Horton

(Eds.), *Verbal behavior and general behavior theory.* Englewood Cliffs, New Jersey: Prentice-Hall, 1968.

McNulty, J. A. The effects of "instructions to mediate" upon paired-associate learning. *Psychonomic Science,* 1966, **4,** 61–62. (a)

McNulty, J. A. The measurement of "adopted chunks" in free recall learning. *Psychonomic Science,* 1966, **4,** 71–72. (b)

Mednick, S. A. The associative basis of the creative process. *Psychological Review,* 1962, **69,** 220–232.

Mehler, J. Some effects of grammatical transformations on the recall of English sentences. *Journal of Verbal Learning and Verbal Behavior,* 1963, **2,** 346–351.

Mehler, J., & Carey, P. Role of surface and base structure in the perception of sentences. *Journal of Verbal Learning and Verbal Behavior,* 1967, **6,** 335–338.

Melton, A. W. Implications of short-term memory for a general theory of memory. *Journal of Verbal Learning and Verbal Behavior,* 1963, **2,** 1–21.

Merikle, P. M., Lowe, D. G., & Coltheart, M. Evidence against left to right processing of input to short-term memory. Paper presented at the meeting of the Canadian Psychological Association, Winnipeg, April, 1970.

Merryman, S. S., & Merryman, C. T. Differential recall of stimuli and responses following paired-associate learning. *Journal of Experimental Psychology,* 1968, **77,** 345–346.

Mewhort, D. J. K. Sequential redundancy and letter spacing as determinants of tachistoscopic recognition. *Canadian Journal of Psychology,* 1966, **20,** 435–444.

Mewhort, D. J. K., Merikle, P. M., & Bryden, M. P. On the transfer from iconic to short-term memory. *Journal of Experimental Psychology,* 1969, **81,** 89–94.

Michon, J. A. On the internal representation of associative data networks. *Nederlands Tijdschrift voor de Psychologie,* 1968, **23,** 428–457.

Middleton, A. E. *All about mnemonics.* London: Pitman, 1887.

Milgram, N. A. Verbal context versus visual compound in paired-associate learning by children. *Journal of Experimental Child Psychology,* 1967, **5,** 597–603.

Miller, G. A. The magical number seven, plus or minus two. *Psychological Review,* 1956, **63,** 81–97.

Miller, G. A. Some psychological studies of grammar. *American Psychologist,* 1962, **17,** 748–762.

Miller, G. A., Galanter, E., & Pribram, K. H. *Plans and the structure of behavior.* New York; Holt, 1960.

Miller, G. A., & Isard, S. Some perceptual consequences of linguistic rules. *Journal of Verbal Learning and Verbal Behavior,* 1963, **2,** 217–228.

Miller, G. A., & McNeill, D. Psycholinguistics. In G. Lindzey and E. Aranson (Eds.), *The handbook of social psychology,* Vol. III. Reading, Mass.: Addison-Wesley, 1969.

Miller, G. A., & Selfridge, J. A. Verbal context and the recall of meaningful material. *American Journal of Psychology,* 1950, **63,** 176–187.

Miller, N. E. Liberalization of basic S-R concepts: Extension to conflict behavior, motivation, and social learning. In S. Koch (Ed.), Psychology: *A study of a science.* Vol. 2. New York: McGraw-Hill, 1959.

Miller, N. E., and Dollard, J. *Social learning and imitation.* New Haven: Yale University Press, 1941.

Milner, B., & Teuber, H. L. Alteration of perception and memory in man: Reflections on methods. In L. Weiskrantz (Ed.), *Analysis of behavioral change.* New York: Harper & Row, 1968.

Mishkin, M., & Forgays, D. G. Word recognition as a function of retinal locus. *Journal of Experimental Psychology,* 1952, **43,** 43–48.

Montague, W. E., Adams, J. A., & Kiess, H. O. Forgetting and natural language mediation. *Journal of Experimental Psychology,* 1966, **72,** 829–833.

Montague, W. E., & Kiess, H. O. The associability of CVC pairs. *Journal of Experimental Psychology Monograph,* 1968, **78** (2, Pt. 2).

Montague, W. E., & Wearing, A. J. The complexity of natural language mediators and its relation to paired-associate learning. *Psychonomic Science,* 1967, **7,** 135–136.

Monty, R. A., & Karsh, R. Spatial encoding of auditory stimuli in sequential short-term memory. *Journal of Experimental Psychology,* 1969, **81,** 572–575.

Monty, R. A., Taub, H. A., & Laughery, K. R. Keeping track of sequential events: Effects of rate, categories, and trial length. *Journal of Experimental Psychology,* 1965, **69,** 224–229.

Moore, T. V. The temporal relations of meaning and imagery. *Psychological Review,* 1915, **22,** 177–225.

Moore, T. V. Image and meaning in memory and perception. *Psychological Monographs,* 1919, **27** (Whole No. 119).

Morelli, G. Pictures and competing pictures as mediators in paired-associate learning. *Perceptual and Motor Skills,* 1970, **30,** 729–730.

Morgan, C. T. *Physiological psychology.* New York: McGraw-Hill, 1943.

Morin, R. E., Konick, A., Troxell, N., & McPherson, S. Information and reaction time for "naming" responses. *Journal of Experimental Psychology,* 1965, **70,** 309–314.

Morris, C. *Signs, language and behavior.* New York: Prentice-Hall, 1946.

Morris, V. A., Rankine, F. C., & Reber, A. S. Sentence comprehension, grammatical transformations and response availability. *Journal of Verbal Learning and Verbal Behavior,* 1968, **7,** 1113–1115.

Mowrer, O. H. *Learning theory and the symbolic processes.* New York: Wiley, 1960.

Mueller, D. J., & Travers, R. M. W. Temporal relations and meaningfulness in paired-associate learning. *Psychological Reports,* 1965, **17,** 491–497.

Mueller, J. H. & Jablonski, E. M. Instructions, noun imagery, and priority in free recall. *Psychological Reports,* 1970, **27,** 559–566.

Mueller, M. R., Edmonds, E. M., & Evans, S. H. Amount of uncertainty associated with decoding in free recall. *Journal of Experimental Psychology,* 1967, **75,** 437–443.

Murdock, B. B., Jr. The immediate retention of unrelated words. *Journal of Experimental Psychology,* 1960, **60,** 222–234.

Murdock, B. B., Jr. The serial position effect in free recall. *Journal of Experimental Psychology,* 1962, **64,** 482–488.

Murdock, B. B., Jr. Auditory and visual stores in short term memory. *Acta Psychologica,* 1967, **27,** 316–324. (a)

Murdock, B. B., Jr. Recent developments in short-term memory. *British Journal of Psychology,* 1967, **58,** 421–433. (b)

Murdock, B. B., Jr. Modality effects in short-term memory: Storage or retrieval? *Journal of Experimental Psychology,* 1968, **77,** 79–86.

Murray, D. J. The role of speech responses in short-term memory. *Canadian Journal of Psychology,* 1967, **21,** 263–276.

Murray, D. J. Articulation and acoustic confusability in short-term memory. *Journal of Experimental Psychology,* 1968, **78,** 679–684.

Murray, D. J., & Roberts, B. Visual and auditory presentation, presentation rate, and short-term memory in children. *British Journal of Psychology,* 1968, **59,** 119–125.

Murray, H. A. *Explorations in personality.* New York: Oxford University Press, 1938.

Neisser, U. An experimental distinction between perceptual process and verbal response. *Journal of Experimental Psychology,* 1954, **47,** 399–402.

Neisser, U. *Cognitive psychology.* New York: Appleton, 1967.

Neisser, U. Visual imagery as process and as experience. Paper presented at the Center for Research in Cognition and Affect, New York, June, 1968.

Neisser, U., & Beller, H. K. Searching through word lists. *British Journal of Psychology,* 1965, **56,** 349–358.

Nickerson, R. S. Short-term memory for complex meaningful visual configurations: A demonstration of capacity. *Canadian Journal of Psychology,* 1965, **19,** 155–160.

Nickerson, R. S. A note on long-term recognition memory for pictorial material. *Psychonomic Science,* 1968, **11,** 58.

Noble, C. E. An analysis of meaning. *Psychological Review,* 1952, **59,** 421–430. (a)

Noble, C. E. The role of stimulus meaning (*m*) in serial verbal learning. *Journal of Experimental Psychology,* 1952, **43,** 437–446; 1952, **44,** 465. (b)

Noble, C. E. The meaning-familiarity relationship. *Psychological Review,* 1953, **60,** 89–98.

Noble, C. E. The familiarity-frequency relationship. *Journal of Experimental Psychology,* 1954, **47,** 13–16.

Noble, C. E. Verbal learning and individual differences. In C. N. Cofer (Ed.), *Verbal learning and verbal behavior.* New York: McGraw-Hill, 1961.

Noble, C. E. Meaningfulness and familiarity. In C. N. Cofer and B. S. Musgrave (Eds.), *Verbal behavior and learning.* New York: McGraw-Hill, 1963.

Noble, C. E., & McNeely, D. A. The role of meaningfulness (*m*) in paired-associate verbal learning. *Journal of Experimental Psychology,* 1957, **53,** 16–22.

Noble, C. E., Showell, F. A., & Jones, H. R. Serial CVC learning with varied *m'* but equal *a* values. *Psychonomic Science,* 1966, **4,** 217–218.

Norman, D. A. (Ed.), *Models of human memory.* New York: Academic Press, 1970.

Nunnally, J. C., & Flaugher, R. L. Psychological implications of word usage. *Science,* 1963, **140,** 775–781.

Oldfield, R. C. Memory mechanisms and the theory of schemata. *British Journal of Psychology,* 1954, **45,** 14–23.

Oldfield, R. C. Things, words, and the brain. *Quarterly Journal of Experimental Psychology,* 1966, **18,** 340–353.

Olson, D. R. Language and thought: Aspects of a cognitive theory of semantics. *Psychological Review,* 1970, **77,** 257–273.

Olton, R. M. The effect of a mnemonic upon the retention of paired-associate verbal material. *Journal of Verbal Learning and Verbal Behavior,* 1969, **8,** 43–48.

Olver, M. A. Abstractness, imagery, and meaningfulness in recognition and free recall. Unpublished master's thesis, University of Western Ontario, 1965.

O'Neill, B. Word attributes in dichotic recognition and memory. Unpublished doctoral thesis, University of Western Ontario, 1971.

Osgood, C. E. Method and theory in experimental psychology. New York: Oxford, 1953.

Osgood, C. E. Motivational dynamics of language behavior. In M. R. Jones (Ed.), *Nebraska symposium on motivation.* Lincoln: University of Nebraska Press, 1957.

Osgood, C. E. Comments on Professor Bousfield's paper. In C. N. Cofer (Ed.), *Verbal learning and verbal behavior.* New York: McGraw-Hill, 1961.

Osgood, C. E. Psycholinguistics. In S. Koch (Ed.), *Psychology: A study of a science.* Vol. 6. New York: McGraw-Hill, 1963.

Osgood, C. E. Meaning cannot be r_m? *Journal of Verbal Learning and Verbal Behavior,* 1966, **5**, 402–407.

Osgood, C. E. Toward a wedding of insufficiencies. In T. R. Dixon and D. L. Horton (Eds.), *Verbal behavior and general behavior theory.* Englewood Cliffs, New Jersey: Prentice-Hall, 1968.

Osgood, C. E. Is neo-behaviorism up a blind alley? Unpublished mimeo, Institute of Communications Research, The University of Illinois, 1969.

Osgood, C. E., Suci, G. J., & Tannenbaum, P. H. *The measurement of meaning.* Urbana, Ill.: University of Illinois Press, 1957.

Oswald, I. The EEG, visual imagery and attention. *The Quarterly Journal of Experimental Psychology,* 1957, **9**, 113–118.

Oswald, I. Number-forms and kindred visual images. *Journal of General Psychology,* 1960, **63**, 81–88.

Oswald, I. *Sleeping and waking.* New York: Elsevier, 1962.

Otto, W. The differential effects of verbal and pictorial representations of stimuli upon responses evoked. *Journal of Verbal Learning and Verbal Behavior,* 1962, **1**, 192–196.

Overton, W., & Wiener, M. Visual field position and word-recognition threshold. *Journal of Experimental Psychology,* 1966, **71**, 249–253.

Paivio, A. Learning of adjective-noun paired-associates as a function of adjective-noun word order and noun abstractness. *Canadian Journal of Psychology,* 1963, **17**, 370–379.

Paivio, A. Generalization of verbally conditioned meaning from symbol to referent. *Canadian Journal of Psychology,* 1964, **18**, 146–155.

Paivio, A. Abstractness, imagery, and meaningfulness in paired-associate learning. *Journal of Verbal Learning and Verbal Behavior,* 1965, **4**, 32–38.

Paivio, A. Latency of verbal associations and imagery to noun stimuli as a function of abstractness and generality. *Canadian Journal of Psychology,* 1966, **20**, 378–387.

Paivio, A. Paired-associate learning and free recall of nouns as a function of concreteness, specificity, imagery, and meaningfulness. *Psychological Reports,* 1967, **20**, 239–245.

Paivio, A. A factor-analytic study of word attributes and verbal learning. *Journal of Verbal Learning and Verbal Behavior,* 1968, **7**, 41–49. (a)

Paivio, A. Effects of imagery instructions and concreteness of memory pegs in a mnemonic system. *Proceedings of the 76th Annual Convention of the American Psychological Association,* 1968, 77–78. (b)

Paivio, A. Mental imagery in associative learning and memory. *Psychological Review,* 1969, **76**, 3, 241–263.

Paivio, A. Imagery and natural language. Symposium address, American Educational Research Association meeting, Minneapolis, March, 1970. (a)

Paivio, A. On the functional significance of imagery. In H. W. Reese (Chm.), Imagery in children's learning: A symposium. *Psychological Bulletin,* 1970, **73,** 385–392. (b)

Paivio, A. Imagery and deep structure in the recall of English nominalizations. *Journal of Verbal Learning and Verbal Behavior,* 1971, **10,** 1–12.

Paivio, A., & Begg, I. Imagery and associative overlap in short-term memory. Research Bulletin No. 163, Department of Psychology, University of Western Ontario, 1970. (a)

Paivio, A., & Begg, I. Imagery and comprehension latencies as a function of sentence concreteness and structure. Research Bulletin No. 154, Department of Psychology, University of Western Ontario, 1970. (b)

Paivio, A., & Csapo, K. Concrete-image and verbal memory codes. *Journal of Experimental Psychology,* 1969, **80,** 279–285.

Paivio, A., & Foth, D. Imaginal and verbal mediators and noun concreteness in paired-associate learning: The elusive interaction. *Journal of Verbal Learning and Verbal Behavior,* 1970, **9,** 384–390.

Paivio, A., & Madigan, S. A. Imagery and association value in paired-associate learning. *Journal of Experimental Psychology,* 1968, **76,** 35–39.

Paivio, A., & Madigan, S. A. Noun imagery and frequency in paired-associate and free recall learning. *Canadian Journal of Psychology,* 1970, **24,** 353–361.

Paivio, A., & Okovita, H. W. Word imagery modalities and associative learning in blind and sighted subjects. *Journal of Verbal Learning and Verbal Behavior,* 1971, in press.

Paivio, A., & Olver, M. Denotative-generality, imagery, and meaningfulness in paired associate learning of nouns. *Psychonomic Science,* 1964, **1,** 183–184.

Paivio, A., & O'Neill, B. J. Visual recognition thresholds and dimensions of word meaning. *Perception and Psychophysics,* 1970, **8,** 273–275.

Paivio, A., Rogers, T. B., & Smythe, P. C. Why are pictures easier to recall than words? *Psychonomic Science,* 1968, **11,** 137–138.

Paivio, A., & Rowe, E. J. Noun imagery, frequency, and meaningfulness in verbal discrimination. *Journal of Experimental Psychology,* 1970, **85,** 264–269.

Paivio, A., & Simpson, H. M. The effect of word abstractness and pleasantness on pupil size during an imagery task. *Psychonomic Science,* 1966, **5,** 55–56.

Paivio, A., & Simpson, H. M. Pupillary responses during imagery tasks as a function of stimulus characteristics and imagery ability. Research Bulletin No. 45, Department of Psychology, University of Western Ontario, 1967.

Paivio, A., & Simpson, H. M. Magnitude and latency of the pupillary response during an imagery task as a function of stimulus abstractness and imagery ability. *Psychonomic Science,* 1968, **12,** 45–46.

Paivio, A., & Smythe, P. C. Word imagery, frequency, and meaningfulness in short-term memory. *Psychonomic Science,* 1971, **22,** 333–335.

Paivio, A., Smythe, P. C., & Yuille, J. C. Imagery versus meaningfulness of nouns in paired-associate learning. *Canadian Journal of Psychology,* 1968, **22,** 427–441.

Paivio, A., & Steeves, R. The relations between personal values and the imagery and meaningfulness of value words. *Perceptual and Motor Skills,* 1967, **24,** 357–358.

Paivio, A., & Yarmey, A. D. Abstractness of the common element in mediated learning. *Psychonomic Science,* 1965, **2,** 231–232.

Paivio, A., & Yarmey, A. D. Pictures versus words as stimuli and responses in paired-associate learning. *Psychonomic Science,* 1966, **5,** 235–236.

Paivio, A., & Yuille, J. C. Word abstractness and meaningfulness, and paired-associate learning in children. *Journal of Experimental Child Psychology,* 1966, **4,** 81–89.

Paivio, A., & Yuille, J. C. Mediation instructions and word attributes in paired-associate learning. *Psychonomic Science,* 1967, **8,** 65–66.

Paivio, A., & Yuille, J. C. Changes in associative strategies and paired-associate learning over trials as a function of word imagery and type of learning set. *Journal of Experimental Psychology,* 1969, **79,** 458–463.

Paivio, A., Yuille, J. C., & Madigan, S. Concreteness, imagery, and meaningfulness values for 925 nouns. *Journal of Experimental Psychology Monograph Supplement,* 1968, **76** (1, Pt. 2).

Paivio, A., Yuille, J. C., & Rogers, T. B. Noun imagery and meaningfulness in free and serial recall. *Journal of Experimental Psychology,* 1969, **79,** 509–514.

Paivio, A., Yuille, J. C., & Smythe, P. C. Stimulus and response abstractness, imagery, and meaningfulness, and reported mediators in paired-associate learning. *Canadian Journal of Psychology,* 1966, **20,** 362–377.

Palermo, D. S. & Jenkins, J. J. *Word association norms: Grade school through college.* Minneapolis: University of Minnesota Press, 1964.

Pear, T. H. The relevance of visual imagery to the process of thinking, I. *British Journal of Psychology,* 1927, **28,** 1–14.

Pelton, L. H. Mediational construction vs. mediational perception in paired-associate learning. *Psychonomic Science,* 1969, **17,** 199–200.

Penfield, W. The permanent record of the stream of consciousness. *Proceedings and papers, 14th International Congress of Psychology,* June, 1954, 47–69.

Perfetti, C. A. Sentence retention and the depth hypothesis. *Journal of Verbal Learning and Verbal Behavior,* 1969, **8,** 101–104.

Perky, C. W. An experimental study of imagination. *American Journal of Psychology,* 1910, **21,** 422–452.

Peters, H. N. The relationship between familiarity of words and their memory value. *American Journal of Psychology,* 1936, **48,** 572–584.

Peterson, M. J. Effects of knowledge of results on a verbal mediating response. *Journal of Experimental Psychology,* 1963, **66,** 394–398.

Peterson, M. J., & Blattner, K. C. Development of a verbal mediator. *Journal of Experimental Psychology,* 1963, **66,** 72–77.

Peterson, M. J., Colavita, F. B., Sheahan, D. B., & Blattner, K. C. Verbal mediating chains and response availability as a function of the acquisition paradigm. *Journal of Verbal Learning and Verbal Behavior,* 1964, **3,** 11–18.

Peterson, L. R., & Peterson, M. J. Short-term retention of individual verbal items. *Journal of Experimental Psychology,* 1959, **58,** 193–198.

Pettifor, J. L. The role of language in the development of abstract thinking: A comparison of hard-of-hearing and normal-hearing children on levels of conceptual thinking. *Canadian Journal of Psychology,* 1968, **22,** 139–156.

Philipchalk, R. The development of imaginal meaning in verbal stimuli. Unpublished doctoral dissertation, University of Western Ontario, 1971.

Philipchalk, R., & Begg, I. Context concreteness and form class in the retention of CVCs. Research Bulletin No. 155, Department of Psychology, University of Western Ontario, 1970.

Phillips, L. W. Mediated verbal similarity as a determinant of the generalization of a conditioned GSR. *Journal of Experimental Psychology*, 1958, **55**, 56–62.

Piaget, J. *Play, dreams and imitation in childhood.* New York: Norton, 1962.

Piaget, J., & Inhelder, B. *L'image mentale chez l'enfant.* Paris: Presses Universitaires de France, 1966.

Pinkus, A. L., & Laughery, K. R. Short-term memory: Effects of pronunciability and phonemic uniqueness of chunks. *Proceedings of the 75th Annual Convention of the American Psychological Association*, 1967, 65–66.

Podd, M. H., & Spear, N. E. Stimulus relatedness and response coding. *Journal of Verbal Learning and Verbal Behavior*, 1967, **6**, 55–60.

Pollack, I., & Johnson, L. B. Memory-span with efficient coding procedures. *American Journal of Psychology*, 1965, **78**, 609–614.

Pollio, H. R. Composition of associative clusters. *Journal of Experimental Psychology*, 1964, **67**, 199–208.

Pollio, H. R. Associative structure and verbal behavior. In T. R. Dixon and D. L. Horton (Eds.), *Verbal behavior and general behavior theory.* Englewood Cliffs, New Jersey: Prentice-Hall, 1968.

Pollio, H. R., Richards, S., & Lucas, R. Temporal properties of category recall. *Journal of Verbal Learning and Verbal Behavior*, 1969, **8**, 529–536.

Polson, M. C., Restle, F., & Polson, P. G. Association and discrimination in paired-associates learning. *Journal of Experimental Psychology*, 1965, **69**, 47–55.

Pompi, K. F., & Lachman, R. Surrogate processes in the short-term retention of connected discourse. *Journal of Experimental Psychology*, 1967, **75**, 143–150.

Posner, M. I. Abstraction and the process of recognition. In Spence and Bower (Eds.), *Advances in learning and motivation.* Vol. 3. New York: Academic Press, 1970, in press.

Posner, M. I., Boies, S. J., Eichelman, W. H., & Taylor, R. L. Retention of visual and name codes of single letters. *Journal of Experimental Psychology Monograph*, 1969, **79** (1, Pt. 2).

Posner, M. I., & Keele, S. W. Decay of visual information from a single letter. *Science*, 1967, **158**, 137–139.

Posner, M. I., & Keele, S. W. On the genesis of abstract ideas. *Journal of Experimental Psychology*, 1968, **77**, 353–363.

Posner, M. I., & Konick, A. F. Short-term retention of visual and kinesthetic information. *Organizational Behavior and Human Performance*, 1966, **1**, 71–86.

Posner, M. I., & Mitchell, R. F. Chronometric analysis of classification. *Psychological Review*, 1967, **74**, 392–409.

Postman, L. Extra-experimental interference and the retention of words. *Journal of Experimental Psychology*, 1961, **61**, 97–110.

Postman, L. The effects of language habits on the acquisition and retention of verbal associations. *Journal of Experimental Psychology*, 1962, **64**, 7–19.

Postman, L. Acquisition and retention of consistent associative responses. *Journal of Experimental Psychology*, 1964, **67**, 183–190.

Postman, L., & Phillips, L. W. Short-term temporal changes in free recall. *Quarterly Journal of Experimental Psychology*, 1965, **17**, Pt. 2, 132–138.

Postman, L., & Stark, K. Studies of learning to learn. IV. Transfer from serial to paired-associate learning. *Journal of Verbal Learning and Verbal Behavior*, 1967, **6**, 339–353.

Potter, M. C., & Levy, E. I. Recognition memory for a rapid sequence of pictures. *Journal of Experimental Psychology*, 1969, **81**, 10–15.

Pound, E. *Literary essays of Ezra Pound*. (T. S. Eliot, ed.) Norfolk: New Directions, 1954.

Pratt, W. (Ed.) *The imagist poem*. New York: E. P. Dutton & Co., 1963.

Prentice, J. L. Intraverbal associations in sentence behavior. *Psychonomic Science*, 1968, **10**, 213–214.

Prentice, W. C. H. Visual recognition of verbally labeled figures. *American Journal of Psychology*, 1954, **67**, 315–320.

Pribram, K. H. A review of theory in physiological psychology. *Annual Review of Psychology*, 1960, **11**, 1–40.

Pribram, K. H. The neurophysiology of remembering. *Scientific American*, 1969, **220** (1), 73–86.

Pritchard, R. M. Stabilized images on the retina. *Scientific American*, 1961, **204**, 72–78.

Pritchard, R. M., Heron, W., & Hebb, D. O. Visual perception approached by the method of stabilized images. *Canadian Journal of Psychology*, 1960, **14**, 67–77.

Prytulak, L. S. Natural language mediation. Unpublished doctoral dissertation, Stanford University, 1969.

Puff, C. R., & Hyson, S. P. An empirical comparison of two measures of intertrial organization in free recall. *Psychonomic Science*, 1967, **9**, 329–330.

Pylyshyn, Z. W., & Agnew, N. M. Coding in perception and immediate memory. Paper read at the 17th International Congress of Psychology, Washington, D. C., August, 1963.

Pylyshyn, Z. W., & Feldmar, A. Grammatical category as mediator. *Psychonomic Science*, 1968, **13**, 115–116.

Quillian, M. R. Word concepts. A theory and simulation of some basic semantic capabilities. *Behavioral Science*, 1967, **12**, 410–430.

Quintilian. The institutio oratoria. English translation by H. E. Butler. Cambridge: Harvard University Press, 1953.

Raab, D. H. Backward masking. *Psychological Bulletin*, 1963, **60**, 118–129.

Ranken, H. B. Language and thinking: Positive and negative effects of naming. *Science*, 1963, **141**, 48–50.

Raser, G. A., & Bartz, W. H. Imagery and paired-associate recognition. *Psychonomic Science*, 1968, **12**, 385–386.

Ray-Chowdhury, K. Imagery and performance tests of intelligence. *Indian Psychological Bulletin*, 1957, **2**, 25–30.

Reed, H. B. Associative aids: I. Their relation to learning, retention and other associations. *Psychological Review*, 1918, **25**, 128–155. (a)

Reed, H. B. Associative aids: II. Their relation to practice and the transfer of training. *Psychological Review*, 1918, **25**, 257–285. (b)

Reed, H. B. Associative aids: III. Their relation to the theory of thought and to methodology in psychology. *Psychological Review*, 1918, **25**, 378–401. (c)

Reed, H. B., & Dick, R. D. The learning and generalization of abstract and concrete concepts. *Journal of Verbal Learning and Verbal Behavior*, 1968, **7**, 486–490.

Reese, H. W. Imagery in paired-associate learning in children. *Journal of Experimental Child Psychology*, 1965, **2**, 290–296.

Reese, H. W. Imagery and contextual meaning. In H. W. Reese (Chm.), Imagery in children's learning: A symposium. *Psychological Bulletin,* 1970, **73,** 404–414.

Reitman, W. R. *Cognition and thought.* New York: Wiley, 1965.

Reynolds, A., & Paivio, A. Cognitive and emotional determinants of speech. *Canadian Journal of Psychology,* 1968, **22,** 164–175.

Reynolds, J. H. Cognitive transfer in verbal learning. *Journal of Educational Psychology,* 1966, **57,** 382–388.

Reynolds, J. H. Cognitive transfer in verbal learning: II. Transfer effects after prefamiliarization with integrated versus partially integrated verbal-perceptual structures. *Journal of Educational Psychology,* 1968, **59,** 133–138.

Richardson, A. *Mental imagery.* New York: Springer, 1969.

Richardson, J. Comparison of S-R and R-S learning of paired-associates. *Psychological Reports,* 1960, **7,** 225–228.

Richardson, J. Latencies of implicit associative responses and positive transfer in paired-associate learning. *Journal of Verbal Learning and Verbal Behavior,* 1968, **7,** 638–646.

Riegel, K. F., & Riegel, R. M. Prediction of word-recognition thresholds on the basis of stimulus-parameters. *Language and Speech,* 1961, **4,** 157–170.

Rimm, D. C., Alexander, R. A., & Eiles, R. R. Effects of different mediational instructions and sex of subject on paired-associate learning of concrete nouns. *Psychological Reports,* 1969, **25,** 935–940.

Roberts, K. H. Grammatical and associative constraints in sentence retention. *Journal of Verbal Learning and Verbal Behavior,* 1968, **7,** 1072–1076.

Robinson, J. S., Brown, L. T., & Hayes, W. H. Test of effects of past experience on perception. *Perceptual and Motor Skills,* 1964, **18,** 953–956.

Roe, A. A Study of imagery in research scientists. *Journal of Personality,* 1951, **19,** 459–470.

Rogers, T. B. Coding instructions and item concreteness in free recall. Unpublished master's thesis, University of Western Ontario, 1967.

Rohrman, N. L. The role of syntactic structure in the recall of English nominalizations. *Journal of Verbal Learning and Verbal Behavior,* 1968, **7,** 904–912.

Rohrman, N. L., & Polzella, D. J. Recall of subject nominalizations. *Psychonomic Science,* 1968, **12,** 373–374.

Rohwer, W. D., Jr. Verbal and visual elaboration in paired associate learning. *Project Literacy Reports,* Cornell University, 1966, No. 7, 18–28.

Rohwer, W. D., Jr. Images and pictures in children's learning: Research results and instructional implications. In H. W. Reese (Chm.), Imagery in children's learning: A symposium. *Psychological Bulletin,* 1970, **73,** 393–403.

Rohwer, W. D., Jr., & Lynch, S. Semantic constraint in paired-associate learning. *Journal of Educational Psychology,* 1966, **57,** 271–278.

Rohwer, W. D., Jr., & Lynch, S. Form class and intralist similarity in paired-associate learning. *Journal of Verbal Learning and Verbal Behavior,* 1967, **6,** 551–554.

Rohwer, W. D., Jr., Lynch, S., Levin, J. R., & Suzuki, N. Pictorial and verbal factors in the efficient learning of paired associates. *Journal of Educational Psychology,* 1967, **58,** 278–284.

Rohwer, W. D., Jr. Lynch, S., Suzuki, N., & Levin, J. R. Verbal and pictorial facilitation of paired-associate learning. *Journal of Experimental Child Psychology,* 1967, **5,** 294–302.

Rosenberg, S. Recall of sentences as a function of syntactic and associative habit. *Journal of Verbal Learning and Verbal Behavior,* 1966, **5,** 392–396.

Rosenberg, S. The relation between association and syntax in sentence production. Studies in language and behavior, Progress Report V. Center for Research on Language and Language Behavior, University of Michigan, 1967.

Rosenberg, S. Association and phrase structure in sentence recall. *Journal of Verbal Learning and Verbal Behavior,* 1968, **7,** 1077–1081.

Rosenfeld, J. B. Information processing: encoding and decoding. Unpublished doctoral thesis, Indiana University, 1967.

Rosenstein, J. Perception, cognition and language in deaf children. *Exceptional Children,* 1961, **27,** 276–284.

Ross, J., & Lawrence, K. A. Some observations on memory artifice. *Psychonomic Science,* 1968, **13,** 107–108.

Rouse, R. O., & Verinis, J. S. The effect of associative connections on the recognition of flashed words. *Journal of Verbal Learning and Verbal Behavior,* 1962, **1,** 300–303.

Rowe, E. J. & Paivio, A. Word frequency and imagery effects in verbal discrimination learning. *Journal of Experimental Psychology,* 1971, in press. (a)

Rowe, E. J. & Paivio, A. Effects of imagery and repetition instructions in verbal discrimination learning. Paper presented at the meeting of the Eastern Psychological Association, New York, April, 1971. (b)

Rugg, H. *Imagination.* New York: Harper & Row, 1963.

Runquist, W. N. Functions relating intralist stimulus similarity to acquisition performance with a variety of materials. *Journal of Verbal Learning and Verbal Behavior,* 1968, **7,** 549–553.

Runquist, W. N., & Farley, F. H. The use of mediators in the learning of verbal paired associates. *Journal of Verbal Learning and Verbal Behavior,* 1964, **3,** 280–285.

Russell, B. *An inquiry into meaning and truth.* London: George Allen and Unwin, 1940.

Russell, W. A., & Jenkins, J. J. The complete Minnesota norms for responses to 100 words from the Kent-Rosanoff Word Association Test. *Technical Report No. 11,* Contract No. N8onr-66216, Office of Naval Research and University of Minnesota, 1954.

Russell, W. A., & Storms, L. H. Implicit verbal chaining in paired-associate learning. *Journal of Experimental Psychology,* 1955, **49,** 287–293.

Ryan, J. J. Comparison of verbal response transfer mediated by meaningfully similar and associated stimuli. *Journal of Experimental Psychology,* 1960, **60,** 408–415.

Sachs, J. S. Recognition memory for syntactic and semantic aspects of connected discourse. *Perception and Psychophysics,* 1967, **2,** 437–442. (a)

Sachs, J. S. Recognition of semantic, syntactic and lexical changes in sentences. Paper presented at Psychonomic Society Meetings, Chicago, Ill., October, 1967. (b)

Sales, B. D., Haber, R. N., & Cole, R. A. Mechanisms of aural encoding III: Distinctive features for vowels. *Perception and Psychophysics,* 1968, **4,** 321–327.

Sales, B. D., Haber, R. N., & Cole, R. A. Mechanisms of aural encoding IV: Hearsee, say-write interactions for vowels. *Perception and Psychophysics,* 1969, **6,** 385–390.

Saltz, E. Compound stimuli in verbal learning: Cognitive and sensory differentiation versus stimulus selection. *Journal of Experimental Psychology,* 1963, **66,** 1–5.

Saltz, E. Thorndike-Lorge frequency and *m* of stimuli as separate factors in paired-associate learning. *Journal of Experimental Psychology,* 1967, **73,** 473–478.

Saltz, E., & Ager, J. W. The role of context cues in learning: A reply to Greeno. *Psychological Reports,* 1968, **22,** 351–354.

Saltz, E., & Modigliani, V. Response meaningfulness in paired associates: T-L frequency, *m,* and number of meanings (*dm*). *Journal of Experimental Psychology,* 1967, **75,** 313–320.

Saltz, E., & Wickey, J. Further evidence for differentiation effects of context stimuli: A reply to Birnbaum. *Psychological Reports,* 1967, **20,** 835–838.

Salzinger, K., Portnoy, S., & Feldman, R. S. The effect of order of approximation to the statistical structure of English on the emission of verbal responses. *Journal of Experimental Psychology,* 1962, **64,** 52–57.

Sampson, J. R. Free recall of verbal and non-verbal stimuli. *Quarterly Journal of Experimental Psychology,* 1970, **22,** 215–221.

Samuels, S. J. Effect of word associations on the recognition of flashed words. *Journal of Educational Psychology,* 1969, **60,** 97–102.

Santa, J. L. & Ranken, H. B. Language and memory: Redintegrative memory for shapes facilitated by naming. *Psychonomic Science,* 1968, **13,** 109–110.

Sassenrath, J. M., & Yonge, G. D. Meaning and transfer of verbal learning. *Journal of Educational Psychology,* 1967, **58,** 365–372.

Saufley, W. H., Jr. An analysis of cues in serial learning. *Journal of Experimental Psychology,* 1967, **74,** 414–419.

Savin, H. B., & Perchonock, E. Grammatical structure and the immediate recall of English sentences. *Journal of Verbal Learning and Verbal Behavior,* 1965, **4,** 348–353.

Scagnelli, P. Relationships among visual imagery, language and haptics in spatial perception. Unpublished doctoral dissertation, Duke University, 1969.

Scapinello, K. F. & Yarmey, A. D. The role of familiarity and orientation in immediate and delayed recognition of pictorial stimuli. *Psychonomic Science,* 1970, **21,** 329–331.

Schaub, G. R., & Lindley, R. H. Effects of subject-generated recoding cues on short-term memory. *Journal of Experimental Psychology,* 1964, **68,** 171–175.

Schlaegel, T. F. The dominant method of imagery in blind as compared to sighted adolescents. *Journal of Genetic Psychology,* 1953, **83,** 265–277.

Schmeidler, G. R. Visual imagery correlated to a measure of creativity. *Journal of Consulting Psychology,* 1965, **29,** 78–80.

Schnorr, J. A., & Atkinson, R. C. Repetition versus imagery instructions in the short- and long-term retention of paired-associates. *Psychonomic Science,* 1969, **15,** 183–184.

Scholtz, D. S. Fundamental principles of form perception in touch. *Acta Psychologica,* 1958, **13,** 299–333.

Schuck, J. R., Brock, T. C., & Becker, L. A. Luminous figures: Factors affecting the reporting of disappearances. *Science,* 1964, **146,** 1598–1599.

Schulman, A. I. Word length and rarity in recognition memory. *Psychonomic Science,* 1967, **9,** 211–212.

Schulz, R. W., Liston, J. R., & Weaver, G. E. The A-B, B-C, A-C mediation paradigm:

Recall of A-B following A-C learning. *Journal of Verbal Learning and Verbal Behavior,* 1968, **7,** 602–607.

Schulz, R. W., & Lovelace, E. A. Mediation in verbal paired-associate learning: The role of temporal factors. *Psychonomic Science,* 1964, **1,** 95–96.

Schulz, R. W., & Weaver, G. E. The A-B, B-C, A-C mediation paradigm: The effects of variation in A-C study- and test-interval lengths and strength of A-B or B-C. *Journal of Experimental Psychology,* 1968, **76,** 303–311.

Schwartz, M. Instructions to use verbal mediators in paired-associate learning. *Journal of Experimental Psychology,* 1969, **79,** 1–5. (a)

Schwartz, M. Instructions to mediate, recall time, and type of paired-associate list. *Journal of Experimental Psychology,* 1969, **81,** 398–400. (b)

Scott, K. G. Clustering with perceptual and symbolic stimuli in free recall. *Journal of Verbal Learning and Verbal Behavior,* 1967, **6,** 864–866.

Segal, S. J. The Perky effect: Changes in reality judgments with changing methods of inquiry. *Psychonomic Science,* 1968, **12,** 393–394.

Segal, S. J., & Fusella, V. Influence of imaged pictures and sounds on detection of visual and auditory signals. *Journal of Experimental Psychology,* 1970, **83,** 458–464.

Segal, S. J., & Gordon, P. The Perky effect revisited: Paradoxical thresholds or signal detection error? Paper presented at the 39th annual meeting of the Eastern Psychological Association, 1968.

Segal, S. J., & Nathan, S. The Perky effect: Incorporation of an external stimulus into an imagery experience under placebo and control conditions. *Perceptual Motor Skills,* 1964, **18,** 385–395.

Seibel, R., Lockhart, R., & Taschman, C. S. The learning of 100 paired associates in a single, self-paced trial. Paper presented at the meeting of the Psychonomic Society, Chicago, October, 1967.

Seidel, R. J. The importance of the S-R role of the verbal mediators in mediate association. *Canadian Journal of Psychology,* 1962, **16,** 170–176.

Semler, I. J., & Iscoe, I. Concept interference and paired associates in retarded children. *Journal of Comparative and Physiological Psychology,* 1965, **60,** 465–466.

Semmes, J. Hemispheric specialization: A possible clue to mechanism. *Neuropsychologia,* 1968, **6,** 11–26.

Senter, R. J., & Hauser, G. K. An experimental study of a mnemonic system. *Psychonomic Science,* 1968, **10,** 289–290.

Shapiro, S. I. Response word frequency in paired-associate learning. *Psychonomic Science,* 1969, **16,** 308–309.

Shaw, E. E. Some imaginal factors influencing verbal expression. *Psychological Review Monograph Supplement,* 1919, **26,** No. 113.

Sheehan, P. W. Accuracy and vividness of visual images. *Perceptual and Motor Skills,* 1966, **23,** 391–398. (a)

Sheehan, P. W. Functional similarity of imaging to perceiving: Individual differences in vividness of imagery. *Perceptual and Motor Skills,* 1966, **23,** 1011–1033. (b)

Sheehan, P. W. A shortened form of Betts' questionnaire upon mental imagery. *Journal of Clinical Psychology,* 1967, **23,** 386–389. (a)

Sheehan, P. W. Reliability of a short test of imagery. *Perceptual and Motor Skills,* 1967, **25,** 744. (b)

Sheehan, P. W., & Neisser, U. Some variables affecting the vividness of imagery in recall. *British Journal of Psychology,* 1969, **60,** 71–80.

Sheffield, F. D. Theoretical considerations in the learning of complex sequential tasks from demonstration and practice. In A. A. Lumsdaine (Ed.), *Student response in programmed instruction.* (NAS-NRS Publication No. 943) Washington, D. C.: National Academy of Sciences-National Research Council, 1961.

Sheffield, F. D. Relation between classical conditioning and instrumental learning. In W. F. Prokasy (Ed.), *Classical conditioning.* New York: Appleton-Century-Crofts, 1965.

Shepard, R. N. Learning and recall as organization and search. *Journal of Verbal Learning and Verbal Behavior,* 1966, **5,** 201–204.

Shepard, R. N. Recognition memory for words, sentences, and pictures. *Journal of Verbal Learning and Verbal Behavior,* 1967, **6,** 156–163.

Shepard, R. N., & Chipman, S. Second-order isomorphism of internal representations: Shapes of states. *Cognitive Psychology,* 1970, **1,** 1–17.

Shepard, R. N., & Teghtsoonian, M. Retention of information under conditions approaching a steady state. *Journal of Experimental Psychology,* 1961, **62,** 302–309.

Shipley, W. C. Indirect conditioning. *Journal of General Psychology,* 1935, **12,** 337–357.

Short, P. L. The objective study of mental imagery. *British Journal of Psychology,* 1953, **44,** 38–51.

Shuell, T. J., & Keppel, G. A further test of the chaining hypothesis of serial learning. *Journal of Verbal Learning and Verbal Behavior,* 1967, **6,** 439–445.

Siipola, E. M., & Hayden, S. D. Exploring eidetic imagery among the retarded. *Perceptual and Motor Skills,* 1965, **21,** 275–286.

Siipola, E. M., Walker, W. N., & Kolb, D. Task attitudes in word association, projective and nonprojective. *Journal of Personality,* 1955, **23,** 441–459.

Simon, H. A., & Feigenbaum, E. A. An information-processing theory of some effects of similarity, familiarization, and meaningfulness in verbal learning. *Journal of Verbal Learning and Verbal Behavior,* 1964, **3,** 385–396.

Simpson, H. M. Inferring cognitive processes from pupillary activity and response time. Colloquium presented at the University of Western Ontario, January, 1970.

Simpson, H. M., & Paivio, A. Changes in pupil size during an imagery task without motor response involvement. *Psychonomic Science,* 1966, **5,** 405–406.

Simpson, H. M., & Paivio, A. Effects on pupil size of manual and verbal indicators of cognitive task fulfillment. *Perception and Psychophysics,* 1968, **3,** 185–190.

Simpson, H. M., Paivio, A., & Rogers, T. B. Occipital alpha activity of high and low visual imagers during problem solving. *Psychonomic Science,* 1967, **7,** 49–50.

Singer, J. L. *Daydreaming: An introduction to the experimental study of inner experience.* New York: Random House, 1966.

Singh, S., Brokaw, S. P., & Black, J. W. Effects of delayed sidetone, noise, and syntactic structure on the level and duration of speech. *Journal of Verbal Learning and Verbal Behavior,* 1967, **6,** 629–633.

Skehan, P. The relation of visual imagery to true-false judgment of simple sentences. Unpublished master's thesis, University of Western Ontario, 1970.

Skinner, B. F. *Science and human behavior.* New York: MacMillan, 1953.

Skinner, B. F. *Verbal behavior.* New York: Appleton-Century-Crofts, 1957.

Slamecka, N. J. An inquiry into the doctrine of remote associations. *Psychological Review,* 1964, **71,** 61–76.

Slamecka, N. J. An examination of trace storage in free recall. *Journal of Experimental Psychology,* 1968, **76,** 504–513.

Slamecka, N. J. Recognition of word strings as a function of linguistic violations. *Journal of Experimental Psychology,* 1969, **79,** 377–378.

Slatter, K. H. Alpha rhythms and mental imagery. *Electroencephalography and Clinical Neurophysiology,* 1960, **12,** 851–859.

Slobin, D. I. Grammatical transformations and sentence comprehension in childhood and adulthood. *Journal of Verbal Learning and Verbal Behavior,* 1966, **5,** 219–227.

Slobin, D. L. Recall of full and truncated passive sentences in connected discourse. *Journal of Verbal Learning and Verbal Behavior,* 1968, **7,** 876–881.

Smith, M. G., & Harleston, B. W. Stimulus abstractness and emotionality as determinants of behavioral and physiological responses in a word-association task. *Journal of Verbal Learning and Verbal Behavior,* 1966, **5,** 309–313.

Smith, R. K., & Noble, C. E. Effects of a mnemonic technique applied to verbal learning and memory. *Perceptual and Motor Skills,* 1965, **21,** 123–134.

Smythe, P. C. The effects of imagery and synonymity in verbal transfer. Unpublished honors thesis, University of Western Ontario, 1966.

Smythe, P. C. Pair concreteness and mediation instructions in forward and backward paired-associate recall. Unpublished doctoral thesis, University of Western Ontario, 1970.

Smythe, P. C., & Paivio, A. A comparison of the effectiveness of word imagery and meaningfulness in paired-associate learning of nouns. *Psychonomic Science,* 1968, **10,** 49–50.

Solomon, R. L., & Howes, D. H. Word frequency, personal values, and visual duration thresholds. *Psychological Review,* 1951, **58,** 256–270.

Spear, N. E., Ekstrand, B. R., & Underwood, B. J. Association by contiguity. *Journal of Experimental Psychology,* 1964, **67,** 151–161.

Sperling, G. The information available in brief visual presentations. *Psychological Monographs,* 1960, **74** (Whole No. 498).

Sperling, G. A model for visual memory tasks. *Human Factors,* 1963, **5,** 19–31.

Sperry, R. W. Hemisphere deconnection and unity in conscious awareness. *American Psychologist,* 1968, **23,** 723–733.

Spielberger, C. D., & DeNike, L. D. Descriptive behaviorism versus cognitive theory in verbal operant conditioning. *Psychological Review,* 1966, **73,** 306–326.

Spielberger, C. D., & Denny, J. P. Visual recognition thresholds as a function of verbal ability and word frequency. *Journal of Experimental Psychology,* 1963, **65,** 597–602.

Spiker, C. C. Associative transfer in verbal paired-associate learning. *Child Development,* 1960, **31,** 73–87.

Spreen, O., Borkowski, J. G., & Benton, A. L. Auditory recognition in relation to meaningfulness, abstractness, and phonetic structure of words. *Journal of Verbal Learning and Verbal Behavior,* 1967, **6,** 101–104.

Spreen, O., & Schulz, R. W. Parameters of abstraction, meaningfulness, and pronunciability for 329 nouns. *Journal of Verbal Learning and Verbal Behavior,* 1966, **5,** 459–468.

Staats, A. W. Verbal habit families, concepts, and the operant conditioning of word classes. *Psychological Review,* 1961, **68,** 190–204.

Staats, A. W. *Learning, language, and cognition.* New York: Holt, Rinehart, and Winston, 1968.

Staats, A. W. Integrated functional learning theory and language development. In D. I. Slobin (Ed.), *The ontogenesis of grammar: Facts and theories.* New York: Academic Press, in press.

Staats, A. W., & Staats, C. K. Attitudes established by classical conditioning. *Journal of Abnormal and Social Psychology,* 1958, **57,** 37–40.

Staats, A. W., & Staats, C. K. Meaning and *m*: Correlated but separate. *Psychological Review,* 1959, **66,** 136–144.

Staats, A. W., Staats, C. K., & Heard, W. G. Language conditioning of meaning to meaning using a semantic generalization paradigm. *Journal of Experimental Psychology,* 1959, **57,** 187–192.

Staats, C. K., & Staats, A. W. Meaning established by classical conditioning. *Journal of Experimental Psychology,* 1957, **54,** 74–80.

Standing, L., Conezio, J., & Haber, R. N. Perception and memory for pictures: Single-trial learning of 2560 visual stimuli. *Psychonomic Science,* 1970, **19,** 73–74.

Standing, L., Sell, C., Boss, J., & Haber, R. N. Effect of visualization and subvocalization on perceptual clarity. *Psychonomic Science,* 1970, **18,** 89–90.

Steinfeld, G. J. Concepts of set and availability and their relation to the reorganization of ambiguous pictorial stimuli. *Psychological Review,* 1967, **74,** 505–522.

Sternberg, S. Two operations in character recognition: Some evidence from reaction-time measurements. *Perception and Psychophysics,* 1967, **2,** 45–53.

Sternberg, S. The discovery of processing stages: Extensions of Donders' method. Paper presented at the Donders Centenary Symposium on reaction-time. Instituut Voor Perceptie Onderzoek, Eindhoven, Netherlands, 1968.

Stevenson, C. L. *Ethics and language.* New Haven: Yale University Press, 1944.

Stewart, J. C. *An experimental investigation of imagery.* Unpublished doctoral thesis, University of Toronto, 1965.

Stoke, S. M. Memory for onomatopes. *Journal of Genetic Psychology,* 1929, **36,** 594–596.

Stolz, W. S. A study of the ability to decode grammatically novel sentences. *Journal of Verbal Learning and Verbal Behavior,* 1967, **6,** 867–873.

Stoyva, J., & Kamiya, J. Electrophysiological studies of dreaming as the prototype of a new strategy in the study of consciousness. *Psychological Review,* 1968, **75,** 192–205.

Street, R. F. *A Gestalt completion test: A study of a cross section of intellect.* New York: Bureau of Publications, Teachers College, Columbia University, 1931.

Stromeyer, C. F., & Psotka, J. The detailed texture of eidetic images. *Nature,* 1970, **225,** 346–349.

Stroop, J. R. Interference in serial verbal reactions. *Journal of Experimental Psychology,* 1935, **18,** 643–661.

Stumberg, D. A study of poetic talent. *Journal of Experimental Psychology,* 1928, **11,** 219–234.

Supa, M., Cotzin, M., & Dallenbach, K. M. "Facial vision": The perception of obstacles by the blind. *American Journal of Psychology,* 1944, **57,** 133–183.

Suzuki, N. S., & Rohwer, W. D., Jr. Verbal facilitation of paired-associate learning: Type of grammatical unit vs. connective form class. *Journal of Verbal Learning and Verbal Behavior,* 1968, **7,** 584–588.

Taylor, A. M., & Black, H. B. Variables affecting imagery instruction in children. Research Monograph No. 6, Audio-Visual Center, Indiana University, April, 1969.

Taylor, A. M., Josberger, M., & Prentice, J. L. Imagery organization and children's recall. Paper presented at the American Educational Research Association Convention, March, 1970.

Taylor, J. A. Meaning, frequency, and visual duration threshold. *Journal of Experimental Psychology,* 1958, **55,** 329–334.

Taylor, J. G. *The behavioral basis of perception.* New Haven: Yale University Press, 1962.

Taylor, R. L., & Posner, M. I. Retrieval from visual and verbal memory codes. Paper presented at the meeting of the Midwestern Psychological Association, Chicago, May, 1968.

Tees, R. C., & More, L. K. Effect of amount of perceptual learning upon disappearances observed under reduced stimulation conditions. *Perception and Psychophysics,* 1967, **2,** 565–568. (a)

Tees, R. C., & More, L. K. Visual disappearances under simplified stimulus conditions caused by auditory perceptual learning. *Perception and Psychophysics,* 1967, **2,** 627–629. (b)

Tejirian, E. Syntactic and semantic structure in the recall of orders of approximation to English. *Journal of Verbal Learning and Verbal Behavior,* 1968, **7,** 1010–1015.

Terrace, H. The effects of retinal locus and attention on the perception of words. *Journal of Experimental Psychology,* 1959, **58,** 382–385.

Thorndike, E. L. On the function of visual images. *Journal of Philosophy,* 1907, **4,** 324–327.

Thorndike, E. L. *Educational psychology.* Volume III. New York: Teachers College, Columbia University, 1914.

Thorndike, E. L., & Lorge, I. *The teacher's word book of 30,000 words.* New York: Bureau of Publications, Teachers College, 1944.

Thurstone, L. L. Primary mental abilities. *Psychometrika Monographs,* 1938, No. 1.

Thurstone, L. L., & Jeffrey, T. E. *Flags: A test of space thinking.* Chicago: Education Industry Service, 1956.

Titchener, E. B. *Lectures on the experimental psychology of thought processes.* New York: Macmillan, 1909.

Tolman, E. C. More concerning the temporal relations of meaning and imagery. *Psychological Review,* 1917, **24,** 114–138.

Tolman, E. C. *Purposive behavior in animals and men.* New York: Century, 1932.

Tolman, E. C. Cognitive maps in rats and men. *Psychological Review,* 1948, **55,** 189–208.

Tolman, E. C. Principles of purposive behavior. In S. Koch (Ed.), *Psychology: A Study of a science.* Vol. 2. New York: McGraw-Hill, 1959.

Tomkins, S. S. *Affect, imagery, consciousness.* Vol. 1. New York: Springer, 1962.

Tulving, E. Subjective organization in free recall of "unrelated" words. *Psychological Review*, 1962, **69**, 344–354.

Tulving, E. Intratrial and intertrial retention: Notes towards a theory of free recall verbal learning. *Psychological Review*, 1964, **71**, 219–237.

Tulving, E. Subjective organization and effects of repetition in multitrial free-recall learning. *Journal of Verbal Learning and Verbal Behavior*, 1966, **5**, 193–197.

Tulving, E. Theoretical issues in free recall. In T. R. Dixon and D. L. Horton (Eds.), *Verbal behavior and general behavior theory*. Englewood Cliffs, N. J., Prentice-Hall, 1968.

Tulving, E., & Gold, C. Stimulus information and contextual information as determinants of tachistoscopic recognition of words. *Journal of Experimental Psychology*, 1963, **66**, 319–327.

Tulving, E., McNulty, J. A., & Ozier, M. Vividness of words and learning to learn in free-recall learning. *Canadian Journal of Psychology*, 1965, **19**, 242–252.

Tulving, E., & Osler, S. Transfer effects in whole/part free-recall learning. *Canadian Journal of Psychology*, 1967, **21**, 253–262.

Tulving, E., & Osler, S. Effectiveness of retrieval cues in memory for words. *Journal of Experimental Psychology*, 1968, **77**, 593–601.

Tulving, E., & Patkau, J. E. Concurrent effects of contextual constraint and word frequency on immediate recall and learning of verbal material. *Canadian Journal of Psychology*, 1962, **16**, 83–95.

Tulving, E., & Pearlstone, Z. Availability versus accessibility of information in memory for words. *Journal of Verbal Learning and Verbal Behavior*, 1966, **5**, 381–391.

Turner, E. A., & Rommetveit, R. Focus of attention in recall of active and passive sentences. *Journal of Verbal Learning and Verbal Behavior*, 1968, **7**, 543–548.

Turvey, M. T. Analysis of augmented recall in short-term memory following a shift in connotation. *British Journal of Psychology*, 1968, **59**, 131–137.

Tversky, B. Pictorial and verbal encoding in a short-term memory task. *Perception and Psychophysics*, 1969, **6**, 225–233.

Uhlenbeck, E. M. Some further remarks on transformational grammar. *Lingua*, 1967, **17**, 263–316.

Underwood, B. J. An evaluation of the Gibson theory of verbal learning. In C. N. Cofer (Ed.), *Verbal learning and verbal behavior*. New York: McGraw-Hill, 1961.

Underwood, B. J. Stimulus selection in verbal learning. In C. N. Cofer and B. S. Musgrave (Eds.), *Verbal behavior and learning: Problems and processes*. New York: McGraw-Hill, 1963.

Underwood, B. J., The representativeness of rote verbal learning. In A. W. Melton (Ed.), *Categories of human learning*. New York: Academic Press, 1964.

Underwood, B. J. False recognition produced by implicit verbal responses. *Journal of Experimental Psychology*, 1965, **70**, 122–129.

Underwood, B. J. Attributes of memory. *Psychological Review*, 1969, **76**, 559–573.

Underwood, B. J., & Ekstrand, B. R. An analysis of some shortcomings in the interference theory of forgetting. *Psychological Review*, 1966, **73**, 540–549.

Underwood, B. J., Ekstrand, B. R., & Keppel, G. An analysis of intralist similarity in verbal learning with experiments on conceptual similarity. *Journal of Verbal Learning and Verbal Behavior*, 1965, **4**, 447–462.

Underwood, B. J., & Erlebacher, A. Studies of coding in verbal learning. *Psychological Monographs*, 1965, **79** (13, Whole No. 606).

Underwood, B. J., & Freund, J. S. Testing effects in recognition of words. *Journal of Verbal Learning and Verbal Behavior*, 1970, **9**, 117–125.

Underwood, B. J., & Keppel, G. Coding processes in verbal learning. *Journal of Verbal Learning and Verbal Behavior*, 1963, **1**, 250–257.

Underwood, B. J., & Postman, L. Extraexperimental sources of interference in forgetting. *Psychological Review*, 1960, **67**, 73–95.

Underwood, B. J., & Richardson, J. Some verbal materials for the study of concept formation. *Psychological Bulletin*, 1956, **53**, 84–95.

Underwood, B. J., & Schulz, R. W. *Meaningfulness and verbal learning.* Chicago: Lippincott, 1960.

Uznadze, D. N. *The psychology of set.* Translated by B. Haigh. New York: Consultants' Bureau, 1966.

Vanderplas, J. M., & Garvin, E. A. The association value of random shapes. *Journal of Experimental Psychology*, 1959, **57**, 147–154. (a)

Vanderplas, J. M., & Garvin, E. A. Complexity, association value, and practice as factors in shape recognition. *Journal of Experimental Psychology*, 1959, **57**, 155–163. (b)

Vanderplas, J. M., Sanderson, W. A., & Vanderplas, J. N. Some task-related determinants of transfer in perceptual learning. *Perceptual and Motor Skills*, 1964, **18**, 71–80.

Vernon, M. Relationship of language to the thinking process. *Archives of General Psychiatry*, 1967, **16**, 325–333.

Walker, H. J. Imagery ratings for 338 nouns. *Behavior Research Methods and Instrumentation*, 1970, **2**, 165–167.

Walkup, L. E. Creativity in science through visualization. *Perceptual and Motor Skills*, 1965, **21**, 35–41.

Wallace, W. H., Turner, S. H., & Perkins, C. C. *Preliminary studies of human information storage.* Signal Corps Project No. 1320, Institute for Cooperative Research, University of Pennsylvania, 1957.

Wallace, W. P. Review of the historical, empirical, and theoretical status of the von Restorff phenomenon. *Psychological Bulletin*, 1965, **63**, 410–424.

Wallace, W. P. Implicit associative response occurrence in learning with retarded subjects: a supplementary report. *Journal of Educational Psychology*, 1967, **58**, 110–114.

Wallace, W. P., & Underwood B. J. Implicit responses and the role of intralist similarity in verbal learning by normal and retarded subjects. *Journal of Educational Psychology*, 1964, **55**, 362–370.

Wallach, H., & Averbach, E. On memory modalities. *American Journal of Psychology*, 1955, **68**, 249–257.

Wallach, H., O'Connell, D. N., & Neisser, U. The memory effect on visual perception of three-dimensional form. *Journal of Experimental Psychology*, 1953, **45**, 360–368.

Walter, R. D., & Yeager, C. L. Visual imagery and electroencephalographic changes. *Electroencephalography and Clinical Neurophysiology*, 1956, **8**, 193–199.

Wanner, H. E. On remembering, forgetting, and understanding sentences: A study of the deep structure hypothesis. Unpublished doctoral dissertation, Harvard University, 1968.

Wapner, S., & Werner, H. *Perceptual development.* Worcester, Mass.: Clark University Press, 1957.

Warren, R. M., Obusek, C. J., Farmer, R. M., & Warren, R. P. Auditory sequence: Confusion of patterns other than speech or music. *Science,* 1969, **164,** 586–587.

Watson, J. B. Psychology as the behaviorist views it. *Psychological Review,* 1913, **20,** 158–177.

Watson, J. B. *Behaviorism.* Chicago, Ill.: University of Chicago Press, 1930.

Watson, J. D. *The double helix.* London: Weidenfeld and Nicolson, 1968.

Waugh, N. C., & Norman, D. A. Primary memory. *Psychological Review,* 1965, **72,** 89–104.

Wearing, A. J. Vividness in the recall of English nominalizations. *Psychonomic Science,* 1971, **22,** 121–122.

Weaver, G. E., Hopkins, R. H., & Schulz, R. W. The A-B, B-C, A-C mediation paradigm: A-C performance in the absence of study trials. *Journal of Experimental Psychology,* 1968, **77,** 670–675.

Weber, R. J., & Bach, M. Visual and speech imagery. *British Journal of Psychology,* 1969, **60,** 199–202.

Weber, R. J. & Castleman, J. The time it takes to imagine. *Perception and Psychophysics,* 1970, **8,** 165–168.

Weisstein, N. A Rashevsky-Landahl neural net: Simulation of meta-contrast. *Psychological Review,* 1968, **75,** 494–521.

Werner, H., & Kaplan, B. *Symbol formation: An organismic-developmental approach to the psychology of language and the expression of thought.* New York: Wiley, 1963.

Whorf, B. L. *Language, thought, and reality.* Cambridge: Technology Press, 1956.

Wickelgren, W. A. Size of rehearsal group and short-term memory. *Journal of Experimental Psychology,* 1964, **68,** 413–419.

Wickelgren, W. A. Acoustic similarity and intrusion errors in short-term memory. *Journal of Experimental Psychology,* 1965, **70,** 102–108.

Wickelgren W. A. Auditory or articulatory coding in verbal short-term memory. *Psychological Review,* 1969, **76,** 232–235.

Wickens, D. D. Encoding categories of words: An empirical approach to meaning. *Psychological Review,* 1970, **77,** 1–15.

Wickens, D. D., Born, D. G., & Allen, C. K. Proactive inhibition and item similarity in short-term memory. *Journal of Verbal Learning and Verbal Behavior,* 1963, **2,** 440–445.

Wickens, D. D., & Clark, S. Osgood dimensions as an encoding class in short-term memory. *Journal of Experimental Psychology,* 1968, **78,** 580–584.

Wickens, D. D., & Engle, R. W. Imagery and abstractness in short-term memory. *Journal of Experimental Psychology,* 1970, **84,** 268–272.

Wicker, F. W. On the locus of picture-word differences in paired-associate learning. *Journal of Verbal Learning and Verbal Behavior,* 1970, **9,** 52–57. (a)

Wicker, F. W. Photographs, drawings, and nouns as stimuli in paired-associate learning. *Psychonomic Science,* 1970, **18,** 205–206. (b)

Wilgosh, L. R. The interaction between pictures and their labels in the memory of four-year-old children. Unpublished doctoral dissertation, McMaster University, 1970.

Williams, J. R., & Levin, I. P. Mediated facilitation in a four-stage chaining paradigm. *Psychonomic Science*, 1968, **12**, 281–282.

Wimer, C. An analysis of semantic stimulus factors in paired-associate learning. *Journal of Verbal Learning and Verbal Behavior*, 1963, **1**, 397–407.

Wimer, C. , & Lambert, W. E. The differential effects of word and object stimuli on the learning of paired associates. *Journal of Experimental Psychology*, 1959, **57**, 31–36.

Wind, M., & Davidson, M. Facilitation of paired-associate learning by language context. *Psychonomic Science*, 1969, **15**, 184–185.

Wing, J. F. Stimulus-trace model of serial acquisition and retention. *Proceedings of the 75th Annual Convention of the American Psychological Association*, 1967, 59–60.

Winnick, W. A., & Bruder, G. E. Signal detection approach to the study of retinal locus in tachistoscopic recognition. *Journal of Experimental Psychology*, 1968, **78**, 528–530.

Winnick, W. A., & Kressel, K. Tachistoscopic recognition thresholds, paired-associate learning, and immediate recall as a function of abstractness-concreteness and word frequency. *Journal of Experimental Psychology*, 1965, **70**, 163–168.

Winograd, E., Karchmer, M. A., & Russell, I. S. Role of encoding unitization in cued recognition memory. *Journal of Verbal Learning and Verbal Behavior*, 1971, in press.

Wirtz, J. & Anisfeld, M. Imagery, synonymity, antonymy, and false recognition of phrases. Unpublished manuscript, Yeshiva University, 1970.

Witmer, L. R. The association value of three-place consonant syllables. *Journal of Genetic Psychology*, 1935, **47**, 337–359.

Wollen, K. A. Effects of relevant or irrelevant pictorial mediators upon forward and backward recall. Paper presented at the meeting of the Psychonomic Society, St. Louis, November, 1968.

Wollen, K. A. Variables that determine the effectiveness of picture mediators in paired-associate learning. Paper presented at the meeting of the Psychonomic Society, St. Louis, November, 1969.

Wolpe, J. *Psychotherapy by reciprocal inhibition*. Stanford: Stanford University Press, 1958.

Wood, G. Mnemonic systems in recall. *Journal of Educational Psychology Monographs*, 1967, **58** (6, Pt. 2).

Woodworth, R. S. *Experimental psychology*. New York: Holt, 1938.

Woodworth, R. S., & Schlosberg, H. *Experimental psychology*. New York: Holt, 1954.

Worchel, P. Space perception and orientation in the blind. *Psychological Monographs*, 1951, **65** (15).

Wynne, R. D., & Cofer, C. N. On meaning, association, and transfer. Unpublished manuscript, 1958.

Yarmey, A. D. Word abstractness, awareness, and type of design in verbal mediation. *Psychology*, 1967, **4**, 24–32.

Yarmey, A. D. The person-image and social mediated learning. *Psychological Record*, 1969, **19**, 123–127.

Yarmey, A. D., & Csapo, K. G. Imaginal and verbal mediation instructions and stimulus attributes in paired-associate learning. *Psychological Record*, 1968, **18**, 191–199.

Yarmey, A. D., & O'Neill, B. J. S-R and R-S paired-associate learning as a function of concreteness, imagery, specificity, and association value. *Journal of Psychology*, 1969, **71**, 95–109.

Yarmey, A. D., & Paivio, A. Further evidence on the effects of word abstractness and meaningfulness in paired-associate learning. *Psychonomic Science*, 1965, **2**, 307–308.

Yates, F. A. *The art of memory*. London: Routledge and Kegan Paul, 1966.

Yin, R. K. Looking at upside-down faces. *Journal of Experimental Psychology*, 1969, **81**, 141–145.

Yngve, V. A model and an hypothesis for language structure. *Proceedings of the American Philosophical Society*, 1960, **104**, 444–466.

Yntema, D. B., & Trask, F. P. Recall as a search process. *Journal of Verbal Learning and Verbal Behavior*, 1963, **2**, 65–74.

Young, R. K. Tests of three hypotheses about the effective stimulus in serial learning. *Journal of Experimental Psychology*, 1962, **63**, 307–313.

Young, R. K. Serial learning. In T. R. Dixon and D. L. Horton (Eds.), *Verbal behavior and general behavior theory*. Englewood Cliffs, N. J.: Prentice-Hall, 1968.

Yuille, J. C. Concreteness without imagery in paired-associate learning. *Psychonomic Science*, 1968, **11**, 55–56.

Yuille, J. C., & Barnsley, R. H. Visual, auditory, and tactual imagery in paired associate learning. Paper read at the 19th International Congress of Psychology, London, England, July, 1969.

Yuille, J. C., & Paivio, A. Latency of imaginal and verbal mediators as a function of stimulus and response concreteness-imagery. *Journal of Experimental Psychology*, 1967, **75**, 540–544.

Yuille, J. C., & Paivio, A. Imagery and verbal mediation instructions in paired-associate learning. *Journal of Experimental Psychology*, 1968, **78**, 436–441.

Yuille, J. C., & Paivio, A. Abstractness and recall of connected discourse. *Journal of Experimental Psychology*, 1969, **82**, 467–471.

Yuille, J. C., Paivio, A., & Lambert, W. E. Noun and adjective imagery and order in paired-associate learning by French and English subjects. *Canadian Journal of Psychology*, 1969, **23**, 459–466.

Yuille, J. C., & Pritchard, S. Noun concreteness and verbal facilitation as factors in imaginal mediation and paired-associate learning in children. *Journal of Experimental Child Psychology*, 1969, **7**, 459–466.

Zajonc, R. B. Attitudinal effects of mere exposure. *Journal of Personality and Social Psychology Monograph Supplement*, 1968, **9**, 1–27.

Zigler, M. J., & Northrup, K. M. The tactual perception of form. *American Journal of Psychology*, 1926, **37**, 391–397.

Zuckerman, C. B., & Rock, I. A reappraisal of the roles of past experience and innate organizing processes in visual perception. *Psychological Bulletin*, 1957, **54**, 269–296.

Name Index

Subject Index

Abilities: convergent and divergent, 494; language, and relation to cognition, 521–522. *See also* Individual differences in imagery; Symbolic habits

Abstract imagery (*see* Schema)

Abstraction, 16 ff., 130

Abstract language: evolution of, 26–27; intraverbal meaning of, 435, 439. *See also* Abstractness-concreteness of stimuli

Abstractness: definitions of, 16–17, 59, 60, 77–78; development of, 18–28; of symbolic processes, 16–28

Abstractness-concreteness of stimuli: measurement of, 77 ff.; relation of, to imagery, 64, 77–80, 201, 257, 266–267; and word class, 272–276, 282. *See also* Imagery vs. verbal processes, relative availability of; specific tasks

Acoustic coding, 53, 317; vs. articulatory coding, 225, 238; confusability and, 224–226, 231–232, 238–239

Afterimages, 12, 70, 89, 99 ff., 130, 481

Associability, 304–305, 308–309

Association(s): commonality of, 74; direct vs. mediated, 294–295. *See also* Language habits; Natural language mediators; Word association

Association value, 4, 45, 77, 187, 189 ff., 223, 269, 309, 334; and use of NLMs, 303–304, 306–307

Associative directionality, 248, 276–285, 320, 346, 408; as related to imagery and concreteness, 276–285

Associative fluency, 190, 494, 517

Associative meaning, 53, 57–59, 93; measures of, 76–77; relation of, to imagery and verbal processes, 57–59, 67. *See also* specific tasks; Verbal associative meaningfulness

Associative overlap, 46–47, 194, 211, 219, 290, 293, 324 ff.; and imagery-concreteness, 231, 290

Associative priming: in perception, 125–127; of verbal mediators, 316, 318

Associative probability theory, 4, 45, 219, 256, 260–261, 316; and adjective-noun order effect, 295; compared to imagery mediation hypothesis, 249–250, 294–295

Associative symmetry (*see* Associative directionality)

Associative variables in languages, vs. grammatical and semantic variables, 410, 420, 424, 465–466

Auditory-motor nature of verbal system, 9, 90, 150, 238–239, 372–374, 479

Awareness, 104, 135, 322–324, 441

Backward association, 248, 276 ff., 320, 346

Backward masking, 137–141

Behaviorism (*see* Imagery, historical background of)

Blindness, 518–520

Categorization, 90, 142, 146. *See also* Conceptual categories

Cell-assembly theory (Hebb), 26, 51, 52, 54, 95, 101–103, 107, 124, 385, 528; and imagery, 15, 71, 87, 531

Cerebral hemispheres: functional asymmetries of, 94–95, 113–115; and verbal-nonverbal distinction, 113–114, 522–523

Chunking, 159, 163, 212, 233, 386, 419–422, 451 ff. *See also* Organization in memory; Unitization

DATE DUE